D1810199

Anthology of Korean Studies
VOLUME V

KOREAN HISTORY:
Discovery of Its Characteristics and Developments

Edited by
Korean National Commission for UNESCO

Hollym
Elizabeth, NJ·Seoul

Anthology of Korean Studies, Volume V

Korean History:
Discovery of Its Characteristics and Developments

Copyright © 2004
by Tae-don Noh

All rights reserved. No part of this book may be reproduced in any form, except for brief quotation for a review or in scholarly essays and books, without the prior written permission of the publisher.

Edited by the Korean National Commission for UNESCO

First published in 2004
Second printing, 2008
by Hollym International Corp.
18 Donald Place, Elizabeth, New Jersey 07208, USA
Phone 908 353 1655   **Fax** 908 353 0255
http://www.hollym.com

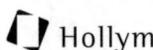 Hollym

Published simultaneously in Korea
by Hollym Corp., Publishers
13-13, Gwancheol-dong, Jongno-gu, Seoul 110-111, Korea
Phone +82 2 735 7551~4   **Fax** +82 2 730 5149, 8192
http://www.hollym.co.kr   **e-Mail** info@hollym.co.kr

ISBN: 978-1-56591-177-2 (Volume V)
Library of Congress Control Number: 2001098683

Printed in Korea

Contents

Foreword   *ix*

Preface   *xi*

Guide to Romanization   *xiii*

PART I: FORMATION OF KOREAN NATION AND
      ANCIENT PERIOD

Theories on the Formative Period of the Korean *Minjok*   *3*
    Noh Tae Don

Formation of the Ethnic Korean Nation and the Emergence   *27*
of Its Ancient Kingdom States
    Kim Jung Bae

Prehistoric Rock Art in Korea: *Ban-gudae*   *37*
    Werner Sasse

Korean-Japanese Relations during the Taika Reforms: *57*
A Perspective of International Cooperation
    Kim Hyun-Koo

A New Interpretation of the Problems of Mimana   *71*
    Chun Kwan-Woo

Hwarang Organization: Its Functions and Ethics   *115*
    Vladimir Tikhonov

Several Questions in Historical Studies of Balhae   *133*
    Song Kiho

PART II: GORYEO PERIOD

Politics and Culture within the Sinic Zone: Chinese   *161*
Influences on Medieval Korea
    Keith Pratt

The Landowning Slave: A Korean Phenomenon   *185*
    Ellen Salem

Social Changes from the Late Goryeo to Early Joseon Periods *199*
    Yi Tae-Jin

PART III: JOSEON PERIOD

The *Gwageo* Examination System during the Goryeo and   *221*
Early Joseon Periods
    Lee Song Mu

Confucian Politics and the *Sallim* Scholars during   *245*
the Joseon Dynasty
    Lee Woo Sung

Perception of Nature in the Joseon Period   *259*
    Yang Bo Kyung

Korean Envoys and Their Relations with Japan   *289*
in the 17th to 19th Centuries
    Yi Chin-Hui

The Role of Hangang River Merchants
and the Commercial Development in
the Late Joseon Dynasty
Kang Man-gil

307

Western Science and Silhak Scholars
Park Seong-rae

327

Dasan's Thought on Western Learning and Confucianism
Keum Jang-tae

363

PART IV: MODERN PERIOD

Was Korea Really a "Hermit Nation"?
Yi Tae-Jin

385

The Peasant War in 1894 and the Growth of
Peasant Society
Lee Young-ho

413

A Comparison of the 1894 Peasant Army Revolution
and the French Revolution
Shin Yong-Ha

429

Korea's Responses to Social Darwinism
Lee Kwang-rin

439

Japanese Challenge and Korean Response, 1870–1910:
A Brief Historical Survey
Lew Young Ick

475

Korea and Tsarist Russia: Russian Interests,
Policy, and Involvement in Korea, 1884–1904
Andrew C. Nahm

499

The Road to Colonization: Korea under Imperialism   525
    Kim Ki-Jung

PART V: COLONIAL PERIOD AND
POST-LIBERATION PERIOD

Korean Resistance to Imperial Japanese Aggression   553
and the Development of the Independence Movement
    Yun Pyong Suk

The Nature and Process of the Korean National Liberation   575
Movement during the Japanese Colonial Period
    Kang Man-gil

Inauguration of the Singanhoe Society and the Establishment   595
of Its Chapters
    Yi Kyun Young

Crisis and Discord in Colonial Korean Agricultural Society   617
during the Great Depression
    Chung Youn-Tae

Deduction of the National Division and the Premise   641
of Reunification of the Korean Peninsula
    Doh Jin Soon

Index-Glossary   665

Foreword

Since the seventeenth century when Hendrick Hamel first introduced Korea to the Western world, many Westerners have been drawn to the study of Korea and its rich cultural, literary, and philosophical history. Although important pioneering works on Korea have been produced, however, much research by Western scholars has been shaped by ethnocentric assumptions and interpretive biases, often reproducing preconceptions and simple misunderstandings about Korea. Many Korean scholars, too, have pursued scholarly aims that fall short of objective analyses. Thus, there has long been a need for a forum to bridge the gaps between Korean and non-Korean scholars, to make space for a multiplicity of voices, and to promote an interdisciplinary academic approach to Korean studies.

The *Korea Journal*, an academic quarterly published in English by the Korean National Commission for UNESCO, aims to act as such a forum. Since its foundation in 1961, the *Korea Journal* has attempted to provide grounded and accurate knowledge of Korea by featuring articles by prominent Korean and non-Korean specialists. Fortunately, an increasing number of Korean and foreign scholars and specialists are tackling the study of Korea with a more rigorous, objective, and open-minded outlook, engaging in critical dialogue with each other. The *Korea Journal* has played an invaluable role in developing and deepening this scholarly dialogue.

In 2001, the *Journal* celebrated its 40th anniversary. To commemorate this occasion, we planned to publish the Anthology of Korean Studies, a series of six volumes in the fields of economics, politics, anthropology, literature, history, and philosophy. All the articles in the series have been carefully selected from previous issues of the *Journal* by the Advisory

Committee, composed of six prominent specialists representing each field. The Anthology will be completed in 2004, marking the 50th anniversary of the Korean National Commission for UNESCO.

It is our hope that the Anthology will serve those who seek a comprehensive understanding of Korean society and culture. We recommend that it be used as a textbook at the university level or a standard reference for anyone teaching, studying, or researching in any area of Korean studies.

I would like to express my sincere gratitude to the members of the Advisory Committee, who took part in a one-year process to select the articles for inclusion in the Anthology: Dr. Kim Won Bae for economics, Prof. Kang Jung In for politics, Prof. Han Kyung-Koo for anthropology, Prof. Hwang Jong-yon for literature, Prof. Yi Tae-Jin for history, and Prof. Lee Seung-Hwan for philosophy. I would also like to recognize the editors and proofreaders who have labored tirelessly for the publication of this series, and the authors who have reexamined and revised their original texts. My thanks also go to the Hollym Publishing Company which has made it possible for our Commission to publish this Anthology, thus ensuring its contribution to the continued development of Korean studies.

Yersu Kim
Secretary-General
Korean National Commission
for UNESCO

Preface

Japanese colonialism robbed Korea of its opportunity to modernize by its own volition. Imperial Japan also propagated a false image of Korea to the outside world from the moment it went to the war against Russia in 1904. Claiming that Korea was a source of calamity in East Asia, the Japanese insisted that their occupation of Korea was inevitable and justifiable. While the Japanese buried Korea's achievements of self-modernization prior to the Russo-Japanese War, they sustained the false idea of Korean incapacity by negatively representing Korean history and racial characteristics. Japan's forced annexation of Korea brought about not only distress to the lives of Koreans but also serious distortions of Korean history.

Since the Liberation of 1945, Korean historians have spent much time restoring the "true" history of Korea while criticizing Japanese colonialist historiography. However, recovering losses already incurred during the forty years of Japanese forced occupation proved to be extremely difficult. Subsequent unstable political situations such as ideological conflict, national division, war, poverty, and dictatorship made consistent academic activity nearly unsustainable. Stable academic activity in Korea did not settle into place until the late 1960s, when Korean studies began to grow and expand. Many articles in this volume, written in the 1970s and later, would not have been possible without that initial boom.

Korean historians, however, are still not free from the concept that their first task is to overcome Japanese colonialist history. Japan damaged and distorted Korea's history to such a serious extent that it was virtually impossible for scholars to construct a true image of Korea. Moreover, Western scholars made this task even more difficult as they followed in the footsteps of Japanese colonialist historians. Considering all these obstacles, achievements in the field of Korean history over the past 30 years have been quite remarkable.

This volume, *Korean History: Discovery of Its Characteristics and Developments*, presents 29 original articles carefully selected from the *Korea Journal* that cover all periods of Korean history. The articles, spanning various fields and chosen under the guidance of Professor Yi Tae-Jin, are arranged into five major periods: 1) Ancient, 2) Goryeo (First Medieval), 3) Joseon (Second Medieval), 4) Modern, and 5) Colonial and Post-Liberation. Though the compilation aims to cover a wide range of fields within each period, it should be noted that the articles published in the *Korea Journal* were originally limited in number and subject. Therefore, it cannot be said that this selection covers all necessary aspects of Korean history presently reflected in the advanced level of current Korean historiography. There are myriad of interesting and important articles worthy of being introduced to Western academic societies through English translation. Still, this volume serves as a display of the endeavors of Korean historians to correct the distorted image of Korean history, and is also meant to encourage and promote the English translation of a more comprehensive surveys of Korean history.

Guide to Romanization

The Anthology uses the new Romanization system proclaimed by the Ministry of Culture and Tourism for terms in Korean. Outline of the Romanization system is as follows.

The Romanization of Korean

1. Basic Principles of Romanization

1) Romanization is based on standard Korean pronunciation.
2) Symbols other than Roman letters are avoided to the greatest extent possible.

2. Summary of the Romanization System

1) Vowels are transcribed as follows:

• simple vowels

ㅏ	ㅓ	ㅗ	ㅜ	ㅡ	ㅣ	ㅐ	ㅔ	ㅚ	ㅟ
a	eo	o	u	eu	i	ae	e	oe	wi

• diphthongs

ㅑ	ㅕ	ㅛ	ㅠ	ㅒ	ㅖ	ㅘ	ㅙ	ㅝ	ㅞ	ㅢ
ya	yeo	yo	yu	yae	ye	wa	wae	wo	we	ui

Note : ㅢ is transcribed as *ui*, even when pronounced as ㅣ.
Long vowels are not reflected in Romanization.

2) Consonants are transcribed as follows:

• plosives (stops)

ㄱ	ㄲ	ㅋ	ㄷ	ㄸ	ㅌ	ㅂ	ㅃ	ㅍ
g, k	kk	k	d, t	tt	t	b, p	pp	p

• affricates

ㅈ	ㅉ	ㅊ
j	jj	ch

• fricatives

ㅅ	ㅆ	ㅎ
s	ss	h

• nasals

ㄴ	ㅁ	ㅇ
n	m	ng

• liquids

ㄹ
r, l

Note 1: The sounds ㄱ, ㄷ, and ㅂ are transcribed respectively as *g*, *d*, and *b* when they appear before a vowel; they are transcribed as *k*, *t*, and *p* when followed by another consonant or form the final sound of a word. (They are Romanized as pronunciation in [ ].)

e.g. 구미   Gumi   영동   Yeongdong
      백암   Baegam   옥천   Okcheon
      합덕   Hapdeok   호법   Hobeop
      월곶[월곧]   Wolgot   벗꽃[벋꼳]   beotkkot
      한밭[한받]   Hanbat

Note 2: ㄹ is transcribed as *r* when followed by a vowel, and as *l* when followed by a consonant or when appearing at the end of a word. ㄹㄹ is transcribed as *ll*.

e.g. 구리   Guri   설악   Seorak
      칠곡   Chilgok   임실   Imsil
      울릉   Ulleung   대관령[대괄령] Daegwallyeong

However, the Anthology follows the principle below when romanizing Korean family name starting with ㄱ and family name 이.

1) For family names starting with ㄱ (e.g., 강, 권, and 김), *K* will be used instead of *G.*
2) When romanizing the family name 이, *Yi* will be used instead of *I.*

The Anthology follows the *pinyin* system as found in the *Xiandai banyu cidian* published by the Institute of the Chinese Academy of Sciences (Bejing Shangwuyin Shuguan, 1978) for terms in Chinese and the romanization system used in the *New Japanese-English Character Dictionary* (Kenkyusha, 1990) for terms in Japanese.

PART I

FORMATION OF KOREAN NATIONS AND ANCIENT PERIOD

Theories on the Formative Period of the Korean *Minjok*

Noh Tae Don

Preface

Minjok (Volk)[1] is one of the most frequently used words in modern and contemporary Korean history. It is so familiar that we assume its meanings as self-evident. However, in reality, the word has multiple definitions and usages, varying according to each academic discipline and to the writer using the word to describe certain concepts. Discussions of the formative period of the Korean *minjok* provide an excellent example.[2] Some people think that the Korean *minjok* was formed as

---

* Originally published in the *Korea Journal*, vol. 37, no. 4 (winter 1997).

Noh Tae Don (No, Tae-don) is Professor of Korean History at Seoul National University. He has written numerous books and papers on ancient Korean history, including *Hanguksa-reul tonghae bon uri-wa segye-e daehan insik* (Essays on the Understanding of "We" and "World" in Korean History) (1998), *Goguryeosa yeongu* (A Study on the History of Goguryeo) (1999), and "Yeoksajeok silche-roseoui Dangun" (Dangun as a Historical Entity) (2000). E-mail: hangawe@snu.ac.kr.

1. I intend to survey the concept and usage of the word *minjok* (民族) in Korean academia. *Minjok* has been defined very differently by Korean scholars. Therefore, in some places in this paper, *minjok* will be used instead of "nation" (which refers more to a particular country and its citizens), "ethnic group" (which is a purely cultural and historical concept), or "race" (which carries a biological meaning). Instead of these English translations, the German word "Volk" has been chosen as having the most similar meaning to the Korean word *minjok*. Therefore, "Volk" will be used throughout this paper, except in those cases where *minjok* is deemed to be more appropriate.

2. Three recently published articles reveal the basic arguments related to concept of *minjok*: Noh Tae Don, "Hanguk minjok-eun eonje hyeongseong doe-eonna?" (When

early as 1000 B.C., while others think this did not occur until after the twentieth century. While the contrast between these opinions is remarkable, it should be noted that this debate is not unique to Korea: similar questions are perplexing scholars in other East Asian countries with long historical traditions.

Differences in opinion about the emergence of the Korean *minjok* may have led to a variety of perspectives in understanding its history. Defining the word *minjok* is quite problematic, and the word is sometimes used to state historical accounts even if its meaning is misunderstood.[3]

So far four theories about the formation of the Korean *minjok* have been established, each adopting a different definition of *minjok*. First is the physical anthropological approach. Second is the theory that a *minjok* is a human group with common life-styles and shared identity perceptions. The third theory regards *minjok* as a product of the modern nation-state and modern nationalism. Finally, the fourth theory, which is based on the second theory, reflects on the historicity by prescribing various stages in which the *minjok* developed. In this article, I will first introduce these four theories, and then examine many problems inherent in each.

The Blood Community and *Minjok*

We often hear the phrase "Koreans are one *minjok*," which is innocuous unless it is underscored to imply ethnic superiority. The phrase can be interpreted to mean either "the Korean nation is one ethnic group" or that "Koreans share the same blood." On the whole, the latter interpreta-

---

Had the Korean *Minjok* Been Formed?), *Yeoksa bipyeong* (Critical Review of History) 19 (fall 1992): pp. 15-101; The Association for Korean Historical Studies, ed., *Geundae gungmin gukga-wa minjok munje* (The Modern Nation-State and the Question of *Minjok*) (Seoul: Jisik Sanupsa, 1995); Hallim Academy of Sciences, *Hanguk minjok-ui giwon-gwa hyeongseong* (The Origin and Formation of the Korean *Minjok*), vols. 1 and 2 (Sohwa, 1996).

3. Discussions about this topic were held in North Korea, China, and Japan. Some works which support this idea include: 歷史研究編輯部 編, 『韓民族形成問題討論集』 (The Discussion on the Formation of the Korean *Minjok*) (Beijing, 1957); "Joseon-eseoui bureujowa hyeongseong-e gwanhan toronhoe" (On the Formation of the Bourgeois in Korea), *Ryeoksa gwahak* (1957); 古田元夫, 「ベトナム史學界とベトナム史像」 (Historiography of Vietnam), 『東京大學教養學部 人文科學紀要』 第 87輯 (1988).

tion has more force because it denotes the blood ties creating the Korean "group" or Volk. Expressions such as "the 70 million brothers" and "one bloodline, one people" are frequently used within Korea. Of course, such notions of fraternity are just another dimension of the Korean consciousness of their blood ties, and do not mean Koreans literally descended from the same ancestor.

However, some people have viewed *minjok* as blood-based communities which have come down from the antiquity. Were that actually the case, we might redate the formative period of the Korean *minjok* to earlier times, as has sometimes been done both in South Korea and certainly in North Korean historical works.

Joseon tongsa (A General History of Korea), published in 1977 in North Korea, was the first work to emphasize blood relations and language as standards for distinguishing the *minjok*. Bloodline and language, it states, are unchangeable attributes, thus concluding that no large-scale population movement into the Korean peninsula has occurred since the ancient times. This premise, naturally, puts the formative period of the Korean *minjok* at a time prior to the Three Kingdoms period. The 1987 edition of the *Joseon tongsa* emphasized this point, clearly stating, "Before the establishment of the Three Kingdoms period, the Ye, Maek, and Han tribes were three branches of one *minjok* who shared basically the same bloodline, language and customs."[4] Moreover, to support the view that *minjok* is equivalent to race, the *Joseon tongsa* supposed the existence of "an archaic Joseon people" from primitive times. Accordingly, it stressed that because a *minjok* is a community sharing a common fate and bound together by blood and language, sacrificing for one's Volk is the uppermost duty and virtue of its members. This idea, as reflected in historical studies, gives precedence to *minjok* even over notions of chronology in interpreting and evaluating historical events.

Blood relations and especially the group's consciousness of those relations are important factors in the formation of a *minjok*. Even though Koreans may not have descended from the same one ancestor, it is possible for one to wonder whether they have physical characteristics different from other Volks, considering the extent of their consciousness of

4. Sahoe Gwahagwon (Institute for Research in Social Science, DPRK), ed., *Joseon tongsa* (A General History of Korea), DPRK Academic Series vol. 1 (Seoul: Owol, 1988), pp. 32-33.

their own consanguinity. If they do, then analyzing these characteristics would be an effective means for pinpointing their identity; and if the analysis of ancient bones should reveal the presence of different characteristics, this would serve to refute the idea of "Koreans are one *minjok*" and also serve as the clue that leads to the solution of the question of how the Korean *minjok* formed.

Studies of the physical characteristics of the Korean people have proceeded in two directions. One has entailed the analysis of ancient human bones, and the other has investigated the physical features of present-day Koreans. Studies concerning the former have been carried out by analyzing human fossils from the Paleolithic period and human bones found in late Paleolithic tombs. This article will not examine the results of these current studies in detail. Briefly speaking, because human fossils from the Paleolithic period are very few in number, such studies can only confirm one thing—whether human beings have lived in Korea since the antiquity. Even in other countries definite results have not been forthcoming in determining certain peoples' traits through studying the Paleolithic bones. This, together with the fact that human fossils are so few, may be due to the fact that nothing beyond racial features had developed by the late stages of the Paleolithic period.

In many cases, unearthed remains of human skeletons from after the Neolithic Age have gone unanalyzed, but the few existing studies on these bones have led to several hypotheses about the origins of the Korean people. For instance, when two normacephalic heads and two brachycephalic heads discovered during the colonial period in Hamgyeongbuk-do province (Songpyeong-dong, Unggi-eup) were analyzed, it was argued that the former reflected Paleo-Asiatic characteristics and the latter was of Altaic origin, which led to a theory of racial immigrations. Another example came from a dolichocephalic head and a skeleton from a tall body excavated in 1962 from a dolmen at Hwangseok-ri, Gangwon-do province. Based on these analyses some scholars have suggested that peoples of Caucasian origin may have migrated from the southern regions to the Korean peninsula during the Bronze Age. However, apart from the accuracy question of these theories, one problem remains in that this conclusion was drawn after analyzing only a small number of bones, thus taking away their persuasiveness. Although a greater number of bones were unearthed from the Three Kingdoms period tombs than from ancient Neolithic tombs, they have been subjected only to limited analysis. Therefore, it is a difficult task to draw conclusions about the origins and formation of the Korean *minjok* through bone analysis. Even though we find the people from murals and other paintings of the Three Kingdoms period possessing similar features as those of modern Koreans, the paintings do not allow us to gather any concrete physical characteristics. Therefore, to identify the physical features of the Korean *minjok*, first of all, it is necessary to examine those of present-day Koreans and then advance the research by comparing them to their premodern ancestors.

Every Korean individual has his or her own differentiating physical features. However, Koreans are considered to possess a degree of characteristics in common. For example, the width of the Korean skull, divided diametrically from the forehead to the back of the head, is shown to be comparatively short. Koreans also have wide faces, protruding cheekbones, yellowish skin, dark brown eyes, thick, straight black hair, and little body hair. Their height is average among East Asians.

According to a recent research, these physical features distinguish Koreans from neighboring peoples. Such research, combined with data on physical proportion, helps us to grasp the distinguishing physical characteristics of present-day Koreans.[5] However, as a nonspecialist in this field, I wonder if such numerical differences are meaningful in analyzing a *minjok* as a consanguineous group. Even setting aside questions regarding the methods used to derive statistical data, the quantity of the data, and the narrow differences among numerical values, a fundamental doubt remains as to even whether an external physical form can actually be inherited.

For example, the shape of the cranium, usually considered to be the most important part of the human body, is determined by cultural differences as well as by hereditary factors. Koreans are said to have brachycephalic heads. Although this was the norm in Korea several decades ago, normacephalic or dolichocephalic heads can nowadays be readily found among the young. This phenomenon has resulted from recent child-rearing methods. It has been assumed that the width from the forehead to the back of the head can be widened to result in a dolichocephalic head if the mother makes the child lie on its face in infancy. This practice reflects the fact that some young Korean mothers prefer Western features to Eastern ones. Changes in cranial shapes are evident,

---

5. Jang U-jin, *Joseon saram-ui giwon* (The Origins of the Koreans) (Pyeongyang: Sahoe Gwahak Chulpansa, 1989), pp. 172-197.

though further research and analysis of these changes are needed. Other physical changes, such as height and stature, have also been readily apparent.

Some physical changes are abrupt, while others are realized over a greater period of time, for example, eye color and shape, hair color and shape, and skin color. Changes in skin color can also be traced to the environment or one's occupation. Giving full consideration to these aspects, it can be concluded that the narrow numerical differences are not very important.

In the future, as people employ more detailed methods of examination such as measurements of gene frequency, even more unusual results might come to light. However, existing research points toward rejection of the uniqueness of Koreans' physical characteristics, especially considering their similarity to those of other Northeast Asian peoples such as Manchurians, Mongolians, the Tungus, etc. While we can easily perceive the differences between northern Europeans and Koreans, it is difficult to find such differences between Koreans and other peoples living in Northeast Asia. The numerical differences seem to result from culture and environment, rather than from genetic makeup.

The Korean people's highly homogeneous physical features are due to their long course of history rather than to their blood lineage. The geopolitical characteristic of the peninsula has made migration from outside and the opportunity to mix physical traits infrequent. Especially after the foundation of the Goryeo, when Korea began to exist as a single state. Only one gene pool[6] was available on the peninsula as "marriage arranged by exchange" prevailed. This, combined with the fact that Korea has possessed a single culture of food, clothing, and shelter, has led to the development of identical characteristics.

Such aspects are also found in discussions of the Korean language system. Arguments about whether Korean belongs to the Altaic language group continue, but even if it is so categorized, the Korean language yet carries many features which mark it as an isolated language.[7]

---

6. Na Se-jin, "Chejil illyuhak-eseo bon han-gugin" (Koreans Seen from Physical Anthropology Perspective), in *Hanguksa* (Korean History), vol. 23 (Gwacheon: National Institute of Korean History, 1978), p. 214.

7. Yi Gi-mun, "Hanminjok: eoneo" (Korean *Minjok*: Languages), in *Hanguk minjok munhwa daebaekgwa sajeon* (Encyclopedia of Korean Culture), vol. 24 (Seongnam: The Academy of Korean Studies, 1991), p. 211.

As summarized above, no grounds exist for thinking that Koreans are a biological unit with the same blood or originated from a single ancestor. Thus, any theory claiming that the Korean *minjok* formed in early antiquity descended from a single ancestor cannot be supported. However, there can be no denying that Koreans possess highly homogeneous features which have amalgamated during their long history and which are one of the major elements leading Koreans to hold a strong consciousness of their blood relations. It is this consciousness which contributes to the maintenance of the Korean *minjok*'s unity.

Consciousness of one's blood relations is one of the main elements constituting a *minjok*. It is basically a historical result created by various social and cultural relationships although actual blood relationship may have had its role here. However, just as untenable are recent notions which consider the Korean peoples' consciousness of their blood relations as dangerous, or deny it by insisting that it is only a ideological product, as is the view that considers this consciousness to be actually connected to biological blood ties. Consciousness of blood relations is a product of a long history, and is thus a precious part of the Korean people's heritage. However, there have periodically been differences in how this consciousness is revealed. It was only in recent times that the idea of blood relations was constructed, often through expressions like "millions of our people, same blood, one *minjok*." Such ideas were in turn projected onto Korean people's understanding of its own history, such as the assertion that Koreans have existed from antiquity as a single race. This consciousness of being an ethnic group was closely related to the formation of the modern Korean political and economic community. I will discuss this topic in the following chapter.

The Cultural Community and *Minjok*

"Volk" is generally defined in the field of cultural anthropology as a community of human beings sharing a common style of living and culture. This concept values objective factors—such as traditional styles of living and the sharing of one language—and, based on these common factors, has tended to emphasize boundary divisions in accounting for Volk distribution. But, we cannot regard a given Volk's shared life-style only as an objective fact; it seems rather to give a certain homogeneity to the normative actions of its members, which in turn affects the value system, and which then forms the "Volk-like" characteristics of a Volk. While life-styles do change in the course of time, they also persist amidst change. If they disappear, the Volk perishes and becomes adapted to other Volks. If a certain group produces new traits in the course of adapting itself to new circumstances, that group will create a new Volk distinct from the old Volk to which it previously belonged. In other words, cultural factors are what enable a Volk to identify itself. Besides, in recent considerations of ethnicity in modern societies, a tendency has been observed which values not only objective factors but also the sub-jective factor of the "we-consciousness" formed through a Volk's rela-tionships with "others."[8]

Let us look at the theory that puts the formative period of the Korean *minjok* at the Bronze Age, at the time when the Ye, Maek, and Han tribes appeared.[9] Korean history textbooks for high-school students accept the idea that the Ye, Maek, and Han tribes, though geographical-ly divided, had the same origins.

The Ye, Maek, and Han, the oldest tribes on record with relation to present-day Koreans, are assumed to be the ancestors of the Korean *min-jok*. Though it is true that later in history the descendants of these three tribes formed a common Volk, it is questionable whether we can actual-ly classify these people as having been one Volk originally. To justify this point, it must be determined whether they formed one cultural commu-nity or considered themselves as one people. We cannot prove that they shared a common blood line, customs, language, or even the concep-tions of a single people. In the end, objective indicators such as similari-ties in material culture must be observed.

We cannot conclude that the Ye, Maek, and Han tribes shared a com-mon style of living, even though they exhibited certain common cultural patterns from the Bronze Age to the early Iron Age. Originally, there were regional differences in burial rituals and artifacts; and through

---

8. Thomas Hylland Eriksen, *Ethnicity and Nationalism: Anthropological Perspectives* (London: Pluto Press, 1993), pp. 1-17.
9. Kim Jeong-hak, "Hanguk minjok hyeongseong sa" (The History of the Korean *Min-jok* Formation), in *Hanguk munhwasa daegye* (Overview on the Korean Culture), vol. 1 (1964); Kim Jeong-bae, "Hanguk minjok-gwa yemaek" (The Korean *Minjok* and the Ye and Maek Tribes), in *Hanguk minjok munhwa-ui giwon* (The Origin of Kore-an National Culture) (Seoul: Korea University Press, 1973).

time, these differences were intensified. However, such differences in the three tribes gradually decreased after the fifth century. Much more precision is needed in drawing conclusions about the graves of the ruling classes of the Three Kingdoms period. In the fifth century, Silla utilized stone mound tombs with wooden chambers (*jeokseok mokgwakbun*) but used stone chambers covered with an earthen mound (*seoksil bongtobun*) after the sixth century. In Goguryeo, too, the earlier periods are marked by stone mound tombs (*jeokseokchong*), but stone chambers covered with an earthen mound were predominant after the fifth century. In Baekje, stone chambers covered with an earthen mound had been established following the use of stone mound tombs. Also, until the fifth century, there were vast differences between Ye tribe graves on the east coast and Ye tribe graves in the northern Sungari river basin in Northeast China. At this same period, people in the Yeongsangang river basin located in the southwestern part of the peninsula maintained their own peculiar burial practice using large jars (*onggwanmyo*). In light of these facts, we cannot say that the Ye, Maek, and Han tribes formed a single cultural community. Of course, similar elements of material culture can be found among different tribes, just as a variety of such elements can be located within a single tribe. Given this, it is not persuasive to define them as a single cultural community based on these material factors. Comparing the Ye, Maek, and Han tribes with other neighboring tribes, we must admit that while their artifacts are quite similar, there are many heterogeneous factors which also must be considered.

This is especially true if we apply the element of "we-consciousness" to this. In this case, it would even be difficult to say that these tribes did not have a consciousness of a single ethnicity within themselves. The Ye people, for example, were spread over a wide area from the edge of the Yeongilman bay in Gyeongsangbuk-do extending to the northern part of the Sungari river in Northeast China. While the ancient Chinese first classified this group as "Ye," people living in one small area of Ye would not have known about other Ye tribes further away. Such would have been the case for the Han tribe as well.

A group's being classified and named as a Volk or a tribe by a third party is not without significance, however. "Naming" results when a group has objective characteristics differentiating it from other groups. These divisions, however, are not meaningful until the people call themselves by this name. When the object which is "named" is identical with the name the object calls itself, we can say that a Volk, or a group that has a common life-style and consciousness of itself, has been formed. From this aspect, it is hard to consider the Ye, Maek, and Han tribes as one Volk, which leads us to the conclusion that the Korean *minjok* was formed at a much later date.

At any rate, regarding a Volk as a cultural community brings out the need for an understanding, at the phenomenal level, of the differences among Volks, which appear from applying synchronic comparisons. However, using this as the sole factor in determining Volks may lead us to ignore the Volk's historicity. Most importantly, we are no longer able to grasp the outstanding differences between Volks of the modern and premodern periods. Discussions of "ethnicity" are also meaningful in terms of raising questions about differences among human groups living in a modern society or nation-state in the same time period. But it unfortunately becomes difficult to understand the way in which the formation of human groups took place in the premodern period and the dynamic historical process from which modern nations evolved. The theory of the modern formation of Volks seriously looks at the dynamic process involved in the evolution of the modern Volks and also evaluates its historicity.

The Political and Economic Community and *Minjok*

In the modern period, the basic category of discourse in world history has been the notion of a nation-state. The nation-state is, among other things, a territorial state having external sovereignty; a political community whose members are controlled by a common set of laws and who also create laws for themselves. Also, it is an economic community operating under a market system or planned economy, as well as a cultural community offering public education (national education) and possessing cultural media. Some argue that the word *minjok* by its own definition refers to members of the nation-state. According to them, a *minjok* is, above all else, a community of people who carry out their rights and duties, participate positively in political and social matters, and feel compatriotism with other members of their nation-state. A community displaying these characteristics is the product of a modern nation-state. This notion of *minjok* follows that of the Western "nation." The West's discourse, particularly England and France, has become the standard by which other discourses on the formation of the nation developed. In adopting this modern nation formation, we compare the specific circumstances of other nations, measuring them using the standard of the English and the French. After the nineteenth century, capitalism created a global economic zone, and Western nation-states became the model to be followed by states in other areas; and in fact the nation-state became the basic unit of world history. Accordingly, we can ascertain that, although the formation processes of each nation may be different, the concept of "nation" has nonetheless begun to be accepted as a universal unit in world history, based both on the fundamental nature of the concept of "nation" and its modernity.

Korea is no exception. On the outset of modernization, Korea freed itself from the world order system centered around China. Doing so, Korea joined a universal system in which all nations base their interrelationships on equality. Culturally, Korea discarded its "Eastern medieval ideology" based on Confucianism, and began to value the uniqueness of its own culture. As its system of social hierarchy collapsed, Koreans began to advocate the principle of equality among human beings. Economically, their agrarian society began to transform into an industrial society. Korea also tried to ward off imperialistic invasions and to protect its own sovereignty and independence. It was under these conditions that the Korean *minjok* was molded. The *minjok* adopted a new historical character entirely different in quality from that of premodern times. There are many different opinions about the concrete formation process of the Korean *minjok*, the dynamics which guided that formation and precisely when the formation occurred. For example, different opinions have centered around the late Joseon's endogenous development and its extent as Joseon was itself entering into the modern age; the consequences of opening the Korean ports; and the socioeconomic changes during the colonial period. These opinions assert that the Korean *minjok* was formed in the throes of modernization after the opening of Korea's ports and during movements of resistance against the Japanese rule.

Great qualitative changes occurred in human communities between the premodern and modern ages. We can examine these changes through the terms used to refer to the *minjok*, and words of similar meanings, such as *dongpo* (compatriots) and *gungmin* which appeared in the editorials and commentaries of early newspapers such as the *Hanseong maeil sinbo* (Hanseong Daily Newspaper). We can also find in the manifestos of the righteous armies terms like "history of 4,000 years," "3,000-*ri* territory," and "twenty million compatriots" used to urge people to rise up against Japanese aggression.[10] In addition, Korean history texts written at that time did not begin with the dynastic origins of Korean history, but rather proceeded from the origins of the Korean *minjok*.[11] There are some contextual differences in which these expressions were used, but such cases were rare and unprecedented in Korean history. Although we cannot conclude once and for all that the Korean *minjok* formed in the modern age, we may nonetheless conjecture about the directions of this extraordinary movement. By this period, slavery had already been abolished by the Gabo Reform of 1894, and Korea was facing the loss of its sovereignty to Japan following the establishment of the Japanese Residency-General in Korea. A movement to promote national identity subsequently spread to foster the resistance against the Japanese, and Koreans began to employ the term *minjok* commonly. Of course, terms such as *gyeore* (compatriots) and *dongpo* had been used during the Joseon dynasty, but these terms did not include all Koreans but referred to only the actual blood relatives. In a stratified society, the use of such expressions was not generally tolerated.

On the other hand, in the theory of "modern formation of nations," people living in the premodern era are said to have had "nationality." When applying this concept to Korea, two views emerge: one view states that formation took place during the Unified Silla period, whereas the other view places formation during the early Goryeo period. The "Silla period theory," which asserts Korean nationality emerged at the end of the Three Kingdoms period, states that various small countries within the three kingdoms' territory broke up and merged into larger ones, thereby enabling each of the three kingdoms to have an economic, cultural, and psychological identity of its own based on common language and shared territory. Therefore, the theory argues, each of the three kingdoms formed its own nationality, and the Korean *minjok* was formed after their unification.[12] The "early Goryeo period theory," on the other hand, focuses on the idea that the people of Goryeo, together with migrants from Balhae who crossed into their border, consisted of

---

10. Hong Sun-gwon, *Hanmal honam jiyeok uibyeong undongsa yeongu* (A Study of the Movement of the Righteous Army in Honam Region at the End of the Great Han Empire) (Seoul: Seoul National University Press, 1994), pp. 336-345.
11. Sin Chae-ho, *Doksa sillon* (A New Reading of History), vol. 1 of *Danjae Sin Chae-ho jeonjip* (The Complete Collection of Sin Chae-ho's Works).
12. Sahoe Gwahagwon, *Joseon tongsa* (1956), pp. 98-102.

one cultural unit and shared a common life-style within the boundary of a single state.

The concept of "nationality" was created by Stalin. He divided up human communities according to qualitative changes in the social formation. *Narodnost* changed into *natsiya* following the rise of capitalism. This concept is translated as "nationality" in English, but the word in this sense is rarely used in English-speaking countries. Some people designated groups prior to "nation" as "ethnic groups" or as "ethnies."[13] Other people have said that countries with long histories like Korea, China, and Vietnam had developed as "historic-nations" before forming "nations."[14] The idea that a nationality usually changes into a nation brings into relief the dynamic process of change in the formation of a *minjok* and helps to make the historicity of *minjok* a distinct concept. That is why we find a logical system in it.

Western nations are products of nation-states. It is not that nations existed before nation-states; indeed, the opposite is true. Korea was divided into north and south after liberation in 1945. Then each country followed the nation-state formations separately. Each has had its own political and economic system—communism and capitalism—over the long fifty years of "national" division. If we contend that nation is equivalent to *minjok*, Korea presents a problem: because the Korean *minjok* extending across North and South Korea has not been unified, the Korean *minjok* cannot be said to have yet been established. This opinion appears to emphasize national unification and therefore the nation-state. According to Stalin's theory, which insists that one of the main attributes of *natsiya* (nation) is a common economy, and which also states that many nations were formed when capitalism rose to its height, we may conclude that the Korean *minjok* was formed following the 1945 Liberation. Since North and South Korea separately developed their own economic structures, there currently exist two nations on the peninsula. Perhaps, it is due to these complications that North Korea gave up determining when the Korean *minjok* was formed, after some attempts in the 1960s.

---

13. Anthony D. Smith, *The Ethnic Origins of Nations* (Oxford: Blackwell, 1986), pp. 21-119.

14. E. J. Hobsbawn, *Nation and Nationalism since 1780* (Cambridge: Cambridge University Press, 1990), p. 137.

Judging from the standpoint of the modern nation formation theory, we can say that the Korean *minjok* was formed by the anti-imperialistic and antifeudalistic national movements prior to the 1945 Liberation. Korea's situation is unique in that after its division, nation-states were formed respectively on each side of the border. This, of course, serves as a valid claim for exploring the means of unification in overcoming the present situation. Aside from this, however, the modern formation theory's assertion that nation and *minjok* are identical, is problematical. Let us consider the following points.

Nation and *Minjok*

First, there is the problem in the terminology. The English word "nation" was translated into Japanese in the late nineteenth century as *minzoku*, which came also to be widely used in China and Korea. If the argument that the idea of a *minjok* could not have existed in East Asia in the premodern age because there was no term referring to it is indeed true, then this supports the theory that *minjok* formed in the modern age. But many academic words in modern East-Asian languages are translations of Western words. For example, class distinctions existed even before the term "class" was introduced in the modern age. The problem lies in how to define various concepts and to ascertain their correspondence with the facts.

The fact that the word "nation" was also translated as *kokka* (Japanese: "state") or *kokumin* (Japanese: "people") is confirmed by a dictionary published in Japan in the late nineteenth century.[15] Since that time, this word has been translated in three different ways. The English phrase "ethnic group" is also translated as *minjok* in Korean. It seems

---

15. In two English-Japanese dictionaries published in 1867 (『英和對譯袖珍辭書』, 江戸) and in 1872 (『英和對譯辭書』, 開拓史) respectively, "nation" was translated into "人民, 國人." However, a Japanese-German dictionary (『和譯獨逸辭書』, 1873) translated "nation" into "國民," English-Chinese-Japanese dictionary (『英華和譯字典』, 1876) "nation" into "民, 國, 邦, 邦國," and German-English-Japanese dictionary (『獨英和 三對字彙 大典』, 1887) "nation" into "國民, 人民" and "Volk, people, nation" into "民, 人民, 國民, 庶民, 萬民, 衆庶." According to a standard Japanese-English dictionary (『スタンソダード和英大辭典』, 1924), *minzoku* (民族) was translated into "people," "race" and "nation."

that when the concepts of "nation" and "ethnic group" were introduced to Korea, China and Japan, they came to be used interchangeably, so that the two dissimilar concepts ended up being translated together as *minjok*. Korea and Japan still do not make a clear distinction between these two words. Furthermore, just as Koreans were deprived of their national rights under Japanese colonization and could not use the word *gungmin* (nation),[16] they still hesitate to use the word *gungmin* today because it cannot include the people from both the North and South. So in many cases, *minjok* replaces the word *gungmin* when expressing the equivalent of the English word "nation," regardless of the fact that *minjok* and *gungmin* are not identical concepts.

Korean people who live in China refer to themselves as "Chinese nationals of Korean ethnicity." Residents of Korea think of these people as Korean *minjok*, but do not consider them a part of the Korean nation. This highlights the discordance between the concepts of *minjok* and nation. If a notion of a "multiethnic state" holds, this situation can be applied to peoples of other states. Of course, "nation" is not a term limited to legal or political matters ensuring citizenship. The people of modern nation-states form not only from political or economic communities, but also share a common culture and have national consciousness due to education and mass media. A nation, however, is not made up of only a single Volk sharing an identical mode of living and "we-consciousness." Koreans living in China have a double identity: one is a "we-consciousness" of being a member of the Chinese nation, the other is that of belonging to the Korean Volk. If so, the people of a nation-state could be referred to as a *minjok* whereas subgroups could be called "ethnic groups" (*jok*) or "races" (*injong*) (race, of course, refers to biology, such as black or white), providing there is general agreement among its members. The word "nation," however, originally meant a political community, of which France after its Revolution is an example. We cannot think of "nation-building" without a nation-state, which is why we call the

---

16. According to the "Twentieth-Century New People" (editorial column of *Daehan maeil sinbo*, 1910), Sin Chae-ho emphasized the elements of freedom, equality, and justice as the basis of those things that all people should have. He also stressed the importance of the economy and the capacity for self-defence. The meaning of the word *gungmin* in this writing was equivalent to that of "nation." However, after Korea's loss of independence, the word *gungmin* was no longer used. It was replaced with the word *minjok*.

international organization of nation-states the "United Nations," not the "United Volks." The main purpose of nationalism serves in a colonial state is to foster the formation of an independent nation-state. In this case, therefore, "nation" can be translated as *gungmin* rather than *minjok*.

Members of a nation-state are eventually supposed to become a Volk culturally and homogeneously in the process of manifold social operations effected through the medium of the nation-state. Citing Western nations as an example, some people have used this argument to make the case for a nation being the same as a Volk. This view is based on the mechanisms of modern civilization, including "Reason" and the functions of the modern state, in which it is assumed that many ethnic groups can be integrated into a single Volk. For example, though China is now one nation with 56 ethnicities, it is China's official position that those ethnicities will merge into a single, great Chinese Volk (*minzu* in Chinese). In fact, in some cases people of various ethnicities do unite as one Volk and form a nation. However, this usually involves the assimilation and unification of disparate groups, cultural assimilation, and identification with the main Volk under the leadership of a central force. This is similar to the principle which believes uniting many languages together rarely leads to the creation of a new language. When disparate languages are combined into one, one of the more influential languages will absorb the others, leading to their extinction. Though not exactly the same as with languages, there are similar problems among ethnicities or Volk.

This is confirmed in the case of Europe, where nation-states were formed early on. For instance, over 150 years since Belgians became independent and formed a nation-state in 1830, they have developed democratic politics and a capitalistic economy, while creating a welfare society. However, recently the nation-state was converted to a federation because of continuous conflict between the "Walloon" in the southern region and the "Flemish" in the northern region. Even the prestigious Louvain University with its long history in Belgium, was divided into two. The "Kataran" and "Basque" in Spain serve as another example. Such situations were intensified after the breakdown of socialism in Eastern Europe and the Soviet Union. Besides that, one can also find similarities in nation-states such as Quebec in Canada. The degree of conflict between ethnic groups taking place within any given nation-state varies according to the degree of the nation-state's economical, political, and ideological strength to ease conflicts of interest between involved groups.

These conflicts are variously manifested as the pursuance of separate states of independence, the extension of autonomy, and elevation in the social status of minorities.

This article does not intend to deal with the problems which occur in the process of national unity and with the so-called "fabrication of the nation-state," but only points out that it is not easy to merge ethnic groups in an ideological or political sense and that awareness of identity and culture involving blood relationships and modes of living in one Volk may vary. These factors are constantly changing. However, identity awareness, more than other factors, is enduring, and cannot quickly be replaced nor easily substituted by any one or several functional policies. Some issues cannot be solved either politically or economically; therefore, distinctions between nation and Volk remain in contemporary society.

Some nation-states are composed of many Volks, while in other cases a single Volk is spread over many different nation-states. For instance, there are more than 5 million Koreans living abroad and over 10 million Chinese in Southeast Asia alone, who for the most part feel bound both to their country and to their blood group. They maintain their cultural identity, taking advantage of long-distance transportation and modern communication and information services. "One Volk" nations are the rarity in the global age. Therefore, there is now increased interest in cultural pluralism and ethnicity.

This point of view sees *minjok* as signifying "nation" in the same sense as used in the modern formation theory. Generally, a *minjok* is defined as a group of human beings sharing a "we-consciousness" grounded in a common life-style and origins. This concept of *minjok* is equivalent to "Volk." Of course, proponents of the modern formation theory have been critical of this definition of *minjok*, saying that the word "nation" should replace "Volk" and that "consciousness of a nation" should replace the "consciousness of a Volk." However, I will avoid further debate on this point as it clearly is beyond the scope of this paper.

In as much as they are different from premodern peoples, perhaps we should regard *minjok* within the context of a nation-state as the product of modernity, and use the measures of cultural difference and "we-consciousness" as ways of distinguishing them. However, in order to clearly reflect differences in the quality of their patterns of existence and the "we-consciousness" in the modern and premodern periods, it has been stressed that *minjok* should be used only to describe modern-day peoples. In contrast to this, there is another argument that sees *minjok* and nation as different categories while it regards *minjok* within the context of a nation-state as the product of the modernity, in as much as *minjok* differs in quality from a premodern group of people. When we compare synchronically *minjok* and nation, we can use the measures of cultural difference and "we-consciousness" as ways of distinguishing them. However, diachronic comparison inevitably brings out remarkable differences in the quality of their patterns of existence and the "we-consciousness" in the modern and premodern periods. In order to reflect these differences, it has been stressed that *minjok* should be used only to describe modern-day peoples. From the point of view of the majority ethnic group within a nation-state, it itself is the nation. For that reason, modern formation scholars strongly insist that nations are products of the modern age and that the modern formation theory is irrefutable.

Their opinion is that only the minorities within a nation-state who emphasize their own originality are likely to resist the majority. In fact, the word "ethnicity" has been used to indicate a minority group or a group of "foreigners" regarded as "them," not as "we."[17] This has led to the opinion that, based on such a definition of an ethnicity or ethnic group, the modern formation theory is valid. Nevertheless, from a different standpoint, the main ethnic group, that is, the majority of the people who claim to be the nation is itself an ethnicity. Here the question is whether the point of view raised by discussions of ethnicity or ethnic groups is valid or not.

In fact, such discussions lack any consciousness of qualitative changes from premodern groups to modern-age groups. However, in speaking of an ethnic group, it is necessary to consider those characteristics which distinguish it both subjectively and objectively from other coeval groups. If we neglect this fact, we can no longer distinguish between nation and *minjok* (or ethnicity) as concepts, nor can we explain how existing ethnic groups live today.

In short, which is more essential in defining *minjok*, the qualitative change of relationships among members of an ethnic group over different periods of time, or the demarcation between coeval ethnicities? If the former is more essential, *minjok* could then only apply to the modern

---

17. Elizabeth Tonkin, Maryon McDonald, and Malcolm Chapman, *History and Ethnicity* (London: Routledge, 1989), pp. 11-17.

period. If the latter is more essential, *minjok* would then be used to describe both the modern and premodern periods. I believe the latter is closer to the truth. If we consider the concepts of nation and *minjok* separately, it is the latter which contains the kernel concept of a *minjok* or an ethnicity. Taking this perspective, the Korean *minjok* seems to have been formed in the premodern age. *Minjok* was formed as a product of history, and changed qualitatively with the progression of history. Therefore, we may further divide *minjok* into "premodern" and "modern." In terms of the relationships among *minjok* members, these are identical in characteristics to those of nation members, though these two categories do not precisely correspond to each other. This supposition, previously excluded from discussions about ethnicity, aids in our understanding of the dynamic process in which a Volk first forms and then gradually transforms into a modern Volk.

On the other hand, considering that all phenomena are historical and change with time and a definition is significant in that it telescopes such changes into a conception, the insistence that Volks have existed from the premodern to the modern age serves to further cloud our perceptions. From this perspective, some have contended that the word "state" can be applied only to the modern state as it is defined in legal terms, and that the word "polity" should be used for premodern times.[18] It seems that they also center their argument on modernity.

The word *gukga* (state) has been used from antiquity using Chinese characters 國家—as seen in such phrases as *godae gukga* (ancient states) or *geundae gukga* (modern states). Therefore, it is unreasonable to limit the use of this word only to modern states. In addition to these linguistic customs, other elements have also endured despite changes in human civilization. For example, whatever definition we give to the "state," the factor of a "power system which has legal force and is formed within the boundaries of a certain area and based on social relationships other than blood ties," is immanent in the concept of state. Even though this factor is meaningful in highlighting the differences between primitive societies and ancient kingdoms, it is not so useful in showing the differences between modern nation-states and premodern states. However, this factor is common to states of all periods. The factors' form and appear-

---

18. Im Ji-hyeon, "Hanguk sahakgye-ui minjok ihae-e daehan bipanjeok geomto" (A Critical Investigation about Understanding of *Minjok* in Academic Circles of Korean History), *Yeoksa bipyeong* (fall 1994).

ances differ with each age and in each country. These differences are represented by which adjective precedes the word "state." Thus, history is both the process of change and accumulation.

Next, some assert that it is problematic to give a premodern date for the formation of the Korean *minjok* because a modern concept of *minjok* was applied to premodern history, resulting in the error of transhistorical interpretation. To some extent, these criticisms are valid. However, what is necessary is not the proof of error in the premodern formation theory, but rather the error inherent in explaining the existing differences between premodern and modern period Volk. At the same time, to ignore the meaning and function of the *minjok* in the premodern age, taking only modern Volk as the standard, is ahistorical. These elements help us to understand East Asia's premodern history, in which the domain of each ethnic group coincided with the territory of each state, and in which for over a thousand years people shared common languages and common ways of life as a historical and cultural unit.

Now, I would like to conclude this article by making some brief comments on the formation process of the Korean *minjok*.

Conclusion

Human groups sharing a similar lifestyle are observable in the clan or tribal stages of a society, so that when we classify a clan or a tribe with similar cultural traits into one unit, someone will call it a *minjok*. However, during the age of hunting and gathering, communities did not have any consciousness of being one Volk. This is because their lives were based on communal relationships, kinships, and marriage relations, and these were central to the fundamental principles that kept their communities moving.

We must consider how the formation of a state contributed to the formation of "we-consciousness," as well as a common culture, by going beyond the idea of kinship. A state is built on the foundation of secondary social relationships, not just on blood relationships existing within a certain boundary. The state integrates residents into its domain, and assimilates their languages and cultures. Symbolic systems such as myths presenting the community's common wishes and rituals were created for this purpose. These systems, coupled with the goal of eulogizing the king's legitimacy and dignity, were even further expanded through grand ceremonies. Through this process, tribes which formed ancient states began to share the "we-consciousness" of being one *minjok*.

However, during the early stages, such consciousness was limited only to the main tribes of the states. Minor groups subjugated under the kingdom's rule were still considered different. This was only a fragmentary and primary step in the formation of a *minjok*. This was true during the Old Joseon and the early stages of the Three Kingdoms period.

As the Three Kingdoms developed, communal relationships in villages and kin groups became severed due to increases in productivity, wars, and other activities. The result was that the kingdoms began to be ruled by law and to be administered by the *gun-hyeon* system—the system in which officials dispatched from the central government govern local administrative units such as prefectures and counties. Also, there was a large mobilization of military forces composed of farmers. Wars frequently broke out. In the meantime, at least as far as material culture goes, common features began to develop between the people residing in each territory. For example, pottery styles were standardized in Silla from the sixth century. On the one hand, from the end of the Three Kingdoms period, customs, institutions, and clothing were nearly identical because of mutual exchanges and territorial shifts. For that reason, people outside of the three kingdoms designated the inhabitants of the three kingdoms as one people and "named" them *sanhan* (Chinese, "three Korean peoples").

Or, it might have been that the consciousness of being the same ethnicity did not exist among the people of the Three Kingdoms. Such a consciousness did begin to arise, however, following a dispute with Tang China after 668, and during the last stages of the unification war. Silla made claims for a single ethnicity out of the realistic necessities accompanying unification under its leadership. This is the consciousness that understood the people of the three kingdoms as one. "Naming themselves" and "being named by others" began to correspond at that time. Under Unified Silla's centralized rule over two hundred years, many common features began to be seen across the peninsula, with the initiation of central governing systems such as the *gun-hyeon* system and the *gyeolbuje* system (system of taxation based on measures of yields and arable land). Cultural fusion took place through exchanges between inhabitants of Unified Silla, and through the spread of Buddhism by building monasteries and advocating an open doctrine of the Buddha-nature. In the process of these changes, "we-consciousness" was diffused. However, the people of Baekje and Goguryeo, alienated politically and economically, could only assume a passive role. More or less, they continued to maintain separate consciousness about their origins. Later, at the end of the Unified Silla period, those emotions erupted in the form of peasant uprisings which marked the beginning of the Later Three Kingdoms period.

Goryeo, which united the Later Three Kingdoms, was established as a joint political regime by the local gentry from local communities throughout the country. That means political participation expanded, which continued as this enabled the wealthy, higher-classes to take the civil service examination. This had great meaning in respect to the spread of "we-consciousness." On the other hand, in early Goryeo, Balhae residents—more than five percent of Goryeo's population—wept into Koryeo. This fact is important, not only because the Balhae people originated from Goguryeo, but because there was never such a massive influx of people after that. Moreover, Korea's fundamental pattern of living space was actually set in the Goryeo era. The dialect of 'the central area of the peninsula came to be the foundation of the medieval language which was to be the direct ancestor of modern Korean. This supports the theory which says the Korean premodern *minjok* was formed in the early Goryeo era.

After this time, it can be said that Korean history was in the process of transition from premodern to modern *minjok*. Both specially and socially, it was also the full integration and expansion of the "we-consciousness."

Spatially, even during the Goryeo period, vestiges of separate consciousness derived from the Three Kingdoms period still remained in the hearts of Goryeo people, though it weakened significantly. These vestiges were eliminated and a new "group-consciousness" was formed during the approximately thirty-year struggle with the Mongols in the late Goryeo period. Included in this new consciousness was the inherited idea that the more than seventy countries of the Three Han were all the offspring of Dangun, as related in the "Dangun bon-gi" (Chronological Narrative of Dangun), which is considered to have been written during the struggle with the Mongols.

Socially, on the other hand, Korean history was in the process of overcoming the discrimination in the social status system. Over time, consciousness of social status was overcome in the process of continuous changes in society as well as through the rapid and painful changes following the opening of the ports to foreign influence, which resulted in the formation of a modern *minjok* in the twentieth century.

Investigating the formation of a *minjok* by using only political changes centered around the upper calss—such as establishment and development of a state, integration between countries, or a change of regime—as bases, may fail to address the oppressed people and their living conditions. In this case, "the advances of fusion into a *minjok*" might be no more than a rhetoric. To supplement such deficiency in discussing the formation of a *minjok*, further study is needed in the field of social history, cultural history, and regional history.

Formation of the Ethnic Korean Nation and the Emergence of Its Ancient Kingdom States

Kim Jung Bae

I

In the discussion of Korea's prehistoric culture and ancient history, much attention has been given to the starting point or the formative process of our nation as a state. Out of proportion to the extent of raised interests, our study has encountered much frustration and difficulty. Under the Japanese rule, for instance, official Japanese scholars not only distrusted the account of *Samguk sagi* (Historical Records of the Three Kingdoms) but chronicled the period of the formation of ancient Korean states in the third to fourth century, in an attempt to obliterate the first part of Korea's ancient history. Again, they lowered the upper ceiling of Korean history by negating or distorting prehistoric culture since the Paleolithic Age.

Despite such distortion, advances made in the field of archaeology and efforts made by concerned scholars in the postliberation era came to affirm and verify the traces of Paleolithic culture on the Korean peninsula. Though the range in chronicle concerning the beginning of Korea's ancient history was thus extended, the question of the origin and formation of the state still remains unanswered.

* Originally published in the *Korea Journal*, vol. 27, no. 4 (April 1987).

Kim Jung Bae (Kim, Jeong-bae) is Professor of Korean History at Korea University. He received his Ph.D. in History from Korea University in 1975. His publications include *Hanguk minjok munhwa-ui giwon* (The Origin of Korean Ethnic Group and Its Culture) (1973), *Hanguk godae-ui gukga giwon-gwa hyeongseong* (The Origin and Formation of the Ancient Korean State) (1986), and "On the Origin of Korean Bronze Culture" (in Korean) (1979). E-mail: chyum@korea.ac.kr.

Paucity in the source of historical and bibliographical materials is one reason. Other reasons may stem from the scholars' attempts to fill in the paucity of historical materials with assumed logic, failure of interpreting the relevant archeological remains, or questionable research methodology still remaining from the Japanese colonial scholarship. An upward extension in the ladder of history's chronicle does not necessarily date back the formation of ethnic Korean nation in the same proportion. Rather, in parallel with strict verification of bibliographical data, meanings of historical relics and remains of the prehistoric age have to be exactly analyzed. As for the issues remaining in ambiguity, theories of related disciplines have to be used for the sake of getting a clearer picture of the beginning of Korea's ancient history.

The writer has endeavored to comprehend the beginning of Korea's history, keeping such points in mind, from such bibliographical materials as the myth of Dangun, Old Joseon, the Three Han and so on. These periods correspond to the dawning of Korea's history in terms of ethnic and cultural bearings, shedding light on the ethnic origin of Korean culture of today. The origin of the states in the history of Korea can be dated either corresponding to or ahead of these periods.

II

In discussing the origin of ethnic Korean culture, one tends to think that a single nation and its culture have uninterruptedly continued since the "founding" by Dangun as described in records as *Samguk yusa* (Memorabilia of the Three Kingdoms). Of course, there is no arguing that Korea, as a single entity, has inherited and developed its culture since the beginning of its history. However, if accounts on Dangun Joseon are not to be regarded merely as a myth, a more detailed examination of this point is required in discussing the Korean ethnic and cultural origin.

In Chinese old sources, Yemaek, Han, and others are listed as the ethnic ancestors of Koreans. The age of Yemaek, either called Ye or Maek according to its geographical distribution as the same ethnic group, corresponds to the Bronze Age in the archeological chronicle. On the other hand, Korea's prehistoric culture started with the Paleolithic Age (Old Stone Age), and Dangun Joseon appears prior to the Yemaek in the historical accounts. In other words, the question raised here is: In case the Yemaek are to be seen as the ancestor of Koreans, the inhabitants and culture that preceded Yemaek may have to be seen as of early settlers in the Korean peninsula. Discussion of the history and culture of a certain area harks back to the culture of the Paleolithic Age, but discussion on the origin and ancestry of a nation as an ethnic group does not regard men of the Paleolithic Age as a straight-line ancestry, for there is a considerable span of time between the Paleolithic Age and the Neolithic Age, with the glacial epoch set in between. In this context, the fact that the period of Dangun Joseon corresponds to the archeological chronicle of the Neolithic Age presents a clue. So far, we have perceived prehistoric relics and remains as directly relevant to the inhabitants who show up in the course of history. Or, due to prejudice or a vague conception of Korea's homogeneous ethnicity since the days of Dangun, we could not surmise the heterogeneous element that might have existed between the two, or the dual structure in the composition of its inhabitants. Surveys of Neolithic Age culture show a wide-ranged geographical distribution of its representative relics and patterned pottery, scattered from Finland to the Korean peninsula via Siberia. Though there is some variation in patterns and styles in the artifacts from one region to another, these relics and sites are located mostly by the riverbanks and seashore, illustrating life patterns based on fishing, hunting, and food-gathering cultures.

V. G. Childe, in his archeological chronicle for Northern Europe and the Near East, characterized the Neolithic Age (New Stone Age) culture as the "Neolithic Revolution" based on the agricultural food production. However, the Neolithic Age in Korea had not reached this stage. Though there are some partial traces of farming, the agricultural food production in Korea took place in the Bronze Age. Thus, I classify the Neolithic people as the primary inhabitants in Korea and as the group that diverged from ancient Asian tribes. Because the comb-pattern pottery culture, found scattered widely throughout Siberia, is also related to that of Korea and such observation is verifiable in the light of the findings made by Russian academic circles which maintain that ancient Asian tribes, still extant today in some Maritime Province of Siberia, are descendants from the Neolithic culture of Siberia.

If the earlier inhabitants of Neolithic Age culture in Korea were to be seen as a branch from the ancient Asian tribes, Dangun Joseon can be understood in this historical context—as an entity that existed in the Neolithic Age. Though the question related to Dangun's "founding of a nation" will be discussed later in relation to the nation origins, the meanings associated with it have to be interpreted as reflecting its contemporary historical time, not merely as a mythical story.

In this case, the bear cult in the Dangun myth attracts our attention. The bear cult shows up in the late Zhou dynasty in China, and is noted as the characteristic of totemism practiced by the ancient Asian tribes of the Neolithic culture. Thus, the Neolithic Age overlaps "nation-founding" of Dangun Joseon. In the light of the similarity between the totemism practiced by ancient Asian tribes of the Neolithic culture and the bear cult in the myth of Dangun, I take them as an entity in Dangun Joseon and as earlier inhabitants in the line of Korean culture. A note of caution is that we must avoid the assumption that the Neolithic Age was culturally primitive. Since the Neolithic Age spanned over many thousands of years, one should not, in oversimplification, regard it operating at a low cultural stage.

The Neolithic Age develops into an entirely different society, called the Bronze Age, by the thirteenth-twelfth centuries B.C. The Bronze Age culture in Siberia was moving from Andronovo to Karassuk culture. It was the time when Yin perished in China and Gija Joseon was established in Korea. As pointed out earlier, the history of China consider the inhabitants in the Bronze Age culture as the Yemaek. Based on this, I name Gija Joseon as Yemaek Joseon and regard its culture as belonging to Bronze Age culture, thus stressing the role-bearers of its culture in the discussion of questions related to Old Joseon.

One of the representative relics of Bronze Age culture is the nondecorated pottery. This pottery, made by other inhabitants separate from the Neolithic people, has been unearthed from the wide hilly terrains of Korean peninsular along with farming tools. This indicates that the Altaic people Yemaek excelled among the ancient Asian tribes in food production, as the bearers of the Bronze Age culture, and were the matrix for Korean ethnicity by accommodating and assimilating those around them.

In this period, a number of social groups were settled within the realm of Korea. What were recorded in history with distinction from among them were the Old Joseon and the Three Han.

The relevance of Chinese culture on the cultures in Korean peninsular may be questioned in the relation between the Bronze Age culture of China's Yin dynasty and the "eastward movement of Gija." Generally, one tends to think that Korean culture was closely associated with that of China since the beginning of its history. However, the comb-pattern or nondecorated pottery excavated in Korean peninsular are different from those of Chinese central regions in their lineage and style. Again, the dolmen tombs (*jiseongmyo*) and stone-cist tombs (*seokgwanmyo*) as the representative burial mode of the Bronze Age do not appear in the central regions of China.

However, distribution of the Yemaek people coincides with that of dolmen tombs, indicating that they must have settled ranging from Shandong to Liaodong, to Manchuria, to the Korean peninsula. The stone-cist tombs they left behind are found concentrated in the northeastern region of the Korean peninsula, and also centered around the Liaodong region. This reveals a cultural lineage separate from that of China, when compared to the Bronze Age culture of Siberia. Furthermore, "violin-shaped bronze dagger" (*bipahyeong donggeom*), "slender Korean-style bronze dagger" (*sehyeong donggeom*), "mold" (*yongbeom*), "polished stone dagger" (*maje seokgeom*) and others unearthed from these tombs are relics originally found in Korea. The fact that zinc is found in bronze articles is quite suggestive that the Bronze Age culture in Korea had its own origin and an independent culture.

In historical accounts, the first clash between Korea and China took place in the period of Yan. From then on, the Iron Age culture of China seems to have entered the Korean peninsula as evidenced from the "earthen tombs" (*togwangmyo*) and "knife-shaped coin" (*mingdaoqian*) belonging to the Warring States period. However, earthen tombs as the representative burial mode of the Iron Age culture of Korea, corresponding to the period of Wiman Joseon, can be verified as belonging to the cultural lineage of Yemaek Joseon rather those of the Iron Age culture of China. Since the unearthing of knife-shaped coin is confined to the northern area of Cheongcheongang river, its presence seems to have been a result of trade with China rather than the influx of Chinese Iron Age culture. Furthermore, findings in current research indicate that the chronicle of the Iron Age for the Maritime Province of Siberia and Heilongjiang river date further back than for China. Again in the light of the northeastern concentrated distribution of the Iron Age in Korea, there will be no needs to compare the chronicle of the Iron Age in Korea to that of China.

After all, the origin of Korean culture and ethnicity may have to be sought in the internal development which must have taken place after Dangun Joseon vis-à-vis the rise of Yemaek Joseon. In other words, the formation of the Korean nation, beginning with the rise of the Yemaek tribes, may date from thirteenth to twelfth centuries B.C.—the opening stage of the Bronze Age—in its accommodating and assimilating of the earlier settlers, maintaining the cultural and ethnic line as a nation. Cultural complexity and dual composition of inhabitants against such backgrounds must have provided the basic foundation of the Korean nation, adhering to the backbone of its ethnic culture through assimilation despite the influx of emigrants and culture from China from then on.

Against the background of the ethnic formation and its cultural heritage, another question to be addressed concerns the origin of the nation as a state. Its political development used to be described in terms of the "tribal states," "tribal confederation," or "ancient states" beginning in the Three Kingdoms period. However, the term, "tribe" (*bujok*) is self-contradictory in that the concept of the "state" (*gukga*) cannot be induced therefrom. Even if we take due consideration of such an evolutionary concept, the stage of "tribal states" or "tribal confederation" cannot be applied to Old Joseon or to the Three Han. Such an erroneous approach seems to ensue either from the unwillingness to see historical data and materials more in the perspective of progress or from an excessive inclination to relate the ideological aspect in the inflow of Buddhism to the state power.

Any discussion of the origin and formation of the state has to start with its definition. There has been no consensus, however, reached on the definition and many views have been developed on the formation of the state based on insufficient materials. Anthropology is applying many modern concepts such as "territory, sovereignty, and people," but they are not absolute determinants applicable to the ancient society.

The theory on the origin of the state offers "conflict" and "integration" on a wider assumption on one hand, and "conquest," "struggle," and "marginal territory" on a narrower scale on the other. However, one particular theory cannot be applied uniformly to all regions and to all ages, since there are variations in regions and periods. Thus, a "state" is defined, in general, in terms of diverse social hierarchy, security, political institutions, territory, performance of external relations, rise of social authority or legitimate exercise of power, execution of administration by bureaucrats and so on.

On the other hand, the archeological chronicle is against placing the formation of the state of ancient society after the Neolithic Age, since the Neolithic culture was at the stage of a full-scale food production. Therefore, discussion of the state origin in the history of Korea has to start, for the time being, from the cultural base of the Bronze Age.

Thus seen, the "nation-founding" in the myth of Dangun, if interpreted as the birth of the nation or as a story holding Dangun as a king, cannot but be an argument beside the point. Likewise, the more than seventy "states" that existed in the Three Han region should not be understood vaguely in the sense of the state without considering their genuine characteristics. For, the origin or the founding process of a state cannot be presented without an account preceding and following its birth. On this point, we have to give more weight to the emerging process than to the mere fact of its emergence.

Then, what stage has to be postulated for the periods preceding the formation of the state in the Korean history? In regards to this point, I have earlier postulated the concept of "chiefdom" employing the theory of E. R. Service. An indiscriminate introduction and the use of foreign theories must be cautioned. Nevertheless, I dared to follow his theory because not only his model of developmental stage was seen applicable to the early ancient society of Korea, but also the term "chief" (*gunjang*) was used in bibliographical records to indicate social loaders, prior to the emergence of kings. In this regard, a term "walled-town state" (*seongeup gukga*) has been proposed as an alternative. The Korean term contains the meaning of "state," and it furthermore insinuates the Western concept of the "city-state." Then, the term needs to be bolstered with practical theory before it is applied to the case of Korea.

With the postulation of the stage of chiefs and chiefdoms placed before the stage of kingdoms, society then can be related to the Iron Age culture, at least, based on the Bronze Age culture. This is the period when the differing dating in the chronicle of, and the differing strength among, groups can be revealed in relics unearthed from such historical sites as stone-cist tombs, and this stage seems to coincide right with the Three Han that appear in records.

According to historical records such as *Sanguozhi* (The History of the Three Kingdoms) there were a little over seventy "states" in the Three Han. There was size variance but in the case of a big "chiefdom," its population seems to have been around 10,000–15,000. Population of this size just corresponds to the size of a chiefdom, and relics unearthed from earthen tombs indicate that the Iron Age culture was set amid remnants of the Bronze Age culture. There is a strong possibility that such big "chiefdoms" were forerunners in forming the state. In the case of Saro, it is understood that a state as a political entity must have bean formed, centering around six influential villages, by handling external relations and internal development via the "chiefdom" stage. After all, chiefdoms in the Three Han seem to have been of such characteristics and their rulers seem to have been those buried in stone-cist tombs, where a set of daggers, mirrors, and jade have been unearthed.

On the other hand, the case of Yemaek Joseon also follows similar rationale. Its verification is possible in relation to the Bronze Age culture even though there is no existing record concerning it in relation to the stage of chiefdoms. Stepping into the Bronze Age, roles are differentiated, among political and religious leaders, and social functions begin to diversify with food surplus resulting from farming and cattle raising.

Furthermore, entering into the latter period of the Bronze Age, bronze daggers, bronze mirrors, and jade were unearthed from stone-cist tombs, and this seems to indicate the enhanced prestige attached to rulers and the practice of a variety of rites that should have been performed.

The change in the title of king, from *hu* to *wang*, in the latter part of Yemaek Joseon means that it had already shifted from the stage of a "chiefdom" to that of a state at the time. Thus, the history of the period centering around King Jun, the latest king of Yemaek Joseon, seems to correspond, in terms of its political stage, to the period of the pristine State. This period should have begun, at the latest, by fourth to third centuries B.C.

If so, the entity of a state in more substantive terms may have to be sought in Wiman Joseon which emerged from driving out Yemaek Joseon by force. According to *Gogi* (Old Record), Wiman Joseon resisted invasion from the Han China, armed in equivalent military power. Its strength, the existence of official functionaries as recorded in bibliographical data, and the fact that a war arose from increased pressure due to population growth within a limited territory of Wiman Joseon—all suffice to picture Wiman Joseon as a conqueror's state. This is the very point we should focus on our discussions about the origin of the state in the course of Korean history.

III

In addition to the foregoing discussions, the question about the horse-riders sometimes arises concerning the early ancient history of Korea. Trappings for carts and horses, as initial relics to be associated with the question on horse riders, are being excavated from earthen tombs and their distribution is clearly divided between the north and the south with the Hangang river as a center. This question may have to be studied, not in terms of the ethnicity, but of a nation as a political entity. Therefore, discussions of the Three Kingdoms should be made not in terms of the nation or the state but in terms of the military system or military tactics.

After all, the origin of the ethnic culture of Koreans has to be sought from the Old Joseon, and the formation of the state has to be considered to have followed the stage of chiefdoms in its internal development and in its conquering character. When historical data and relics are examined in this light, meanings hidden in the data and the distribution map of unearthed relics may coincide with chronological compilation and with the regional territory in the early ancient history of Korea.

Prehistoric Rock Art in Korea:
Ban-gudae

Werner Sasse

Every visitor to Korea who has enough sense to leave the hustle and bustle of the metropolitan city of Seoul, where the special features of the Korean culture are sometimes too difficult to detect under the surface of this modern international city, will as the next "must" on his itinerary travel to Gyeongju. There, in the ancient capital of Silla, which flourished until the tenth century, he will much more easily find glimpses of the charm and artistry of Korea's glorious tradition. The sheer number and the splendor of the colorful temples, the tumuli graves of majestic size, the works of sculpture like the buddhas or the zodiac animals in human clothing, the parks and castles, will make the visitor understand why his Korean friends are so proud of their history and long cultural heritage.

Information and tourist guidance will be easily available for the visitor to Gyeongju. But neither the friends who may have advised him to visit Gyeongju, nor a travel agent or the tourist guide will normally direct the visitor to a place nearby where he could see two monuments of a different and much earlier art in Korea, which are still fairly unknown outside specialists' circles and which actually should be made known to the world as outstanding examples of their kind: the rock art panels of Ban-gudae and Cheonjeon-ri.

---

* Originally published in the *Korea Journal*, vol. 36, no. 2 (summer 1996).

Werner Sasse is Head of Korean Studies Section, University of Hamburg, Germany. He has written many monographs, articles, and book reviews on Korean philology, including "Dialect Studies in North Korea" (1980), "Minjung Theory and Culture" (1988) and "The Silla Stone Inscription form Naengsuri, Yonggil-gun" (1991). His present research interests lie in comparing Korean with German cultural history. E-mail: Werner.Sasse@ uni-hamburg.de.

The monuments in question are presumed to be Neolithic or early Bronze Age rock art. True, these works of art are in a way only loosely related with Korean culture, because they are prehistoric and have been left by a people whose culture in later times underwent many revolutionary changes before the Korean culture we know today was created. It may even be that the people who created these masterworks became extinguished when the forefathers of today's Koreans moved into the peninsula, at least they were completely absorbed during the formation of the Korean people. From this point of view, this early rock art could be labeled non-Korean or, rather, pre-Korean art. Viewed from another perspective, however, the prehistory is still somehow connected with the later Korean people. The Neolithic and Bronze Age settlers formed the basis for later developments, and therefore evidence of the material culture and art still surviving today should be taken best care of and held in high esteem, and should also be presented with pride to tourists traveling with an interest in Korea's cultural monuments.

When the visitor has seen the Silla and later monuments, parks, ponds, temples, and mountain fortresses of Gyeongju he could, for instance, take a bus or a train heading south and proceed to the small town of Eonyang, from where it will be a twenty-minute taxi ride to Cheonjeon-ri, and slightly less to Ban-gudae.

Ban-gudae is located at the upper end of the Sayeondam lake, which was built to supply water for the nearby industrial city of Ulsan. With their tranquility and natural beauty, the steep valleys formed by the Taehwagang river and its tributaries, cut deep into wooded mountains, were a favorite place of reclusion among the literati during Goryeo and Joseon times, and scribbling engraved on some rocks in the area attest to already members of the Silla nobility having come here for leisure: an area famous through all of Korea's history.

But with respect to the prehistoric rock art at Ban-gudae a warning is due. The area is worth visiting for its natural beauty all year round, but anyone coming specifically to see the rock art should choose late winter or spring for his visit. The reason is that only when the waters of the Sayeondam are low the rock art can be seen, while the rains of summer filling the dam will put this outstanding example of prehistoric art some one or two meters below water!

I

Before introducing the panel at Ban-gudae in greater detail, a summary of all rock art sites in Korea may be helpful. In these short introductory notes on the rock art of Korea I will purposely concentrate on sites with larger panels carrying motifs in many variations. Additionally to the sites to be introduced here there are also a number of similar but much smaller pieces of rock art. For the time being, however, they would ask for separate treatment before they can be compared with the rock art presented here. The motifs are different, small geometric patterns, cup marks, or pictures of a dagger, and also the size and occasionally the setting is different, because some of them are carved on rocks used in the construction of dolmens. For these reasons they may not fit into the same category as large panels on rocks which are left unmoved in their natural surroundings.

Up to now 9 sites with larger panels of rock art have been found, which can be grouped according to the motifs depicted. They are usually referred to by the names of the small administrational areas where they are situated,[1] of which the full addresses are shown in Table 1.

Table 1. Sites with Prehistoric Rock Art in Korea[2]

A. motif I:	animals, human figures, hunting
	#1. Gyeongsangnam-do, Ulju-gun, Eonyang-myeon, Daegok-ri, Ban-gudae
B. motif II:	lozenges, spirals, concentric circles, zigzags, and other more or less geometrical patterns (with animals, human figures and Chinese characters added at a later period).
	# 2. Gyeongsangnam-do, Ulju-gun, Dudong-myeon, Cheonjeon-ri
C. motif III:	face-like, mask, anthropoid or sun god figures
	# 3. Gyeongsangbuk-do, Goryeong-gun, Gaejin-myeon, Yangjeon-ri
	# 4. Gyeongsangbuk-do, Goryeong-gun, Ssangnim-myeon, Anhwa-ri
	# 5. Gyeongsangbuk-do, Yeongju-si, Gaheung-dong
	# 6. Gyeongsangbuk-do, Yeongil-gun, Heunghae-eup, Chilpo-ri
	# 7. Jeollabuk-do, Namwon-gun, Daesan-myeon, Daegok-ri
	# 8. Gyeongsangbuk-do, Yeongcheon-gun, Cheongtong-myeon, Boseong-ri
	# 9. Gyeongsangbuk-do, Gyeongju-si, Seokjang-dong

---

1. Sites # 1 and # 7 are both situated in the Daegok-ri region. Site # 1 is generally identified as Ban-gudae, which is a small local area within the Daegok-ri region.
2. The addresses in Korean and Sino-Korean scripts are as follows:

Figure 1. Location of rock art sites on the Korean peninsula

When we look at the geographical distribution of the rock art found in Korea up to now, we can observe that all of them are found in the two southern provinces of Gyeongsang-do and Jeolla-do, and the only site in Jeolla-do is situated very close just behind the provincial boundary between the two. It is obviously only the southeastern part of the penin-

---

#1 경상남도 울주군 언양면 대곡리 반구대 慶尙南道 蔚州郡 彦陽面 大谷里 盤龜臺
#2 경상남도 울주군 두동면 천전리 慶尙南道 蔚州郡 斗東面 川前里
#3 경상북도 고령군 개진면 양전리 慶尙北道 高靈郡 開津面 良田里
#4 경상북도 고령군 쌍림면 안화리 慶尙北道 高靈郡 雙林面 安和里
#5 경상북도 영주시 가흥동 慶尙北道 榮州市 可興洞
#6 경상북도 영일군 흥해읍 칠포리 慶尙北道 迎日郡 興海邑 七浦里
#7 전라북도 남원군 대산면 대곡리 全羅北道 南原郡 大山面 大谷里
#8 경상북도 영천군 청통면 보성리 慶尙北道 永川郡 靑通面 甫城里
#9 경상북도 경주시 석장동 慶尙北道 慶州市 錫杖洞

sula, and more precisely the Nakdonggang river basin, where rock art has been found. Another observation points to the vicinity of rivers which seems to be connected with the sites, but it is not quite clear whether this has simply to do with the geographical features of the area concerned, or whether this is of significance when an interpretation of the pictures as to their meaning or economical and social setting is attempted.

Comparisons of styles and techniques have led to the generally accepted theory that the Korean rock art dates from Neolithic and Bronze Age cultural layers, but the comparisons do not yet seem to be based on sufficient data and there is still room for doubt.

In this connection it is especially the so-called "x-ray style" found in Ban-gudae, which could engender rethinking, and therefore this article puts special stress on this site (Fig. 2).

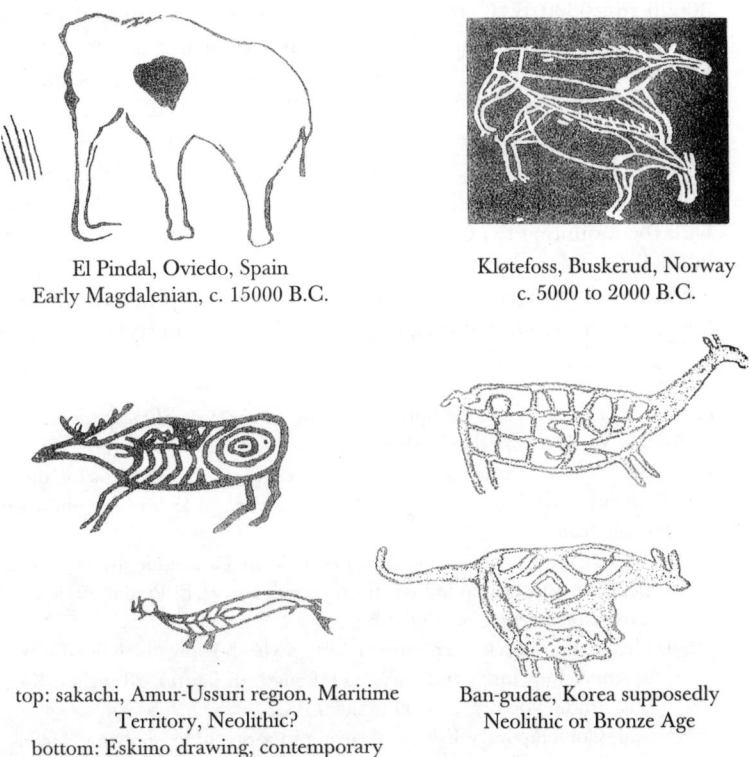

El Pindal, Oviedo, Spain
Early Magdalenian, c. 15000 B.C.

Kløtefoss, Buskerud, Norway
c. 5000 to 2000 B.C.

top: sakachi, Amur-Ussuri region, Maritime
Territory, Neolithic?
bottom: Eskimo drawing, contemporary

Ban-gudae, Korea supposedly
Neolithic or Bronze Age

Figure 2. Animals in x-ray style

The x-ray style, i.e. an outline with lines and lined patterns inside, has been said to have started in Spain as early as in Paleolithic, and not Neolithic, times about 15.000 B.C., and spread practically all over the world, where it is still in use in various art traditions from Eurasia, America, and Africa.

One interesting summary of two extensive West-East migrations from Europe via Siberia to America will engage the attention of anyone researching into the prehistory of Korea, because elements of early Korean culture can be connected with the main cultural characteristics of both migrations mentioned:[3]

> During the relatively warmer season of the so-called Aurignacian Oscillations, from c. 40000 to 30000 B.C., the rising waters of the Pacific submerged the landbridges, and both America and Australia, as well as Japan, were for a time cut off. However, with the return of the cold, c. 30000 to 20000 B.C., the ocean levels dropped again and the landbridges reappeared. The oldest known site in northeastern Siberia, Ust'Nil' (59° 45′ N, 133° 00′ E), in central Yakutia, is radiocarbon-dated to this period (c. 33400 to 28000 B.C.). And it was then that tools of Mousteroid type were carried to America. But at the maximum of this increasing freeze, c. 18000 B.C. (Map 11, p. 35), the American glaciers closed the corridor from Alaska to the Plains; and it was only with the mounting temperatures of the terminal Pleistocene, c. 11000 to 8000 B.C. (Map 12, p. 35), that the passage opened again and an advanced Aurignacoid industry was brought in, presently to be followed by the creators of rock engravings in the x-ray style.

---

3. The quote is from Joseph Campbell, *The Way of the Animal Powers*, vol. 1 of *Historical Atlas of World Mythology* (Nashville, Tenn.: Vanderbilt University, Dept. of Environmental & Water Resources Engineering, 1988), p. 133. Except for the examples from Ban-gudae the illustrations are taken from *ibid.*, p. 132. In full quote the respective captions read:

    227. Earliest known intimation of x-ray style in Paleolithic art. Mammoth (or elephant, Elephas antiquus), from corridor cave El Pindal, Oviedo, Spain. Early Magdalenian, c. 15000 B.C.

    229. Elks mating. Rock engraving in x-ray style showing "lifeline" (from mouth to stomach or lung) and vertebrae. Length of figures, 28 inches. Kløtefoss, Buskerud, Norway, c. 5000 to 2000 B.C.

    230. Seal. Contemporary Eskimo drawing in x-ray style, showing "lifeline" and ribs. Alaska.

    231. Reindeer. Rock engraving in x-ray style, showing ribs. Sakachi, Amur-Ussuri region, Maritime Territory, USSR.

Thus there were two distinct tool traditions carried across northern Asia and through Beringland to the Americas during and immediately following the long course of the Riss-Würm glaciation: the first, a Mousteroid tradition, and the second, Aurignacoid. With the first there must have traveled knowledge of the Neanderthal cult of the Master Bear, for it has left its unmistakable traces the entire length of the way. And with the second, we must assume, there traveled not only an interest in the x-ray style of animal art, but also knowledge (or at least some portion of knowledge) of the shamanistic myths and rites of the great French and Spanish caves out of which that art style took its rise. For like the bear cult, shamanism is an essential constituent of the lore of the Hyperboreans—those Dwellers beyond the North Wind who remained settled along the Arctic way from Lapland, Norway, and Finland to Kamchatka and Alaska.

The bear cult of the first migration may be connected with the Dangun myth, today the most important foundation myth of Korea, and in respect to the second migration, shamanism is still alive in Korea today, and the x-ray style can be found at Ban-gudae (but only here in such a great variety!). The interesting question is: is Korea the southern most extension of the great prehistoric cultural unit of the Arctic Circle known up to now? This question will be left open for the moment, but the immense importance of Ban-gudae, Korea's only rock art panel with x-ray style, cannot but make it necessary to save the monument from destruction.

Roughly speaking there are two styles in Korean rock art: the first may be called "silhouette" style. In this style the full area of the motif is covered, sometimes with an outline carved deeper than the area of the silhouette. The second style, figures drawn with an outline and some lined pattern within, has been called "x-ray style". These two styles may come in the same panel, but in that case they usually have a tendency to be spread unevenly over the panel and form clusters in one part of the composition. It is not yet clear whether both styles were employed at the same time, or whether they may turn out to have been used at different periods (Fig. 3).

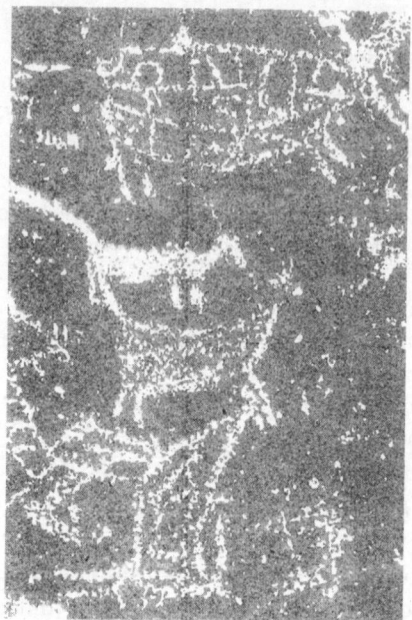

Figure 3. Stone rubbings of "silhouette" style (center) and
"x-ray" style (top and bottom). From Ban-gudae

With regard to techniques, there are three different ones employed in
Korean prehistoric art: pecking, grinding and engraving. Pecking, normally about 1 cm deep, was used both for filling the silhouettes and for
carving lines, 1-3 cm wide, c. 1 cm deep and U-shaped. The lines of the
engraving technique are thinner, not more than 1 cm wide, and usually
less than 1 cm deep. They may be U-shaped or V-shaped, in which latter case probably a metal tool was used. Grinding was used for lines
only, normally much rougher and resembling the techniques used for
cup marks on some rocks and some dolmen, which are distributed over
the entire peninsula.

Much more detailed research is necessary with respect to styles and
techniques, but in a preliminary and general way the distribution can be
summarized as Table 2.[4]

---

4. Im Se-gwon, "Hanguk seonsa sidae amgakhwa-ui seonggyeok" (The Nature of Rock
   Art in the Prehistoric Age of Korea) (Ph.D. diss., Danguk University, 1994), p. 24.

Table 2. Styles and Techniques Found in Rock Art on the Korean Peninsula

	silhouettes		x-ray style		
	pecking	grinding	pecking	grinding	engraving
# 1.	x		x	x	
# 2.	x		x	x	x
# 3.		x	x	x	
# 4.			x		
# 5.				x	
# 6.			x	x	
# 7.				x	
# 8.			x		
# 9.	x		x		

Of these techniques pecking and grinding seem to stem from prehistoric times, and it is not clear yet whether they were employed at the same time. Only the engraving of thin lines seems to be a later technique to judge from the motifs (e.g. the dresses can be dated) and the sketchy execution of the pictures, cf. the following detail from Cheonjeon-ri. In addition to that there are also inscriptions in Chinese characters engraved in thin lines, which by definition do not date from prehistoric times (Fig. 4).[5]

Figure 4. Details from Cheonjeon-ri in sketchy thin lines

5. Hwang Su-yeong and Mun Myeong-dae, *Ban-gudae ambyeok jogak* (Rock Sculptures on Ban-gudae) (Seoul: Dongguk University Press, 1984), p. 178 f.

The motifs on the panels of Group C (#3–#9) are the ones that are most difficult to interpret, and all the suggestions made have an air of arbitrariness. However, they definitely seem to be variations of the same idea, as can be seen from a chart comparing basic forms (Fig. 5).[6]

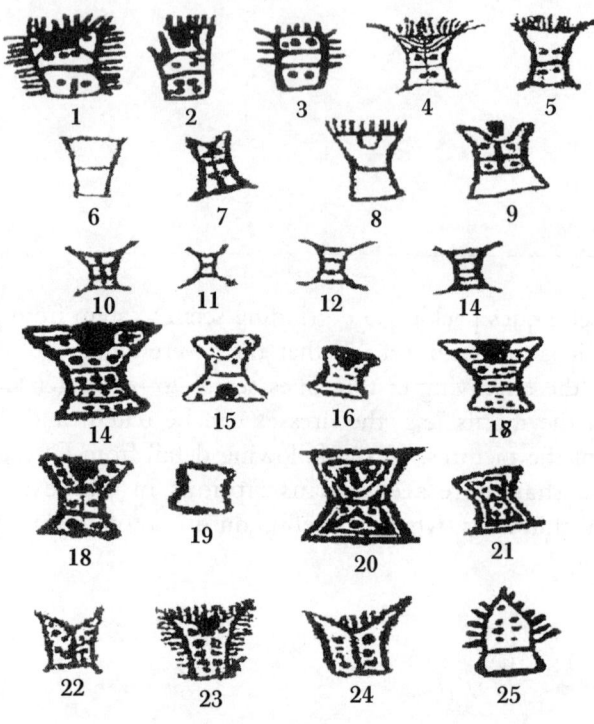

Figure 5. Comparison of basic forms of motif III
(face-like, mask, anthropoid or sun god figures)

1– 3 : # 3. Gyeongsangbuk-do, Goryeong-gun, Gaejin-myeon, Yangjeon-ri
4– 7 : # 8. Gyeongsangbuk-do, Yeongcheon-gun, Cheongtong-myeon, Boseong-ri
8– 9 : # 4. Gyeongsangbuk-do, Goryeong-gun, Ssangnim-myeon, Anhwa-ri
10–13 : # 5. Gyeongsangbuk-do, Yeongju-si, Gaheung-dong
14–19 : # 6. Gyeongsangbuk-do, Yeongil-gun, Heunghae-eup, Chilpo-ri
20–24 : # 7. Jeollabuk-do, Namwon-gun, Daesan-myeon, Daegok-ri
25   : # 9. Gyeongsangbuk-do, Gyeongju-si, Seokjang-dong

---

6. Im Se-gwon, op. cit., p. 125.

There is a certain resemblance of some of these motifs with engravings found, for instance, in dolmen or passage graves in France and other parts of Western Europe (Fig. 6).[7]

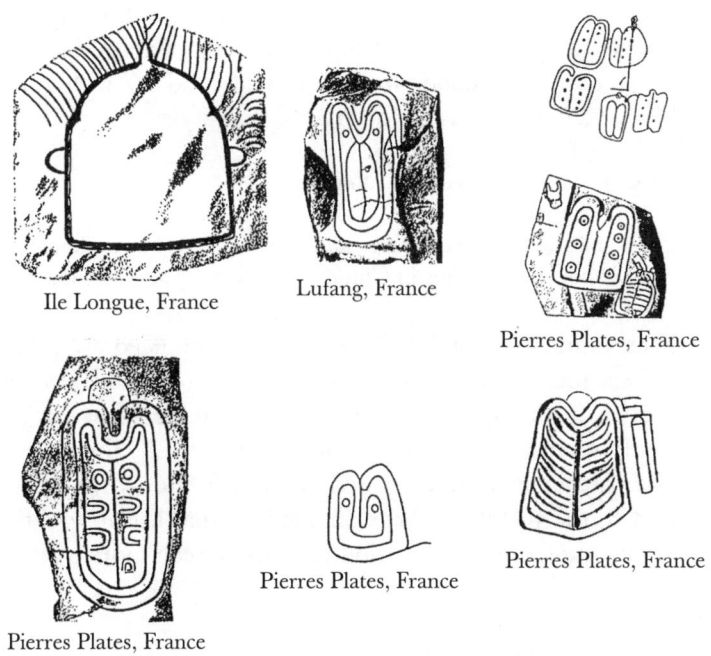

Ile Longue, France

Lufang, France

Pierres Plates, France

Pierres Plates, France

Pierres Plates, France

Pierres Plates, France

Figure 6. Motifs from dolmens in France

Obviously further comparative research is necessary, because there does not seem to be an easy explanation for this similarity. Is there a direct connection possible between the extreme West and the extreme East of Eurasia in prehistoric times? Or do we have a case of one basic idea, which was obvious at a certain time of mankind's intellectual or emotional development, or the representation of an imagination we no

---

7. Albrecht Meyer, *Gavr'inis* (Stuttgart: Verlag Freies Geistesleben, 1974), pp. 18, 30-32.

longer understand, which may have been conceived independently in two areas far apart and possibly at different times?

However, we are at the moment concerned with background information only, and we will therefore not pursue this interesting question for the time being and turn to the motifs of Group B (# 2), the geometric petroglyphs at Cheonjeon-ri. Here a huge rock, lying at the edge of the same river next to which only 1 km downstream Ban-gudae can be found, carries a panel of similar size (9.5 m wide and 2.7 m high). The panel can be divided according to four motifs and styles:

1. thick lines forming geometrical patterns
2. animals in silhouette style
3. animals, scenes with human beings and ships in thin sketchy lines
4. names and short inscriptions in Chinese characters (thin lines like 3).

While numbers 3 and 4 are definitely later, they again need not necessarily be from the same period. In any case, they are confined to the lower half of the panel. In the upper part the geometric patterns in thick lines are fairly evenly spread over the whole of the panel, while the animals in silhouette style are mainly concentrated at the left end of the panel. In Figures 7 and 8, the panel has been divided so that the four different motifs and techniques and their distribution can be seen more easily.[8]

Figure 7. Neolithic geometric patterns and later Chinese character
inscriptions in Cheonjeon-ri

---

8. Im Chang-sun, *Seonsa sidae* (The Prehistoric Age), vol. 1 of *Hanguk geumseok jipseong* (Codification of Korean Epigraphy) (Seoul: Iljisa Publishing Co., 1984), p. 17.

Figure 8. Neolithic silhouette animals and later thin lined animals
in Cheonjeon-ri

The silhouette style animals resemble the ones at Ban-gudae, although they are smaller, and there are similar ones in all of Northern Eurasia. The geometric patterns, rows of lozenges, concentric rings, zigzags, and even the masks, again are in no way unique to Korea, but can be compared with similar ones in Siberia and Europe.

II

After introducing the sites of Groups B and C, we will now finally turn to Ban-gudae, which is definitely the most striking site of prehistoric rock art on the Korean peninsula. About 500 m from the end of the small road to Ban-gudae, there is a path passing over a hill from which in winter and spring one can see the Taehwagang river, which was blocked downstream to create the Sayeondam lake, in its original bed bending towards the right around a ridge (while in summer and autumn the whole area is covered with water, 3-5 m deep and ca. 100 m wide). Almost towards the end of the ridge around which the river originally bent, there is a hanging cliff of shale in reddish-brown color rising directly from the river, and here on a panel 3 m wide and 10 m long, almost 200 animals, human figures and geometric designs can be seen, some of them not larger than the span of a hand, but some up to 1 m in length (see Fig. 9).

Figure 9. The Ban-gudae rock art panel

Table 3. Summary of motifs in Gyeongsangnam-do, Ulju-gun, Eonyang-myeon, Daegok-ri, Ban-gudae

88 land animals:	deer	41
	tiger, leopard or wild cat	14
	boar or pig	10
	cow	3
	rabbit	1
	weasel or dog	2
	others	17
75 water animals:	whale	48
	seal or sea lion	5
	sea turtle	6
	fish	14
	others	2
8 human figures:	single figures	6
	faces or masks	2
10 hunting or fishing scenes:	whale hunting, fishing, boat	4
	net hunting	2
	fence hunting	
1 bird		
10 unidentified motifs		

Closer inspection will reveal that land and water animals are represented in nearly even numbers (Table 3).[9]

As can be seen, land and water animals can be found distributed over the whole of the panel, but not evenly. There are more sea animals in the left half and more land animals on the right (Fig. 10 and Fig. 11).

The identification and classification of the animals is actually still quite preliminary and a definite identification of many animals will probably be disputable for a long time to come.

For instance, similar figures like the ones identified as sea turtles have in other parts of the world been identified as representations of human figures and actually compare to one figure at Ban-gudae which has been

Figure 10. Distribution of water animals at Ban-gudae

Figure 11. Distribution of land animals at Ban-gudae

9. Adapted from Hwang and Mun, *op. cit.*, p. 211.

identified as a human being. One can wonder how much tail there actually is with the turtles, and then one should return to the other rock art sites in order to find out whether any tail had simply been overlooked there (Fig. 12).

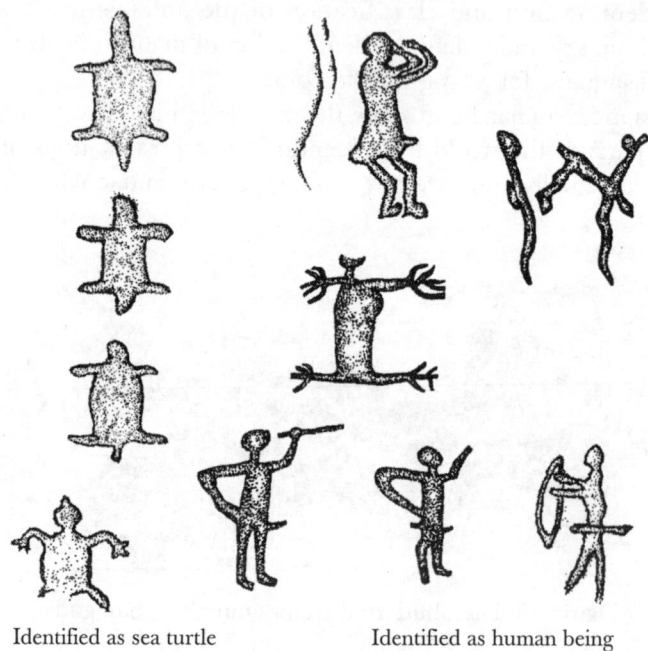

Identified as sea turtle   Identified as human being

Figure 12. Comparison between figures from Ban-gudae identified
as sea turtles and as human beings

A comparison between the motifs in silhouette style and in x-ray style and the representation of land and sea animals raises some interesting questions.

When we compare the animals we can find that whales and other water animals with few exceptions are in silhouette style, mainly with their head upward or occasionally sideward, and the only representation head downwards is in lines. As with most observations in research into rock art in Korea, this poses another question, which cannot yet be answered. The question is whether it will be possible to find a relative chronology with, for instance, the whale in x-ray style being of later date, or whether both styles were used at the same time.

Land animals come in both styles, but the majority is not in silhouette style but drawn as an outline with some lined pattern within, the x-ray style. It catches the eye, with most land animals placed to the right.

Unfortunately, the distribution of animals and styles does not by itself give a clue towards a relative chronology, because we can assume that land animals have been hunted all through the ages, and whales are reported to have been hunted by people from the nearby shore until the beginning of last century.

Another observation is also difficult to interpret as temporal succession. Net hunting and fence hunting are in x-ray style, while the boats are in silhouette style. In this case, I would suggest, it is the motif itself which seems to be the significant factor in the choice of style: fences and nets naturally come in lined style, and boats, set possibly against the horizon, seem to naturally lead to a representation as silhouettes. The latter motif, by the way, especially resembles rock art from Scandinavia (Fig. 13 and Fig. 14).

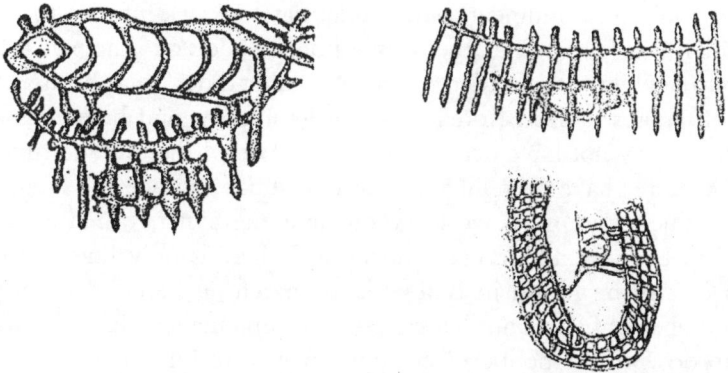

Figure 13. Traps and net hunting or animals behind fences

As we have seen, Ban-gudae has been often compared with similar rock art in the northern maritime zones, Manchuria, Mongolia, but also as far as Scandinavia and the rest of the world. Further research is called for, because observing the motifs and the style in a very selective manner only has made these similarities. Comparison with other sites, referring to techniques in greater detail, natural surroundings, and other archaeological data, may reveal better results and enhance our under-

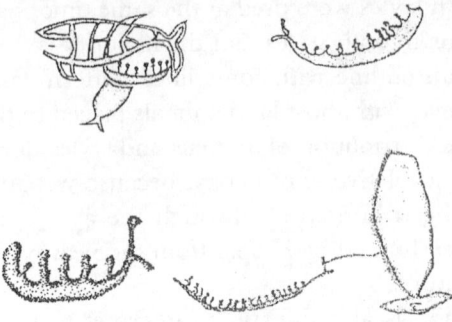

Figure 14. Boats and whale hunting

standing of the Ban-gudae style. But this will only be possible if research can be carried out before the seasonal coming and going of the water in the summer, or the wind, rain and ice attacking the unprotected surface in winter have destroyed this valuable prehistoric monument forever!

Only comparative research into the techniques used might eventually help to date the monument, which may have taken centuries to reach the state it was left in when the people stopped adding to the panel. Dating up to now has been settled for late Neolithic times up to Bronze Age, but rock art research in Korea is still in its infancy, and here again the final word may not have been spoken, yet. Two of the three techniques found in Korea have been identified at Ban-gudae: surface and line pecking and line grinding. If we leave out line engraving, which we have argued to be a technique used much later, there is only line grinding, which cannot be found in Ban-gudae. Therefore, Ban-gudae with its large number of figures and its variety of techniques—which most likely have to do with the period of creation—may with further research lead to a relative chronology of rock art in Korea—again, only if this monument can be saved from destruction!

III

Climb a mountain, and when you look around, all details of the landscape will have disappeared. They will have merged into some kind of over-all picture, where only a few elements can be distinguished, and these seem to be connected and interrelated. Modern man likes to follow a fantasy that is both analytic and synthetic and perceives this kind of picture as layers of structures. Rivers run through mountain ranges, roads connect towns and villages, and lakes may form centers. Some outstanding elements that catch our eye are analyzed and interpreted, and then connected into an imagined system that seems to make sense.

Looking back into the times before the beginning of historical memory will always result in something similar. The details have disappeared, some destroyed by nature or by man and some simply not yet recognized, but some extant elements are analyzed, interpreted, and then connected to form an imagined system, which seems to make sense.

But there is one important difference. The mountain climber can verify how much sense the structures he perceives really make, and all he has to do to test them is to climb back down and walk along the roads and rivers, or swim across the lake. No such experiment is possible for those who take delight in prehistoric research. They will always perceive some details to be important, give some interpretations and then connect these elements, and the result of this process will constitute what we "know" about prehistoric times, but there is no ultimate way of testing. Therefore the theories that seem most plausible today will look ridiculous tomorrow (and a scholar in my opinion should actually learn this lesson as most likely the only definite result of any historical research).

It seems all the more important to put the utmost effort into preserving as many works of art transmitted from these prehistoric times of humanity, and to preserve them as much as possible in their original shape, by which I mean the state these works of art are in when they draw our attention. Later generations will look at the same artifacts and come to entirely different conclusions—but only if we allow them to do so by not destroying these works of art.

And with this aspect we have now, after a very sketchy introduction to rock art in Korea, arrived at the main reason why I have written this article. This time it was not so much my head but rather my heart that led my pen. I wanted to call the attention of the readers of the Korea Journal to this outstanding monument of prehistoric art, which has been found in Korea, but which is in great danger of being destroyed, thereby denying future generations to find the conclusions necessary or suitable for their times.

As with similar cases in many places of the world, a most welcome twentieth-century industrial development is the reason why this monument is in danger of being destroyed. An artificial lake, the economic importance of which cannot be challenged, had to be built near the Ulsan Industrial Complex, and now its waters cover the monument in question for most of the year. However necessary this sacrifice may look at first sight, I still want to beg you to give this seemingly unchangeable fate a second thought.

With all the technical development of this century, should there not be a way of saving the monument? Can we not try to see that destruction comes naturally with many technical developments, but using technical development for constructive purposes outside of the economic sphere is only possible if man decides of his own free will to apply the new techniques to saving the monuments of our past?

With all the economic development of Korea during the second half of last century, should there not be the money to save this monument? Here again, the necessary money seems to have been accumulated, but someone in possession of this money must decide of his own free will to use part of it for saving such an important document of the history of mankind.

Experts in rock art and other archaeologists or art historians have stressed the uniqueness of the Ban-gudae site, and especially local, but also national, newspapers have sporadically carried articles pointing out its importance and reporting that various groups of citizens have already formed a kind of loose movement aiming at saving Ban-gudae from destruction. Various ways can be imagined, but all of them need financial support. Can we find a sponsor? Korea is admired all over the world for the "Miracle of the Hangang River," but a s ponsor who would save Ban-gudae could set another positive example for the world. I may be a romantic dreamer, but then dreaming is one way of giving the future a desired direction!

Korean-Japanese Relations during the Taika Reforms:
A Perspective of International Cooperation

Kim Hyun-Koo

Question

The period from the Three Kingdoms to Unified Silla bears the greatest importance throughout history in discussing Korea-Japan relations, as supported by written records and remaining relics.

The existing studies of early Korea-Japan relations have been, however, mainly concerned with Baekje-Japan relations. Indeed, it cannot be denied that Baekje and Japan had a deep relationship. In the sixth and seventh centuries, powerful clans under the Yamato government such as Mononobe, Kose, Ki, and Shinano sent their sons to Baekje to function as bureaucrats. Among them, Mononobe Makibumuraji was promoted to commander in one local region in Baekje to oversee Japanese soldiers. In fact, he even took part in a war against Silla.[1] Baekje also dispatched many professionals to Japan, such as technicians in metal processing, saddle making, cloth weaving, dress making, and irrigation, doctors in divination, calendar makers, Chinese scriptures (*ogyeong baksa*), and per-

---

* Originally published in the *Korea Journal*, vol. 29, no. 10 (October 1989).

Kim Hyun-Koo (Kim, Hyeon-gu) is Professor of History at Korea University. He obtained his Ph.D. in History from Waseda University in 1986. His publications include *Imna ilbonbu yeongu* (A Study of Mimana) (1992), *Kim Hyeon-gu gyosu-ui ilbon iyagi* (Prof. Kim Hyun-Koo's Story of Japan) (1996), and *Baekje-neun ilbon-ui giwon-in-ga* (Is Baekje the Origin of Japan?) (2002). E-mail: Hyunkoo@Kuconx.Korea.ac.kr.

1. Kim Hyeon-gu (Kim Hyun-Koo), chap. III-3 in 『大和政權の對外關係研究』 (A Study of Foreign Relations of the Yamato Government), vol. 1 (Tokyo: Yoshikawa Kobunkan, 1985).

sons of Buddhist priests, temple architects, and tile-making specialists. They made a contribution in elevating the Japanese culture and in forming the ancient state in Japan. In addition, many royal family members and royal princes from Baekje went to Japan. Many of them returned to Baekje and ascended to the throne. They included King Dongseong, Munyeong, and Pung. These facts clearly testify that the two countries were in a special relationship.

Silla, too, formed relations with Japan as close as Baekje due to its geographical proximity. *Samguk sagi* (Historical Records of the Three Kingdoms) mentions more than fifty encounters between Silla and Japan, some of them described as hostile ones. The same book, however, describes more than ten encounters between Baekje and Japan, which began in 379 A.D. This was because Silla was closer geographically to Japan than Baekje. In *Nihon shoki* (Chronicles of Japan), on the other hand, it is stated that Sosen Meimei, a Silla god, emigrated to Izumo (presently Shimane Prefecture) together with his son Izumo Kami. This story suggests that there may have been some population movements from Silla to Japan in ancient times. This can be supported anthropologically and archaeologically.[2] Population movement is often accompanied with cultural diffusion. It was clarified that the region centered around Izumo accepted the Silla culture, especially blacksmithing techniques and Buddhism.[3] It is clear that there was a geographical route of cultural transmission for Silla, from the southeastern section of the Korean peninsula to the Sanin coastline across the strait. This was different from Baekje cultural transmission route from northern Kyushu to Yamato by way of the Setonaikai.

Despite the fact that Silla-Japan relations were as close as those between Baekje and Japan, even Korean scholars, not to mention Japanese scholars, have been accustomed to considering ancient Korea-Japan relations only in the context of Baekje and Japan connections. This can be interpreted as their inability to free themselves from the colonial historiography of imperialist Japan, which overlooked the *Nihon shoki*. If we are to overcome the colonial historical outlook, we must examine Silla-Japan relations on a par with that of Baekje-Japan. We must clarify

---

2. Mizuno Hiroshi, 「出雲のなかの新羅文化」 (Silla Culture in Izumo), in 『日本のなかの朝鮮文化』 (Korean Culture in Japan), vol. 28 (1978).

3. Mizuno Hiroshi, 『古代の出雲』 (Izumo in Acient Times) (Tokyo: Yoshikawa Kobunkan, 1972).

the structure of the relationship between individual states within Korea and Japan. It will be meaningful to examine the Silla-Japan relationship immediately before and after the Taika Reforms (Taikano Kaishin) in 645 A.D., which ushered in great changes throughout the region.

Korea-Japan Relations prior to the Taika Reforms

The Korea-Japan relations in the sixth and seventh centuries are described in the *Nihon shoki* in a relatively minute detail. These, however, are almost omitted in Korean historical literature. The chapter on Emperor Keitai (r. 507-531 A.D.), a part of the *Nihon shoki* with a relatively high degree of creditability, mentions interactions between Korean states and the Yamato government from the year when Gara or Gaya (or Mimana as it is called by the Japanese) was destroyed, all the way to the 23rd year of Emperor Kinmei's reign (562 A.D.). It states that Goguryeo and Silla each sent envoys to Japan on one occasion, Mimana on five occasions, and Baekje on twenty-three occasions. The Yamato government, however, did not send any envoys to either Goguryeo or Silla, but sent two to Mimana and fourteen to Baekje.[4] Although the accuracy of this material is questionable, the frequency of envoys may suggest the degree of closeness between the Korean states and the Yamato government. If so, it can be concluded that contacts between Korea and Japan at that time involved mainly the relationship between Baekje and Japan. What matters most is the essence of the relations between Baekje and the Yamato government.

Among the twenty-three dispatches of envoys by Baekje to Japan, the purpose of the trips were clarified on only thirteen occasions. On five occasions the purpose was to discuss problems in connection to Mimana. On eight other occasions envoys were dispatched in order to request military assistance from Japan. The dispatch of Baekje envoys to the Yamato government presupposed Japanese rule of Mimana. However, the Yamato government had never ruled Mimana. The Yamato government responded favorably to Baekje's request for military assistance by providing aid on nine occasions. The Yamato government dispatched envoys to Baekje on fourteen occasions, all in connection with its request for Baekje scholars and advanced Baekje social and cultural

---

4. Kim Hyeon-gu, 『大和政權の對外關係研究』, p. 15.

institutions. In response to these requests, Baekje reciprocated by send-ing scholars on nine occasions. We may then conclude that Baekje and the Yamato government exchanged advanced institutions and military assistance on only nine confirmed occasions. Since the military aid took the form of mercenary soldiers, the relations between Baekje and the Yamato government can be defined as a mercenary relationship.[5]

Was Baekje alone among the three Korean kingdoms in employing mercenary troops sent by the Yamato government? Goguryeo, Baekje, and Silla competed with each other on the Korean peninsula at that time. All three sought military assistance from outside the peninsula. Japan, on the other hand, as it was still in a formative stage, needed advanced continental institutions. It can be presumed that Japan pur-sued its relationship with Baekje because it had developed a higher level of culture than the two other Korean states due to its interchange with the Southern Dynasties in China.[6] The Soga clan, which had special relations with Baekje, played a pivotal role in this process and finally occupied the hegemonic position in the Yamato government.[7]

The mercenary relationship between Baekje and the Yamato govern-ment began to undergo a series of changes in the second half of the sixth century, and it was entirely transformed from the last years of the sixth century to the first half of the seventh century, when peace prevailed on the Korean peninsula. During this period, Baekje sent its envoys to the Yamato government on seven occasions, Silla on seven, and Goguryeo on six. The Yamato government, in return, sent its envoy on one occa-sion each to Baekje, Goguryeo, and Silla. Compared with the first half of the sixth century, the intensity of Japan's relations with Baekje declined while its relations with both Silla and Goguryeo improved greatly. This indicates that the three Korean states generally had equal relations with the Yamato government.[8] This indicates that the Yamato government

---

5. Refer to Kim Hyeon-gu, chap. I in 『大和政權の對外關係研究』 for the relations of mer-cenary employment between Baekje and the Yamato government.

6. The fact that Baekje led others in introducing advanced institutions from the South-ern Dynasties in China is clarified in the article of King Seong's 19th year (541 A.D.) in "Baekje bon-gi" (Annals of Baekje) of *Samguk sagi* and in the "Xinluozhuani" (Biography on Silla) of *Liangshu* (History of the Liang Dynasty).

7. Refer to Kato Kenkichi, 『蘇我氏と大和政權』 (The Soga Clan and the Yamato Govern-ment) (Tokyo: Yoshikawa Kobunkan, 1983).

8. Kim Hyeon-gu, chap. I-1 in 『大和政權の對外關係研究』, part 3.

replaced its heavily Baekje-centered diplomacy with multilateral diplomacy with equal attention given to all three kingdoms on the Korean peninsula.

It is probable that the Yamato government shifted to multilateral diplomacy because the tripartite struggle on the Korean peninsula entered into a brief halt. However, there may be a more significant reason. With the fall of the Southern Dynasties in China in the second half of the sixth century, the political and cultural center moved to northern China, thus weakening the relationship between Baekje and China. On the other hand, the area near the Hangang river, which was a gateway to China, was taken over by Silla. Thereafter, relations between Silla and China became much closer.[9] Japan, which had formerly adopted advanced institutions, including Buddhism, only from Baekje, now sought them mainly from Silla and Goguryeo.[10]

As a result of implementing multilateral diplomacy toward the Korean kingdoms, the Yamato government could receive and adopt advanced institutions including Buddhism not only from Baekje but from Silla and Goguryeo. Ignoring the rivalry between Baekje and Silla on the Korean peninsula, Japan could accommodate both the Baekje Buddhism represented by Hokoji temple (Asukadera temple) and the Silla Buddhism that was represented by Koryuji temple (Katsunoji temple) during the reign of Emperor Suiko (r. 593–628).[11] Though Goguryeo influence began to emerge in Japan as well,[12] this period is mainly marked as the first formal dissemination of Silla culture to Japan.

In the process of transforming its mercenary relationship with Baekje for multilateral diplomacy, the Soga clan, which had wielded real power in the Yamato government, lost the ability to lead the new diplomatic

---

9. Tamura Encho, 『古代朝鮮佛教と日本佛教』 (Ancient Korean Buddhism and Japanese Buddhism) (Tokyo: Yoshikawa Kobunkan, 1980), pp. 113-114. According to him, only two Baekje monks went to China on two occasions from 553 A.D. when Baekje's marine route to China was brought under Silla control to 660 A.D. In the meantime Silla sent more than twenty monks to China on eleven occasions during the same period.

10. Kim Hyeon-gu, chap. II-2 in 『大和政權の對外關係研究』, part 3.

11. Hirano Kunio, 『大化前代社會組織の研究』 (A Study of Social Organization prior to the Taika Reforms) (Tokyo: Yoshikawa Kobunkan, 1969), p. 195.

12. According to Kadowaki Sadaji, 『新版飛鳥』 (New Edition of Asuka) (Tokyo: Nihon Hososyuppan Kyokai, 1977), pp. 101, 118, Asukaji temple received influence from Goguryeo.

policy, mainly due to its special relationship with Baekje. Therefore, Prince Shotoku, who was deeply related to Goguryeo and Shilla, emerged as the regent. Multilateral diplomacy was possible because there was a brief period of peaceful coexistence among the three Korean states. In the mid-seventh century, however, the rivalry among the three kingdoms on the Korean peninsula intensified again and disputes arose in the Yamato government which was not entirely unconnected with the antagonism in Korea as to its future foreign policy.

The Soga clan which was deeply connected with Baekje was still in power in Japan despite the multilateral diplomacy. There was a steady increase in the number of Japanese students returning from Tang China through Silla in this period. On the basis of a recommendation submitted by Keinichi and others, they asserted the importance of establishing new relations with Tang in 623.[13] The pro-Baekje faction, represented by Nakatomi Murajikuni, and the pro-Silla faction, led by Tanaka Tomi, confronted each other in open rivalry over the issue of whether to take a pro-Baekje policy or a pro-Silla policy.[14] A Tang envoy named Gao Biaoren visited Japan in 632 with Keinichi, the first Japanese envoy to Tang, and a Chinese monk named Min, and bluntly asked Japan to sever relations with Baekje and adopt a pro-Silla policy.[15]

One thing worthy of note is that both Keinichi, who advocated a pro-Silla policy, and Gao Biaoren, who forced a pro-Silla policy on the Yamato government, were guided to Japan by Silla officials through Silla.[16] There were two routes from China to Japan: one was to go through Baekje, and the other through Silla. Tang sent the delegates through Silla on purpose, as it supported the policy of forcing Japan to take a pro-Silla stance.

The contention over a pro-Silla or a pro-Baekje policy put the Soga clan, which maintained close relations with Baekje, in a difficult situation. To accept the Tang demand and take a pro-Silla stance would turn

---

13. *Nihon shoki*, July of the 31st year of Emperor Suiko's reign.
14. *Nihon shoki*, Sesaijo of the 31st year of Emperor Suiko's reign.
15. Kim Hyeon-gu, 「初期の日唐關係する─『日本書紀』 "高表仁の來日" 記事を中心に」 (An Inquiry into Early Japan-Tang Relations—Centering on the Records on Gao Biaoren's Visit to Japan in *Nihon shoki*), 『日本歷史』 (History of Japan) 413. The process in which Gao Biaoren asked the Yamato government to take a pro-Silla policy is described in detail in this paper.
16. *Nihon shoki*, July of the 31st year of Emperor Suiko's reign and August of the 4th year of Emperor Jomei's reign.

the hegemony in the Yamato government over to persons who were closely linked to Tang or Silla. To refuse their demand and adhere to a pro-Baekje policy would result in abandoning the clan's leadership in the government and isolating itself. It was inevitable that the Soga clan, whose basis of power was rooted in relations with Baekje, would return to a pro-Baekje policy. This position presented itself in the form of rupture of relations with Tang in 632.[17] This marked the end of Soga power and delineated its limited role in the Yamato government.

Students sent to Tang such as Takamuko Kuromaro and Minabuchi Shoan returned to Japan with the Silla envoys. The pressure on the Yamato government from Tang and Silla grew steadily.[18] Removing the Soga clan from power was the only recourse for the Yamato government in reaction to the mounting pressure from Tang and Silla. Students such as Monk Min and Takamuko Kuromaro, who were returning from Tang and Silla, played an important role in this historical juncture. These are known as the Taika Reforms (645 A.D.) led by Nakatomi Kamatari, Prince Naka no Oe (later Emperor Tenji), and Prince Karu Ouji (later Emperor Kotoku) with the help of National Consultants Monk Min and Takamuko Kuromaro.

The Taika Reforms and the Establishment of Cooperative Relations among Silla, Japan, and Tang China

The Japanese government after the Taika Reforms was pro-Silla, as amply confirmed by the personnel in leading government positions, its changed foreign policies, and the newly selected routes for accepting advanced cultures.

The leading figures in the reform government were Prince Karu Ouji, who acceded to the throne as Emperor Kotoku after the overthrow of the Soga clan, Prince Naka no Oe, who was named Prince Imperial, Abeno Uchimaro, Soganokura, Yamada Ishikawamaro, and Nakatomi Kamatari, who were appointed left, right, and prime ministers, and Takamuko Kuromaro and Monk Min who, as National Consultants, formulated policies for the reform government.

Takamuko Kuromaro and Monk Min represented the character of the

---

17. Refer to Kim Hyeon-gu, 「初期の日唐關係する―『日本書紀』"高表仁の來日"記事を中心に」.
18. *Nihon shoki*, October of the 12th year of Emperor Jomei's reign.

reform government most clearly. The two National Consultants formulated policies for the new government. They were sent to Tang China and returned to Japan through Silla together, with Silla envoys. As they returned to Japan via Silla from Tang China,[19] it is not unreasonable to assume that they stayed in Silla for a considerable period of time. Takamuko Kuromaro was the very person who visited Silla in September 646 immediately after the Taika Reforms (645) and returned to Japan together with Kim Chun-chu in order to draw up a system of cooperation among Silla, Japan and Tang.[20] Monk Min led the movement to introduce Silla Buddhism in opposition to Baekje Buddhism during the Taika period (645-649).[21]

Both Prince Naka no Oe and Nakatomi Kamatari—the real force behind the Taika Reforms—were the disciples of Minabuchi no Shoan, who studied in Tang and returned home through Silla.[22] Nakatomi Kamatari had once studied under Monk Min.[23] Emperor Kotoku was also influenced by Monk Min. Abeno Uchimaro, who was one of pillars supporting the Taika Reforms as left prime minister, was of Silla descent and had been shouldering the mission of guiding relations with Shills for a long time.[24]

Leading figures in the Yamato government, as we have seen, were all directly or indirectly related to Silla. It was inevitable, therefore, for the Yamato government to take a pro-Silla stance, as expressed in its foreign policy.

What were the relations between the Korean kingdoms and the Yama-

19. *Ibid.*
20. Kim Hyeon-gu, "Ildang gwan-gye-ui seongnip-gwa nail dongmaeng—Ilbon seogi Kim Chun-chu-ui doil gisa-reul jungsim-euro" (Establishment of Japan-Tang Relations and Silla-Japan Alliance—Centering on Records on Kim Chun-chu's Visit to Japan in *Nihon shoki*), *Junggukhak nonchong* (A Collection of Treatises on Chinese Studies) (Seoul: The Publication Committee of A Collection of Treatises on Chinese Studies, 1983). The process leading to the establishment of a three-nation system of cooperation and the role played by Takamuko no Kuromaro is described in detail in this paper.
21. The relations between Silla Buddhism and Monk Min are described in detail in Tamura Encho, 『古代朝鮮佛教と日本佛教』, pp. 108-130.
22. *Nihon shoki,* January of the 3rd year of Emperor Kokyoku's reign.
23. *Kaden* (Family Transmission).
24. That Abe clan was a descendant of Silla is described in detail in Mizuno Hiroshi, 『古代の出雲と大和』 (Ancient Izumo and Yamato) (Yamato Shoban, 1975).

to government during the Taika period (645–649) prior to the power shift in the government? Japan did not send any envoys to Baekje or Goguryeo and the two Korean states also did not send any mission to the Yamato government. On the contrary, Silla sent envoys to the Yamato government every year, including Kim Chun-chu's visit. The Yamato government sent envoys and students to Silla every year, including the visit of Takamuko Kuromaro.

It is crucial to note one thing. Takamuko Kuromaro returned to Japan together with Kim Chun-chu. Takamuko visited Silla in 646 and promised Silla that Japan would sever formal relations with Baekje and provide military assistance to Silla. This was the decision Tang and Silla had persistently asked Japan to make since the Tang envoy Gao Biaoren visited Japan in 632. Kim Chun-chu accompanied Takamuko in 647 and confirmed the establishment of new relations between Silla and Japan. He also visited Tang in 648, carrying with him a Japanese declaration to that effect, thereby normalizing relations between Tang and the Yamato government.[25]

Established here was a three-nation system of cooperation among Silla, Japan, and Tang. This, in one sense, can be considered a direct result of a change in international political circumstances. In another sense, however, this can be considered a fruit of Silla's diplomatic efforts to lead the Yamato government to a pro-Silla policy.

Silla culture was introduced to Japan in earnest with the emergence of a pro-Silla government in Japan for the first time.[26] However, a power struggle erupted in the reform government between Emperor Kotoku and Prince Naka no Oe, In efforts to gather opposition to the emperor, the crown prince sided with elements of the old pro-Baekje faction, and for a brief period, the Yamato government returned to a pro-Baekje policy and the introduction of Silla culture was temporarily suspended. However, the return to a pro-Baekje policy and the suspension of the introduction of Silla culture were only short-term phenomena caused by the power struggle. Emperor Tenji (formerly Prince Naka no Oe) and Nakatomi Kamatari sent presents to King Munmu and Kim Yu-sin of Silla after its defeat at a battle along Baekchongang river in 663 in efforts to reopen formal relations with Silla.[27] The succeeding Tenmu regime

---

25. See note 15.
26. Kim Hyeon-gu, chap. III in 『大和政權の對外關係研究』, part 4.
27. *Nihon shoki*, September of the 7th year of Emperor Tenji's reign.

returned to a pro-Silla policy and actively introduced Silla culture.

Immediately after its establishment, the reform government equipped itself with a centralized administrative organization in order to readjust various institutions. This is represented by the *hyo* system. The *hyo* was not only an administrative unit but a military unit as well. An early form of the *hyo* (*pyeong* in Korean) as an administrative unit can be found in Goguryeo's *naepyeong* and *oepyeong*,[28] and as a military unit in Silla's *takpyeong*.[29] The question is: Which one did the reform government adopt as its model? While the reform government had hostile relations with it and had no interactions at all with Goguryeo, Japan had friendly relations with Silla and interchange took place frequently between the two. Doubtlessly Japan adopted Silla's *takpyeong* which was military in its nature.

With progress in readjusting administrative organization and developing a decree-governed state, Japan came to feel the necessity of training bureaucrats. An important task facing the new government in Japan was the establishment of schools. The forerunner of Japanese schools was a private institute opened by leaders of the reform government before the Taika Reforms.[30] The official title "doctor" (*hakase*) emerged immediately after the reform.[31] A comparison of Silla's Gukhak (National Confucian College) system with Japan's educational decrees promulgated in the Taiho (701) and Yoro (718) eras (undergoing revisions on several occasions) discloses several similarities between the two educational systems, which included the following: the title of the college was Taigaku (Taehak in Korean). Tang's three departments—*guozi*, *daxue*, and *siwen*—were integrated into one department, *mingjing* (the study of Confacian classics). Optional subjects in its curriculum were *Liji* (Book of Rites), *Chunqiu zuozhizhuan*, *Maoshi* (Mao's Odes), *Zhouyi* (Book of Changes), *Shangshu* (Book of Documents), and *Wenxuan* (Selected Lit-

---

28. Ikeuchi Hiroshi, 「高句麗五部族及び五部考」 (A Study of the Five Tribes and Five Sections of Goguryeo), in 『滿鮮史研究—上世編』 (Studies of Manchurian-Korean History— Part of Antiquity) (Sokokusha, 1951), p. 395.

29. Suematsu Yasukalu, 「梁書新羅傳考」 (A Study of the Biography of Silla in *Liangshu*), in 『新羅史の諸問題』 (Various Problems in the History of Shilla) (Tokyo Bunko, 1944), p. 342.

30. *Kaden* reports that Monk Min and Minabuchino Shoan already opened their private school before the Taika Reforms.

31. *Nihon shoki* carries an article that Monk Min and Takamuko no Kuromaro were appointed *hakase* before the coronation of Emperor Kotoku.

erature). Compulsory subjects were the *Lunyu* (Analects of Confucius) and *Xiaojing* (Classic of Filial Piety). *Chunqiu gongyangzhuan, Chunqiu guliangzhuan* and *Laozi* were excluded.[32] This an eloquent reminder that the education system of the reform government in Japan was an imitation of Silla's. This was a result of human exchanges between the two. The introduction of Silla's educational system became important in creating a new educational system in Japan.

Religion, in a similar light, was not only a form of faith in the antiquity but it also bore a great political significance. Among ten priests ordained in accordance with the first priest-official system adopted in Japan after the establishment of the reform government were Keiun, Seian, Reiun, and Monk Min.[33] The reform government moved its seat to Nanpa in December 645 to complete the construction of Shitennouji temple. Presents, including a gold pagoda, from Silla's King Jinpyeong were kept there. It inherited the tradition of Silla Buddhism to pray for the well-being of the reform government.[34] It was Monk Min who drew up a Buddhist policy for the reform government. Since Japan sent its students to Silla exclusively during the Taika period,[35] the reform government apparently had great confidence in Silla Buddhism and expected to learn much from it.

As we have examined so far, the introduction of advanced institutions from Silla and Japan's pledge of military assistance to Silla were the results of the three-nation system of cooperation among Silla, Japan and Tang, established mostly by Kim Chun-chu and Takamuko Kuromaro. However, Japan's reception of advanced institutions from Silla was interrupted briefly because Prince Naka no Oe sided with the pro-Baekje faction to back up his struggle for power against Emperor Kotoku prior to Japan's defeat at Baekchongang river. Silla – Japan relations were reopened with Emperor Tenji and Nakatomi Kamatari's presentation of ships to Silla King Munmu and Kim Yu-sin through a Silla envoy named

---

32. Toga Shugoro, 『唐代教育史の問題』 (Problems concerning History of Tang Education) (Humaido Shoten, 1943), pp. 123-134; Wako Mitsuo, 『律令制とそ周邊』 (The Decree System and Its Environment) (Keiogijuku Hogakukenkyukai, 1967), p. 11.

33. *Nihon shoki*, August of the 1st year of Emperor Kotoku's reign.

34. Tamura Encho, 『古代朝鮮佛教と日本佛教』, pp. 108-130.

35. The article from February of Kotoku Tenno's 4th year of Taika described that student-monks were sent to Three Han in Korea. That Three Han meant Silla is explained in detail in Kim Hyeon-gu, chap. II-1 in 『大和政權の對外關係研究』, part 4.

Kim Dong-eom in 668.

Gifts from the reopening of relations with Silla were the establishment of an observatory in Japan and the adoption of an eight-surname system (*yatsuseisei*) during the reign of Emperor Tenmu (672–686) and the adoption of the practice of cremation during the reign of Emperor Bumbu (697–707).

While the Cheomseongdae Observatory was erected during the reign of Queen Seondeok (632–645) in Silla, the first observatory was built in Japan in the 4th year of Emperor Tenmu (676).[36] A certain Kim from Silla was named the astronomer.[37] The fact that an astronomer emerged in relation to Silla demonstrates the existence of close relations between Silla's Cheomseongdae Observatory and Japan's astronomical observatory or that the latter originated from the former.

The eight-surname system readjusted the traditional Japanese family names in the 13th year of Emperor Tenmu (685), placing the imperial family at the top. It seems that Japan's eight-surname system had some connection with Silla's bone-rank system (*golpumje*). The *seonggol* (holy-bone) class ceased to exist in Silla with King Munmu (r. 661–681) as the last member, allowing the *jin-gol* (true-bone) class to become the highest class. In Japan's eight-surname system, the imperial family was given the highest title of *shinjin*. In Silla's bone-rank system, classes below the fifth *pum* did not exist. In Japan's eight-surname system, no clauses were provided for persons below the *doushi* holding the fifth rank. These similarities showed that Japan's eight-surname system was not without connection to Silla's bone-rank system.[38]

The first example of cremation in the Silla royalty occurred with the funeral of King Munmu in 681. In Japan, cremation first occurred with the funeral of Emperor Jito in 703. Both King Munmu and Emperor Jito left imperial wills. They were similar in that they both expressed the wish for simple funeral ceremonies. A connection with Silla cannot be denied in Japan's adoption of cremation for the imperial family.

The influence of advanced institutions from Silla can be found not only in the examples stated above but in all cultural realms including the compilation of historical records and in the acceptance of Buddhist culture.

---

36. *Nihon shoki*, January of the 4th year of Emperor Tenmu's reign.
37. Hirano Kunio, 『大化前代社會組織の研究』, p. 180.
38. *Ibid.*, p. 180.

Japan's relations with Silla are well reflected in the myths and imperial genealogy contained in the *Nihon shoki*, which began to be compiled in the second half of the seventh century and completed early in the eighth century. If the migration of Sosen Meimei, a god originating in Silla, and his son Izumo Kami to the Izumo and Kii regions was a story created in the stage of political myths immediately before the compilation of *Nihon shoki*,[39] this must be considered a reflection of the relationship with Silla in the second half of the seventh century. In the imperial genealogy, the change from a sun goddess to Amaterasu Omikami (Sun Goddess) is similar to the change in Silla from Seonghan to Bak Geoseogan.[40] The two were closely interconnected in the composition of the royal genealogy.[41]

Silla produced noted scholar-monks including Uisang, Woncheuk, and Gyeongheung in the second half of the seventh century. In the meantime, Japan sent Chiryu (returning home in 687),[42] Meiso, and Kanchi (in 689)[43] to Silla for studies. This indicates the existence of a perception that there was much to learn about Silla Buddhism at that time.

In the general cultural fields, the Silla influence was clearly evident. Tiles bearing telltale Silla arabesque patterns were unearthed in the Kyokuzojishi temple site of the Hakuho period. Ruined temple sites of the Tenpyo period include the site of the Tarusuihaijishi temple.[44] Bricks of the Silla style dating to 698 were unearthed in the site of the Kansenonji temple in Chikuzendazaihudo as well.[45]

The above facts indicate that this was a turning point in relations with Silla during the Tenmu era (672–686). This is confirmed by the fact that Japan sent envoys to Silla on nine occasions and Silla sent envoys to Japan on 20 occasions from the last year of the Tenji era (669) to the

---

39. Inoue Hideo, 「日本書紀の新羅傳説考」 (Articles on Silla Legends in *Nihon Shoki*), in 『日本書紀研究』 (A Study of *Nihon Shoki*), vol. 4 (Tachibana Shobo, 1970), p. 240.

40. Kinoshita Norihito, 「八世紀たおける王統系譜の形成」 (Formation of the Royal Genealogy in the Eighth Century), in 『日本書紀研究』, vol. 4 (Tachibana Shobo, 1970), p. 322.

41. Ibid., p. 324.

42. *Nihon shoki*, August of the 1st year of Emperor Jito's reign.

43. *Nihon shoki*, March of the 3rd year of Emperor Jito's reign.

44. Hirano Kunio, 『大化前代社會組織の研究』, p. 200.

45. *Ibid.*, p. 201.

first year of the Taiho era (701), whereas Japan did not send any envoys to Tang during this period.[46]

Conclusion

When the three kingdoms in the Korean peninsula competed with one another for dominance, Japan was in the process of forming itself as a state for the first time. The ruling class considered it its supreme task to monopolize the importation of advanced institutions in attempts to secure and maintain its power. It naturally sought relations with one of the three Korean kingdoms that possessed the highest degree of cultural development. The result was that at one time Japan affiliated itself with Baekje and then sought an approach to all of the three Korean states with multilateral diplomacy. Thus, it established a three-nation system of cooperation with Silla and Tang.

In this process, a powerful faction that was close to one of the three kingdoms came into power in the Yamato government. This faction, however, fell from its power because it failed to adapt itself to the new changes taking place in the international arena and, as a result, a new force came to the fore. This was exemplified by the fall of the Soga clan, which failed to terminate its special relationship with Baekje, as well as the Taika Reforms, led by students who returned from Tang or Silla, along with the emergence of a three-nation system of cooperation among Silla, Japan, and Tang. After the establishment of a pro-Silla government as a result of the Taika Reforms, advanced institutions from Silla began to be officially introduced to Japan, where their influence reached all sectors of Japanese society. Silla's influence finally reached as far as imperial genealogy, even influencing the creation of political myths in the *Nihon shoki*.

---

46. Kinoshita Norihito, 「八世紀たおける王統系譜の形成」, p. 324.

A New Interpretation of the Problems of Mimana

Chun Kwan-Woo

Introduction: Gaya and Mimana

Although the period known as the Three Kingdoms in Korean history refers to the time when the Silla, Goguryeo, and Baekje kingdoms vied for power, two other states also had considerable power during this period: Buyeo and Gaya. The first was located to the north of Goguryeo on the great Manchurian plain, and was conquered by Goguryo in 494; Gaya, which was in the southern part of the peninsula on the basin of Nakdonggang river, was annexed by Silla in 562.

In the Japanese document, the *Nihon shoki* (Chronicles of Japan), the Japanese name of Mimana (Imna in Korean) is used to refer to Gaya. According to this same document, the country was occupied and ruled for over two centuries (365–562) by the Wai (the old name for Japan; the name "Japan" only appeared at the beginning of the seventh century).

On the same subject, Korean documents state that the Wai raided the Silla coast (the south-western part of the peninsula), but all the attacks (between 30 and 40) were immediately suppressed by the Silla troops.

* Originally published in the *Korea Journal*, vol. 14, no. 2 and no. 4 (February/April 1974).

The late Chun Kwan-Woo (Cheon, Gwan-u) had a varied career as a journalist as well as a scholar. He was the chief editor of the *Dong-a Ilbo*, a member of the National Institute of Korean History, a member of the Cultural Properties Protection Committee, etc. He published many books and articles in the field of Korean history, including *Samhansa yeongu* (A Study of the Three Hans), *Hanguksa-ui jaebalgyeon* (Rediscovery of Korean History), *Geunse joseonsa yeongu* (A Study of the History of Modern Joseon).

There is no proof in the Korean sources to absolutely support the claim that the Wai armies occupied the peninsula for such a long period. Only the inscription on the tombstone of the King of Goguryeo, Gwanggaeto (391–413), refers to the several years of the Wai army's stay on the Baekje peninsula during the period of military confrontation between Baekje and Goguryeo. This army is recorded as having been beaten and routed by the forces of King Gwanggaeto.

Korean and Japanese documents concerning Gaya, then, completely contradict one another. Over the centuries, Korean historians have paid little attention to this issue, while Japanese historians, especially since the Meiji Restoration (1853–1871) have spent much effort in claiming the legitimacy for Japanese occupation of the peninsula in the ancient times. This line of historical inquiry coincides with the birth of Japanese imperial aspirations and expansionism in continental Asia.

This article's main purpose is to prove the fictional nature of the arguments supporting the Japanese domination of Mimana.

The Problems of Mimana in Japanese Documents

In the *Nihon shoki*, the first set of references to Mimana are in the articles concerning the 65th year of Emperor Sujin's reign (ca. 33 B.C) and the second year of King Suijin's reign (ca. 28 B.C.); records state that the people of Mimana were Wai subjects, but the description is full of exaggerated expressions intended to enhance Wai authority. For example: "The King of Mimana paid tribute to the Wai king," or "The Mimana presented a gift of red silk to Wai" etc. In any case, the *Nihon shoki* constantly comments on the Three Kingdoms of Korea in a similar manner. Since ancient Japanese history permeates with legends, such grandiose assertions do not merit serious consideration.

Mimana does not appear at all in the *Nihon shoki* for the next two or three hundred years. According to the section on the 49th year of Queen Jingu's reign (249 or 369 according to the system worded out by Japanese scholars) the Wai[1] of Yamato sent the first expedition against Mimana. There are several other brief references to Mimana in this sec-

---

1. Wai is a generic name applied to various tribes on the Japanese archipelago; e.g. the Wai of Yamato; those of northern Kyushu.

tion. According to this document, the Wai of Yamato also conquered Baekje and exacted a promise of tribute from Baekje people, whom the Wai called the Western barbarians. Subsequently, the Wai continued to send armies to the southern part of the peninsula, and in particular to Mimana, where they set up a colonial organization called the *mikotomoji* (literally meaning "a person who carries out the king's command") or *yamato no mikotomoji*. This organization and the King of Mimana governed Mimana: the organization was also given the name of *miyake* sometimes written *tonso*, which means territory governed directly by the Wai of Yamato or territory where the population was subject to taxation by the Wai. This Japanese document therefore seems to provide a proof of the Wai domination of Mimana and the submission of Baekje. This situation is supposed to have lasted until the year of 562 when Silla completely defeated the *miyake* in Mimana, which coincides with the Korean accounts of Silla's conquest of the Dae (Great) Gaya.[2] Thus this theoretical Wai domination over Mimana supposedly lasted for about two centuries, from 369 until 562. Furthermore, Japanese scholars maintain that even after the Wai had been completely driven out of Mimana territory by Silla, either Silla or Baekje continued to pay tribute to Wai in Mimana's name until about 646.[3]

The Japanese claim that it had the administration of southern Korea is principally based on Queen Jingu's supposed conquest of the Three Han Kingdoms, and on the Yamato expedition against Mimana. The first premise is too fictitious even for Japanese historians to support it, but the second is now considered an irrefutable historical fact by almost all Japanese scholars. The Mimana problem is one of the central themes in the study of ancient Japan, since the resources obtained during this period of "occupation" enabled the Japanese, according to Japanese historians, to manufacture an abundant amount of arms and agricultural implements, ultimately leading to the unification of Japan.

What is the exact meaning of "administration"? Even among the Japanese scholars supporting the theory on the southern Korea administration, there are some who admit the difficulty in proving the existence of the *mikotomoji* in Mimana, either with regard to its function or to its dates, and therefore find it difficult to recognize it as a permanent orga-

---

2. The Greater Gaya, which existed in present-day Goryeong, was a tiny kingdom belonging to the Gaya federation.
3. The collapse of Baekje dates from 660.

nization with overall control. The mistaken assumption that there was some type of Japanese administration ruling Gaya, similar to the colonial administration of 1910–1945, is widespread among the Japanese public, with the primary school history texts stating it as a fact. Why do Japanese still use the term "administration" to describe this ambiguous presence of Japanese power in the southern part of the peninsula during this period?

Was the Japanese Expedition against the Peninsula Possible?

First, let us examine the problem from a general viewpoint: was it possible for the Wai of Yamato to launch an armed expedition against Mimana, and to occupy the southern region of the peninsula for a considerable period? The historical development of East Asia during the two centuries (360–560), when the question of Mimana is mentioned in the *Nihon shoki*, will be considered.

1) During the period 360–560 or even earlier, cultural exchanges between mainland China, Korean peninsula and Japanese archipelago were one sided, and the cultural development in these three regions formed a hierarchy. If one started from the Chinese continent, he had to pass through the Korean peninsula before reaching the Japanese archipelago. Through the migration of people from the Three Kingdoms, Korea exercised considerable cultural as well as political influence in the Japanese archipelago. Moreover, people from the Korean peninsula played an important role in the Japanese royal succession. Therefore, if one must insists on the words "administer" or "rule," it can reasonably be argued that the Korean descendants in Japan "ruled" the western part of Japan. Therefore, the question of the Wai "administration" of the southern Korean peninsula naturally arises.

To prove this theory, some Japanese scholars have examined Chinese historical texts such as the *Houhanshu* (History of the Later Han) or the *Weizhi* of *Sanguozi* (The History of the Three Kingdoms) in order to find supporting arguments. Since ancient times, they have argued that the Wai had been superior to the peninsular peoples, and very likely have exacted tribute from them. The Chinese texts on which this hypothesis is raised are much older than the Korean or Japanese documents such as the *Samguk sagi* (Historical Records of the Three Kingdoms) or the *Nihon shoki*. In addition, their treatment of Korean-Japanese relations might have been expected as relatively objective and unbiased. These texts, however, cannot be considered completely impartial on all points.

For example, even the *Dongyizhuan* (Account of the Eastern Barbarians) of the *Weizhi*, the most important of these texts, lends itself to criticism for the following reasons: i) The chronology of the text is sometimes clearly erroneous. For example, the text describes its relations with countries to the east of China, in a limited way by only recording the primitive standards of life and culture of those countries even though the event took place in 250 A.D. not too long before the writing of the text. ii) This text is also biased against each nation it mentions. For example, as one can see from the comparison between Goguryeo and Buyeo or between Byeonhan (one of the Three Han States) and Mahan, the text describes the regions relatively well-known to the Chinese as being highly civilized, while the hostile or little-known regions are dismissed as barbaric. This applies even more to the *Dongyizhuan* in the *Houhanshu*, which follows the *Sanguozi* almost to the letter.

In documents such as the *Worenzhuan* in the *Weizhi*, it states that the Wai had been in contact with China since ancient times, but this does not necessarily signify that the Wai was more advanced or developed than the Three Han States or their successor, Baekje, Silla and Gaya. Even if one considers the Wai somewhat more advanced, there is no evidence that they were developed to a level to exact tribute from foreign states or to launch a military expedition and establish a colony.

Japanese historians have also attempted to favorably interpret archaeological evidence such as the *chiljido* or the tomb inscription of King Gwanggaeto, as well as certain other fragments of Chinese texts as supporting Japanese administration in Korea. This attempt to support their theory is, however, far from convincing.

2) At this point, we must consider whether the Wai of Yamato in the central part of Japan (Kinai) would have been capable of sending a large expeditionary force to the Korean peninsula. The following events help us to gain a clear understanding of the unification process of Japan: the great Taika Reforms in 646; the first promulgation of the codes in 701; and the transfer of the capital in 710. Could the Wai of Yamato have been capable, several centuries before this political centralization, of bringing such regions as Jugoku or Northern Kyushu, under their control? Without first doing so, they could not have subdued the peninsula.

In considering this point, I will summarize the theories of Yi Jin-hui, a Korean historian resident in Japan. Japanese scholars generally believe in the Wai's capability of launching a military expedition against the peninsula based on the discovery of tombs in western Japan. These tombs, square at the front and round at the back, are believed to be from fourth to fifth centuries when the Yamato government had strong centralized power. However, there is no proof that these tombs were first constructed in central Japan. On the contrary, tombs of this type, but probably from a much earlier period, also exist in the western regions such as Kyushu and Jugoku. It would seem therefore that the western Wai (of Korean descent) advanced towards the central regions, contrary to the assertions made by Japanese historians. Even if one assumes the tombs to be from the same period, there is no evidence to suggest that war took place thus subduing the region from Kanto to Kyushu.

In this connection, two facts draw our particular attention: i) it was after the second half of the fifth century that the number of Yamato government *miyake* increased over a very wide area; ii) a basic change also took place during that period in the construction style of tombs and the buried objects, especially those made of iron. From this it can be inferred that the Wai of Yamato carried out a policy of centralization during the second half of the fifth century, but that it would have been very difficult for them to have dispatched armies to the Korean peninsula.

Some Japanese scholars believe that the Wai of Yamato set up a federal government, combining the regional powers. These scholars argue that the Wai of Yamato managed to gain almost complete control, if not absolute power. Some further argue that the government sent military expeditions overseas into neighboring territories to subdue regional principalities. The argument continues that the iron, slaves and the techniques acquired from their expedition to the peninsula enabled them to win the war on the Japanese archipelago. However, with regard to this supposed federal government, it probably was merely a coalition of regional powers in central Japan, rather than a federation extending throughout the archipelago. Even if there had been such a federation, the Yamato government's military expedition overseas could not be carried out unless the strong regional powers were utterly subdued. if one accepts the fact that the advanced iron culture in Japan was as a result of the military expedition to Korea, the qualitative change in japanese iron culture must have taken place after the period 450–500.

Even in the *Nihon shoki* one can find evidence that the Wai of Yamato were not yet in control of the Kyushu region during the period 360–370 when the supposed military expedition against Mimana took place. The famous Iwai revolt of 527 well illustrates this point. At this time, Keitai, the King of Yamato, intended to invade Silla with 60,000 troops under the pretext of the "reconquest of Mimana." One of the great provincial lords, Iwai, who opposed the project, started a revolt against the central government. First, he succeeded in halting the advance of the expeditionary force by bribing its commander, then he occupied the regions of Hi, now Saga and Toyo, now Oith. He held out stubbornly against the Yamato armies for a year and a half before finally succumbing to defeat. Following this revolt, the *miyake* of Gaska (now Fukuoka prefecture) came under Yamato's control.

It is clear that even after 500 A.D. there was a provincial power strong enough to challenge Yamato for a year and a half, and that the power of Yamato extended over northern Kyushu only after then. Moreover, in Yame of Jukuoka prefecture, there is a tomb presumed to be that of Iwai. The style of this tomb is not truly Japanese, but Korean (as it incorporates stone statues of a man and a horse). This indicates that Iwai governed groups of migrants from the peninsula. Furthermore, we can conclude from the Iwai revolt that a military expedition could have been launched by the Wai of northern Kyushu (of Korean descent) but not by the Wai of Yamato.

3) Thirdly, one must consider the size of the Japanese expeditionary force at the time of the supposed rule in the south of the peninsula. We shall also limit ourselves to the accounts of Yi Jin-hui on this point. According to the *Samguk sagi* and the inscription on the tomb of King Gwanggaeto, there were between 30,000 and 50,000 soldiers under arms in the Three Kingdoms some time during the latter half of the 4th century. Therefore, the Japanese armies, whether of Yamato or northern Kyushu, must have been exceedingly large to have occupied the south of the peninsula for an extended period. Japanese forces however, had only small boats, even after the fifth century. It is doubtful, therefore, that the Japanese would have been possible to transport such armies in these crafts.

Furthermore, during the period 350–400, the power of the peninsular cavalry reached a considerable level. A certain historical source indicates that it was after the period 450–500, under the influence of Korean military art (the techniques of knightly combat), that Japanese armour, such as the helmet, the breast-plate, the sabre and the lance changed to follow the Korean style. Could the Wai of Yamato have defeated the people of Korean peninsula? Could they, with the knowledge of military arts and weapons, have kept the Nakdonggang river basin for more than a century?

4) We do not however deny the possibility of a military expedition by some force from the Japanese archipelago. Since ancient times, people traveled between the Three Han States or the Three Kingdoms and the Japanese archipelago. The *Samguk sagi* records show that the Wai often raided the peninsula, but it probably was the Wai of northern Kyushu, rather than of Yamato. Even if a Japanese military campaign took place, they probably were not able to take the southern peninsula under control.

Some Japanese historians have argued the following hypothesis:

A Wai tribe originally inhabited the Korean peninsula, along with other major role in the "administration" of Mimana. The Wai of the Three Han States / Three Kingdoms were related to the inhabitants of the peninsula, but it is scarcely credible that the Wai tribe alone crossed the seas to settle in the Japanese archipelago. And it is probable that the people of the Three Han States and the Three Kingdoms only became known as "Wai" after their migration to Japan. There are also some Chinese texts, e.g., the *Shanhaijing* which state that the Wai inhabited the north-eastern part of China. However, it is hardly feasible that there should have been any real communication between these Wai and those who may have lived on the peninsula.

Various Opposing Theories

The claim of Yamato rule in southern Korean peninsula seems highly fictitious. Nevertheless, Japanese historians are still attempting to interpret various historical documents and archaeological findings in such a way to support their theory.

Before examining their studies, however, it would be more fruitful to look at some Korean scholarship on this topic. A systematic examination of the Mimana question has yet to be undertaken in Korea. Few Korean scholars who have approached the problem have done so simply, dismissing the military expedition as one of the Japanese raids, or have explained the "organization" set up in Mimana as a commercial operation to that of a later time. Other scholars have ignored the matter altogether by asserting that Japanese arguments are too preposterous to engage in an academic debate. Such arguments, however, do not add any constructive elements to Japanese scholarship.

Several papers have been published in Korea since the 1960s. One argues that all the references to Mimana in the Japanese historical texts refer to one of the communities on the Japanese archipelago which had set themselves up in the name of the Three States of the Three Kingdoms. Another paper places Mimana on the island of Tushima, not on the Korean peninsula. Due consideration must be given to these explanatory attempts and one should certainly not underestimate their painstaking and well-founded research. Regrettably, however, these studies are not sufficient enough to solve the Mimana puzzle.

Let us now examine them a little more closely.

Clearly, one cannot deny the existence of regional principalities formed by people of Korean descent, as is quite evident from the following passage: "In the 22nd year of the reign of King Ojin, Silla soldiers launched a raid against Japan, and advanced as far as the village of Akasinoura, a hundred leagues from Osaka. The Japanese cut the throat of a white horse as a sign of peace, which they swore on oath to respect the peace west of Akaseki. The tumulus of this white horse still exists." It is mentioned in the *Haedong yeoksa* (History of Korea) and in the *Dongsa gangmok* (Annotated Account of Korean History), which quotes the Japanese book, *Nendaiki* (Chronicles). On the other hand, however, it is difficult to accept this account without reservations. For example, a Chinese text, *Yangzhi gongtu* cites as small satellite communities of Baekje: Banpa, Tak, Dara, Sanggimun, and Hachimna, but it is not feasible to imagine that these names are entirely unconnected with the place-names: Hahe, Tokujun (or Toku), Tara, Komon and Tomutare which were, according to the *Nihon shoki*, in Mimana.

The theory of the island of Tushima has been put forward on the basis of the passage in the *Nihon shoki*: 「任那者去筑紫國＿千里北阻海以在？林之西」. Japanese historians have traditionally translated this as: "Mimana is a thousand *li* (leagues) to the north of Sukusi (northern Kyushu) and the sea separates it from the latter. . . ." But some Korean historians have interpreted this as: "Mimana is 2,000 *ri* from the country of Sukusi and it is bounded on the north by the sea. . . ." But the Japanese interpretation is possible. Therefore, this passage cannot really be taken as tangible proof for the Tushima Island theory. As can be seen in the passage from the chapter of King Silsong of Silla of the *Samguk sagi*:

"The Wai occupied the island of Tushima, built up stores of arms and ammunition, and prepared to invade us." Tushima certainly played an important role as a military base, but it is so small and barren and so thinly populated, that it could not have been Mimana.

In this connection, it can be confirmed that the facts concerning Mimana reported in the *Nihon shoki* are entirely the outcome of the mis-representation of Japanese history which runs throughout this work; the facts concerning the relations between Baekje and Imna (Mimana in Japanese) were transposed and adapted in the *Nihon shoki* to describe relations between Japan and Mimana. Bearing this in mind, one can solve many of the problems relative to Mimana, and moreover, one can also reconstruct a considerable part of the history of Gaya, hitherto obscure. Concerning the history of Gaya, the only information we have refers to the founding and disappearance of some Gaya states, border incidents with Silla, and the period of the Gaya kingdom.

An Overall View of the Mimana Problems

Let us now look at the basic problems concerning Mimana.

In the first place, did Mimana actually exist? In the *Nihon shoki*, the name of Mimana is mentioned several hundred times, and the book on Kinmei in particular is full of page-long references to Mimana and to Baekje.

According to Chinese documents, a Chinese emperor offered the Wai king the right to control all the armies of six or seven peninsular states including Mimana. As we shall see later, this does not necessarily attest to the existence of Mimana: the Chinese emperor recognized this right simply in response to a request from the Wai king; China was certainly not in control of the states in question. But a Chinese historical text dat-ing from the time of the Silla unification of the peninsula, *Hanyuan*, reports that Silla destroyed Imna, quoting the word of an old man of Silla: "Gara-imna was destroyed long ago by Silla," a remark which is particularly significant.

Korean documents also mention Mimana, albeit rarely and in a very fragmentary manner: i) the indication by the inscription of the tomb of King Gwanggaeto that the Goguryeo armies pursued the Wai forces to the territory of Imna Gaya; ii) according to the inscription on the tomb of the great Silla monk Jin-gyeong, he was born of a royal family of Imna; iii) according to the *Samguk sagi*, Gangsu descended from Imnagaryang. On the evidence of these documents, it is impossible to deny that there was a place called Imna on the Korean peninsula. Even if one accepts the hypothesis that Imna (Mimana) was in the Japanese archipelago or on the island of Tushima, one must still find solutions to the existence of Imna on the Korean peninsula.

Secondly, where exactly was Imna on the Korean peninsula? According to the *Nihon shoki*, when the people of Mimana went to Japan for the first time, the Wai gave them a place-name: Mimana from the name of the Emperor Mimaki (King Sujin). Now, certain Japanese scholars assert that King Mimaki was an emigrant from Gaya. Therefore, one can also say that the name of King Mimaki came from the Gaya word, *mimana*. Although there are several explanations of the etymology of the word *mimana*, we shall here adopt the opinion which identifies the country of Mima (*na* probably means "country") with the country of Mioyama of Byeonjin (cf. *Haedong yeoksa*). Mioyama occupied the region which is now Goryeong and was replaced by the Greater Gaya.

Imna was also originally in present-day Goryeong. Further the name Mimana in the *Nihon shoki* refers sometimes to the region of Goryeong (Dae Gaya), sometimes to that of Gimhae (Geumgwan Gaya), sometimes to that of Haman (Anra Gaya); or even to all the Gaya states in the Middle as well as the lower Nakdonggang river area.

Thus the Mimana of the *Nihon shoki* corresponds roughly to the Imna of Korean documents concerning the Three Kingdoms. We shall therefore make no distinction between the terms Mimana and Gaya, except where this distinction must be maintained.

Thirdly, did the Wai in fact launch a military expedition against Mimana, and was a Japanese colonial government, the *mikotomoji* of Mimana or the Yamato no Mikotomoji actually set up in the Korean peninsula? These are the really essential questions concerning the existence of Mimana.

Before developing our arguments in detail, we shall sum up our conclusions on these questions:

1) Mimana Gaya, which, according to Japanese documents, fell under the control of the Wai, was under Baekje influence from the year 396 (the date when according to the Japanese texts the first Wai military expedition was launched). From about the year 500, the little Gaya states were occupied one after the other by Silla (cf. article 527, 21st year of the reign of King Keitai, in the *Nihon shoki*). The statement that Gaya was under Baekje influence means that Gaya had her own government

and a certain measure of political autonomy, but that she was affected to some extent by political and military developments in Baekje.

2) The *mikotomoji* of Mimana or the *miyake* of Mimana (Japanese texts even mention the *miyake* of Baekje), which are supposed to have existed from 463, are utterly fictitious. Japanese scholars are generally of the opinion that even the *miyake* on the Japanese archipelago did not appear until the first half of the seventh century and yet in reference to the supposed *kanka* set up in Mimana-Baekje, they say only that it has the same pronunciation as the *miyake* of the Japanese islands, but that the two organizations were different. In other words, they are unable at this time to define the nature of the *kanka*.

If one must account for an organization like the supposed Mimana *mikotomoji* being set up in Gaya territory, it would be feasible to imagine the existence of a permanent Baekje delegation in Gaya. It is therefore absurd to discuss the functions of the Mimana *mikotomoji*.

3) According to the *Samguk sagi*, the Wai often raided the Silla coast. Moreover, in addition to these raids, on the evidence of the tomb-inscription of King Gwanggaeto, they remained for some time in Gaya territory. This fact is accepted even by scholars who place Mimana on the Japanese archipelago.

4) The Wai armies sent to the Gaya region were a support force for Baekje against Silla and Goguryeo. In other words, the Wai armies were not hostile to Baekje but were sent by the Wai at Baekje's request. They were part of the allied forces of Baekje, Gaya and Wai (and naturally the Baekje and Gaya troops outnumbered the Wai). Further, we are of the opinion that the Wai expeditionary force was perhaps not sent by the Yamato government, but by the provincial government of the people of northern Kyushu, who came originally from Baekje or Gaya.

5) Wai troops remained on Gaya soil from the year 399. According to the tomb inscription of King Gwanggaeto, they were utterly routed by the Goguryeo armies in about 407. Even if one supposes that some of them survived, it is obvious that the development of relations on the peninsula would have precluded the permanent stationing of Wai troops.

The Problems of Mimana and the Nihon shoki

The domination of Mimana by the Wai is still one of the principal questions unsolved in the history of Korean-Japanese relations in ancient times. As we have seen above, there are great differences between the opinions of Korean and Japanese scholars. They do not even agree in their interpretation of archaeological material.

The divergence between the explanations offered by the Korean and Japanese scholars also stems from the fact that both groups have relied on only their own documents, although the documents of the two sides often provide contradictory information. For example, excepting a few obscure passages quoted in the Japanese documents, texts on the Three Kingdoms do not mention the Wai domination on Imna, whereas the Japanese texts are full of often contradictory indications, thick with legend.

One may ask why the information in the Korean texts is diametrically opposed to that in the Japanese texts.

First possibility: the writers of the documents relating to the Three Kingdoms deliberately played down the Mimana question. But the *Samguk sagi* and the *Samguk yusa* (Memorabilia of the Three Kingdoms) often report raids by the Wai. These two texts are so impartial in their accounts that they report the fact that the Baekje crown prince Jeonji and the Silla crown prince Misaheun were held hostage by the Wai. It is therefore highly unlikely that these writers would have omitted to mention the Wai occupation for reasons of patriotism. Moreover, before the attempted Mongol conquest of Japan, and before the Japanese pirate raids on Goryeo, Goryeo indubitably enjoyed good relations with Japan.

Second possibility: the writers of the Korean texts, considering the historical event in question to be of little importance, make no mention of it, and conversely, the writers of the Japanese texts refer to it many times and attribute great importance to this event. If, however, the extensive Nakdonggang river region was really under their domination, as the japanese texts would have us believe, it is not possible that the Korean texts would fail to mention it. If Mimana was on the island of Tushima, then they might not have done so, but, as we have seen, there was definitely an Imna on the Korean peninsula.

We are thus led to think that the historical facts concerning Mimana, as set down in the Japanese texts are false.

This possibility arises from the following arguments:

1) Only the *Nihon shoki* describes in relative detail the supposed conquest of the Three Han States by Queen Jingu and the domination of Mimana by the Wai. However, it should be noted that the *Kojiki* (Notes on Past Events, 712), a work almost contemporaneous with the *Nihon shoki* (720), hardly mentions the domination of Mimana although it goes

into great detail about the conquest of the Three Han States. Regarding other historical events, the *Kojiki*, a government publication, covers a period of several decades after 562 (the year, according to the *Nihon shoki*, of the Silla conquest of Mimana).

So what is the significance of these differences and discrepancies in the dates? Why does the *Kojiki* attach so little importance to this supposedly great event which exercised such great influence over the subsequent historical development of the Japanese archipelago?[4]

2) The *Nihon shoki* constitutes, for Japanese scholars, absolute and irrefutable proof of the occupation of southern Korea by the Wai. Now even Japanese historians have long pointed out that this work has little historical validity and its authenticity is debatable, for its authors almost certainly misrepresented the history of their country in order to enhance the prestige of the Yamato kings, who had just established their centralizing power. It is odd that these historians, who admit to the misrepresentations relevant to the history of Japan itself, nevertheless insist on the truth of the information in the same text when it concerns Mimana.

Regarding the history of Baekje, Imna and Mimana, we are sure that the writers of the *Nihon shoki* falsified historical fact. For example, according to this text, the Wai government "conceded" to Baekje, on several occasions, a large part of the peninsular regions they had conquered. It may sometimes have happened in the history of the world that a conquering power has recognized the political autonomy of the conquered country. However, the greatest power of this period, China, never granted to another country the right to control a region she had subjugated, even if such a country had good relation with her.

Moreover, this false report is a clear indication of the spread of Baekje power. This is a case which illustrates how the *Nihon shoki*'s misrepresentations often give a clue to the true situation. To take a further example, the passage concerning the Japanese expedition to Mimana is full of discrepancies, even if one takes a literal reading, that is if one believes that the Japanese military operations did in fact take place on the peninsula.

If one believes, on the other hand, that these operations were carried out by Baekje troops, a fairly reasonable interpretation can be put forth regarding most of the passages referring to Mimana. So we are dealing

---

4. Note particularly that this event of such great national importance to the Japanese did not come to an end until 150 years before the *Kojiki* was written.

with a straight adaptation, which has transplanted to the history of Japan the events taken from the history of Baekje.

This misrepresentation of the truth explains why historians, instead of seeing the matter clearly, have fallen deeper and deeper into irrationality. The misrepresentation started after the *Nihon shoki* first appeared, and has continued over the centuries in an effort to sort out the contradictions and discrepancies inherent in the original work.

Ingenious as it was, various traces of the falsification remain: it is not feasible that, according to the *Nihon shoki* this time quoting a Baekje document in an attempt to seem authentic, Baekje should have referred to the country of the Wai using terms such as "the celestial Empire" or "their honored country," in speaking of the Wai to a third country.

3) The *Nihon shoki* contains many pages about Mimana and Baekje, and quotes abundantly from Baekje texts such as the *Baekje gi* (Book on Baekje), the *Baekje sinchan* (New Compiled Book on Baekje) and the "Baekje bon-gi" (Chronological Narratives on Baekje) (These texts probably furnished an important source for the *Nihon shoki* concerning Wai relations with Baekje and Mimana). Strangely, however, there are very few documents in Korea about Baekje and Gaya. This odd phenomenon probably means that most of the documents concerning these states have gone to Japan.

Indeed, the "Baekje bon-gi" is but a small part of the *Samguk sagi*. This work familiarizes us with at least a broad outline of the historical development of Goguryeo, the other country conquered by Silla. On the subject of Baekje, the *Samguk sagi* limits itself to a few of the principal events concerning the period of its foundation, such as the conquest of Mokjiguk of Mahan by the founder-king of Baekje, Onjo. On the other hand, the book on Silla in the *Samguk sagi* contains several fragmentary passages referring to Gaya (border incidents), while the book on Baekje contains scarcely anything relating to Mimana or Gaya.

For several decades, Japanese scholars have been carrying out ingenious documentary research on the place-names and dates in the *Nihon shoki*. Among this research, some of the results await further verification, and there must be some doubt as to some of the conclusions. However, if one has recourse to the results of the research on the assumption that the historical events described took place on the peninsula and not in Japan, one can arrive at relatively reasonable solutions to several of the problems which arise in the course of the study of Korean-Japanese relations in ancient times.

All this serves to confirm that the information concerning Mimana and Baekje provided by the *Nihon shoki* is not purely fictitious, but an adaptation made to enhance the glory of the Yamato kings, based on events which took place between Baekje and Gaya.

4) Why, in the *Nihon shoki*, should the misrepresentation of history have applied to the subject of the relations between Baekje and Gaya? Although the reply to this question must as yet remain hypothetical, one can offer the following explanation.

It is known that the editor of the *Nihon shoki* was a member of the Wai royal family. But as with all government publications, his function was limited to managing the publication of the work. There were historians directly responsible for actually doing the writing. One can be fairly certain about the names of these writers. Now, we believe that the Baekje scholars who had migrated to Japan played the principal role among these writers. It may be that these Korean writers took with them numerous Baekje people who were very hostile, not only toward Silla (which had conquered Baekje) but also probably toward the whole of the peninsula which had been unified by Silla. Certainly, they had little affection for the peninsula where they had been born, just at the moment when the national spirit was growing stronger in Japan, the young and recently unified new state. The desire at the Japanese court to enhance the prestige of the emperor, the hostility which the Baekje immigrants felt towards Silla and even towards their vanquished fatherland, and the constant exchanges between Baekje, Gaya and the Wai, all contribute to the belief that the falsification of Japanese history by the writers of the *Nihon shoki* attempted to give the impression that Baekje and Gaya had long been subject to the political and military influence of the Wai.

5) A Japanese archaeologist, Mori Koiji, remarks that there are no written documents attesting to the colonization of England by the Romans for several centuries, and that archaeological evidence alone provides sufficient proof of it. Now regarding Korean-Japanese relations in ancient times, there is little archaeological evidence to show the influence of Japanese culture on the peninsula, while there are thousands of archaeological remains in Japan to which we can turn to establish the extent of Korean influence on Japan.

If such a strange document as the *Nihon shoki* did not exist, most of the questions concerning Mimana would certainly have been answered without such controversy, or would never have arisen. If, despite various researches assiduously undertaken, it has not been possible to furnish sufficiently precise answers to these questions, it is due to the existence of this curious document, and also because in the course of the Japanese historical and archaeological studies of these problems, assumptions have been considered as irrefutable facts.

An Analysis of Objective Evidence Attesting to the Japanese Conquest of Mimana

The Supposedly Objective Evidence

The *Nihon shoki* is the only history of Japan containing passages on the conquest of Mimana by the Wai. But as we have seen above, even Japanese historians admit that this work has little value as a historical document. This is why Japanese scholars have been at pains to discover objective proofs to corroborate the theory on the domination of Mimana. The proofs put forward are: i) the inscription engraved on the sword shaped like a bough with seven branches (*chiljido*), which is in the Isikami sanctuary near Nara; ii) the inscription on the tombstone of King Gwanggaeto at Tungkuo; iii) the title of *totoku mimana shogunji* (post of which the function is to control the armies of Mimana) which the Chinese emperor conferred on the king of the Wai; iv) the letter to the Chinese court from the Wai King Bu (according to this letter, King Bu crossed the seas and conquered 95 countries to the north of the ocean).

But none of these pieces of evidence lend credence to the assertion made by Japanese scholars that Mimana corresponds to Gaya. On the contrary, one of them confirms the fact that the Wai were subject to Baekje.

Before attempting to analyze in greater detail the information given by the *Nihon shoki*, we must examine these so-called objective proofs.

The Chiljido

The sword in the form of a bough with seven branches made in the kingdom of Baekje is preserved in the Shinto shrine of Isikami in the town of Tenri near Nara. The inscription on this sword in the only one in Japan engraved on a metal or stone object which tells of relations between Baekje and the Wai. The scholars, who attempt to explain the problems of Mimana by reference to archaeological material, consider it to be of great importance because the inscription shows that the sword was made in 369, the year when the first military expedition was launched by the Wai against Mimana. According to the *Nihon shoki*, an envoy from Baekje offered a *chiljido* to the Wai king in 372.

The following passages from the inscription on the *chiljido* have drawn particular attention from scholars: i) As this *chiljido* has a magical power enabling its bearer to evade the blows of a sharp sword, we sent it to the king of a vassal state (literally, "it would be good that a gift should be made of it to a vassal state"); ii) The crown prince of Baekje (whom one presumes to be Konkyushu 近仇首)[5] made it for the king of the Wai (or, according to the wishes; or, according to the request of the king of the Wai). Certain Japanese historians would have us believe that since a member of the royal court of Baekje dedicated the sword to the Wai king, Baekje was probably a vassal state of the Wai of Yamato. However, 「供候王」 means, without any doubt, "to send to the king of a vassal state." One cannot interpret it in the opposite sense of "dedicate it to the king of a suzerain state." The passage: 「爲倭王旨造」 means "to make it for the king of the Wai (being the name of a person)" or perhaps "to make it according to the wishes (旨) or at the request (旨) of the king of the Wai." It is impossible to translate it as "to make it on the command of the king of the Wai." At all events, since the donor was the prince of Baekje, and the recipient the king of the Wai, it is certain that the king of the Wai and the prince of Baekje were not equals. One Japanese scholar attempts to interpret the passage: 「百滋王世子奇生聖音」 in the following way: the king and the crown prince of Baekje owe their lives to the grace of the king of the Wai. What a fanciful interpretation!

The fact that the king of Baekje sent a gift to the king of the Wai simply demonstrates that the relations between the two countries were friendly. Japanese scholars, however, insist on considering this gift as evidence to support the claim that the king of Baekje was a vassal of the king of the Wai. If the relationship between these kings must be clearly defined, it is clear from this passage that the king of the Wai was a vassal of Baekje.

On the other hand, one cannot be certain that, because the *chiljido* is

---

5. According to the *Nihon shoki*, the prince of Baekje is pronounced like *sesimu* (the crown prince), like *koni sesimu*.

preserved in Nara prefecture, the recipient was necessarily the king of the Wai of Yamato. On the contrary, it is likely that the Wai of Korean stock occupying northern Kyushu penetrated the Kinai (Nara) region. It was not until after 450–500 that the Wai of Yamato, having unified Japan, were able to set up official ties with Baekje. All these points preclude the conclusion that the *chiljido* is a very important piece of evidence. It tells us that King Geunchogo of Baekje, who extended his rule as far as the south coast of Jeolla-do, was in contact with the king of the Wai of northern Kyushu, and also that the king of Baekje treated the king of the Wai of northern Kyushu (perhaps of Baekje origin) as a king of a vassal state.

The Tombstone of King Gwanggaeto

King Gwanggaeto is considered one of the great kings of Korean history. During the twenty years of his reign, he succeeded, from his capital Tungkuo on the Yalu (Amnokgang river), in extending Goguryeo territory to the west as far as Liaohe. He defeated the Khitan-Tartars tribe who inhabited Daxinganling. He gained control over the Buyeo of the Changchun region in the north and the Wuji in Northern Manchuria. To the south he inflicted heavy defeats on the allied troops of Baekje, Gaya and Wai, as well as subjugating Southern Manchuria and all the northern region of the Korean peninsula.

Two years after his death, a great tomb with a huge tombstone was erected at Tongguo to commemorate his deeds. The stone was discovered in 1880 and captured the attention of historians from China, Japan, Korea and France. On the stone are passages concerning the military confrontation with the Wai. Japanese scholars assert their argument of the conquest of Mimana by the Wai based on this stone.

Recently, however, scholars are coming to recognize that in 1884, after the discovery of the stone, a Japanese officer named Sako falsified the inscription by coating several parts of it with lime and modifying several characters. Research on this inscription must now be carried out exclusively with the help of prints, since the site of the stone is in the People's Republic of China. We are just beginning to find out how the inscription was modified and the characters changed by Sako. It is also said that the Chinese obliterated some characters in this inscription. If the Japanese or the Chinese changed this inscription, it must mean that they were attempting to conceal passages unfavorable to themselves, and that they falsified the inscription on the stone so that it would help to embellish their national histories. On the other hand, since the surface of the stone has undergone the depredations caused by the elements of nature, several characters are illegible. And, in particular, the passages concerning the relations between Goguryeo and the Wai lend themselves to ambiguity. In deciphering these passages there are several possible interpretations. It is thus difficult, on the basis of this stone, to reconstruct completely the history of Korean-Japanese relations in ancient times.

In this article, we shall confine ourselves to a summary of our own conclusions concerning the deciphering of the tomb inscription of King Gwanggaeto.

1) The character "Wai" appears in the legible part of the inscription nine times. Two of these characters are scarcely legible, but the seven others are quite clear. Hence it cannot be denied that the Goguryeo armies confronted the Wai troops on the peninsula.

2) From the lines decipherable at present, it is learned that the Wai armies were first sent to the peninsula in 391. If one takes this date as a criterion in examining relations between Goguryeo and the Wai, even the inscription presents a contradiction. Also, it is made clear in the *Samguk sagi* and the *Nihon shoki* that the first Wai military expedition to the peninsula was organized in 399 A.D.

3) The Wai forces were completely destroyed by those of Goguryeo in 404, and after that date, the relation between the Three Kingdoms entered a new phase, that of the alliance between Baekje and Silla (433), which put an end to the Wai military intervention in peninsular affairs.

4) It follows that the operations by Wai forces in the peninsula were carried out during the period 399–404, which lasted for six years. They were completely brought to an end with the defeat of the Wai in 404 by the Goguryeo armies.

5) According to the lines decipherable at present, Wai military activity in the peninsula started with the conquest of Baekje. At that period, however, Baekje was a great power second only to China in northeast Asia, and had been opposing Goguryeo for about thirty years. It is absolutely not possible that Baekje was conquered by the Wai. In 396, Baekje was in such a dangerous situation as a result of attacks from Goguryeo, that the capital, Gwangju, had to be abandoned to the enemy. To overcome the crisis, Baekje asked the Wai for reinforcements, and it was in response to Baekje's request that Wai military expedition was launched in 399.

6) The Wai soldiers dispatched to the peninsula at that time fought with the troops of Baekje and probably with Gaya soldiers as well. A maximum of 30,000 soldiers were mobilized for the Baekje forces; there were a mere few thousand soldiers in the Wai expeditionary force.

7) In the Japanese archipelago at that period there were two representative provincial governments: that of the Wai of northern Kyushu, and that of the Wai of Kinai. The military expedition under discussion was organized by the Wai of Kyushu, who maintained very friendly relations with Baekje, and whose country, moreover, was founded by descendants of Baekje and Gaya immigrants. In 404–405, the Baekje royal court sent two scholars, Ajikgi and Wangin, to Wai. These two figures took to the Japanese archipelago the so-called "*hanja* culture" (the culture which was based on Chinese characters). This exchange took place against the background of the friendly relations between Baekje and the Wai of northern Kyushu. On the other hand, the Wai of Kinai were friendly with Goguryeo and Silla.

8) The six year period of Wai military operations in the peninsula, confirmed by the inscription under discussion, bears no relation to the conquest of Mimana to which the Japanese historians refer. This also figures in the *Nihon shoki*, where it is reported that the Wai military expedition launched against the Goguryeo forces retreated immediately.

9) Only the six years of Wai military activity mentioned on King Gwanggaeto's tombstone are confirmed in documents concerning the period of the Three Kingdoms. If one includes the pirate raids on the coast or the intervention, during border incidents, of small detachments which retreated immediately, the Wai incursions on the peninsula amount to between 30 and 40, according to the *Samguk sagi*. But as far as military expeditions of a more important nature are generally concerned, there are only two: the Wai expedition cited by the King Gwanggaeto inscription, and the expedition launched by Japan in 663, which took place just after the fall of Baekje and at the end of the period of the Three Kingdoms. As we shall see below, the frequent expeditions against Baekje and Gaya described in the *Nihon shoki* are purely fictitious.

The Wai Command of the Mimana Armies

Let us now look into the relationship between Baekje, Imna and the Wai, with reference to the titles bestowed by the Chinese kings on the kings of these states.

According to Chinese documents such as *Jinshu, Songshu, Nanqishu,* and *Liangshu,* the Wai Queen Himiko made direct contact with the Chinese court around 240. This contact was interrupted for a certain period, then in 413 the Wai paid tribute to Eastern Jin and for about 90 years until 501, the Wai paid tribute to the Chinese court in the names of the kings San, Chin, Sai, Ko, Bu, etc. These Kings were given various titles by the Chinese kings. In particular, the Wai King Zhen, giving himself the title of Totokuwai, General Andong, Wai King, etc., requested the consent of the Chinese king. In response, the Song court named him only as General Andong and Wai King and it was not until 451 that it granted to the title of commander of the armies of six states, including Gara in place of Baekje (it appears that the Wai requested Chinese consent after dividing Mimana into Ninto and Gara so as to keep the same number while omitting Baekje). Later, the Wai King Bu stubbornly petitioned the Chinese king to grant him the title of *totoku shichikoku shogunji* (commander of the armies of seven states including Baekje), but in the end his wish was not granted.

However, Japanese scholars claim that the Wai actually governed the south of the Korean peninsula, since the Chinese king granted the Wai king the right to command the armies not only of the Wai but also of five peninsular states.

In this connection, the following observations must be made:

1) The titles which the Chinese king gave to the kings of neighboring countries were bestowed according to the requests of the recipients. Thus they were merely formal titles, and had nothing to do with actual power in those countries. This is clear in the case of the Wai King Bu, who did not manage to obtain the title he wanted. In this connection, a further example can be cited. According to a Chinese historical text, *Nanqishu,* the emperor of China bestowed Chinese titles on high officials of Baekje in accordance with the wishes of the Baekje court. Moreover, the Wai King mentioned above asked for the right to control states which had already been conquered by Silla and had disappeared, namely, Mahan and Jinhan. He even claimed that Silla, which was constantly warring with the Wai of northern Kyushu, was under his domination.

Not only were the Wai kings given titles by the Chinese emperor, but other king as well. King Jangsu of Goguryeo was also named in 422 by the Song.[6] In fact at that time Yingzhou (the region around Dalinghua)

---

6. 「都督營・平二州 諸軍事, 征東大將軍, 高句麗王」.

and Pingzhou (the region around Luanhua) were not under the domination of Goguryeo and quite outside the political influence of the Song of Nanhan. At that time too, King Gumisin of Baekje was designated as General Jindong.[7] Later, high officials of Baekje were named directly by the Chinese king, not to mention the prefects of Joseon and Daebang, and the prefects of the Guangyang, Guangling, Qinghua and Chengyang regions in the north of the Chinese continent and quite outside the control of the court of Nanji (479–494).

2) One can classify the title conferred by the emperors of China on the kings of Goguryeo, Baekje and the Wai. Clearly, the king of Goguryeo received a title superior to that of the king of Baekje, and the latter a title superior to that of the Wai king. To be more specific, the kings of these three states were ranked as follows:

    a) The King of Goguryeo
        General Jeongdong → General General Chagi (or General General
        Pyogi) → General Mudong[8]
    b) The King of Baekje
        General Jindong → General Jeongdong[9]
    c) The King of Wai
        General Andong → General Jindong → General Jeongdong[10]

At that time, Silla had no relations with the dynasties of southern China.

As seen above, the Wai could not govern Baekje. It is not true that the king of Wai actually exercised his right to control the armies of Baekje, Silla or Imna even though he was appointed commander of these armies by the Chinese. Therefore, this title cannot be put forward as proof of domination of the southern part of the peninsula by the Wai.

The Letter from the Wai King Bu to the Emperor of China

The letter in question was sent by the Wai King Bu in 476 to the Emperor Song. In this letter, quoted by the *Yimanzhuan* of the *Songshu*, the Wai king entreated the Chinese emperor to launch a military expedition

---

  7. 「都督百濟諸軍事，鎭東大軍，百濟」.
  8. 征東將軍→車騎大將軍 (or 驃騎大將軍)→撫東將軍.
  9. 鎭東將軍→征東將軍.
 10. 安東將軍→鎭東將軍→征東將軍.

against Goguryeo. According to this letter, the Wai often wished to send messengers to the Chinese court, but Goguryeo prevented them from doing so.

In particular, Japanese historians quote the following passage:

> . . . since our ancestors, dressed in their armour, traversing the mountains and crossing the rivers, without a moment's rest, made subject to us 55 uncivilized countries to the east, 60 barbaric countries to the west, and to the north of the seas, having crossed the seas, conquered 95 countries . . .

The countries referred to in the passage, namely, 55 countries to the east, 60 countries to the west, and 95 countries north of the seas, merely correspond to villages or castles as in the *Dongyizhuan* of the *Weizhi*. Therefore, although this letter speaks of several dozens of countries, it must not be concluded that it concerns an immense region.

It seems to us that the 95 countries to the north of the seas correspond to a small part of the Korean peninsula, and that "cross the seas and conquer" is the exaggerated description of the six years of military operations mentioned on the tombstone of King Gwanggaeto. Actually, from the geographical point of view, it would have been difficult for Goguryeo to be an obstacle to the sending of Wai envoys to the Song court, whose capital was Nanjing. In any case, the letter mentioned above is full of hostility towards Goguryeo. One can imagine that this misrepresentation or exaggeration was prompted by the memory of the severe defeat inflicted on the Wai armies by those of King Gwanggaeto. Certain Japanese scholars assert that this letter suggests the fact that the Wai opposed the great power of Goguryeo, and were ignorant of the other two Kingdoms, Baekje and Silla. But this mistaken view displays both and ignorance of the general situation in the peninsula at that time and a lack of knowledge concerning the style in which diplomatic documents were couched during that time.

In conclusion, we would like to repeat that the letter of the Wai King Bu cannot possibly, as we have seen, be put forward as a document proving the domination of Mimana by the Wai.

Analysis of the Articles on Mimana in the *Nihon shoki*

The Falsifications in the Nihon shoki *and in the Interpretation of the* Nihon shoki

Thus far, we have shown that the Japanese domination of Mimana cannot be proved by the objective evidence such as the *chiljido* or the tomb stone of King Gwanggaeto, or by Chinese historical documents. On the contrary, as we have seen, some of this evidence confirms the fact that the Wai were inferior to the peninsular powers.

At this point, to refute the falsifications made from the *Nihon shoki* onwards, we shall examine in some detail the articles concerning the administration of Mimana by the Wai. Since there are about fifty of these articles, there will not be space to analyze every one of them. We shall, therefore, limit ourselves to a study of the most important.[11]

Our task is twofold. First, we must specify the falsifications in the *Nihon shoki* itself, and secondly we must correct the errors of the Japanese scholars in their interpretation of these articles, paying particular attention to the geographical location of ancient place-names. Regarding the documentary research by Japanese scholars on these place-names, it must be said that they were not simply mistaken, but consciously orientated by definite prejudice. The appearance of these erroneous interpretations coincided with the birth of Japanese expansionism at the end of the last century.[12]

The First Articles Mentioning the Japanese Domination of the Southern Part of the Korean Peninsula

The fiction of Wai rule over the southern part of the peninsula starts with the legend of Queen Jingu, which is briefly as follows:

The 14th king of the Wai, Chuai, died while attempting to invade Silla (ca. 320 A.D.). His wife, Queen Jingu, carried on with his plan and

---

11. For more details, see the four volumes of *Sin Dong-a* (December 1972, January 1973, February 1973, and March 1973) where our theory on Mimana was developed at greater length.
12. Map 1 illustrates: (a) the development of Mimana reconstructed by Japanese historians and (b) the development of Gaya. It makes clear the error of the reconstruction by the Japanese historians.

succeeded in conquering Silla. At that time, Goguryeo and Baekje were also subject to Wai. Queen Jingu designated the Three Han States *ujis miyake* and returned to her own country.

According to the *Nihon shoki*, "the queen named the king of Silla *mimakai* (official in charge of livestock) . . . and established the *ujis miyake* in the Three Han States," and according to the *Kojiki*, "Silla was designated as *mimakai* (the place where horses are kept) and Baekje as *watano miyake*."

Actually, the terms 官家, 屯家, 屯倉 which are all pronounced *miyake* mean: "territory governed directly by the Wai king," or "territory where the inhabitants are subject to taxation by the Wai king." As we have already pointed out, Japanese historians, with the exception of a few ultrachauvinists, do not believe that the Wai king conquered the Three Han States or set up any colonial administration of this type in 320. But to substantiate their theory of Japanese domination over the southern part of the peninsula, Japanese scholars generally turn to and quote the article summarized as follows:

In 369 (the 49th year of the reign of Queen Jingu) the Wai launched a military expedition against the peninsula. The Wai troops, having assembled at Tokujun (Daegu or Gyeongsan), destroyed the Silla forces and conquered the seven states: Hisiho (Changnyeong), Nam Gara, Tokunokuni (Gyeongsan or Daegu), Anra (Haman), Dara (Hyeopcheon), Tokujun, Gara (Goryeong). Moving westwards, they attacked a barbaric country in the south, Tomutare (Gangin or Jejudo island), and presented it as a gift to Baekje. King Shoko (Geunchogo) of Baekje and his son, prince Kuis (Geun-gusu) came with their own armies to meet the Wai. At that point, four villages—Hiri (Gongju or Naju), Heju (Gimje), Homuki (Gongju, Yugu), and Hanko (Naju, Bonnam)—surrendered without a struggle. The king of Baekje and his son rejoiced at meeting the Wai general, and then returned to Baekje territory with a Wai envoy. The king of Baekje and the Wai envoy climbed to the summit of a mountain and the king swore an oath to pay tribute to the king of the Wai twice a year, in spring and in autumn, as did the Western barbarians. The following year, the general and the Wai envoy went back to their own country.

It was thus, according to Japanese documents, that the Wai subjugated the middle and lower basin of the Nakdonggang river as well as the provinces of Jeollanam-do, Jeollabuk-do and Chungcheongnam-do. This is the basis of the claim to the Japanese domination of Mimana or the southern part of the peninsula.

However, the theory concerning the supposed Japanese domination of Mimana is clearly fictitious. In fact, if the articles summarized above are closely examine, several matters are debatable. In the first place, it is unthinkable that the Wai armies could have conquered Silla so easily. In the next place, the fate of Silla following the defeat is not mentioned at all. Furthermore, no clear reason is given concerning why the Wai armies invaded the six states surrounding Gaya and the present-day Jeolla provinces. And it is unlikely that the Wai troops would have massed inland at Daegu (or Gyeongsan), rather than at a port.

In any case, it would not have been possible in 369 or thereabouts for the Wai, having crossed the sea, to have carried out military operations over such an extensive area, and to have conquered Baekje as well, exacting from Baekje an oath to pay tribute to Wai.

Baekje was ruled over at that time by King Geunchogo. This king had put to route twenty thousand Goguryeo soldiers (including a number of knights) who had invaded Baekje, and had succeeded in extending his territory to the Yeseonggang river. Subsequently, with thirty thousand soldiers he attacked Pyeongyang, the capital of Goguryeo, and killed the king of Goguryeo, Gogugwon, in battle. It was thus at this period that Baekje reached the peak of its power.

In contrast, as we have seen above, it was not until the period 450–500 that Kinai (the Nara and Osaka regions) managed to form a unified state including the central and western parts of the Japanese archipelago. It was only after Iwai's revolt in 527 that they gained control of northern Kyushu.

If it is presumed that it was the Wai of northern Kyushu who sent troops to the peninsula, it is not certain that they were much more powerful than the Wai of Kinai. Moreover, we have already noted that the Japanese navy, even after the time of the peninsular wars, when Baekje had 30,000 men under arms, had only small vessels capable of transporting 40 or 50 soldiers at the most.

So what lies behind these realistic accounts in the *Nihon shoki*, featuring the names of actual historical people and places? In our opinion, King Geunchogo of Baekje dispatched part of his forces to pursue the Mahan armies into the present-day Jeolla provinces by way of the Nakdonggang river area, leading the rest of his troops in a direct attack on these provinces.

If this was so, one can reasonably assume the following facts: 1) The

Map 1

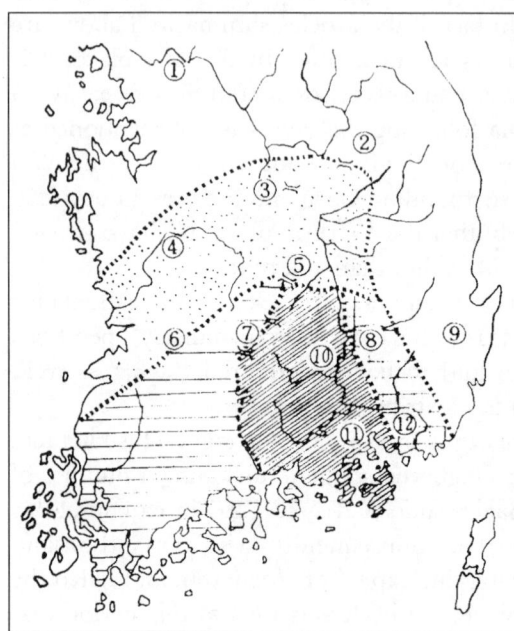

A. Mimana according to Japanese Historians
1. Gwangju
2. Jungnyeong
3. Joryeong
4. Gongju
5. Chupungnyeong
6. Jeonju
7. Machi
8. Daegu
9. Gyeongju
10. Goryeong
11. Haman
12. Gimhae

▦ Mimana in the first period of Wai occupation

▨ Mimana in the final period of Wai occupation

B. Gaya according to Korean Historians
1. Gwangju
2. Jungnyeong
3. Joryeong
4. Gongju
5. Chupungnyeong
6. Hamchang
7. Machi
8. Seongju
9. Daegu
10. Goryeong
11. Changryeong
12. Gyeongju
13. Jinju
14. Haman
15. Goseong
16. Gimhae

▦ The first Gaya period

▨ The final Gaya period

armies of Baekje (of which the capital was Gwangju) crossed the Sobaek mountain range and first assembled at Daegu; 2) Tomutare (which I calculate to be present-day Gangjin) was called the Barbaric Place in the South; and 3) this village was the base for the Baekje expeditionary force.

Concerning this, we can raise an objection as follows: even if we accept that the military operations described in the *Nihon shoki* were carried out by the Baekje armies, we can place a coherent and reasonable interpretation on the articles in question. The positive proof to support this interpretation, however, can be found in the Japanese text itself.

According to the article on King Kinmei (July 541, second year of his reign), the king of Baekje declared, speaking of Mimana, that "his ancestors, King Shoko (Geunchogo) and Kuis (Geun-gusu), made peace with the Kanji (the chieftains of the little Gaya states) and that they swore to come to each other's aid like brothers." So it is even reported in the *Nihon shoki* that Mimana was under the influence of Baekje not the Wai.

So how do Japanese scholars explain their conclusion that Mimana was situated in present-day Jeollabuk-do and Chungcheongnam-do provinces? Research carried out by Korean historians (including Dr. Yi Byeong-do) indicates that the villages in question were in present-day Jeollanam-do province, which was actually, under the sway of Mahan: Hiri, Homuki, Hamuko are the names of little communities in the Naju region, and Heju corresponds to the present-day Boseong.

The First Articles Mentioning the Mikotomoji *or* the Yamato no Mikomoji *of Mimana*

The articles for the seventh and the ninth years of King Xiong (462 and 464) are the first that mention the supposed colonial organization set up in the Mimana territory. However, this does not necessarily mean that the organization in question was established for the first time in those years. According to the Japanese document, it was in 369 that the Wai armies conquered the six states of Mimana, and in 320 that Queen Jingu set up the *ujis miyake*.

But well-documented studies show that the post of *mikotomoji* was first instituted at the time of the great Taika Reforms (646). It is therefore impossible for a *mikotomoji* to have been appointed well before that time in a region overseas. Furthermore, with regard to the *yamato no mikomoji* the name of the country "Japan" (Nihon) does not appear before 600

A.D. it is therefore inconceivable that this organization bearing the name of "Nihon" should have been set up in the peninsula. If one takes *mikotomoji* (a person who carries out the king's orders) or *yamato no mikomoji* to mean a Wai delegation resident in Mimana, and if one supposes that the term "Nihon" in the expression "Nihonfu" is a homonym for the name "Japan," little credence can be put in the articles in question.

First, let us examine in detail the article concerning the Mimana *mikotomoji*:

As the wife of Tasa was beautiful, the Wai king, who desired her, sent Tasa to Mimana as *mikotomoji*. Tasa attempted to organize a revolt with his son Otokimi who had come to invade Baekje.

Reading this article, it is odd to find that Otokimi, who had been ordered by the king to attack Silla, attempted to conquer Baekje, and finally stayed in Baekje instead of attacking it, to take part in the revolt organized by his father.

If one takes the hypothesis that Tasa and his son were of Baekje origin, the passage becomes a little less confusing. In other words, one should, on the one hand, consider Tasa, the supposed *mikotomoji*, to have been a Baekje military leader sent to Gaya (Mimana), who felt some resentment against his king; and on the other hand, it would be reasonable to believe that his son Otokimi, who stayed in Baekje, attempted to rise against the royal authority, along with other rebels both in the country and abroad.

Next, let us look at the article which first mentions the *yamato no mikomoji* in Mimana. According to the *Nihon shoki*, the king of Silla, retreating before the Goguryeo army, asked for help through the king of Mimana, from the general staff (*ikusanokimi*) of the *yamato no mikomoji*; the Wai generals, bringing reinforcements, inflicted a severe defeat on the Goguryeo troops.

In 433 Baekje and Silla concluded a military alliance against Goguryeo. It is reported in the *Samguk sagi* that the allied forces of Baekje, Silla and Gaya (Gaya was at that period subject to Baekje) won a great victory over the Goguryeo armies. Moreover, even the *Nihon shoki* states that relations between Silla and Wai were always hostile. It is therefore out of the question that Silla should have asked the leaders of the Wai forces for help in repelling Goguryeo's attack. The general staff of the Mimana *yamato no mikomoji* was actually that of the Baekje armies stationed in Mimana territory.

Is it true that Baekje troops were stationed in the Mimana region? No mention of it is to be found in the *Samguk sagi*. However, since the history of Mimana is largely obscure, one cannot deny absolutely that Baekje troops occupied Mimana just because it is not reported in the Korean document. On the other hand, one could piece together the history of Mimana on the basis of the *Nihon shoki*, which furnishes plenty of information about Mimana. The stationing of Baekje troops in Mimana is a typical example of facts which can be reconstrued in this way.

It seems to me that the area around present-day Jirye in the administrative district of Geumneung was the region of Mimana occupied by Baekje troops in about 463–465, the date when the existence of the *mikotomoji* or *yamato no mikomoji* is first acknowledged in the *Nihon shoki* (see Map 3).

According to the article recording the year 397 (4th year of the reign of King Ojin) in the *Nihon shoki*, Baekje troops were occupying the three regions of Kennan, Sisimu and Kokuna. Japanese historians maintain that the latter two correspond respectively to Hongseong in present-day Chungcheongnam-do province and Gokseong in present-day Jeollanam-do province, or Goksan in present-day Hwanghae-do province. Research so far has not established the locality of the first.

However, Kennan means the region near the southern slopes of the Sobaek mountains, Sisimu is present-day Jirye, and Kokuna is present-day Jangsu. It follows that the regions in question were situated in the area between Jangsu and Geumneung around the Sobaek mountains.

Regarding this matter of location, it is not possible to find irrefutable answers relying solely on the method based on the phonological similarities between the two languages. Our analysis below will confirm the hypothesis on the four *hyeon* (county)[13] and two regions, such that the first regions to fall under Baekje correspond to the area around present-day Geumneung.

The Articles on the Four Hyeon and Two Regions Supposedly Conceded to Baekje by the Wai King

In corroborating the theory asserting Japanese domination of Mimana, Japanese historians also refer to the information in the *Nihon shoki* concerning the four *hyeon* and two regions supposedly conceded to Baekje by the Wai. In the articles for the 6th and 7th years (512–513 A.D.) of

---

13. A *hyeon* is a unit of the administrative division of territory in ancient Korea.

Map 2. Location of Historical Places according to the Articles of the 49th Year of Queen Jingu's Reign (ca. 369 A.D.) in the *Nihon shoki*

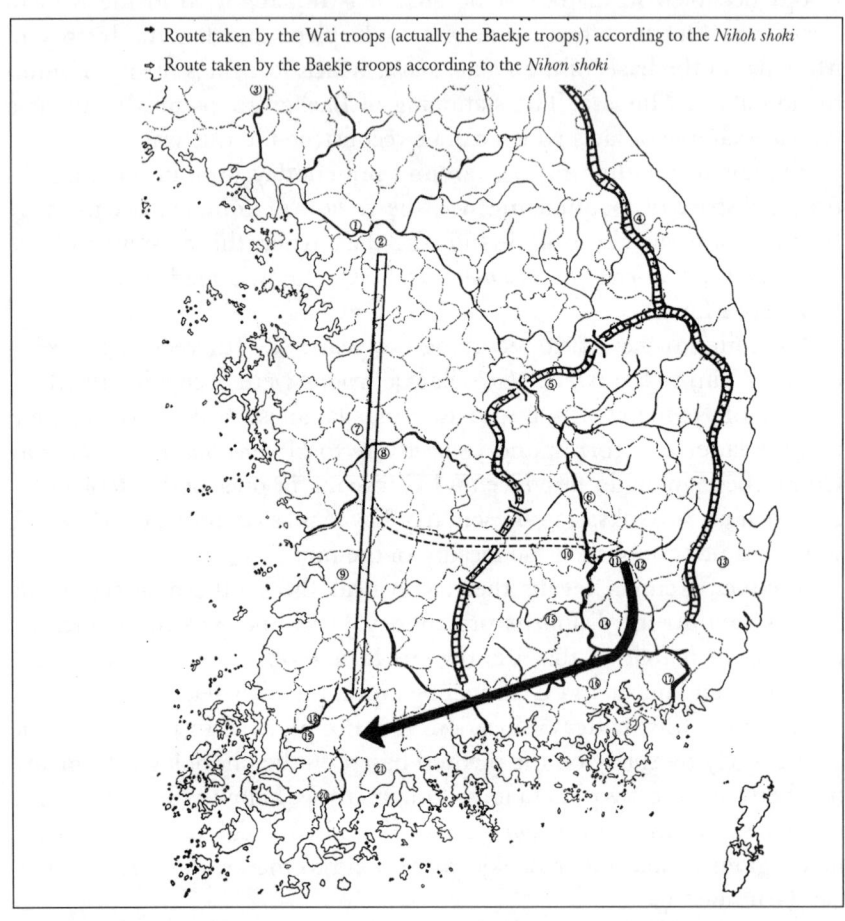

1. Present location of Seoul
2. Gwangju: capital of Baekje
3. Yeseonggang river
4. Taebaeksan mountain range
5. Sobaeksan mountain range
6. Nakdonggang river
7. Yugu (Homuki in Japanese history)
8. Gongju (Hiri in Japanese history)
9. Gimje (Heju in Japanese history)
10. Goryeong (Kara in Japanese history)
11. Daegu (Tokujun in Japanese history)
12. Gyeongsan (Tokunokuni in Japanese history)
13. Gyeongju: capital of Silla
14. Changnyeong (Hisiho in Japanese history)
15. Hapcheon (Tara in Japanese history)
16. Haman (Ara in Japanese history)
17. Gimhae (South Kara in Japanese history)
18. Naju (Hiri and Homuki according to Korean historians)
19. Bannam (Hamuko)
20. Gangjin (Tomutaro)
21. Boseong (Haeju according to Korean historians)

the reign of King Keitai, it is written that Baekje requested King Keitai to deign to give Baekje four *hyeon* such as Upper and Lower Tari, Sata, and Muro, and the request was granted. It is also reported that Baekje later requested the return of the former Baekje territory of Komon, which had been occupied by Hahe, and that the king of Wai also conceded Komon and Tasa to Baekje.

Was it really within the power of the king of the Wai to give Baekje these four *hyeon* and two regions as it pleased him? As we have noted above, world history has no such examples of power which concedes the right to control part of its territory to another state. Moreover, if one takes the information at face value, the Wai king gave Baekje the Tasa region, which had not even been requested. Did the king of Wai throw it in for good measure? This fanciful, trumped-up report does, however, point to the truth of the situation. It indicates that Baekje gained control of these four *hyeon* and two regions.

Where can one localize the areas in question? The conclusions of Japanese research are as follows:

1) Upper and Lower Tari = the area between Gwangju and Yeongam bank of the Yeongsangang river in Jeollanam-do province
2) Muro = the area around Yeonggwang and Muan, the western coastal region of Jeollanam-do province
3) Komon = the area around Sunchang and Namwon, the upper Seomjingang river region;
4) Sata = the area around Gurye, the central Seomjingang river region;
5) Tasa = the area around Hadong, the lower Seomjingang river region.

Briefly, these areas include almost the whole of Jeollanam-do province. According to historians, the Wai lost these territories in 512–513, the first stage of the decline of the Wai power in the peninsula.

But it is a grave error on the part of Japanese scholars to localize the four *hyeon* and two regions in present Jeollanam-do province and to place the three villages mentioned above (Hiri, Heju and Homuki) in the provinces of Jeollabuk-do and Chungcheongnam-do. Does this mean that these areas of present-day Jeollanam-do province, to say nothing of those in the provinces of Jeollabuk-do and Chungcheongnam-do, were under the control of Baekje from the conquest in 369 by Baekje of Maha, which occupied these regions at that time? In any case, the Japanese research on these questions has no solid basis. The one which appears most convincing is the localization of Komon, which the Japanese scholars place in the Sunchang and Namwon area, basing their assumption on the hypothesis that the Kimonsen (基汶川) in the *Hanyuan* corresponds to Komonsen (己汶川). But in the geography book of the *Samguk sagi*, it is written that Komon was originally Konmochi. Hence it is more reasonable to associate Komon with Konmochi rather than with Komonsen which the pronunciation would seem to relate to Komon. Again according to the geography book of the *Samguk sagi*, Konmochi corresponds to Eohoi-hyeon in the administrative district of Gaeryeong (present-day Eohoi in the administrative district of Geumneung). We have already localized Sisimu at Jirye in the district of Geumneung, which was under Baekje control around 400 A.D. Similarly, we believe that Eohoi in the district of Geumneung also came under Baekje control at about the same date. In about 510 this region was invaded by the armies of Hahe (now Seongju), but subsequently always belonged to Baekje.

So the localizing of Komon can serve as the point of departure for research on the other places, which can be logically placed in the Nakdonggang river region and not in the present-day Jeollanam-do province.

On this basis, the results of the attempts at localization are as follows:

1) Muro = Yecheon
2) Tari = Dain in the administrative district of Uiseong
3) Sata = Indong in the administrative district of Chilgok
4) Tasa = Habin and Dasa, in the administrative district of Dalseong

Thus, the four *hyeon* and two regions occupied by Baekje correspond to the upper and middle parts of the Nakdonggang river—Yecheon, Dain, Indong, Dasa—and in the center of which is the region of Geumneung. This localization is also justified, albeit indirectly, by the following historical fact:

Originally, as far back as 150–250, Silla occupied the upper and middle basin of the Nakdonggang river (Uiseong, Geumneung, Gaeryeong, Seongju); however, in 523–524, Silla gave particular attention to those areas, establishing a secondary capital[14] at Asichon (present-day Anpye-

---

14. In the Silla period, a secondary capital was established in a militarily or politically important region.

ong, in the administrative district of Uiseong) and a *gunju*[15] at Sangju. Might this have been because Baekje troops were invading these areas?

At any rate, to say that the Wai made a gift of four *hyeon* and two regions to Baekje is to indulge in pure fiction. As we have shown, both Baekje and Silla were trying to gain control of these regions at the same time. Only Komon was the subject of dispute between Baekje and Gaya.

The Articles on the Supposed Yamato no Mikomoji of Ara

According to the *Samguk sagi*, Baekje was advancing towards the upper and middle Nakdonggang basin in 512–513. Silla attempted to repel these attacks from the year 524 (the 11th year of the reign of King Beopheung) and reoccupied the Sangju region. On the other hand, according to the *Nihon shoki*, at roughly the same period, Silla extended its territory to Gyeongsan, Daegu and Sangju areas in the central Nakdonggang region, and as far as the Gimhae region in the lower Nakdonggang basin. On the basis of all this information, one may conclude that Silla was militarily active all along the natural line of the Nakdonggang river (see Map 3).

Thus among the Gaya regions of the Nakdonggang river area, the upper basin was occupied by Silla from 150-250, but it was once invaded by Baekje. The other regions, around the middle and ower Nakdong, seem to have centered respectively on Geumgwan Gaya (capital: Gimhae) and Dae Gaya (capital: Goryeong). This is why Geumgwan Gaya was also called Nam Gaya (South Gaya) or Ha Gaya (Lower Gaya), and Dae Gaya was also known as Buk Gaya (North Gaya) or Sang Gaya (Upper Gaya).

But when Gimhae came under Silla control, the Gaya capital was transferred to Haman (Ara Gaya: Anra in the *Nihon shoki*) and all the small Gaya states were divided into two groups—Dae Gaya and Ara Gaya.

According to the *Nihon shoki*, after 527 (the 21st year of the reign of King Keitai) the Wai king gave particular attention to a plan for the reconquest of the territories lost to and occupied by Silla—Nam Gara (Gimhae) and Tokukoton (Daegu or Gyeongsan). At this point, it is

---

15. A military chief of staff in the Silla period who was put in command of the armies of each province (*ju*).

scarcely necessary to repeat that this was a plan of the king of Baekje, who wished to reconquer these regions. Still referring to the *Nihon shoki*, it is reported in detail that the various Gaya tribes (Dae Gaya and Ara Gaya), allied with Baekje, were attempting, at about this date, to confront Silla militarily. In articles concerning this period, there is a reappearance of the expression, "*yamato no mikomoji* of Mimana," which had not figured in the chronicle for some time. In one article there appears the term "*yamato no mikomoji* of Ara." What was this *yamato no mikomoji* of Mimana or Ara in the last days of the history of Gaya? In our opinion, it was a sort of general staff of the Baekje troops sent to the Ara Gaya region, that is Ara or Anra Gaya of Haman.

Although the *Samguk sagi* makes no mention of the Baekje military expedition to the Haman region, one can, with the information in the *Nihon shoki*, formulate the following conclusions about the Baekje territorial expansion:

1) In the Japanese text, it is written that the Wai king made a gift to Baekje of Dasa (Han Dasa and So Dasa, the latter corresponding to Hadong). Actually, it was Baekje which occupied Hadong.

2) According to the article for the year 531, the Baekje armies reached Ara and built the castle of Kotoku. It is thus clear that Baekje advanced as far as Haman and built a castle at Jinju. The ancient name for Jinju was Geotaseong, which would correspond to Kotoku. The *Dongguk yeoji seungnam* (Augmented Survey of the Geography of Korea) also tells us that Jinju was occupied by Baekje until the unification of the Three Kingdoms by Silla. It says, "Jinju was originally Geotaseong in Baekje; King Munmu of Silla conquered Jinju and set up a province there."

Baekje had to cross the Sobaek mountain range to invade the Gaya regions around the Nakdonggang river. The main routes across the Mountain range are:

    a) Jungnyeong[16]
    b) Joryeong
    c) Chupungnyeong
    d) Machi
    e) Yuksimnyeong
    f) Pallyangchi

---

16. *Ryeong* (嶺) or *chi* (峙) means mountain-pass.

The history of the Baekje conquest of Gaya falls roughly into three periods:

1) The first period: Around 400 A.D., Baekje troops had already raided the Geumneung region, crossing the Machi, by route (d). The Sisimu (Jirye) mentioned in the *Nihon shoki* corresponds exactly to this region. Komon (Eohoi) also seems to have come under Baekje control at just this time. It is our opinion that the *yamato no mikomoji* of Mimana mentioned in the *Nihon shoki* was a general staff of the Baekje troops stationed in the Geumneung region.

2) The second period: In about 510, using Geumneung as an advance base, Baekje occupied the upper and middle regions of the Nakdonggang river basin, (Yecheon, Dain, Indong, Dasa), which originally belonged to Silla. The four *hyeon* and two regions, Muro, Tari, Sata, Tasa mentioned in the *Nihon shoki* correspond to these places (although Komon is rather far from the Nakdonggang river). There is scarcely any reference to the Mimana *yamato no mikomoji* in the *Nihon shoki* articles referring to this period.

3) The third period: The Baekje forces which had advanced to the upper and middle Nakdonggang regions retreated before the Silla attacks and then, from the year 530, started to invade the southern coastal regions, Hadong, Jinju and Haman, where one can localize Tasa or the castle of Kotoku of the *Nihon shoki*. As we have noted above, the *yamato no mikomoji* of Mimana or Ara denotes the general staff of the Baekje armies, which were occupying these southern coastal areas. Gaya finally disappeared completely when Dae Gaya of Goryeong was destroyed by Silla in 562.

The Articles on the Japanese Governors of Mimana

We have hazarded that the supposed colonial organization, the *yamato no mikomoji* of Mimana, was actually the general staff of the Baekje troops stationed in the Gaya regions. To support this theory, we must turn to yet another analysis of the information in the *Nihon shoki*.

Concerning this organization, the *Nihon shoki* merely mentions certain titles, hardly reporting any material facts about the administration. On the other hand, the *Nihon shoki* does mention four persons, supposedly officials appointed to deal with the various regions of Mimana. We shall now examine who these people actually were.

1) Mokurakonsi: According to the *Nihon shoki*, this man was the chief of the Japanese expeditionary force sent to the peninsula in 369, at the

time of the first conquest of the seven states of Mimana. A little later, in 382, when another Wai general attempted, in a rebellion against the king, to invade Gara, he came again to ask that country to support him. In the first place, the conquest by the Wai of the seven states of Mimana was in fact the conquest of the Gaya region by the Baekje forces, who were going to attack Mahan in Jeollanam-do province. Further, it is extremely significant that in the *Nihon shoki*, Mokurakonsi is referred to as being a Baekje general. Finally the report that the Wai, having conquered Gara, tried to restore it can be interpreted as the re-establishment by Baekje of Gaya, which had previously been conquered by the Wai. It was Mokurakonsi who was made responsible for the restoration of the kingdom of Gara. The name Mokura (木羅) corresponds to Mok (木) which is one of the eight great family names of Baekje.

As we examine the second example, it will become more evident that Mokurakonsi was from Baekje.

2) Mokumanji: This man was the son of Mokurakonsi; his mother was a Silla woman. Thanks to his father's eminent position, he was called upon to deal with Mimana affairs, and finally became a high Baekje official. Still according to the *Nihon shoki*, he was recalled in 414 for having made a number of mistakes. But according to the *Samguk sagi*, in 475 when Goguryeo forces seized Gwangju, the Baekje capital, the king of Baekje, Gaero, was killed in the battle. His son, King Munju, decided to establish a new capital at Gongju, and turned to the task of building up his country again. And the central figure in this project was Mongnye-manchi.

Comparing the two texts and on the assumption that Mokumanji was born when his father was in Gaya, this would have made him more than 100 years old when the capital was transferred to Gongju, which means that there has been some error in chronology. But in any case, the two persons in question were indubitably of Baekje origin.

3) Kionoiwa: The *Nihon shoki* states that this was "a man who wished to become king of the Three Han States, exercising his power in Mimana and maintaining relations with Goguryeo. In 487, by building the castle of Sitoromure and blocking the route eastward, he prevented the Baekje troops from transporting military supplies." Baekje attacked, and Kionoiwa lost the battle and retreated to his own country (see Map 3).

However, he was also from Baekje. Japanese historians place the castle of Sitoromure at present-day Taein. But how would it have been possible

Map 3. Location of Places during King Keitai's Reign (512–513 A.D.) according to the *Nihon shoki*

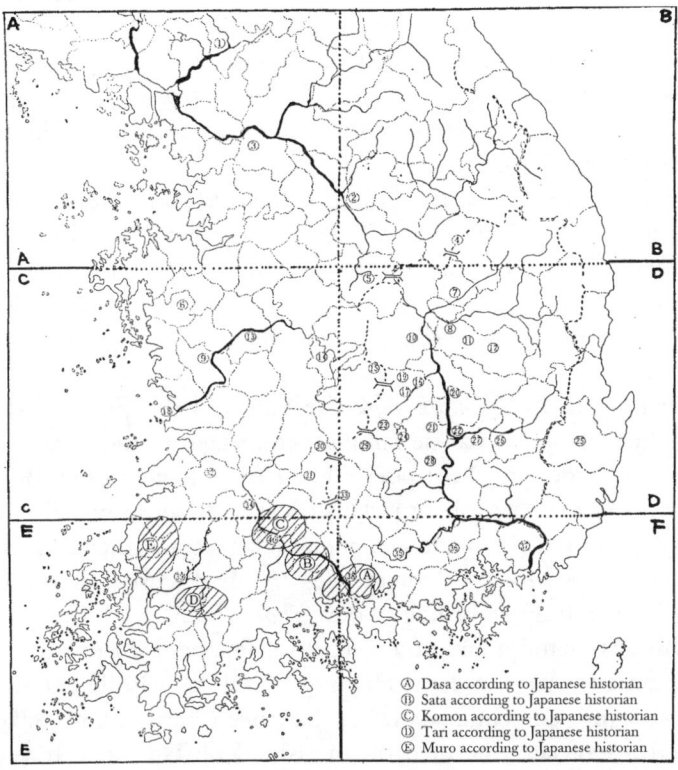

Ⓐ Dasa according to Japanese historian
Ⓑ Sata according to Japanese historian
Ⓒ Komon according to Japanese historian
Ⓓ Tari according to Japanese historian
Ⓔ Muro according to Japanese historian

1. Bukhangang river
2. Namhangang river
3. Gwangju
4. Jungnyeong
5. Joryeong
6. Sisimu in Japanese history
7. Muro according to the author's research
8. Tari according to the author's research
9. Geumgang river
10. Sangju
11. Anpyeong
12. Uiseong
13. Gongju
14. Okcheon
15. Chupungnyeong
16. Gaeryeong
17. Geumneung
18. Entrance of Baekgang river
19. Komon according to the author's research
20. Sata according to the author's research
21. Seongju
22. Sata according to the author's research
23. Sisimu according to the author's research
24. Sitoromure according to the author's research
25. Gyeongju
26. Gyeongsan
27. Daegu
28. Goryeong
29. Machi
30. Yuksimnyeong
31. Kokuna according to the author's research
32. Sitoromure in Japanese history
33. Pallyangchi
34. Seomjingang river
35. Kotoku
36. Ara
37. Gimhae
38. Tasa
39. Yeongsangang river
40. Kokuna in Japanese history

at Taein, in the coastal region of Jeollabuk-do province, to have "blocked the route eastward" and "prevented the Baekje troops from transporting military supplies"? Taisan actually corresponds to the Dosan area of the administrative district of Seongju which is between Seongju and Jirye. This is the site of the fortress of Dogyong. It was there that Sitoromure was built to cut the line of communication between the Baekje troops and the capital. Only it is likely that he went into exile in the Japanese archipelago after his defeat.

Further, Kinosno-noskune (紀角宿稱) referred to in the *Nihon shoki* is written Kinosnonoskune (木角宿稱) in another Japanese historical document, the *Kokenki*. According to this text, he was also an ancestor of the Ki (木) family. Thus it becomes evident that the family name Ki (木) is identical to another name Ki (紀), which has the same pronunciation in Japanese.

According to the *Samguk sagi*, the Hai and the Jin (眞) who were among the eight great Baekje families, connected to the royal family on the maternal side, and held power for a considerable time. But hardly any members of the Mok (木) clan, except Mongnye-manchi occupied important positions or made any remarkable achievements. It is significant that all the Moks (木) or the Kis (紀) had close connections with Mimana, albeit only according to the *Nihon shoki*.

4) Ominoke-naminomi: According to a Japanese document, this personage came to Anra (present Haman) in 529 to help that state recover Nam Gara (present Gimhae) which had been occupied by Silla. But a year and a half later, he died on the island of Tsushima, having gone back home after doing great harm to Anra. It seems that he was of Wai origin, as opposed to others who originated from Baekje. Indeed, if one supposes Ominoke-namionmi to have been of Baekje, Silla or Gaya origin, it is difficult to find a reasonable explanation for the information about him contained in the *Nihon shoki*. Moreover, ancient Japanese historical documents state that he played an important role in Japan at the time when the Wai of Kinai suppressed the Iwai revolt in northern Kyushu. We are not led to believe that he was in command of the armies, but merely that he quickly escaped when he was beseiged by the Silla forces. He was sent to Anra to represent the Wai, and probably had a hand in the development of Wai political diplomacy towards Mimana. But he did not play any part in the supposed Wai administration of Mimana. As it was the period just after the Wai of Kinai had gained control of northern Kyushu, Gaya should have received this Wai delegate in

a different manner from the way it had received previous Wai envoys.

Wai Military Expeditions Unrelated to the Supposed Domination of Mimana

To confirm the non-validity of the theory which asserts the administration of Mimana by the Wai, it is useful to review the information given concerning Wai military expeditions against the peninsula over the two centuries in question.

The *Samguk sagi* makes no mention of the invasion of Gaya or Baekje by the Wai but reports thirty or forty raids by the Wai on the Silla coast. According to this document, the Wai who carried out these raids were always immediately repelled. According to a study of relations between Korea and Japan in ancient times, emigrants of peninsular stock set up several communities in the Japanese archipelago in the name of the Three Han States or the Three Kingdoms. These communities made a considerable contribution to the development of ancient Japan, exercising great cultural, political and military influence.

Therefore, it is not at all strange that the Wai should have come in the opposite direction to make numerous raids on the coast of the peninsula. We are merely concerned with establishing whether or not full-scale military expeditions were carried out by the Wai on the Korean peninsula, lasting a considerable period of time and over a vast area of peninsular territory.

1) The tomb-inscription of King Gwanggaeto refers to the Wai military activities lasting for a period of six years (399–404). But it is remarkable that not only the *Samguk sagi* but even the *Nihon shoki* makes no mention of this at all.

According to this inscription, Baekje requested reinforcements from the Wai of northern Kyushu, during the wars against Goguryeo and Silla. After the defeat of the Wai reinforcements, the situation on the peninsula changed, and Baekje and Silla started a period of collaboration which was to last 120 years.[17] The *Nihon shoki* describes other military expeditions by the Wai, but analysis of the text proves that these were actually military operations carried out by Baekje forces.

---

17. It was in 433 that a military alliance was concluded which put the seal on the collaboration between the two countries.

2) In 533, after the break between Baekje and Silla, Baekje found itself isolated, it turned again to Wai for help.

The *Nihon shoki* states that 4,000 Wai military operations on the peninsula existed, which is also confirmed by the inscription on the tomb of King Gwanggaeto. But given the small size of this force, this cannot really be termed a full-scale military expedition. In any case, as soon as these Wai troops reached the peninsula, they were routed by the Silla forces.

The Silla troops, led by King Jinheung, carried out a great battle against Baekje at Okcheon in 554 and inflicted a heavy defeat on Baekje. According to the *Samguk sagi*, Baekje troops killed in this battle numbered 30,000. It is easy to assess the insignificance of the role of the Wai reinforcements, who did not number above one thousand.

After the battle of Okcheon, Baekje was not able to regain its former power although it attempted to win back the border regions along the frontier with Silla. But these military operations effected no change in the peninsular situation.

3) On the other hand, Silla's policy toward the Tang of China brought positive results. In 651 the Tang, in a seeming effort to bring about a reconciliation between Baekje and Silla, suggested that Baekje should cease its attacks on Silla. The Tang even implicitly threatened Baekje that they would come to the aid of Silla should the Baekje attacks on Silla territory not cease. Baekje, once more in difficult straits, called on the Wai a third time for help. This corresponds to the following fact in the *Samguk sagi* in the article on the 13th year of King Uija's reign, it is stated that King Uija sent a delegation to Wai. This was in 653, seven years before the collapse of Baekje and one year before the great Taika Reforms.

In 660, the allied troops of Tang and Silla mounted a great offensive against Baekje. The *Samguk sagi* states one hundred and thirty thousand troops were mobilized by the Tang and fifty thousand by Silla for this war, but there is no way of telling how many men Baekje had under arms. At all event, Buyeo, the capital of Baekje, immediately fell to the allied troops. At that point Prince Pung, who had been held hostage by the Wai, ascended to the throne and took the offensive against the allies. In consequence, Tang had to send reinforcements of seven thousand soldiers. In 663 Baekje also received reinforcements from Goguryeo and the Wai.

According to the *Nihon shoki*, the Wai soldiers sent at that time numbered about 27,000, but one cannot be sure of the accuracy of this fig-ure. According to the *Samguk sagi*, four hundred Wai boats were burnt at the mouth of the Baekgang river (now Geumgang river) when the Baekje and Wai troops were routed by those of Silla and Tang. It is clear that this third Wai expeditionary force was of little use to Baekje.

4. As we have seen during the Three Kingdoms Period, the Wai sent armies to the aid of Baekje three times:

a) the first expedition (399–404) is reported by the tomb-inscription of King Gwanggaeto;
b) the second expedition took place at the time of the battle of Okcheon in 554;
c) the third expedition was defeated at the battle of the mouth of the Baekgang river in 662.

Each expedition ended in the defeat of the Wai expeditionary force. Since these three expeditions were sent as reinforcements for Baekje, one might assume that Baekje and the Wai maintained a permanent relation, and that these facts reflect the domination of the south of the Korean peninsula by the Wai.

However, these expeditions took place quite independently of one another each time Baekje found herself in an internationally isolated sit-uation. Moreover, it is clear that the first expedition was carried out by the Wai of northern Kyushu, and that the second and third were orga-nized by the Wai of Kinai, who had succeeded in setting up one sole government in the Japanese archipelago.

Conclusion

The following passage is an extract from *The History of Japan*, a Japan-ese high-school textbook published prior to 1945:

Since only a narrow strip of sea separates the Korean peninsula from our country, there has since time immemorial been communication between the two peoples. In ancient times this peninsula was settled by the Mahan, Byeonhan and Jinhan tribes. Later, it was divided into Three Kingdoms: Silla, Goguryeo and Baekje. The region between Silla and Baekje admired the virtue of our (Japanese) court and submit-ted to our country. This was the region called Mimana. Our country ruled this region, setting up a *yamato no mikomoji.*

The following passage is also an extract from a Japanese high-school textbook, published in 1965, twenty years after the end of Japanese colonialism in Korea:

> In the *Kojiki* or the *Nihon shoki*, edited in the eighth century, it is reported that Queen Jingu, with her naval forces, subjugated the southern region of the Korean peninsula.
>
> When the court of Taika (the Wai of Kinai) had achieved unification (in Japan) on the Korean peninsula, where the Chinese occupation had only just come to an end, there was a confrontation between Goguryeo, Silla and Baekje. At the end of the fourth century, with Mimana as a base, the Japanese court sent armies to southern Korea, waged war against Baekje and Silla, and fought Goguryeo. The administrative organization set up in these regions was called the *yamato no mikomoji.*

It is thus that the supposed conquest of the Three Han states by Queen Jingu, considered a legend even by Japanese historians, is still described as an actual fact in certain Japanese secondary-school books. These textbooks are founded on erroneous opinions and misrepresentations which maintain that the history of Korea started with Chinese occupation, and that Silla and Baekje were subjugated by Japan. These are serious mistakes that cannot be passed over in silence.

The Japanese theory concerning the domination of the southern region of the Korean peninsula has been clearly revealed as a complete fiction with no solid basis. Since the Japanese consider that the manpower and material resources acquired in the course of this occupation contributed greatly to the unification of Japan, the problems concerning Mimana present one of the major questions in the study of Japan. This is why it is fitting that historians in Korea, which is in a sense the victim of this theory, should carry out research and bring to light the true character of Korean-Japanese relations at that time.

We have been at pains to find the exact answer to these problems by formulating the theory that the historical facts contained in the *Nihon shoki* concerning the relations between the Wai and the peninsula were in fact merely a transposition of events which took place between Baekje and the rest of the peninsula.

Hwarang Organization:
Its Functions and Ethics

Vladimir Tikhonov

Along with Dangun, the legendary progenitor of the Korean race, Great King Sejong (r. 1418–1450), the inventor of Hangeul, and the illustrious admiral Yi Sun-sin (1545–1598) Silla's *hwarang* (literally "flower boys") organization has become one of the most popular symbols of Korean ethnic identity.[1] In fact, keen interest in the history of the *hwarang* persisted among Korean intellectuals of successive dynasties for several cen-

* Originally published in the *Korea Journal*, vol. 38, no. 2 (summer 1998).

Vladimir Tikhonov is currently teaching in the Oslo University, Norway. The theme of his doctoral dissertation is "Political and Diplomatical History of the Gaya Proto-States from mid-5 c. to 562" (Ph.D. in History, Moscow State University, 1996). He has written a number of articles on Korean ancient history and Buddhism, including "Epigraphical Sources on the Official Ideology of Unified Silla—On Material of the Inscription on King Munmu's Tomb Stele" (2000), "Social Darwinism in Korea and Its Influence on Early Modern Korean Buddhism" (2001). E-mail: vladimir.tikhonov@east.uio.no.

1. Kim Dong-uk argues that "the Way of the *hwarang*" (*hwarangdo* 花郎道) fully represents the traditional Korean spirituality, in much the same way that the concept of "gentlemanliness" reflects the essential features of the modern Western psyche, and the doctrines of *shidao* (道士) and *bushido* (武士道) contain the gist of traditional Chinese and Japanese philosophies respectively. Cf. Kim Dong-uk, "Hwarangdo-wa sinsado-wa seonbido" (The Way of *Hwarang*, the Gentlemanship and the Way of the Literati), in *Hwarang munhwa-ui jaejomyeong: Silla munhwaje haksul balpyohoe nonmunjip, je 8 jip* (New Research on the *Hwarang* Culture: The Collection of Papers Presented at the Academical Conference held on the Occasion of the Festival of Silla Culture, vol. 8) (Seoul: Silla Munhwa Seonyanghoe, 1989), pp. 15-33. The thesis of "The Eternal Spirit of *Hwarang* as the Driving Force of the Nation's Perpetual Struggle against External Enemies," containing visible chauvinistic traits, was extensively elaborated on by Yi Seon-geun, an influential ideologue of the past. Cf. Yi Seon-geun, *Hwarangdo yeongu* (The Research on the Way of the *Hwarang*) (Seoul: Haedong Munhwasa, 1950).

turies.[2] Among the factors contributing to *hwarang* prominence today, a variety of their functions can be enumerated, such as the pluralistic and non-sectarian character of their religious and philosophical beliefs, and the pan-national, non-class-bound structure of their organization.[3]

The same factors are probably accountable for one interesting feature of *hwarang* studies in present-day South Korea: scholars cannot agree on which of the various beliefs and functions of *hwarang* were primordial. Most mainstream historians hold that, being a successor to the youth leagues of the primitive society, the *hwarang* organization was, at least at the time of Silla's unification wars in the late sixth and early seventh century, primarily an elite corps d'armée which provided the state with well-trained warriors in times of emergency. Historians have also usually stated that the organization was a kind of "springboard" for upward social mobility, carrying the function of a training center for would-be high-ranking state cadres.[4] It is also widely accepted that the *hwarang*

---

2. A detailed description of the *hwarang*'s activities can be found in such well-known Goryeo (918–1392) chronicles as *Samguk sagi* (History of the Three Kingdoms, 1145) by Kim Bu-sik (1075–1151), *Haedong goseungjeon* (Lives of Eminent Korean Monks, 1215) by Gakhun and *Samguk yusa* (Memorabilia of the Three Kingdoms, 1285) by Iryeon (1206–1289). Leading intellectuals of Goryeo—Yi Gyu-bo (1168–1241), the author of *Dongguk Yi Sangguk jip* (The Collection of Writings by the Chancellor Yi of the Eastern State), Yi In-ro (1152–1220), the author of *Pahanjip* (Collected Works of Yi In-ro), Yi Gok (1298–1351), the author of *Dongyugi* (The Records of Travels to The East), and many others were fascinated by stories of Silla's "Four *hwarang*," who used to cultivate their virtues in mountains near Samilpo lake (Goseong-gun county of Gangwon-do province). Interest in the four *hwarang* was also expressed by certain Joseon literati, such as Kim Jong-jik (1431–1492), his disciple Nam Gon (1471–1527), great Silhak scholar Yi Su-gwang (1563–1628), to name only a few. So, the nationalist historians, like Sin Chae-ho (1880–1936), who often emphasized the "*hwarang* spirit," have taken up, in some sense, a Joseon "*hwarang*ophilic" tradition. Cf. Kim Sang-hyeon "Goryeo sidae-ui hwarang insik" (The Perception of the *Hwarang* in Goryeo Period), in *Hwarang munhwa-ui jaejomyeong*, pp. 217-243.

3. According to Yi Gi-baek and Yi Jong-uk, even plain commoners could join the ranks of *hwarang* disciple. Cf. Yi Gi-baek, *Hanguk-ui jeontong sahoe-wa byeongje—Hanguk sahak-ui banghyang* (Traditional Society and Military System in Korea—The Trends of Korean Historiography) (Seoul: Ilchogak Publisher's Co., 1978), pp. 194-201; Yi Jong-uk, "Silla hwarangdo-ui pyeonseong-gwa jojik, byeoncheon" (The Structure of Silla *Hwarang* Order and the Changes in its Organization), in *Hwarang munhwa-ui jaejomyeong*, p. 255.

4. In *Samguk sagi* by Kim Bu-sik it is stated that "[When the state] began to support *wonhwa* (the female predecessors of the *hwarang*), [it was for the reason that] first the

organization was basically an educational institute, where a wide range of native traditions—ethical, religious, moral, poetical, etc.—were taught to adolescents.[5] At the same time, historians cannot help but agree that *hwarang* also performed some religious functions.[6] Some younger researchers even consider these religious functions to have been the most important for the *hwarang* organization as a social institution.[7] As to the essence of the *hwarang* teachings, leading historians maintain that, as a military training unit, *hwarang* "order" mostly taught its disciples self-sacrifice for the sake of the state.[8] But serious attention is also being paid to the role of Buddhist faith and the Maitreya cult in *hwarang* philosophy,[9]

King and [his] ministers were in anguish over their ignorance concerning the men [of ability]. So, they decided to assemble [young people] into a group and let them enjoy themselves together, all the while interested in seeing how moral their behavior was, and then recommending [the best] for official appointments. . . . So, it became possible to know the merits and demerits of these people and to choose the right persons to recommend to the Court. That is why Kim Dae-mun wrote in his *Hwarang segi* (Annals of the *Hwarang*): "Wise ministers and loyal servants came from among them; talented generals and brave soldiers were produced by them." (Chapter 4, 37th year of King Jinheung. In the original: "始奉源花 初君臣病無以知人 欲使類聚群遊 以觀其行義 然後舉而用之 (…) 因此 知其人邪正 擇其善者 薦之於朝 故金大問花郎世記曰 賢佐忠臣 從此而秀 良將勇卒 由是而生.")

5. Kim Bu-sik's *Samguk sagi* also mentions the *hwarang*, saying that "they helped each other to practice their moral virtues and entertained each other with songs and music; they ranged over the mountains seeking amusement and there were no remote places they did not reach" (Chapter 4, 37th year of King Jinheung. In the original: "相磨以道義 或相悅以歌樂 遊娛山水 無遠不至").

6. Yi Gi-baek, *Hanguksa sillon* (New History of Korea) (Seoul: Ilchokak Publishing Co., 1989), p. 72; Yi Gi-dong. *Silla hwarangdo-ui sahoehakjeok gochal—Silla golpumje sahoe-wa hwarangdo* (Sociological Study of the *Hwarang* Order in Silla—The Bone-Rank System in Silla Society and the *Hwarang* Order) (Seoul: Ilchokak Publishing Co., 1984).

7. Choe Gwang-sik, *Godae hanguk-ui gukga-wa jesa* (The State and the Sacrificial Rites in Ancient Korea) (Seoul: Hangilsa Publishing Co., 1994), pp. 272 297.

8. Sin Hyeong-sik, "Hanguk godaesa-e natanan chunghyo sasang" (The Ideology of the Loyalty and Filial Piety in the Ancient History of Korea), *Seongsin yeodae nonmunjip* 11.11; Sin Hyeong-sik, *Sillasa* (The History of Silla) (Seoul: Ewha Womans University Press, 1993), pp. 180-183.

9. Kim Sang-gi, "Hwarang-gwa mireuk sinang-e daehayeo" (On the *Hwarang* and Maitreya Belief), in *Hanguk sahak nonchong: Yi Hong-sik baksa hoegap ginyeom* (The Collection of Papers on Korean History: In Honour of Dr. Yi Hong-sik's 60th Birthday Anniversary), ed. Commemoration Committee for Dr. Yi Hong-sik's 60th Birthday (Seoul: Shin Gu Publishing Co., 1969); Kim Yeong-tae, "Mireuk seonhwago" (The Study of Maitreya-turned-*hwarang*), *Bulgyo hakbo* 3-4 (1966); Yi Gi-baek, *Silla*

and continuous attempts are also being made to grasp the practical character of its synthesis of Buddhism, Confucianism and Daoism.[10]

Doubtlessly, all the above-mentioned aspects of *hwarang* organization
and ideology are important for our understanding of this unique historical phenomenon. Basically, the *hwarang* inherited the traditions of tribal
youth leagues where the customs and ethics of the ancestors were handed down to young men of initiation age. It is undeniable that, like all
able-bodied Silla men of that epoch, the *hwarang* had to join the army in
wartime. It is also very probable that some kinds of psychophysical
training, received during the time of their *hwarang* discipleship, helped
*hwarang*s-turned-soldiers to fight fearlessly and effectively. It is only logical that in the time of ceaseless wars against Baekje and Goguryeo any
state-supported organization—and the *hwarang* were definitely patronized by the state—could not but become a bit militaristic. But could the
hwarang, even in the time of the Unification Wars, have been called a
"primarily military organization"? Can the still prevalent notion about
the *hwarang* organization itself as being the elite corps of the Silla army
in the early seventh century and the "*hwarang* spirit" as being a "philosophy of self-sacrifice for the sake of the state" be corroborated by historical records? Let us try to assess the extent of the *hwarang*'s military participation throughout their history.

Biographies of the *hwarang* who died at the battlefield can be found in
Kim Bu-sik's *Samguk sagi*, but interestingly enough these are missing in
Iryeon's *Samguk yusa*, with prominent exceptions of *hwarang*-turned-
generals Kim Yu-sin (595–673) and Jukji (seventh century)'s biographies
mentioned in both sources.[11] Furthermore, neither source gives any

---

    sidae-ui gukga bulgyo-wa yugyo (The State Buddhism and Confucianism in Silla
    Epoch) (Seoul: Hanguk Yeonguwon, 1978), p. 85.

10. Kim Chung-yeol, "Hwarang ogye-wa samgyo sasang-ui hyeonsiljeok guhyeon"
    ("Five Mundane Precepts" of the *Hwarang* and Practical Realization of the Ideas of
    Confucianism, Buddhism, and Daoism), in *Hwarang munhwa-ui jaejomyeong*.

11. Excluding Kim Yu-sin and Jukji, the *Samguk yusa* mentions such *hwarang* as:
    1) Nammo (南毛) and Gyojeong (姣貞), both women, who were leaders of the
       women's age-group, *wonhwa*, the predecessor of the *hwarang*. Cf. 「彌勒仙花 · 未尸
       郎 · 眞慈師條」 (The article on Maitreya-turned-*hwarang*, whose name was Misi, and
       Preceptor Jinja).
    2) Misi (未尸), who lived in the time of King Jinji (576–579) and who was thought to
       be an incarnation of Maitreya. His disciple, Jinja (眞慈), or Jeongja (貞慈), was a
       Maitreya devotee—even the last character of both variants of his name is thought
       to be taken from the Sinified name of Maitreya, Ja-ssi (慈氏; A Merciful One). Cf.

「彌勒仙花 · 未尸郎 · 眞慈師條」 (The article on Maitreya-turned-*hwarang*, whose name was Misi, and Preceptor Jinja).

3) Hose (好世), who lived in the time of King Jinpyeong (579–632). His disciple, Hyesuk (惠宿), was a well-known monk, famous for his "marvels." Cf. 「二惠同塵條」 (The article on monks Hyesuk and Hyegong, who concealed their virtues and mingled among the common people).

4) Gucham (瞿旵), who lived in the same period and was known as a keen hunter. Cf. 「二惠同塵條」 (The article on monks Hyesuk and Hyegong, who concealed their virtues and mingled among the common people).

5) Geoyeol (居烈), Silcheo (實處; or Dolcheo, 突處), and Bodong (寶同), who lived in the same period. They are known for their trips to the Diamond Mountains, or Geumgangsan. They were helped by Yungcheon (融天), a monk-poet. Cf. 「融天師 · 彗星歌 · 眞平王代條」 (The article on Preceptor Yungcheon of the time of King Jinpyeong, who wrote "The Song of the Comet").

6) Burye (夫禮) and his disciple Ansang (安常), who lived in the time of King Hyoso (692–702) and who also travelled to mountains in today's Gangwon-do province; once they were captured by "barbarians," but then were marvellously saved. Cf. 「栢栗寺條」 (The article on the Baegyulsa temple).

7) Yeong (永, or Junyeong, 俊永) and his disciples Jinjae (眞才) and Beonwan (繁完), who presumedly lived in the same period. Cf. 「栢栗寺條」 (The article on the Baegyulsa temple).

8) Deugogok (得烏谷), a disciple of Jukji, who lived in the same period and was known as a poet. Cf. 「孝昭王代 竹旨郎條」 (The article on Jukji, a *hwarang* of the time of King Hyoso).

9) Gipa (耆婆): Chungdam (忠談), a famous monk-poet during the time of King Gyeongdeok (742–765), is presumed to have been his disciple. Cf. 「景德王 · 忠談師 · 表訓大德條」 (The article on Preceptor Chungdam and Honourable Preceptor Pyohun, of the time of King Gyeongdeok).

10) Wolmyeong (月明), a famous monk-poet and Maitreya devotee of the same period, once introduced himself as a *hwarang* disciple. Cf. 「月明師兜率歌條」 (The article on "The Song of Tuśita Heaven" by Precepor Wolmyeong).

11) Kim Eung-ryeom (金膺廉) was a *hwarang* leader, who became King Gyeongmun (861–875) upon the wise advice of his disciple, monk Beomgyo (範教). In the time of his reign, *hwarang* Yowon (邀元), Yeheun (譽昕), Gyewon (桂元) and Sukjong (叔宗), known as poets and travellers to mountains in today's Gangwon-do province, were active. Cf. 「四十八 · 景文大王條」 (The article on the 48th King of Silla, Great King Gyeongmun).

12) Hyojong (孝宗) was a *hwarang*, who lived in the time of Queen Jinseong (887–897) and who was known for his merciful acts towards a poor, but filial girl. Cf. 「貧女養母條」 (The article on the Poor Girl Who Supported Her Mother).

As we can see from the above list, Iryeon had information mostly about *hwarang* from the time of Kings Jinpyeong, Hyoso, Gyeongdeok and Gyeongmun. He largely disregarded the military aspect of *hwarang* activity, but emphasized the role of monk-*hwarang*, *hwarang* poetry and travels to mountains which probably had strong religious character. He also linked a lot of *hwarang* (Misi, information on the military aspect of *hwarang* training. Military details of the *hwarang* biographies, included in *Samguk sagi* and *Samguk yusa*, also give some ground for doubt.

The earliest *hwarang* leader to be mentioned in *Samguk sagi*, Kim Sadaham,[12] did participate, followed by a large group of his disciples, in the annexation of Dae Gaya in 562. Being 15-16 years old at that time, however, he could go to war only on receiving special royal permission, which was given quite reluctantly. He and other *hwarang* could not take part in the war as a separate detachment: Sadaham was commissioned as a deputy commander of a regular territorial unit of Sangju county (later renamed into "precious corps") and aid to the famous general Isabu, the operation's chief commander. The sources do not mention any serious bloodshed during that operation—Dae Gaya was weakened and demoralized to the point of voluntarily surrendering after being shaken following a sudden raid by Sadaham's unit. The operation must have seemed so insignificant that it was not even recorded in Isabu's "Biography" in Chapter 44 of *Samguk sagi*. And last but not least, concerning the nature of Sadaham's personality, the author of the original version of his "Biography" (probably, Kim Dae-mun, a contemporary of the *hwarang*) seems to have most highly praised not his hero's blood-thirstiness, but his merciful attitude towards Dae Gaya prisoners of war and abstemiousness in questions of property. All these peculiarities do not well befit the picture of a *hwarang* leader as a ferocious fighter, nor the organization itself as a separate elite military detachment. In the mid-sixth century, *hwarang*'s participation in war still seems to have been the

---

Jinja, Hyesuk, Burye, Ansang, Wolmyeong) to the stories of Buddhistic "marvels," thus underlining the depth of their Buddhist devotion.

12. *Samguk sagi*, chapter 4, 23th year of King Jinheung (562), September and *Samguk sagi*, chapter 44, Biography of Sadaham.

Interestingly enough, the name "Sadaham" itself seems to be derived from the Sinified form, 斯陀含, of the Sanskrit Buddhist term "Sakrdagamin," meaning the second category of "Šravaka"—saints, who liberated themselves from 6 out of all 9 possible "anxieties" and so have to incarnate only one time before ultimate Nirvana. Such a name suggests certain Buddhistic connections for Sadaham. Given the Buddhistic zeal characteristic of the time of King Jinheung reign, this hypothesis looks quite plausible, but our only source, *Samguk sagi*, does not offer any data on doctrinal basis of Sadaham's presumed Buddhistic faith. In *Samguk yusa hwarang* leader Gucham (瞿旵), whose name also sounds rather Buddhistic, is mentioned too (Cf.: Footnote 9). "Gucham" seems to be a spelling variant of 瞿曇, (or 瞿譚)—Chinese transliteration of "Gautama," one of Buddha's names.

exception rather than the rule.[13]

The next record of *hwarang* involvement in military affairs is Kim Yu-sin's participation in the battle of Nangbiseong (629). According to *Samguk sagi*, Kim Yu-sin became a *hwarang* leader in his 15th year, i.e. about 610 (according to *Samguk yusa*, and his *hwarang* membership began in his 18th year, i.e. about 613). It seems quite possible that in 629 Kim Yu-sin had already retired from *hwarang* leadership and was no longer directly connected with the organization: at least, no facts of his involvement with the *hwarang* are recorded in the sources from that time. It is still doubtless that Kim Yu-sin had once been a *hwarang* leader, although he first bloodied his sword in serious battle almost 20 years before.

But the accounts of his *hwarang* training and experience found in *Samguk sagi*'s "Biography of Kim Yu-sin" (Chapter 41-43) and *Samguk sagi*'s article on Kim Yu-sin in its first volume, do not seem to fully support the still prevailing concept of Yu-sin's *hwarang* as a highly militarized youth "order."

First, Kim Yu-sin is described as a master of fencing.[14] But this would only indicate that swordmanship was not really that common among the *hwarang*; otherwise this detail would not have been recorded separately.

Second, one semi-military adventure from Kim Yu-sin's *hwarang* period is recorded in *Samguk yusa*: a failed intelligence-gathering raid to Goguryeo and Baekje, undertaken by Kim Yu-sin on the advice of his disciple Baekseok, as Goguryeo spy, tried to entrap Yu-sin and kill him.[15]

---

13. At the same time, Kim Bu-sik must have viewed Sadaham as a military hero par excellence. Otherwise he would not have put Sadaham's "Biography" into Chapter 44 of his *Samguk sagi*, alongside biographies of military commanders like the illustrious Eulji Mundeok or Jangbogo. But I do not think that Kim Bu-sik, who, for example, only rarely mentioned *hwarang*-monks (mostly found in *Samguk yusa*), was flawlessly objective in his interpretation of *hwarang* organization.

14. "修劍得術," *Samguk yusa*.

15. "時有白石者 不知其所自來 屬於徒中有年 郎以伐麗濟之事 日夜深謀 白石知其謀 告於郎曰 僕請 與公密先探於彼 然後圖之何如 郎喜 親率白石夜出行" 云云 ("At that time there was a fellow called Baekseok. Nobody knew where he was from. Still, he belonged to [Yu-sin's] disciples for a long time. [At that time] Yu-sin exerted his mind all day long on the matter of chastising Goguryeo and Baekje. Baekseok knew about his plans and [once] said to him: 'I ask [to be allowed] to spy on those [hostile states] with you first and after that to make plans on the matters [of expedition against the enemy powers]. Yu-sin was glad [to accept it] and, attended by Baekseok, he went out at night. . . ." *Samguk yusa*).

But this bunglesome raid seems to have been undertaken individually by Kim Yu-sin and Baekseok, without any recorded participation of other *hwarang* or the *hwarang* as an organization. And, most importantly, the above-mentioned raid culminated in a succession of mystical experiences—Kim Yu-sin's encounter with state-protecting mountain goddesses, who disclosed the treacherous intentions of Baekseok, followed by Baekseok's revelations about the Goguryeo rulers' perception of Yu-sin as an incarnation of a calumniated and executed Goguryeo diviner.[16] Basically, mystical experiences of the same sort constitute the main content of Kim Yu-sin's *hwarang* education as described in Kim Yu-sin's "Biography" in *Samguk sagi*, Chapter 41 (see below). Clearly, the ultimate purpose of his experiments with the mystical was to become a "general able to chastise Baekje and Goguryeo," but methods of self-cultivation he had to use as a *hwarang* partake more of Buddhistic or Taoist magic than conventional forms of military exercise.

Third, as many Korean scholars have reasonably pointed out long before, the name *yonghwa hyangdo* (fragrant disciples of Maitreya's naga-puspa tree) given to the *hwarang* body led by Kim Yu-sin, suggests that the organization was somehow connected with the Maitreya cult.[17]

---

16. 娘等便現神形曰 我等奈林 穴禮 骨火等三護國之神 今敵國之人誘郎引之 郎不知而進途 我欲留郎 而至此矣 言訖而隱 公聞之驚 再拜而出 宿於骨火館 謂白石曰 今歸他國 忘其要文 請與爾還家取來 遂與還至家 拷縛白石 而問其情 曰 我本高麗人 (…) 我國群臣曰 新羅庾信 是我國卜筮之士楸南 也" 云云 ("The ladies assumed their divine form and said: 'We are the three state-protecting goddesses of Mt. Naerimsan, Hyeolyesan, and Golhwasan. Now a man from a hostile state enticed You here. But You did not know about it and went ahead. So, we wished to stop You and that is the reason we came here.' On saying this, they disappeared. Having heard their words, Yu-sin fell down in astonishment. After that, he bowed twice and went away. While staying in a house on Mt. Golhwasan, he said to Baekseok: 'Going to the foreign country now, we forgot an important document. Let us return home together, fetch it and come again.' On coming home together, he tied Baekseok up and demanded the truth. [Baekseok] said: 'I am a native of Go[gu]ryeo. . . . Our King and his ministers said that Silla's Yu-sin is [an incarnation of] Chunam, a diviner from our country'. . . ." *Samguk yusa*). "Golhwagwan," or "the house on Mt. Golhwasan" seems very much to have been a kind of a shrine dedicated to the sacred Mt. Golhwasan, object of nation-held sacrifices (located in today's Yeongcheon-gun county of Gyeongsangnam-do province).

17. The tradition of the Maitreya cult was probably inherited by Kim Yu-sin from an earlier *hwarang* group, whose leader, Misi, was thought to have been an incarnation of Maitreya, and to which Jinja, a Maitreya devotee monk, had belonged (cf. *Samguk yusa*, chapter 3). It is also important to remember also, that another *hwarang* of Kim Yu-sin's time, Jukji, a noted general and statesman who was described in *Samguk*

Fourth, as a mighty nobleman, Kim Yu-sin had an impressive brigade of personal retainers, some of whom received official ranks for their bravery, and were even honored with separate biographies in 47th "warrior"'s chapter of *Samguk sagi* (Binyeongja, Yeolgi, Gugeun and others). In *Samguk sagi* it is said that in 642, when Kim Yu-sin's closest friend and ally, Kim Chun-chu (who later became King Taejong-Muyeol, r. 654–661), went on a mission to Goguryeo and was detained there, Kim Yu-sin mustered—probably, as his own "private militia"—three thousand "brave and strong men," who took the oath to rescue Kim Chun-chu even at the price of their lives (Chapter 41, Biography of Kim Yu-sin). Probably, the character or training of these bands of Kim Yu-sin's personal followers had something in common with the *hwarang*'s. But, strictly speaking, none of these personal vassals was said to have been a *hwarang* member. So, it is still not clear whether Kim Yu-sin's *hwarang* followers, *nangdo*, and the band of his military retainers represented the same entity or not.

So, it is clear that from his *hwarang*'s days Kim Yu-sin's ultimate objective was "to militarily chastise" Silla's two rival states, Baekje and Goguryeo, and to consolidate the position of his clan, the Gaya Kims,

---

yusa as "having unified the Three Kingdoms in the capacity of Kim Yu-sin's subordinate" (chapter 2), was also thought to be a reincarnation of a Buddhist lay devotee (Skt.: Kulapati, 居士) linked to Maitreya. The Maitreya cult seems to have been a specific feature of the *hwarang* milieu in the late sixth and the early seventh century.

Besides, Kim Yu-sin seems to have been more interested in "practical" magic elements of Silla Buddhism. He used Buddhist magic very widely, especially in the critical time of the culmination of the Unification Wars (660–668), when Silla fought Goguryeo and remnants of the Baekje army at the same time. First, as recorded in his "Biography" in *Samguk sagi* (chapter 42), he resorted successfully to Buddhist prayer during the siege of Bukhansan fortress (in today's Seoul) by Goguryeo troops in 661. Then in 662 he used his magic talents to provide secure transport of forage to the Tang army engaged with Goguryeo. His magic spells were also thought to have helped to put down the remnant Baekje troop's resistance in 664 (chapter 43). A detailed, but undated record of Kim Yu-sin's usage of Buddhist magic against Baekje's remaining loyalists can be found in *Samguk yusa*, chapter 1 (an article on King Taejong-Muyeol). Probably, all these conjurings were extraordinary measures which Kim Yu-sin, an offspring of Gaya Kim clan, which initially did not belong to Silla's ruling *jin-gol* aristocracy, necessarily had to resort to in order to make his way into the highest echelons of Silla's nobility. As to the source of Kim Yu-sin's magic abilities, we can suspect his supposed friendly ties with Milbon, a well-known esoteric monk of the seventh century, recorded in *Samguk yusa* (chapter 5, article on Milbon).

through the strengthening of the central government's autocratic power. Those aims seemingly left the mark of patriotic militarism on the activity of Kim Yu-sin's *nangdo* band. But as long as Kim Yu-sin and his followers were inheritors to the *hwarang* tradition, their activity could not but become colored by native and Buddhist mysticism. These mystical trends must have been, in fact, nothing more than tools in Kim Yu-sin's power play, but their pervasiveness in Kim Yu-sin's *hwarang* and adult life suggests that they could have belonged to the very essence of the *hwarang* tradition.

In the time of the Unification Wars, three prominent *hwarang* members—Kim Yu-sin, his younger brother Kim Heum-chun (or Heum-sun) and his subordinate Jukji—were among Silla's top military leaders. Still, we do not have any records suggesting that other noted generals and statesman of Silla of that time—such as above-mentioned Kim Chun-chu, Kim In-mun (629–694), Kim Yang-do, Jinju, Cheonjon, Pumil, Chungsang and others—belonged to the *hwarang*. So, it is hard to say whether *hwarang* membership was really common among Silla's military and state elite at the time. Among lower grade warriors, Pumil's son, *hwarang* Gwanchang (or Gwanjang), became widely known as a hero at the battle of Hwangsan (660) with Baekje, which resulted in a definite victory by Silla and dealt a lethal blow to Baekje forces. Along with Kim Heum-chun's son, Ban-gul (whose *hwarang* membership is not recorded), Gwanchang had stirred up the morale of the Silla soldiers through his sacrificial single-handed raid into the enemy's camp (cf. his biography in chapter 47 of *Samguk sagi*). Gwanchang's bravery probably resulted from his *hwarang* training, but Gwanchang himself participated in the battle not as a *hwarang*, but as a deputy commander of the regular army; besides, no participation of his fellow *hwarang* in the battle is recorded. Interestingly enough, ordering his son to launch the fatal raid, Pumil appealed not only to the traditional *hwarang* virtue of unconditional bravery, but also to the duty of glorifying one's name and elevating the status of the family.[18] It suggests that the ideological background of Gwanchang's heroism encompassed not only the *hwarang* virtue of self-sacrifice specifically, but also the Silla's aristocratic tradition of fami-

---

18. "父品曰謂曰 爾雖幼年有志氣 今日是立功名 取富貴之時 其可無勇乎" ("His father, Pumil, said: 'For all your young age, you have a [strong] will and spirit. Today is the time you [can] perform a glorious deed and acquire wealth and noble status. How can you not be brave?'" *Samguk sagi*, chapter 47, Biography of Gwanchang).

ly loyalism.

The only other *hwarang* trainee whose heroic self-sacrifice during the Unification Wars is recorded in the sources is Kim Heum-un, a disciple of the *hwarang* Munno. Kim Heum-un lost his life in a battle with Baekje in 655. But in this case too we have to note that Kim Heum-un participated in the battle not in the capacity of a *hwarang* disciple, but as an officer (*daegam*) in charge of a regular unit, *nangdang*.[19] As it was probably also the case with general Pumil's son Gwanchang, Kim Heum-un, hailing from the aristocratic *jin-gol* class, must have felt obliged by his social position to participate in war anyway, irrespective of his *hwarang* membership. In *Samguk sagi*, it is recorded that three other Silla officers, Yepa, Jeokdeok and Boyongna, followed Kim Heum-un and preferred heroic death to disgraceful retreat, but still, it is not mentioned that the three brave officers were *hwarang* disciples too (cf. *Samguk sagi*, chapter 47, biography of Kim Heum-un).

Two other heroic Silla warriors who are thought by some historians to have belonged to the *hwarang* are Gwisan and Chuhang, both known for their self-sacrificial deaths in the battle with Baekje in 602 and in connection with the famous "Five Mundane Precepts" (*sesok ogye*) of Priest Won-gwang. Still, in the absence of any records confirming both warriors' *hwarang* membership, we cannot connect them to the *hwarang* organization unequivocally.[20]

The role of Kim Heum-un and Gwanchang as symbols of sacrificial intrepidity in inspiring the Silla soldiers in countless battles with Baekje and Goguryeo must not be undervalued. Still, their real contribution somehow pales before that of non-*jin-gol*, non-*hwarang* warriors also honored with biographies in chapter 47 of *Samguk sagi*, such as Chandeok, Haeron, Simna, Sona, monk Chwido, Nulchoe and his slave,

---

19. According to Kim Bu-sik's description of Silla's military structure, *nangdang* was one of the "nine corps" (九誓幢) of the Silla army. It was established in 625 by King Jin-pyeong (cf. *Samguk sagi*, chapter 40).

20. In the Biography of Gwisan in *Samguk sagi* (chapter 45) it is said that both Gwisan and Chuhang "wanted to saunter together with the noble persons," and so they had "to cultivate their mind and body first in order not to be disgraced" ("我等期與士君子 遊 而不先正心修身 則恐不免於招辱"). Taking into consideration that *hwarang* leaders were mostly of noble *jin-gol* birth and were well-known to have had a penchant for roving their country's mountains, we can probably surmise that Gwisan and Chuhang wanted to join the *hwarang* ranks. Still no conclusive evidence to support this theory has been put forth so far.

Jukjuk, Yongseok and many others. These numerous instances well prove that the militaristic spirit of the time best expressed by Sona's adage that "man must die in a battlefield, not in a bed tended by his wife" ("丈夫固當兵死 豈可臥牀席死家人之手乎," Biography of Sona) was the common ethos of the epoch, not the exclusive mentality of the *hwarang*. All able-bodied Silla men were obliged to serve and felt proud of their military service, and the *hwarang* were no exception; but this does not mean that either the *hwarang* organization or its teachings were essentially or primarily militaristic.

Above, records concerning the six *hwarang* (Sadaham, Kim Yu-sin, Kim Heum-chun, Jukji, Kim Heum-un and Gwanchang), whose participation in wars can be corroborated, have been briefly analyzed. It is possible to conclude that glorious military records of all the six *hwarang* war participants can be ascribed to social obligations connected with their noble *jin-gol* origin rather than to a supposedly "war-like" *hwarang* "spirit." As shown above, none of the above-mentioned six *hwarang* are indicated to have received military training in the *hwarang* ranks in the sources available to us. Most probably they owed their military prowess to their family background: at least, the fathers of Kim Yu-sin, Kim Heum-chun and Gwanchang were well-known as generals. All of them took part in war as commanders of regular military units, not as *hwarang* leaders. There is a direct indication in sources that Sadaham was followed by his numerous *hwarang* disciples when he went to the battlefield. The same thing can probably be conjectured in the cases of Kim Yu-sin and Kim Heum-un, but positive proof is lacking. The magnitude of the contribution of several *hwarang* groups in Silla's war efforts should not be belittled, but their casual participation does not seem to have played a decisive role in the success of Silla's unification. And, most importantly, the militaristic spirit characteristic of Silla's Unification Wars period definitely influenced the *hwarang* in so far as they were Silla subjects, but this war-like mentality should not be confused with the essential spirituality of the *hwarang*, which was deeply entrenched in mysticism and religious ethics, as exemplified by the cases of Sadaham and Kim Yu-sin. Admittedly, the critical period of the Unification Wars had witnessed some militarization of the *hwarang* organization and philosophy, but it is acknowledged by most historians that in the ensuing peaceful period of Unified Silla the *hwarang* quickly changed into an educational and recreational organization primarily concerned with matters of Confucian education, ritual poetry, music and mountaineering.[21] For the *hwarang* organization, launched as an organ for education and the promotion of talent and which eventually turned into a congregation for literary and sport activities, the military feats of the six previously mentioned *hwarang* were a minor episode.

So, if not infused with militaristic ideas, what was the real essence of the *hwarang*'s training, education and organizational life? If, as the prevalent view maintains, the *hwarang* "order" was basically an instrument of selecting and educating young talent, what was the fundamental content of the *hwarang* "curriculum"? As was mentioned above, ritual and sacramental functions of the *hwarang* as mediators between the human and spiritual worlds seem, at least in the case of Kim Yu-sin, to have been of a serious matter. So, we are led to basically agree with the time-honoured assumption of Misina Syoei, who contended that, as a successor to tribal "men's houses" and men's secret societies, the *hwarang* organization specialized in educating youngsters in matters of native religion.[22] Still, we should not underestimate the degree of complexity of *hwarang* cults and beliefs. In the case of the earliest known *hwarang* with expressed religious inclinations, Jinja (circa reign of King Jinji, 576–579) focused his devotion pointedly at Maitreya, but in the course of his efforts to make Maitreya reincarnate as a *hwarang* he also once sought the assistance of the deity of Mt. Cheonsan.[23] The fact that

---

21. See, for example, Yi Gi-dong, "Hwarangsang-ui byeoncheon-e gwanhan gakseo" (The Notes on the Changes in the *Hwarang*'s Image), *Silla munhwa* 5 (1988). Participation of such *hwarang* leaders, as Myeonggi and Allak, and their disciples, in the quelling of the Kim Heon-chang's rebellion in 822, was recorded in *Samguk sagi* (chapter 10) as an obvious exception.

22. Misina Syoei (三品彰英), 『新羅花郎の研究』 (A Study of Silla's *Hwarang*) (Tokyo: 三省堂, 1945). We can not agree with all contentions of Misina's work. He seems to have grossly exaggerated the role of the vestiges of primitive organizations in the Silla culture of the 6th–7th centuries. The roots of the *hwarang* certainly can be traced to primitive "males' leagues," but the state-supported *hwarang* organization of 6th-7th centuries embraced much more sophisticated beliefs (including elements of Confucianism and Buddhism) and was, to some extent, a part of Silla's complex state apparatus.

23. "寺僧 (…) 乃曰 此去南隣有千山 自古賢哲寓止 多有冥感 歸彼居 慈從之 至於山下 山靈變老人 出迎曰 到此奚爲 答曰 願見彌勒仙花爾 老人曰 向於水源寺之門外 己見彌勒仙花 更來何求" 云云 ("A monk from the temple said at last: 'To the south of this [temple], not that far from here, there is Cheonsan mountain, from older times [known as] the abode of the wise and sagacious. Many miracles have taken place there. [You] should go there.' [Jin]ja followed [the advice] and went to the said mountain. The mountain god took the shape of an old man and welcomed him, asking why he has come

the "reincarnated" Maitreya, Misi, was said to have been found under a "tree standing near the street" ("路傍樹, also was known as "Sayeosu," 似如樹, or Inyeosu, 印如樹) suggests Misi's connections to Silla's ancient cult of the "cosmic tree" manifested in worship of the "sacred forest," Gyerim, and the tree-like design of golden crowns found in the "Tomb of the Heavenly Horse" (Cheonmachong, sixth century) or the Seobongchong Tomb (fifth century). It seems that in the case of Jinja, the Buddhist worship of Maitreya inseparably merged with the local shamanistic concept of the world centered around a "cosmic tree" and cults of the mountain spirits. Then, Kim Yu-sin, to whom Jinja's tradition of Maitreya worship seems to have been handed down, was said to have worshipped almost the whole known pantheon of Silla, including female mountain deities, star deities and heavenly spirits. Interestingly enough, in two different articles in *Samguk yusa* he is said to have been a reincarnation of a Goguryeo diviner, that is, a representative of native religion (chapter 1, article on Kim Yu-sin), and a reincarnation of "a man from the Trayastrimša Heaven," i.e., a Buddhist deity (chapter 1, article on King Taejong—Prince Chunchu). Such a "double descent" represents very well the complex and syncretic nature of Yu-sin's religious beliefs.

But the syncretism of the times of Jinja and Yu-sin seems to have waned in the period after the Silla unification as the position of Buddhism as the state religion and Confucianism as the state ideology became increasingly strengthened. A typical *hwarang* of the ninth century, Kim Eung-ryeom (who later became King Gyeongmun, r. 861–875), for example, was remembered as a subtle and keen connoisseur of Buddhist metaphysics and Confucian ethical values. One of his recorded Seon dialogs with well-known Seon Master Muyeom (801–888) reads as follows.

> The king asked: " . . . It was said that to think about staying in reality and defending the Void at the same time is to further aggravate the prejudiced theory. I rather want to reach the True Fountain, where the domain of *prajñâ* ends. Can you tell me what the ending of the domain means?" Master replied: "The domain has already ended. Reason is

---

there. [Jinja] replied that he wanted to see Maitreya-turned-*hwarang*. The old man said: 'You have already seen Maitreya-turned-*hwarang* outside the gates of the Temple of Suwonsa last time. What are you seeking again?' (. . .)" *Samguk yusa*, chapter 3, article on Maitreya-turned-*hwarang*, whose name was Misi and Preceptor Jinja).

also the Void, and nothing more. The Seal [of *seon* self-cultivation] is to be realized in silence only."[24]

Nothing strange that such a degree of Buddhist spiritual progress forced Master Muyeom to speak about the special spiritual ties that existed between him and the *hwarang*-turned-King.[25] The example of Kim Eung-ryeom shows very well that in the later period of Silla history, the *hwarang*, celebrants of native gods from a tribal past, eventually became erudite proponents of lofty metaphysical truth. Similar phenomena such as primitive orgies and Dionysian and Orphical mysticism have been seen in the mystagogues of Ancient Greece.

As stated above, the religious element of *hwarang* teaching seems to have undergone a similar course of transition with the Silla religion itself.[26] But one other component of *hwarang* education seems, on the contrary, to have demonstrated surprising stability. By this I mean the ethical code of the *hwarang*, salient features of which were mercifulness towards living creatures, indifference to material temptations, and, most importantly, a calm and optimistic attitude towards death, free of fear or Hamletian misgivings about the Beyond. The *hwarang* chose death with ease and readiness, almost joyfully and often at a very early age. This inclination to smile in the face of death was not the banal bravery of battle, for the voluntary death of *hwarang* was not necessarily that of the battlefield. Sadaham was said to have died at 17, bewailing the death of a friend with whom he earlier established a relationship of "friends in

---

24. "上曰 (⋯) 有言曰 滯有守無 徒銳偏解 欲詣眞源 其般若之絶境則 境之絶者或可聞乎 大師對曰 境旣 絶矣 理亦無矣 斯印也默行爾." From "The inscription on the monument of the Stupa of the Hidden Light of the Bright Moon, dedicated to the monk, posthumously given the name of Daenanghye, who served as National Preceptor to two Kings of the state of Silla in time of Tang Dynasty," by Choe Chi-won (崔致遠撰 有唐 新羅國 兩朝國師 敎 諡 大朗慧和尙 白月光之塔碑銘).

25. "(⋯) 顧與吾君 有香花因緣 (⋯)" From "Inscription. . . ."

26. All changes in the state-approved cult seem to have had a heavy influence on the *hwarang* simply because of their position as a state-run and aristocracy-led institution. For example, in the end of the seventh century, one of the Three National Treasures of Silla, "The Flute Calming Ten Thousand Waves" (which seems to have had deep connections with the Buddhist cult), has been held in great esteem and thought to be a divine protector of the state. Consequently, a legend came into existence, in which the flute miraculously saved a *hwarang* leader and his devoted disciple from captivity (cf. *Samguk yusa*, chapter 3, Article on Baegyulsa Temple).

death." Such a relationship probably entailed an oath to die together. Sadaham was said to have been widely admired for his decision to set free all Gaya prisoners of war bestowed on him by the King and to hand out other royal grants, namely arable land, to the soldiers (cf. *Samguk sagi*, chapter 4, 23rd year of King Jinheung, and chapter 44, Biography of Sadaham). All such actions demonstrate the "unworldly" attitude of Sadaham towards most "worldly" things: social position, property and, finally, life itself. It is tempting, of course, to try to link this kind of charitable and disinterested behavior to two kinds of metaphysical philosophy which began penetrating into the Korean Three Kingdoms about that time, namely Buddhism and Taoism. The complete absence of any textual evidence for Sadaham's familiarity with either or these foreign teachings forces us to think that his disinterest in "this-worldly" things was a prominent feature of Silla's native worldview and as such became a part of the *hwarang*'s philosophy.[27]

---

27. It seems almost impossible to determine what exactly Silla's native understanding of the world was, since most historic records pertaining to the earlier part of Silla history (before mid-6th century, when the first historic book of Silla was said to have been written) are heavily embellished both literarily and ideologically. For example, in the time of Isageum Naehae (196–230) certain military merits of Mulgyeja were flatly disregarded because of his commander's personal animosity against him. Mulgyeja was said to have chosen to blame his own deficient war efforts. He did not complain about the partiality of his commander and, finally left this world for sequestration in the mountains (cf. *Samguk sagi*, chapter 48, Biography of Mulgyeja; *Samguk yusa*, chapter 5, article on Mulgyeja). Such a pattern of behavior was known as early as the first half of third century and confirms the view that a transcendentalist attitude towards "this-worldly" values was part of native ideology from earliest times. Still, the speeches of Mulgyeja, as they are put in both *Samguk sagi* and *Samguk yusa*, are so interspersed with citations from Chinese classics which the Silla people of that time simply could not have known, that the authenticity of the story itself seems quite dubious to some scholars. Another unworldly personage in early Silla history, poor musician Master Baekgyeol of the time of Maripgan Jabi (458–479), was known for his adage, "Life and death depend on predestination, wealth and nobleness depend on Heaven's will; we can not hinder them from coming or prevent them from going," which well could become the motto of Sadaham and those like him (cf. *Samguk sagi*, chapter 48, Biography of Master Baekgyeol). Still, it is said that Baekgyeol adhered to a Chinese anchoret of Confucius's time, Rong Qiji, although this figure was hardly known in Silla in the time of Baekgyeol. So, various records give us some ground to think, that the *hwarang*'s disinterested patterns of conduct were deeply rooted in the Silla native world view, but later historians' penchant to embellish earlier documents with Chinese citations renders it almost impossible to investigate in depth this part of indigenous Silla spirituality.

Following Sadaham was Geomgun, who in 628 consciously drank poison given him by his vicious colleagues because he wished not to harm them by disclosing acts of theft they had committed. He did not care about his life or escape. Explaining his unwillingness to join in profitable theft, he was said to have cited neither Buddhist nor Confucian canons but postulates of the *hwarang* teaching. Then Geomgun was said to have reluctantly informed his *hwarang* teacher, Geunnang, about his decision to die. The teacher did try to dissuade his disciple, but, as a result, let him carry out his decision, thus showing some kind of approval for this sort of behavior (*Samguk sagi*, chapter 48, Biography of Geomgun). All this demonstrates to us that abstemiousness in questions of wealth, career, life and death pertained to the very essence of *hwarang* ethics.

Death, an object of fear for most human beings, was for the *hwarang* nothing short of an object of their passionate desire: Kim Heum-un, for example, was said to have cried out in admiration when he heard of someone dying honorably in battle (*Samguk sagi*, chapter 47, Biography of Kim Heum-un). The death of a *hwarang* was as smooth and lucid as his life, clear of anguish and attachment to "this-world." For example, the face of Gwanchang after he died in battle was said to have been "as if he was alive; he had no remorse, for he could die for [his] sovereign's cause" (*Samguk sagi*, chapter 47, Biography of Gwanchang). Kim Yu-sin was said to have predicted his impending death from some bad omens boding it, but there are no records suggesting that the prospect of his death worried the old general in any way (*Samguk sagi*, chapter 43, Biography of Kim Yu-sin). Treating life and death as two sides of the same coin, the *hwarang* could virtually transcend the limitations of normal mortals' fear of the Beyond because of their love towards friends (Sadaham), associates (Geomgun), or their monarch (Gwanchang, Kim Heum-un, and Kim Yu-sin). In the light of the *hwarang's* proven readiness to die, the warning, a *hwarang*-monk of the ninth century, Priest Beomgyo, once made to the contemporary *hwarang* leader, Kim Eung-ryeom, does not seem to be a simple joke or an emotional exaggeration. When Kim Eung-ryeom said that he would like to marry the second daughter of King Heonan (857–861)—a step, Beomgyo knew, that would deprive Kim Eung-ryeom of prospects of ascending the throne—Beomgyo replied: "If you take the second princess, I will definitely die in your presence." Because Kim Eung-ryeom eventually followed Beomgyo's advice—in defiance of his own parents' will—we can judge that the warning was taken very seriously. Otherwise Beomgyo really could have taken his life on the spot (*Samguk yusa*, chapter 2, article on 48th King Gyeongmun). To be psychologically able to dispose of one's life whenever it is deemed necessary—that was the essence of *hwarang* education.

In conclusion, we can say that, being basically an educational and training institution and having succeeded an earlier tradition of male and female adolescent leagues, the *hwarang*, as a state-supported and aristocracy-led organization, faithfully followed the social, ideological and religious trends of Silla society. From the very beginning, *hwarang* organization was designed to teach youngsters moral, ethical and religious basics of the adult life. A defiant attitude towards death was one of the highly praised values of the Silla community from earliest times and it soon became a kind of a "trademark" of the *hwarang*. At the time of the Unification Wars, bravery in battle emerged as one of the prevailing virtues—and the *hwarang* produced a number of fearless warriors. Still, the organization itself did not transform itself into a military unit. Its war contribution was not crucial or decisive. Noblesse oblige- and highborn *hwarang* did battle to maintain and raise the dignity of their clans, not because of their *hwarang* membership. At the same time, however, their well-trained fearlessness helped them (in some cases) to set patterns of military bravery for others. After the Unification Wars came to an end, the *hwarang* quickly returned to their original role in society and, in accordance with Unified Silla society's steady turn toward accepting advanced continental culture, it became the proponent of Confucian moral education and Buddhist self-cultivation. Besides, as a provider of properly-educated talent to the state's bureaucratic machine, the *hwarang* were an inseparable part of the centralized power structure. With the crash of the centralized state in the late ninth century the *hwarang* virtually collapsed too. However the traditional art of "free play" with life and death which the *hwarang* had cultivated so thoroughly seems to have etched a deep mark on the Korean spiritual life for future dynasties.

Several Questions in Historical Studies of Balhae

Song Kiho

Preface

The study of the history of Balhae (Ch. Bohai) in the history of Korea has been very inactive. This may be because access to it by South Korean historians is impossible since the territory of Balhae was once located in the northeastern region of China, North Korea, and the Maritime Province of Siberia. A shortage of written materials constitutes a fundamental cause of the inactivity as well. The same situation, however, faces historians in China, Japan, the Soviet Union, and other countries, and so it cannot be said to impede Korean historians alone. Nearly 500 treatises and papers on the history of Balhae have been accessible to the public from 1900 to date.[1] China claims 236, almost half of the total; and Korea—South and the North combined—72, about one-seventh of

---

* Originally published in the *Korea Journal*, vol. 30, no. 6 (June 1990).

Song Kiho (Song, Gi-ho) is Professor of Korean History at Seoul National University. He received his Ph.D. in ancient Korean history from Seoul National University in 1995. He has authored several books on ancient Korean history, especially on Balhae history, including *Gangwondo-ui seonsa munhwa* (Prehistory of Gangwon-do Province) (co-authored with Ro Hyeok-jin et al., 1986), *Balhae jeongchisa yeongu* (A Political History of Balhae: Research in Development Process of Balhae History and Phase of Country) (1995), and *Balhae-reul dasi bonda* (Collective History on Balhae History) (1999). E-mail: songkh@snu.ac.kr.

1. Wang Chengli, *Balhae-ui yeoksa* (History of Balhae), trans. Song Gi-ho (Chuncheon: Asian Cultural Research Institute, Hallim University, 1987); originally published as *Bohai jianshi* (Heilongjiang Renmin Chubanshe, 1984).

the total. The percentage written by South Korean historians is rather small. This inactivity apparently made it almost impossible to conduct any systematic research on the history of Balhae and to undertake any examination of written materials in depth. It is evident, then, that we cannot convince scholars that the history of Balhae should be included in the frame of Korean history regardless of how much we assert its rightful place. This paper will discuss perspectives from which to examine the history of Balhae based on Korean history.

We will first examine the origin of Dae Jo-yeong (Ch. Dazuoying), the founder of Balhae, and investigate the group of persons who were led by Dae Jo-yeong to establish the new kingdom. We will then present a counterargument to the common opinion that Balhae and Silla were continuously pitted against each other for more than 200 years. We will make it clear that their relations, as with relations between any other two countries, alternated between amity and enmity in the midst of complex international relations affecting all countries in the region. Their respective domestic circumstances must also be considered. Third, we will discuss questions concerning the culture of Balhae. Finally, is no doubt that Balhae was a country composed of many different races under the leadership of both emigrants from Goguryeo after its fall and the Malgal (Ch. Mohe) people. It is not tenable to assert that only one or the other existed in Balhae culture, but some historians have emphasized Goguryeo elements or Malgal elements alone. This paper will point out these errors and discuss how we can understand Balhae culture, properly in the future. If, as is asserted by Korean historians, the history of Balhae must be described within the frame of Korean history, the question arises: With what terms must we date the period? Fourth, this paper will clarify why I was not able to use exact terms in describing this connection and propose to use positively the concept of "the Period of Southern and Northern Kingdoms" (*nambukguk sidae*). Afterwards this paper will examine the question of how to evaluate the historical significance of the unification of the Three Kingdoms on the Korean peninsula by Silla in connection with the existence of Balhae.

This paper will only cursorily answer these questions and more detailed examinations will be made in the future.

Dae Jo-yeong and Group of Balhae Founders

Origin of Dae Jo-yeong

Little is clear about the founding of Balhae due to the weakness of the written records. Records about the origin of Dae Jo-yeong, the relations between Dae Jo-yeong and Geolgeol Jungsang, the process of establishing Balhae, and its foreign relations immediately after its founding differ to some degree. None of the records clarify these questions in a proper manner. One thing that is certain is that Balhae was founded in the Dongmosan (Ch. Dongmoushan) mountain region: the tomb of Princess Jeonghye (737–777), the second daughter of King Mun or Dae Heummu, the third monarch of Balhae, was discovered together with a tombstone on Liudingshan mountain in Dunhua county, Jilin province, China, in 1949. This fact was confirmed with the discovery that the Odong Castle of Balhae was located near Dongmosan mountain.

Discussions were most active concerning the origin of Dae Jo-yeong, as researchers believed that they would be able to determine where this state belonged to. For this reason, this chapter will be devoted solely to this question.

Studies about Dae Jo-yeong were conducted long ago. Whether he was a descendant of Malgal or a descendant of Goguryeo is not yet resolved. Major Chinese records disagree over the origin of Dae Jo-yeong or are vague. Which records are fallacious have yet to be determined. Scholars have differing opinions depending on the source of their assertions.

Dae Jo-yeong is described in *Jiutangshu* (Old Book of Tang) as being "originally from Goguryeo." *Xintangshu* (New Book of Tang) states that he was "originally a man of the Songmal Malgal race but later belonged to Goguryeo." On the other hand, *Wudai huiyao* (An Outline of Five Successive Dynasties) describes him as "a Goguryeo man" while *Silla gogi* (Old Notes on Silla) excerpted from *Samguk yusa* (Memorabilia of the Three Kingdoms) describes him as "an old general of Goguryeo" and *Jewang un-gi* (Songs of Emperors and Kings) likewise.

The essence of discussions on the origin of Dae Jo-yeong revolves around descriptions in the *Jiutangshu* and the *Xintangshu*. Most Japanese and Chinese scholars, with a few exceptions, side with the *Xintangshu*, asserting that the founder of Balhae was a man of the Malgal race. Korean historians, however, assert that he was a Goguryeo man. That historians of different nationalities offer different views on the origin of Dae Jo-yeong is an issue that is closely connected with the question of Balhae's origin. This question will be examined further below.

Most Japanese scholars proposed the view that he was a Malgal during and after the period of Japanese rule of Korea. The same view is held by Chinese historians at present. Ikeuchi Hiroshi stated that "the Balhae people were Balhae Malgal and no other than Malgal (as Jurchens were)."[2] Wada Kiyoshi interpreted the meaning of "a derivative" in *Jiu-tangshu* as "a man who was not a genuine descendant" and agreed with Dae Jo-yeong's origins as described in *Xintangshu*. He attempted to argue that Dae Jo-yeong was a man of the Songmal Malgal.[3] It is questionable to interpret the meaning of a "derivative" as a "person who belonged to an entirely different race." His view is not convincing.

There is another view that sees Dae Jo-yeong as a Malgal but not a man of the Songmal Malgal race. Instead he is viewed as a man of the Baeksan Malgal race, who lived near Baekdusan mountain. Tsuda Sokichi found that Dongmosan mountain, where Balhae was first founded, was located in Oruha, northeast of Baekdusan mountain, a region where Baeksan Malgal lived, and that Dae Jo-yeong was native to this region. For this reason, he concluded, Dae Jo-yeong returned to this area and founded his kingdom there. He assumed that Dae Jo-yeong was a man of the Baeksan Malgal based on this reasoning. Toriyama Kiichi saw Dae Jo-yeong as not pure Malgal but from the Malgal race and brought up in the sphere of Goguryeo influence, and concluded that he was a man of the Baeksan Malgal race.[4] On the other hand, the dominant view in China is that Dae Jo-yeong was a man of the Songmal Malgal race. For example, Wang Chengli asserted that the emergence of Balhae was an inevitable outcome of historical development achieved by the Malgal who lived in the northeastern section of China for a long time.[5] He saw Dae Jo-yeong as a man of the Songmal Malgal race.[6]

---

2. Ikeuchi Hiroshi, "Tetsuri ko" (On the Tieli Tribe), in *Mansen chiri rekishi kenkyu hokoku* (A Report on Studies of Manchurian and Korean Geography and History), no. 3 (Tokyo: Teikoku University, 1916), p. 66.

3. Wada Kiyoshi, "Bokkaikoku chiri ko" (On Balhae Geography), in *Toashi kenkyu* (Studies of East Asian History), part on Manchuria (Toyo Bunko, 1955), p. 59.

4. Toriyama Kiichi, *Bokkaishijo no shomondai* (Problems in Balhae History) (Kazama Shobo, 1968), p. 32.

5. Wang Chengli, *op. cit.*, p. 31.

6. *Ibid.*, p. 55.

That Dae Jo-yeong was a Goguryeo man is an old position to take. Matsui Hitoshi thought Dae Jo-yeong was a Goguryeo man.[7] On the basis of records contained in *Ruishu kokushi* (A Collection of Anecdotes in National History), Shiratori Kurakichi opined that Dae Jo-yeong was a Goguryeo man, and asserted that Geolgeol Jungsang and Geolsa Biu were chieftains of Malgal tribes.[8] In the 1960s, after Korea's liberation from Japanese rule, Bak Si-hyeong elaborated the view that Dae Jo-yeong was a Goguryeo man, claiming: "Even though Dae Jo-yeong was not in any blood relationship with the Goguryeo royalty, he was at least a man of Goguryeo."[9] He also added, however, that "*dae* 大 of Dae Jo-yeong signifies something big and high like *go* 高 of the Goguryeo royalty and that *dae* is, in fact, the same as *go*."[10]

We have briefly laid out the two major arguments concerning Dae Jo-yeong's origins. In recent years, however, another standpoint has emerged that tries to refrain from drawing a conclusion, and tries to strike a compromise between the two conflicting views rather than siding with either of them. Furuhata Toru said: "As it is not clear whether Dae Jo-yeong was a man of Goguryeo or a man of the Malgal race as long as we rely on books of history, it is necessary to withhold any conclusion as to his origin in this paper."[11] Interpreting "derivative" as a "branch from the main stock," No Tae-don advanced the view that "Dae Jo-yeong was more akin to the central segment of Goguryeo people and more closely adhered to the Goguryeo court than Geolsa Biu who was a man of a Goguryeo-ized Malgal race."[12] He concludes with the sugges-

---

7. Matsui Hitoshi, "Bokkaikoku no koiki" (The Territory of Balhae), in *Manshu rekishi chiri* (History and Geography of Manchuria), vol. 1 (Minami Manshu Tetsudo Kabushikigaishya, 1913), p. 408.
8. Shiratori Kurakichi, "Bokkaikoku ni tsuite" (On Balhae), *Shigaku zasshi* (History Magazine) 44.12 (1933): p. 1584.
9. Bak Si-hyeong, "Balhaesa yeongu-reul wihayeo" (For Studies of Balhae History), *Yeoksa gwahak* (Science of History) 1 (1962): p. 4.
10. Ibid.
11. Furuhata Toru, "Bokkai kenkoku kankei kiji-no saikento: Chugokugawa shiryo no kiso kenkyu" (Re-examination of Papers Concerning the Establishment of Balhae: A Study of the Basis of Historical Materials from the Chinese Side), *Chosen gakuho* (Bulletin of Korean Studies) 113 (1984): p. 41.
12. No Tae-don, "Balhaeguk-ui jumin guseong-gwa balhaein-ui jogwon" (Composition of People in Balhae and Racial Origin of Balhae People), *Hanguk godae-ui gukga-wa sahoe* (Ancient States and Societies in Korea), comp. The Korean Historical Association (Seoul: Ilchokak Publihing Co., 1985), p. 274.

tion that Dae Jo-yeong was one of the Goguryeo people who lived in a frontier district of Goguryeo along the Songmalsu (present Songhwa-gang river).[13] He compromises the descriptions in the *Jiutangshu* and the *Xintangshu*.

It seems that the question of Dae Jo-yeong's origin will not continue to be resolved until new materials are found. It is now more important for us to investigate Dae Jo-yeong's cultural background, regardless of his racial origins, if we are to more fully understand the history of Balhae.

That Dae Jo-yeong was a Goguryeo general can be inferred to a certain extent from records in histories including the *Silla gogi*. After Goguryeo was destroyed, Dae Jo-yeong must have kept contact with many emigrants from Goguryeo in the then internationalized city, Yingzhou. From this, we can say that he grew up and launched activities in the sphere of Goguryeo culture. It can also be assumed that when Dae Jo-yeong rose up against the Tang after he moved to the Dong-mosan mountain region, a number of Malgal people, as well as a number of Goguryeo people, assembled under him to join in the resistance. If we take the Goguryeo influence into consideration, we can understand the explanation in *Jiutangshu* that he was a "derivative from Goguryeo."

We can also confirm that Dae Jo-yeong had close relations with Goguryeo through archeological materials. The tomb of Princess Jeong-hye, which was discovered in 1949, consists of a road leading to the grave site, a corridor from the entrance to the chamber where the coffin is placed in state, and the burial chamber itself. The ceiling above the burial chamber is comprised of squares, a style found commonly in Goguryeo tombs. Her tomb resembles a Goguryeo tomb that has a stone chamber. Her tombstone discloses that she was interred three years after death, suggesting a close relationship with Goguryeo culture, since the three-year funeral was a custom practised uniquely in Goguryeo and Baekje. This leads us to assume that the Princess was a descendant of Goguryeo. Unlike other cultural elements, the tomb structure and funeral system are customs which do not change easily. If Princess Jeonghye had no relations with Goguryeo at all, it is unlikely that a Goguryeo funeral arrangement would be adopted upon her death. If the princess was a descendant of Goguryeo, Dae Jo-yeong, her great-

---

13. Ibid., p. 282.

grandfather, must have been a Goguryeo descendant. On the other hand, we can imagine the possibility that her body was buried with her husband's in one grave site and that their funeral followed Goguryeo tradition. To date, however, no evidence of their burial together has been found and the inscription on her tombstone refers to no one else.

In conclusion, the assumption that Dae Jo-yeong was from Goguryeo or related to Goguryeo is based on evidence in the *Silla gogi* as well as the tomb of Princess Jeonghye.

Founder Group and Ruling Class

More important for understanding the history of Balhae is examining the group that founded it. Written records say that the group divided into subgroups after it moved to the Dongmosan mountain region from Yingzhou. One subgroup was led by Geolgeol Jungsang, another by Dae Jo-yeong himself (Goguryeo descendants), and a third by Geolsa Biu (Malgal). Balhae, therefore, was founded mainly by two groups which migrated to the eastern section of Manchuria—namely Malgal—who had been living in Manchuria for a long time, along with immigrants from Goguryeo. We can assume that most of those who were included in the ruling class after the foundation of Balhae were those who moved to Manchuria from Yingzhou together with Dae Jo-yeong. If so, it is possible to clarify the nature of the early group of persons who established Balhae by examining its ruling class.

It is recorded in the first volume of *Songmojiwen* (Observations by Songmo) written by Hong Hao of Southern Song that surnames of Balhae kings included, besides Dae, Go, Jang, Yang, Du, O, and Yi. Persons identified as Balhae people or descendants from Balhae numbered 335 to date. Jin Yufu counted 331 in "Liezhuan" (Biographies of Important Men) in his *Bohai guozhi zhangpian* (A Long History of Balhae). But we must add four persons to the list. They are Princess Jeonghye, whose name appears on her tombstone, Princess Jeonghyo, who is also identified on her tombstone, Ha Su-gyeom who is mentioned in the tombstone of Zhang Jianzhang, and Dae Bong-ye, who is mentioned in a document by Choe Chi-won. Among these, persons named Dae number 100, persons named Go 59, persons named Jang 21, persons named Yang 9, persons named Ha 3, persons named O 11, and persons named Yi 11. Persons with the surname of Dae, as previously indicated, can be considered descendants of Goguryeo. There is no doubt that most persons named Go were of Goguryeo origin. Although persons connected with the Malgal race were included among Gos, they were very few.[14] The origin of the other surnames cannot be confirmed by name alone.

An analysis of the above materials allows us to conclude that the Goguryeo descendants in the royal family and the influential aristocracy, which constituted the uppermost class in Balhae, were a dominant majority. We can also infer that most of those who migrated from Yingzhou to the eastern section of Manchuria were descendants of Goguryeo. On the other hand, however, the *Ruishu kokushi* records that "there are many Malgal and few natives among people of Balhae," and adds that "all natives can become chieftains." Here Malgal and natives are titles that contrast with one another. Ikeuchi wrote that their relations were similar to the relations between commoners and *yangban* (the upper class) in the Joseon period in Korea.[15] This is not, however, an appropriate comparison. In the case of Balhae, the people must be divided into the Goguryeo group, which was the ruling class, and the Malgal group, which was ruled by it. The "natives" referred to in the above description must be interpreted as indicating people of Goguryeo origin who were ethnologically different from Malgal. Balhae, therefore, must be viewed as a society in which people of Goguryeo descent, who are referred to as "natives," formed the mainstream of the ruling class.

Our thinking is based on the *Songmojiwen* and *Ruishu kokushi*, which were compiled in 892, when Balhae was still in existence. If we accept this analysis, we can understand why Japan, in messages sent to Balhae on behalf of the Emperor, called Balhae "Goryeo (Goguryeo)" and its king "King of Goryeo (Goguryeo)."

Balhae's Relations with Silla and Goryeo

The 229-year Balhae period (698–926) coincides with the period of Unified Silla (676–935) in Korea. During this time, the two kingdoms were contiguous to each other, Silla located in the south and Balhae in the north. Their borderlines were the Niha river (present Yongheunggang river) in the east and the Daedonggang river in the west.

---

14. Shavkunov, *Balhae and Its Cultural Remains in the Maritime Province* (in Russian) (Leningrad, 1968), p. 69; Wang Chengli, *op. cit.*, p. 126.
15. Ikeuchi Hiroshi, op. cit., p. 66.

What sort of relations did the two countries maintain over this long period? Up to now, people generally thought that the two maintained continuously hostile relations. This is a fundamentally problematic assumption. Even from a common-sense point of view, it is hard to see why the two would maintain hostile relations for more than 200 years, for no particular reason. Both in ancient times and modern, relations between any two countries become amicable or hostile depending on changes in the international situation.

It is necessary for us to examine what has led to this false conception. First, there is a shortage of materials on relations between Balhae and United Silla. After Balhae perished, its territory was usurped by the Liao dynasty that immediately succeeded the kingdom. There were no historians to put the history of Balhae in order. In 928, two years after the fall of Balhae, its people were forced by the Khitanese to migrate to the Liaodong peninsula region. Donggyeongseong, the capital of Balhae, was burned to ashes in a great fire.[16]

All written materials that remained were destroyed. Emigrants from Balhae had no time to preserve the materials. Although some Balhae people who fled to Goryeo may have brought documents with them, they probably disappeared on the Goryeo side.

The *Samguk sagi* (Historical Records of the Three Kingdoms), for example, contains only a very few fragmentary descriptions of Balhae. It can be assumed, however, that contact between Balhae and United Silla must have been far more frequent. We assume that when Kim Bu-sik wrote the *Samguk sagi*, he omitted references to Balhae[17] but failed to omit them all. Some survive to this date.

When they studied the history of Balhae based on the fragmentary records remaining in Chinese literature, Japanese historians of the occupation period concentrated on diplomatic relations between Balhae and Japan, or among the Tang, Balhae, and Japan, as well as matters directly concerning themselves. They treated relations between Silla and Balhae as a secondary matter. Toriyama was representative of these Japanese

---

16. Archeological Team, Heilongjiang Province, "A Report on Excavations of Remains in Eastern and Western Corridors in the First Building in the Balhae Palace in Its Capital" (in Chinese), *Wenwu* (Cultural Relics) 11 (1985): p. 51.
17. Yi U-seong, "Samguk sagi-ui guseong-gwa goryeo wangjo-ui jeongtong uisik" (Composition of *Samguk sagi* and Consciousness of Orthodoxy of Goryeo Dynasty), *Jindan hakbo* 38 (1974): p. 206.

historians. In his study, Toriyama stressed the antagonism between Balhae and Silla that resulted from the war among the Tang, Balhae, and Silla (732–733) during the reign of Balhae King Mu. He developed the theory using the Tang royal messages sent to the Silla court, which was aimed at "inducing one barbarian to hit another barbarian." That antagonism continued between Balhae and Silla fostered by the skillful maneuverings of the Tang.[18] He also cited several incidents originating in rivalry with Silla in the second half of the Balhae period, which he claimed showed continuous antagonism between the two kingdoms.

The results of studies made during Japanese rule were generally accepted without question after the liberation because investigations of Balhae were dormant at the time. Relations between Balhae and Silla were not always antagonistic, however. For instance, one of Balhae's major diplomatic routes, as recorded in *Xintangshu*, passed through Silla. This fact confirms that Balhae treated Silla as one of its major trade partners along with the Tang, the Khitan, and Japan. It can also be assumed that their mutual exchanges were considerably frequent. According to *Gogeum gun-gukji* (Notes on Old and New Countries in the Country) referred to in *Samguk sagi* and *Samguk yusa*, there were a total of 39 stations from Cheonjeonggun (present Deogwon), a frontier town of Silla, to Donggyeong Yongwonbu in Balhae. This tells us that there was trade on a permanent basis between Balhae and Silla.

I will now summarize transitions in diplomatic relations between the two countries in five phases on the basis of this information fragmentary though it is.

The first phase corresponds with the reign of Dae Jo-yeong (698–719),[19] when Balhae was busy solidifying its foundation immediately after its establishment, while Silla began to enjoy a peak of prosperity following its success in unifying the Three Kingdoms on the Korean peninsula. This was only a few years after Silla fought wars of unification with the Tang. We cannot deny entirely the possibility that Silla extended some support, albeit indirectly, to Dae Jo-yeong, who, rising in revolt against Tang policies, fled to the east and established a kingdom.

---

18. Toriyama Kiichi, *op. cit.*, pp. 64-65.
19. The tombstone of Princess Jeonghye discovered recently indicates that Balhae adopted the system of counting the reign of a king from the year of his coronation. Sun Yuliang, "Bohai jinian dingbu" (Revised Balhae Chronology), *Shehui kexue zhanxian* (Social Science Front) 1 (1982).

As Balhae was far inferior to Silla in terms of national strength at that time, Silla was presumably not greatly worried about the foundation of Balhae. We can catch a glimpse into the situation of the time with the aid of Choe Chi-won's statement in the "Sabulheo bukguk geosangpyo" and *Dongsa gangmok* (Annotated Account of Korean History) by An Jeong-bok (vol. 4, upper section). According to these records, Dae Jo-yeong sent an envoy to Silla in 700 immediately after the establishment of his kingdom. Silla, in return, bestowed on him the title of *daechan*, a fifth-rank position. The second phase covers the period from the reign of Dae Muye, the second king of Balhae, to the middle part of the reign of Dae Heum-mu, 719 to 762. The task of conquest undertaken by Dae Jo-yeong was inherited by Dae Muye. He subjugated the old territory of Buyeo in the west, the old land of Solbin in the east, the old land of Yemaek in the northeast, and the old land of Okjeo in the south. These expansionist achievements naturally made Silla wary. In July 721 (the 20th year of King Seongdeok's reign), Silla mobilized 2,000 young men in Gangneung and ordered them to construct a castle along the northern borderline in order to defend the country against the Balhae force.

The Heuksu Malgal race, however, feeling threatened by the foreign conquest carried out by Dae Muye, seceded from Balhae and joined the Tang. This incident caused hostilities between Balhae and the Tang beginning in 732. Tang induced Silla to war against Balhae in 733. Four Silla generals including Kim Yun-jung and Kim Yun-mun, grandsons of Kim Yu-sin, who played the leading role in the unification, were ordered to attack the southern frontier of Balhae. It was very cold and it snowed heavily. The mountain paths were very rugged and slippery. More than half of their soldiers died and they had to withdraw their troops.

Balhae's expansionist activities stalled with the war as a turning point. Balhae formed formal diplomatic relations with Japan in 727, immediately before the war with Silla in an effort to relieve itself from opposition to the Tang, the Heuksu Malgal race, and Silla, and from the isolation caused by the antagonism. In the meantime, Emperor Xuanzong of the Tang ceded the land south of Daedonggang river to Silla in return for a dispatch of troops. Pursuing a northward advance from that time, Silla established 14 counties and subcounties, including Daegok Castle, in 748.[20] Encouraged by the massive An Lushan Rebellion in Tang in the

---

20. Wang Chengli, *op. cit.*, p. 76.

mid-eighth century, Balhae and Japan worked out a plan to attack Silla in alliance with one another. In May 762, Silla constructed a castle along the western frontier bordering on Balhae in preparation for a forthcoming attack.

The third phase began in the second half of the reign of Dae Heum-mu, the third monarch of Balhae (cir. 762 to 794). Removing its capital from the present-day Dunhua to Sanggyeong Yongcheonbu, Balhae laid a foundation for further development. It made efforts in domestic administration and expansion of its territory. The title of "King of Balhae County" bestowed on Dae Heum-mu by Tang at the time of his coronation in 738 was changed to "King of Balhae State" in 762. Balhae could for the first time since Dae Jo-yeong equip itself with all the accoutrements required of a state. It was also the first time that Dae Heum-mu was recognized as the king of an independent country, though in form only.

We assumed that Balhae and Silla opened permanent channels of trade at that time. As stated earlier, the *Xintangshu* mentions that Balhae operated five major routes for foreign trade. The area southeast of Yongwonbu faced the sea and so it could serve as a route to Japan; Namhaebu was a route to Silla; Amnokbu a route for paying tributes to the Tang court; Jangnyeongbu a route to Yingzhou; and Buyeobu a route to Khitan. As one of the five major routes was connected with Silla, it is clear that trade between Balhae and Silla was frequent.

That there was a permanent route of trade between the two countries is attested to by records contained in *Gogeum gun-gukji*, excerpts of which are contained in the *Samguk sagi* (*gwon* 37). According to the records, there were 39 stations (about 1,170 *ri*) between Chaekseongbu (Donggyeong Yongwonbu) of Balhae and Cheonjeonggun (Deogwon) of Silla. The fact that stations were established along a route between Donggyeongseong, the capital of Balhae, and a frontier town of Silla enables us to confirm again that the route of trade operated on a permanent basis.

Silla dispatched envoys to Balhae on many occasions through the route and Balhae returned the gestures. As pointed out above, however, records concerning Balhae were struck out in the *Samguk sagi* and other books of history. Only two fragmentary references can be confirmed now. According to *Samguk sagi* (*gwon* 10), Silla sent Baegeo (of the *ilgilchan* rank) to a northern country (Balhae) in March 790 (sixth year of King Wonseong's reign) and sent Sungjeong (holding the *geupchan* rank) in September 812 (fourth year of King Heondeok's reign).

The fourth phase began after the reign of Dae In-su, the 10th king of

Balhae (818–830). Dae In-su subjugated many villages north of present Xingkai lake, to hold a vast territory. He established a complete bureaucratic system extending from the capital to local regions, comprising 5 *gyeong*, 15 *bu*, 62 *ju*, and 3 *dokjuju*. Silla, on the other hand, was in a period of political confusion typical of the corrupt age that characterizes the end of dynasties. Finally, in 822 a revolt broke out under the leadership of Kim Heon-chang. Though King Heondeok subdued the revolt, Silla's national strength became weaker and weaker as years passed. Balhae now outpaced Silla in national strength.

It is recorded in *Liaoshi* (History of Liao) that Balhae, capitalizing on Silla's weakness, attacked it during 818–820, capturing part of its territory and establishing many counties and towns there. Silla decided to defend itself against Balhae. In July 826, Baegyeong, governor-general in Ujam, was ordered by the Silla court to mobilize 10,000 young men in many provinces and countries north of Hansan mountain and construct a long castle along Daedonggang river. The *Samguk sagi* (*gwon* 10) mentions that the castle was 300 *ri* long. Dae In-su expanded his territory by capitalizing on the confusion that crippled both the Tang and Silla during this period. The collision between Balhae and Silla developed following the former's expansion of its territory.

Balhae experienced a period of peak prosperity after this. Silla was so worn out that an age of disruption commenced with the emergence of the Later Three Kingdoms. In Tang, in the meantime, a dispute arose between a Balhae envoy and a Silla envoy over which one would occupy a higher position at the Chinese court. Dae Bong-ye, a prince of Balhae who visited Tang as an envoy, asked the Chinese court to give him a seat higher than the Silla envoy. The Balhae envoy claimed that his country was now stronger than Silla. His demand was not accepted. As a token of thanks to Tang, Silla had Choe Chi-won compose "Sabulheo bukguk geosangpyo."

Another issue followed this dispute which concerned ranking in announcing successful candidates at the foreigner's civil service examination in China. There were two instances. The *Goryeosa* (History of Goryeo) indicates that a dispute arose between Osodo from Balhae and Yi Dong from Silla toward the close of the ninth century.[21] At that time Osodo's success was announced before the man from Silla. The other dispute over ranking at a Tang civil examination broke out in 906

---

21. "Choe Eon-wi," in *Goryeosa, gwon* 9.

between Choe Eon-wi from Silla and Ogwangchan, a son of Osodo, from Balhae, on the grounds that Choe was placed above the man from Balhae in a list of successful candidates.

The fifth phase corresponds with the reign of Dae In-seon, the last king of Balhae (906–921), when the country finally fell to ruin.[22] In 907 the Tang died out and was replaced by the Later Liang. The Age of Five Dynasties began. Khitan, which came into being along the Siramuren valley, gradually expanded its influence, posing a threat to Balhae in the east and finally annexing it. On the Korean peninsula, the Later Baekje and Taebong (Goryeo) emerged as rivals after the confusion-ridden Later Three Kingdoms period. Khitan expanded its influence by capitalizing on the confusion on the Korean peninsula, on the Chinese continent, and in Balhae during this period. Foreign relations in this part of the world were becoming more and more complicated.

Balhae formed diplomatic relations with Khitan in the early period of its emergence. In 918 Balhae sent an envoy to Khitan. Feeling a threat in the eastward advance of Khitan in later years, however, Balhae treated it with hostility. When the Khitanese looted the Balhae people and took them to Liaoyang in February 919, Balhae dispatched troops to attack Liaozhou in Khitan in May 924. The Balhae troops killed the governor, Zhang Xiushi and kidnapped a number of people.

A record that Balhae, alarmed by Khitanese pressure, secretly contacted Silla and other countries in its region in 911 is contained in volume 1 of *Xiedan guozhi* (History of Khitan). When the founder-king of Khitan personally commanded his troops in an assault on Balhae in December 925, however, Silla instead extended support to the Khitanese troops instead for some unknown reason. After destroying Balhae, according to the *Liaoshi*, Khitan presented awards to many countries including Silla to acknowledge their service in conquering Balhae.

That Goryeo and Balhae entered into matrimonial or diplomatic relations of a similar degree sometime during the period from 918 to 925 is recorded in the *Zizhi tongjian* (General Mirror for the Aid of Government) (vol. 285). If the record is reliable, we may be able to easily under-

---

22. Concerning this period, refer to the following treatise: Song Gi-ho, "Balhae myeol-manggi-ui daeoe gwan-gye: georan, husamguk-gwaui gwan-gye-reul jungsim-euro" (Balhae's Foreign Relations in the Period of Downfall: Centering on its Relations with Khitan and Later Three Kingdoms), *Hanguksa ron* (Treaties on Korean History) 17 (1987): pp. 47-97.

stand the background of a series of policies Goryeo took toward Balhae after it unified the Later Three Kingdoms on the Korean peninsula. Goryeo refused to receive an envoy sent by Khitan and rather scolded Khitan for its breach of alliance with Balhae because it ran counter to reason. They hanged the envoy's camel under the Manbugyo bridge, creating the Manbugyo Incident. The fact that Goryeo received emigrants from Balhae continually after its fall and, especially, bestowed *wang*, the surname of the Goryeo royalty, on Dae Gwang-hyeon from Balhae and listed him in the royal family register can be interpreted as a result of matrimonial relationships formed between Goryeo and Balhae during the reign of Taejo.

We have summarized diplomatic relations between Balhae and Silla. Balhae and Silla maintained friendly relations in the first and third phases of diplomatic transitions. They were pitted against each other, however, in the second and fourth phases. The two countries traded with each other or stood in opposition according to the ebbs and peaks of their national strength, or according to the international situation surrounding them.

Most of materials that are extant today tell of their mutual antagonism. Yet it is evident that the "Silla Road" was open on a permanent basis between the two countries and that many stations were established along it. Trade between the two must have been brisk. Nevertheless, Balhae left no records about this and many Silla records on Balhae were deleted when the *Samguk sagi* was compiled. The result is that records concerning their normal exchanges are unavailable and only fragmentary records of diplomatic incidents between the two remain. This must be taken into consideration when we examine relations between Balhae and Silla.

The Nature of Balhae Culture

The Balhae culture is as complicated as its racial composition. Balhae's cultural features which are revealed through archeological findings are a mixture of Goguryeo, Tang, Malgal and indigenous elements, with traits that evolved within Balhae itself. Some features are emphasized more than others, depending on teleological perspectives. Malgal elements tend to be emphasized when the history of Balhae is seen from the standpoint of the Malgal. If Balhae is considered as part of Chinese history, the focus is usually placed on how Tang culture influenced and civilized the barbaric Malgal race. If one sees Balhae as a successor to Goguryeo, s/he would be tempted to emphasize Goguryeo elements alone. If we are to understand the history of Balhae objectively, we must, first of all, eschew prejudice and examine each feature before deciding which factors played the leading role in forming Balhae culture.

Let us first review the Japanese evaluation of Balhae culture. Through studies of Balhae castles, tombs, Buddha statues, tiles and bricks, Japanese scholars view it as follows: In the first place, Balhae castles were patterned after the Chinese castle in Changan, the capital of the Sui and the Tang. Balhae stone burial chambers for aristocrats were of the Tang style, but it is in the tradition of Goguryeo tombs that structures were erected above tombs. Balhae Buddha statues, while showing aspects of the Southern and Northern Dynasties period of China, reveal a strong Goguryeo influence. Among patterns on tiles, the lotus flower pattern (*lianhua*) discloses a Goguryeo style. However, the green glaze (*luyou*) richly reflects an influence from Tang culture.[23] The Japanese saw Balhae as established by the uncivilized Malgal race and nothing but a cultural colony subordinate to Tang and Goguryeo cultures. They attached greater importance to Balhae's relations with Japan, the Tang, and Goguryeo rather than to the history of Balhae itself.[24]

After a considerable amount of archeological data on Balhae were accumulated in China after the liberation in 1945, Chinese scholars began to evaluate Balhae culture itself in earnest. The official view of Balhae in China today is as follows: "Balhae was a local feudal regime established in a vast territory in the northeastern section of our fatherland by the Songmal Malgal race during the Tang period and it existed from 698 to 926."[25] In short, Chinese scholars understand the history of Balhae as a unified multiracial state in which many races merged together, with the Chinese functioning as its core. Their main concern is how the sophisticated culture of the Tang exerted influence on Balhae, a country in a remote region. Consequently, any influence from Goguryeo culture was treated passively or ignored entirely by Chinese scholars,

---

23. Nishikawa Hiroshi, "Bokkai kokogaku no seka to minzoku mondai" (Results of Balhae Archeology and Racial Problems), *Sanin kokogaku no shomondai* (Various Problems in Sanin Archaeology) (Publication Society for Treatises in Commemoration of Dr. Yamamoto Kiyoshi, 1986), p. 4.
24. Ibid., pp. 4-5.
25. Ibid., p. 14.

more so than the Japanese historians.

Wang Chengli, for instance, held that although Balhae culture inherited the cultural tradition of the Malgal race and was influenced by Goguryeo culture, the highly developed feudal culture of the Chinese race in the center of the continent penetrated Balhae deeply and, as its history developed, Balhae finally entered into the sphere of Tang culture.[26] Whereas Wang gave some minor recognition to Goguryeo's cultural influence, other Chinese scholars such as Li Zhanfu, Wei Cuncheng, Zhu Guochen, and Liu Zhenhua did not raise the question.[27]

Scholars from the Soviet Union understand Balhae as a country established by the Malgal but assert that its culture was a composite of Japanese, Tang, Goguryeo, Silla, Uighur (from the inner region of the Asian continent), Turkish and Nestorian elements.[28] Shavkunov stressed that elements of Silla and Goguryeo cultures were the most abundant in Balhae culture and explained why Balhae culture was most closely connected with Goguryeo culture. He argued that when Goguryeo was destroyed by the Tang army, a number of Goguryeo people, including handicraftsmen, fled in search of Malgal protection, finally formed the nucleus of urban handicraftsmen in the southern district of Balhae after the Malgal people established their own independent country. On the contrary, Okladnikov stressed the composite nature of Balhae culture in which many cultural elements were mixed, along with Balhae's unique cultural traits. He cited the shapes of tiles as an example.[29]

Studies of Balhae in North Korea reveals its ultranationalist perspective. North Korean historians emphatically assert that Balhae was a country established by Goguryeo people and inherited Goguryeo in all respects. Accordingly, elements of Chinese culture or indigenous Malgal culture cannot be found at all in Balhae culture.

Ju Yeong-heon states the following:

> That Balhae was a successor to Goguryeo can be attested to not only with written records but with archaeological relics and remains.

---

26. Wang Chengli, *op. cit.*, p. 231.
27. Nishikawa Hiroshi, op. cit., p. 13.
28. Okladnikov, *Shiberia no kodai bunka* (Siberian Ancient Culture), trans. Kato Kyusaku and Kato Shinpe (Kodansha, 1974), pp. 200-201, 203.
29. *Ibid.*, pp. 203-205.

Tombs, housing sites, and city sites dating to the Balhae period, and various small and large relics and remains brought to light there including vessels, tiles, bricks, weapons, and Buddha statues clearly indicate a relation of succession between Goguryeo and Balhae.[30]

Bak Yeong-hae substantiated their assertion with written records.[31] This assertion is not their individual opinion but is common to all scholars in North Korea.

Taking Balhae culture as a successor to Goguryeo culture, they believe that Balhae culture was a bridge linking Goguryeo culture with Goryeo culture and that its role as such was stronger and more direct than Silla culture. For example, they say that Goguryeo ceramics and handicraft pieces such as tiles and bricks were inherited directly by Balhae and exerted strong influence on Silla. The influence, according to their findings, became stronger as cultural exchanges between Balhae and Silla progressed.[32]

How do South Korean historians view Balhae? It is generally held here that Balhae culture was formed with Goguryeo culture as its base, but accepted Tang culture willingly. Yi Yong-beom believes that Balhae was established by emigrants from Goguryeo along the Dumangang river after they fled Yingzhou to the east and that they were eager for Tang culture. Their 30-year life in Liaoxi region can be regarded as a period when China-based culture among the Goguryeo upper class had growing in fluence.[33] Balhae culture was formed not only by the upper class from Goguryeo but by ordinary emigrants as well from fields where advanced techniques were required such as iron tool making, rice farming, weaving, and trading. Yi further argued that relics clearly testify not only to the China-based culture of the Goguryeo upper class but

---

30. Ju Yeong-heon and Choe Taek-seon, *Balhae munhwa* (Balhae Culture) (Pyeongyang: Sahoe Gwahakgwon, 1971), p. 148.
31. Bak Yeong-hae, "Balhae-neun goguryeo-reul gyeseunghan gukga" (Balhae Was a Country That Succeeded Goguryeo), *Yeoksa gwahak* 3 (1986).
32. Sahoe Gwahagwon (Institute of Social Sciences), *Joseon gogohak gaeyo* (An Outline of Korean Archeology) (Pyeongyang: Gwahak Baekgwasajeon Chulpansa, 1977), p. 292.
33. Yi Yong-beom, *Godae-ui manju gwan-gye* (Relations with Manchuria in Ancient Times), Chunchu mun-go, no. 20 (Seoul: Hankook Ilbo Sa, 1976), p. 150; Yi Yong-beom, *Jungse dongbuk asiasa yeongu* (A Study of Medieval Northeast Asian History) (Seoul: The Asian Culture Press, 1976), pp. 24-27.

also to the existence of major industrial sectors.[34] Yi Man-yeol, too, cited several examples demonstrating the Goguryeo nature of Balhae culture.[35]

We have so far reviewed a number of divergent opinions of Balhae culture among scholars of different nationalities. They attempted to understand Balhae culture but stressed some of its features over others, due to national bias. As pointed out earlier, we must divide elements of Balhae culture into several types, in consideration of its composite nature, if we are to understand the kingdom objectively. It is necessary for us to consider Goguryeo elements, elements brought in from Tang, indigenous Malgal elements, elements from Central Asia, elements from Japan, and elements of the culture Balhae people created for themselves after establishing their country. Through this process can we examine more objectively how elements of Goguryeo culture and Malgal culture laid the foundation of Balhae culture and how its people developed their own culture while absorbing and digesting Tang, along with other foreign cultures.

The composite nature of Balhae culture can be found in the tombs of Princess Jeonghye and Princess Jeonghyo. The structure of the tomb of Princess Jeonghye and her funeral rites, namely, a three-year funeral process, followed the Goguryeo tradition. On the other hand, the custom of arranging stone lions and a tombstone around the tomb reflects Chinese influence. In the case of the tomb of Princess Jeonghyo, its structure closely followed Chinese tradition, with the slight influence of the Buddhist funeral tradition. The tombstones also reflected Confucian ceremonial attributes. Once we understand the composite nature of Balhae culture, we can more accurately analyze it and trace transitions that took place within it.

Theories on the South-North Period and the System of Korean History

Koreans generally believe that Balhae history is part of Korean history. Yi Gi-baek, for instance, states that Balhae was a country founded by

---

34. Yi Yong-beom, *Godae-ui manju gwan-gye*, p. 155.
35. Yi Man-yeol, "Balhae," in *Hanguksa yeongu immun* (An Introduction to Korean Historical Studies) (Seoul: Jisik Sanupsa, 1981), pp. 157-158.

immigrants from Goguryeo in a land that was originally Goguryeo territory; consequently, if Goguryeo history is treated in Korean history,[36]
Balhae history should be accorded the same treatment in Korean history. Ko Byeong-ik states that whereas the Malgal race, which constituted
the majority of people in Balhae, disappeared from history after the
country perished, immigrants from Goguryeo who are believed to have
formed the ruling class remained even after its fall. Moreover, he points
out, the Balhae king was called the "Goryeo (Goguryeo) king" by Balhae people themselves in national messages exchanged between Balhae
and Japan. For this reason, he says, Balhae history can only be treated as
part of Korean history.[37]

The concept of dating in common use at present does not properly
place Balhae in history. In the case of dating based on dynasties, the age
of Unified Silla is usually placed beside the age of the Three Kingdoms.
Balhae history is included within the Unified Silla. Since Balhae cannot
be neatly included within the Unified Silla period, historical descriptions
concerning this period must be ambiguous. Theories on the "Period of
Southern and Northern Kingdoms" asserted admission of Balhae history
to the frame of Korean history positively by recognizing the questions
mentioned above. The term "Period of Southern and Northern Kingdoms" suggests Silla as a southern country and Balhae as a northern
country. This assertion is not new but was made long ago.

According to the *Samguk sagi*, Silla called Balhae a "northern kingdom" when it sent an envoy to Balhae on two occasions. The title
"northern dynasty" appears in *Jiriji* (Book of Geography). In his famous
writing denouncing Balhae, Choe Chi-won called it a "northern kingdom." In view of these facts, it is clear that Silla called Balhae a northern
country. On the basis of the record in "Bohaizhuan" (History of Balhae)
in the *Xintangshu* stating that "Namgyeong Namhaebu is the starting
point of a road leading to Silla," Bak Si-hyeong argued that it was not
entirely groundless to assume that Balhae may have called Silla a southern kingdom or a southern dynasty.[38] Arguments still continue, however, as to whether the titles were used because both Balhae and Silla
regarded the other as part of their common nation, or whether they

---

36. Cheon Gwan-u, comp., *Hanguk sanggosa-ui jaengjeom* (Points in Dispute in Korean
    Ancient History) (Seoul: Ilchokak Publishing Co., 1975), p. 20.
37. *Ibid.*
38. Bak Si-hyeong, op. cit., pp. 9-10.

were used merely as a concept of defense.[39] It was An Jeong-bok of the Joseon dynasty period who recognized the northern country recorded in *Samguk sagi* as Balhae.

That both Jeong Yak-yong and Hong Seok-ju overlooked Balhae was noted by Kim Taek-yeong in his *Dongsa jimnyak* (An Outline of Eastern History), vol. 5.

It is well known that Yu Deuk-gong first proposed the idea of establishing the Period of Southern and Northern Kingdoms. He introduced his view of Balhae in the preface to his *Balhaego* (On Balhae, 1784):

> As Goryeo did not compile a history of Balhae, it is evident that its national influence was not so strong . . . After Buyeo (the royal family of Baekje) went to ruin and the Go (the royal family of Goguryeo) also perished, Kim (the royal family of Silla) came to possess the south and Dae (the royal family of Balhae) took possession of the north. They were the southern and northern kingdoms and their history should have been written. However, Goryeo did not compile it and this is a mistake.

He considered the establishment of the Period of Southern and Northern Kingdoms and compilation of their history as a prerequisite for recovering the land connected with Korea.

Kim Jeong-ho used the concept of southern and northern countries in his *Daedong jiji* (Geography of Korea, 1864), vol. 31.

> Many countries in the land of Han united themselves to give birth to three kingdoms. They were Silla, Gaya, and Baekje. Gaya was destroyed later and Goguryeo advanced to the south to open a period of three kingdoms again. In 50 years after the fall of Goguryeo and Baekje, Balhae inherited the old land of Goguryeo. The northern kingdom (Balhae) and the southern kingdom (Silla) continued to exist for more than 200 years . . . .

Jang Do-bin and Kwon Deok-gyu accepted this assertion during the Japanese rule of Korea. Jang wrote an essay on "The Three Kingdoms

---

39. Yi Yong-beom, *Jungse dongbuk asiasa yeongu*, p. 27; Sakaki Masashi, "Bokkai kokka no shiteki tenkai-to kokusai kanke" (Historical Development of Balhae and Its Foreign Relations), in *Chosenshi kenkyukai ronbunshu* (A Collection of Treatises by the Korean History Study Association), no. 16 (1979), p. 34 n. 4.

Period and the Southern and Northern Kingdoms" and Kwon devoted a separate chapter to "Southern and Northern Kingdoms" treating Silla and Balhae on an equal footing.[40]

Despite the fact that he recognized Balhae history as part of Korean history after the liberation of Korea, Yi Yong-beom nevertheless did not use the term "southern and northern kingdoms." On the contrary, Yi U-seong developed his own theory about the Period of Southern and Northern Kingdoms enthusiastically.

> The Period of Southern and Northern Kingdoms which is not so widely used an as expression for the period of the Three Kingdoms was originally a historical period and occupies a clear position in our history. It is, therefore, proper to treat the Period of Southern and Northern Kingdoms with the same degree of importance as the period of the Three Kingdoms in dating historical periods in the common sense of the term. Yet to date, it has not been commonly used. This responsibility should be borne by Kim Bu-sik, the author of the *Samguk sagi*. Even those scholars who criticize Kim Bu-sik do not readily approve of theories supporting the establishment of the Period of Southern and Northern Kingdoms. This was a result of pressures exerted on them by government-patronized Japanese scholars.[41]

The Period of Southern and Northern Kingdoms was asserted by Han Gyu-cheol as well.[42]

It is very rare, however, that the Period of Southern and Northern Kingdoms is applied in descriptions of Korean history. Most books outlining Korean history describe the history of Balhae in chapters dealing with the period of Unified Silla. In his *Hanguksa daegwan*[43] (A Grand View of Korean History), Yi Byeong-do inserted "Chapter 12: Unification by Silla and Establishment of Balhae" in "Phase 4: Peroid of Unified

---

40. Han Gyu-cheol, "Silla-wa balhae-ui jeongchijeok gyohyo gwajeong: Nambukguk-ui sasin pagyeon-eul jungsim-euro" (The Process of the Political Contact of the Silla and Balhae Kingdoms Centering on the Dispatch of Envoys by the Southern and Northern Countries), *Hanguksa yeongu* (Studies of Korean History) 43.1 (1983): p. 131.

41. Yi U-seong, "Nambukguk sidae-wa Choe Chi-won" (The Period of Southern and Northern Kingdoms and Choe Chi-won), *Changjak-gwa bipyeong* (Creation and Criticism) 10.4 (winter 1975): p. 244.

42. Han Gyu-cheol, op. cit.

43. Yi Byeong-do, *Hanguksa daegwan* (A Grand View of Korean History) (Seoul: Orient Publishing Co., 1983).

Silla." Han U-geun established "Chapter 3: Cultures of Balhae and Unified Silla" in "Part 3. Antiquity (II): Unified Silla" in his *Hanguk tongsa* (A General History of Korea).[44] Han withdrew his former standpoint in the revised edition. In the original edition, he devoted Chapter 3 to the "Establishment of Balhae and Cultures of Southern and Northern Kingdoms," even though he dated historical periods in such a manner as to include "Part 3. Ancient United State: United Silla." As Yi Gi-baek based his dating on the process of changes in the ruling class in *Hanguksa sillon* (A New History of Korea), he juxtaposed Silla and Balhae without using the term "Period of Southern and Northern Kingdoms."[45]

Unlike these scholars, Byeon Tae-seop devoted Chapter 3 to the "Development of Southern and Northern Kingdoms" in *Hanguksa tongnon* (A General Discourse on Korean History),[46] adding to it the "Historical Nature of Southern and Northern Kingdoms" in an effort to supplement his theory on the two countries. Yi I-hwa recently established a chapter with the subject "An Age of Southern and Northern Kingdoms Opens" in *Uri nara yeoksa* (History of Our Country).[47] In *Hanguk munhak tongsa* (A General History of Korean Literature),[48] Jo Dong-il conceived a chapter for "the situation during the Period of Southern and Northern Kingdoms and its literature" and made it the first book to deal with the literature of Balhae.

There are, however, many opinions opposed to the establishment of the Period of Southern and Northern Kingdoms. Ko Byeong-ik claims that it is highly questionable to employ the Confucian idea of establishing an orthodoxy of dynasties in our modern age.[49] Yi Gi-baek pointed out defects in dating historical periods on the basis of dynasties like the period of the Three Kingdoms and the Goryeo period.[50] However, considering

---

44. Han U-geun, *Hanguk tongsa* (A General History of Korea) (Seoul: Eul Yoo Publishing Co., 1987).
45. Yi Gi-baek, *Hanguksa sillon* (A New History of Korea) (Seoul: Ilchokak Publishing Co., 1981).
46. Byeon Tae-seop, *Hanguksa tongnon* (A General Discourse on Korean History) (Seoul: Sam Young Sa, 1986).
47. Yi I-hwa, *Uri nara yeoksa* (History of Our Country) (Seoul: Yeogang Publishing House, 1987).
48. Jo Dong-il, *Hanguk munhak tongsa* (A General History of Korean Literature) (Seoul: Jisik Sanupsa, 1982).
49. Cheon Gwan-u, *op. cit.*, p. 20.
50. Yi Gi-baek and Yi Gi-dong, *Hanguksa gangjwa* (A Discourse on Korean History), vol. 1 (Seoul: Ilchokak Publishing Co., 1982), p. 306.

that it is customary to base the names of historical periods on the names of dynasties—as seen in the name "Three Kingdoms Period" commonly used in Korea or the name "Period of Southern and Northern Dynasties" that is current in China—it is reasonable to use the name "Period of Southern and Northern Kingdoms" in detailing Korean history.

In the meantime, *Joseon tongsa* (A General History of Korea), which was published in North Korea in 1962, devoted its Chapter 6 to the "Unification of the Southern Part of Our Country by Silla and Establishment of Balhae in the Old Land of Goguryeo" and Chapter 7 to the "Development of Silla and Balhae." *Joseon jeonsa* (A Complete History of Korea) consisting of 5 volumes, also published in North Korea in 1979, describes the "History of Balhae and Later Silla," reflecting the intention of accepting the history of Balhae into Korea's national history. North Korean historians, however, did not use the term "Period of Southern and Northern Kingdoms" but juxtaposed Silla and Balhae.

We have examined questions concerning theories on the Period of Southern and Northern Kingdoms. Needless to say, we agree with the idea that Balhae history should be brought into the frame of Korean history and support the idea that the age of the coexistence of Balhae and Silla should be called "the Period of Southern and Northern Kingdoms."

The significance of the unification of the Three Kingdoms by Silla must be discussed in connection with theories on the Period of Southern and Northern Kingdoms. The more we emphasize the ultimate aim of Silla's unification, the weaker the position of Balhae in Korean history becomes; on the contrary, the more we emphasize Balhae history, the weaker the significance of Silla's unification becomes. We generally assert that Silla's unification of the Three Kingdoms was the first national unification. In order to include Balhae history in Korean history, we must downplay the significance of Silla's unification. We must consider that even though Silla laid a unified cultural foundation in uniting the Three Kingdoms, it failed to encompass the territory of the new united state, Manchuria, which was once a domain of Goguryeo people. It was, in other words, an imperfect unification. After we recognize its incompleteness, we will be able to recognize the significance of Balhae history more clearly. Yi U-seong agreed that "the Goryeo dynasty could achieve a united national state by incorporating the territory of Silla in the south and absorbing people and institutions of Balhae in the north."[51] He pro-

---

51. Yi U-seong, "Samguk sagi-ui guseong-gwa goryeo wangjo-ui jeongtong uisik," p. 205.

posed a reevaluation of Goryeo's unification. He understood that Goryeo's unification of the Later Three Kingdoms and the absorption of immigrants from Balhae could supplement Silla's unification to some extent.

The North Korean-style evaluation of Silla's unification of the Three Kingdoms and Goryeo's unification of the Later Three Kingdoms which overemphasizes Balhae history must be reconsidered as well. North Korean scholars regard Silla's unification of the Three Kingdoms as an integration that only affected the southern part of the country. They do not consider Silla's achievement as "unification" in a true sense but opt for Goryeo's unification of the Later Three Kingdoms as the first national unification.[52] They use "Later Silla" in the place of "Unified Silla." We find it difficult to accept this North Korean interpretation of history. We must have a correct understanding of both the significance and limitations of Silla's unification of the Three Kingdoms and positively evaluate Goryeo's unification of the Later Three Kingdoms and its absorption of immigrants from Balhae because they supplemented the imperfectness of Silla's unification.

Conclusion

I have pointed out several problems affecting an understanding of Balhae history and offered some opinions which we hope will clarify some pertinent issues in the discussion. To summarize:

Although there are many different views as to the origin of Dae Jo-yeong, there is no doubt that he grew up and acted within the sphere of Goguryeo influence. This can be confirmed by records in the *Silla gogi* and the tomb and tombstone of Princess Jeonghye. We have also examined the composition of the group of persons who founded Balhae under the leadership of Dae Jo-yeong and found that descendants of Goguryeo formed the majority. With these facts we can better understand why the terms "Goryeo or Goguryeo" and "Goryeo king or Goguryeo King" were used in national communique between Balhae and Japan. These facts also allow us to understand why Balhae considered itself a successor to Goguryeo after it was established. Here Balhae

---

52. Sahoe Gwahagwon (Institute for Research in Social Science, DPRK), ed., *Joseon jeonsa* (A Complete History of Korea), vol. 6 (n.p., n.d.), p. 29.

history stands as part of Korean history.

Many Korean historians have uncritically accepted that Balhae maintained relations of mutual antagonism with Silla for more than 200 years. It makes little sense that two neighboring countries could remain continuously antagonistic for the entire duration of their relationship. We have documentation to prove that the relationship alternated between conflict and exchange. Their relations were examined in five phases: Periods of amity and exchange in the first phase (region of Dae Jo-yeong) and the third phase (period of downfall, reign of Dae In-seon), and periods of opposition in the second phase (reign of Dae Muye and the first half of the reign of Dae Heum-mu) and fourth phase (reign of Dae In-su and thereafter).

Since Balhae was a multiracial country established mainly by immigrants from Goguryeo and Malgal, its culture too was a complex amalgam of different ethnic traits. This is especially evident in Balhae relics found in archeological excavations as well as in other remains. To emphasize elements of only one culture or another found within Balhae distorts the historical picture. In order to study Balhae with objectivity, we must free ourselves from one-sided observations. Mindful of the many different elements that formed Balhae culture, we must examine how Goguryeo culture and Malgal culture laid their foundation and how Balhae developed its own unique culture after its establishment by absorbing foreign cultures such as the Tang and others in parts of Central Asia.

Lastly, if it is right and proper to include Balhae history in the frame of Korean history, we must adopt a name to indicate the period that embraces both Balhae and United Silla together. The term "Unified Silla period" is too vague a term to use when discussing Korean history. The term "Period of Southern and Northern Kingdoms" is more accurate, though it too is not unproblematic. We consider Silla's unification of the three kingdoms the first national unification; however, we also point out that it was imperfect. Unification was more complete in Goryeo's unification of the later Three Kingdoms, which included acceptance of immigrants from Balhae.

We have strived to clarify several problems that affect the study of Balhae history. These themes will be probed in greater depth in the future.

## PART II

GORYEO PERIOD

Politics and Culture within the Sinic Zone:
Chinese Influences on Medieval Korea

Keith Pratt

I

Korea formed one of the most important parts of the Chinese culture zone—Fairbank's "Sinic Zone"—within which it was "umbilically tied to China by cultural bonds such as the Chinese written language and Confucianism."[1] From the Han dynasty at least, Chinese culture flowed almost uninterruptedly into the peninsula, making Korea "the second most civilized nation in ancient East Asia."[2] Politically, the Korean acknowledgement of Chinese supremacy was not as whole-hearted. "The Korean peninsula has been a son of dagger pointed at the side of China. The ruler of the Chinese mainland must have obtained the consent of Korea, by force or negotiation, to accept it as the administrative apex of the Asian continent."[3] That consent was not always forthcoming, especially during the medieval period, and the Song Chinese were

---

* Originally published in the *Korea Journal*, vol. 20, no. 6 (June 1980).

Keith Pratt is Professor Emeritus of Chinese at the University of Durham. He also presently serves as President of the British Association for Korean Studies. His publications include *China: An Index to European Visual and Aural Materials (1973)*, *Korean Music: its History and its Interpretation* (1987), and *Korea: A Historical and Cultural Dictionary* (coauthor, 1999). E-mail: keith.pratt@durham.ac.kr.

1. J. K. Fairbank, ed., *The Chinese World Order* (Cambridge, Mass., 1968), p. 3.
2. Kim Won-yong, "Some Aspects of the Interrelation of Korean, Chinese, and Japanese Arts," *Korea Journal* 17.11 (November 1977): p. 14.
3. Ibid.

obliged to reevaluate the power traditionally ascribed to *wen* (letters) and *te* (virtue). According to the *Songshi* (History of Song China), these had attracted foreign countries from all directions as recently as the reunification in 960, but within less than half a century politicians were reassessing foreign relations in more pragmatic terms.

This did not mean that they foresaw any change in the system, now known as the tribute system, which had already formed the basis of an international order in the Far East for a thousand years, suiting foreigners as well as it did the Chinese. However, as Professor Fairbank has pointed out, "in modern parlance alone we cannot comprehend the international order. As in all historical research, to understand it in our own modern terms in English we must first find out how it was understood by Chinese and other East Asian peoples in their own languages at the time."[4] In the case of the Koreans, we cannot do this so easily because their written language was fundamentally that of their political and cultural overlords, classical Chinese; and those who had been trained to write in this language might reasonably be assumed to reflect many of its mental and political premises too. We may try and read between the lines to discover any streak of independence or challenge, but the best clues to the Koreans' feelings are more likely to be found in an analysis of their actual political behavior and their cultural development, either of which might from time to time exhibit satisfied compliance with Chinese instructions and models or a readiness to tread their own paths.

H. J. Chun has said that in the Qing dynasty "the tributary system was not designed for direct cultural influence,"[5] but that the Koreans were "already fully sinicized," and in Korea, acceptance of Confucian culture underpinned the essential object of the tribute system, which was the maintenance of Chinese political authority. In the Goryeo period this was not so. The Koreans were not yet as fully sinicized as they became after the triumph of Neo-Confucianism in the early Joseon dynasty, and the Song rulers, for their part, were still trying to exert cultural influence over politics by means of the tributary relationship. In this they were only moderately successful, and if we evaluate the success of their efforts, we may come to a clearer understanding of what it meant to live

---

4. H. J. Chun, "Sino-Korean Tributary Relations in the Qing Period," in Fairbank, *op. cit.*
5. *Cefu yuangui* (冊府元龜), 975.17a.

in a "barbarian" society and be on the receiving end of a Chinese cultural relationship.

When Emperor Xuanzong (r. 712–756) dispatched a senior minister to Korea in 737 A.D. with his apparently genuine condolences on the death of King Seongdeok (r. 702–736), he did so with these words: "Korea is known as the "country of gentlemen," where they know the *Shijing* (Book of Songs) and *Shujing* (Book of Documents) and respect scholars. Be careful how you behave there and observe the standards shown in the Classics, so that they will appreciate the perfection of our country's scholarly teachings."[6] The words "a country of gentlemen" were to pop up again on later occasions, both when Sino-Korean relations were good and when they were in need of improvement. Xu Jing, who accompanied another mourning embassy to Korea in 1123 and stayed there for thirty days, called its people the most civilized of the Eastern barbarians, a feeling echoed by the author of *Wuzazu*, who said that "of all the barbarian countries none is more [conscious of] rites and righteousness than Korea."[7] Xu Jing called their government *ren*. In words reminiscent of Xuanzong's injunction, he noted with approval that they honored scholars and thought it shameful to be illiterate.

A note of doubt about the extent of sinicization is struck however by the Korean envoy Kwak Won, who on his visit to China in 1015–1016 says simply that Korean customs are similar to those of China.[8] Xu Jing, whose book is a mine of information about Korean culture and society, provides many examples to show that however civilized he thought the country might be, its ways were often not Chinese ways. He comments favorably on some of them and less favorably on others. "There is an old story that Korean habits are clean, and this is still so. They laugh at the Chinese for being dirty and greasy. They wash before going out in the mornings. In the summer months they wash many times every day in the streams. Men and women together take off all their clothes on the river bank and bathe. They see nothing strange in undressing in front of each other."[9] But, "after dressing a corpse, not even for a king or a mem-

---

6. *Haedong yeoksa* (History of Korea), p. 425.

7. *Ibid.*, p. 420.

8. *Gaoli tujing* (Illustrated Account of Goryeo), *juan* 23. This story was refuted in 1487 by a Chinese envoy to Hanyang (Seoul), Dong Yue.

9. *Ibid.*, ch. 22. Goryeo coffins were fastened down with decorative wooden wedges, unlike those of Silla which were nailed down. Han China had used similar wedges, but by the Song, nails were used.

ber of the nobility do they hammer down the coffin. For the poor without burial means they place [their coffins] exposed in the fields, unsealed and unplanted [with grass etc.]. Nobody thinks it wrong to abandon them for ants and birds of prey to eat them."[10] A comment by Zhu Xi probably summed up the view of many Song dynasty Chinese about the Koreans: "Someone asked whether Korean customs were good. I replied, 'In the last resort they include some barbarian habits.'"[11]

II

After Tang assistance in the unification wars in which Silla defeated Baekje (660) and Goguryeo (668), relations between Korea and China became good. To see the ups and downs of the Northern Song-Goryeo period in perspective, we should first consider the trustful and fruitful relationship of the previous three hundred years.

Before Unification, all three kingdoms had been fairly diligent about sending tribute to Changan, and once things had settled down, the new government at Gyeongju continued this duty. Only four missions were sent before the end of the seventh century, but sixty-three are recorded for the eighth and thirty-one for the first half of the ninth. They went for a variety of reasons, such as the presentation of New Year and birthday greetings, condolences and congratulations on imperial deaths and accessions, the announcement of their own royal succession, thanksgiving for imperial appointments and gifts, and of course the offering of tribute. This included many unusual and desirable items.[12] Most valuable were the finely made gold and silver goods, for which Silla was as renowned as Tibet in early medieval times. Silks and other cloth were frequently sent, a particularly famous example being a polychrome silk woven with a poem in honor of Emperor Tang Gaozong (r. 650–683) after the defeat of Baekje.[13] Among other contributions to courtly life came miniature horses, hunting birds, peacocks, sealskins, walrus ivory and books, including a set of sutras and an illustrated description of edi-

---

10. Quoted in *Haedong yeoksa*, p. 425.
11. E. Schafer, *The Golden Peaches of Samarkand* (Berkeley, 1963) gives more details of this subject.
12. *Cefu yuangui*, 962.15a.
13. *Tanghuiyao*, 86.1571.

ble herbs and fungi known to the Koreans. The significance of the latter and of the superior Korean ginseng and other drugs such as the "physic nut" *latropha jampha, bezoar*, etc., will be mentioned below. Foodstuffs sent as tribute included seafood and edible pine seeds, and Korean paper was highly prized among Tang poets for its high quality.

One other important type of Korean donation to the service of their suzerains was the human one. Thousands of Koreans had been captured and enslaved during the wars on the peninsula in the early seventh century. Korean girls were justly famed for their beauty and were employed in well-to-do Chinese houses, though an unpleasant trade in them was officially stopped in 692 after protests from the Silla government.[14] Many of them were kept at court as singing girls. Musicians and dancers from Korea along with others from countries of South and Central Asia and the Middle East formed orchestral groups in court employment, foreign music being especially popular in the seventh and eighth centuries. In 771, the King of Pohai offered eleven Japanese dancing girls.[15] Most importantly, however, even after good relations were established between the two capitals, the Chinese sometimes detained leaders of visiting missions, often kings' brothers or other relatives, as hostages. They were treated well, given official ranks and gifts, but they might not be allowed to go home for many years, and the Korean court occasionally had to ask for the return of important persons whom it had not seen for a very long time. When a hostage died in China, as Kim In-mun did for example in 694 after twenty-two years in detention, the Chinese court showed some sign of embarrassment through the attention which it paid to funeral and mourning expenses.[16]

Koreans with high military rank in the Chinese army frequented the capital, and for quite different reasons, so did Buddhist monks.[17] Also at court were Korean students, of whom some returned to official posts in Korea while others stayed and obtained positions in China. Best known is the famous poet Choe Chi-won (b. 857), but surely one of the longest residents in the Flowery Kingdom was Choe Eon-wi (d. 944), who was

14. *Cefu yuangui*, 972.3b.
15. *Dongguk tonggam* (Comprehensive Mirror of the Eastern Kingdom), p. 219.
16. Ennin stayed in a Korean monastery on the Shandong peninsula during his eventful trip to China from 838 to 847. See E. O. Reischaluer, Ennin's Travels in Tang China (New York, 1955).
17. *Dongguk tonggam*, p. 306.

honored by the Goryeo court when he returned after forty-two years abroad.[18] A total of eighty-eight Koreans passed the Tang examinations.

The largest section of the Korean community in Tang China was the merchant one. Their ships controlled the north China seas, virtually monopolizing trade between China, Korea, and Japan. They lived in large wards with extraterritorial rights in the towns of Chuzhou and Liangshui, and they sailed the Chinese inland waterway system.

Chinese visitors to Korea were considerably fewer. Some monks and other teachers are recorded in Korean sources, but it was official envoys from the court who most frequently crossed the sea to present the imperial calendar, mourn the passing of kings and invest their successors with appropriate titles and gifts.

Clearly there were plenty of opportunities for cultural diffusion in both directions between China and Korea, but as yet Korean culture had little to offer China apart from its music. Such was the strength of Tang culture and its preference for the highly developed arts of India, Central Asia and the Middle East that the transmission between China and Korea was entirely in an eastward direction.

The twin pillars of the sinicized way of life that was so characteristic of the ruling classes in Silla society were the Chinese written script and Buddhism. The system of *idu* for putting Korean sounds into Chinese characters had been invented in the late sixth century. In 682 King Sinmun (r. 681–691) established a state school for the advancement of Chinese culture and political science. Among the subjects studied there were the Confucian and Taoist classics, poetry, law, calligraphy, music and medicine. The government at Gyeongju, the capital city which was itself laid out on a rectangular plan in imitation of Changan, was modelled on the Tang Six Boards. It used the Chinese calendar and it used Chinese music at court, where the division of music into *dangak* (Tang music) and *hyangak* (native music) was based on the Chinese court's classification of *yayue*, *suyue*, and *huyue*.

While the great revival of Confucianism was not yet taking place even in China, it could hardly be apparent in Korea, and as the Buddhist church on the mainland headed towards its calamitous apogee in 842–845, Buddhism in Korea was well launched into its own millennium of

---

18. The most widely traveled was Hyecho, who reached India by sea and returned by way of Changan in 729.

philosophical and artistic progress. Mahayana was preferred to Hinayana, though not exclusively. Monks who traveled to China and beyond were given national honors on their return.[19] The scriptures were copied and printed.[20] Buddhist chant (*beompae*) and dances were introduced from China, and great temples and hundreds of stone pagodas, both big and small, were built across the hillsides. The glorious confidence and assurance of the Buddhist devotee, the wealthy patron and the humble craftsman burst forth in an outpouring of artistic expression that was almost as Chinese as it was spectacular. By the 670s, "the dynamic naturalism of early Tang sculpture was fully dominant in the ateliers of Gyeongju."[21] Whereas gold had been the medium for outstanding craftsmanship in pre-Unification Silla, stone and bronze came to the forefront in the Unified period, and iron was to be preferred in the early Goryeo. Examples of direct Chinese inspiration can be seen in the rock niche figures of Buddha, Shizhi and Kwanyin at Palgongsan mountain near Gyeongju and the bronze seated Buddha of c. 700 A.D., now in the National Museum at Seoul, which imitates a limestone stele from Bao Qing Su in China. But the Korean sculptors were not simply imitators. They achieved heights of artistic perfection of their own, notably in the perfect symmetry and balance of their stone lanterns and pagodas.

The liking for the Chinese style in sculpture does not imply that other Korean culture was lacking in native originality in the Silla period and earlier. Its pottery has been called "the most genuinely indigenous of all Korean forms,"[22] and although we know too little about early Korean music, a similar claim might be made on its behalf, stressing especially

---

19. The world's oldest extant printed text, the *Dharani Sutra*, was found in 1966 inside the 5-story pagoda at Bulguksa temple, Gyeongju. It was printed some time between 712 and 751.
20. C. W. Kim and W. Y. Kim, *The Arts of Korea* (Londong: Thames & Hudson, 1966), p. 142. The influence on Korean statuary can be seen from the sixth century onwards.
21. *Ibid.* p. 53.
22. The peculiar stylistic feature of the Korean bell is the cylindrical knob on its crown. Its unique decorative features are its two flying devas and the two lotus medallions which indicate the striking points of the bell. Perhaps the best example, and one of the biggest, is at the Sangwonsa temple, Gangwon-do province. Made in 725 A.D. its flying devas are both playing musical instruments, one a *gonghu* harp and the other a *saeng* mouth organ.

the outstanding instruments, the *gayageum* and *geomun-go*. The enormous bronze bells that were cast for use in the temples differed in style and decoration from Chinese bells.[23] Finally, royal tombs, in imitation of Chinese style, show a change from the earlier wooden chamber to a stone vault entered through a sloping passage. However, the tomb mounds were surrounded by protective columns decorated with the twelve zodiac images, which, though Chinese in inspiration, were peculiarly Korean in manufacture.

III

In the mid-tenth century, it looked as though the old Tang-Silla relationship would be reestablished once the political situation in China had been resolved. Trade continued, the Korean court used a number of Chinese calendars[24] and it accepted investiture from Later Jin and Zhou emperors. In 943, a royal edict said, "In the old days only we in the East admired Tang habits, culture, rites and music, and thoroughly respected its laws. Other regimes had different ways. Their nature was different in every case." And it continued, "We should not respect and imitate the Khitan. Theirs is an animal kingdom. Their habits and speech are different. We should be careful not to imitate their dress habits."[25] In 956, the court adopted Chinese official dress.

We shall not describe in detail the events that shook Korean allegiance to China from the late tenth century onwards,[26] but we must first outline the pattern of that allegiance, since the resulting exchange of missions contributed to the adoption of Chinese rites and styles in Gaeseong. In the first thirty-two years of the Song dynasty, Korea sent twenty embassies to Kaifeng, receiving sixteen in return. Most of the latter were for routine feudal purposes, investing kings, distributing ranks etc., the main exception being in 985, when China sought Korean help for an attack on Liao, which they said was a threat to trade and official tribu-

---

23. 933 Later Tang, 938 Later Jin, 948 Later Han, 951 Later Zhou.
24. *Dongguk tonggam*, p. 303.
25. For further information on these see M. C. Rogers, "Sung-Koryo Relations, some Inhibiting Factors," *Oriens* 11 (1958); "Factionalism and Goryeo Policy under the Northern Song," *Journal of the American Oriental Society* 79 (1959).
26. *Goryeosa* (History of Goryeo) 3, 6a ff.

tary communications.[27] The help was approved but never sent. In 994, the position was reversed, Korea vainly sent ambassador Won Uk to China for aid.[28] The Koreans must have been prepared for the failure of their request: four months previously, they had already adopted the Liao calendar and over the next two years, they sent twenty students to learn the language in the Liao Empire. They sent presents of singing girls (who were declined), eagles, and maps in 1002, while apparently trying to protect their interests on both sides by sending a further six missions to China between 994 and 1003. The Chinese did not reciprocate, and in 1005, Korea congratulated Liao on its victory over Song.

When King Hyeonjong (r. 1009–1031) tried to reopen relations with China in 1014, sending gifts of horses and saddles and seeking a return to vassaldom as before, the Emperor had a hostel opened at Dengzhou for Korean envoys. In 1016, Gaeseong readopted the Song calendar, but it was too late, for in that year the Middle Kingdom was again forced to submit to Liao. After its own defeat in 1020 Korea returned to the Liao calendar in 1022 and officially communicated with Kaifeng five more times before the complete breakdown of relations in 1030.[29] The Chinese sent no embassies back, there being, in fact, a long gap of altogether seventy-nine years during which no Chinese officials went to Korea on imperial business (see Appendix). It was on Chinese initiative that communications were eventually restored. Emperor Shenzong (r. 1067-1085), being reminded by his minister Luo Zheng that Korea was a "country of gentlemen," sent a message in 1068 by way of the merchant Huang Shen indicating his willingness to reopen relations.[30] The Koreans seemed glad to respond. The Emperor sent textiles and two doctors with the returning Korean ambassador in 1072; in 1073, the Koreans asked for more doctors as well as Chinese painters and sculptors, and

---

27. *Goryeosa* 3, 26b-27a.
28. This breakdown did not mean the total severance of contacts nor a welcome political ostracization on either side. In 1021, the Emperor had sent books to Korea by way of the returning ambassador and according to one source (*Yeosa jegang*), the Koreans tried to send a mission in 1036, but the ship was wrecked. In 1058, King Munjong (r. 1046–1083) was dissuaded from building ships to communicate with Song partly on the grounds that it would offend Liao, and that since trade with China continued to flourish anyway, there was no justification for upsetting the Khitans (*Goryeosa* 8, 11a-b; *Dongguk tonggam*, p. 404).
29. *Goryeosa* 8, 32a; 8, 35a.
30. *Goryeosa* 9, 10a.

Luo Zheng was given the job of recruiting them;[31] in 1077, the Korean government opened a hostel for Chinese envoys, and the first Chinese embassy on a grand scale was headed by An Dao in 1078. Its specially built ships were loaded with textiles, clothing, belts, horses, whips, tea, teapots, wine warmers, silver vessels, bowls, candles and musical instruments.[32] It was given a rapturous reception in Korea, and tribute was promptly sent back consisting of clothing, belts, horses, saddles, gold, silver, and rice.[33]

The last thirty years of this century were a prolific period for the exchange of official gifts, and it may be appropriate here to say something about the substance of these. Three categories of gifts in particular, those of ritual goods, books, and music may be said to have contributed to the cultural life of the Korean court. A complete list of gifts exchanged in the Northern Song period is as follows:

(a) *China to Korea.* Silk, textiles, clothing, belts; gold, silver, and jade articles; sacrificial and mourning items; wine warmers, bowls, teapots, candles; tea, wine, and fruit; sheep, horses, saddles, whips, bows and arrows; medical supplies; books, paintings, Lohans and Buddhist relics; musical instruments and texts.

(b) *Korea to China.* Textiles, wool and other cloth, clothing, gold belts, furs, rugs, furnishings, and covers; gold, silver, and copper objects; wine pourers; rice, pine seeds, ginseng, aromatic drugs, aromatic oils, and sulphur; horses, saddles and fittings, one carriage, armour, weapons, swords and fittings, bows and arrows, military items; screens, scrolls, paper, ink, religious texts and images, books.

During the tenth and eleventh centuries there was a roughly even balance in the number of missions sent by each country which are recorded as bearing gifts, thirteen from Korea and seventeen from China.[34] Unfortunately not all of them arrived. The sea between Dengzhou or Mingzhou and the west coast of Korea was notoriously rough and a number of ships were wrecked. When the ship bearing Lu Duan and Lu

---

31. *Goryeosa* 9, 18a, *Songshi* (History of Song China) 487.13a.
32. *Goryeosa* 9, 22a.
33. See Keith L. Pratt, "Some Aspects of Diplomatic and Cultural Exchange between Korea and Northern Song China," in *Dongyang eumak nonchong* (Collection of Papers on Oriental Music) (Seoul, 1976).
34. *Haedong yeoksa*, p. 592.

Youzhi was hit by a storm in 988 and the boatmen were terrified, Lu Duan calmed them by reading books to them. He had been loaned 500,000 cash from the palace treasury to do business, but a storm blew up on the return voyage, and they had to throw overboard everything they had bought.[35]

Some time later, a ship was being loaded for Li Shiheng and Yu Ying. The latter, fearing that his personal goods would be damaged by water seeping into the bottom of the hold, had Li's put underneath and his own on top. During the voyage, however, there was a storm and his belongings were the first to be thrown overboard.[36]

The most serious loss was surely in 1080, when a ship laden with textiles, clothing, belts, gold washing vessels, silver objects, screens, scrolls, paper, ink, armor, bows and arrows, horses, saddles, gold boxes, dishes, wine pourers, furnishings, swords, cloth, ginseng, pine seeds, aromatic oils, and a Japanese carriage was almost overturned before it reached China and half its cargo was lost.[37]

In addition to the gift bearing missions, the Chinese court gave presents to Korean envoys and sent presents back to their king. Of all the items sent to Korea the wide variety of textiles was probably the most costly, though the large quantities of tea sent in 1078 and drugs in 1079 are also impressive.[38] Nevertheless, the value of Korean tribute to China seems to have outweighed that of the Chinese gifts, though it is hard to

---

35. *Haedong yeoksa*, p. 592-593.
36. *Goryeosa* 9, 27b ff; *Songshi* 487.13a; *Dongguk tonggam*, p. 413; *Wenxian tongkao* (文獻 通考) 2560a.
37. *Goryeosa* 9, 19a ff; *Goryeosa* 9, 24a; *Songshi* 487.13a; *Wenxian tongkao*, 2560a.
38. This refers only to the value of the goods exchanged, however, not to the total economic cost of maintaining the tribute system nor to the balance of mercantile trade. Diplomatic missions were sometimes very large; those sent by Korea in 1021 and 1030 consisted of 179 and 293 men. There was also the cost of building and staffing official hostels, both in China and Korea. Su Dongpo was particularly vehement in condemning both the economic and political harm which he thought resulted from Song-Goryeo relations. It should be remembered that both China and Korea were also involved in tributary relations with Liao. In 1004, China had agreed to pay 100,000 taels of silver and 200,000 lustring per annum, increased in 1042 to 200,000 taels and 300,000 lustring. Korea sent 23 tribute missions to Liao between 994 and 1110. K. A. Wittfogel & C. S. Feng, *History of Chinese Society: Liao* (New York, 1948) lists the contents of this tribute and some of the items received in return, including camels, sheep, horses, carriages, weapons, wine, silk, fruit, etc.

be sure about this since the records are not specific about the quantities of objects sent, such as gold dishes and other costly items. In economic terms, the balance of tributary exchange appears to have been in China's favor.[39]

In the first quarter of the twelfth century, the situation changed and China sent eleven embassies with gifts recorded for only two in return. One reason for this was the fact that in 1110, Emperor Huizong (r. 1100–1126) granted Yejong (r. 1105–1122) the status of a "true king" (*zhenwang*), absolving him from his feudal obligations in view of what he caned the hundred years of good relations between their countries and their own brotherly feelings.[40] Yejong continued however to be enfeoffed to Liao and China continued to worry about Korean loyalty.

The second reason was the advance of the Jurchen, which prompted the possibility of an alliance with them against the Khitan but also the danger of their recognition by Goryeo at Song's expense. A steady flow of Khitan, Xi, Pohai, and Chinese refugees arrived in Korea, some of the Khitans entertaining the King with music, dancing, and plays in 1117.[41]

Perhaps it was unlikely that Yejong would agree to Huizong's suggestion that Koreans should bring Jurchen representatives to Kaifeng, but his ambassador Yi Ja-ryang, to whom the idea was put confidentially in 1116, rejected it on his behalf. He called the Jurchen the most savage of barbarians with whom there was no question of the Chinese communicating. Some of the Emperor's courtiers said that all sons of Jurchen valuables went to Korea as trade and that Yi Ja-ryang's refusal to cooperate was through unwillingness to risk these profits. The Koreans, unfaithfully turning their backs on the Emperor's paternal love for their country, should not be encouraged any further to contact their northern neighbours to the possible detriment of peace and order.[42]

The rejection of the Emperor's suggestion and the subsequent Korean advances to the Jurchen were pan of a major failure on China's pan to exert cultural influence in support of political goals. Before putting his proposal to Yi Ja-ryang, Huizong had sent Yejong two outstanding and costly gifts of instruments and music, one in 1114 and the second in

---

39. *Goryeosa*, 13.14a.
40. *Goryeosa*, 14.23b-24a.
41. *Goryeosa*, 95.11b-12a; *Dongguk tonggam*, p. 472.
42. See Keith L. Pratt, "Music as a Factor in Sung-Koryo Diplomatic Relations, 1069-1126," *Toung bao* LXII (1976).

1116. The ambassador was, in fact, in Kaifeng to thank him for the second of these.[43]

Even when the power of ritual music seemed to have no effect, the Emperor did not give up hope, using the importance of other rites to try and convince the Koreans of their allegiance to him. When King Yejong died in 1122, he sent gins of mourning objects, saying that his hopes for the continuity of the rites in Gaeseong and the receipt of imperial messengers there had suddenly been put at risk. There were numerous instances of China's conferring mourning honors. It was right for him to wear respectful mourning and for the new King to pay eternal obedience to his duties as a feudal prince. When King Injong (r. 1123–1146) went to the temple to make sacrificial libations the Chinese envoys said, "We have heard that formerly when a king died the mourning king was too busy conducting business, so he would send officials to perform these rites, and the commands and funeral orations were all written by the Emperor himself in a personal letter. . . . Now our generous etiquette is quite different, emphasizing the favors of a father to his son. Since the edict of 1110 [the Emperor] has specially abjured his rights in giving [the King] the rites of a true king. Formerly King Yejong was enfeoffed by Liao so he was out of touch. But now the Liao mandate has been broken and you may request the mandate to go to court." King Injong replied, "From the beginning our country has taken pleasure in and admired Chinese customs. From the beginning [of my reign] I especially should strive to "serve the great" (*shida*) according to the rites and go to court out of loyalty. Though you are over the sea you constantly have us in mind, so you see clearly [what happens here] and frequently send us favors. Now for [the Emperor] himself to write a funerary oblation shows exceptional kindness to his servant. For the Emperor to abjure his rights even though he should first have tested me, how could a small person [such as I] be worthy of this? The so-called investiture mandate (*ceming*) by which the Emperor confers rewards is the great statute (*datien*) of the feudal lords. Now Liao institutions have not yet ended [but I shall] hurriedly seek this great statute from [the source of] righteousness. I have not yet got over my agitated spirit. I hope to send envoys to you next year to offer thanks and bring myself to your attention."[44]

---

43. *Goryeosa*, 15.4a ff; *Dongguk tonggam*, p. 484.
44. *Goryeosa*, 15.11b; *Dongguk tonggam*, p. 491.

The envoys were sent in 1124, but Injong refused to join an alliance against the Jurchen, and in June 1125, a mission left for the Jin capital. On May 5, 1126, the Goryeo court pledged its submission to Jin, the King having being persuaded by Yi Ja-gyeom in the face of strong opposition that this was the new interpretation of "serving the great."[45] Shortly afterwards, a Chinese mission with over sixty members made a last unavailing attempt to persuade the King of the value of the ritual connection with Song.[46]

Had King Injong really been sincere in suggesting that he would serve Kaifeng or was it a piece of deliberate subterfuge on his part? Certainly a strong argument went on at court between the advocates of independence and those who urged submission to either Song or Jin. Was the young King tugged backwards and forwards? Xu Jing's assessment of his character indicates that he was quite capable of taking tough decisions for himself. He calls him intelligent, well-educated, strict and hard on his officials who feared him despite his youth, indeed "a virtuous king among the Eastern barbarians."[47] However, the authority exercised at court by the Yi clan, especially Yi Ja-gyeom, suggests that Xu Jing was only repeating an "approved" view of the fifteen-year old monarch.

One other incident in the battle of wits between Song, Liao, Jin, and Goryeo is described by several sources but with differing dates and details. According to the *Goryeosa*, *Dongguk tonggam*, and *Gaoli tujing*, it was King Yejong, and according to *Songshi*, *Wenxian tongkao*, and Zhu Xi's *Yulei*, King Injong who sent a request to Emperor Huizong for doctors.[48] The number mentioned varies between two, five and seven, and *Dongguk tonggam* tells us that they were to deal with a swelling on the Crown Prince's artery. They arrived, either in 1118 or 1123, and were treated politely but not asked for any medical advice. When they expressed surprise, the King told them that he wanted them to take a message that he thought might not reach the Emperor secretly if it were sent by an official envoy. He had heard, he said, of the Emperor's plan to make an agreement with the Jurchen against the Liao. In his opinion, no attack should be considered on Liao, who were fraternal neighbors.

---

45. *Goryeosa*, 15.14a.
46. *Gaoli tujing*, ch. 1.
47. *Goryeosa*, 14.27b, 14.30b; *Dongguk tonggam*, p. 475; *Gaoli tujing*, ch. 16; *Songshi*, 487.15a; *Wenxian tongkao*, 325.1560a-b; *Haedong yeoksa*, p. 196.
48. *Dongguk tonggam*, p. 306.

The Jurchen, though complimented for their good military tactics in Zhu Xi's version of the story, were tierce tigers with whom there should be no contact. There seems little doubt as to the actual date of this event. It clearly followed the return of Yi Ja-ryang with his account of the Emperor's suggestion to him in 1116, and though it might have been another piece of camouflage on Injong's part while he contemplated the merits of a Jurchen alliance, the fact that the 1123 mission was that of Xu Jing himself and that he says the doctors went to Korea in 1118, must conclusively prove the *Songshi* wrong.

So far we have discussed only the exchange of official missions at court level, neglecting incidentally the occasional visits by local officials, especially from the main point of embarkation for Korea at Mingzhou. Before going on to consider the nature and extent of Chinese cultural transmission in the Northern Song period, however, we should not over-look the other classes of people who might have been partly responsible for it.

As in the Silla period, Korean students and monks traveled to China, returning after varying lengths of time with the fruits of their Confucian and Buddhist labors. The record for swift success seems to be held by Kim Haeng-seong, who took only one year to obtain his *jinshi* in 976–977.[49] Four particularly famous monks were Jegwan, who went to China in 960 in answer to a Chinese request for scriptures to replace those lost during fighting in China,[50] Yeoga in 989,[51] Uicheon (or Seungtong) in 1085[52] and his disciple Suga in 1089.[53] Uicheon was the brother of King Sukjong (r. 1095–1105) and went to offer condolences on the death of Emperor Shenzong, so he also counts as an official envoy. Suga's mission was partly to give two gold stupas to the Song Empress from the Korean Queen.

The foreign community in Gaeseong included refugees from over the northern frontiers, occasionally large parties of visitors such as the hun-

49. *Haedong yeoksa*, p. 512.
50. *Songshi*, 487.5b; *Wenxian tongkao*, 325.2559a; *Goryeosa*, 3.14b.
51. *Songshi*, 487.14a; *Wenxian tongkao*, 325.2560a; *Goryeosa*, 10.5b.
52. *Songshi*, 487.14a.
53. *Goryeosa*, 5.4a, 5.6a. Other evidence for Middle Easterners living in Korea is to be found in the poem "Ssanghwajeom"; see Yi Hye-gu, *Hanguk eumak seoseol* (Introduction to Korean Music) (Seoul: Seoul National University Press, 1967), pp. 125-139; Peter H. Lee, *Poems from Korea* (London: George Allen & Unwin: 1975), p. 54.

dred Arabs who arrived in 1024 and those in 1025,[54] foreign musicians resident at court,[55] and Chinese merchants. These settled in Korea by the hundred, and although the *shibosi* at Quan Zhou and Ban Qiao which were to encourage Korean trade were not opened until 1087 and 1088, merchants had not been deterred by the absence of diplomatic contacts through the mid-eleventh century. At a time when trade with Southeast Asia seemed to be falling, the big new Chinese ships, the largest able to carry ave or six hundred men, plied regularly across the north China Sea.[56] The Fukienese were particularly active,[57] their voyages taking seven to twenty days. Su Dungpo, an ardent critic of the revival of the Goryeo alliance who attacked Chinese merchants for undermining economic and strategic interests in their lust for personal gain, said that "the entire province of Fukien makes its living by the practice of seaborne commerce."[58] Significantly, Fang Dacong commented on the high degree of literacy among Fukienese merchants: "In my own county every family is adept at music and the chanting of texts . . . . Every peasant, artisan, and merchant teaches his son how to read books."[59]

It is unlikely that much scholarship rubbed off on the Koreans with whom they came into contact. They lived in official hostels, and though commerce was plentiful, it was not organized with the regularity and efficiency that it was in China. Mostly it was conducted at irregular fairs, and though some Chinese undoubtedly knew the Korean language, there is nothing to suggest a degree of fraternization between

---

54. *Goryeosa*, 72.24b mentions groups of 18 from India, 40 from Bokhara, and 16 from Turfan.
55. See Keum Sang-gi, *Dongbang munhwa gyoryusa non-go* (A Study on History of Cultural Exchange in East Asia) (Seoul: Eulyoo Publishing Co., 1955). On the basis of Korean records a total of over 1,200 Chinese merchants visited Korea between 1030 and 1069.
56. Y. Shiba, *Sodai shogyshi kenkyu* (Commerce and Society in Song China) (Tokyo, 1968), pp. 341-342, has a table listing those who visited Korea between 1013 and 1161.
57. Y. Shiba, *Commerce and Society in Song China*, trans. M. Elvin (Ann Arbor: Michigan, 1970), p. 187.
58. *Ibid.*, p. 182.
59. Two exceptional instances should be mentioned here. In 1027, a merchant from Jiangnan presented 597 books to the Korean court, and in 1087, the merchant Xu Jian presented printing blocks for *Xinzhu huayanjing*.

merchants and Koreans that would have led to cultural exchange, except of course through the goods that were bartered, notably porcelain.[60]

The Korean habit of barter was mentioned by Xu Jing, the only exceptions to it being in the cloth and drugs trade. A monetary economy was developing rapidly in Northern Song China, and when Uicheon returned after his fourteen-month stay there, he urged his brother to encourage the use of coinage in Korea. A mint was established in 1097, and with another issue of coins in 1102 (*haedong tongbo*) the first public tavern was opened in Gaeseong to try and popularize them, but only the silver coins used by the upper classes achieved any degree of acceptance.

IV

Three types of religious observance were practised by members of the Goryeo court: Confucian, Buddhist and shamanist. Confucianism provided most of the state ritual and ceremony, and the Koreans did their best to ensure that the rites were kept up to date by Chinese standards. In 1111, for example, Kim Yeon was sent to China to check on the performance of the sacrificial rites,[61] and after the death of the Queen Mother two years later, An Jik-sung went on a similar mission.[62] It was he who was given the first of the two historic musical gins. There had been no diminution of Chinese ceremonial influence while diplomatic relations were at their low ebb. Chinese historical precedents continued to be quoted in court arguments[63] and Chinese ritual was still used. Xu Jing complimented the Koreans on the splendor of their rites and the diligence with which they took care of them, noting both similarities and differences with Chinese usage.[64]

The growth of Confucian influence is plain in royal pronouncements during early Goryeo. The state examination system had been set up in 958 with the assistance of a Chinese official from the Later Zhou empire, Shuang Ji, who had been detained in Korea through illness.[65]

---

60. *Goryeosa*, 13.21a.
61. *Goryeosa*, 13.29b-30a.
62. See, for example, *Goryeosa*, 7.25b-26a.
63. *KLTC*, ch. 24.
64. *Dongguk tonggam*, p. 310.
65. *Xiaojing citu, Huangling xiaojing, Yuewang xiaojing xinyi, Biexu xiaojing. Dongguk tonggam*, p. 174.

The first two grades, *gong* and *geo*, were based on *si* and *bu* poetry and the *jinsa* on the Classics. In 992, the National University, the Gukjagam, was opened for the children of officials, teaching Chinese classics and literature. The following year, a request was sent to China for editions of the Nine Classics to help in the teaching of scholars and in 1091, Kwak Won urged that more attention should be paid to the *Liji* in the *jinsa*. In 1118, King Yejong instituted a series of discussions held over the next four years at which selected scholars presented papers on sections of six classics, the *Shijing*, *Shujing*, *Yijing*, *Liji*, *Zhongyong*, and *Laozi*.

In particular, we might note the royal emphasis on filial piety. In 959, four books on this subject were sent to China.[66] When King Seongjong (r. 981–997) established the Royal Library in 990, ordering its members to copy out books, his edict drew an analogy between the need of Han dynasty China to recreate books destroyed by Qin and his own desire to rescue books lost in the conquest of Silla. He ordered that unemployed *sujae* should hold discussions on the Classics in order to appreciate the customs of the feudal states (Qin, Han, Zhou, and Lu), and to understand the constancy of a father's compassion and a son's filialness and the virtue of an elder brother's love and a younger brother's respect.[67]

In the following year, local officials were ordered to make a survey of illness within their districts,[68] following an edict of 987 which had established twelve *baksa* to study medicine. This edict said that since the time of the Chinese Three Dynasties (Xia, Shang, and Zhou), education had stressed the ethics of the father-son and minister-subject relationship.

---

66. *Goryeosa*, 3.22a; *Dongguk tonggam*, pp. 332-333.
67. *Dongguk tonggam*, p. 333.
68. *Dongguk tonggam*, p. 328; *Goryeosa*, 3.11a ff. We should note here the inaccuracy of the *Songshi* assertion (quoted in *Haedong yeoksa*, p. 420) that the Koreans did not understand medicine until King Yejong asked for doctors in 1122. Xu Jing (*Gaoli tujing*, ch. 16) said that in the past they knew nothing about medicine but just relied on serving the spirits with oaths and sacrifices. All this came to an end with King Muniong's request for doctors in 1078 which resulted in the big Chinese medical expedition of 1079. After Yejong's request, says Xu Jing, there was an influx of doctors. A medical office was opened to the east of Jinjae-sa with officials in charge of it. Certainly there was some truth in the Chinese claim that it was their medical knowledge that was at the basis of the Koreans, but we have noted above that the Koreans almost certainly had some experience of herbalism in the Silla period, and that they studied Chinese medicine then and in the early Goryeo.

The King was overwhelmed by the plethora of sagely wisdom and books on rites, music, poetry, and history which had been produced in China even before the institution of kingship had originated in Korea. In aiming to transform the lives of the people, nothing was more effective than medicine, for "the care of materials and what can be made from them in the service of one's lord and king is the beginning of loyalty, and the care of the body and the establishment of a reputation in the honoring of one's parents is the culmination of filial piety."[69]

State ritual and official pronouncements apart, it was Buddhism that maintained the strongest hold on the royal family and court circles. Wang Geon, founder of the Goryeo dynasty, left a will of Ten Admonitions, three of which gave encouragement to Buddhism. So well were these observed that Buddhism was the principal influence both at court and throughout the countryside in the early Goryeo period. Members of the upper classes observed its rites and festivals and many of their sons entered the church, whose leadership was as much of an elite as was the civil leadership. We have already mentioned Uicheon, brother of King Sukjong. On his return from China in 1086, he reinstated the suppressed Cheontae (Tiantai) Sect and established a printing office at Heungwangsa. Here, he published a four thousand roll set of the Tripitaka compiled from the best Chinese, Liao[70] and Japanese editions.

The subject of book collection, publishing and authorship is too big to be covered here, but it was stimulated greatly by Chinese influence and by Confucianism and Buddhism in particular. The ability to read and write Chinese characters was a *sine qua non* for the intelligentsia. In 995, local officials were required to submit regularly *si* and *bu* on subjects chosen by Hallim Academy scholars.[71] Thousands of Chinese books were imported either by purchase or donation and book production in Korea was encouraged. Xu Jing goes so far as to talk of the proliferation of bookshops even in the alleyways of local villages, though this might be doubted. The Chinese believed that Korean libraries had good copies of books that had been lost in China and sent a request for 118 titles in

---

69. Liao presented Korea with printed sets of the Tripitaka in 1063 and 1073, Korea reciprocating by sending copies of other Buddhist texts. Liao, Korean and Japanese editions were generally better than the current Chinese editions. See Wittfogel & Feng, *op. cit.*

70. *Goryeosa*, 3.28a.

71. *Ibid.*, 10.23a ff.

1091.[72] The Korean answer was that they had not enough scholars available to copy them and that if the Chinese wanted them, they must send copyists. They may have had good reason for not wishing to embark on such a large task themselves. In 1056, it had been reported that handwritten copies of texts for advanced students in the capital contained too many mistakes, and all private libraries with editions of the Classics, histories, *belles lettres*, books on medicine, divination, geography, and mathematics were asked to have one copy of each printed and sent in.[73] How efficiently this was done is not recorded, but the copying and printing industry must have been at fun stretch for some time.

The records contain frequent references to titles that were sent from China to Korea and vice versa. The *Haedong yeoksa* (*gwon* 44) contains a list of Chinese books known in Korea though it is not complete. Sometimes restrictions were placed on books which could be presented or bought. In 1085, Korea asked to buy *Xingfa wenshu*, *Taiping yulan*, *Kaibao tongli* and *Wenyuan yinghuaji*. Only the last of these was permitted. Following the Chinese request in 1091, ambassador Hwang Jong-gak was sent to China with just one work, *Huangdi zhenjing*, and the rather tactless request to buy a large number of books himself. He was only allowed to buy *Cefu yuangui*.[76] Su Dongpo claimed that the book trade could be of military disadvantage to China and urged in 1093 that it should be stopped altogether. Some relaxation in the official attitude followed, however, and in 1101, the new Emperor Huizong released copies of *Shenyi pujiu fang* and *Taiping yulan* (1,000 *juan*). The accompanying message might even have been a little tongue in cheek:

> We have heard that your king likes literature and that literary things have recently prospered greatly in Korea. The memorials which you have submitted have been excellent and the court has found them very beautiful.

King Sukjong expressed his thanks, especially for the Taiping yulan,

72. *Ibid.*, 7.38b.
73. *Songshi*, 17.4b; *Wenxian tongkao*, 325.2560a.
74. *Ibid.*, 17.18b, 487.14b; *Wenxian tongkao*, 325.2560a.
75. For a thorough account of Su Dongpo's views on the Korean book trade and other commerce see M. C. Rogers, op. cit.
76. *Gaoli tujing*, ch. 17.

which he said he had long wanted and not been able to obtain. In the view of Michael Rogers, however, Song restrictions on the book trade "must have engendered a cynical attitude" among the Koreans, affecting "the movements, purchases and personal contacts" of official embassies.

Despite the Confucian-inspired interest professed by the early Goryeo kings in their subjects' welfare, it is unlikely that the latter had any interest in Confucianism. Buddhism affected their lives more, as it did the lives of the Chinese lower classes. Truly popular religion in Korea, however, was shamanistic. In Xu Jing's opinion, "It is their habit to make excessive sacrifices to the spirits."[77] At times, the court and even the kings were unwilling to dispense with the shaman's services.[78] The shamanistic Palgwanhoe (Festival of the Eight Vows) ceremony became an annual national rite.[79] Originating in the old Goguryeo village sacrificial rite Dongmaeng (Jumong foundership), banned in 981 as uncanonical and too noisy, it was reintroduced in 1010 and frequently attended by kings. After attending one such occasion in the 11th moon of 1115, King Yejong stayed outside the Hammun Gate, ordering his players to sing and dance until the third drum. He was rebuked by the Chief Censor.[80]

Yejong was a colorful, extravagant, extrovert monarch. He had genuine literary taste and particularly enjoyed poetry. He liked traveling, feasting, drinking, singing, and fraternizing generously with his officials and artisans. He was strong-willed: on becoming besotted by two female musicians, he was admonished by Ko Hyo-chung in a poem entitled "Gami nyeosi," recalling Han Yu's poem about Emperor Xianzong's (r. 805–820) love for two birds. Instead of taking the point, the King dismissed the unfortunate official.[81] He sent to the provinces another who tried to persuade him that the Classics and history were more fit pursuits for the court than poetry.[82] It was he who, on sending five students to China in 1115, said that "in using Chinese ways to change barbarians one avails oneself of the teachings of the Former Kings."[83] He who was

---

77. Yi Hye-gu, *op. cit.*, pp. 299-336.
78. *Goryeosa*, 69.12a ff. records the participation of Song merchant leaders (*dougang*) and other foreigners in Palgwanhoe ceremonies.
79. *Dongguk tonggam*, p. 467.
80. *Ibid.*, p. 476.
81. *Ibid.*, p. 468.
82. *Goryeosa*, 14.4b.
83. This may be seen particularly in examples of Goryeo metal-work in the National

favored with the *yayue* (*aak*) in the following year and with an imperial inducement of a different kind in 1120, the gift of Buddha's teeth and bones in a golden casket.

V

We could go on giving examples of the Chinese cultural presence in Goryeo Korea, of Chinese employed in the Korean bureaucracy, of Koreans renowned for their skills in Chinese literature, of gifts of imperial calligraphy and painting, of the Korean imitation of Chinese historiography. But this might, after all, be to beg the question of the effect of the Chinese example on Korean society as a whole, or even of the degree of its acceptance by the tiny, elite pan of society that was the apparently sinicized ruling class.

It is doubtful whether in the years before the Yi dynasty the bulk of the population, the peasantry, had any sense of connection at all with their feudal relatives across the sea in China. In the National Folklore Museum, Seoul, the rooms devoted to the upper class way of life constantly reflect Chinese education and interests, while those showing the life of ordinary people do so hardly at all. Even the upper class, for all its Chinese-ness, maintained its own cultural integrity to some extent. It played and appreciated native music (*hyangak*) with apparently as much enjoyment as it derived from imported Chinese *zi* tunes or the more formal Chinese ritual music (*aak*). It preferred its own stringed instruments, the *gayageum* and *geomun-go*, to the Chinese *cheng* and *qin*. Though it liked and imitated the great Tang poets, it perfected in the *sijo* form its own distinctive style of expressing its love of nature. It patronized craftsmen who made artifacts that in no way aped Chinese style or taste,[84] and at the same time by giving them the encouragement to copy the best Chinese imports, the celadon wares of the ten and eleven centuries, it spurred them on to surpass the techniques of the Chinese potters. In later centuries, the game of Korean independence and originality might be dimmed, but in the medieval period it still burned quite brightly.

Museum in Seoul. The tradition of fine metal craftsmanship, inherited from the Three Kingdoms period, was especially strong.

84. See Evelyn McCune, *The Arts of Korea* (Rutland: Charles E. Tuttle Co., 1962).

APPENDIX

Missions between China and Korea in the Period 960–1126*

A.D.	a	b	A.D.	a	b	A.D.	a	b	A.D.	a	b
960			993	★	★	1026			1097		
961			994	★		1027			1098	★	
962	★	★	995	★		1028			1099	★	
963	★	★	996			1029			1100	★★	
964			997	★		1030	★		1101		
965	★		998			1070			1102		
966			999	★		1071	★★		1103		★
967			1000	★		1072		★	1104	★	
968			1001			1073	★		1105		
969			1002			1074		★	1106		
970			1003	★		1075			1107		
971			1004			1076	★		1108	★★	
972			1005			1077			1109		
973			1006			1078		★	1110		★
974			1007			1079		★	1111	★	
975			1008			1080	★★	★	1112	★	
976	★	★	1009			1081	★		1113	★	
977	★		1010			1082			1114	★	
978	★	★	1011			1083		★	1115	★	
979		★	1012			1084			1116	★	
980	★	★	1013			1085	★★		1117		★
981	★		1014	★		1086		★	1118	★	★
982	★	★	1015	★		1087			1119		
983		★	1016			1088			1120		★
984	★		1017	★		1089	★		1121		★
985		★★	1018			1090	★★		1122	★	★
986	★	★	1019	★		1091	★		1123	★	★
987			1020	★		1092	★		1124	★	
988	★	★	1021	★		1093	★		1125	★	
989	★★		1022			1094			1126	★	★
990	★★	★★	1023			1095					
991	★		1024			1096					
992	★	★	1025								

* This table is a revision of that given in Keith L. Pratt "Some Aspects of Diplomatic and Cultural Exchange," where references to most missions are given. It is based on *Songshi, Wenxian tongkao, Xu zizhi tongjian, Goryeosa, Haedong yeoksa, Goryeosa jeoryo, Dongguk tonggam,* and *Yeosa jegang.*

** a. Goryeo-Song b: Song-Goryeo

The Landowning Slave:
A Korean Phenomenon

Ellen Salem

Slavery in Goryeo was an extraordinary, if not unique institution in the annals of human society. The ordinary factors that are generally assumed to set the slave apart from his owner, such as racial differentiation[1] or social pollution, did not apply. Nonetheless, that institution formed an integral, important and highly viable part of the Goryeo social fabric. As such, it presents a fascinating problem, both in terms of human values and the mechanics of social stratification.

It was my original intent to investigate this topic in a rather orthodox manner. That is, my intention was to gather all the information available in the sources to first define the parameters of that institution in Goryeo, and, beyond that, to integrate the Korean historical experience with that of other societies, particularly in the Western hemisphere.

While I did not abandon this approach, I have added another dimension. What started out as a sociological query has become a human and conceptual one. The prime reason for this is that as I undertook a parallel investigation of slavery in Goryeo and the West, it became clear that many of the attributes of slavery generally assumed to be unique to Korea are indeed not. Still, the totality of that institution is unprecedent-

---

* Originally published in the *Korea Journal*, vol. 16, no. 4 (April 1976).

Ellen Salem is the Vice President & Deputy Executive Director of the Korea Society Quarterly. She obtained her Ph.D. in History from Columbia University.

1. "No group uses their own members permanently as slaves. At any rate such types of slavery do not create hereditary strata." Egon Ernest Bergel, *Social Stratification* (New York: The McGraw-Hill Companies, 1962), p. 71. The validity of this hypothesis is negated by the Korean experience.

ed by any other society, be it Eastern or Western. Thus, it became apparent that mere descriptive analysis, no matter how detailed, was simply begging a far more fundamental question: What defined slave? On what grounds did the men of Goryeo rationalize the subordination of one group to another, to the point of appropriating themselves the authority to buy and sell other individuals? In other words, before one can even begin to comprehend slavery in Goryeo, one must come to terms with certain components of the basic premises of the society that gave rise to this unique variant of a universal institution. One must, in the final analysis, suspend such concepts as freedom, equality and equal rights before the law.[2] While this suspension is necessary, it is not a panacea. But, hopefully, I will, in the next several pages, be able to explain—and ultimately convey the ability to understand—a portion of the Korean reality through a study of slavery in Goryeo.

For the purposes of this essay, slavery is defined as a non-kinship relationship in which one individual is subject to the will of another individual or group, to the extent that he can be bought or sold as property. This definition, culled from a number of sources, is not meant to be a definitive one.[3] Rather, it is a working definition and one that may or may not be refined as my study of slavery progresses.

It should be pointed out, moreover, that any attempt to define slavery in terms broad enough to encompass the almost infinite variations of that institution must be so general as to render the definition meaningless. A general, succinct and universally applicable description of slavery is impossible.[4]

While I would not totally deny the utilitarianism of an attempt to define in universal terms, I cannot help but wonder if the present pen-

---

2. For a discussion of legal capacity and the concept of "rights" in premodern Korea, see Bak Byeong-ho, "Hanguk-ui jeontong sahoe-wa beop" (Korean Traditional Society and Its Laws), *Seouldae beophak* (Seoul National University Law Journal) 15.1 (1974): pp. 99-102.

3. See Bergel, *op. cit.*, pp. 71-76; Paul Bohannan, *Social Anthropology* (New York: International Thomson Publishing, 1965), pp. 179-183; David Brian Davis, *The Problem of Slavery in Western Culture* (Ithaca: Cornell University Press, 1966), pp. 30-35; William L. Westermann, *The Slave Systems of Greek and Roman Antiquity* (Baltimore: JH Furst Company, 1955), p. 1; and C. Martin Wilbur, *Slavery in China during the Former Han Dynasty* (New York: Russell and Russell, 1943), p. 63.

4. "No single definition has succeeded in comprehending the historical varieties of slavery or in clearly distinguishing the institution from other forms of involuntary servitude." Davis, *op. cit.*, p. 35.

chant for "universality" does not impede cross-cultural understanding. What we must come to terms with, and try to understand, are those elements that make one culture different from another. There is a tendency today (which is not limited to Western scholars) to define a culture in terms of the elusive god of "modernization." Thus, eccentrics who ran counter to the norms of their society—Sin Don for example—can easily become modern-day heroes if for no other reason than that certain of the ideas they fought for against societal norms have become the norms of modern, and, in too many cases, Western societies.

To many of my readers, the point I am trying to make may be self-evident, particularly in the context of slavery. But, on the other hand, I think it must be stressed that not only does each generation rewrite its own history, but in so doing, each tends to obfuscate the basic integrity and values of the past, particularly when those values are at odds with its own present values. The ascription of different values has become, regrettably, a value judgment. All too often it leads to the imposition of a Western model, a model that was devised to explain the logic behind the development of a capitalistic, industrial society, subsequently superimposed upon the facts of Korean history.

The men of Goryeo were different. Unless we attempt to understand their society in their terms, sources such as the *Goryeosa* (History of Goryeo) are, at best, a hodgepodge of unconnected data and, at worst, sheer gibberish. The premises upon which these men acted were not ours. Nor, basic humanity aside, were many of their values our own. In particular, concepts such as freedom and equality were totally meaningless.

The words freedom and equality (or parallel concepts) were not a part of the Chinese vocabulary until the mid-nineteenth century—a good five hundred years after the fall of Goryeo. Nor does there appear to have been any term in pure Korean to express that concept. The world, and indeed, the world order, was envisioned in a hierarchical configuration. All men may have been brothers under heaven, but to extend that fraternity to everyday life could only disrupt society. And despite the lip service given to equality in the West, is not inequality far easier to discern than equality? Heretical as it may be to suggest, it is not self-evident that all men are created equal.

While it is beyond the scope of this paper to explore, at any length, the philosophical underpinnings of Goryeo society, it should be stressed that social equality was never an issue. In Silla, one's place in society was determined by birth—the *golpumje* (bone-rank system). The gradual acceptance of Confucian dictums had, by mid-Goryeo, added another element: moral qualifications. The most important manifestation of this was the implementation of the examination system. Fundamentally, it was a system devised to screen men on the basis of their moral qualifications to hold office. Thus, as I will discuss at some length later, it was of paramount importance to exclude the "base" from office, or if they somehow managed to assume office, it was necessary to prove that they were morally unfit for such a post. The basic assumption that social hierarchy was part of the universal order is nowhere so clear as in the legal statutes contained in *Goryeosa* and, most specifically, in the *Gyeong-guk daejeon* (National Code). Law was, in effect, a device to ensure that each man retained his "place" in society. The penalties that applied to the *yangban* did not apply to the slave. Law was a discriminatory tool devised to perpetuate a hierarchical order.

Even more pertinent to the question of slavery is freedom. Slavery, for the Westerner is the antithesis of freedom. While I do not wish to bela- bor the point of "Western definition," the social sciences are totally dom- inated by formulations and concepts that are the product of the Western historical experience. Therefore, implicit in the minds of many today, be they Korean or American, is the assumption that slavery is the absence of freedom, the denial of the right to act independently of other men, a violation of human dignity.[5] This was not the case in Goryeo. Men—be they *yangban* or slave—saw themselves as part of a social whole. His role was predicated by his place in society, and to act independently of that framework, with its obligations, responsibilities, benefits, and securi- ty would not merely have been alien, it would have been unthinkable.

The problems involved in determining the parameters of slavery in Goryeo are manifold. The greatest obstacle, however, lies in the sources themselves. The problems caused by the paucity of remaining records written prior to the Imjin War cannot be discounted. But it is the tenor of the records themselves, rather than their scarcity, that frustrate the social historian. For the study of slavery I am almost entirely limited to two official histories, compiled after the fact—the *Goryeosa* and the

---

5. Two particularly insightful articles on the question are Victoria Cuffel, "The Classi- cal Greek Concept of Slavery," *Journal of the History of Ideas* 27.2 (April-June 1966), and Arnold A. Sio, "Interpretations of Slavery; The Slave Status in the Americas," *Comparative Studies in Society and History* 7.3 (April 1965).

Goryeosa jeoryo (Essentials of Goryeo History). Aside from a section appended to the penal code in the *Goryeosa*, these histories deal with slavery only incidentally. References to slaves or slavery are not absent from their pages; if anything the reverse is true. But ninety-nine references to the fact that a certain *yangban* was accompanied by his slave tell us little except that it was common for *yangban* to own slaves.[6]

The problem lies in the mind-set of the upper classes, both during Goryeo itself and in the early years of the Joseon dynasty. The activities of the lower classes, whether commoner or slave, were of interest to the ruling stratum only when they caused trouble or could have been a source of potential social imbalance. As a result, it is only by inference that one can describe the daily life of the slave. On the other hand, I can describe in great detail the changes in the law concerning the inheritance of slave status.

Official records aside, the various literary collections have been a total and unanticipated disappointment. With the exception of poetic references to the peaceful countryside with slaves working in the fields, the sum total of information in the literary collections Goryeo notables has been nil. Stone inscriptions, too, have, with one very fortuitous exception, yielded very little aside from items such as how many slaves a merit subject received. My final source, the *Gyeongguk daejeon* has been,

---

6. Professor C. Martin Wilbur, primarily dependent upon two dynastic histories for his study of slavery in Han China, says: "Because mention of slaves is incidental, the slaves appear chiefly in association with important people or events. The important people were those connected with the state (noblemen and high officials), or those who by their acts or accomplishments either influenced the course of national events or won some niche in the historian's hall of fame. About the slaves of these people we are comparatively well informed; but about slaves belonging to "unimportant" people, those who were only somewhat wealthy, somewhat successful in business and scholarship, or somewhat important as administrators, there is little information. Of the common folk and slaves, virtually nothing is known about them. This lack of information may greatly distort the picture of Han slavery, especially in regard to its extent and economic importance." Wilbur, *op. cit.*, p. 54. The dynastic histories utilized in Wilbur's study, Sima Qian's *Shiji* (Historical Records) and Fan Ye's *Houhanshu* (History of the Later Han), were the prototypes for the *Goryeosa* (History of Goreyo). See *Goryeosa*, "Beomnye," pp. 1-3. For an informative discussion of the historiographic principles that informed the *Goryeosa*, see Charles S. Gardiner, *Chinese Traditional Historiography* (Cambridge: Harvard University Press, 1938). For a history of the *Goryeosa* and *Goryeosa jeoryo* (Essentials of Goryeo History), see National Institute of Korean History, comp., *Hanguksa* (Korean History), vol. 11 (Gwacheon: National Institute of Korean History, 1974), pp. 78-79.

more than anything else, insightful. Though compiled in the early years
of the Joseon dynasty, it reflects, in many respects, society at the closing
years of Goryeo.[7] Here is a document of discrimination, and nowhere
else are the tensions inherent in a society where discrimination did not
imply segregation so evident.

In sum, then, my sources are entirely the product of the upper, ruling
segment of society. Rarely is the slave allowed to speak for himself. This
omission would not be so disturbing if I did not feel that history, as a
record of man's hopes and endeavors, accomplishments and failures,
must, at the very least, attempt to incorporate all men, be he king or be
he slave.

Unfortunately, in dealing with Goryeo, one is faced with a stone wall.
The sources I want do not exist. All that remains for us are records written by the upper class for the upper class. As a result, our understanding
of slavery in Goryeo can only be informed by the worldview of the
upper and ruling echelon of that society.

For one member of that stratum, "[s]laves, though they be base are
still heaven's people. In speaking of law or precedent they are property.
They are calmly bought and sold or exchanged with an ox or horse.
One horse will give you two or three people and still it is not sufficient
repayment. Thus it is fate that an ox or a horse is considered more important than a person."[8]

This definition of a slave is, by the way, the only one I have been able
to find in all the references to slaves in the sources. Such a phenomenon
is not uncommon. Rather, in societies where slavery was an integral part
of the social network, there is an almost universal disinclination to
define the institution in sociological terms. Discussion about slaves, however, can be either virtually interminable or almost non-existent.

Slaves in Goryeo occupied the lowest level of that highly stratified
society. In simplest terms, in that society, a person was either "good"
(*yang*) or "base" (*cheon*).[9] The "good" people included the *yangban* and

---

7. For an evaluation of the *Gyeongguk daejeon* as a source for late Goryeo institutional
   history see *Hanguksa*, vol. 9, pp. 236-267.

8. *Goryeosa*, 85:39:45b.

9. "Base" is the term most commonly used to translate *cheon*, and "good" to translate
   yang. They are inadequate translations at best, But for the present, we are stuck with
   them. I have not been able to come up with satisfactory English equivalents because
   such words with all of their cultural connotations cannot be expressed in English.
   The best I can do now is to describe "base."

commoners. The "base" consisted primarily of slaves, although individuals engaged in occupations considered foul in Buddhist philosophy, such as butchers or nonsedentary workers (traveling or professional entertainers and peddlers), were also "base." Baseness was heritable and, most importantly, in order to become an official, it was theoretically necessary to prove that one had no "base" ancestors for eight generations.[10] The stigma of baseness was of such gravity that Kim Bu-sik was concerned about the enslavement of *yangban* involved in a rebellion, a punishment applicable to all convicted of treason.[11]

This schematization is, to say the least, an overly simplified one and is meant only to place slaves in the broadest of social contexts. It should be pointed out that the gap between the "good" *yangban* and "good" commoner was far wider than that between the "good" commoner and the "base" slave. Indeed, avenues of social mobility open to slaves were closed to commoners because these avenues resulted from the proximity of the slave to his master, who was almost always a *yangban*.

There were many sources of slaves in Goryeo. Some were the descendants of those who had been enslaved in earlier periods, either as prisoners of war in the unification of Silla, criminals, or descendants of common people forced into slavery. Others were newly enslaved, either as punishment for crime, self-enslaved for economic reasons, or coerced into slavery by powerful local magnates. Slaves could be public or private, depending upon the agent or agency controlling them. Public slaves were property of the government or royal family and private slaves the property of an individual or family.

The conditions under which slaves lived and worked varied greatly. Public slaves were attached to all government offices and performed a variety of functions ranging from clerical work to janitorial services. They appear to have been able to set up their own households, and within their own domestic establishments, possessed a fair degree of autonomy. Other public slaves, particularly those belonging to the royal family, were agricultural workers on the large estates owned by the Goryeo royal house. Some of these slaves, however, were given positions of responsibility tantamount to estate managers. Some public female slaves worked for the royal family and government as domestics, entertainers or courtesans.

---

10. *Goryeosa*, 85:39:44a.
11. *Goryeosa*, 98:11:17a-b.

Private slaves, too, in certain instances, lived apart from their owners. Again, some functioned as country estate managers for their absentee owners. Many, of course, did live with their owners and the variety of tasks required of them seems to have depended upon the predilections and needs of their owners. Temple slaves, for example, engaged in a variety of industrial tasks such as weaving and brewing because Buddhist commercial activities were so extensive in Goryeo.

Some slaves were treated well, while others were not. Escape was not uncommon, but only after a slave had fled his master three times would he be branded on the face. Indeed, one is struck by the leniency in the punishments of slaves.[12] One particularly striking example concerns the public slave, Seonhwa, who killed a pregnant woman in a quarrel over grain. Her punishment, contrary to my expectations, was not execution, but banishment.[13] While a cynic might remark that it would have been uneconomical to kill an expensive investment, it should be pointed out that leniency in punishments was a hallmark of the Goryeo legal system.

Slaves were not cheap. In 986, a male slave between the ages of fifteen and sixty cost one hundred bolts of material while those below fifteen and over sixty cost half that amount. A female slave above fifteen and under fifty was worth one hundred and twenty bolts, whereas those younger or older were worth sixty.[14]

The above sketch of the slave system, in and of itself, does little to set the Goryeo slave apart from slaves in other societies. The enslavement of prisoners of war was a virtually universal practice throughout the world. Though slavery as a punishment for crime is not universal, it too has its parallels. One lies in China for one, where enslavement as punishment for rebellion is said to have its origins in late Zhou. Self-enslavement, because of dire economic straits, was common in both Han China and the Ancient Near East. In Greece, as in Goryeo, the variety of tasks to which a slave could be assigned to was almost unlimited. Also, in Greece and medieval Spain, slaves could live apart from their owners. And in Greece, a distinction was made between public and private slaves, though a third category—temple slaves—was added. Even the

---

12. This sketch is drawn primarily from the subsection on slavery appended to the Penal Code of the *Goryeosa*, 85:39:40-47; section two of the Penal Code, 85:39:1-40; and the Penal Code of the *Gyeongguk daejeon, gwon* 5.

13. *Goryeosa*, 84:38:46b.

14. *Goryeosa*, 85:39:42b.

fact that slaves were ethnically undistinguishable from their masters has its parallel in ancient Babylonia and Assyria.[15]

What is unusual, however, is that by mid-Goryeo, slaves appear to have been permitted to own and dispose of property, i.e. land, and, by late Goryeo, even other slaves. The *Gyeongguk daejeon* stipulates that should a slave die without descendants, his land and slaves were to revert to the public domain.[16] Nowhere in the *Goryeosa* have I found any suggestion that a slave owning property would upset the social order. What was objected to, however, was a slave using his property to appropriate for himself the trappings reserved for the *yangban*. Sumptuary laws abound; a slave must dress and act like a slave.

This authority to own and dispose of property is, particularly for the Westerner, startling. For many, it negates the "slaveness" of the Korean slave. Has materialism so warped our thinking that liberty is interpreted as the liberty to make money and own property?

Be that as it may, in Goryeo, "slaveness" had a moral, not a material, connotation. A slave, no matter what his position, was not as good as other men. This attitude towards slaves is made quite explicit in an anecdote included in the funerary tablet of Choe An-do, who was himself the son of a slave, written by Choe Hae. Choe Hae had reason to call on a slave who had found favor with the king, acting in effect as a private secretary. Scholars and gentry were so in awe of his power that they bowed from the knee when he entered the room. Choe Hae was outraged and berated the assembled, saying that it was unfitting for anyone to bow to a slave. The slave, incidentally, was none too pleased with this and

---

15. For China, see Wilbur, *op. cit.*, especially pp. 72-98. For the Middle East, Issac Mendelssohn, *Slavery in the Ancient Near East* (New York, 1947), p. 14. For Greece, Westermann, *op. cit.*, p. 12. For medieval Spain, Davis, *op. cit.*, particularly the section on the slave laws incorporated into *Las Siete Partidas del Rey Don Alfonso el sabio*, promulgated in 1265. Though enslavement of groups ethnically indistinguishable from the masters existed in Ancient Greece, China, and the Near East, the enslaved did not form hereditary classes. Once they were manumitted, there appears to have been no legal hindrances to their advancement. Conversely, in societies where the slave was racially different from the owner, such as in the United States, manumission did not imply full legal rights. To cite one striking example, in the American South during the Reconstruction period, the freed man was, through a variety of legal maneuvers, denied the right to own land, to say nothing of the right to vote.

16. *Gyeongguk daejeon*, *gwon* 5, p. 11. If he was a private slave, his owner was permitted to dispose of his property.

abruptly mounted his horse and galloped away.[17]

In Goryeo, then, there existed a class of people who could be bought and sold and whose status was heritable. They were forbidden by law to intermarry with "good" people and the offspring of such unions—a rather frequent occurrence—followed, in theory at least, the status of their mother. Conversely, a slave could own property and appropriate power to himself. A few, in fact, actually held office. By and large, moreover, they seem to have been as well off, if not better, than the rest of the general populace.

What then, if any, would be the benefits of manumission? On one hand, the slave could no longer be bought or sold. This, most certainly, was important psychologically although there appears to have been a strong disinclination to sell slaves or break up a family because of sale. Rather, the law fostered the retention of slaves by members of a lineage.[18] On the other hand, by becoming a commoner, the slave—particularly the private slave—had the burden of government taxes and *corveé*, a burden that had caused many to sell themselves into slavery in the first place. Thus, improvement of one's economic lot was questionable prospect at best. However, over the course of time—and probably far less than eight generations—the descendants of the former slave could lose the stigma of "base" and become eligible for office. This, more than anything else, was the benefit of manumission.

As I mentioned before, the sources, with few exceptions, do not let the slave speak for himself. In one of the rare instances when a slave does speak for himself, the slave Manjeok, the leader of a slave rebellion in 1198, is very explicit about what he considers to be the benefit of manumission:

> . . . each of us will kin his master and burn the slave registers. When we eliminate *cheonmin* from the Three Han we will be able to become nobles and ministers.[19]

The denial of access to official posts was not only of crucial importance to the slave but to his master as well. The *Goryeosa* is replete with the fears that manumitted slaves would become officials. A striking example

---

17. *Joseon geumseok chongnam* (A Comprehensive Survey of Monument Inscriptions in the Joseon Period), vol. 1 (Seoul: Kyung In Publishing Co., 1974), pp. 625-626.
18. *Gyeongguk daejeon, gwon* 5, particularly pp. 11-16.
19. *Goryeosa*, 129:42:12b.

of this—one of many—was contained in the letter King Chungnyeol sent to the Yuan Emperor in order to counter the Yuan envoy's insistence that Goryeo change its slave laws.

Of old Our Founder handed down precepts to his descendants that said: In all cases involving those who are of a base category, their kind is different. Take care and do not let this kind become good. If they are permitted to become good then afterwards they win inevitably fill government offices and gradually demand that they become officials and will plot to disturb the country. If you disregard this precept the altar of the soil and grain grin be in peril.[20]

It must be emphasized that the demonstrable proof of one's "goodness" was holding office. To permit a "base" person to do so would, in effect, negate the moral justification for social stratification. This point becomes very clear when one examines the biographies of men of base origin—either slaves or sons of slaves—who held office in Goryeo.

For the compilers of the *Goryeosa*, and the contemporaries of these "base" office holders as well, it was essential to prove that these men were morally unfit for the posts they held. These officials ranged from Choe An-do, who was responsible for convincing the Yuan government not to turn Goryeo into a province of China,[21] to Bae Jeon, who received his initial post because of the sexual predilections of King Chunghye.[22] The biographies of both men, however, are included under the category of "catamite." Indeed, there is a suspiciously high percentage of men of base origins included in the biographical sections on "catamites," "eunuchs" and "rebels." In several instances in the section on catamites, the moral defects of men such as Choe An-do and Kang Yung[23] do not set them apart from many of the officials deemed virtuous by the compilers of the *Goryeosa*.

All efforts, however, are made to present both men in the most unfavorable light. The tale of Kang Yung's revenge on Kim Gae-mul,[24] who cursed him as a slave is told with unnecessary detail, while Choe's greed and misuse of power are emphasized to the point of absurdity.[25]

---

20. *Goryeosa*, 85:39:43b-44a.
21. *Goryeosa*, 124:37:25-28.
22. *Goryeosa*, 124:37:13b-14a.
23. *Goryeosa*, 124:37:12a-b.
24. *Goryeosa*, 124:37:12a-b; 108:19:20b-21a.
25. *Goryeosa*, 124:37:25-28a.

With obvious villains, such as Yi Ui-mun[26] or the charlatan and revolutionary Sin Don,[27] biography becomes little more than a collection of
anecdotes that serve no purpose other than to demonstrate the "baseness" of the subject. In the case of Yi Ui-mun, biography becomes a
bawdy tale, at times highly comical. Sex, violence and impropriety are
almost invariably key elements in the many biographies of men of base
origins.

This dependency on stereotype would not be so telling or significant
if such a technique were not one of the main elements of the Sino-Korean historiographical tradition. The *Goryeosa*, in particular, was modeled
on Chinese dynastic history, informed by the Confucian worldview. For
the Confucianists, history had a didactic purpose. This didactic demand
was not fulfilled by extensive exposition of the writer's point of view,
but rather by the content and emphasis of the record. Thus, stereotype
becomes a medium for expressing the attitudes and values of the mold-
ers of public opinion in premodern Korea.

My reliance on these biographies to generalize about the preconceived
attributes of slaves was not a matter of choice, but dictated by necessity.
Ideally, somewhere in the historical or literary collections, I thought that
there would have been at least one document, letter or poem about
slaves—not a rebel leader or one audacious enough to attain a high position—but a typical slave who lived out his life under the stigma of
"base." Such was not the case.

Perhaps the most important fact emerging from the biographies is that
baseness is a moral attribute and is indeed hereditary. By extension,
moral deficiency is sufficient justification for enslavement. Because the
social schema was founded on a moral premise, certain privileges, such
as owning property or other slaves, could not contradict or negate the
baseness of slaves.

In every society where slavery has been important, slavery has been
justified on the basis of inferiority, and efforts were made to differentiate
slave from master. The basis of that differentiation was predicated upon
what was considered important for the maintenance of the upper segment of society. In all societies, that differentiation is a reflection of the
prerogatives that the upper classes assumed for themselves. Might

---

26. *Goryeosa*, 128:41:19-25.
27. *Goryeosa*, 132:45:1-12.

became right and was documented as such. Thus, a conceptualization of slavery in Goryeo can only be drawn from sources written by the upper classes for the upper classes. By denying slaves the opportunity to speak for themselves, the totality of human experience was denied.

Social Changes from the Late Goryeo to Early Joseon Periods

Yi Tae-Jin

I

The late Goryeo to early Joseon periods represents one of the most significant transitional times in Korean history. This period saw several important changes. First, newly rising scholar-officials (*sinheung sadaebu*) coming from the class of medium and small landlords emerged as a new ruling class. Second, a strong, centralized bureaucratic system became the model of political organization. Third, the landlord-tenant system was developed at economic levels. Fourth, political and economic changes brought about changes in the estate system. Fifth, Neo-Confucianism was adopted as a new ideology by the ruling class.

This research also inquired into the implications of these changes for the process of development of Korean history. In debates concerning the periodization of Korean history, these changes were defined as the beginning of the medieval age in some cases, or as one of the stages in the course of medieval development in other cases. Some scholars, on the basis of their view that these changes indicated a more advanced stage when compared with the medieval society of Europe, asserted that it was desirable to regard the period as the beginning of the premodern

* Originally published in the *Korea Journal,* vol. 23, no. 5 (May 1983).

Yi Tae-Jin (Yi, Tae-jin) is Professor of Korean History at Seoul National University. He has published many books, including *Joseon yugyo sahoesa ron* (Discussion on the History of the Neo-Confucianist Society in the Joseon Period) (1989) and *Joseon hugi-ui jeongchi-wa gunyeongje baldal* (Politics and the System of Central Army Garrisons during the Late Joseon Dynasty) (1985). E-mail: tjyi@plaza.snu.ac.kr.

age. Such differences in viewpoints imply that there is room for further discussion concerning this question, and these discussions indicate the importance of this transitional period.

Although considerable progress has been made identifying the social changes that occurred in the late Goryeo to early Joseon period, understanding of the causative factors and roots of such changes is still incomplete. Arguments have focused narrowly on the political sphere. The new political force made up of newly rising scholar-officials has been emphasized as the source of all changes. Research has not yet questioned what made the emergence of the new scholar-officials possible. Furthermore, it has not been made clear whether the transition from the late Goryeo to early Joseon period started from the age of coups d'état of military officials or from any other point of time. This paper is designed to contribute to the structural understanding of the changes in this transitional period while trying to supplement what previous studies have overlooked.

II

It is essential to first pinpoint the earliest possible beginning of the transitional period. There have been few arguments other than the one that sees the transition's origins in a military coup d'etat. One good example of this argument is the view that the literati "well versed in letters and competent as officials" who emerged under the military regime are the origin of the "newly rising scholar-officials."[1]

At the economic level, the relationship between private land and manors (*nongjang*) is interpreted as a causal one where the former was the origin of the latter, without, however, drawing a clear borderline between the two. The Goryeo period was studded with internal disturbances and foreign invasions that took place after the military coup d'etat. It seems that researchers found it difficult to read changes in the confusion of succession. As a consequence, it came to be accepted generally that the tumult and confusion of the military coup d'etat was the starting point of social changes.

---

1. Yi U-seong, "Goryeojo-ui sa-e daehayeo" (Concerning Literati Officials of the Goryeo Period), *Yeoksa hakbo* (Journal of History) 21 (1964).

This interpretation, however, raises a number of questions. First of all, the span of over 220 years from the military coup d'etat (1170) to the establishment of the Joseon dynasty (1392) is much too long to be seen as one stage of social evolution. Second, the similarities between the literati who were "well versed in letters and competent as officials" under the military regime and the newly rising scholar-officials are too weak for us to regard the former as the progenitor of the latter. Although both were regarded as literati, the literati in the later period are defined by their Neo-Confucianist character, which the literati in the Goryeo are missing.

The political power of the newly rising scholar-officials manifested itself clearly during the reign of King Gongmin (r. 1352–1374) toward the end of the Goryeo period. Thus, research into those who rose to power during this period may help to reveal the starting point of the transitional late Goryeo to early Joseon period, though this focuses too narrowly on the political aspect. The political activities of the newly emerging group during the reign of King Gongmin, were aimed primarily at eliminating the pro-Yuan group and reforming the administration that was detrimental to the land and people. However, it has been made clear that two parallel reforms to these were pursued earlier during the reigns of both King Chungseon (r. 1309–1313) and King Chungmok (r. 1344–1348). Anti-Yuan political reforms had already been attempted, focusing on the Sarimwon (Secretariat of Letters) during the reign of King Chungseon and on the Jeongchi Dogam (Office of Maladministration Reform) during the reign of King Chungmok.[2] In substance, these two reforms were the same as those undertaken during King Gongmin's reign and, furthermore, they were related in terms of time. Therefore, it may seem proper to date the origins of the transitional period back to the early part of the fourteenth century. Having established the starting point, then, it is next essential to examine what factors emerged or were created to generate social changes.

In view of the fact that, toward the close of the twelfth century, rebel-

---

2. Yi Gi-nam, "Chungseonwang-ui gaehyeok-gwa sarimwon-ui seolchi" (The Reform of King Chungseon and the Establishment of Sarimwon), *Yeoksa hakbo* 52 (1971); Min Hyeon-gu, "Jeongchi dogam-ui seolchi gyeongwi" (The Process of Establishing the Jeongchi Dogam), in *Gungmin daehak nonmunjip* (Kookmin University Collection of Dissertations) 11 (1977), and "Jeongchi dogam-ui seonggyeok" (The Nature of the Jeongchi Dogam), *Dongbang hakji* 23/24 (1980).

lions staged by peasants and menials spread on a wide scale at the same time the military coup d'etat was staged, it is obvious that Goryeo society already underwent one great change. Those changes, however, took place after political stability was established under the leadership of the Choe clan and continued during the 50-year military regime. This could represent one distinctive age. The situation at the beginning of the fourteenth century, however, was different from the military regime period. The social system led by pro-Yuan aristocrats had already existed for half a century under Mongol intervention after a treaty of capitulation to the Mongols, which followed the fall of the military regime led by the Choe family. A crucial task of the time was to root out the structural contradictions created by the foreign forces. For this reason the anti-Yuan reform politics could be executed through the fourteenth century. Therefore, the strong impetus for political reform must rightly be accepted as the basic factor of social changes at that time. It is important, however, to examine the reasons which helped the ultimate success of the reform.

The anti-Yuan reforms in the final years of the Goryeo period have been highly acclaimed not only because they were successful in spite of many difficulties but also because they brought about significant social development. But the research on the social development of the period has lately begun to focus on the improvements related to ownership and distribution of land and to the estate system. On the one hand, it is generally recognized that these improvements were made possible because the new ruling class came not from the class of large-scale landlords but rather from medium and small-scale landlords. On the other hand, credit was also given to the active efforts of the ruled classes to elevate their status.

The achievements in agricultural technique at this time are additional factors in the development of this period.[3] The *Nongsa jikseol* (Straight Talk on Farming) attest to the agricultural developments in the early part of the Joseon period. As outlined in this text, farming of this time was not restricted by the practice of fallowing. According to the *gongbeop*,

---

3. Refer to Yi Tae-jin, "14/15 segi nongeop gisul-ui baldal-gwa sinheung sajok" (Development of Agricultural Technology and the Newly Emerging Scholar-Officials during the 14th and 15th Centuries), *Dongyanghak* 9 (1978); and "Simnyuk segi cheonbang (bo) gwan-gae-ui baldal" (The Development of Irrigation in River Areas in the 16th Century), in *Han U-geun baksa jeongnyeon ginyeom sahak nonchong* (Seoul: Jisik Sanupsa, 1981).

a new law of land rents and taxes enacted during the reign of King Sejong, fallowing was not allowed in any case to *jeongjeon* (lands allocated to male adults) or land which was once registered in the cadastre.[4] This represents a great change from the middle-Goryeo period, when farms lying fallow were widely scattered throughout the country.

According to the regulations concerning the grading of farmlands legislated in March 1054 (eighth year of King Munjong's reign), farms that were cultivated every year were regarded as best; farms that were cultivated after one year of lying fallow were regarded as medium-quality; and farms that were cultivated after two years of fallowing were regarded as the poorest quality. According to the same regulations, one *gyeol* (unit of land area) of farmland on mountain slopes without fallowing corresponded to one *gyeol* of farmland in the plains; two *gyeol* of farmland on mountains with one year's fallowing corresponded to one *gyeol* of farmland in the plains; and three *gyeol* of farmland on mountains with two years' fallowing corresponded to one *gyeol* of farmland in the plains.[5] The fact that farmland graded as medium or lowest quality occupying the majority had to be fallowed a year or two, indicates that the method of fallowing was universal. Yi Je-hyeon (1287–1367), who was active mainly in the first half of the fourteenth century, pointed out in his commentaries on initiating a system of providing land and firewood for officials during the reign of King Gyeongjong (r. 975–981) that "the south areas of the Amnokgang river (Yalu in Chinese) are filled generally with mountains, the land is poor, and so there is almost no land that is not laid fallow."[6] An official, while debating on the law of land taxes during the reign of King Sejong, said, "the fact that there were lands that lay fallow a year or two in old times tells us that it was necessary to raise the productivity of the land."[7] This is a good example showing the agricultural technique of the preceding age.

The restrictions of fallowing originated in limitations of fertilization technique. Specifically, it is not possible to fertilize whole fields when

---

4. *Sejong sillok* (Annals of King Sejong), *gwon* 107, first month, 27th year of King Sejong's reign. "A royal message was sent to the Ministry of Taxation, reminding that the law of land rents and taxes stipulates that both those who hold the registered farms and those who hold fallow land shall be obligated to pay the taxes . . ."

5. "Sikhwa," in *Goryeosa* (History of Goryeo), *gwon* 77.

6. Yi Je-hyeon, "Sachan gyeongwang pyeon" (Remarks on the Section of King Gyeongjong), in *Ikjae nan-go* (Complete Works of Ikjae Yi Je-heyon).

7. *Sejong sillok*, *gwon* 112, 6th month, 28th year of King Sejong's reign.

there is no effective means of weeding during the ploughing stage. It was therefore inevitable to lay land fallow every other year for the restoration of fertility. *Nongsa jikseol* describes detailed studies on the technique of fertilization used in early Joseon when farms were free from the restriction of fallowing.[8]

The beginnings of the agricultural techniques that were free from the restriction of fallowing as shown in *Nongsa jikseol* are unclear. However, it is clear that a succession of cultivation of crops was put into practice in the early part of the Joseon period, implying that the shift to successive planting took place toward the close of the Goryeo period. The last years of the Goryeo period, then, demand further examination.

A memorial submitted to the throne by Jo Jun points to corruption accompanying the manor system in the fourteenth century: "Wicked persons hold large estates which sometimes reach the boundaries of countries and are demarcated by the natural features such as mountains and rivers, claiming them as bequeathed by their ancestors. Thus five or six persons lay claim to a small tract of land, with one preying upon another."[9] He also exposed that land rent is fixed unfairly, so that "one *gyeol* of land is assessed as many as three or four *gyeol*."[10] This indicates the extent of corruption in ownership and exploitation. There remains, however, the question of how such exploitation could occur without a collapse of the system itself; in other words, how those who were so exploited were able to bear the burden. Part of the answer lies in the changes that led to the obsolescence of fallowing.

Once fertilization techniques were improved, not only was it no longer necessary to lay farms idle but the productivity of land was greatly increased. This can be confirmed by comparing the output from one *gyeol* in the early part of the Goryeo period with the early part of the Joseon period. Calculating the output from one *gyeol* of public land in 970 (11th year of Goryeo King Seongjong's reign) on the basis of the principle of collecting one fourth of the output as land tax from one *gyeol* of public land, results range between 6 and 11 *seok*.[11] According to a

---

8. Yi Tae-jin, "14/15 segi nongeop gisul-ui baldal-gwa sinheung sajok," pp. 337-338.

9. "Sikhwa (食貨) 1," in *Goryeosa, gwon* 78.

10. *Ibid.*

11. This is given a detailed explanation in *ibid.*, p. 332. The uppermost ceiling of 11 *seok* and two *hop* was pointed out as a mistake of 15 *seok* and two *hop* in the original text in Kang Jin-cheol, "Joseon jeon-gi-ui gongjeon, sajeon-gwa geu-ui chayulsu joyul-e dae-

document from 1430 (12th year of Joseon King Sejong's reign), "the paddies along the Gyeongsang and Jeolla coastal areas turned out an output exceeding 50 to 60 *seok* from one *gyeol* and the lowest harvest never declined below 30 or 20 *seok*. Even dry fields, being extremely fertile, produce a great deal."[12]

In spite of employing the same method in farming, there must have been a difference in productivity between the fourteenth century when non-fallow planting was first tested and the fifteenth century when it actively employed. In view of the wide disparity between the output before and after fallowing techniques were used, one can conclude that a rapid increase in productivity brought about exploitation.[13]

At this point, it is crucial to examine the fact that lawsuits involving land ownership emerged as a significant problem at this time. Although most of the land suits were brought up by land seizure of large-scale landlords, the problem, as explained in the memorial by Jo Jun cited above, was serious. The following record attests to the extent of the problem: "the Pandosa (Office of Census Registration) and the Jeonbeopsa (Office of Legal Administration) in the central government and the provincial magistrates and supervisors listen to land suits every day, and are unable to perform their main job." It seems, then, that the whole country was affected by this problem. Once improved agricultural techniques rendered the practice of fallowing unnecessary, they also opened up new problems in land ownership. Once fallowing was no longer necessary for the soil to refertilize itself, it was natural that a household would ask others to cultivate a part of its land which would have been taken care of by its own family members. This way, it is natural that disputes concerning land ownership occurred.

It is important to remember that at this point, systems of remuneration for services of soldiers and local officials, such as *jokjeong* and *banjeong*, were no longer in effect. In return for service, such people were

---

hayeo" (Public and Private Farms in the First Half of the Goryeo Period and Their Graded Rates of Taxation), *Yeoksa hakbo* 29 (1965). Here the original text was adopted.

12. *Sejong sillok, gwon* 49, 8th month 12th year of King Sejong's reign.

13. Kim Yong-seop, "Goryeo sigi-ui yangjeonje" (The System of Land Survey during the Goryeo Period), *Dongbang hakji* 16 (1975): p. 84. He presented an almost identical explanation. However, this dissertation is based on the opinion that cultivation of other kinds of crops was limited to a small number of farms on mountain slopes and most of the other farms did not shift to other kinds of crops. In this respect there is a wide disparity between his opinion and this writer's opinion.

given 17 *gyeol* per person. This is a generous amount, considering that in the early part of the Joseon period, "farmers, in most cases, own one or two *gyeol* of farm,"[14] and "farmers who till more than 10 *gyeol* of farm could be considered wealthy and not a small number of farmers own a mere three or four *gyeol* each."[15] The disparity disclosed in this comparison shows that the fixation of the remuneration for professional service at 17 *gyeol* was made in consideration of the possibility that farms had to be laid fallow for a year or two. But with the advent of constant cultivation in the fourteenth century, the need for such an extravagant remunerative structure ceased. In the process of collapse of the traditional system, it seems, the distribution of the surplus related to agricultural manpower brought about many lawsuits. Private land also developed at the same period. Its development was partly due to reclamation and partly due to the extinction of idle land. The development of private land resulted from an increased consciousness of ownership in addition to quantitative expansion. Constant cultivation may have exerted great influence on such an increased consciousness.

III

As we have examined so far, a change in the agricultural technique took place in the fourteenth century by overcoming fallowing. And logically, significant social changes followed this development. Besides the extinction of remuneration and the development of private land, many other changes must also be explained.

It is most likely that the improvement of agricultural technique, another product of the development of private land, provided an important basis for the growth of owner-farmers, frequently pointed out as a notable phenomenon of this period. The landlord-tenant relationship developed into a more stabilized one with increased productivity due to the advance of agriculture. It is on the basis of the development of agriculture that the Joseon period, from the macroscopic point of view, was able to strengthen its state conscription system and more effectively enforce its policy of securing commoners who responded to the conscription decree. The extinction of special administrative units such as *hyang,*

---

14. *Sejong sillok, gwon* 112, 6th month, 28th year of King Sejong's reign.
15. *Sejong sillok, gwon* 83, 11th month, 20th year of King Sejong's reign.

so, and *bugok* can be identified as one of the more important social changes of this period. As in the case of those who lived in ordinary *gun* (county) and *hyeon* (subcounty), inhabitants of *hyang* and *bugok* made their living through farming. The major difference between them was that heavier taxes were imposed on the latter due to the fact that the areas in which they lived were treated as special administrative units and their inhabitants treated as menials. However, it became unnecessary to maintain this discriminatory system once the new agricultural techniques boosted the economic strength of the society as a whole. Another factor in its disappearance is that the discrimination tended to weaken the motivation to work and produce. Such social changes can be seen most clearly with the extinction of *so* (所) as places where specific tribute-supplies were assessed. As far as new possibilities in agriculture are concerned, it seems that the situation changed in such a way that it became more profitable to invest manpower into agriculture than other traditional occupations.

Another important change took place in the local administrative system related to agricultural development. The encouragement of agricultural production in the early and middle parts of the Goryeo period was among the duties of the *allyeomsa* (governors) in seven provinces and the *gamchangsa* (superintendents of granaries) in five provinces. The only mention made of their practices in *Goryeosa* (History of Goryeo) states that, "though the system of sending agriculture encouragement supervisors was established, the system was abolished and returned to previous condition in 1286 because it might harm the people."[16] In the Joseon period, a rule was created where men of *hallyang* (out of government service) title were appointed to the post of *gwonnongsa* (officer in charge of the encouragement of farming) in each *myeon* (township), in all subcounties, counties, cities, and provinces.[17] This change signals the grow-

---

16. "Sikhwa 2," in *Goryeosa* (History of Goryeo), *gwon* 77.
17. *Taejo sillok* (Annals of King Taejo), *gwon* 8, 7th month, 4th year of King Taejo's reign. "Jeong Bun-jin said that an essential thing for encouraging agriculture is to build embankments and asked that governors order city, county, and subcounty chiefs to appoint gentlemen out of government service to the position of *gwonnong sa*."; *Seongjong sillok*, *gwon* 245, 9th month, 21st year of King Seongjong's reign, "Yun Hyo-son submitted a memorial to the throne asking to unite every five households and fix a chief to administer the unit . . . and to station one agriculture encouragement supervisor at each *myeon*."

ing importance of the encouragement of farming. Furthermore, changes were made in the official duties of local officials. There was nothing concerning agriculture among the six duties of magistrates of the Goryeo kingdom which were based on the Tang system.[18] In the Joseon kingdom, however, "encouragement of agriculture and sericulture" occupied the first position among the seven duties of the magistrate.[19] During the Goryeo period, when there was no clear prospect for agricultural development within the limitations of fallowing, all the affairs related to farming were entrusted to *hyangni* or clerks in local authorities, while the central government paid no special attention to it.

On account of internal and external unrest, farming techniques did not progress smoothly in the fourteenth century. It seems that, although a change had already begun, there was no time to extend it into the political arena. The invasion of Japanese pirates after the mid-fourteenth century dealt an especially devastating blow to the progress that had already been made. After the establishment of the new dynasty, reclamation was encouraged and a land survey project launched, signaling a determination to restore previous achievements as the situation stabilized. The *Nongsa jikseol*, based on the farming techniques of the three southern provinces, was compiled between 1428 and 1429. This compilation project, besides rearranging the achievements in farming techniques, was designed to propagate the most advanced techniques of the three provinces according to the northern districts' standard, particularly Pyeongan-do and Hamgyeong-do provinces. The two provinces had not yet overcome the need for fallowing, and were disadvantaged compared with the three southern provinces. The compilation of the *Nongsa jikseol* was designed to eliminate these disparities in farming techniques. It was also aimed at standardizing agricultural techniques, and at the same

---

18. The six articles which were legislated newly in the 9th year of King Gyeongjong's reign: 1) Investigate diseases and sufferings of the people; 2) Investigate the competency of officials; 3) Investigate theft, robbery, and adultery; 4) Investigate whether the people violate prohibitions; 5) Investigate whether the people are faithful to their parents, friendly with their brothers, and honest; and 6) Investigate whether officials embezzle government money and grain "Seon-geo (選擧)," in *Goryeosa, gwon* 75.

19. "Ijeon" (Code of Government Officials), in *Gyeongguk daejeon* (National Code), *gwon* 1. The seven articles are as follows: 1) Promotion of agriculture and sericulture; 2) Increasement of households; 3) Expansion of schools; 4) Arrangement of the military administration; 5) Making the labor conscription fair; 6) Making the procedure of trials simple; and 7) Elimination of wicked practices.

time, at revising the taxation system. In December of the year when *Nongsa jikseol* was published, King Sejong ordered his officials to examine the *gongbeop* as a new law of taxation. A final decision was made on the law after 14 years of deliberations and tests. The law gained fame because it lowered tax rates from one-tenth to one-twentieth, reflecting the advancements in farming methods. With its passing, the laying of registered farms in fallow was no longer recognized, and the grades of land were subdivided from three to six. The subdivision of land was necessitated by the fact that the disparity of productivity among farms grew due to the development of farming techniques. In short, the task of rearranging the system to accommodate the changes in farming techniques since the fourteenth century was brought to a successful conclusion.

Changes in agricultural techniques were usually accompanied by corresponding changes in society. The *hyangdo*, or bier bearers union as community organizations occupied a very influential position in the history of village communities in Korea. According to a pagoda inscription in Gaesimsa temple in Yecheon, two groups of bier bearers, one in the county of Yecheon and the other in the subcounty of Dain, which were prime movers for the erection of the pagoda, were so large that they embraced almost all the inhabitants.[20] A record states that, "lanterns are customarily lit (by two bier bearer unions) for nights from the fifteenth day of January in all places ranging from the royal palaces and the capital to local towns,"[21] showing that the *hyangdo* were unions that performed rituals such as the Yeondeunghoe (Lantern Festival) and Palgwanhoe (Festival of Eight Vows) which throve at that time and retained their descendants as a form of *sangdukkun*, the members of a burial society. According to a royal message issued in 1168 (22nd year of King Uijong's reign), "the Palgwanhoe festival at the two capitals (Gaegyeong and Seogyeong) have recently been losing their dignity and the inherited ancient customs have been gradually weakening."[22] This shows the changes in customs dating to the early part of the Goryeo period.

---

20. Yi Tae-jin, "Yecheon gaesimsa seoktapgi-ui bunseok: goryeo jeon-gi hyang-do-ui illye" (Analysis of the Inscription of a Pagoda in Gaesimsa Temple in Yecheon: One Example of the *Hyangdo* in the First Half of the Goryeo Period), *Yeoksa hakbo* 53/54 (1982).

21. "Yeji" 2, in *Goryeosa, gwon* 69.

22. *Goryeosa, gwon* 18, 3rd month, 22nd year of King Uijong's reign.

Because of the lack of relevant historical data, we know nothing about how the custom transformed and progressed under the military regime. Nevertheless, the *hyangdo* unions represented an aspect of the fourteenth century that was entirely different from the previous age. After the fourteenth century, members of the unions were united generally for services to honor the guardian deities of natural villages. Their numbers shrank greatly as they became societies for natural village rituals.[23] The transformation of the *hyangdo* unions may be regarded as having indicated the increased importance of the individuality of natural villages, at the same time the natural villages were given the administrative name of *ri*.

The transformation of the *hyangdo* unions, the essence of village communities, reflected a process of transition from large social units to smaller ones. Furthermore, the achievements in agricultural technique since the fourteenth century are the most fundamental factor of the transition. The low yields of fallow-field farming necessitated the reclamation of larger tracts of land more so than in continuous farming systems in order to secure the maximum social product. It was inevitable under these circumstances that great manpower be mobilized at once and the method of mobilization be collective. The large scale of the *hyangdo* groups in the first half of the Goryeo period may have reflected the above fact. The local *gun-hyeon* societies were led by local officials during the early and middle parts of the Goryeo period, revealing the tendency for local administration to center heavily on counties and subcounties. It can be pointed out that, under these circumstances, the community villages were more valuable as a unit than natural villages.[24] The social structure during the early and middle parts of the Goryeo period was connected with the large scale of the *hyangdo* organizations. As for the authority of mobilizing the labor force, it was entrusted directly to local officials more frequently than at any other time. Unlike extensive agriculture, the management of intensive farming became more important than the size of the acreage under cultivation. In other words, timing the different stages of farming was more important than the simultaneous mobilization of the labor force.

23. Yi Tae-jin, "Sarimpa-ui yuhyangso bongnip undong" (The Movement of the Faction of Scholars out of Government Service to Revive the Yuhyangso) 1, *Jindan hakbo* 34 (1972): pp. 9-12.
24. Yi U-seong, "Reodae baekseong go" (A Study on the Commoners during the Goryeo Period), *Yeoksa hakbo* 14 (1961).

Management of intensive farming for a long period could result in a drastic reduction in the size of the acreage under cultivation, naturally enabling a household as a unit of management to cultivate its land with only the labor provided by its own members. This kind of farming that took the natural household as a unit meant that social formation might not need its previous structure which was based on the level of natural villages. There might, of course, be other factors generating this change in the social composition, but advances in agricultural technology must have been one of the most fundamental factors. The growth of individuality of natural villages was founded on the enforcement of the *ri* chief system, which was effected as a means of pursuing a centralized administration system.

Lastly, the changes in the ruling classes and their interest in agricultural techniques is another significant aspect of the social changes taking place during the late Goryeo and early Joseon period. A new force of scholar-officials, made up of local small and medium-scale landlords, emerged as the new ruling class toward the close of the Goryeo period. The fact that there were more members of the new ruling class coming from the three southern provinces is related to the development of agricultural technology in the three provinces at that time.

Research has been conducted which analyzes the surnames of officials who advanced to the capital from the reign of King Taejo to the reign of King Uijong, arranging them according to ancestral origin.[25] The research, utilizing histories of influential families contained in the *Goryeosa* (History of Goryeo) and extant epitaphs, deals with surnames of officials who held the third rank or higher, and classifies them into two groups: surnames that turned out more than three such officials and those that turned out less than two such officials. The former group includes 54 surnames and the latter group includes 53 surnames. An examination of the ancestral origins of the surnames discloses that only 20 among 54 surnames, or slightly more than one-third, had their ancestral origins in the three southern provinces, while those coming from the northern districts were far superior in numbers. In the case of the latter group, 25 among 53 surnames had their ancestral origins in the three southern provinces, failing to attain the majority. This situation underwent a great change after the fourteenth century.

---

25. Yi Su-geon, "Goryeo sidae saseong yeongu" (A Research on Native Surnames during the Goryeo Period) 1, *Asea hakbo* 12 (1976).

No research has been conducted to examine the regional origins of the newly rising scholar-officials who made their debuts in the central government after the fourteenth century. The *Deunggwarok* (Records of State Service Examinations)[26] lists names of those who passed the examinations during the Goryeo period. The ancestral origins of successful candidates after the late thirteenth century are listed in greater detail than records for the preceding period. These records make it possible to grasp the situation in general. Until the end of the Goryeo period, the ancestral origins generally corresponded to areas from which officials came or their domiciles.[27] The scope of this paper will start from the coups d'etat by military officials as a sequel to the above research.

According to the documentary record, before the establishment of military regime, the ancestral origins of only 51 of the 120 successful candidates were noted, less than half the total (Table 1). This low accounting rate is due to special conditions that existed when the *Deunggwarok* was compiled, and provides a striking contrast with the high rates, topping 80 percent, of later periods. The disparity, as pointed out at the outset of this paper, may reflect differences between the two ages. Be that as it may, an examination of recorded ancestral origins reveals that among the total of 51 ancestral origins, those in the southern three provinces numbered 25, a slight and uncritical increase compared with King Uijong's reign. During the reigns of Kings Wonjong and Chungnyeol, however, the ancestral origins in the three southern provinces began to show a rising tendency, making up 62 percent of the total known origins. Despite a considerable decrease in the overall number of successful candidates from King Chungseon's reign to that of King Chungmok, the rate for those who hailed from the southern provinces shot up 80 percent. And while the total number of successful candidates increased rapidly from the reign of King Gongmin to the reign of King Gongyang, candidates from the three southern provinces retained a superior position, constituting 77 percent of the total.

Of course, it cannot be said that those who passed the *gwageo* enjoyed numerical superiority among government officials. However, as they

---

26. Concerning the nature of the *Deunggwarok*, refer to Heo Heung-sik, *Goryeo gwageo jedosa yeongu* (A Research on the History of Goryeo's *Gwageo* System) (Seoul: Ilchokak Publishing Co., 1981), pp. 241-243.

27. Heo Heung-sik, *Goryeo sahoesa yeongu* (A Research on the Social History of Goryeo) (Seoul: The Asian Culture Press, 1981), pp. 420-421.

Table 1. An Examination of the Ancestral Origins of Successful Candidates of the State Service Examinations during King Myeongjong (1171–1197) to King Gongyang (1389–1392)

Years	Total Number of Successful Candidates	Number of Recording the Ancestral Origins	Number of Ancestral Origins of Southern Three Provinces
Myeongjong (1171–1197)	38	15	7
Sinjong (1197–1204)	8	3	0
Huijong (1204–1211)	9	5	4
Gangjong (1213–1259)	4	1	0
Gojong (1213–1259)	51	22	14
Subtotal	120	51	25
Wonjong (1259–1274)	25	19	11
Chungnyeong (1274–1308)	83	58	39
Subtotal	108	77	59
Chungseok (1306–1313)	4	3	3
Chungsuk (1313–1329)	19	17	15
Chunghye (1330–1332)	10	7	6
Chungsuk (1332–1339)	5	4	3
Chunghye (1339–1344)	9	6	5
Chungmok (1344–1348)	7	7	5
Chungjeong (1349–1351)	0	0	0
Subtotal	54	44	37
Gongmin (1351–1374)	210	118	87
U (1374–1388)	203	141	112
Chang (1389)	65	30	27
Gongyang (1389–1392)	33	10	8
Subtotal	511	299	234
Total	793	471	346

were considered elites among officials, any trend appearing among them can be taken as a reflection of the condition of their time. The higher number of representatives from northern areas, including Gyeonggi-do province, from the early part of the Goryeo period to the reign of King Uijong can be explained primarily by the fact that they provided the basis for the power that established the Goryeo dynasty.

Other conditions must be considered for better understanding of this political transformation that, once established, continued unchanged for two and a half centuries. In this context, we must consider agricultural economy of the period.

As mentioned earlier, the restrictions imposed by the method of fallowing could not be overcome during the early and middle parts of the Goryeo period. Under the restricted agricultural conditions of that time, dry fields occupied far more land than paddy fields. In view of the fact that active paddies occupied less than 30 percent of the total farms until as late as the reign of Joseon King Sejong,[28] we can safely assume the predominance of dry field farming during the early and middle parts of the Goryeo period. More importantly, the mountain slopes were more profitable than plains for dry field farming within the limitations of fallowing. Since mountain slopes had richer grass than plains, they would become far more profitable in terms of soil fertility once they were reclaimed.[29] In grading farms during the reign of King Munjong, the ratio between farms in plains and those on mountain slopes was clarified. The *Gaoli tujing* (Illustrated Account of Goryeo), written by Xu Jing of Song China in 1123, notes that since plains are insufficient, people choose mountain slopes in reclamation, and that it is extremely laborious to till farms on mountain slopes because they have to climb up and go down.

Since farms on mountain slopes throve with the predominance of dry fields in farming during the early and middle parts of the Goryeo period, it is obvious why those who had their ancestral origins in areas

---

28. 宮嶋博史 (Hiroshi Miyajima), 「朝鮮農業史上における十五世紀」 (The 15th Century in the History of Korean Agriculture), 『朝鮮史叢』 3 (1980): pp. 46-47. Here his inquiry is based on the figures of reclamation contained in the section of geography, *Sejong sillok* (Annals of King Sejong).

29. A geographical research on farms on mountain slopes during the Goryeo period is Kim Sang-ho's *Ijo jeon-gi-ui sujeon nongeop yeongu* (A Research on Paddy Farming in the Early Joseon Period) (published in the book form with a subsidy for academic researches provided by the Ministry of Education in 1969), pp. 29-30.

north of Gyeonggi-do province retained continuous superiority. As the farming of the north including Gyeonggi-do province was by no means inferior to that of the three southern provinces under these agricultural conditions, the position acquired by the former for political momentum could not be undermined. When the agricultural conditions became entirely different after the fourteenth century, however, a significant change began to take place.

Dry fields predominated even into the fourteenth century when changes in agricultural technology came into effect. Conditions for dry fields transformed as soon as the restrictions imposed by the method of fallowing were overcome and complete fertilization became possible. In other words, farms became more profitable in plains than on mountain slopes.

During debates on the method of collecting land rents and taxes during the reign of King Sejong, one discussant noted that "Farms in plains are divided into three grades and those on the top and waist of mountains are also divided into four grades: this is our law concerning land."[30] As mentioned earlier, the method of grading farms on mountains is an indication of their long tradition. More importantly, farms on mountaintops were already distinguished from those in the plains. Another remark dating to the early part of the Joseon period recounts that "because of the formerly imposed limit pertaining to classifying farms into three grades, farms on the top, on the waist, and below mountains are worth double of ordinary farms."[31] This indicates the trend of treating mountain farms as different from ordinary farms. This was an obvious transformation from the situation existing during the early and middle parts of the Goryeo period when farms on mountain slopes were prevalent. It is highly likely that when mountain farms were more numerous, farms in plains were utilized for rice cultivation or as paddies. After overcoming the method of fallowing, farms in the plains, which were apt to be irrigated, continued to develop as paddies. It can also be assumed that a large number of farms in the plains were utilized as dry fields. Considering the development of dry fields in the plains, the prevalence of such dry fields must still have been high after the fourteenth century. It is safe to presume that the people in the three southern provinces, which had far more plains than areas north of Gyeonggi-do

---

30. *Sejong sillok, gwon* 113, 7th month, 28th year of King Sejong's reign.
31. *Sejong sillok, gwon* 109, 7th month, 27th year of King Sejong's reign.

province, could promote their economic power on the basis of their dry field farming. The obvious increase in the number of the southerners in the central government after the fourteenth century may have been caused by their reinforced economic power.

An important facet of social change during the period is the fact that the newly rising scholar-officials who advanced to the central government on the winds of agricultural advancement in the fourteenth century demonstrated considerable concern for the development of agricultural technology.[32] This new interest is reflected in the publication by a group of scholar-officials of a Chinese book on farming and sericulture, in an easier version in a smaller square type. The *Nongsang jiyao* (A Synopsis of Agriculture and Sericulture) was brought home by Yi Am from Beijing, Yuan China, where he had escorted King Chungjeong who was enthroned as a new ruler in 1349. Even though the text, which dealt mainly with the traditional dry field farming practices of northern China, failed to reflect the most advanced Chinese technology in a perfect manner, Goryeo scholar-officials saw fit to publish it in a popular edition for easier propagation. Such effort illustrates their interest and desire to contribute to the development of Goryeo's agricultural technology.

In 1362 (11th year of King Gongmin's reign), Baek Mun-bo proposed that it be necessary to learn the merits of the farming methods practiced south of the Yangzi River (Jiangnan), the most advanced in China at that time, and that the water-wheel be spread in Goryeo. These techniques were the foundation for the development of paddy farming in China.[33] In short, the newly rising group of Goryeo scholar-officials took a keen interest in the situation of its neighbor, China, in order to develop and transform the home agriculture in a more effective manner. In their academic and philosophical studies, these scholars reflected on a system of Neo-Confucian tenets to encourage agriculture as follows: "As a tenant feeds his family members which he owns to his landlord, he should not encroach upon his lord; as the landlord could enrich upon his lord; as the landlord could enrich his domestic economy owing to his tenant, he should not maltreat his tenant." This recognition of the mutually supplementary relations between landlord and tenant cannot be

---

32. Yi Tae-jin, "14/15 segi nongeop gisul-ui baldal-gwa sinheung sajok," p. 345.
33. "Sikhwa 2," in *Goryeosa, gwon* 79.

found in any other system of thought in Chinese history and so can be seen as a historical achievement of Neo-Confucianism. The new recognition by Zhu Xi owed much to the achievements reaped in the agricultural method of Jiangnan which, centering on paddy farming, overcame the limit of fallowing completely in the Song, especially Southern Song period. As productivity was elevated greatly by dint of the new technical improvements in agriculture and as the economic power of the whole society expanded, it was recognized that the landlord was not independent but in a mutual relationship with his tenant. Taking this fact into consideration, it is apparent that Goryeo's new ruling class began to adopt the Neo-Confucian outlook owing to the new technical achievements in agriculture in the fourteenth century. However, they were not able to obtain the high productivity of paddy farming in Jiangnan provinces, where, compared with Goryeo, land tax rates were lowered significantly by the newly rising scholar-officials to enforce the Confucian "people-first" principle. The reform of the land system was based fundamentally on the expansion of economic power as a result of technical development in agriculture. In an epilogue to the Korean edition of *Nongsang jiyao*, Yi Saek argues that the book had merits in its suggestions for the "right method for sublimation of living."[34] How to make a contribution to "sublimation of living" was one of the most important tasks facing the new ruling class of Goryeo.

The important tasks in agricultural economy during the fourteenth century included the question of how to eliminate contradictions in the relations of land control and how to rearrange the problems that accompanied the development of agricultural technique. The former task was resolved as soon as *gwajeonbeop* (Rank Land Law) was put into operation. The latter task, however, was resolved with the legislation of a new law governing the collection of land rents and taxes during the reign of King Sejong. In other words, all the tasks of the fourteenth century were brought to conclusion in the mid-fifteenth century.

---

34. Yi Saek, "Nongsang jibyo huseo" (An Epilogue to *Nongsang jiyao*), in *Mogeun mungo* (Complete Works of Mogeun Yi Saek).

## PART III

JOSEON PERIOD

The *Gwageo* Examination System during the Goryeo and Early Joseon Periods

Lee Song Mu

Preface

The *gwageo*, a state examination system administered in the selection process of bureaucrat officials, was enforced only in China, Korea, and Vietnam. This system was employed first in China about 1,400 years ago during the reign of the Sui Emperor Wenti. Sui was a centralized autocratic state which unified China for the third time after Qin. Emperor Wenti adopted the state examination system to strengthen the centralized ruling structure, with the emperor in the center, by restraining the influence of the aristocrats. Designed to select officials on the basis of their individual ability, the *keju* (imperial examination system; *gwageo* in Korean) was deemed as the most appropriate means of curbing the hereditary transmission of power traditionally enjoyed by the aristocrats who held the lineage of their families or clans in high esteem.

China's *keju* system was first introduced to Korea in 958 (ninth year of King Gwangjong's reign of Goreyo), about four centuries after its implementation in China. The state examination system was thereafter enforced in Korea continuously for 936 years until it was abolished in 1894.

---

* Originally published in the *Korea Journal*, vol. 21, no. 7 (July 1981).

Lee Song Mu (Yi, Seong-mu) currently serves as the Chairman of the National Institute of Korean History. He obtained his Ph.D. in History from Seoul National University in 1979. He published many books and articles in the field of Korean history, including *Hanguk-ui gwageo jedo* (*Gwageo* System of Korea) (1976), *Hanguk yeoksa-ui ihae* (Understanding of Korean History), 3 vols. (1994–2001), and *Joseon-ui sahoe-wa sasang* (Joseon Society and Its Thought) (1999). E-mail: leesm@nhc.go.kr.

Korea was late in adopting the system in comparison to China because of the sociocultural disparities between the two countries, and due to the fact that a unified state emerged in the Korean peninsula relatively late. Silla unified the Three Kingdoms in 669 and the *dokseo sampum gwa* (state service examination in the reading of texts in three gradations; hereafter, the "three-gradation reading examination") was established in 788, but the prevailing social system, *golpumje* (bone-rank system) clashed with the examination system, preventing the *gwageo* from functioning properly. The *gwageo* system was not enforced, therefore, until as late as in 958.

In order to establish a firm centralized bureaucratic structure by liquidating the bone-rank system, the Goryeo dynasty attempted to suppress the influence of aristocrats and powerful families in the provinces and enlist them as officials of the central government through state examinations. The aristocrats' deep-rooted influence in the provinces was not easily undermined, however. In addition, those who did pass the examinations successfully began acquiring desire for power, and were turning into aristocrats as well. Two appointment systems were employed: *eumseo*, according to which one son of an official of the fifth rank or above was allowed to receive an official appointment, thus maintaining the importance of family lineage; and the *gwageo* system, which emphasized individual ability. While the *eumseo* system attenuated, however, the *gwageo* system became increasingly strong.

While it was impossible to control the influence of the local gentry altogether, the *hyanggeoriseon* (Ch. *xiangju lixuan*), a system of recommending applicants for the *gwageo* by local offices, was enforced together with state examinations given at the capital. During this period, military examinations were administered as a part of the state examinations in order to weaken the military power of the local gentry. The *gwageo* was a state examination system enforced by an autocratic sovereign who unified the country by force of arms with the purpose of fortifying the principle of civil rule by training competent civil officials. Later, in the early part of the Joseon period, the examinations were readjusted to include both civil and military examinations. The centralized *yangban* (upper class) bureaucratic system was firmly established at the same time.

Korea's *gwageo* system is closely related to the development of the *yangban* bureaucratic system during the Goryeo and Joseon periods. In order to understand the history and culture of these periods, therefore, it is necessary to examine the contents of the *gwageo* system in detail. This paper limits the object of its research to the *gwageo* system in the periods before the establishment of the Joseon dynasty, because this period is sufficient in providing an overall understanding of the characteristics of Korea's *gwageo* system.

The *Gwageo* System and the *Eumseo* System

The late Silla period to the early Goryeo period represents one of the most turbulent times in Korean history. The most significant changes taking place during this period was a shift from the implementation of Silla's bone-rank system, which attached importance to lineage, to the implementation of Goryeo's bureaucratic system that valued individuals' ability.

Opinions vary as to the origins and structure of Silla's bone-rank system.[1] The bone-rank system was a caste system dividing kinsfolk in and around Gyeongju into royalty and nobility and was readjusted and strengthened in order to reorganize the status of those conquered by Silla in the process of unification. When the territory under Silla expanded with unification, it became impossible for the kingdom to maintain itself with its existing government structure. The result was the expansion of *gyeongwi*, the central government ranks, and the disappearance of *oewi*, the provincial government ranks. The provincial ranks were Silla's primordial ranks bestowed on local gentry.[2] They were established unofficially before unification, but in 674 they were officially established.[3] The provincial ranks integrated with the central government after unification and with the strengthening of the central government. It became necessary to define how the provincial ranks corresponded to the seventeen central ranks. There was a clearly defined limit as to the level of promotion among the seventeen central government ranks. Members of the *jin-gol* (true-bone) class could advance to

1. Yi Gi-dong, "Silla golpumje-ui hyeonhwang-gwa geu gwaje" (The Present Situation of Research on Silla's Bone-Rank System and Its Tasks), *Yeoksa hakbo* (Journal of History) 74 (June 1977): pp. 105-153.
2. Sachio Takeda, "Silla's Golpumje Society" (in Japanese), *Rekishigaku kenkyu* (Journal of Historical Studies) 299 (1965): pp. 3-12.
3. Kim Cheol-jun, "Hanguk godae gukga baldalsa" (The History of Development of Korea's Ancient States), in *Hanguk munhwasa daegye*, vol. 1 (Seoul: Institute of National Culture, Korea University, 1964), p. 514.

the highest official rank (that of *ibeolchan*); those of the *yukdupum* (head-rank six) only to the sixth office rank (*achan*); those of the *odupum* (head-rank five) only to the tenth office ranks (*daenaema*); and those of the *sadupum* (head-rank four) only to the twelfth office rank (*daesa*).

This presents a good contrast to the *gigaje* (family-based system), modeled after the Nine Rank System (Ch. *jiupin guanrenfa*) enforced in China during the periods of the Wei, Jin, and Southern and Northern Dynasties, which fixed provincial and central ranks on the basis of seniority.[4] In the Nine Rank System, provincial ranks were first determined according to family status, and central rank was fixed on the basis of the provincial rank. In the bone-rank system, on the contrary, the promotion was limited according to the status of bones with the same starting point. The Nine Rank System regulated personnel affairs in order to incorporate officials of the Later Han into the Wei system of government after Wei destroyed the Later Han. In contrast to this, when Silla unified the Three Kingdoms, its measure did not go beyond simply retaining its bone-rank system while making minor readjustments to include its conquered people.[5]

After unification, however, a new system of personnel administration evaluating individual ability, the "three-gradation reading examination," was created which still adhered to the traditional bone-rank system. It was designed to recruit officials from among the National Confucian College (Gukhak)[6] graduates. The National Confucian College enrolled sons of aristocrats who ranked under *daesa* or had no rank at all and graduated them when they reached the ranks of *naema* (eleventh office rank) or *daenaema* after nine years of study.[7] As those holding *daehaeja*

---

4. Miyazaki Ichisada, *Kyuhin kanninho no kenkyu* (Research on the Nine Rank System) (Kyoto: Dohosha, 1956).

5. The Nine Rank System developed into the *keju* (*gwageo*) system during the Sui and Tang periods, but in Korea the limits imposed by the bone-rank system were passed on to the *eumseo* system with the implementation of civil and military examinations during the Joseon period.

6. Gukhak is a National Confucian College established in 602 during the Silla period. Around 750 this state institution was renamed the Taehakgam (National Confucian University). Gukhak in the early Goryeo period is translated as National Academy, to differentiate its character from that of Silla period. It was abolished as the Gukjagam (National University) was established in 992 (11th year of King Seongjong's reign). This institution was renamed as the Gukhak in 1275 (first year of King Chungnyeol's reign).

7. "On Official Positions 1," in *Samguk sagi, gwon* 38.

rank could be promoted only to the fifth head-rank, graduates of the National Confucian College must have come from families of the sixth head-rank or from the *jin-gol* classes permitted to rise up to the rank of *daenaema* or above. The National Confucian College was an educational institute for sons of the *jin-gol* class or aristocrats holding the sixth head-rank and the "three-gradation reading examination" was the state examination system administered for their employment. It is only in the later years of the Silla period that a system of employing officials on the basis of their ability instead of their lineage was created.

As Silla's central government weakened in its waning years, provincial magnates' personal strengths increased, and power struggles among them resulted in the emergence of the Later Three Kingdoms. In the war among the three, Wang Geon absorbed Silla in 935 (18th year of his reign) and the Later Baekje in 936, thereby establishing a unified country in Korea for the second time. The unification by Goryeo, however, was incomplete, because the local gentry, with their semi-independent spheres of influence, were still scattered in the provinces. The Goryeo dynasty merely united them, but the result was more like an allegiance of the local gentry. In order to strengthen royal authority, Goryeo had to suppress the influence of military commanders and local gentry, which grew stronger in the process of unification, and firmly establish a centralized bureaucratic system in the kingdom. For this purpose, Goryeo tried to absorb military commanders as loyal civil officials by enforcing the *gwageo* system in 958 (ninth year of King Gwangjong's reign) and enforcing the civil and military examinations in 995 (14th year of King Seongjong's reign). Goryeo's *gwageo* examinations did not include military examinations, but offered only civil and miscellaneous examinations (*japgwa*) in order to control the militaristic semi-independent influence of the local gentry.[8] Most importantly, the qualifications for applying for the state examinations were limited to community chiefs with surnames listed in the records of noted clans kept at the capital in the first half of the period.

It was impossible for Goryeo to remove the deep-rooted influence of local magnates at once because a new group of its own aristocrats was still in the process of forming. As a result, the *eumseo* system, which emphasized the lineage of clans or families, was administered simultane-

---

8. The *mugwa* (military examinations) was not administered during the Goryeo period in order to reduce the militaristic nature of local magnates.

ously with the *gwageo*, which emphasized individual ability.[9] The *gwageo* supported the bureaucratic system while the *eumseo* retained the aristocratic system. With time, however, aristocracy weakened while the bureaucracy strengthened its basis. Although both Goryeo and Joseon were bureaucratic societies, which espoused *gwageo*-first policy, they were also ruled by the estate system. They were not aristocratic societies in which several aristocrats monopolized political power but *yangban* bureaucratic societies which advocated rule by a wider upper class through the *gwageo* system.[10]

The *yangban* bureaucratic system was established gradually, in four stages: (1) The early part of the Goryeo period when civil aristocracy was enforced; (2) Mid-Goryeo when military officials assumed the reign of government; (3) Late Goryeo when Goryeo was subjugated to Yuan and then the Yuan dynasty was replaced by Ming China; and (4) Early Joseon when the *yangban* bureaucratic system was established.

Even though Silla's bone-rank system was liquidated in the early part of the Goryeo period, the foundation for a bureaucratic system was still feeble. Many measures were taken by the government to strengthen the autocratic regal authority and bureaucratic system, such as adoption of the *gwageo* system, promotion of public schooling, and enforcement of the *gun-hyeon* system (a system of centrally controlled local administration). And yet Goryeo was still obliged to enact laws guaranteeing privileges for civil aristocrats due to the deep-rooted influence of aristocrats and local gentry. It was on this account that the Goryeo government placed sons of those who held the fifth rank or above in government positions, granted them farms and forests in recognition of the meritorious service rendered to the state by their ancestors, promoted the Twelve Private Schools, and enforced the *gonggeoje*[11] and the *jwaju munsaeng je*.[12]

---

9. The theory that Goryeo was an aristocratic society was pitted against another theory that it was a bureaucratic society. Both conclusions are extreme views; the two had mutually supplementary relations, forming one characteristic of the *yangban* bureaucratic system.

10. Yi Seong-mu, *Joseon chogi yangban yeongu* (Research on the *Yangban* in the Early Joseon Period) (Seoul: Ilchokak Publishing Co., 1980), p. 43.

11. A system of state examinations in which the official in charge, called *jigonggeo*, selected successful applicants at his own discretion.

12. A system of recognizing the formation of academic cliques between the examiners functioning as teachers and successful applicants as their pupils; lit., "a system of the leader questioning the students."

By mid-Goryeo (12–13th century B.C.) when the military regime was established, the aristocratic dominance had waned considerably. While military officials of humble birth rose to the status of aristocrats, newly rising scholar-officials who were formerly provincial clerks and who were well versed in both literature and government administration advanced in rank through the state examinations alongside sons of noble families. As a result, the number of people who were placed in government positions on account of meritorious service rendered to the state by their ancestor was decreased to include only sons of those who held the third rank or above. The advancement of provincial clerks to the central government infused new blood into the existing group of *yangban* bureaucrats.

When the military regime crumbled and Goryeo was subjugated to Mongol rule, the newly rising scholar-officials became more active in politics. When the Yuan (Mongol) empire began to rule Goryeo, a new trend of evaluating individual skill over lineage gained in influence. With the accelerated introduction of Chinese institutions, Goryeo experienced cultural changes.[13] These changes included the acceptance of Neo-Confucianism and import of Neo-Confucian books, introduction of the "three-stage state examination system" (*keju sanzhengfa*), the promotion of public schooling, and the development of printing. Scholar-bureaucrats trained in Neo-Confucianism who advanced through the *gwageo* began to emerge. The number of officials further increased as a result of the creation of new positions. The ruling class reached a saturation point in the closing years of the Goryeo dynasty and great restrictions were imposed on local clerks to qualify for the *gwageo* examination. When the Ming dynasty replaced the Yuan in China, the ruling class was split into the pro-Yuan old aristocratic faction and the pro-Ming new aristocratic faction. It was the latter faction that finally founded the Joseon dynasty.

With the establishment of the Joseon dynasty, a new *yangban* bureaucratic system took root, guaranteeing benefits and privileges for the upper class on a broader scale. The system of civil and military examinations, public schooling, central government positions, and centrally-controlled local administration were readjusted, while the ruling class

---

13. After Goryeo was subjugated to Mongol rule, many opportunities arose for Koreans to visit Yuan, both voluntarily and not. Their frequent visits resulted in active introduction of Chinese institutions.

was divided into *yangban* on top and *jungin* (middle people) beneath them.[14] The state examination system changed from the *gonggeoje* to the *gosigwanje* (a system of selecting candidates by multiple judges), and the Twelve Private Schools and the *jwaju munsaengje* were discontinued. At the same time, illegitimate sons and those born to mothers who remarried were barred from applying to the state examinations. On the other hand, hereditary positions in recognition of meritorious services rendered by ancestors and the rank land (*gwajeon*) system granted to hereditary fiefs were not abolished even in the early Joseon dynasty. Such rewards were granted continuously, even though their scope and amount were curtailed.[15]

After the 500-year Goryeo period, a *yangban* bureaucratic system was ready to finally be established in the early Joseon dynasty. Both Goryeo and Joseon were agricultural societies whose main constituents were rural clans with longstanding traditions. Most of the rural clans, however, consisted of impoverished owner-farmers and tenants. The state therefore had no means other than to increase its revenue, face alien aggression, and carry out projects in irrigation, transportation of tax-grain, construction of fortresses, and city planning for the capital. These projects provided the very foundation on which the autocratic royal authority could establish itself during the Goryeo and Joseon periods.

The sovereign dominated the entire country, demanding unconditional loyalty. The relationship between sovereign and subjects, based on confucian ethics, was likened to that between father and son, meaning

---

14. Yi Seong-mu, *op. cit.*, p. 39.
15. According to the article on descendants benefited by the meritorious service of their ancestors, of "Ijeon" (On Government Officials), in *Gyeongguk daejeon* (National Code), *gwon* 1, persons to be appointed for this reason were limited to the following: (1) Sons, grandsons, son-in-law, younger brothers, and nephews of meritorious retainers and officials holding the second rank or above (sons and grandsons in the case of secondary meritorious retainers); (2) Sons and grandsons of officials in service at the third rans; and (3) Sons of officials who served important positions with clean records in the Ministries of Personnel and Military Affairs, Office of City Administration, Office of the Inspectior-General, Office of the Censor-General, Office of Special Advisers, and as generals and royal messengers. It was stipulated in the Rank Land Law (*gwajeonbeop*) that no land was granted to petit officials. The New Rank Land Law provided that land could be granted to *yangban* bureaucrats in active service; the provision was revised into a system of government management and granted after King Seongjong. It was abolished during the reign of King Myeongjong (Yi Seong-mu, *op. cit.*, p. 294).

that all actions that undermined his authority were subject to severe penalties. On the other hand, a king was expected to work always towards the benefit and welfare of his people and thus the king needed the bureaucrats to assist him in statecraft. On their part, the bureaucrats tried to advance into aristocracy by increasing their freedoms and rights. The king therefore devised various measures to limit the bureaucrats' provincial force. Among the measures taken included a limit on the tenure of office in any single position; the prohibition of employment in one's native place; the strengthening of censorship; strict evaluation of service records such as the *gogwa beop* (a rule of performance rating), the *popyeom beop* (a method deciding promotion or demotion based on evaluation of an official's service), and the *sunja beop* (a method of deciding promotion or demotion based on length of service); and the reinforcement of the state examination systems such as the *gwageo* and *chwijae* (an examination for the selection of lower-level officials). Also, the *yangban* officials who were policy makers and the *jungin* officials who were at the working level were separated and made inspectors of each other through the Yuhyangso (local government advisory committee), *hyangyak* (village code), and the *bumin goso beop* (the law for filing grievances against magistrates' misdoings). During the Goryeo period, the curricula of the state examination centered heavily on Confucian ideology and literature that had little connection with the practical affairs of state administration. No training was provided in martial arts, whereas Confucian education was offered at public schools and the *mun-gwa* (civil examinations) was valued over the *mugwa* (military examinations).

The military officials were also considered subjects of the king. They were allowed to maintain strength only enough to support the king. As a result, when faced with foreign invasion, the government was compelled to mobilize peasant troops. Professional knowledge was entrusted to specialists with hereditary professions and estates. And in places beyond the reach of royal authority, the magistrates and local clerks collected tax-grain. Local clerks were authorized to transmit their official duties to their offspring, but magistrates were replaced frequently to prevent their power from increasing to the extent of threatening royal authority.

To preserve his power, then, the king destabilized the bureaucrats in order to limit their personal rights, and also promoted an atmosphere of competition, distrust, and mutual surveillance. With this imbalance of power, partisan wrangling erupted and the dignity of the king declined as the strife became violent. Even though there were written law, all acts of legislation were subject to the king's decision, and all laws enacted by the preceding kings were observed as legislated constitution.

However, the king could not completely eradicate the bureaucrats' privileges. On the contrary, the king granted hereditary positions in recognition of meritorious service rendered bureaucrats' ancestors and "rank land" as hereditary fiefs in exchange for the loyalty displayed by *yangban* bureaucrats. By transferring official positions and rank land to their offspring, the *yangban* bureaucrats undermined autocratic regal authority as hereditary officials holding high rank. They made it inevitable for the monarch to recruit newly emerging bureaucrats in order to form a new corps of officials to be placed under his direct command.

After the establishment of the Joseon dynasty, the power of the subjects became stronger than regal authority. The *yangban* class wanted the royal authority to be firmly established and the state examinations to be carried out in a fair manner in order to secure their own coexistence. Men of the *yangban* class did not tolerate any of the king's arbitrary politics. For this purpose there were lectures to the crown prince and the king, remonstrance to the sovereign by officials and royal historians, and memorials to the throne open to all. Although it was true that important decisions on policies, personnel administration, military affairs, and the state examinations required final approval by the king, these decisions were actually controlled by the *yangban* bureaucrats. Even though the king officially ruled the land and its people, he was in actuality a chief of state representing the *yangban* class.

In Korea, private land and private slaves were recognized since early times and the autocratic royal authority was established on the basis of this recognition. The public powers of the sovereign and the private powers of his subjects coexisted mutually. The king's position as an autocratic ruler was guaranteed by the *yangban* bureaucrats, and there was a certain limit to his authority.[16] For this reason *yangban* bureaucratic system was considered to rule Joseon society. The Goryeo period is regarded as a transitional or preparatory stage for the establishment of the *yangban* bureaucratic system.

---

16. If the notion that all land was royal possession had been prevalent, it would not have been necessary for the royal household to strive to hold royal property (i.e., manors and palaces in Goryeo and land managed by the Naesusi, bondmen and bondwomen, and long-term interests).

According to Max Weber, countries where the state is regarded as the sovereign's hereditary property and there is no distinction between public law and private law and between sovereignty and ownership are called power-centered bureaucratic countries based on family property.[17] When these countries expand, the retainers who are situated between the chieftain (the king) and the general constituents (the people) come to monopolize the power of rule, and they are called estate-centered bureaucratic countries based on family property.[18] Although the power-centered bureaucratic system based on family property was regarded as an ideal in Goryeo and Joseon, it was an estate-centered bureaucratic system based more on family property. Although all the land and people were nominally subject to the rule of the king during Goryeo and Joseon, there existed private land and private slaves. For this reason, it cannot be simply defined as a bureaucratic system based on family property. This can be said to be one characteristic of the *yangban* bureaucratic system of the two periods.

Qualifications for Application for the *Gwageo*

The National Confucian College (Gukhak) of Silla admitted sons of aristocrats holding the capital rank of *daesa* (12th) or below and graduated the students when they rose to the capital rank of *daenaema* (10th) after nine years of study. The "three-gradation reading examination" corresponded to a graduation examination.[19] As the *daenaema* was the highest rank to which persons holding the *odupum* were permitted to rise, those students who were entitled to apply for the "three-gradation reading examination" must have been sons of aristocrats who held at least a *yukdupum* rank or above.

Due to the restraints imposed by the bone-rank system, the "three-gradation reading examination" system of Silla could not openly recruit officials. The Goryeo dynasty, which came into existence on the basis of provincial magnates, felt the need to adopt a system of recruiting competent persons on a wider scale and in an open manner. It was for this pur-

---

17. Hideo Aoyama, *Max Weber's Social Theory* (in Japanese) (Tokyo: Iwanami Shoten, 1950), pp. 164, 166.
18. *Ibid.*, p. 167.
19. "On Official Positions," in *Samguk sagi, gwon* 38.

pose that the *gwageo* system was enforced in 958 (ninth year of King Gwangjong's reign). Nevertheless, it was impossible to loosen the qualifications to apply for the state examinations even from the beginning. This is because it was necessary to enroll local magnates and their followers to the group of central bureaucrats with priority. The qualifications to apply for the *gwageo* gradually expanded their scope in proportion to the degree of firmness with which the centralized *yangban* bureaucratic system was being established.

Persons who were qualified to apply for the *gwageo* during the Goryeo period can be broadly divided into three groups. The first were those recommended by local offices; second, National Academy (Gukhak) students in the capital who were recommended by the central government; and third, officials in service.[20] When the state examination system was first enforced, people recommended by local offices (as well as National Academy students with recommendations) were authorized to apply for the main examination (*daegwa*) without passing preparatory tests. After 1024, however, those who were recommended by local offices were permitted to sit for the main examination, *dongdanggamsi*,[21] after passing the *gyesugwansi*.[22] After the coronation of King Deokjong in 1031, people who aspired to enroll in the National University (Gukjagam) were required to pass the *gukjagamsi* examination.[23] After 1147 National University students were required to go through the promotion examination called *seungbosi* if they were to be admitted to the Chiljae (seven special courses at the Gukjagam).[24] Stu-

---

20. Xu Jing, *Xuanhe fengshi gaoli tujing* (Illustrated Record of the Chinese Embassy to the Goryeo Court during the Xuanhe Era), vol. 19.

21. *Dongdanggamsi* was also called *dongdangsi*. *Dongdang* means the place where the king evaluates the results of the *gwageo* examination in person.

22. The *gyesugwansi* was a local examination given at the nearest designated counties. *Gyesugwan* refers to the "head official of the border region," i.e., the chief administrator of a region along the main road or provincial border. This examination accepted three applicants from a prefecture with a male population of more than 1,000 and two applicants from a county with a male population of less than 500. This measure was designed to strengthen the power of the sovereign by evenly selecting able persons from all districts (*Goryeosa, gwon* 73).

23. An examination conducted at the National University for the selection of *jinsa* (literary licentiate) in the Goryeo period. The *gukjagamsi* examination was first established in the tenth month of the lunar calendar during the year of King Deokjong's crowning (*Goryeosa, gwon* 5).

24. "Seon-geo 2," in *Goryeosa, gwon* 74.

dents were also required to study at the National University for a total of 300 days in three years before they obtained the qualifications to apply for the main examination.[25] Officials in active service were qualified to apply for the main examination directly. Toward the close of the Goryeo dynasty, the *gaeseongsi* examination,[26] which was a *chosi* examination[27] for the civil examinations, was established solely for these officials.

In the early part of the Goryeo period, only community chiefs whose surnames were listed in the records of notable clans kept at the capital were authorized to apply for the *gwageo* examinations. A regulation was promulgated in 1048 to the effect that only descendants of community deputy chiefs and local clerks holding higher ranks and sons of aides to the community deputy chiefs or local clerks of higher rank were permitted to apply for the *jesureop* (composition examination course) or *myeonggyeongeop* (classics examinations course). It was further issued to the Supreme Council (Naesa Munhaseong) in 1055 that "people whose surnames are not listed in the records of clans are prohibited from applying for the *gwageo*."[28] Those who did not have surnames which were confirmed and listed in the records of clans compiled by the central government were not permitted to apply for the state examination. Those who had ruling surnames at that time were members of the Goryeo royalty, Silla nobility, and local magistrates. It was necessary for the state to confirm these leading clans by listing their surnames in the records of clans. The government presumably recruited officials and soldiers on the basis of the clan records. These clans included members who were entitled to become local clerks and members qualified to become soldiers.[29]

---

25. "Seon-geo 1," in *Goryeosa, gwon* 73.

26. *Gaseongsi* was a preliminary examination conducted at Gaeseong, capital of Goryeo, also called *gaegyeongsi*.

27. *Chosi* is the "first-stage examination" of the *daegwa* (the main examinations that awarded the *mun-gwa* degree), taken by classics licentiates and literary licentiates who passed the *sogwa* (the preliminary examination that offered *saengwon* or *jinsa* degrees).

28. "Seon-geo 1," in *Goryeosa, gwon* 73.

29. Kim Gwang-su, "Ramal yeocho-ui hojok-gwa gwanban" (The Powerful Clans and the Province Government Officials of the Silla-Goryeo Transitional Period), *Hanguk-sa yeongu* 23 (1979): pp. 140-141; Yi Gi-baek, *Goryeo byeongjesa yeongu* (A Study of the History of the Goryeo Dynasty's Military Systems) (Seoul: Ilchokak Publishing Co., 1968), pp. 284-285.

This meant the establishment of a new class system comprising *munban* (civil official order), *muban* (military officer order), *namban* (court functionary order), *gunban* (soldier order), etc. The class system was transformed into a system of roles with the development of the two-class system dividing the *yangban* into the civil class and the military class.[30]

In the meantime, even commoners were authorized to apply for miscellaneous examinations such as the *ui-eop* (medical examination). Totally excluded from all sorts of state examinations were political and ethical offenders such as those who committed the five acts of treason, disloyalty, and undutifulness to parents, people engaged in the five despicable occupations, privately employed soldiers of local magnates, musicians, and officials of the lowest rank.[31] As the *yangban* bureaucratic system developed, the scope of qualifications to apply for the state examinations also expanded. After 1125, commoners were permitted to apply for the military and miscellaneous examinations in the *gwageo*, with limited promotion. Those who passed the civil examinations could rise only to the fifth rank and those who passed the miscellaneous examinations only to the seventh rank.[32]

Alongside the development of the *gwageo* system, low-ranking provincial clerks came to possess their own surnames; and all people who possessed surnames were, in principle, granted the right to sit for the *gwageo*. Therefore, the expansion of the scope of qualifications to apply for the state examinations took place generally in proportion to the diffusion of surnames. The king certainly wanted to strengthen his royal powers by selecting officials from as wide a range of social classes as possible. As more men of the low class endeavored to apply for the *gwageo* by whatever means possible, the scope of the qualifications for the *gwageo* also had to be expanded.[33] Due to various social, economic, and cultural conditions, however, it was mostly local clerks who applied for the state examinations during the Goryeo period. *Yangban* bureaucrats during the Goryeo period were outfitted by the local clerks. As the ruling

---

30. Yi Gi-baek, *Minjok-gwa yeoksa* (Nation and History) (Seoul: Ilchokak Publishing Co., 1971), pp. 94-95.
31. "Seon-geo 1," in *Goryeosa, gwon* 73.
32. *Goryeosa, gwon* 75.
33. One example may be that King Munjong recognized the success in the examination of Yi Sin-seok who passed it although he was not registered in the record of clans. Refer to "Choe Chung," in *Goryeosa, gwon* 95.

class expanded in the last years of the period, some restrictions were imposed on the local clerks who were applying for the *gwageo*. For example, a local clerk could send only one among his three sons (aged 16 to 60) to take the miscellaneous examinations.[34] The "sons" of the local clerks were restrained by *yangban* bureaucrats in terms of the *gwageo* qualifications.

According to the *Gyeongguk daejeon* (National Code), the local clerk was authorized to send only one among his three sons to the miscellaneous examinations which excluded the civil examinations, military examinations, and the preliminary examinations (*sogwa*) for the title of *saengwon* (classics licentiate) or *jinsa* (literary licentiate) if they had rendered meritorious service in war to the state.[35] Many other restrictions were attached. For example, if local clerks wanted to apply for the preliminary examinations, they were required first to obtain approval from the magistrates in their respective counties.[36] Before applying for the *boksi* (the second-stage examination) for the title of *saengwon* or *jinsa*, they were required to go through a test in *Xiaoxue* (Lesser Learning) and *Zhuxi jiali* (Family Rituals of Zhu Xi) in addition to being tested in the Four Books and one of the Three Classics of Confucianism.[37] Before applying for the preliminary examinations for the military examinations, they were required to score better than "coarse" on a test on the Seven Books of Martial Arts.[38] These measures are closely associated with the degradation of local clerks' social position in the early part of the Joseon period.[39] Illegitimate sons and those born to mothers who remarried were prohibited from applying for the civil examinations and preliminary examinations for the title of *saengwon* or *jinsa*.[40] A law unique to the Joseon dynasty, this was a phenomenon of self-selection imposed by

---

34. *Goryeosa, gwon* 75.
35. "Ijeon," in *Gyeongguk daejeon, gwon* 1.
36. *Taejong sillok* (Annals of King Taejong), *gwon* 1, 3rd month, first year of King Taejong's reign.
37. Song Jun-ho, *Ijo saengwon, jinsasi-ui yeongu* (Research on the Joseon Dynasty's *Saengwon* and *Jinsa* Examinations) (Seoul: National Assembly Library, 1970), p. 31.
38. "Byeongjeon" (Military Code), in *Gyeongguk daejeon, gwon* 4.
39. Yi Seong-mu, "Joseon chogi-ui hyangni" (Local Clerks in the Early Joseon Period), *Hanguksa yeongu* 5 (March 1970): pp. 69-100.
40. "Yejeon" (Code of Rites), in *Gyeongguk daejeon, gwon* 3. According to *Gyeongguk daejeon juhae*, only sons and grandsons of women who remarried were prohibited from applying for the *gwageo*, whereas all descendants of illegitimate sons were forbidden to apply for the state examinations throughout the generations.

the *yangban* class on itself. Most of the sons of specialists applied for the miscellaneous examinations.

Even in the Joseon period, commoners were entitled to apply for the *gwageo*, and, some of them, in fact, succeeded in the state examination. Nevertheless, it was difficult for impoverished commoners to prepare for the *gwageo* which required 25 to 30 years on the average; and it was also difficult for them to acquire the necessary books. The procedure of applying for the state examination was complicated for commoners and their rate of success in the state examination was therefore very low.[41] The reason the Joseon government, while imposing restrictions on application for the *gwageo* on local clerks and illegitimate sons of *yangban*, did not restrain the application of commoners is that local clerks and illegitimate sons were most formidable rivals of the *yangban*. The *yangban* and commoners were distinguished by their family background. Family background was evaluated according to the following criteria: (1) Whether there was mixed blood in the family; (2) How many successful candidates a family produced at state examinations; (3) Marital connections to other prestigious families; and (4) Prominent positions held by the father, grandfather, great grandfather and maternal grandfather.[42]

Menials could not apply for the state examination in the Joseon period. This is because menials, whether they were subordinate to others or not, were regarded as persons who were not free and consequently denied rights as human beings. There is an example of a private slave who elevated his status and successfully passed the state examination, but this was a very rare exception.[43]

Whereas *chamsanggwan* (officials of the third to the sixth grade junior) in Goryeo were prohibited from applying for the state examination, officials of the Joseon dynasty who were below the lowest rank held by the lower-level officials titled *danghagwan* (officials of the third grade senior or lower ranks) were permitted to apply. This was on the condition that the civil examinations and the *jungsi* (a special examina-

---

41. Yi Seong-mu, "Joseon chogi mun-gwa-ui eungsi jagyeok" (Qualifications for Application for the Civil Examination in the Early Joseon Period), *Gungmin daehak non-munjip* (Kookmin University Collection of Dissertations) 9 (1976).
42. Ibid., p. 63.
43. A private bondman of Prince Suyang named Jo Deuk-nim became his meritorious retainer and Jo's son applied for the *gwageo*. Refer to *Gyeongguk daejeon*, *gwon* 4, "Byeongjeon," pp. 81-82.

tion to encourage those who passed the state examination) were open to officials below the lowest rank held by the *danghagwan* and the preliminary examinations for the title of *saengwon* or *jinsa* to officials below the rank of the *tongdeok rang* (an honorific phrase for officials of fifth grade senior). Why did the Joseon government expand the scope of qualifications for officials in active service to apply for the *gwageo*? Whereas the state examinations of the Goryeo dynasty were designed primarily to incorporate local clerks into the group of central bureaucrats, the *gwageo* system of the Joseon dynasty which had already developed its *yangban* bureaucratic system to a considerable degree was aimed primarily at promoting officials through the *choja* (a method of promotion which allowed one to advance several ranks at a time) and the *chojik* (a method of promotion which allowed one to advance one rank at a time).[44]

Applicants for the civil examinations, in the meantime, had to enter the Seonggyungwan (National Confucian Academy) after passing the preliminary examinations for the title of *saengwon* or *jinsa* and score more than 300 points (one day's attendance at school giving one point) before applying for the *gwansi* (academy examinations) or the *hyangsi* (local examinations), while officials in active service were entitled to sit for the *hanseongsi* (a kind of preliminary examination conducted at the Prefecture of Seoul). The same was applied to students of the four national colleges in Seoul and to other students who were enrolled by virtue of the meritorious service rendered by their ancestors.[45] Therefore, people who passed the civil examinations during the Joseon period included both those who had already passed the preliminary examinations for the title of *saengwon* or *jinsa* or repeaters who were preparing for the state examinations. In the early part of the period, about 80 per cent of those who passed the civil examinations were holders of the *saengwon* or *jinsa* title. This percentage gradually declined. After the reign of King Yeongjo, repeaters occupied 80 per cent among those who passed the civil examinations.[46]

44. "Ijeon," in *Gyeongguk daejeon*, *gwon* 1. *Taejong sillok*, *gwon* 3, 1st month, second year of King Taejong's reign.
45. Yi Seong-mu, "Seoncho-ui seonggyungwan yeongu" (A Study on the Seonggyung-wan in the Early Joseon Dynasty), *Yeoksa hakbo* 35 (1967): pp. 219-268.
46. Song Jun-ho, *op. cit.*, p. 37.

The *Gwageo* System and the School System

Schools were educational institutes training competent personnel, and the *gwageo* system was designed to select competent personnel who had been trained at schools, through examinations for the purpose of recruiting officials. Even though the two did not necessarily correspond to each other, they were closely interrelated. In many cases, examinations given at schools were aimed more at preparing their students for the state examinations. This was more so in the case of public schools. The two examinations were so closely interrelated that Wang Anshi of the middle period of the Northern Song proposed a reform plan which was designed to assign schools the double mission of training and selecting competent personnel by reinforcing the school system.[47] If this reform plan had been implemented, graduation examinations at schools would have become the state examinations.

However, it is not always proper to consider the training of competent persons and selection of government officials on the same basis. Besides educating candidates for officialdom, schools served the important purpose of cultivating characters. The state examinations laid more emphasis on the quality and ability of examinees as officials rather than on their characters. Although the two seemed to correspond to each other, there existed a strict distinction between the two. Whereas it was desirable for schools to educate as many students as the national budget permitted, the state examinations had to limit the number of successful applicants because of the restricted number of government positions available. Therefore, it was most desirable to select competent officials after schools produced a large number of able persons.

As public schools were operated wholly at state expenses, the number of students had to be limited. Those students who were excluded from government scholarships had to be entrusted to private schools for their education. Private schools were therefore promoted despite the existence of public schools. Furthermore, because the operation of public schools required a large expense, the government was unwilling to provide them with continuous financial support. Government schools were promoted only immediately after the founding of a dynasty or when the royal authority had been strengthened at whatever cost. When the *yangban*

---

47. Miyazaki Ichisada, *Kakyo: Chugoku no shiken jigoku* (The Civil Service Examinations of Imperial China) (Tokyo: Chuo Koronsha, 1963), p. 4.

bureaucrats assumed power, private schools developed as personal educational mediums to prepare their own sons and kinsmen for state examinations. In other words, public schools were dominant when royal power was strengthened and new bureaucrats advanced to the political world, and private schools flourished and the state examinations suffered irregularities when the *yangban* aristocrats became influential.[48]

There are concrete examples of the relationship between the school system and the *gwageo* system in Korean history. In 788, about 180 years after the establishment of the National Confucian College, Silla enforced the "three-gradation reading examination." However, the system failed to provide good results due to the restraints imposed by the bone-rank system and the development of the *bin-gong gwa* (a civil service examination for foreigners). While the National Confucian College in the capital was in poor condition, autonomous educational institutes operated by local gentry thrived,[49] later becoming the basis for which the Goryeo dynasty, during the reign of King Gwangjong, could enforce its *gwageo* system.[50] King Seongjong, too, made an effort to promote school education with the view of enforcing the *gwageo* system. The Twelve Private Schools operated by the nobility were established after the reign of King Gwangjong; and seven special courses were initiated in the National Academy during the reign of King Yejong, thus establishing the social and cultural foundation for the enforcement of the *gwageo* system.

In the early part of the Goryeo period, however, school examinations as a preparatory step toward the state examinations did not develop sufficiently. As a result, National Academy students in the capital and persons who were recommended by local offices as holders of the title of *jinsa* were entitled to apply for the main state examinations. As the centralized ruling system gradually prescribed more conditions and as competition at the *gwageo* became keener, various preliminary examinations were administered before the main state examinations. They included the *dongdanggamsi* examination enforced in 1024 and the *gukjagamsi* examination in 1147.[51] The *gukjagamsi*, an entrance examination to the

---

48. The early Goryeo period, the reign of King Gongmin, and the early Joseon period belong to the former and most of the other periods to the latter.
49. Kim Gwang-su, "Ramal yeocho-ui jibang hakgyo munje" (Local Schools of Late Silla and Early Goreyo Period), *Hanguksa yeongu* 7.1 (1972): p. 130.
50. *Goryeosa, gwon* 74.
51. *Goryeosa, gwon* 73.

National University, known also as the *seonggyungwansi* or *namseongsi*, corresponded to the *jinsasi* examination of the Joseon dynasty. Under Mongol rule, the *gukjagamsi* examination was replaced with the *gujae-saksi* examination given by the Twelve Private Schools (in 1327 or the fourth year of King Chungsuk's reign) or by the *geojasi* examination (1320).[52] The *seungbosi* was an examination that students of the National University, colleges, and four groups of private schools were required to pass if they were to be promoted to the Seven Special Courses of the National University. The *seungbosi* examination used the Confucian classics as its curricula, and for this reason, the compilers of *Goryeosa* (History of Goryeo) considered it to be similar to the *saengwonsi* examination of the Joseon dynasty. Those who passed the *gukjagamsi* and *seungbosi* examinations were admitted to the National University, where they studied for 300 days during next three years. After that, they were required to pass the main examination together with persons from local areas who had passed the *dongdanggamsi* examination and a re-examination given at the National University before applying for the second-stage examination. The second-stage examination was not held regularly, and was discontinued after 1120 (15th year of King Yejong's reign).[53]

Military examinations were not given during the Goryeo period.[54] Education in Confucianism and miscellaneous knowledge was provided through the National University. Those that completed their prescribed courses were authorized to take an examination in their respective departments at the Dongdanggam. After the reign of King Injong, a direct application system was initiated for National University students, enabling them to sit for the middle or final round of the main examination depending on their academic achievements and their conduct.[55] The relationship between these schools and the *gwageo* examination is illustrated briefly in the figure below.

---

52. *Ibid.*
53. It was in 983 (second year of King Seongjong's reign) that the *boksi* examination was first enforced. The *Goryeosa* notes that the *boksi* was last held in 1120 (15th year of King Yejong's reign).
54. Martial arts education was provided and the military examinations were given for 24 years from 1109 (fourth year of King Yejong's reign) until the Seven Special Courses was established at the National University in 1133 (11th year of King Injong's reign).
55. *Goryeosa, gwon* 74.

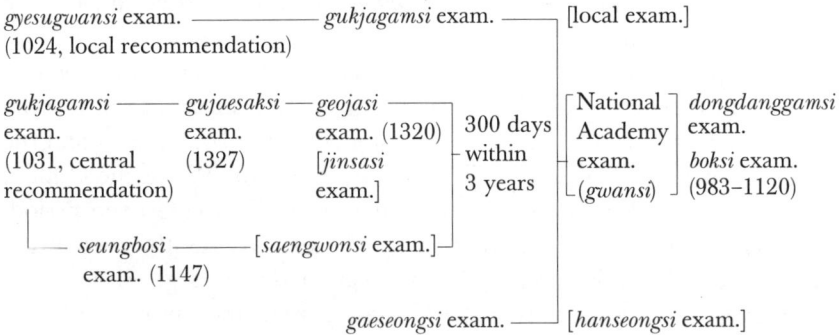

Figure 1. Relationship between Schools and the *Gwageo* Examination

With the enforcement of the "three-stage state examination system" in 1369, the second-stage examination was replaced by the so-called "palace examination" or *jeonsi* (the final examination of civil examinations, taken in the presence of the King); the main examination by the *hoesi* (the second-stage examination); and the first-stage examination by other preliminary examinations such as *hyangsi, gyesugwansi, gwansi,* and *gaeseongsi.*

Differences between the *gwageo* systems of Goryeo and Joseon can be summarized as follows. (1) Examinations for the title of *saengwon* or *jinsa* were conducted separately from rural schools and capital colleges. (2) More weight was placed on the position of the civil examinations. As competition at the examination intensified, the examinations for the title of *saengwon* or *jinsa* were divided into the *hyangsi* and *boksi* examinations, in which the examinees were first tested in *Xiaoxue* and *Zhuzi jiali.* (3) During the Goryeo period, education was provided at the National University in the department, while the examinations in martial arts and miscellaneous knowledge were given in separate departments at the Dongdanggam. During the Joseon period, martial arts education was discontinued, while the literary department (Confucianism) was taught at the Seonggyungwan and miscellaneous knowledge at respective government agencies. In the state examinations, the civil examinations were handled by the Ministry of Rites (Yejo); the military examinations by the Ministry of Military Affairs (Byeongjo); and the miscellaneous examinations by respective government agencies. (4) Whereas the *dongdanggam-*

si (the main examination) and the *gonggeoje* were in effect during the Goryeo period, the "three-stage examination system" and the *gosigwanje* were adopted in the Joseon period. (5) Whereas the main emphasis was placed on letters and the Five Classics of Confucianism in the Goryeo state examinations, the emphasis was shifted to the Four Books and the Classics of Confucianism in the Joseon period. (6) While the *hyangsi* was administered with the county as its unit during the Goryeo period, the examinations were conducted with the province as the unit in the Joseon period. (7) Whereas the state examination was given generally once every two years during the Goryeo period, they were conducted with the province as the unit in the Joseon period (excepting occasional

Table 1. The Gwageo *System in Joseon Dynasty*

Curricula			chosi	hoesi	jeonsi
Civil (*mun-gwa*)	Preliminary	*saengwonsi* exam.	local exam. (500) — hanseongsi exam. (200) —] (700)	*saengwonsi* (100)	
		jinsasi exam.	local exam. (500) — hanseongsi exam. (200) —] (700)	*jinsasi* (100)	
	main (*daegwa*)		*Seonggun-gwansi* { (sangjaesaengsi) / saengwonsi / jinsasi / seungbosaengsi / (hajaesaengsi) } score 300 [local exam. (150) / academy exam. (50) / hanseongsi exam. (40)	success (33)	success (33)
	Military (*mugwa*)		local exam. (120) — hullyeonwonsi exam. (70) —] (190)	success (28)	success (28)
Miscellaneous (*japgwa*)	Translation	Chinese	local exam. (22) — sayeogwonsi exam. (23) —] (45)	(13)	
		Mongolian	*sayeogwonsi* exam. (4)	(2)	
		Japanese	*sayeogwonsi* exam. (4)	(2)	
		Manchurian	*sayeogwonsi* exam. (4)	(2)	
	Medical		*jeonuigamsi* exam. (18)	(9)	
	Cosmology	Astronomy	*gwansanggamsi* exam. (10)	(5)	
		Geography	*gwansanggamsi* exam. (4)	(2)	
		Divination	*gwansanggamsi* exam. (4)	(2)	
	Law		*hyeongjosi* exam. (18)	(9)	

examinations). (8) Applicants for the departments of thesis writing and versification, scriptural studies and miscellaneous knowledge were not clearly distinguished during the Goryeo period, but in the Joseon dynasty, members of the *yangban* class mainly applied for the civil and military examinations while specialists applied to miscellaneous examinations. This was closely related to the polarization of the ruling estates which took place in the early part of the Joseon period.

Conclusion

I will conclude this paper by talking about characteristics of Korea's *Gwageo* System.

First, Korea's *gwageo* system was closely tied to its social classes. Although all people, excluding illegitimate sons and local clerks were, legally speaking, entitled to apply for the state examination, mostly men from the *yangban* class applied for the civil and military examinations while the *jungin* class applied for miscellaneous examinations.

Second, Korea's *gwageo* system was not directly connected to the school system. School examinations did not necessarily provide an adequate level of preparation for the *gwageo*. School education required a large expense, and the government relied heavily on the less expensive *gwageo* system in selecting officials. For example, the preliminary examinations for the title of *saengwon* or *jinsa* were separated from local schools and colleges in the capital, and repeaters were permitted to sit for the state examination.

Third, civil examinations were held in such esteem that they came to be considered equivalent almost to the *gwageo* itself. This was a result of the influence of the principle of civil rule upheld during the Goryeo and Joseon periods.

Fourth, Korea's *gwageo* system was significant on two accounts: to select freshman-officials and to promote officials in service in ranks and positions. The former were valued more highly during the Goryeo period with a view of incorporating as many local clerks as possible into the group of central government officials. In the Joseon dynasty the latter were valued more for the purpose of accelerating the promotion of officials who were already bound by complicated rules of promotion.

Fifth, Korea's *gwageo* system restricted promotion. The civil examinations could be applied for by officials whose ranks were below the senior third, and the preliminary examinations for the title of *saengwon* or *jinsa* could be applied for those whose ranks were below the senior fifth. While civil officials could rise to the first grade senior, specialists could not advance higher than the third grade senior.

Finally, the civil and military examinations were given frequently as a means of soothing complaints from the *yangban* class. As a result, the number of occasional examinations was far larger than that of the regular examinations (officially scheduled examinations). The civil examinations selected thousands of successful candidates at a time.

Confucian Politics and the *Sallim* Scholars during the Joseon Dynasty

Lee Woo Sung

Introduction

According to the old saying, "One queen is unrivalled by ten prime ministers, but one *sallim* outdoes ten queens." This saying subtly illustrates how much the ruling class of the late Joseon dynasty needed *sallim* scholars in order to maintain their power.

That one queen was unrivalled by ten prime ministers alludes to the fact that in the late Joseon dynasty, the ruling class was dominated by a queen's relatives. Those members of the ruling class related to the queen exercised political influence to the extent that they could dismiss a prime minister from office and exile him at will when they were so inclined. This means that the power of a prime minister was virtually nil in comparison with the queen's.

The saying also notes that a *sallim* is more important than ten queens. It is an exaggeration, to be sure, but we cannot ignore the pointed meaning contained in this phrase. It alludes to the fact that the role of a *sallim* was indispensable at a certain time during the late Joseon dynasty. The *sallim* was actually in a position to settle various issues outside the queen's authority. They were competent in solving controversial government issues with their scholarly dignity and judgement. Their judge-

* Originally published in the *Korea Journal*, vol. 23, no. 4 (April 1983).

Lee Woo Sung (Yi, U-seong) is presently Professor Emeritus of Sungkyunkwan University. He is also serving as President of the Korea Research Association for Practical Learning. His publications include *Hanguk-ui yeoksasang* (Images of the Korean History) (1982), *Hanguk jungse sahoe yeongu* (A Study of Korean Medieval Society) (1991), and *Hanguk gojeon-ui balgyeon* (Rediscovery of Korean Classic Literature) (1995).

ments adhered to Confucian teachings, and their role held vital political power, especially in settling cases involving succession to the throne.

Strangely, this important role of *sallim* in the history of Joseon dynasty has seldom been dealt with by Korean historians. This is probably due to the general tendency for historians to view the history of Joseon dynasty within the framework of the history of party strife. Of course, the question of party strife cannot be overlooked in the examination of the *sallim* scholars. Nevertheless, there is room for us to consider *sallim* beyond the realm of party strife and to attempt a new analysis of *sallim* from the angle of political history. Doing so will enable us to understand the politico-social structure of the Joseon dynasty in general and the realistic situation of the late Joseon dynasty in particular. This paper will attempt to consider the importance of *sallim* and how they were associated with the political history of the late Joseon dynasty that was dominated by Confucianism as a political instrument.

The Meaning of *Sallim*

Sallim, literally meaning the mountains and forests, is the antithesis of *josi*, which means the court and city. Unlike the officials serving at the court and city offices, *sallim* lived a life of a hermit or a *cheosa* in the countryside and maintained high moral standards and a highly disciplined conduct, refusing to seek fame or power. *Josi* officials can often be corrupted, but *sallim cheosa* remained noble and disciplined, thus in general given higher regard.

Confucian ideals were aimed at achieving moral integrity, self and family discipline, and ultimately successful administration of the nation and world. The *sadaebu*, or class of scholar-officials, were devoted to studying and government service in accord with Confucian teaching.[1] In this respect, the ideals of the *sallim cheosa* were probably not derived from Confucian teaching.

The *sadaebu* of the Joseon dynasty were called *yangban*, or men of the noble class, and took part in civil or military service.

The respect for *sallim* hermits who remained in the countryside despite their remarkable scholarly caliber can be partly traced to the public disappointment over heated partisan dissension. But more impor-

---

1. "Yangbanjeon" (Tales of Yangban), in *Yeonamjip* (Collected Works of Bak Ji-won).

tantly, it was directly related to the corruption in the state examination system called *gwageo* which all government servants of higher posts had to pass. In the late Joseon dynasty, however, the *gwageo* system became extremely corrupt and was the target of public criticism. Dasan (Jeong Yak-yong, 1762–1836) wrote the following about the *gwageo* examination system:

> Today, *seonbi* or thoughtful scholars are ashamed of the *gwageo*. In the early Joseon dynasty, respected scholars applied for the examination and Jo Jeong-am and Yi Toe-gye were among them. Since the reign of King Injo, however, no men of self-respect have considered taking the examinations.[2]

Maecheon (Hwang Hyeon, 1955–1910) made a similar remark:

> Entering the late period of Joseon dynasty, government practices became disorderly to the extent that the *gwageo* examination hall was like a marketplace. Many people derided the situation. This is why men of pride refused to apply for the examinations.[3]

An increasing number of proud *seonbi* denounced the *gwageo* system. This brought about changes in the political system of the period. In this connection, Dasan points out that "Those who remained in the *sallim* circles alone were revered as men of learning and virtue, but those career officials who passed the *gwageo* examination could no longer take pride in their status as Confucian scholars."[4] This social trend was certainly unprecedented in the Joseon society. The term "Confucianist" equipped with the Confucian learning and virtue became applicable to the *sallim* scholars who had nothing to do with *gwageo*. The *sallim* scholars were respected above those officials who won *gwageo* degrees.

It is important to remember, however, that the *sallim* scholars did not necessarily denounce politics, though they did denounce the *gwageo* exams. If they had remained as hermits throughout their lives, without having participated in politics, their role would have been of little histori-

---

2. *Jeungbo yeoyudang jeonseo* (Collected Works of Jeong Yak-yong, expanded edition), *gwon* 5 (Seoul: Gyeongin Munhwasa, 1971), pp. 288-289.

3. *Maecheon yarok* (Personal Account of Hwang Hyeon), *gwon* 1 (Gwacheon: National Institute of Korean History), p. 35.

4. *Jeungbo yeoyudang jeonseo*, *gwon* 5, pp. 288-289.

cal importance. There were two reasons why they could not belittle politics. In the first place, it was natural for a Confucian state to appeal to the services of great Confucianists, so the government had to treat them well in whatever form. Secondly, although they lived in mountain retreats, they had the Confucian moral obligation to not betray their country and could not completely detach themselves from the fate of their nation.

Thus the *sallim* participated in politics, without abandoning their *sallim* status. They must remain physically in *sallim* or countryside or at least stay faithful to "the spirit of *sallim*" even if they had to leave the countryside to take part in political affairs. For if they chose to leave their hermitages and became career officials, they would lose their qualification as Confucianists.

At first, the Confucianists who cultivated themselves in the countryside, aloof from the secular city life, were generally called *sallim hakja* (scholars in hermitage) or *sallim yangdeok jisa* (gentlemen accumulating virtue in the mountains and forests). The title was shortened to *sallim*. Later, only those who received various special privileges as they responded to the call of the government were called *sallim*. Then the term *sallim* was no longer applicable to ordinary scholars in the countryside. Just as *sadaebu* or Confucian scholars who became career officials through the *gwageo* system could no longer be regarded as true Confucianists, those ordinary country scholars could not become *sallim* because they had not been called upon by the government. This defined a paradox.

Political Importance of *Sallim*

Maecheon traced the beginning of the *sallim*'s participation in politics to Jeong In-hong (1535–1623)

> When Yi I-cheom came to power during the reign of King Gwanghae, he made Jeong In-hong a prime minister and made full use of him as a political instrument for his own power on the pretext that Jeong In-hong was a Confucian sage. Following his suit, subsequent strongmen chose a scholar in hermitage and made him a puppet leader. Every man in power invariably used a *sallim* to exploit his own fortune.[5]

---

5. *Maecheon yarok, gwon* 1, p. 12.

After the reign of King Gwanghae, however, with the downfall of the Northerners (Bugin), Jeong In-hong was dismissed from office and exiled. This brought disgrace to him, and he was never again able to restore his honorable status of *sallim*. The *sallim* rose to power after the reform in 1623. Yeongjae (Yi Geon-chang, 1852–1898) explains the new situation:

> After the Injo Reform, the reformists who dethroned an incompetent king secretly agreed among themselves to continue their relations with the court by marriage and to put *sallim* into important government positions.[6]

This shows that the reformists, the vassals of the Westerners (Seoin), tried to keep both the queen and *sallim* by their sides for political purposes. By maintaining kinship with the king through marriage, they could enjoy power with the support of the queen. At the same time, they needed political support from *sallim* to secure their political stability. Yeongjae further wrote: "When Song Si-yeol rose to fame as a virtuous Confucian scholar, such vassals as Kim Ja-jeom, Won Du-pyo and Yi Hu-won competed amongst themselves to recommend him to the king to the position of their party leader." The leader was sometimes called *gamju*. Choe Myeong-gil (1586–1647) explained the role of *gamju* in his letter of appeal to the king:

> Since the beginning of partisan strife, the government structure was based on Jeonjo (Office of Personnel Administration) and three offices dealing with political affairs—Hongmungwan, Saheonbu and Saganwon. The *gamju* was selected from among competent officials of these government branches. He alone decided on personnel affairs and political controversies within the count.[7]

The three vassals all attempted to entrust such an important position to Song Si-yeol since he was a reputed Confucian scholar of the *sallim* school. This illustrates well the political weight of the *sallim* during the late Joseon dynasty.

---

6. *Tangui tongnyak* (History of Factional Strife during the Joseon Dynasty) (Joseon Guangmunhoe).

7. *Ibid.*

Rise of the *Sallim* and the New Government System

The government created new posts in order to provide *sallim* scholars with privileged treatment. The first to be installed was a post called *sa-eop* in Seonggyungwan (National Confucian Academy). The *Jeungbo munheon bigo* (Reference Compilation of Documents) states:

> Such scholars as Kim Jang-saeng, Jang Hyeon-gwang and Bak Ji-gye were brought to Seoul by government horses and were given privileged official treatments during the first year under the reign of King Injo. One was appointed to the post of *sa-eop* at Seonggyun-gwan, the other to a post in Saheonbu, or to a teaching post responsible for the education of the crown prince. Kim Jip, Song Si-yeol and Song Jun-gil were also recommended to such posts.[8]

The Editor of the *Injo Sillok* (The Annals of King Injo) made a note on the importance of this new system: "Confucianism was more respected after the reform, and an unprecedented new post of *sa-eop* was installed in Seonggyungwan. Kim Jang-saeng was appointed to this new post and made responsible for training Confucian students."[9]

At the suggestion of Kim Sang-heon, a deputy prime minister, during the 24th year under the reign of King Injo, new official posts were created in Seja Sigangwon (institute for the education of the crown prince), namely, *chanseon*, *jinseon*, and *ja-ui*. The new posts were installed for the *sallim* scholars with no *gwageo* degrees. Two years later, one *sallim* scholar after another were appointed to these posts:[10]

> Kim Jip was appointed to *chanseon*, Song Si-yeol to *jinseon*, and Kwon Si to *ja-ui*. Song Si-yeol and Kwon Si were especially reputed as Confucian scholars, though they held no official positions. Government horses were made available to all three. This was exceptional perk given to *sallim* scholars because there were few horses left after the Qing invasion of 1636.[11]

---

8. *Jeungbo munheon bigo* (Reference Compilation of Documents), *gwon* 199 (Gojeon Ganhaenghoe), p. 313.
9. *Joseon wangjo sillok* (Annals of Joseon Dynasty), *gwon* 34, p. 524.
10. *Jeungbo munheon bigo*, *gwon* 225, p. 621.
11. *Joseon wangjo sillok*, *gwon* 35, p. 337.

Im Dam was once appointed to a cabinet minister, but under pressure he had to concede the office to Kim Jip. The rise of *sallim* became active as Kim Jip took over the post. *Sallim* scholars were given one high government post after the other. They included Song Jun-gil, Song Si-yeol, Yun Seon-geo, and Yi Yu-tae among the Westerners, and Kwon Si, Heo Mok, and Yun Hyu among the Southerners.[12]

The rise of *sallim* scholars invited the resentment of career officials, such as Sin Myeon and his group. Sin Myeon was from a reputed family and Song Si-yeol had informed him of his desire to serve in the government. Sin Myeon wondered what *sanin* (mountain people) would do for the government. Song Si-yeol's side declared: "We pledge to revenge ourselves on Qing for our disgrace at Namhansanseong fortress and the death of Kang Bin (the wife of crown prince Sohyeon)." In response, Sin Myeon's side wrote:

> You are like the phoenix. You will be loved by people for the sound alone and are welcome to make your occasional flight in the secular world. But you would be derided by women and Confucianists alike if you stayed in this world and made noise like some domestic fowls.[13]

This remark angered the *sallim*.

Thus the *sallim* group itself came to be regarded as a political faction. It was labeled as *sandang* (mountain party) or *handang* (*han* party). Yeongjae wrote of this:

> The *sandang* was headed by Kim Jip and supported by Song Si-yeol and Song Jun-gil. They were all from the mountainous region of Yeonsan and Hoedeok. Meanwhile, the *handang* was led by Kim Yuk and Sin Myeon both from Seoul.[14]

Sin Myeon and his friends were aristocratic bureaucrats residing in Seoul, hence the name *handang*, and Song Si-yeol and his group came from the countryside of Hoedeok and Yeonsan, hence the name *sandang*.

Sandang and *handang* were antagonistic toward each other for some time. When Sin Myeon was accused of having collaborated with Qing

---

12. *Ibid.*, the chapter dealing with the year of Eulsa.
13. *Tangui tongnyak* , p. 18.
14. *Ibid.*

and flogged to death, people thought this was a result of the animosity held against him by the *sandang* faction.[15] But both factions belonged to the Westerners, and they allied with each other when threatened by the Southerners. In the long run, *handang* had to compromise with the powerful *sallim* group, and gradually the *sandang* and *handang* factions disappeared. This made the political influence of *sallim* group even stronger.

The need for more new government posts arose with the promotion of the *sallim*'s political status. The official post of *jeju* was created in Seonggyungwan during the ninth year of the reign of King Hyojong. While *sa-eop*, established in Seonggyungwan before, ranked fourth in the government hierarchy the newly installed *jeju* ranked third. *Jeju* was the highest post given to the *sallim* group and became a synonym for *sallim*. The head of Seonggyungwan was *daesaseong*, which held the same rank as *jeju*. But *jeju* exercised a stronger political and social influence than *daesaseong*, who came up via the *gwageo* examination. The honorable post of *chanseon* at Sigangwon held by *sallim* also ranked third, but *jeju* was considered to be the more honorable government position to offer to a *sallim* scholar. The position was held first by Song Jun-gil and next by Song Si-yeol. *Jeju* was a special post and not restricted by ranks. Even the prime minister, who ranked first in the government, was allowed to serve concurrently as a *jeju*. During the year in which King Hyeonjong was enthroned, there was a debate as to whether Song Si-yeol should remain as *jeju* while serving at a lower rank. But he was allowed to remain at the post of *jeju* by consensus.

Jeju was used to be called "*joeju*" to suggest that it has a special function and was like a pronoun of the powerful *sallim* school. Its honor, power, and prestige increased with time. A man who had once served as *jeju* was called *jeju* even when he was promoted to higher position.

Changes in the Character of *Sallim*

The prestige of the *sallim* was at its height between 1650–1720 during the reigns of King Hyojong, King Hyeonjong and King Sukjong. At the same time, this period witnessed the most serious factional strife. During the second year of the reign of King Sukjong, Yeong-pyeong-jeong, a relative of the king, tearfully read the following before the king. "The fac-

---

15. *Ibid.*

tional dissension started from Song Jun-gil and Song Si-yeol, and then from Heo Mok and Yun Hyu. This has come to threaten the fate of the nation."[16]

The four mentioned above were all members of the *sallim* group. But Song Jun-gil and Song Si-yeol were politically the Westerners, while Heo Mok and Yun Hyu were the Southerners. They were all leaders of their political factions. On the surface, their antagonism was a simple dissension among the *sallim* group. But their strife was rooted in political antagonism. The most controversial issue concerned the official memorial costume of the queen mother of a deceased king. It concerned ceremonial affairs, but it came from the difference in the political stand of the two groups. An understanding of the dissension requires a complex explanations and will not be discussed here.

The Southerners, led by Heo Mok and Yun Hyu, temporarily succeeded in taking power by winning the ceremonial issue, but could not overcome the persistent counterattack of the Westerners. As we have already seen, the Westerners maintained kinship with the king and solidified its traditional power with support from the queen. They occasionally retreated from the forefront, but they easily restored their power. But the Southerners collapsed at the time of the Gapsul Hwan-guk Incident of 1694. From this time onward, the *sallim* group was dominated by the Westerners.

During the reigns of Hyojong, Hyeonjong and Sukjong, the principal figure in the *sallim* group was no doubt Song Si-yeol. He was revered widely as a *daero* (the great authority). He became a victim of factional strife when he was 80 and lost power, but many of his disciples dominated both political and academic circles and his fame grew even greater after his death.

Having risen to power, the Westerners were divided into the Old Doctrine (Noron) and Young Doctrine (Soron) factions. The Old Doctrine faction was the mainstream of the Westerners that had high regards for Song Si-Yeol. The followers of Song Si-yeol naturally dominated the *sallim* group.

Unlike Song Si-yeol, however, his followers did not take part in politics. Times changed and with the rise of the Old Doctrine faction the role of *sallim* also suffered alterations. The following record explains the new situation:

16. *Hansagye, gwon* 4, p. 6.

The king offered a position of *u-uijeong* (a deputy prime minister) to Kwon Sang-ha (1641–1721) because Kwon was respected as the most distinguished disciple of Song Si-yeol. Time and again, Kwon refused every high office offered to him. The king was even more impressed and offered him the office of the prime minister. Kwon refused again. Thereafter, the *sallim* scholars did not enter the government even when they were offered high posts.[17]

Even though the *sallim* scholars avoided a call by the throne to high official positions, they did not lose their authority. In 1728 (fourth year of King Yeongjo's reign), Yi Se-jin of Saganwon proposed to King Yeongjo that two high officials of the *sallim* group, Bak Pil-ju and Yang Deuk-jung be relieved of their positions on the grounds that they had no intention of appearing at a national mourning ceremony. Thereupon, the King reprimanded Yi Se-jin for having belittled respectable Confucian scholars. The King emphasized: "Treating *sallim* scholars with respect has been our royal tradition. Our national fate depends on the Confucian learning."[18]

King Yeongjo's remark points to the fact that he did not expect policy planning from the *sallim* scholars, but rather the *sallim* scholars should be treated with respect as symbolic figures, and in that context he treated them with full courtesy.

Jeongjo, the succeeding king, was a distinguished ruler like his predecessor, King Yeongjo. The two kings were remarkable administrators, and thus factional strife gradually declined during their reign. The *sallim* scholars' prestige in this period was not as great as it had been in the period of Song Si-yeol, but they did enjoy the king's high respect. The status of the *sallim* scholars began to wane as the King's maternal relatives gained power, following King Sunjo's reign. No longer were they accorded with equal respect, as they had been before. Dasan wrote about the situation of this period:

> A man of high scholarly achievement and moral standard should have been selected from among *sallim* scholars through a regular channel and promoted to a higher position and even to a post of prime minister if qualified. This was not the case at the time. Only a few were selected and called Confucian sage or *sallim* and were treated as *binsa* (honor-

17. *Ibid.*, p. 14-15.
18. *Joseon wangjo sillok, gwon* 42, p. 97.

able master) and thereby assigned to a post responsible for Confucian worship. They showed humility at the beginning but later became arrogant as a *binsa* and were ridiculed by everyone. Finally, they were unable to maintain their honor when they were found to be unqualified.[19]

Discussing Neo-Confucian doctrine (Seongnihak) in his *Ohak ron* (The Theory of Five Sciences), Dasan wrote of *sallim*.

In the old days, a man devoted to learning was defined as a *sa*, implying a man who serves. Today, those who study Neo-Confucian doctrine consider themselves *eun*, a term that can be interpreted as hermits. Even those who had been reared in Seoul were called *sallim* if they studied Neo-Confucian doctrine and refused to serve in the government. They were only made to lecture on the Confucian classics or to take part in the education of the crown prince. When the government tried to assign them to the posts dealing with finance, defense, law or diplomatic posts, many people objected to the idea insisting that such treatment could hardly be adequate to "respectable Confucian scholars." Then where could the king use them? *Sallim* scholars would say, "I follow the teachings of Zhuzi. Was the teaching of Zhuzi ever like this?[20]

Dasan criticized the symbolic gesture of the government that ridiculed *sallim* scholars, and at the same time criticized the *sallim* scholars for their attitude towards the nation and society that had become unrealistic and useless.

As Dasan stated, a few Confucian scholars were selected from among *sallim* scholars as symbolic leaders. Scholars of the *sallim* group had the title *sallim* attached to their surnames, namely, Kim *sallim* or Song *sallim*.

Many of the *sallim* scholars were the descendants of Song Jun-gil and Song Si-yeol. Maecheon commented:

Sallim scholars in the recent years were represented by the Noron group, and members of Song family from Eunjin alone dominated the *sallim* group generation after generation. The Song family from Eunjin was comparable to the Jang family from Lungu Mountain, who domi-

19. *Jeungbo yeoyudang jeonseo, gwon* 5, p. 50.
20. *Jeong Dasan jeonseo* (Complete Works of Jeong Yak-yong), *gwon* 1, p. 227.

nated the Taoist group.[21]

In order to maintain their status, the *sallim* scholars had to compromise with the people in power. Maecheon gave examples:

> *Sallim* scholars were invariably associated closely with people in power. When they had to deal with national protocol affairs, they had to consult people in power and followed their opinions. Song Deok-sang was regarded as a member of Hong Guk-yeong's *sadang* (blood pledge party), Hong Jik-pil as a henchman of Kim Byeong gi and Im Heon-hoe as a confidant of Min Gyu-ho.[22]

Song Deok-sang, Hong Jik-pil and Im Heon-hoe were renowned Confucian scholars of the *sallim* group around the end of the Joseon dynasty. Song Deok-sang ended his life unhappily with the downfall of Hong Guk-yeong. But Hong Jik-pil and Im Heon-hoe were able to survive as *sallim* by the power of their respective protectors, the Kim family from Andong and the Min family from Yeoheung. Hong Jik-pil played an important role in the prince's succession to the throne. When King Heonjong died and about to be succeeded by King Cheoljong in 1849, the Kim family from Andong planned to have Cheoljong succeed King Sunjo in lineage instead of King Heonjong for fear that the Jo family from Pungyang, who were Heonjong's maternal relatives, might rise to power. In this regards, Kim Taek-yeong worte:

> At the time of Cheoljong's rise to the throne, Kim Hong-geun insisted to Queen Sunwon (Queen of King Sunjo from the Kim family): "The new king is an uncle of Heonjong and should therefore succeed Sunjo, in respect to the order in royal lineage." Hong Jik-pil supported Kim Hong-geun's idea to please him. Kwon Don-in, then the prime minister, objected to Kim Hong-geun's contention, saying: "The succession to the throne is unlike private family matters and has little to do with seniority in blood relations and therefore Cheoljong should succeed Heonjong." But Kwon Don-in was exiled to Bukcheong for having disagreed with Kim's opinion. Kim Jeong-hui was also exiled to Bukcheong on the pretext that Kwon's idea came from Kim Jeong-hui."[23]

---

21. Hwang Hyeon, *Ohakimun* 1, p. 2.
22. *Ibid.*
23. *Hansagye, gwon.* 5, p. 18.

Hong Jik-pil displayed his scholarly authority in such important matters of royal lineage, and had a hand in the exile of the prime minister. By this time, the *sallim* had degenerated into a political tool for the people in power. But the *sallim* scholars had their own complaints. Hong Jik-pil (1776–1852), called Hong *sallim* during the reign of Cheoljong (1850–1863), spoke wistfully of the *sallilm's* degenerated status: "When the dynasty was prosperous, important government affairs were dealt with by *sallim*. The fate of the nation was dependent on *sallim*."[24] He has tormented on the fact that he had no free will to speak, so he decided it was best not to speak at all. This can be seen in the record of his words, written later by Im Heon-hoe (1811–1876), one of his disciples who succeeded him as a *sallim* scholar:

> If a scholar were to survive in troubled world, he should not be involved in a debate that might endanger him. A man should read widely, discipline himself and his family, cultivate a farm, please his parents and worship his ancestors. There is little else to say about the conduct of a learned man.[25]

One can understand his feelings when one reads a few lines of his memoir. One can also understand that both Hong *sallim*, who were closely associated with the powerful Kim family from Andong and Im *sallim*, who were likewise associated with the Min family from Yeoheung, were in no position to refuse to speak up and act in favor of their protectors.

---

24. *Maesan jip* (Collected Works of Hong Jik-oil), *gwon* 52, p. 50.
25. *Gosan jip* (Collected Works of Im Heon-hoe), *gwon* 19, pp. 17-28, *Jamnok Maesan eorok.*

Perceptions of Nature in the Joseon Period

Yang Bo Kyung

Introduction

Since ancient times, people have used their own perception and structuralization to understand their surrounding environment, thereby establishing their worldview. Such views of nature or views of the world as an underlying philosophy influenced human history, science and technological development, and our way of life. As societies changed, views of the world also changed. However, underlying such changes is an archetypal ideological structure that has provided the basis for those changes.

Systematic research on how nature or the environment has been viewed in Korea is limited, and this lack has been a major obstacle to the understanding of our traditional culture, society, and history. This is mainly due to the discontinuation of our "traditional geography," a field of study that once organized and systematized our traditional views of nature. In modern times, people tend to equate "traditional geography" with *pungsu*, a traditional geomancy, and still think that our traditional beliefs about geography and topology are the same as *pungsu*. As one of the basic geographical theories held by our ancestors, *pungsu* once clearly reflected their deepest beliefs about nature. Because it played such a

* Originally published in the *Korea Journal*, vol. 37, no. 4 (winter 1997).

Yang Bo Kyung (Yang, Bo-gyeong) is Assistant Professor of Geography at Sungshin Women's University. She received her Ph.D. in Geography from Seoul National University in 1987. She published a number of articles on history of Korean cartography and Korean traditional geography, and also co-authored many books such as *Seoul-ui gyeonggwan byeonhwa* (Changing Landscape of Seoul) (1994), *Hanguk-ui munhwa yusan* (Cultural Heritage of Korea) (1997), and *Maps of Korea: Past, Present and Future* (2000). E-mail: ybk@cc.sungshin.ac.kr.

significant role in premodern society, the necessity and importance of research into *pungsu* is all the more pressing. Yet, *pungsu*, as people know it today, is greatly misunderstood since many believe "traditional geography" to be identical to *pungsu*, a belief that eliminates any chance for the revitalization of "traditional geography" and its limitless potential.

Expressions of Korea's traditional geography can be divided into geographical records, mapping, *pungsu*, and Silhak (Practical Learning) geography. The first three sub-categories developed throughout the Joseon Period and existed in a complementary relationship, thereby creating a solid mainstream field of "traditional geography." "Shilhak geography" was a new branch of "traditional geography" that flourished after the seventeenth century, during the latter part of Joseon dynasty. Quantitatively, "Shilhak geography" is less known than the other three fields of geography; but qualitatively, its active and leading presentation of the changes in our society and locality, as well as the development of geography as a science, were enough to signal a major shift in the status quo of mainstream geography.

This paper was written to explore the manner in which the people of the Joseon dynasty understood their country and its surrounding environment. Today, our understanding of land and surrounding environment is completely different from the way our ancestors understood it, and this difference signals that somewhere there was a discontinuation from an earlier, traditional view; the present view is not a development or outgrowth from it, as one might expect. On the other hand, people currently studying our traditional geography mistakenly think it was based only and primarily on *pungsu*. This narrow view of geographical history prevents them from gaining a more complete understanding of the land as it was dealt with in "traditional geography." In this paper, I would like to comprehensively review the kind of perception of this land and its features held by the people of the Joseon Period through geographical records, maps, and Silhak geographical works. The way a people view its land and their relationship to it are widely reflected in geography and mapping, but these are especially detailed in the Silhak geography, a structurally better presented source. This paper discusses the results of research into this Silhak geography.

Overview of Perceptions of Nature

Following the establishment of the Joseon dynasty, the nation's capital was moved from Gaeseong to Hanyang. During King Taejong's reign, the areas for the government's administrative districts were streamlined, while from King Taejo's reign through King Sejong's reign, new settlements were established in the reclaimed land around the Amnokgang and Dumangang rivers. As the restructuring and streamlining of local government structures progressed in the new dynasty, the government required accurate information regarding the population and products from all regions. For this reason, the publication of maps and geographical material began flourishing since the early days of the new dynasty. As we know well, the reigns of Kings Sejong and Sejo witnessed great developments in science and map production skills, which resulted in more detailed discovery and recording of geographical information for every region of the country.

After the sixteenth century, local records were published for each regional area and a wider variety of more sophisticated information became available. During the sixteenth and seventeenth centuries, local area records were actively published by interested individuals, while in the eighteenth century, government-produced local records were widely published, establishing the mainstream of the Joseon dynasty's geographical studies. Accordingly, people were able to receive detailed information about different areas and to become aware of any regional changes. Moreover, after the eighteenth century, as local area publications began to include detailed maps of their surrounding areas (*gun/hyeon*), and as map production skills developed further, a detailed and three-dimensional view of local areas became possible.

The Japanese and Manchurian Invasions of 1592 and 1636, respectively, reawakened people to the need to learn about their surrounding environment and geography. The wars also brought an increase in migration within the nation. As a result, the nation's governmental districts were restructured. In addition, people's awareness of geography was renewed following the development of Silhak geography in the early seventeenth century, as well as following the importation of geographical awareness and knowledge of the Western world. Furthermore, as the border dispute with Qing China escalated at the end of the seventeenth century, more people became aware of geographical boundaries and land ownership. Thus, increased geographical awareness came about amid profound social and economic changes in the late Joseon period; these changes, in turn, influenced people's perceptions of the land and the national environment.

Today, there are no known complete geographical records showing the manner in which people perceived nature in the early Joseon dynasty. We can only glimpse at the overall picture by looking at extant parts of these maps and writings available today. But, on the evidence we have, we can infer that there was no structured field of geography in the early years of Joseon dynasty, as there was to be by the latter days of the period. Map 1-1 is an excerpt from the oldest world map in existence in Korea today, which is the *Honil gangni yeokdae gukto jido* (Unified Territorial and Chronological Map of National Lands). It shows the charted mountains and rivers in the Joseon area. It is considered a valuable historical heritage, as it was created in 1402 by the order of King Taejong, only ten years after the establishment of Joseon. Upon comparing this map with maps of the latter days of Joseon dynasty, one can see several distinctive differences in the portrayal of the country's mountains and rivers between the two.

First, Baekdusan mountain, greatly emphasized in maps produced after King Sejong's period, is not labeled on this map. The opinion that Baekdusan mountain is the place of Korea's origin has been long held. It was particularly popular and widespread during the Goryeo dynasty, when *pungsu* was widely accepted and people called the mountain the "root" of Korea.[1] It seems odd then that Baekdusan mountain is not marked in this map and even the routes of the Amnokgang and Dumangang rivers are unclear. Some argue that this is because the region around Baekdusan mountain and the Amnokgang and Dumangang rivers had not been part of Korea since the Unified Silla period. This reason appears somewhat plausible, but since the map's purpose here is not to designate national borders, it is inadequate. The more probable explanation for such a map would be that the general attitude regarding Baekdusan mountain changed between the early and late Joseon dynasty. If we look at the directionality of the mountain ranges, we see that the map does not depict Baekdusan as the starting point, but rather as part of a mountain range begining in the northeastern region of

---

1. *Seongho saseol* and other publications use Doseon's *Ongnyonggi* (玉龍記), written during the Unified Silla period, which states, "all the mountain ranges of our country begin at Baekdusan mountain and end at Jirisan mountain."

Hamheung, a region lying further south than Baekdusan mountain, which reaches down to the Jirisan mountain area.

More important than the existence or lack of Baekdusan mountain, is the way the map shows the mountain ranges that branch out of the major mountain range, which constitutes the backbone of the land. There are four major branches toward the west depicted on this map, considerably less than the number of branches depicted in maps in the late Joseon period. The northernmost mountain range must surely be today's Jeogyuryeong mountain range, but it appears to be disconnected in several places on this map. The second mountain range is the largest, with branches reaching toward Gaeseong, the capital of the Goryeo dynasty. The third is a smaller mountain range that stopped in Gapyeong, east of Hanyang (today's Seoul) and the fourth is the mountain range that includes today's Sobaek and Noryeong mountain ranges, reaching toward Naju, in Jeolla-do province. The most noticeable difference between this map and later ones is that this one emphasizes the mountain range reaching toward Gaeseong, but not all the way south to Hanyang, the capital of Joseon. This fact is significant in that it reflects the people's view of their environment at the time, a view still centered around Gaeseong.

In comparison, *Honil yeokdae gukto gangni jido* (Unified Chronological and Territorial Map of National Land) (map 1-2),[2] which is presumed to have been published in the mid-sixteenth century, places great emphasis on Baekdusan mountain. Its mountain range clearly reaches all the way down to Hanyang. Although even at this time, the country's border is not yet well defined, the map reveals that Baekdusan mountain and Hanyang had become focal locations of Joseon.

This dual concept of considering Baekdusan mountain as the root and Hanyang as the "center" is a belief held by the Korean people since the sixteenth century, a fact which can be documented through various maps and geographical publications. Maps 1-3 and 1-4 are taken from *Yeojido* (A National Atlas), which was published at the end of the eighteenth century, as well as from *Daedong yeoji jeondo* (A Complete Detailed Map of Korea), which was published at the end of the nineteenth century. Both maps reflect the Baekdusan mountain and Hanyang-centered society of the time and show evidence of the progressive development of map making through detailed representation and structuralization.

---

2. Yi Chan, *Hanguk-ui gojido* (Old Maps of Korea) (Seoul: Bobmu Sa, 1991), pp. 13-15.

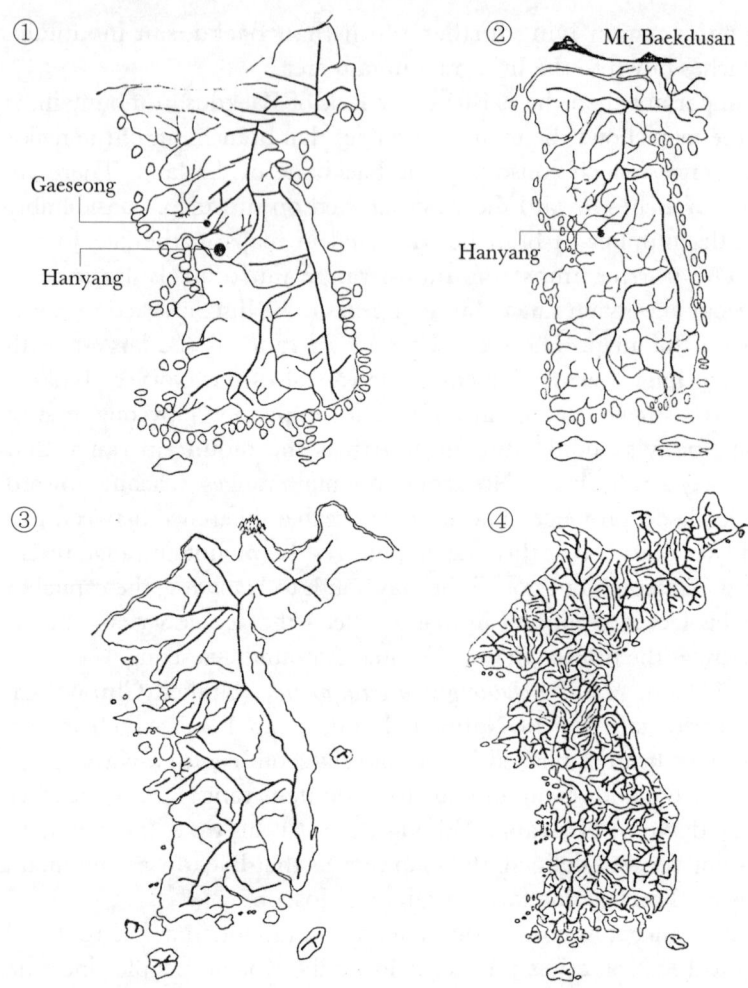

Map 1. Structure of Mountain Ranges and Rivers as Seen in the Early and Late Joseon Dynasty

Map 1-1: Joseon's mountain ranges and rivers as shown in *Honil gangni yeokdae gukto jido* (1402)

Map 1-2: Joseon's mountain ranges and rivers as shown in *Honil yeokdae gukto gangni jido* (Mid-sixteenth century)

Map 1-3: Joseon's mountain ranges and rivers as shown in *Yeojido* (End of the eighteenth century)

Map 1-4: Joseon's mountain ranges and rivers as shown in *Daedong yeoji jeondo* (End of the nineteenth century)

Koreans had held Baekdusan mountain in awe for centuries, and their awe continued throughout the Joseon dynasty. Various facts exist that lend support to the deification of Baekdusan. First of all Taejo, the first king of the Joseon dynasty, was born in the Hamgyeong-do region, at the foot of Baekdusan mountain. Also, during the seventeenth century, the Jurchen tribe, whose origin was near Baekdusan, established Qing China. The Jurchen began holding ceremonial rites at the Daeji lake (today's Cheonji) on the mountain's top, making it even more sacred. As China and Joseon began having border disputes around the mountain, its role as a holy place grew stronger. And, toward the end of the Joseon dynasty, interest in the region increased in accordance with its growing population and economic importance as a mining area.

The nation's focus on Baekdusan as dominating the country's environmental structure was probably quite natural, considering its topography. Baekdusan mountain has always been the highest and the most unapproachable, and its snow-capped peaks and mountain-top lake add to its mystique. To place Baekdusan mountain at the center of the nation in terms of geographical importance reflects a natural rather than an intellectual understanding, viewed from a popular level rather than a national one. Furthermore, the Korean people have traditionally tended to think only in terms of the tangible aspects of nature, and so, this view assumed it to be absolute and unchanging. As mentioned earlier, the Baekdusan mountain-centered view is typically represented on all Korean maps with an emphasized importance, depicted as very big and colored with white or gold. The most representative book showing this conceptualization is the *Dongguk munheon bigo* (Reference Compilation of Documents on Korea). *Taengniji* (Ecological Guide to Korea), written by Yi Jung-hwan, is also based on this concept.

Viewing one's country as having its capital at the center is a typical point of view in a traditional society. The capital where a king lived and where a kingdom originated functioned as a nation's political and cultural center. Understandably then, the capital where the sacred and the mundane coexisted was the center of our ancestors' small universe. Their belief could be seen in the directional markers which placed the capital at the center of various national and local maps, as well as many other geographical publications.[3] Sin Gyeong-jun's *Sansugo* (A Land-

---

3. Yang Bo Kyung (Yang, Bo-gyeong), "Joseon sidae eupji-ui seonggyeok-gwa jirijeok insik-e gwanhan yeongu" (Research on Characteristics of Local Records and Geo-

scape Study) is a good example of how we structure our understanding of the environment by placing the capital as the center. In comparing such a conceptualization with a Baekdusan mountain-centered notion, the capital-centered concept is based on reasoning rather than nature, defining a subjective perspective that may change if the capital were to be relocated. In addition, a capital-centered concept is directly reflective of merchandise distribution systems in transportation, political, and business systems as well as of a people's movements, giving it critical importance in a realistic world.

In addition to these two faceted concepts, other dual notions of the Korean landscape were established in the late Joseon period; one was a mountain-based concept and the other was a river-based one. The most representative book of the mountain-based concept was the *San-gyeong-pyo* (A Chart of Mountain Ranges), while the most representative of the other was the *Daedong sugyeong* (Rivers in Korea), which was written by Jeong Yak-yong, a famous Silhak scholar of the time. The mountain-based concept, an investigation into how mountain chains link and branch off from one another, focuses on the "range" of mountains stemming from Baekdusan mountain and extending down through the rest of the country. This reflected the Korean people's archetypal conception of Baekdusan mountain as the center of the territory, as well as the traditional belief that the mountain was sacred. At the same time, mountains structured regional borders and divided smaller localities. In everyday life, a mountain-based concept signified division rather than unification.

A river-based concept of the terrain centered on the rivers that flowed through the valleys and basins between the mountains. This concept was a method of understanding nature through the lives of everyday people. Such people built settlements along the rivers, and the mountains were the borders between these settlements. Therefore, this river-based concept was based on a harmonious relationship with nature rather than abject awe of it. Table 1 shows the basic characteristics of these dual faceted systems.

---

graphical Awareness during Joseon Dynasty) (Ph.D. diss., Seoul National University, 1987).

Table 1. The Structure of People's Perception of Nature
during the Joseon Dynasty

Center of Structure	Characteristics				
Mt. Baekdusan	Natural	Popular	Archetypal	Root	Absolute
Hanyang	Cultural	National	Realistic	Center	Relative
Mountain	Holy	Centered on the *gi* of the land	Ideological	Supernatural	Dividing
River	Humanistic	Centered on human life	Realistic	Harmonious	Unifying

Of the two systems, the dual faceted system of Baekdusan mountain and the Hanyang-centered structure was established first. The second system, with its foundation in the mountain and river-based concept, surfaced after the eighteenth century. Whereas the Baekdusan mountain and Hanyang-centered structure was an archetypal, ideological concept, the mountain and river-based concept reflected a realistic understanding of nature attained through life experience. Of these two, the mountain-based concept of the landscape was conceptualized first, and the river-based one followed thereafter.

Thus far, we have examined the way the general environment was conceptualized during the Joseon dynasty. Now we will review in detail the research results of geographical studies conducted during the latter days of the Joseon dynasty. First, we will discuss the structure of Joseon's mountains and rivers, while reviewing the books written on that subject.

Systematization of the Perceptions of Nature

Sin Gyeong-jun (1712–1781), one of the most outstanding geographers during the Joseon period, produced numerous works,[4] the most famous

---

4. He was noted for being a Korean linguist rather than a geographer, but his most famous books are on geography. They are *Sansugo, Ganggyeji, Sayeon-go, Dorogo, Gunhyeonji je, Chajechaek,* and *Garamgo.* He was also knowledgeable about maps and produced them.

of which were the *Sansugo* and "Yeojigo" (A National Topography), which was one volume of the *Dongguk munheon bigo*. These books were the first geographical publications to organize Korea's mountains and rivers as the backbone of our country, and discuss the people's view of nature in relation to them. In this paper, we will concentrate only on *Sansugo*, a book aimed at systematizing conceptions of nature during the late Joseon dynasty.

The *Sansugo*,[5] included in Sin Gyeong-jun's anthology *Yeoam jeonseo* (Compete Works of Yeoam Sin Gyeong-jun), begins as follows:

> What divides into thousands from one origin is a mountain; what thousands make up by unifying into one is a river. [Korea's] Mountains and rivers are arterial, the mountains originate from Baekdusan mountain and divide into twelve, which further divide into eight roads (provinces). The water in these eight roads becomes twelve rivers, which in turn combine to become the ocean. In them we clearly perceive the harmony of rise and flow and the marvels of division and unification.

In this paragraph we can see the author's motive for writing the work, as well as the wellspring from whence the "mountains and rivers" theories derive. It clearly shows that Sin Gyeong-jun saw mountains and rivers, the foundation of this nation, in terms of unification and division. He understood this concept as a part of *yin-yang*, which signify the dual-sided notions of contrast and harmony. It is very notable that Joseon's key mountains and rivers are divided into twelve. This is reflective of the people's view of nature and the universe in terms of a singular totality. In looking at the flow of nature, one year is made up of twelve months, and there is a *yin-yang* in everything in the universe. In this way, the laws of time mirror those of Korea's natural environment, which contains, as it does, twelve mountain ranges and rivers. It is also an environment in which the forces of division and unification harmoniously coexist, along with the rise and flow of mountains and rivers in nature. It is in this view of the environment that we see the people's

---

5. For more information on Sin Gyeong-jun, his *Sansugo* and *San-gyeongpyo*, see Yang Bo Kyung, "Sin Gyeong-jun-ui *Sansugo*-wa *San-gyeongpyo*: gukto-ui sancheon-e daehan chegyejeok ihae" (Sin Gyeong-jun's *Sansugo* and *San-gyeongpyo*: Structural Understanding of the Nation's Nature), *Toji yeongu* (Korea Land Development Association) 3.3 (1992): pp. 135-145.

view of Joseon as a small but complete universe.

Sansugo lists twelve names of mountains and rivers. The twelve mountains are 1) Samgaksan, 2) Baekdusan, 3) Wonsan, 4) Nangnim-san, 5) Duryusan, 6) Bunsuryeong, 7) Geumgangsan, 8) Odaesan, 9) Taebaeksan, 10) Songnisan, 11) Yuksipchi, 12) Jirisan. The twelve rivers are 1) Hangang, 2) Yeseonggang, 3) Daejingang, 4) Geumgang, 5) Saho, 6) Damgang, 7) Nakdonggang, 8) Yongheunggang, 9) Dumangang, 10) Daedonggang, 11) Cheongcheongang, 12) Amnokgang. In this list, Sam-gaksan is the most outstanding mountain while Hangang is the most notable, allowing the capital to take on more importance. Although Sin Gyeong-jun notes in the preface that Joseon's mountains originate from Baekdusan mountain, he lists Hanyang's Samgaksan first when he describes mountain distribution, indicating his feeling for both Baekdu-san and the capital.

In describing the mountains, he lists Samgaksan first, then continues with Baekdusan and moves southward. In listing rivers he lists the Han-gang first and then moves outward from there to the Yeseonggang river, Geumgang river, Nakdonggang river, Dumangang river, Daedonggang river, Cheongcheongang river, and Amnokgang river. A short descrip-tion of *Sansugo* follows below:

> *Sansugo* 1: "San-gyeong" discusses the twelve major mountains and their relationship to one another, and to various smaller surrounding mountains, the direction of mountain ranges, affects on local govern-ments, regions included in major mountains, and the range of rivers fed by the major mountain ranges. "San-gyeong" analyzed the pulse and flow of the mountain ranges, and the regions divided by them, based on the formation of rivers. In particular, this book outlined the order of the mountains and mountain ranges, showed the scope of the regions surrounded by the mountains, and analyzed regional character-istics in terms of natural geography, establishing the system of moun-tain ranges.
>
> *Sansugo* 2: "Sanwi" and *Sansugo* 3: "San-gyeong" contain such infor-mation as the names of the main mountains in each district, their loca-tion, smaller branches of the mountains, and the annual rainfall by dis-trict. *Sansugo* 1 was organized to provide a deeper understanding of the branches of the mountain ranges and large areas surrounded by them on a national scale. *Sansugo* 2 and *Sansugo* 3, on the other hand, provided a closer look at individual mountains. They listed, by district, the names of all the mountains, the relationships among them, the

main mountain location in each district, and how people used it.

Sansugo 4: "Sugyeong" begins with the Hangang and records major rivers around the nation. It shows their origins, the major sites they passed through, and locations where they merged, the separate branches that fed them, and finally the location where the branches merged with the major rivers.

Sansugo 5 and *Sansugo* 6: "Suwi" list the names of each district's rivers, gulfs, lakes, docks, and ports. Also included are their locations and anecdotal information recorded by famous scholars. This book presented an accurate analysis of the geographical distribution of rivers within a small regional area.

Sansugo became the fundamental reference guide for books published in the late Joseon dynasty related to Korea's topography. It is difficult to believe that Sin Gyeong-jun completed such a comprehensive and encompassing publication without some referential assistance. He might have had opportunities to study other national archive documents, which would have been difficult for ordinary people to access, when he edited such publications as *Yeoji pyeollam* (A General Survey of Korean Geography) and *Dongguk munheon bigo* under the King's order. Of the numerous available publications, he probably referenced *Sinjeung dongguk yeoji seungnam* (A Newly Supplemented and Augmented Survey of the Geography of Korea) and *Yeojiji* (A National Geographical Survey) by Yu Hyeong-won, and local records of all the particular towns. This is evident in the frequent references to local maps in *Sansugo*. In other words, Sin Gyeong-jun was probably able to establish his topography on a national scale due to the active publication of local records after the sixteenth century. These allowed Sin Gyeong-jun to vividly depict the natural and cultural environment of Korea. In particular, the *Yeoji doseo* (A Detailed Survey of Korean Geography), which was published from 1757 to 1765 in 55 volumes and contained almost all local records of the entire country, must have been a valuable reference to him.

As seen above, the *Sansugo* is a reference volume that analyzed the nation's mountains and rivers from a macroscopic viewpoint and explained the locations of villages and towns in relation to them. This book provides evidence that Joseon's geography was structured into "San-gyeong," "Sanwi," "Sugyeong," and "Suwi" in the second half of the eighteenth century. It systematically depicted the nation's geographical environment and local regions that developed naturally from it by noting the main mountain ranges and rivers (*gyeong*) as well as regional details and characteristics (*wi*). Such a systematic analysis of this land by Sin Gyeong-jun can be evaluated as a systematization of the traditional topology or physical geography. Thus, in the *Sansugo*, which tried to treat geography professionally and approach it through natural occurrences, we see aspects of geography's diversification and systematic geography, as well as evidence of modern geographical analyses.

Following the *Sansugo* and "Yeojigo" of the *Dongguk munheon bigo*, there is evidence of further systematization within geographical publications. Instead of simply providing information about mountains and rivers, later publications concentrated on one topic only, each one being treated in separate volumes. The *San-gyeongpyo* is the book on mountain ranges and the *Daedong sugyeong* by Jeong Yak-yong is the representative book on rivers and surrounding regions. Let us examine each book below.

A Mountain-Based Perception of Nature and Its Special Characteristics

San-gyeongpyo is a geographical publication that charted Korea's mountain ranges and branches, and the locations of each mountain. The book has been copied under various titles such as *Salligo* (A Survey of Mountains and Villages), *Gibong bangyeokji*, and *Yeoji pyeollam*. It has been generally believed that Sin Gyeong-jun was the author of the *San-gyeongpyo*.[6] Although it is acknowledged that the *San-gyeongpyo* was based on

---

6. *San-gyeongpyo* (Seoul: Pureunsan, 1990). In this book, Bak Yong-su confirms that writer of *San-gyeongpyo* is Sin Gyeong-jun and its publication date as 1769. This information is based on the data currently with the Academy of Korean Studies. In *Yeoji pyeollam* (2 volumes) the subtitle is "*San-gyeongpyo*" and in 1769 King Yeongjo asked Sin Gyeong-jun to edit *Yeoji pyeollam*. However, *Yeoji pyeollam* which appears in Seikido Bunko in Japan is an entirely different six-volume atlas of Joseon. Accordingly, it is possible that they may be two different books with the same name. Also when King Yeongjo explained the publication process of *Dongguk munheon bigo*, he mentioned that *Yeoji pyeollam*'s preface is similar to China's *Wenxian tongkao* (文獻通考). However, *Yeoji pyeollam* currently at the Academy of Korean Studies is a book of maps dissimilar to *Wenxian tongkao*. As such, it may be difficult to assume that *Yeoji pyeollam* currently at the Academy of Korean Studies is the same book that King Yeongjo asked Sin Gyeong-jun to edit. Accordingly, it is difficult to assume Sin Gyeong-jun as the author of *San-gyeongpyo*, and there should be further efforts to clarify this matter.

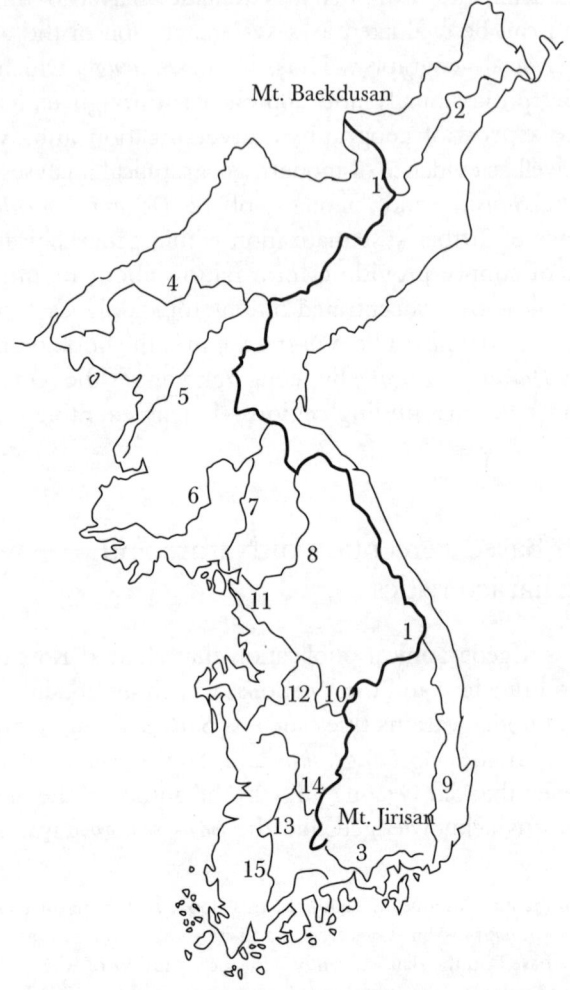

Map 2. Structure of Mountain Ranges in *San-gyeongpyo*

1. Baekdu Daegan
2. Jangbaek Jeonggan
3. Nangnam Jeongmaek
4. Cheongbuk Jeongmaek
5. Cheongnam Jeongmaek
6. Haeseo Jeongmaek
7. Injinbuk Yeseongnam Jeongmaek
8. Hanbuk Jeongmaek

9. Nakdong Jeongmaek
10. Hannam Geumbuk Jeongmaek
11. Hannam Jeongmaek
12. Geumbuk Jeongmaek
13. Geumnam Honam Jeongmaek
14. Geumnam Jeongmaek
15. Honam Jeongmaek

Sin Gyeong-jun's *Sansugo* and "Yeojigo," the authorship of this publication still remains to be verified.

The mountains in the *San-gyeongpyo* start at Baekdusan mountain and show one *daegan* (primary mountain range), one *jeonggan* (major mountain range), and thirteen *jeongmaek* (secondary mountain ranges). The following list shows fifteen mountain ranges listed in *San-gyeongpyo*.

1. Baekdu Daegan: begins from Baekdusan and reaches southward to Jirisan mountain. This primary mountain range vertically crosses the peninsula from north to south.
2. Jangbaek Jeonggan: begins from Jangbaeksan and crosses Hamgyeong-do province from east to west.
3. Nangnam Jeongmaek:[7] begins south of Jirisan and reaches eastward and is a mountain range located between the Namgang and Nakdonggang rivers to the south.
4. Cheongbuk Jeongmaek: begins at Nangnimsan of Baekdu Daegan and reaches westward, it goes through the northern region of the Cheongcheongang river, thus giving it the name Cheongbuk (north of Cheongcheongang).
5. Cheongnam Jeongmaek: begins from Nangnimsan and reaches toward the southwesterly direction. The southern region of Cheongcheongang river belongs to this mountain range.
6. Haeseo Jeongmaek: goes through Hwanghae-do province.
7. Injinbuk Yeseongnam Jeongmaek: is located between Imjingang and Yeseonggang rivers, goes through the city of Gaeseong and reaches toward Pungdeok.
8. Hanbuk Jeongmaek: begins at Bunsuryeong of Baekdu Daegan and reaches out in a southwesterly direction to the north of Hangang river.
9. Nakdong Jeongmaek: begins at Taebaeksan, reaches southward and stays to the east of Nakdonggang river.
10. Hannam Geumbuk Jeongmaek: begins at Songnisan and goes through Cheongju, Goesan, Eumseong, and Juksan in Chungcheong-do province.
11. Hannam Jeongmaek: begins at Chilhyeonsan in Juksan, Gyeonggi-do province and goes in the northwesterly direction toward Gimpo. It is in the southern region of the Hangang river.
12. Geumbuk Jeongmaek: begins at Chilhyeonsan in Juksan and

---

7. In *Yeoji pyeollam* in Jangseogak of the Academy of Korean Studies, the name of this mountain range is Nangnam Jeonggan.

reaches toward Taean. It is confined to the northern region of the Geumgang river.

13. Geumnam Honam Jeongmaek: begins at Janganchi of Baekdu Daegan and reaches southwesterly to Jinan and Namwon in Jeolla-do province.

14. Geumnam Jeongmaek: begins at Maisan in Jinan and reaches north toward Gongju and Buyeo in Chungcheong-do province, staying to the south of Geumgang river.

15. Honam Jeongmaek: begins at Maisan in Jinan and goes through Jeonju, Jeongeup, Jangseong, and Suncheon in Jeolla-do province and when it reaches Baegunsan mountain in Gwangyang, it takes on an "L" shape.

The characteristics of mountain ranges in the *San-gyeongpyo* are as follows:

First, the text systematized the mountain ranges' types and names. It classified them into one *daegan*, one *jeonggan* and thirteen *jeongmaek* and assigned names to all the mountain ranges. Although Sin Gyeong-jun's *Sansugo* and "Yeojigo" discussed the mountain ranges and their geographical features, in descriptions they were not as systematic and clear as the *San-gyeongpyo*, which separates the mountain ranges into 15 groups and assigns them names.

However, after the eighteenth century, there were many maps and publications that showed the topography of the nation's mountain ranges. In "Cheonjimun" included in Yi Ik's *Seongho saseol* (*gwon* 1) there is a section that mentions the "Baekdu Jeonggan." It says that the "Baekdusan mountain is the root of this country's mountain ranges. A large, vertical mountain range started at Baekdusan, became Taebaeksan in the middle and ended at Jirisan." The title of this section is, as I mentioned, "Baekdu Jeonggan" and although this name does not match with the Baekdu Daegan noted in the *San-gyeongpyo*, it is only the term *jeonggan* which differs. On maps such as the *Gwangyeodo*, published in the late Joseon period, other terms such as *daemaek*, *naemaek*, and *nangmaek* are also used.

Second, the structures of the mountain ranges are divided according to the river systems. The names of the mountain ranges reflect this. For example, Cheongbuk Jeongmaek and Cheongnam Jeongmaek define the Cheongcheongang river, Cheongnam Jeongmaek and Haeseo Jeong-maek define the Daedonggang river, Haeseo Jeongmaek and Imjinbuk Yeseongnam Jeongmaek define the Yeseonggang river, Imjinbuk Yeseongnam Jeongmaek and Hanbuk Jeongmaek define the Imjingang river, Hanbuk Jeongmaek and Hannam Jeongmaek define the Hangang river, Geumbuk Jeongmaek and Geumnam Jeongmaek define the Geumgang river, and Honam Jeongmaek defines Yeongsangang and Seomjingang rivers. As seen here, rivers are the means of distinguishing the different mountain ranges from one and other. However, Baekdu Daegan and Jangbaek Jeonggan are not distinguished by any river system. They are affixed by the names *daegan* and *jeonggan*, terms used to refer to the mountain ranges dividing the smaller rivers in the region south of Hamgyeong mountain range and east of Taebaek mountain range. In this way, they are differentiated from *jeongmaek*, the term indicating a mountain range a single region around a river.

In reality, when we need to trace the flow of a mountain range, the flow of its rivers becomes the standard. Yi Ik wrote as follows, showing that the flow of the river determines the flow of a mountain range.

> While the main branch of Baekdusan mountain runs south along the ocean, Cheollyeong became a narrow and dangerous valley in Bukgwan (Hamgyeong-do province) and Joryeong became a high and dangerous peak in the southeast. In the region north of Cheollyeong, mountains move toward the west. To follow the flow of the mountain range again, one must depend on the flow of the river again. . . . Between two rivers there is always a mountain range. For example, one mountain range, named Cheongseongnyeong, is located between Seogang and Jeotan rivers and acts as a natural boundary between Gyeonggi-do and Hwanghae-do provinces. Another mountain range in Jeongbangseong is located between Jeotan and Daedonggang rivers and provides a natural boundary between Hwanghae-do and Pyeongan-do provinces.[8]

While the natural boundaries such as the major rivers and side rivers divide the land into different regions, they also simultaneously act as a gateway connecting the different regions. For example, the banks of the Seomjingang river, Hadong in Gyeongsang-do province, and the Gurye and Gwangyang in Jeolla-do province, show evidence of acclimated cultural characteristics and active trading among the towns. The fact that major rivers are the standard for dividing the regions means that moun-

---

8. "Seodo gwanae," in "Cheonjimun," in *Seongho saseol, gwon* 1.

tain ranges are not simply looked upon as natural boundaries, but rather that they are seen as cultural boundaries contributing to the formation of a regional zone of life centering around the river. This notion reflects the Korean traditional view of nature that does not consider nature and humans separately but as one, as a single coexisting entity.

Third, *San-gyeongpyo* categorizes the mountain ranges by using classificatory divisions like *daegan*, *jeonggan*, and *jeongmaek*, which distinguish them by rank. *Gan* is the major stem of mountain ranges with *maek* as the branch that separates out of *gan*. Such ranking categorization is probably based on the size, height, and breadth of the mountains and mountain ranges, and their other physical and observable characteristics. It can also be viewed as a classification system for nature and the environment based Neo-Confucianism, a medieval way of thinking, characterized by discrimination and ranking.

Fourth, from the description of the mountain ranges in *San-gyeongpyo*, we see that the distribution and location of mountains and mountain ranges are seamlessly continuous, having no breaks in their flow. We view individual mountains in a row as mountain ranges today as well, but the *gan* and *maek* in *San-gyeongpyo* are seamless in their continuity. Just as an arterial vein branches into many smaller ones, the mountain ranges are all connected, and there are major mountains at key locations. Because today's depiction of mountain ranges is based on geological structure, the connecting relationship among them is not considered important. So, today, individual mountain ranges are depicted as standing separately and not as continuing ranges. Moreover, the geological features in the North and the South are different and the result is a discontinuance of the mountain ranges between the two sides. This is very significant because the land connected with *maek* is inseparable and has one root, with common characteristics throughout. However, today's portrayal of mountain ranges does not depict the Korean peninsula as one inseparable entity but as a collection of natural features, each possessing different origins and characteristics.

Fifth, *San-gyeongpyo* considered Baekdusan to be the center or origin of the land. Traditionally, the general social trend was to consider the capital where the king resided as the center of the land.[9] As noted earlier, Sin Gyeong-jun's *Sansugo* places considerable importance on Baekdu-

---

9. Yang Bo Kyung, "Joseon sidae eupji-ui seonggyeok-gwa . . . ," p. 131.

san and also places Hanyang as the center. The *San-gyeongpyo*, which views the land in terms of mountain ranges, structures and justifies this view by placing Baekdusan mountain at the center.

The most noteworthy aspect of *San-gyeongpyo* is that it presented a mountain-based conception, but its classification of mountain ranges was entirely based on rivers.

A River-Based Conception of Nature

If the *San-gyeongpyo* was a book that structured the land according to its mountains, then the *Daedong sugyeong* was a book that did so according to its rivers. Jeong Yak-yong, the most famous Silhak scientist of the late eighteenth century and early nineteenth century, was deeply interested in geography and considered it a very important field. He said, "Geography is a field that a Confucian scholar must study and a King must seek."[10] He authored many geographical publications, including the *Abang gangyeokgo* (Historical Geography of Korea), *Abang bieogo* (Korean Geography for National Defense), and *Daedong sugyeong*.[11] Of these, *Daedong sugyeong* is the most comprehensive, systematic geographical publication and deepens our understanding of this land. According to the *Huam seonsaeng yeonbo* (A Chronological Record of Huam),[12] edited by Jeong Gyu-yeong (Jeong Yak-yong's direct descendent) the *Daedong sugyeong* was completed in 1814 while Jeong Yak-yong was in exile in Gangjin. This book was written by Jeong Yak-yong and annotated by Yi Cheong. However, from the contents of the book we can see that it was still being edited after 1822.[13]

Jeong Yak-yong had long been interested in geographical records, particularly in books on the flow of rivers. In 1789 when he was 28 years old, he wrote "Jirichaek" to answer King Jeongjo's questions. In this writing, he pointed out the importance of geography and geography

10. "Jirichaek" (地理策), in "Simunjip" (Collection of Literary Works), *mun* (文), in *Yeoyudang jeonseo* (photoprinted), *gwon* 1, p. 157.
11. In addition to single volume books there are many other shorter papers such as "Chirichaek," "Jigu doseol," "Pungsu ron," "Goguryeo ron," "Baekje ron," etc.
12. Song Jae-so, *Dasan si yeongu: bu Dasan yeonbo* (Research of Dasan's Poetry: A Genealogy of Dasan) (Seoul: Changjaksa, 1986).
13. Yang Bo Kyung, "Jeong Yak-yong-ui *Daedong sugyeong*," *Toji yeongu* 4.6 (1993).

education and expressed his disappointment in the publications of the time. He emphasized the need for a new geographical study and even revealed his plan for it. He insisted that Joseon should publish more factual and detailed geographical works that were more sophisticated than the existing geographical records of the day, books like *Samguk sagi* (History of the Three Kingdoms), *Goryeosa* (History of Goryeo), *Dongguk yeoji seungnam* (Augmented Survey of the Geography of Korea), and *Dongguk munheon bigo*.[14] He suggested in "Jirichaek" that the King should "select qualified scholars to write *Dongguk sugyeong* based on Sang Qin's *Shuijing* (The River Classic) and Li Daoyuan's *Shuijingzhu* (Commentary on the River Classic). In making this suggestion, he recommended a book be published with detailed information on the flow and structure of Joseon's rivers. In his recommendation, Jeong Yak-yong asserted that Joseon's geographical records be based on the Chinese geographical records *Daiming yitongzhi*, *Shuijing* and *Shuijingzhu*. This was partly because Jeong Yak-yong's ideology matched closely with the ideology in these books. However, there is probably a more fundamental reason for his recommendation. He personally believed that with the demise of the Ming dynasty in China, Joseon had inherited Ming's culture and tradition.

Jeong Yak-yong had expected the geographical publications to be national projects. However, with the death of King Jeongjo, Jeong Yak-yong saw that the publication of geographical works as a government project was hardly going to be realized. As a result, he published his geographical work independently.

Daedong sugyeong is a factual book that recorded the flow of major and branch rivers as well as other pertinent factual information surrounding those rivers. In this book, the flow of the major rivers is the main topic while the branch rivers and various historical facts are additional annotations. However, upon examination of the book, one is aware that the details constitute the main portion of the content.

The most notable characteristic of *Daedong sugyeong* is that it covers only the rivers north of the Imjingang river. Jeong Yak-yong was born

---

14. *Jeongjo sillok, gwon* 27, 5th lunar month, 13th year of King Jeongjo's reign. Immediately after that, King Jeongjo ordered Gyujanggak to edit a supplementary volume of the *Yeoji seungnam*. He also ordered the civil ministers to collect the local records and Yegak to reedit them. In this manner, he tried to accomplish geographical projects including publishing new maps but never completed them.

near the Hangang river and was familiar enough with it to use its nick-
name Yeolsu. He probably was also aware of its importance. However,
in *Daedong sugyeong* there is no record of the Hangang or any other
rivers south of it. It is difficult to believe that Jeong Yak-yong intentional-
ly omitted the descriptions on rivers in the central and southern regions
of Korea, since he named his book *Daedong sugyeong* (Rivers in Korea)
and did not indicate the work as "unfinished" as he did with other
works which he did consider unfinished when he listed his writings in
his epitaph.[15] *Daedong sugyeong* literally describes the structure of all
rivers in Korea. Accordingly, *gwon* 2 of *Daedong sugyeong* is a geographical work that describes the factual details of Joseon dynasty rivers. If this
is so, it is likely that the parts describing the central and southern
regions were not finished by Yi Cheong when he edited the book or had
been lost after he completed his work.

The main sections of the *Daedong sugyeong* describe the flow of major
rivers like the Amnokgang, Dumangang, Cheongcheongang, Daedonggang, Yeseonggang, and Imjingang rivers from their origins to the towns
and regions they passed through, up to the point where they merged
with the ocean. The notes provide the exact names of towns and villages
the rivers flowed through, historical facts, and other excerpts from related books. It is a geographical work that provides an overall view of the
rivers as well as of details at a glance. The *Daedong sugyeong* has several
important features.

First, the work has a particular, predesignated topic and audience. It is
unlike the traditional geographical works that had been published until
that time. It is the only such work based on the structure of rivers and
its attention to detailed description is very significant. The mountains
and valleys where the rivers begin, the fields and villages the rivers flow
through, the origins and paths of all the branches that merge with the
main rivers, as well as historical sites are clearly detailed. Instead of simply listing the river's path, this book also described historical events that
occurred along the river as well, thereby providing the details of how
Joseon's history had unfolded.

Second, Jeong Yak-yong tried to systematize Joseon's rivers by assigning new names to them. He renamed the Amnokgang river as Noksu,

---

15. For example, "*Gyeongse yupyo, gwon* 48, was unfinished," "*Abang bieogo, gwon* 30, was
    unfinished," etc.

Dumangang river as Mansu, Cheongcheongang river as Salsu, Dae-donggang river as Paesu, Yeseonggang river as Jeosu, Imjingang river Daesu, Jangjingang river as Jangsu, Donggeongang river as Dongsu, and Daejeonggang river as Jeongsu.

> The Amnokgang river was called Noksu in Jeong Yak-yong's *Sug-yeong*. In ancient days, *gang* (江; *jiang* in Chinese) and *ha* (河; *he* in Chinese), which both currently mean river, referred to different bodies of water. If a river originated from Kunlunshan mountain, it was called *he*. If it originated from Minshan mountain, it was called *jiang*. These names, according to numerous ancient books, were never used interchangeably. In *Shijing*, *ha* is described as being broad while *gang* is described as being long. . . . Following China's Han and Jin dynasties, the rivers in the northern region were called *ha* and the rivers in the southern region were called *gang*. This is how bodies of water were classified in China. Outside of China, however, *ha* and *gang* were not so differentiated. In Joseon, all bodies of water, regardless of their locations, were called *gang*. Furthermore, Ganggye, Gangdong, and Gangseo were located in the northern region, while Cheongha, Hadong, and Hayang were in the southern region, exactly opposite from the case of the names in China. Additionally, there were many redundancies in the names of rivers such as Imjingang, Dongjingang, Dalcheongang, Cheongcheongang, Sinyeongang, and Sahogang. Therefore, Jeong Yak-yong decided to issue new names to the rivers in Joseon, as we can see in *Sugyeong*. In this book, he called Amnokgang river Noksu, and Dumangang river Mansu. All the rivers in this region used this example.[16]

While China used names of *he* (河) for northern rivers and *jiang* (江) for southern rivers, Jeong Yak-yong wanted to unify all of Joseon's rivers with *su* (水). In this way he hoped to differentiate Joseon's rivers from China's rivers and establish an independent environmental system. In order to establish such a system, he tried to call the rivers by names which represented the features of the rivers.

Third, *Daedong sugyeong* can be seen as a historical geographical record comparing information on rivers from Chinese, Japanese, and Korean books. Jeong pointed out errors in each book and set matters

---

16. "Noksu 1," in *Daedong sugyeong, gwon* 1; quoted in *Yeoyudang jeonseo, gwon* 4, p. 385.

straight from his own knowledge. For example, in the book *Daiming yitongzhi*, it says "The height of Zhangbaishan (Mt. Jangbaeksan) is 200 *ri* (1 *ri* = 12,885 ft.), with a large lake at the peak. The lake is 80 *ri* around and the water flows south to become the Ayagoha (a different name for the Dumangang) river." Commenting on this, Jeong Yak-yong wrote "There is no definitive proof that the water from Cheonji lake flows south in three branches to become three rivers. Also, the perimeter of the lake has not been proven to be 80 *ri*. Nor does the water from the lake feed the three rivers directly. The rivers do not originate from Cheonji lake, but stream from various sources in the mountain that merge together to form them." He points out that the size of the Cheonji lake noted in the *Daiming yitongzhi* is inaccurate, and denies the claim that the Amnokgang river, Dumangang river, and Sungari river originate from the Cheonji lake. In fact, his refutation was correct: Dumangang does not originate from Cheonji lake but from various smaller sources in the mountain that merge to become the river.

In addition to the representative names of famous locations in Joseon, this book also provides different names for the same locations as well as the origin of the names, thereby aiding in clarifying the names of various locations in this country. For example, the Amnokgang river was also known as the Majasu, Paesu, Aegang, and Samgang. Yeomnansu was also known as the Donggagang, Tonggagang, Tonggiragang, Pajeogang, Pajegang, and Pojugang. Dumangang river was also known as the Tongmunsu, Domunsu, Ayagogang, Tomungang, and Aehogang.

Jeong Yak-yong's efforts at elaboration are more evident in historical geography related to rivers. This is probably due to the difficulty he faced three years prior to writing the *Daedong sugyeong*, when he was writing the *Abang gangyeokgo*. He came across the names of mountains and rivers that had been named or located differently in each book. As a result, he had to carefully sort out the different names and places mentioned in various books. For example, he demonstrated that Salsu is another name for Cheongcheongang river in Anju, and Paesu for the Daedonggang river in Pyeongyang. Also, Gungnaeseong is the name of the merging point of the Amnokgang and Yeomnansu rivers.

Fourth, Jeong Yak-yong bolstered his theory in the *Daedong sugyeong* by using many maps in addition to literature. He particularly favored maps by Jeong Hang-nyeong,[17] son of Jeong Sang-gi, as well as Yun Du-

---

17. Jeong Hang-nyeong is Jeong Sang-gi's son. Jeong Sang-gi published *Dongguk jido* in

seo,[18] and used them often in his book, along with additional river-related details. This comparison of other maps was only possible because of the development of map production skills and the growth of geographical knowledge as the eighteenth century progressed. Furthermore, the *Daedong sugyeong* is proof that by the end of the eighteenth century, detailed and accurate maps were available, allowing Jeong Yak-yong to verify the names of various locations. He used these maps as references without actually visiting all the places he wrote about. Thus, the *Daedong sugyeong* could be geographically accurate without its author having actually surveyed all its relevant locations, thanks to the development of cartology in the eighteenth century and the knowledge accumulated from local records since the seventeenth century. Also, maps provided the people of that period with a clearer and more accurate spatial perception.[19]

The *Daedong sugyeong*, which is a geographical work surveying the nation's rivers, shows the development of geography in the late Joseon dynasty. It reflects a Joseon-centered notion of space, on the basis of which Jeong Yak-yong gave new names to all the rivers in the nation. He had thereby created an independent system for naming rivers that was now distinguishable from that of China. The *Daedong sugyeong* is a geographical work that carries out the investigation of historical documents and creates a historio-geographical approach by utilizing historical records, geographical works and literary works that creates an accurate perception of space through the use of maps.

On the other hand, the real significance of the book is the geographi-

---

the mid-eighteenth century. This book, which is the first to use accurate scaling of a large area using Korea's traditional measurement unit, is considered to have played a vital role in the development of Korea's map production skills. Jeong Sang-gi's son, Jeong Hang-nyeong, and grandson, Jeong Won-nim, followed his footstep to create maps. Although the original has been lost, there are copies of his book in existence today. Some of the titles are *Dongguk jido*, *Paldo jido*, *Jwahae jido*, and *Joseon paldo jido*.

18. Jeong Yak-yong's mother was the granddaughter of Yun Du-seo, a famous scholar and artist. Yun Du-seo was a descendent of Yun Seon-do. Yun Du-seo's map is currently known as *Dongguk yeoji jido*.

19. 「上仲氏(辛未冬)」, "Simunjip" (Collection of Literary Works), *seo* (書), in *Yeoyudang jeonseo, gwon* 1, p. 428. In a letter to Jeong Yak-jeon, his brother, Jeong Yak-yong wrote of his surprise at the accurateness of geography after reading *Seonggyeong jido* and Yun Du-seo's *Ilbon jido* (Map of Japan).

cal mode of thought that served as the basis for the verification of spatial structures of the land by focusing on its rivers. Understanding geography according to the locations of rivers was clearly a different way of structuring the view of geographical terrain than that found in *pungsu*. This effort not only reflects Jeong Yak-yong's opinion of *pungsu*, but also highlights his own philosophy that history and life evolve around rivers. At the same time, the *Daedong sugyeong* also reflects socioeconomic changes after the eighteenth century, including the development of commerce and industry, and the growth in trade and distribution that accompanies that development. Socioeconomic changes in the late Joseon dynasty occurred regionally as roads and other transportation networks increased. People became aware that rivers were an important method of transportation and aided inter-regional exchange. The *Daedong sugyeong*, insofar as it reflected a river-centered view of nature, can be seen as the fruit of Silhak geography. In this way, we may say that Jeong Yak-yong shaped people's views of topography and ultimately influenced economic development.

The Discontinuation of Traditional Perceptions of Mountains and Rivers

Map 3 shows the current structure of Korea's mountain ranges. When compared with Map 2, which shows a traditional mountain range structure, one can discern many differences. The current mapping of mountain ranges is based on their geological structure. Japan became interested in Korea's geological features around the time when it tried to acquire the developmental rights to Korea's mines. In 1879, when Hanabusa Yoshitada came to Korea to request that Wonsan Port be opened to Japan, he requested the acceptance of seven conditions in reparation for the previous year's "Taxation Issue surrounding Japan's Consular Office" in Busan. One of the seven conditions read, "If a Japanese national requests travel throughout Joseon to research mining ore or for geological study, Joseon must give permission." Though this condition was rejected by the Joseon government, beginning in the 1880s, the Japanese frequently and carefully performed geological and mining expeditions in Korea. And in the 1890s, the Japanese government carried out geological expeditions with geologists and mining specialists on the expedition team. Nishiwada Hisagaku was the most

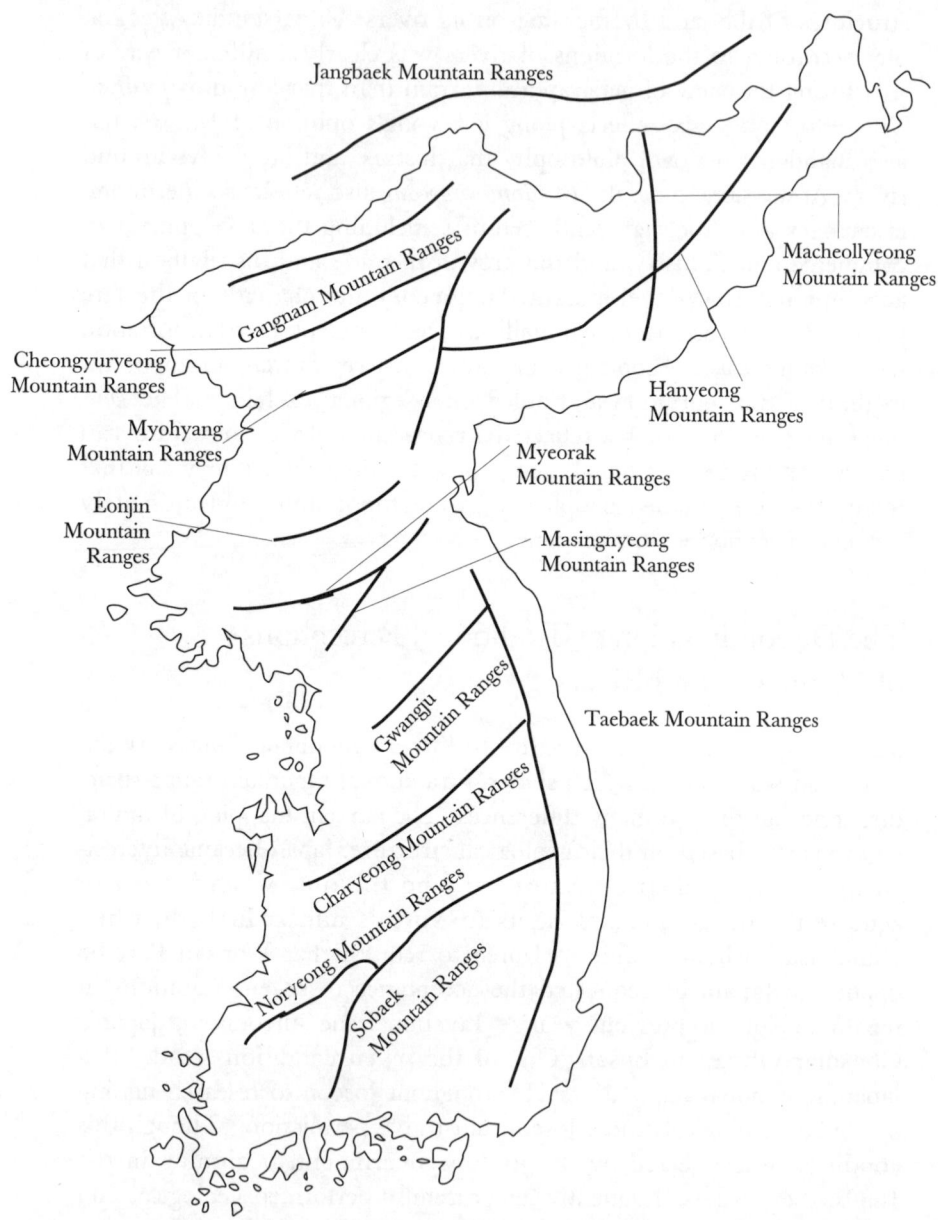

Jangbaek Mountain Ranges

Macheollyeong
Mountain Ranges

Gangnam Mountain Ranges

Cheongyuryeong
Mountain Ranges

Hanyeong
Mountain Ranges

Myohyang
Mountain Ranges

Myeorak
Mountain Ranges

Eonjin
Mountain
Ranges

Masingnyeong
Mountain Ranges

Gwangju
Mountain Ranges

Taebaek Mountain Ranges

Charyeong Mountain Ranges

Noryeong Mountain Ranges

Sobaek
Mountain Ranges

Map 3. Current Structure of Mountain Ranges

famous of the expedition team members.[20]

The method of Japan's mountain range classification system for Korea's mountains, still in use today, can be traced to a paper presented in 1903 by Koto Bunjiro, a geologist with Tokyo University. Koto Bunjiro visited Joseon twice between 1900 and 1902 to study Joseon's geology and geography, reporting his findings in his paper,[21] entitled "Chosen sangaku ron" (An Orographic Sketch of Korea), which was published in the journal *Tokyo teikoku daigaku kiyo* in 1903. In this paper, he mapped out Joseon's mountain ranges. This depiction greatly influenced future books and perspectives. *Kankoku chiri* (The Geography of Korea), published in 1904 by Yasu Shoei in Tokyo, was based on the same ordering as well. By 1905, when Japan's colonization of Joseon had begun in earnest, the contents of Joseon's textbooks were under the control of the Japanese government. Joseon's geography textbooks followed Japan's geological premises for mountain classification, leading to the distortion of Joseon's traditional system.

Japan's classification system of mountain ranges was based on their geological structures, as analyzed by Japanese geologists, rather than on geographical premises. The biggest difference between any geological system and Joseon's traditional geographic system was that whereas Joseon's system considered the features of the mountains and rivers above ground, Japan's system was based on geological structures beneath the ground. The latter emphasis was not concerned with the relationships between terrain and people's lives, nor the shaping of societies. This geological system also divided the Korean peninsula into north and south along the geological divide between Wonsan and Ganghwa. Furthermore, the Baekdu Daegan, which people understood to range from Baektusan to Jirisan mountains, was separated into the Macheollyeong mountain range, part of the Hamgyeong mountain range, Nangnim mountain range, and the Taebaek mountain range. Baekdusan, the spiritual and holy mountain of Joseon, thus became just

---

20. Yi Bae-yong, *Guhanmal gwangsan igwon-gwa yeolgang* (Mining Rights and Western Powers at the End of the Joseon Dynasty), vol. 50 of *Hanguk yeongu chongseo* (Seoul: The Institute of Research on Korea, 1984), p. 163.

21. Koto Bunjiro, "Kankoku nanbu no chisei" (Geographical Picture of Southern Korea), *Chigaku* (Earth Science) 13.34 (1901): pp. 413-434; "An Orographic Sketch of Korea," *Todaiki* 19.1 (1903): pp. 1-61; "Journeys Through Korea," *Todaiki* 26.2 (1909): pp. 1-207.

another mountain. The same fate befell Hanyang, the capital of Joseon, as well as the mountain range that connected Baekdusan with Hanyang.

Another major difference between the two theories was that Japan's theory ignored the directionality of rivers. Even discounting the *Sansugo*, which considered both mountains and rivers as belonging together, the *San-gyeongpyo*, which considered only the physical structure of the mountain ranges, showed distinctive differences in its systematization compared to those found in Japanese theory. The structure of the mountain ranges shown in the *San-gyeongpyo*, although it was supposed to be limited to the mountains, included the structure of rivers. At times, the configuration of the rivers was actually the standard. In understanding geography, the difference between whether or not to include the people living on the land, or whether to exclude the people and focus on geological features, greatly influenced the way the people understood the land. Joseon's understanding of nature was based upon the people and the rivers upon which they organized their societies. As such, this can be defined as a humanistic physical geography. Unfortunately, this traditional perspective changed as more Western theory was imported via Japan, evolving into a geography or topology that ignored human interaction. In particular, this imported view insisted on the geological aspect of Korea's mountain ranges.

This geological view of Korea was not readily accepted by Koreans. Therefore, to correct this view, educational efforts were begun on a popular level under Japanese colonial rule. The Joseon Gwangmunhoe (Korean Institute of Classics) was established in 1910 in an attempt to recover Joseon's stolen land and history from Japanese revisionism. The main goal of this institute was to collect, edit, and maintain important data in Joseon's important books and documents and distribute them to the public. This institute published its third geographical work entitled *San-gyeongpyo* in 1913, following the publication of *Taengniji* and *Dori dopyo* (A Complete Map of Districts and Provinces). In the "Forward" section, the association explained the philosophy of this book as follows.

> Upon careful reflection, works on Joseon geography should devote a considerable amount of effort to a discussion of its mountains; however, unfortunately, they are unsystematic in their organization. "Yeoji-go," published by Sin Gyeong-jun, only describes the branches of the mountains and their history. "San-gyeong," a part of "Yeojigo," details how a mountain has peaks and valleys, and how it provides basins for

villages. It is a book that accurately details the origins and roots of mountains. *San-gyeongpyo* is based on "San-gyeong" and provides further details. It also provides clear measurements of regions and their borders so that they are clearly mapped out for the reader. As a result, *San-gyeongpyo* is a valuable addition to "San-gyeong" and a beacon in Joseon's geographical studies.

The association, as we see, considered *San-gyeongpyo* to be a standard geographical record that accurately described mountain ranges, their branches, and their direction. Unfortunately, the Japanese geology-based stance regarding Joseon's mountain ranges took hold in Joseon during Japan's colonial rule and Joseon's own geographical system of study was discontinued.

Conclusion

The traditional perspective on the nation's landscape during the Joseon dynasty can be summarized as follows. Since the early days of the Joseon dynasty, dual faceted perspectives holding Baekdusan and Hanyang as the centers of Joseon coexisted. The Silhak scholars of the late Joseon dynasty period began to categorize the mountains and rivers; Sin Gyeong-jun's *Sansugo* was the first of such efforts. *Sansugo* is a work that systematically structured the mountains and rivers into twelve main divisions and unions. It analyzed the nation's landscape based on its mountains and rivers, but it also showed that landscape as an intrinsic part of human life. After the mountains and rivers were categorized, theorists began to further classify each mountain and river in depth. The *San-gyeongpyo* delineated mountains and their ranges. On the other hand, the *Daedong sugyeong* structured the land according to the nation's rivers. The *San-gyeongpyo* was based on the *Sansugo*, but also included additional categories and clearly defined the structure of the mountain ranges. Since the rivers flowed from the mountains, The *Daedong sugyeong* did not ignore the existence of mountains by name. However, Jeong Yak-yong's "idea of placing importance on the structure of rivers" was based on his understanding that people's lives were largely dependent on and intertwined with the rivers. This can also be viewed as the result of increasing importance of rivers to the people as methods of transportation. As commerce among various regions increased and distribution and the economy developed further, rivers that served as a means of connecting different regions, rather than mountains that served as a means of dividing regions, became more important to people.

The content and level of knowledge at a given period are created from within not only the structure of people's lives, but also the accumulation of related knowledge. The change in people's awareness of nature during the Joseon dynasty was a direct reflection of the change in people's lifestyles and the accumulation of knowledge during that time. By the end of the Joseon dynasty, scholarly efforts to clarify the importance of nature became very active. Such efforts were based on rivers and a humanistic physical geography, with its emphasis on people's livelihood. This movement was presided over by Silhak geographers who had become aware that dynamic social changes in the late Joseon period were closely related to the changes in spatial perceptions of varied regions. Indeed, the whole country strove to maintain its original structure. These efforts represented the diversification of geography and the professionalization of systematic geography, and they presented a prefiguring of modern geography.

Understanding the archetype of a culture and its features can be a basis for projecting how well the past, present, and future will harmonize. Creation and development begin with a comprehensive understanding of origin. Accurate knowledge of our archetypal understanding of the land is that much more urgent for modern Koreans, who have suffered through such extreme discontinuations from our traditional culture and the views it embodied.

Korean Envoys and Their Relations with Japan in the 17th to 19th Centuries

Yi Chin-Hui

I

The Japanese distortion of school textbooks has created social upheaval in the past few years in Korea, China, and many Southeast Asian countries. The distortion of events presented by the Japanese has created great indignity among the former victims of Japanese aggression. Inside Japan, movements have risen in criticism of the approval of the textbooks by the Ministry of Education, and many authors began working with the aim of educating Japanese youth as well-informed leaders in the international community.

Japanese textbooks have been wrong in dealing with Japanese aggression ranging from the twelfth century until the late nineteenth century and particularly in dealing with the relations between Korea and Japan. The textbooks even omitted the facts regarding amiable relations between the two nations, further misleading Japanese readers in their view of Korea. For instance, high-school world history and Japanese history textbooks described the Korean peninsula as having been repeatedly subjected to aggression by neighboring nations. The textbooks did not make it clear that Koreans were successful in protecting their national dignity and sovereignty.

* Originally published in the *Korea Journal*, vol. 25, no. 12 (December 1985).

Yi Chin-Hui (Yi, Jin-hui) is Professor Emeritus at Wako University. He received his M.A. in Anthropology from Meiji University, Japan in 1957. His publications include *Hanguk-gwa ilbon munhwa* (Cultures of Korea and Japan) (1982), *Hanguk sok-ui ilbon* (Japan Present within Korea) (1986), and *Kankoku do nihon no koryushi* (The History of Exchanges between Korea and Japan) (1994).

The misinformation in Japanese textbooks was deliberate, and served as a means of justifying the Japanese colonial rule of Korea. Japanese historians fabricated the image of the Korean people so that Korea would appear as a completely backward nation. Japanese historians argued that the Korean people were primitive and unable to maintain their own history because they were constantly subjected to alien aggression. Under such premise, there was no room to mention that relations between Japan and Korea had actually been quite amiable during the Muromachi period between the fifteenth and sixteenth centuries, as well as the amiable relations that continued for 260 years after the Hideyoshi invasion. The history textbooks skip to the 1868 Meiji Restoration and the Japanese advocacy of conquest of Korea.

It is now common knowledge in Japan that the Edo period was a period of national seclusion. During the Edo period for over 200 years, Japan lived in isolation, avoiding all diplomatic relations with foreign countries. Their only window to European civilization was the one port of Nagasaki. In 1633, the ruling Tokugawa shogunate issued an Order of National Seclusion to the local magistrate in Nagasaki with the following guidelines:

1. Prohibition of voyages abroad upon pain of death.
2. Strict suppression of Christianity in order to facilitate its extinction in Japan.
3. Permission of foreign trade ships to enter and leave only through the port of Nagasaki, under strict supervision.

According to the above order, the Japanese people were forbidden to make voyages abroad, and foreigners were strictly prohibited from entering Japan, with the exception of Nagasaki. This order, however, was in fact applied only to merchants from Qing China and the Netherlands. In contrast, normal relations were maintained between the Korean Joseon dynasty and Japanese Tokugawa shogunate in 1607, secured by a trade agreement signed in 1609. According to this trade agreement, a Japanese office (*waegwan*) was opened in Busan, occupied constantly by five to six hundred Japanese working in shifts. Japanese trade ships continued to enter Busan, at an average rate of fifty visits per year.

In addition, a Korean mission of 475 members visited Edo, the seat of the Tokugawa shogunate in 1636, immediately after the promulgation of the Order of National Seclusion, traveling through the Japanese archipelago. The Korean envoys secured ties with the Japanese men of letters, scholars of Chinese classics, medical students, and artists they encountered on their way. It is impossible, therefore, to consider the Edo period as one of complete seclusion.

II

The Japanese invasions of Korea of 1592 and 1597, have also been repeatedly distorted in high-school textbooks. Most texts describe the invasions in great detail, and include relevant maps. While the textbooks describe the advance of Japanese troops as far as Pyeongyang in the west and the Dumangang river in the east, there is no mention at all of the circumstances that compelled the Japanese army to retreat southward back to Hanyang (Seoul) 11 months later. In addition, when describing the Japanese re-invasion starting in the year of Jeongyu, there is no mention that the Japanese forces had to retreat back to the shores of the southern coast after several months. Textbooks excuse the Japanese retreats by explaining that the armies withdrew from Korea following the death of Toyotomi Hideyoshi, a statement that is blatantly erroneous. The withdrawal of Japanese forces to Hanyang on March 20, 1593, proceeded as follows.

Troops Leaders	Regular Strength	Actual Strength	Number of Decrease	Rate of Decrease (%)
Yukinaga Konishi	18,700	6,626	12,074	64.57
Kiyomasa Kato	10,000	5,492	4,508	45.08
Naoshige Nabeshima	12,000	7,644	4,356	36.30
Yoshitsugu Otomo	6,000	2,052	3,948	65.80
Yoshinari Mori	2,000	1,425	575	28.75

The Konishi force—the first army corps—lost 64.57 percent of its regular strength while the Kato force—the second army corps—used up 45.08 percent of its regular strength. As these statistical figures tell, the invading army lost half of its frontline force eleven months after hostilities broke out. The Japanese navy, in the meantime, suffered a devastating debacle in engagements with the Korean navy led by Admiral Yi Sun-sin.

Also, the Japanese army was driven to a defensive position merely three months after the start of the Jeongyu re-invasion, and the Kato forces, besieged at Ulsan castle, suffered near starvation. The claim that the Japanese withdrew from the Korean peninsula because of the death of Hideyoshi is erroneous. In fact, the Japanese forces in Korea had dwindled to 75,000 men from 147,000 by May 1598 (three months before Hideyoshi's death), and were unable to continue.

In the war of aggression raged by the Japanese in the sixteenth century, rural areas of Japan were devastated, and the Japanese army suffered a staggering loss of life. It took Japan, in fact, over one hundred years to recover from the war. The Toyotomi regime had lost most of its elite units, and its generals blaming each other for defeat. The Toyotomi forces then suffered an appalling defeat in the battle of Sekigahara in September 1600. The reckless war of aggression in Korea cost the Toyotomi regime its rule and brought about the tragic end of the Toyotomi clan.

This seven-year war also caused indescribable calamity on the Korean peninsula. The loss of human life was immense. Many Korean scholars, technicians, and farmers were taken to Japan, leaving behind a devastated land. It took many years for Korea to recover from the destruction. Toyotomi Hideyoshi and Kato Kiyomasa became targets of hatred, and Korean distrust of Japan followed for a long time after the invasions. Sin Yu-han, who visited Japan in 1719 roughly 120 years after the war declared in his memoirs titled *Haeyurok* (Record of a Sea Voyage to Japan) that "Toyotomi Hideyoshi has been our enemy for a century. A righteous man should not share heaven with his enemy." The Japanese war of aggression left a deep, long-lasting scar on the Korean peninsula.

Tokugawa Iyeyasu, in contrast to Toyotomi Hideyoshi, presented a more loyal account of Korea. He objected to the Hideyoshi invasion on various pretexts. As soon as Iyeyasu emerged as ruler of Japan after defeating the Toyotomi forces in September 1600, Tokugawa issued instructions to So Yoshitoshi of Tsushima to start negotiations with the Joseon dynasty with the aim of restoring diplomatic relations with Korea.

So Yoshitoshi was sent as an envoy to Korea in February 1601 offering an apology to the Korean government for the crimes committed by Toyotomi Hideyoshi and asking for amicable relations. In response, however, the Korean court, still firmly suspicious of Japan, declined the offer. Thereafter Japan had to send numerous envoys to Korea before the Korean government dispatched a mission led by Great Monk Samyeong (Yujeong) to Japan in August 1604 as an envoy probing into the "situation of the enemy." Tokugawa Iyeyasu, upon receiving Great Monk Samyeong and his entourage, expressed his intentions as follows:

> The war of aggression was committed solely by Toyotomi and I did not send a single man among my troops. There is no reason why the Joseon dynasty and the Tokugawa shogunate should hate each other. I am eager, therefore, to restore amicable relations with Korea as soon as possible.

Tokugawa, who was opposed to the war, seems to have been sincerely eager to overcome the emotions of the past. He may have believed it to be in the best interests to the safety of his new Tokugawa shogunate to restore diplomatic relations with Korea.

For the Koreans, Tokugawa's usurpation of the Toyotomi regime served as a kind of catharsis for the grudge held against the Japanese. It was also necessary to reduce tensions between Korea and Japan in order to rehabilitate the war-stricken nation. And the sincere request as presented by Iyeyasu and Hidetada allowed the Joseon dynasty to maintain face and dignity.

Following Great Monk Samyeong's report, the Korean court demanded that Japanes submit an official national apology (later known as Iyeyasu's letter) for Hideyoshi's invasion, and to hand over the criminals who had unearthed royal tombs in Korea and stolen articles contained in them. In response, a Japanese envoy carrying an official apology arrived at the port of Busan in November 1606 and handed over the criminals involved in the ravaging of royal tombs. Thereupon the Korean court sent Yeo U-gil and a party of 461 people to Japan in 1607 as an "envoy for returning courtesies." Diplomatic relations were restored formally between the two countries and continued for 260 years until the Meiji Restoration in 1868.

Working-level diplomatic affairs between the two countries were entrusted to the Dongnae magistrate in Korea and the Tsushima clan lord So in Japan. Liaison between the two remained close until the establishment of the Meiji government. Korean and Japanese envoys visited Busan and Tsushima respectively on occasions of either happiness or ill that affected the Joseon dynasty and Tokugawa shogunate. In addition, Japan sent envoys to Korea reporting on events affecting the Tsushima clan or incidents in Japan, and officials whose mission was to prepare for the reception of formal envoys. The Japanese envoys were called *cham-*

pansa (envoys to the vice-minister), and the diplomatic messages they carried were addressed to the civilian *champan* (vice-minister). They were sent to Korea on more than fifty occasions, and Korean envoys sent to Japan in return visited Izuhara, main town of Tsushima island, on more than fifty occasions.

During the above-mentioned period, the Joseon dynasty would also dispatch an envoy to Beijing, Qing China on a yearly basis. The information gathered by these Korean envoys on Chinese politics, science, culture, and the European world was forwarded to the Tokugawa shogunate whenever a Japanese mission visited Korea. Korea passed on to Japan details concerning, for example, the takeover of Ming by Qing China in the early seventeenth century, the shipwreck in Korea of Hamel, a Dutch sailor, and his escape, a rebellion masterminded by Yi In-jwa in the eighteenth century, and the invasion of Ganghwado island by a French fleet in 1866. Incidents in Japan reported to Korea included the famine during the Kyoho period and the fire in Edo. Such information reached the capital within three months. So it was thanks to its diplomatic relations with Korea that Japan was able to obtain information and knowledge on China and Europe. The Edo period can not be considered, therefore, an age of national seclusion.

III

One practice that symbolizes the friendly relations between Japan and Korea is the mutual envoys whenever a king was enthroned in Korea or a new shogun assumed his position in Japan. Korea sent such envoys on twelve occasions. On three of such occasions, the envoys were sent under the title *hoeryesa* (envoys for returning courtesies) or *hoedap gyeom swaehwansa* (envoys for returning courtesies and promoting the repatriation of kidnapped Koreans). On nine occasions the envoys were called *tongsinsa* (ambassadors to Japan).

The last Korean ambassador mission was sent to Japan in 1811. When Iyeyoshi, the 12th shogun, assumed his position in 1837, Japan invited a Korean mission. Similar invitations were extended when new shoguns came to power, but the confusion in Japan in the closing years of the Tokugawa period and the economic situation in Korea during that period prevented further envoys.

A Japanese mission of more than 300 members arrived at Busan in

1609 in order to extend congratulations to the Korean government on the occasion of restoration of formal relations between the two countries, but the Korean court refused its entrance to the capital. Instead, the Korean court dispatched high-ranking officials to Busan to receive the delegates from Japan. Voices objecting to a Japanese visit to Seoul argued that during Hideyoshi's invasion of Korea, Japanese soldiers had advanced to Seoul in only twenty days, along the same three main roads the Japanese missions would need to utilize to reach the capital. Because of this precedent, all subsequent Japanese missions were received in Busan and sent back to Japan without obtaining permission to go up to Seoul. Korea kept the Japanese at a friendly but cautious arms' length.

The procedure through which Korean envoys were sent to Japan was complex. When a new shogun came to power, the shogunate sent one envoy to report to Korea and another with the mission of asking the Korean government to dispatch a goodwill envoy to Japan. Both envoys were limited to Busan. When the Korean vice-minister returned a letter of approval of the new shogun to Japan, the Tokugawa shogunate would appoint the *roju* (Supervisor of Government Affairs), the highest official in charge of state administration, to the senior position responsible for receiving the goodwill envoy from Korea. In preparation for an envoy, Lords whose territories would be passed through coordinated plans with the lord of the Tsushima clan, and lodgings to accommodate the Korean guests were constructed or repaired. Fleets of escort and towing vessels were formed and harbor facilities rearranged. The logistics of mobilization of overland journeys with laborers and horses was carefully planned to prevent serious blunder, and those responsible for mistakes were expected to commit suicide by disembowelment.

When the Joseon dynasty, on the other hand, was asked by a visiting Japanese envoy to send a Korean envoy to Japan, it embarked on the construction of six ocean-going vessels and the selection of three envoys (senior, deputy, and assistant envoys) and attendants. The senior envoy was chosen from among top bureau chief-level officials of the Ministry of Civility (*yejo chamui*). Others were chosen from among top-level compilers, clerks, artists and physicians in preparation for interchanges with Japan. The party was often comprised of as many as 470 to 500 persons, including interpreters, military officers as escorts, officials in the capacity of guards of honor, sailors, and boys who would render various services. The delegation also had to collect various gifts (wild ginseng, cultivated ginseng, etc.) for the shogun and other ranking personnel and lords of clans in many areas, to whom they would be indebted during the trip. A large sum of money was needed. The three envoys, compilers, and clerks would inspect records and diplomatic documents their predecessor envoys had left behind while studying diplomatic precedents and keeping a close eye on the situation in Japan.

A Japanese envoy would arrive in Busan to escort the Korean delegation about six months after the shogunate asked for its dispatch. The three envoys entered the royal palace and bade farewell to the king. Then the Prime Minister hosted a farewell party for the delegation outside the South Gate in Seoul. Arriving at Busan, the party performed a ritual to honor the Dragon God, praying for a safe voyage. The day was chosen while calculating the winds, waves and tide, and the envoys set sail at dawn and entered Sasuna or Waniura on the northern tip of Tsushima island at dusk.

The approach and safe arrival of the goodwill envoy (aboard six ships) and the party of Japanese delegates sent to Korea was indicated to the lord of the Tsushima clan in Izuhara through signal-fire set atop a mountain peak. The lord reported the arrival to other lords in the neighboring areas and to the shogunate by liaison boats. Their movements thereafter were also reported immediately by liaison boats. After the welcoming ceremony provided by the Tsushima clan, the party would proceed toward Edo under the guidance of the ship on which its lord would be aboard. Escorting the Korean mission were more than 800 clansmen from Tsushima. The ships carrying the envoys from Korea were guarded in the front and rear by the ships the clansmen were aboard, mainly towing vessels and guard ships. The next port of call was Katsumoto on Ikinoshima island. The senior envoy's ship hoisted a flag with the character 正 dyed in red on a blue background, the deputy envoy's ship a flag had 副 dyed in red on a yellow background, and the ship the assistants were aboard a flag had 從 dyed in blue on a red background. The ship with gifts and food provisions from Korea hoisted a flag with predetermined colors. This measure was taken in order to help the escort ships easily discern the vessels they were assigned to.

The next port of call after Katsumoto was Ainoshima. From here the Korean delegation was entrusted to reception by the Fukuoka clan. According to *Chosenjin raiheiki* (Notes on Calls of Koreans, 8 vols.), which contains records on the 1719 reception, a period of six months was needed to construct twenty-four new lodgings for the envoy and party from Korea and repair signal-fire stands at seven points. More than five hundred ships and 3,060 sailors were involved, including towing boats guiding the fleet of ships from Korea to Ainoshima, indicator boats deployed around swift currents, and guard boats stationed along coasts. The host would receive more than 500 guests from Korea and 800 members of the Tsushima clan. According to a Fukuoka clan record, the reception of the Korean envoys was so enormous a project that it could potentially exhaust a clan's finances. Nonetheless, it was considered a courteous event that provided an opportunity for the Japanese to cultivate both body and mind.

The Korean mission then called on Shimonoseki and Kaminoseki to receive a welcome by the Mori clan. The next ports of call were Kamakari, Tomonori, and Ushimado in the Setonaikai Inner Sea. Each clan in the port of call, as in the case of the Fukuoka clan, prepared towing vessels. The Ikeda clan in Ushimado posted 516 boats (in addition to 102 reserve boats) and mobilized 3,707 sailors. 264 guards were stationed in lodgings for the Korean envoys, and 146 others were stationed in lodgings for members of the Tsushima clan. Also posted were 92 fire fighters, odd-job men, and palanquin bearers. Leaving Ushimado, the Korean mission would enter the estuary of the Yodo River in Osaka by way of Murotsu and Hyogo (today's Kobe). This would mark the end of the long journey.

IV

At the estuary of the Yodo River, the party transferred to gorgeously decorated flat-bottom river boats prepared by the Tokugawa shogunate and big clans in western Japan. Navigating upstream along the Yodo, the party landed near today's Naniwa Bridge. The envoy and entourage were led to Nishi Honganji, their designated lodgings. According to the memoir *Haeyurok*, both banks of the Yodo River were filled with spectators. Brilliantly decorated boats passed along the river. Sin Yu-han, a compiler who visited Japan in 1719, described the scene as follows:

> Spectators, men and women, stood like walls on both sides . . . . Those nearby occupied boats anchored on both banks, spreading out their mats so closely that the sleeves of their clothes touched each other. Those who were shoved away from the boats crowded the banks. They climbed walls of houses and railings of bridges. Some sat on brilliant silk mats, enjoying wine, rice, and drinks.

When the news of an impending visit of a Korean envoy reached them, inhabitants of Osaka and nearby communities assembled with blankets and iron pots to look on. The same sight could be observed on the highways along the mission's path.

Relieving themselves of fatigue after the long sea voyage at Nishi Honganji, the envoy would take decorated boats for a journey upstream along the Yodo River until they landed at Yodo, south of Kyoto. This was followed by a two-week overland journey to Edo. They stayed at Kyoto for the night and entered their longings in Moriyama by way of Otsu. On the following day they took the road along the eastern bank of Lake Biwa at Yasu and went northward to enter Hikone.

The Hama Highway became known as the "Korean Highway." The highway came by the name when Tokugawa Iyeyasu, who became the virtual ruler of Japan by winning the Sekigaha war in September 1600, entered Kyoto along this road. The Tokugawa clansmen called it an "auspicious road." Whenever a shogun went up to Kyoto, he followed this road, barring anyone else from travelling it. Only the envoys from Korea were entitled to use this road, and thus is acquired its name. Such is one example of the prestige with which the Korean envoys were treated by the Tokugawa shogunate.

Spending the night at Hikone, the Korean mission stayed at Ogaki and then at Nagoya for the night. Then the party traveled the Tokaido Highway and proceeded toward Edo. Special floating bridges were prepared at rivers such as Ibi, Nagara, Kiso, Tenryu, Fuji, Sakawa, and Banyu. The floating bridge consisted of barges connected together with wooden boards covering the surface, and was taken apart after the Korean visitors would leave. The Tokugawa shogunate prohibited laying bridges over these rivers in order to maintain the security of Edo, and an exception was only made when the Korean envoy had to cross those rivers.

Lodgings and resting houses for the visitors from Korea were constructed or repaired, and roads would be readjusted by covering them with sand. Withered roadside trees were replaced with fresh ones and trimmed so as not to obstruct the passage of flags, spears and swords. Unattractive areas were covered with screens or thatches. New roads were laid where existing ones were too steep. The Satta Ridge in Shizuoka prefecture is one good example. One hundred sailors among the members of the Korean party were told to stay in Osaka, and those who joined the party heading for Edo exceeded 370 to 400. Some 800 members of the Tsushima clan guided and escorted the party. It was a long process consisting also of 1,000 palanquin bearers and laborers, 800 horses, and 800 horsemen mobilized from all clans along the highways.

The following instructions were issued in Edo with a view to controlling spectators along the roads:

1. All passers-by, high and low, are ordered to stand still on both sides of the road when the Korean envoys pass. In case of emergency, they are allowed to cross the road through a rift in the procession only when the reason is recognized as acceptable.
2. Spectators are prohibited from shouting loudly, laughing loudly, or pointing with their fingers. Men and women are also prohibited from intermingling.

The last lodgings were provided at Shingawa on the way to Edo. The envoys and members of the Korean mission formed a long procession in formal attire. Taking the lead were 20 cavalry horses sent by the shogun. The senior envoy was preceded by a flag emblazoned with the characters 清道旗, military officers, and a band. A palanquin containing a message from the Korean king to the shogun followed them. Palanquins carrying the senior envoy, the deputy envoy, and the assistants followed in that order. The Tsushima lord and his men formed the rear of the precession. The guesthouse for the Korean mission in Edo was newly constructed in the compound of Higashi Honganjin in Asakusa. The guesthouse was located originally in Honseiji but was removed after a fire destroyed the temple. It was an independent structure connecting many buildings with corridors, capable of accommodating several hundred guests, including the lodging for the senior envoy, another one for the deputy envoy, and others for assistants. The grounds were covered by gardens.

Ranking officials from the shogunate would wait at the guesthouse, to receive the envoys courteously. Acting on behalf of the shogun, the *roju* paid a courtesy call on the guests from Korea on the first morning after their arrival. The dinner for the three envoys was very luxurious. Breakfast and dinner consisted of seven dishes in the first course, five in the second course, and three in the third course. Lunch consisted of five dishes in the first course, five in the second course, and three in the third course. The food alone indicates how careful the Japanese were in receiving the goodwill envoys from Korea and the act that they spared no expense on their reception.

The most important job awaiting the Korean envoy in Edo was to meet the Tokugawa shogun and deliver to him an official message from the Korean king, which extended congratulations upon the shogun's assumption of power. Escorted by Japanese officials, the three envoys would enter Edo Castle, where they were personally received by the shogun.

Waiting in the main hall of the castle were the shogun, ranking officials of the shogunate, and lords of clans from various parts of Japan, all clothed in formal attire. The chief interpreter led the group of visitors holding a box containing the message from the Korean king. The chief interpreter handed the message to the lord of the Tsushima clan, who in turn passed it to a high official from the shogunate, who then placed it on a desk by the shogun. Then the ranking officials of the shogunate and lords of various clans bowed to the message. Two ranking officials of the shogunate led the three envoys from Korea to the shogun. The envoys offered four bows to the shogun. After the delivery of the national message was over, the envoys entered a welcoming party hosted by the shogun. Thus would the ceremonies confirming the trust and friendship in this mutual relationship conclude.

V

Diplomatic formalities were strictly followed not only in the ceremonies of official message delivery, but in the ceremonies in which gifts were exchanged. Wild ginseng and cultivated ginseng—gifts brought by Korean families of the Tokugawa clan—were actually gifts from the vice-minister of civility to the *roju* even though they were sent in the name of the Korean king or from a bureau director of the Ministry of Civility to the *bugyo* under the *roju*. Gifts to the lords of clans bore the name of a section chief.

About two weeks after the official message delivery ceremony, another ceremony was held to deliver the Japanese official message or shogun's personal letter. In the interval, great cultural interchanges took place between scholars and men of letters of the two countries. The three envoys met the head of Shoheiko, the shogunate's university, compilers, and clerks. Japanese Confucian students and men of letters coming from all parts of the country befriended high-level members of the Korean party. Professor Eiko Nakamura describes the scene as follows:

When the Korean mission entered the country, Japanese men of culture vied with each other to interview the foreigners, who were using the same writing system (Chinese characters). They shared the joy of exchanging Chinese poems, and the Japanese requested calligraphy works and paintings from the Korean visitors. The Japanese learned about the political situations in China and Korea, inquired about Korean history and customs, and engaged in questions and answers in many academic fields including Chinese classics and history by means of writing. (*Chosen*, Yoshikawa Kobunkan)

The compilers in particular were so busy that they could hardly pay attention to other affairs. Sin Yu-han, a compiler who visited Japan as compiler in 1719, had the following report to make in *Haeyurok*:

I was so busily engaged in my duties that I could not set aside time to exchange poems with regular Japanese poets who wanted to see me or engage in a leisurely talk with them by means of writing. This made me sad . . . . I was obliged to write a preface to an anthology of poems, a theme on a painting, a panegyric over a portrait, and compose poems portraying things, while receiving persons who wanted my seal.

The visitors from Korea had to keep themselves busy to receive guests not only in Edo but also in places where they stayed for the night during their sojourn in Japan. They had little time to sleep, for they had to exchange poems with Japanese guests and talk with them through writing. Japanese Confucianists were interested in particular in the scholarship and personal tastes of Yi Toe-gye, while showing extraordinary concern for his descendants. Their studies of Toe-gye were so deep that even the noted Korean Confucianist Yi Dong-gwak, a compiler who visited Japan in 1711, was surprised at their questions.

It was Kang Hang, a Korean who was kidnapped to Japan during the Hideyoshi invasion, who introduced the learning of Yi Toe-gye to Japan. His disciple, Seika Fujiwara, became the forerunner of Neo-Confucianism in Japan. Fujiwara's disciple was Hayashi Razan, and he and his descendants served as the dean of the shogunate university for generations to come. This respect of Yi Toe-gye enhanced Japanese scholars' friendliness toward Korea. Japanese scholars rejoiced at the visits of the Korean mission as a rare opportunity, which could provide a chance for the Japanese not only to have academic and cultural interchanges, but to form real friendships between kindred minds.

Another important point of exchange in these visits was medical science. Japanese physicians were required to always carry medical manuals brought from Korea, up until the propagation of Dutch medicine. Among these were *Uibang yuchwi* (Classified Collection of Medical Prescriptions), *Chijong jinam* (Guidebook to Curing Tumors), and *Dongui bogam* (Exemplar of Korean Medicine). The preface to the Japanese reprint of *Exemplar of Korean Medicine* published in 1723 reads:

> Its descriptions are minute and elaborate and devoid of fabrications. In addition, the prescriptions are clear so that they prevent disease in advance. . . . This book eliminates the futile labor of studying other miscellaneous books of medicine for a score of years.

As the Japanese began to pay greater attention to Korean medicine, the Tokugawa shogunate requested the attendance of physicians as members of the Korean missions. Koreans then brought along first-rate physicians. Kwon Do-jok, one such physician, was interviewed by many Japanese physicians in 1719. Tsukiyama interviewed Baek Heung-jeon, another excellent physician from Korea, at his lodging in Osaka. The interview resulted in the compilation of *Sokan washoshu*, a three-volume collection of questions and answers. Tsukiyama. Kitao, who met Ki Du-mun in 1714, published *Sokan idan* and Yamada, who met Yi Jwa-guk in 1764, authored *Sokan hitsugo*. These books won great acclaim as introductions to Korean books of medicine.

Significant also was the central importance of Korean ginseng. This tonic herb occupied a great position in trade between the two countries in the fifteenth and sixteenth centuries. Korea exported 1,500 to 2,000 *gwan* (equivalent to 3.75kg) of ginseng to Japan annually after the seventeenth century. The growing export volume was due to the wondrous effect of ginseng. *Nihon jinsenshi* records that, "Korean ginseng saved many lives by healing serious diseases which even the best physicians could hardly cure."

As the popularity of the Korean ginseng grew, the Tokugawa shogunate decided to cultivate the plant in Japan and named Uemura as supervisor. The lord of the Tsushima clan was ordered to obtain ginseng roots from Korea. However, all attempts to grow ginseng in Japan ended in failure, with one exception. The Japanese sowed seeds in Imaichi, Tochigi Prefecture, and succeeded in growing the plant. Ginseng cultivation spread to other parts of the country and the amount of ginseng imported from Korea decreased drastically.

The Korean envoys were accompanied by first-rate painters. Yi Hong-gyu, Yu Seong-eop, and Yi Eon-hong went to Japan in 1607, 1617, and 1624 as "government-employed painters." In 1636, Kim Myeong-guk, the foremost representative of Korean art in the seventeenth century, visited Japan. He too accompanied the Korean mission as a government-employed painter in 1643, and painted "Portrait of a Dharma," in Japan, where the painting remains even today.

Yi Gi-yong, too, visited Japan in 1643 and left behind *Songam bijodo* (Pine Rocks with Flying Birds). Han Si-gak, who went to Japan in 1655, bequeathed two paintings of bamboo trees. Ham Je-geon was known for his *Jukgukdo* (Bamboo and Chrysanthemum) in 1682. Bak Dong-bo, who visited Japan in 1711, left behind *Maeng Ho-yeon bangmae* (Maeng Ho-yeon Visits Plum Trees) and Ham Se-hwi left behind *Sansudo* (Landscape) and *Buyong bongdo* (Peony Peaks) in 1719.

Yi Seong-rin bequeathed *Saro seunggudo* (Wonderful Views on the Waterways), an album of paintings, in 1748 (now in the collection of the National Museum in Seoul). Choe Buk left five paintings including *Cho-ok sansu* (Landscape with a Thatched Cottage). Four paintings executed by Kim Yu-seong, another government-employed painter from Korea, in Japan in 1764 are kept at present at Seikenji Temple in Shimizu. *Yi Sin-won sasaengcheop* (An Album of Sketches by Yi Sin-won), which Yi Ui-chun (Sinwon) painted in Japan in 1811, included in the collection of the Gansong Gallery in Seoul, contains *Daemado bujungdo* (A Sketch of the Tsushima Government Office). Japanese painters drew portraits of Korean envoys, paying heed to the visit of the Korean mission. Representative are a portrait of Bak An-gi, a compiler who visited Japan in 1644, painted by Kano Tanyu, and a portrait of Jo Tae-eok, the senior envoy in 1711, painted by Kano Joshin. The Japanese artists also painted a scene showing a fleet of ships with Korean envoys aboard navigating upstream along the Yodo River and a scene showing a procession of Korean envoys taking an overland journey. Other noted painting include "Chosen tsushinshi toshosha sannyuzu" (Korean Envoys Paying Respect to Toshosha Shrine) by Kano Tanyu, "Chosen kokushi kantaizu" (Welcoming Korean Envoys) by Kano Ikushin, and "Chosenjin raichozu" (Koreans Visiting Japan) by Hagawa Toei.

VI

Economic exchange throve between the two countries in the seventeenth century, encouraged by their friendly relations. In evidence, the Treaty of the Year Giyu concerning trade was concluded in 1609, as follows:

1. Japanese trade ships to Korea will be limited to those which are authorized by the Japanese king (Tokugawa shogun), Lord So of Tsushima, or Tsushima officials.
2. The number of Japanese trade ships from the Tsushima clan will not exceed 20 annually.
3. The "Tsushima officials" will be limited to those who rendered service to promoting friendship between the two countries during or after the Hideyoshi invasion and invested with government positions by the Korean government.

In accordance with the agreement, Korea established a Japanese office in Busan and Japan opened Waniura in the northern tip of Tsushima Island as a trade port. However, Korean merchants did not enter the port because they could settle all accounts in Busan.

The Japanese office in Busan was opened originally in Dumopo but removed to a 100,000 *pyeong* site surrounding the present Yongdusan Park in 1678. The director of the office led a staff of 500 to 600 Japanese who worked there in shifts for two to three years engaging in diplomacy and trade.

According to a record of the Japanese office dating to the eighteenth century, about 50 Japanese trade ships entered Busan annually. The trade followed three patterns. In the first pattern, the lord of Tsushima paid "tribute" including items such as black pepper and tropical wood, dyestuffs such as alum, colored ink stones, and gilt screens. The gifts in return included ginseng, honey, tiger fur, leopard fur, white hemp cloth, white cotton cloth, and pine nuts.

The second pattern was official trade of goods. Korea imported copper, zinc, black pepper, tropical wood, and buffalo horns, and silver was added to the list from the latter half of the seventeenth century. In return, the main export item to Japan was cotton cloth. According to *Tongmun gwanji* (Records of the Bureau of the Interpreters of Foreign Languages), the barter rates were 610 rolls of cotton cloth for 100 *gwan* of copper, 100 rolls of cotton cloth for 100 *gwan* of black pepper, and 33 rolls of cotton cloth for 100 *gwan* of tropical wood.

Private trade took place between Korean Dongnae and Japanese Tsushima merchants at a market opened inside the Japanese office six times a month. The Japanese purchased ginseng, Chinese raw silk, and silk clothes and paid in silver.

Cotton cloth was the central item of export to Japan. 60,000 rolls of Korean cotton cloth went to Japan annually until the early eighteenth century when Japan could provide its own cotton. The raw silk Korea purchased in Beijing and sold to Japan was larger in quantity and cheaper in price than the Chinese raw silk that entered Nagasaki. Japanese silver, on the other hand, was carried to Beijing by Korean merchants who accompanied the Korean mission to the Chinese court and was exchanged there for raw silk. Silver amounting to 18,000 *gwan* flowed to Beijing from Korea on the average annually until the early eighteenth century. Thus, Silver and raw cotton successfully connected these three countries in East Asia.

The friendly relations between Korea and Japan promoted economic exchange between the two countries. Tobacco, red pepper, and potatoes played a great role in facilitating this cordial relationship. Tobacco, red pepper, and pumpkinseeds were introduced from Japan, together with their methods of cultivation, in 1616 or 1617, immediately after diplomatic relations with that country were resumed. Tobacco was propagated at an unexpectedly rapid pace and tobacco won soon an important item among Korean exports to Qing China. Red pepper became popular in the eighteenth century and became an indispensable ingredient in Korean food by changing the palate of Korean people after it found its way to *gimchi*.

It was in 1764 that potatoes entered Korea for the first time. Many people died of starvation in a great famine that ravaged Japan in 1732 but the inhabitants of Tsushima were able to survive by subsisting on potatoes. The mighty effect of potatoes soon spread to Korea when Jo Eom, who visited Japan as a Korean envoy in 1764, learned the art of growing potatoes and brought his knowledge home. Potatoes transplanted to Korea thus saved many lives during the repeated famines in Korea in the nineteenth century.

VII

Although peculiar domestic situations in both countries prevented the

Korean mission from visiting Japan after 1811, a staff of 500 to 600 Japanese was stationed at the Japanese office in Choryang, Busan. Close contact was kept between the Dongnae magistrate and the Tsushima lord at all times and missions traveled back and forth regularly between Busan and Tsushima. When a French fleet invaded Ganghwado island in 1866, for instance, the Korean government immediately informed Japan of this incident and advised her to draw up appropriate measures against possible imperialist aggression from Europe. Such was the nature of the relationship between Japan and Korea until two years before the 1868 Meiji Restoration in Japan, when the Meiji government disrupted the relations that had continued for more than 260 years.

This year (1985) marks the twentieth anniversary of the normalization of diplomatic relations between Korea and Japan. A special exhibition on the Korean goodwill envoys is scheduled in Tokyo from late October to commemorate the anniversary. It is significant to seek ways of developing new friendship between the two neighbors.

The Role of Hangang River Merchants and the Commercial Development in the Late Joseon Dynasty

Kang Man-gil

Preface

Research from a variety of perspectives has been conducted on merchants of various types who were active in Joseon dynasty prior to the opening of Korean ports for external commerce. Early research was largely concerned with middlemen in provincial towns called *gaekju* (inland market brokers) or *yeogak* (coastal trade brokers). Recently the focus of research has shifted to *gongin* (tribute men), *siin* (marketeers), *songsang* (merchants of Gaeseong), *yeokgwan* (government translators and interpreters), and *nanjeonin* (owners of unlicensed shops). The activities of these merchants prior to the opening of the ports can be grouped into two categories, as defined by the research. The first can be understood simply as commercial activities long rooted in history. The second can be expressed as activities that played a role in creating prerequisite conditions for breaking the foundations of feudal society and promoting the development of the capitalist mode of production in the process of the collapse of feudal society and emergence of capitalist

---

* Originally published in the *Korea Journal*, vol. 19, no. 3 (March 1979).

Kang Man-gil is President of Sangji University. He obtained his Ph.D. in Korean history from Korea University in 1975. He is the author of many books on Korean history, including *Bundan sidae-ui yeoksa insik* (Historical Perceptions of the National Division Period) (1978), *Haebang jeonhusa-ui insik* (Recognition of History before and after Liberation) I, II, III (1979), and *Hanguk jabonjuui-ui yeoksa* (History of Korean Capitalism) (2000). E-mail: bbdbej@korea.com.

society.

Needless to explain, we shall not encounter any problems if we limit the merchant's activities to the former category. If we want to extend their role to the latter, however, we need more positive research and a more sound theoretical footing. Research on the history of commerce during this period will bear fruit only with in-depth analysis of various groups of merchants who were active during that time. Such analysis will more clearly elucidate both the universality and particularity of the commerce and economy of Joseon society in general prior to the opening of its ports.

On the basis of this understanding, this paper will delve into the activities of the merchants called *gyeonggang sangin*, the scope of whose activities was broader and more conspicuous than other groups of merchants active prior to the opening of Korean ports. They have not been rigorously examined by prior research. These merchants were based in areas bordering the Hangang river which flows through the capital city of Seoul. They transported the grain paid to the government as tax, engaged in commercial activities utilizing boats, or carried on various types of commerce in Seoul while settling themselves along the Hangang river. The merchants appear in various historical materials concerning this period under names such as *gyeonggang sangin* (Hangang river merchants), *gangsang* (river merchants), *gyeongsang seonin* (Hangang river boatmen), and *gyeonggangin* (Hangang river men). Although these different names may indicate slight differences in their main occupations, they will be referred to as "Hangang river merchants" in this paper. For while these groups may have differed from each other in the scope of trade and the nature of their commerce may have varied, they formed a distinctive commercial sphere along the Hangang river throughout the Joseon period and held an important position in the history of Joseon dynasty commerce. A major aspect of that history will be examined in this paper through delving into the activities of these merchants.

Accumulation of Capital through Transportation of Grain

The original method of accumulating capital by Hangang river merchants was transportation of grain by boat. The most important trade was transportation of tax grain paid to the government and farm-rents in kind paid to the landlord-*yangban* class throughout the Joseon period.

The Joseon kingdom, following the example of Goryeo, enforced the System of Oarsmen immediately after its establishment, utilizing only government-owned rowboats and naval vessels. Given that a system of hiring private boats, which was also enforced for transportation of tax grain, is mentioned frequently in early Joseon period literature,[1] it is likely that shipping business with private vessels developed considerably. However, we have no data with which to confirm whether the Hangang river merchants owned all the private boats rented for transportation of tax grain. Nevertheless, we may presume that merchant boats led river shipping in the first half of the Joseon period, given that the Hangang river was the center of river shipping throughout the Joseon period and that private vessels were more active there than were those owned by the government.[2]

It was, however, in the latter half of the Joseon period or, more precisely, after the seventeenth century, that the Hangang river merchants could connect their grain transportation business with the accumulation of capital. It also seems that committing various irregularities in the course of transporting grain, rather than connecting freight charges, was their central means of amassing wealth. In various government documents on the latter half of the Joseon period, we find a number of cases of irregularities by the Hangang river merchants in the course of shipping grain. Most widely known among these were *hwasu* (mixing water), *tuksik* (stealing), and *gopae* (scuttling ships on purpose). They poured a certain amount of water into the grain to swell it to a larger size and pocketed the surplus of grain that exceeded its original measurement before swelling.[3] Theft of tax grain occurred on a relatively large scale.[4] Hangang river merchants embezzled a part or the whole of

---

1. *Taejong sillok* (Annals of King Taejong), *gwon* 5, *sinhae* day of the 6th lunar month, 3rd year of King Taejo's reign, and *gwon* 24, gapsin day of the 11th lunar month, 12th year of King Taejo's reign.

2. *Sejong sillok* (Annals of King Sejong), *gwon* 102, *gyeongsin* day of the 10th lunar month, 25th year of Sejong, and *Sejo sillok* (Annals of King Sejo), *gwon* 5, *imjin* day of the 12th lunar month, 2nd year of King Sejo's reign.

3. *Bibyeonsa deungnok* (Records of the Border Defense Council), *gwon* 9, 23rd day of the 4th lunar month, 8th year of King Yeongjo's reign.

4. *Seungjeongwon ilgi* (Diaries of the Royal Secretariat), *gwon* 532, 17th day of the 7th lunar month, 1st year of Gyeongjong, and *Bibyeonsa ilgi* (Daily Records of the Border Defense Council), *gwon* 139, 21st day of the 12th lunar month, 36th year of King Yeongjo's reign.

the tax grain, including rice collected under the Daedongbeop (Uniform Land Tax Law), which they were forwarding under contract with the government. Their method of scuttling boats on purpose after loading the grain to their secret storage was quite clever. This practice continued to thrive throughout the latter half of the Joseon period in spite of strong government measures against it, inflicting heavy damage on the people and government.

The various irregularities committed by Hangang river merchants brought about a serious decline in the government's tax revenue. They took almost exclusive charge of transporting tax grain from the three southern provinces of Jeolla, Chungcheong, and Gyeongsang, which constituted the most important financial source of the state throughout the latter half of the Joseon period. Thereupon, the government studied, from a variety of perspectives, effective measures to improve methods of shipping tax grain. As an alternative, the System of Oarsmen was studied again and placed into partial effect, mobilizing government-owned ships and coastal inhabitants for the corvee of transporting the tax grain. The system, however, met active opposition and resistance by the Hangang river merchants who bribed ranking officials and even assisted them in committing irregularities if necessary, thereby causing trouble on many occasions. One such example is that of collusion between the merchants and the chief of the Saganwon (Office of the Censor-General), Kim Yang-sim in 1774 (50th year of King Yeongjo's reign).[5]

The persistent and aggressive moves of the Hangang river merchants to frustrate the enforcement of exclusive government shipping were effective because the authorities were not in a position to deprive the merchants arbitrarily of their monopolized right to transport tax grain. Further, the government did not foresee that conversion to the new system would bring about greater convenience and greater profit than continuing to pay freight charges to the merchants for their transportation service.

We may generally cite three reasons why the Joseon dynasty government could not strip Hangang river merchants of their shipping rights. First, their position as merchants and their relations with the government had already become so firm that the government was unable to deprive them arbitrarily of their right. Second, the government foresaw

---

5. *Bibyeonsa deungnok, gwon* 156, 18th day of the 12th lunar month, 50th year of King Yeongjo's reign.

that if Hangang river merchants were forced to abandon their tax grain transportation service, there would be no way of forwarding farm rents to landlords residing in Seoul. Third, the government also foresaw difficulty in mobilizing a sufficient number of boats if the system of using Hangang river merchants to transport tax grain was discarded and replaced by a system of direct shipping. We may even cite a fourth reason: the system of direct transportation by the government proved less profitable than entrusting the service to the merchants. This was explained in "Yeongnam joseon byeontong ji chaek" (A Measure for Improving Shipping Service in the Yeongnam District), which an official named U Jeong-gyu proposed to the government in 1788 (12th year of King Jeongjo's reign) through his *Gyeongje ya-eon* (Unofficial Notes on Economy). He proposed that the service of transporting tax grain from the Yeongnam district be awarded to Hangang river merchants. According to his arguments, the measure would help the government economize in terms of the overall cost of transportation and would result in nine other advantageous points for the government.[6] Even though not all of U's proposals were accepted by the government, the position of the Hangang river merchants was, as a result of U's proposals, raised to a higher level than it had been under the System of Oarsmen. The merchants also began to enjoy the right to transport tax grain to a steadily increasing number of local offices. They were granted these rights because they were excellently skilled in ship navigation and they were well-equipped with the proper transportation gear, advantages they held over other groups of public forwarding agents.

In short, grain transportation with private vessels had been rapidly developing since the early years of the Joseon dynasty, and the grain transportation service by the Hangang river merchants with their private boats became particularly active in the latter half of the dynasty period. In the seventeenth and eighteenth centuries and thereafter, Hangang river merchants won contracts for forwarding most of the tax grain sent to the central government in Seoul from the three southern provinces and most of the farm rents to the bureaucrat *yangban* class in the capital. In fact, they firmly secured their position as the largest forwarding agents in the country.

---

6. U Jeong-gyu, *Gyeongje ya-eon* (Unofficial Notes on Economy). "Yeongnam josen byeontong ji chaek" (A Measure for Improving Shipping Service in the Yeongnam District).

The tax paid in kind to the government and the farm rents paid to landlords began to be replaced gradually by cash payments in the latter part of the Joseon period, presumably entailing a decrease in the quantity of grain transported from the provinces to the capital. Even under such circumstances, the position held by Hangang river merchants in nationwide gain transportation was impressive and they enjoyed a relatively high rate of capital accumulation.

Commerce by Ship and Development of Wholesale Trade

Hangang river merchants conducted various commercial activities as additional means of accumulating capital. The scope of their commercial activities covered almost the whole of the country; grain, fish, and salt constituted the major types of merchandise they handled. Among the three, grain was the most important item as they supplied the majority of the grain consumed by the inhabitants of Seoul. As Seoul gradually transformed into a commercial metropolis from the seventeenth century onwards, the position of Hangang river merchants as grain dealers became firmer, with the result that the sphere of their commercial activities and the scope of their capital expanded. This growth ultimately enabled them to launch wholesale trade through their monopoly on certain goods.

Foremost among the commercial activities conducted by Hangang river merchants was trade by ship. They purchased goods where they were produced, transported them by ship to areas along the Hangang river, and sold them either to marketeers or directly to end-users. It is not clear in this case whether all of the Hangang river merchants were independently engaged in the trade utilizing their own craft and capital, or they were hired by financiers and acted merely as their agents. Presumably, however, both kinds of arrangements existed. In some cases merchants formed a close connection with financiers, frequented production centers in the provinces, bought goods they wanted, carried them to the Seoul area utilizing ships provided by the financiers or their own craft, and sold them to the financiers along the Hangang river who operated markets. In other cases, the Hangang river merchants, with their own considerable capital, commanded their own vessels and transported to Seoul the goods they bought in person at provincial production centers. In either case, the Hangang river merchants who brought their merchandise from the provinces by ships could set up one market after another along the Hangang river to dispose of their commodities. Gradually they were able to organize wholesale trade or monopolize goods for commercial purposes, further expanding the scope of their capital. One good example can be found in the salt trade. According to the *Sipye*, a book recording evil practices in the Seoul market business, published in 1753 (29th year of King Yeongjo's reign), several guards from the signal fire stand on Namsan mountain in Seoul began to engage in the transportation of commercial salt in 1740 or thereabouts. Their business had grown so enormous by that time that they could make use of more than ten large ships in transporting a large quantity of salt from where it was made to Seoul. Their direct sale of salt on the Hangang river posed a great threat to the government licensed salt market in Mapo.[7]

This example shows many aspects of the friction between the Hangang river merchants who were settled along the Hangang river as boat merchants and the owners of the government-licensed markets inside the fortress walls of Seoul. Existing alongside the Hangang river since the early years of the Joseon dynasty were government licensed markets trading in fish, salt, fire-wood, and rice. Some of them operated independently; others were subordinate to their head markets inside the walls, bound as subsidiaries or through harsh terms of taxation.[8] The relationship between the riverside markets and the Hangang river merchants was also close. The boat merchants had to sell their commodities to the riverside markets when they brought the goods from where they were produced to the river, for they were not allowed to retail their goods directly to consumers given the monopoly rights of government licensed marketeers. However, the boat merchants who were previously guards at the signal stand, as referred to earlier, gradually evolved into settled merchants along the Hangang river and secured their position through severe competition with the government licensed marketeers. As shown in this example, the monopoly rights of the markets began to crumble. After the adoption of a measure removing the favoritism, called the Sinhae Tonggong (Commercialization Equalization Enactment of 1791), in 1791 (15th year of King Jeongjo's reign), the trend became so

---

7. *Sipye, gwon* 3, "Mapo yeomjeon jo" (On the Salt Market in Mapo).
8. *Sipye, gwon* 3, "Yongsan daejamok jeon" (On the Fire-Wood Market in Yongsan) and "Seogang mijeon jo" (On the Rice Market in Seogang).

conspicuous that the boat merchants were able to work free of the system of the government-licensed retail monopoly. This phenomenon illustrated the process by which the boat merchants, after liberating themselves from not only economic, but non-economic subordination to the marketeers, gradually secured their own independent sales mechanisms and networks.

At around this time, financiers along the Hangang river, and the ship owners and middlemen, who had accumulated wealth through transportation of tax grain, came to be engaged in riverside commerce in competition with the licensed marketeers, securing their commercial foothold in the process.

According to written records, they too were obligated to pay a tax for their infringement on the monopoly rights of the licensed riverside merchants and downtown marketeers, as in the case of those Hangang river merchants who converted to become boat merchants.[9] Overcoming the noneconomic infringement by the licensed marketeers with the influence of their capital, they, too, gradually expanded their commercial sphere. According to a record dating to the early part of the nineteenth century, those who posed the greatest threat to the government-licensed markets were these ship owners and financiers based on the Hangang river. In short, three groups of merchants—boat merchants; financiers, ship owners and middlemen; and licensed riverside merchants—launched brisk commercial activities along the Hangang river in the latter half of the Joseon period. With Seoul in the background, the scope of their commerce gradually reached the extent to which they could commence wholesale trade.

Let us now examine the reality of the wholesale trade engaged in by the Hangang river merchants, the causes that led to its rise, and its character.

The wholesale trade of the Hangang river merchants developed especially in the rice sector. In addition to the small quantity of rice that flowed into the capital from farming villages in its suburbs, most of the rice needs of Seoul citizens was met with the grain that the government gave to gongin (tribute men) in payment for their work, called gongmi, and the grain that the Hangang river merchants purchased from rural areas, called gangsangmi. The gongmi, or tax rice, which the government collected with the enforcement of the Uniform Land Tax Law, flowed

---

9. *Sipye, gwon* 3, "Seogang mijeon jo."

into the rice markets in Seoul through the *gongin* and was sold to general consumers. The *gangsangmi*, too, flowed into the rice markets through boat merchants and rice dealers based on the Hangang river. When a group of merchants with a considerable financial strength bought up rice that flowed into the capital through the above-mentioned two channels, the price of rice in Seoul skyrocketed. By making monopoly of the market on rice brought to Seoul from the provinces, Hangang river merchants could manipulate its price at will.

Of the total amount of rice needed by Seoul inhabitants yearly, stock for three to four month periods was supplied from places of production along the periphery of the capital, brought in either by farmers directly, or by rice dealers via overland routes. The rest of the demand was met with rice released by the government, including *gongmi*. However, the quantity of government rice was limited and, furthermore, kept decreasing as tax rice was gradually replaced by payment in cash. All this meant, finally, that almost all the rice needed by Seoul citizens was met with the grain boat merchants purchased and brought from Jeolla-do, Hwanghae-do, and other provinces.

According to records in *Bibyeonsa deungnok* (Records of the Border Defense Council), Hangang river merchants sold the rice they had bought up on the river not only in Seoul but also in small and large provincial cities and even in rural villages whenever rice became scarce due to bad harvests, sending its price soaring. This was enabled by their substantial capital, which in turn allowed then to hoard rice for long periods of time. Further, their commercial networks had expanded so much that they were able to foresee any fluctuation in the price of rice promptly and on a broad scale.

Figures concerning the rice transported to and stored along the Hangang river would reveal the scope of the Hangang river merchants' commercial activities and the power of their capital. Unfortunately, the materials with which we can measure it are only fragmentary. What we know is that the population of the capital within the fortress walls amounted to about 200,000 as of the latter half of the eighteenth century[10] and the amount of rice consumed per year can be estimated at about 300,000 *seok*. Given that three to four months stocks were sup-

---

10. *Jeongjo sillok* (Annals of King Jeongjo), *gwon* 28, *sinmi* day of the 12th lunar month, 13th year of King Jeongjo's reign, contains statistics according to which the population of Seoul was recorded to be 189,153.

plied from farming villages on the periphery of the capital and that the rest was met with *gongmi* and *gangsangmi*, we may guess with a certain degree of accuracy the amount of rice collected and distributed by the Hangang river merchants as well as the scope of their rice monopoly.

Besides the rice and salt that were the major items in their wholesale trade, Hangang river merchants also dealt, on a relatively broad scale, in firewood, lumber, and ice (which they picked up from the Hangang river during winter). Firewood and lumber were the most important commodities in their commerce by boat, next to rice and salt. Household firewood and lumber for construction consumed in Seoul were cut down in mountainous areas in Gangwon-do province from which the Hangang river takes its rise and ferried or rafted to the capital and sold there, with the Hangang river merchants making profits through monopoly. As firewood, like rice, was an indispensable item of daily necessity which the city dwellers could not produce themselves, the Hangang river merchants who were in near sole possession of lumber supply routes had a direct connection with the life of Seoul inhabitants. As virtually all of the lumber sent to Seoul from upstream was transported by the so-called *yujeonja* (the persons who have money), even the government-licensed lumber dealers (*jangmokjeon*) with the right to retail it had to rely on these "persons" for its supply.[11] The "persons who have money" were merchants who were not admitted to the gild of government-licensed markets in Seoul and were based on the Hangang river. By isolating the Seoul market lumber dealers, who were admitted exclusive rights to sell lumber by the government, from the boat merchants who brought in lumber to Seoul, these persons could secure their position as middlemen. Having amassed significant capital, they were able to buy up all lumber brought in to Seoul and to restrain or even exert pressure upon the government-licensed lumber dealers.

Additionally, the *bingdogo* (icehouse), where the river merchants stored ice they collected from the Hangang river in winter for sale in the summer to preserve fish, became another important sector of their wholesale business developed on the river. The *bingdogo* dealers, holding a certain duty to the government to supply ice for public use in summer, like the licensed markets, were entitled to sell ice to fishing boats

---

11. *Sipye, gwon* 2, "Mun oe jangmok jeon jo" (On the Cotton Cloth Market in and outside Seoul).

scattered on the Hangang river. Small-scale icehouses were gradually closed down through competition and this business came to be monopolized by a few dealers. By 1786 (the 10th year of King Jeongjo's reign) the number of these icehouses declined from more than 30 to only 8.

In short, the wholesale trade on the Hangang river developed in the latter half of the Joseon period as a result of a number of factors. First, Seoul, as the hub of river commerce, was urbanized gradually and came to function more as a consumer market. Second, wealth had accumulated along the Hangang river since the early years of the Joseon dynasty through transportation of tax gain for hire. Third, coastal shipping by Hangang river merchants became active through the tax grain transportation, though limited to nearby waters, and their commercial activities utilizing ships developed commensurately. Marine transportation proved far more profitable, with the Hangang as the artery, than land carriage to Seoul. Fourth, wholesale trade made rapid progress in the general commercial world, centering on the government-licensed Seoul markets in the second half of the Joseon period. The large-scale merchants were able to amass great wealth in the process, which in turn put pressure on small, petty merchants—a phenomenon common among Hangang river merchants as well.

There are many records containing frequent discussion by the government of a measure to ask Hangang river merchants to employ as workers those people who wandered the country homeless and were on the verge of starvation as a means of providing them with relief. We can therefore presume that the Hangang river merchants, who had accumulated significant wealth in the latter half of the Joseon period, ran operations that were so extensive as to require considerable hired labor.

Extension of Wholesale Trade and Antagonism by the Consumer Class

The wholesale trade that pervaded the commercial world in the second half of the Joseon dynasty period grew more extensive over time, giving rise to serious ill effects, which, in turn, elicited antagonism from many sectors.

The wholesale trade of Hangang river merchants was no exception, expanding over the years with the rice trade occupying the central position. We may cite a number of factors in this growth. First, as referred to above, as Seoul grew more urbanized, the trend of grain being replaced gradually by cash in paying the land tax to the government and farm-rents to the bureaucratic *yangban* class became more conspicuous. This resulted in an increase in the amount of rice to be sold in the capital. Second, the trend toward cash payment led to the situation in which the scope the Hangang river merchant's commercial activities narrowed in the sector of gain transportation, while it broadened in the sectors of marine commerce and rice sales. Third, their successful performance in wholesale business brought about a rapid expansion in their capital, such that they could further seize all rice markets in Seoul including the government-licensed market by applying their substantial resources.

When Hangang river merchants' wholesale rice trade expanded and the merchants had seized virtually the entire market in Seoul, the impact was promptly and significantly brought to bear upon those who pur-chased a majority of the rice, namely commoners or members of the lower classes. This finally touched off a relatively large-scale "rice riot."

We can examine the character of the wholesale trade engaged in by the Hangang river merchants in the nineteenth century by studying the cause and progress of the "rice riot," which broke out in Seoul in 1883 (33rd year of King Sunjo's reign).

The riot erupted 22 years after the Hong Gyeong-nae Rebellion and 29 years before the Jinju Uprising. Although all three were resistance movements during the last years of the same medieval society, we may make clear distinctions between them. Whereas the Hong Gyeong-nae and Jinju rebellions can be defined as resistance by those men of the *yangban* class whose fortunes were crumbling, as well as medium- and and small-scale merchants, and peasants opposed to government corrup-tion and harsh exploitation by local officials, the "rice riot" was staged by consumers in the capital who, not owning their own land, had to buy their food-grain—mostly poverty-stricken people in low social estates. Although the cause of the rice riot can be examined from various angles, it is the position of this paper that it was touched off more by the resent-ment of the class of urban consumers for merchants, who were based largely in the Hangang river and indulged in the practice of monopoly, than by the general friction between privileged merchant classes and medium- to small-scale urban merchant classes in the medieval society. The roots of the riot can be more clearly revealed when it is examined in connection with the growth of commercial capital and the problem of commercial monopoly in the latter half of the Joseon period. We can also see what should have been the proper method of solving the problem by first examining the measures the Joseon government took against the rice riot.

As soon as the riot broke out, the Joseon government meted out indiscriminate punishment against rioters while, on the other hand, dealing severely with rice dealers. The government possessed enough insight to realize that the practice of monopoly by rice dealers was the cause of the disturbance.

Concluding that profiteering by owners of rice markets, together with price manipulation by Hangang river merchants, made it impossible for citizens, even those who had the money, to buy the staple grain. The government asserted that the incident was caused by a secret conspiracy between the rice marketeers and the Hangang river merchants. Also making it clear that it would have been unreasonable to leave marketeers intact while punishing the rioters, the government condemned leading marketeers to exile and prohibited rice monopoly on the river, while emphasizing the need to put merchants under stricter government surveillance.[12]

In spite of its admission that the rice riot was caused by a conspiracy between rice marketeers and the Hangang river merchants, the government held only the marketeers inside Seoul heavily accountable for the incident, condemning their heads to exile while limiting punitive action against the river merchants to a ban on rice monopoly.

On the other hand, however, the Ministry of Punishment expressed in a report that a heavier penalty be meted out to the river merchants. According to a report in the *Sunjo sillok* (Annals of King Sunjo), a larger amount of rice was brought that year (1832; 33rd year of Sunjo's reign) to the Hangang river than in ordinary years, such that its price declined in the middle of February, thereby stabilizing the feelings of the people. Concerned that the price of the rice they kept in storage would not rise, the report continued, the river merchants made *yeogak* and *gaekju* transport the rice in Seoul back to the countryside and pressured the marketeers inside Seoul to hike prices. Thus, *gangsanggok* (grain that is dealt by the Hangang river merchants) could not be brought in to Seoul after the end of February, and rice prices subsequently rose to twice the previous level

---

12. *Sunjo sillok* (Annals of King Sunjo), *gwon* 33, *sinmi* day of the 3rd lunar month, 33rd year of King Sunjo's reign.

on March 6. Two days later the riot finally broke out as the poor, now unable to buy rice, with all rice shops in Seoul having shut down, rose up in desperate protest.[13]

On the basis of this report, we can estimate the scope of the Hangang river merchant's wholesale trade to some extent. The financiers of the rice wholesale on the river were Hangang river merchants. As examined thus far, they manipulated provincial middlemen and rice marketeers in Seoul, through monopoly for commercial gains on the basis of their superior power of their capital. Important to note here is the fact that their wholesale trade was enabled more by their economic superiority than by any privilege they may have enjoyed. Social privileges shrunk in importance in the commercial world.

Emphasizing that the rice riot was caused by the conspiratorial practices of the Hangang river merchants, the ministry report furthermore pointed out that it was unreasonable for the government to have executed as many as seven riot leaders while the heaviest penalty meted out to the rice marketeers was exile, with not a single one of the Hangang river merchants having been punished. The report went on to recommend that the government, in compliance with the overwhelming opinion of Seoul citizens, investigate those who monopolized the rice market in the largest quantities, those who closed their shops and refused to sell rice in Seoul, and that they be executed.[14]

Ultimately in this incident, which is the only urban rice riot that broke out in the last stage of medieval Korean society, several river merchants and Seoul marketeers were put to death and several others banished to remote areas.[15] Although this incident was caused by a complex of factors, one of the most serious was monopoly on the Hangang river.

In sum, this incident showed us the process of deepening in the wholesale trade along the Hangang river and the degree of growth of their commercial capital that backed it. It also provided us with a glimpse of one aspect of the commerce of that time as shown by the rise of an anti-wholesale movement in the wake of the deepening in wholesale business.

---

13. *Sunjo sillok*, *gwon* 33, *gyemi* day of the 3rd lunar month, 33rd year of King Sunjo's reign.
14. *Ibid.*
15. *Sunjo sillok*, *gwon* 33, *imja* day of the 4th lunar month, 33rd year of King Sunjo's reign.

The Shipbuilding Monopoly and Its Meaning

We can easily imagine that, as the Hangang river had been the center of river shipping and commerce by boat since the early years of the Joseon dynasty, the river naturally formed a close connection with shipbuilding. It is very difficult, however, to obtain data showing when, in what scope, and in what form shipyards began to operate along the Hangang river. We can utilize only various official documents dating to the second half of the dynasty with which to trace the several methods by which Hangang river merchants came to possess ships. From these documents we can also learn of the relations between their wholesale business and shipbuilding and form an idea of the degree of development in their wholesale trade.

One method employed by Hangang river merchants to possess ships was to buy them. As an example we can cite a report submitted to the central government by a royal secret inspector sent to Chungcheong-nam-do province, who exposed an irregularity committed by a local magistrate there. According to the report, the local official gathered ship-building lumber from different areas of his subcounty and had three large and small ships illegally built, selling the large ones to a Hangang river merchant for 280 *ryang* each and the small one to a merchant from Cheongpung for 60 *ryang*.[16] Nevertheless, it would be difficult to conclude that such cases arose frequently. It is also unthinkable that the subcounty concerned and other towns for that matter were equipped with special shipyards.

Another method of possessing ships employed by Hangang river merchants was to procure second-hand ones which had been used for a considerable time. This method it seems, became quite universal among the river merchants. In 1736 (12th year of King Yeongjo's reign), a local official proposed to extend for ten more years the official retirement age for military vessels. He based his proposal on the fact that Hangang river merchants, after purchasing ten-year-old ships, repaired and used them for ten more years. On the basis of this observation, the official proposed a measure not to hand decommissioned naval boats over to Hangang river merchants but to repair and use them again.[17] According

---

16. *Seungjeongwon ilgi*, gwon 429, 10th day of the 4th lunar month, 32nd year of King Sukjong's reign.
17. *Bibyeonsa deungnok*, gwon 99, 17th day of the 6th lunar month, 12th year of King

to a record dated 1710 (36th year of King Sukjong's reign), Hangang river merchants purchased decommissioned military ships from one local government and sold them to another. We can safely presume, further, that they possessed marine repair workshops. This helps us to conclude that Hangang river merchants, who obviously relied on ships for most of their commercial activities, such as grain shipment on hire and trade by ship, had been engaged in various phases of shipbuilding since long before.

Several examples can be cited to bolster this claim. In 1731 (7th year of King Yeongjo's reign), the government selected 33 Hangang river merchants whose ships had been sunk and sent them to lumber-rich areas in the Honam district. They were directed to build 33 ships with lumber taken from wind-hewn trees on mountains, where intentional felling was prohibited, and to transport rice collected under the Uniform Land Tax Law with the vessels they constructed.[18] The government disbursed a sum of 100 *ryang* per vessel in addition to living expenses, thereby providing a handsome profit for the boatmen. The lucrative gains not withstanding, the river merchants from the Seoul area, taking advantage of their assignment to shipbuilding, utilized the ships they built for private purposes, inflicting damage on the government. This exposed them to adverse criticism.[19] According to another record dated 1737 (13th year of King Yeongjo's reign), orders were issued to Hangang river merchants to construct five vessels to transport tax grain collected in Jinju, Gyeongsang-do province. However, before the shipbuilding funds were released, the magistrate in Jinju was replaced and the newly appointed one did not disburse the funds, thereby incurring public reproach.[20]

The examples cited above all indicate that the government gave both shipbuilding lumber and funds to those Hangang river merchants who did not own vessels, made them build their own ships, and placed the ships on the state registry while, nevertheless, assigning to them the mis-

---

Yeongjo's reign.

18. *Bibyeonsa deungnok*, *gwon* 90, 27th day of the 12th lunar month, 7th year of King Yeongjo's reign.

19. *Seungjeongwon ilgi*, *gwon* 75, 20th day of the 11th lunar month, 8th year of King Yeongjo's reign.

20. *Bibyeonsa deungnok*, *gwon* 102, 28th day of the 11th lunar month, 13th year of King Yeongjo's reign.

sion of transporting tax rice with the ships they constructed. The last example does not show clearly to which side the vessels belonged legally. It is certain, however, that the Hangang river merchants who were sent to Jinju built the ships there and carried the tax rice to Seoul by utilizing those ships. Hence, it can hardly be said that they operated shipyards in the real sense of the term along the Hangang river.

On the other hand, however, there must have been some among the Hangang river merchants who gradually switched their major occupation to shipbuilding. This is evidenced by the fact that lumber brought from mountains on Anmyeondo island and other areas throughout the country where felling was prohibited was sold to Hangang river merchants for shipbuilding[21] and, more notably, by the fact that wholesale posts were set up along the Hangang river for shipbuilding lumber.

By the latter half of the Joseon dynasty period the wholesale dealers had become powerful enough to monopolize the repair and construction of the *jinseon* (ferry boats) which provided the most important transportation means along the Hangang river. Nevertheless, it is not clear whether the work of the lumber dealers was confined to supplying only lumber or whether they further supplied ships constructed with that lumber. However, we can say definitely that the Hangang river merchants who took charge of constructing ships utilized their wholesale posts as shipyards. This is based on records concerning the construction of *chamseon* (river boats), created when *joseon* (coastal ships) and river boats which were utilized for transporting tax grain were built and when they were repaired. According to the records, riverboats underwent partial repair seven years after construction and complete repair fourteen years after construction. The wholesale lumber dealers based in the Hangang river area constructed and supplied ships with funds disbursed by the local governments that paid tax grain.[22]

It is also not clear whether the wholesale posts operated by the Hangang river boatmen specialized in shipbuilding alone or they were engaged in sale of rice and shipbuilding lumber in addition. We should find considerable significance in the fact that the lumber wholesale busi-

---

21. *Bibyeonsa deungnok*, *gwon* 158, first day of the 6th lunar month, 1st year of King Jeongjo's reign.
22. *Ilseongnok* (Records of Daily Reflection), 13th day of the first lunar month, 12th year of King Jeongjo's reign.

ness grew up to engage in shipbuilding in the Hangang river area which was one of the most notable commercial centers in the second half of the Joseon period. The fact that Hangang river merchants relied on ships to make their living while engaging in commercial activities on board vessels and shipping tax grain on errands for hire is not sufficient to explain the reason why they could develop wholesale business for shipbuilding to such an extent. The main reason must have been that the development of wholesale trade along the Hangang river culminated in accumulating commercial capital to a considerable degree in the latter half of the Joseon period.

Wholesale trade was one characteristic form of commerce of the latter Joseon period and shipbuilding by wholesale dealers was a notable phenomenon in connection with the nature of wholesale business in general. Commercial activities became very brisk as a whole in the latter half of the Joseon period, resulting in the development of wholesale commerce as engaged in not only by the licensed Seoul marketeers but by Gaeseong and Hangang river merchants. Their wholesale activities were not confined to the practice of making a profit through monopoly; but the capital they amassed by cornering was, in the case of Hangang river merchants, invested in shipbuilding. Those who operated shipbuilding establishments were generally speaking ship owners and middlemen based in the Hangang river area who accumulated wealth through shipment of tax gain commercial activities by utilizing ships and wholesale trade along the river. Presumably they first operated shipbuilding lumber wholesale establishments and later explored the business of shipbuilding by employing shipbuilding technicians who lived along the Hangang river.

In short, Hangang river merchants developed wholesale trade along the river through the process of shipment of tax grain at first and commercial activities by utilizing ships next, and after succeeding in accumulating a certain amount of capital, launched the business of shipbuilding. These indicate one aspect of the change that took place in the commercial activities along the Hangang river in a narrow sense and throughout the country in a broad sense in the latter half of the Joseon dynasty period.

Conclusion

Among the groups of merchants that formed within districts or through various organizations throughout the Joseon dynasty, the Hangang river merchants who engaged in commercial activities in the capital sphere were the most characteristic. Early in the Joseon dynasty they began to transport tax grain on errands for hire. By the second half of the period, their transportation business had expanded so much that they shipped most of the rice collected under the Uniform Land Tax Law. Their network of forwarding services, further, came to cover almost all parts of the country. The enormous amounts of grain the merchants received as freight rates and the freedom to set freight rates empowered them to manipulate the price of rice in Seoul. However, they also resorted to illegal means in order to accumulate their wealth. In spite of these irregularities, the Hangang river merchants gradually monopolized the transportation of tax gain and farm-rents by taking advantage of their collusion with ranking officials and their superiority in terms of navigational skills and equipment.

Besides the transportation of grain, the Hangang river merchants also engaged in commerce in salt and fish. The scope of their activities in this line of business was large, connecting Seoul with all provincial production centers. Some of the merchants came to settle along the Hangang river, securing wholesale establishments. In the wholesale business the Hangang river merchants at first were subjected to restrictions exercised by government-licensed Seoul marketeers; they were, however, able to overcome this problem through their significant economic strength. The development of wholesale trade stimulated accumulation of capital by the Hangang river merchants, so much that some of them were called *gyeonggang busang* (wealthy merchants on the Hangang river) or *gyeonggang geobu* (men of great wealth on the Hangang river). In around the eighteenth century, the commercial world witnessed a great development of wholesale trade, whether it was dominated by the marketeers or by other merchants. In the process of its expansion, many problems ensued in all sectors of the economy. From the second half of the eighteenth century to the first half of the nineteenth century, discussions arose denouncing the wholesale business; the public denunciation was ultimately translated into action in the form of public movements. Finally, in 1883 consumers in Seoul rose up in a "rice riot."

The rice riot unleashed by urban consumers in the last stage of our medieval society can be interpreted as an indicator of the seriously deepening process of wholesale business engaged in by the Hangang river merchants, although we may examine its causes from many angles. It will also help us understand the nature of the period's wholesale commerce as a whole.

The wholesale activities of the Hangang river merchants were not confined to dealing in grain and other commodities of daily necessity; rather, they developed production establishments of their own. The foremost among these were shipyards, where they built ships for wholesale, another phenomenon bearing economic significance. Their ship wholesale was evidence of the fact that the capital the Hangang river merchants had accumulated through transportation of grain on errands for hire, commerce by boat, and wholesale trade, had been invested in the production sector, though on a small scale and in an unorganized fashion.

Western Science and Silhak Scholars

Park Seong-rae

Changes in Korean society at the end of the Joseon dynasty have been studied in various fields, particularly in the history of agriculture, commerce and industry, and the social hierarchy. Again, in the history of thought, Silhak (Practical Learning) represented a turning point. It has been pointed out by many scholars that the science of the West, which Koreans in the latter half of the seventeenth century began to accept, was an impetus for that turning point in the thought of Koreans.

Hong I-seop pinpointed Silhak as an important subject for study in the history of science, saying that the study of the Silhak school in the "scientific history of Korea" is "an important task for Korean historians of science to tackle in the future."[1] Cheon Gwan-u (Chun Kwan-Woo) recently remarked on the same need, saying:

> In those days when specialized knowledge in public administration was seen as "affairs of government functionaries" and technique for production as "talented craft," the study of natural science or technique itself, lying outside the general interest of intelligentsia, was a sign of an attitude to modernization and in this sense, the realm of science and tech-

* Originally published in the *Korea Journal*, vol. 26, no. 3 (March 1986).

Park Seong-rae (Bak, Seong-rae) is Professor of History of Korean Science at Hankuk University of Foreign Studies. He also currently serves as a member of the National Institute of Korean History. He obtained his Ph.D. in History from the University of Hawaii in 1977. He authored many books, including *Hanguk gwahaksa* (History of Korean Science) (1982), *Hangugin-ui gwahak jeongsin* (Koreans' Scientific Mind) (1994), and *Dasi boneun minjok gwahak iyagi* (Essays Reviewing the National Science) (2002). E-mail: parkstar@unitel.co.kr.

1. Hong I-seop, *Joseon gwahaksa* (History of Joseon Science) (Seoul: Jeongeumsa, 1949), p. 24, n. 2.

nique has to be noted as an important ingredient of Silhak in the latter part of the Joseon dynasty.[2]

Despite this recognition, a number of studies so far on Silhak or the modern history of thought have been lopsided considerations of the history of social and economic thought without due regard to science. Of course, there has been some progress—the theory of the rotating earth of Kim Seok-mun was unearthed, and the scientific thought of Yi Ik and Hong Dae-yong has been publicized.[3] But most of the rest in the realm of science was in the form of partial references made either in individual studies of Silhak scholars or in research on the landing of Catholicism in Korea, falling far short of depicting the genuine picture of science in the body of Silhak.

How did science emerge as an important component in Silhak? This occurred because Korean scholars widely accepted the science of the West, which had been brought to China mostly by Jesuits from the early seventeenth century. From the end of Ming and the beginning of Qing, a number of Western missionaries centering around Matteo Ricci exerted great influence on China with the introduction of new science and technology from the West.[4] Books on Western science and technology in Chinese translation, which began to be published in quantity in China, formed the very foundation of science in Silhak. And these books began to be brought to Korea by Korean envoys who were to visit Beijing at least once a year.

This paper attempts to measure the latter-period Joseon intelligentsia's interest in Western science, centering around the records of envoys who had been to China in the closing days of Ming and the early days of Qing (the records in the days of Ming were called *Jocheonnok* and of

---

2. Cheon Gwan-u, *Hanguksa-ui jae balgyeon* (Rediscovery of Korean History) (Seoul: Ilchokak Publishing Co., 1975), pp. 174-175.

3. A number of scholars such as Min Yeong-gyu, Yi Yong-beom, Cheon Gwan-u, and Jeon Sang-un published some papers on this question. At the second academic seminar where this paper was presented, a Japanese Kokawa Haruhisa, participating at the meeting, published "Hong Dae-yong's View on Infinity of the Universe" (Tokyo: Institute of Comparative Cultural Research, Tokyo Women's University, 1975) and Bak Seong-rae wrote "Hong Dae-yong's Idea of the Rotating Earth" in English for the *Journal of the Scientific Society of Korea* (an inaugural issue, 1979), pp. 39-46.

4. Refer to Bak Seong-rae, comp. *Jungguk gwahak-ui sasang* (Chinese Scientific Thought) (Seoul: Chon Pa Kwa Hak Sa, 1978), pp. 105-131.

Qing Beijing travelogues). Yi Ik, Hong Dae-yong, and Jeong Dasan will be surveyed as Silhak scholars who showed the keenest interest in the science of the West. Also, the case of Choe Han-gi will be examined in detail.

The biggest handicap in this study is that the whole picture of Western science is not available. Most Western science books translated and published in China seem to have been imported to Korea by Korean envoys to Beijing. However, there is no way of knowing as yet when these books were first introduced into China and how widely they were read in China. Furthermore, there is also no way of knowing what sort of science books they were, although they were imported to Korea in great quantities in those days. Accordingly, references to Western science in this paper will be limited only to those which Silhak scholars recognized as so themselves, or those which I judge to be so through my own knowledge of science.

Western Science in Beijing Travelogues

Records of tribute left by Korean envoys who had been to Beijing in Ming and Qing days total more than 100 titles.[5] A meager part has been published by the Daedong Cultural Institute at Sungkyunkwan University in two volumes as *Yeonhaengnok seonjip* (Selected Works of Beijing Travelogues), part of which was recently translated into Korean. Most of the rest are still neglected in the libraries with no bibliographical study made as yet.

Korea was first really exposed to the civilization of the West when Jeong Du-won brought back from Ming in 1631 (ninth year of King Injo's reign) a few Western science books in Chinese translation in such subjects as astronomy, calendric calculation, and geography. In addition, he also carried back such goods as a telescope, alarm clock, astronomical chart, and a canon. However, the science of the West seems to have been known to Korean scholars piecemeal even prior to this time. For instance, Yi Su-gwang (1563–1629) not only made a short comment on Matteo Ricci's *True Principles of Catholicism* in his book, *Jibong yuseol*

5. Hwang Won-gu, *Dong asea yeongu* (Historical Study of East Asia) (Seoul: Ilchokak Publishing Co., 1976), pp. 277-290.

(Topical Discourses of Jibong), which seems to have been written in 1614 but praised the precision of the world atlas which was brought back by a Korean envoy from Beijing in 1603.[6] In the seventeen-eighteenth century, Crown Prince Sohyeon, Kim Yak, Yi I-myeong, and others endeavored to learn astronomy and the calendric calculation of the West either by direct negotiation with Western missionaries or by sending in questions for detailed knowledge.[7]

Against this intellectual climate, Korean men of learning, on their visits to China, naturally called at the Astronomical Observatory or Catholic churches in Beijing and some other places. Interested as keenly as Hong Dae-yong in Eastern science, they called on Western missionaries in person for a conversation by writing. Kim Yuk (1580-1658), who had been to Ming in 1636, is noted in history for having done his best in accommodating the Western calendar system, but no noteworthy remarks are found in his travelogue.[8]

Yi I-myeong (1658–1722), who was in Qing in 1704, left behind letters addressed to Western missionaries in his collected works.[9] But these letters are not recorded in his Beijing travelogue, which merely mentions that the Westerners Joseph Suarez and Ignatius Koegler called on him at the House of the Envoys. He asked about Catholicism and the calendar, but did not get clear explanations from them and left it for another opportunity for clarification.

Among Beijing travelogues Kim Chang-eop's (1658–1721) *Nogajae yeonhaeng ilgi* (Beijing Travelogue by Nogajae) is rated as the most representative, along with those by Bak Ji-won and Hong Dae-yong. Kim Chang-eop accompanied the envoy in 1712 and left behind an account of his visit to Catholic churches and to the Astronomical Observatory in February the next year while in Beijing. He saw the statue of Jesus at the cathedral and wrote a detailed account of an armillary sphere and a clock he saw there. However, he merely wrote that it was at the residence of a Western envoy, Thomas Pereira, and he seems to have not

---

6. Yi Su-gwang, "Jegukbu" (Foreign Nations), in *Jibong yuseol* (Topical Discourses of Jibong).

7. Hong I-seop, *op. cit.,* pp. 235-246.

8. Kim Yuk, *Jogyeong illok* (Daily Records of Travel to Ming Capital), in *Yeonhaengnok seonjip* (Selected Works of *Yeonhaengnok*), vol. 1 (Seoul: Daedong Cultural Institute, Sungkyunkwan University, 1976), pp. 201-230.

9. Hong I-seop, *op. cit.,* pp. 244-245.

been quite interested in seeing him or in knowing about science or the religion of the West.[10] A few days later, he called at the Astronomical Observatory and, seeing a bronze instrument about four feet high standing in the courtyard, he wrote that he did not know what it was. He wanted to go up to the observatory but was refused entry by a gatekeeper. On his way out, he looked up at the observatory and saw two armillary spheres and another instrument between them on the top of the observatory. But he wrote in his record that he did not know what they were.[11]

Yi Ui-hyeon (1669–1745), back from Beijing observing a sundial and a clock at a Catholic church during his short stay there in 1720, again visited the Catholic cathedral in his visit to Beijing in 1732 and met a Western with a Chinese family name Mai (賣). He is recorded to have asked that foreigner—aged 60 years old at the time—how far it was from Beijing to his native land. Their relationship seems to have deepened beyond that. Shortly afterward, that Westerner sent a gift pack to Yi Ui-hyeon that included two books titled *Sanshanlun xueji* and *Zhuzai qunzheng*, 15 pictures, small and large, a poison-absorptive stone, six "bitter-fruits," four sheets of color paper and ten sheets of white paper. He explained in detail that the poison absorptive stone was effective in eliminating many kinds of poison, healing swellings and that "bitter-fruits" were a panacea for all sorts of diseases ranging from women's hard labor in child delivery to acute gastroenteritis and malarial fever.[12]

A generation later, there is a travelogue of Hong Dae-yong (1731–1784), titled *Damheon yeon-gi* (Beijing Diary of Travel by Damheon) (1765–1766) and a little more later, Bak Ji-won's (1737–1805) *Yeolha ilgi* (Jehol Diary) (1780). There are not many noteworthy records in the diary of Bak Ji-won but Hong Dae-yong paid a visit three times to Augustin von Hallerstein, a third-rank official, and Anton Gogeisl, a sixth-rank official, at the South Cathedral. He left behind records showing that there could have been no other scholar better versed in the science of the West. Meeting these foreigners along with Yi Deok-seong, a calendric official, he asked many questions about astronomy and the calendar and recorded the proceedings in detail in "Questions and Answers

---

10. Kim Chang-eop, Diary of February 9, the Year of Gyesa, *Nogajae yeonhaeng ilgi* (Beijing Travelogues by Nogajae), *gwon* 6.
11. Kim Chang-eop, Diary of February 15, the Year of Gyesa, *ibid.*, *gwon* 7.
12. Yi Ui-hyeon, *Dogokjip* (Collected Works of Dogok), 30:22b, 30:31a-b, 30:34b-35b.

with Hallerstein and Gogeisl."[13] Hong Dae-yong also stayed at the East Cathedral and the Astronomical Observatory, observing instruments and gadgets there.[14] "Questions and Answers with Hallerstein and Gogeisl," revealing the scientific knowledge of Hong Dae-yong most vividly, seems to have been compiled after his visit to Beijing while under the influence of talks there.

The record of Yi Gap (1737–1795) in Beijing in 1777 also described many things about the civilization of the West, introducing astronomy, the calendar, musical instruments, clocks, wines and other small accoutrements. He says, "There are hospitals and orphanages in the West and the teaching of Christianity is said to be similar to that of the Mojiao but I am not sure."[15] However, he was not much interested in the science of the West and he did not care to meet Western missionaries. This attitude was true of Bak Ji-won, who left behind his travelogue *Yeolha ilgi* following his visit to Beijing in 1780. The same was also true of Yi Deok-mu (1741–1793), who went to Beijing two years before, receiving a farewell party from Bak Ji-won and Yu Deuk-gong. Unlike Hong Dae-yong, he did not care to observe the science of the West in person. According to his travelogue in 1778, he went to a Catholic church, but the two Westerners were not there since they were on duty at the Yuanmingyuan (The Garden of Perfection and Light). He could not enter the building where the instruments were kept since the gatekeeper refused entry. He went inside the church and saw holy pictures only.[16]

Seo Ho-su (1736–1799), in Beijing in 1790, in the capacity of a vice envoy as Minister of Rites, seemed to have been interested in astronomy and the calendar as much as Hong Dae-yong. He was the son of Seo Myeong-eung and the father of the famous Silhak scholar Seo Yu-gu. He was accompanied by Bak Je-ga and Yu Deuk-gong on the mission. Arriving in Beijing he met a protocol officer, Tie Bao, and upon showing him his book, *Hon-gae doseol jipjeon*, asked whether he could find any mistakes there. He also asked who the specialists in China were in this field. Recommended by Tie Bao to Weng Fanggang and Li Yan, he sent a

13. Hong Dae-yong, *Damheonseo* (Writings of Damheon), 7: 9-15.
14. *Ibid.*, 9:17a-18b.
15. Yi Gon, *Yeonhaeng gisa* (Accounts of Beijing Travelogues), in *Yeonhaengnok seonjip* (Selected Works of *Yeonhaengnok*).
16. Yi Deok-mu, Diary of June 14, 1778, *Cheongjanggwan jeonseo* (Collected Works of Yi Deok-mu), vol. 16.

copy of his book to Weng Fanggang, to obtain an epilogue for it. But Seo Ho-su seems to have been quite displeased with the epilogue he received a week later. He said that though Weng Fanggang was recommended for his detailed knowledge of calendric science, his writing of the epilogue revealed his total ignorance of the astronomy of the West. His harsh criticism went further, saying that China's literati were only mindful of self-publicity through rhymes, calligraphy and painting. He regretted he did not meet the Observatory official, Xi Chang and a Westerner named Andreas Rodriguez, who were said to be specialists in astronomical phenomena. However, the text did not explain why Seo could not see Rodriguez.[17] It is strange that Seo Ho-su could not meet Rodriguez, who was the topmost astronomer of the time and later became an official of the Astronomical Observatory.

Yu Deuk-gong (1748–1807), who accompanied Seo Ho-su and conveyed Seo's book to Weng Fanggang, left behind his account of the journey,[18] though without mention of astronomy or of the Western missionaries. He visited Beijing in 1796 and again in 1801 but his account of these visits made no mention of astronomy or of Western science. Korean visitors to Beijing, who had been quite enthusiastic in calling on Catholic churches or at the Observatories at the end of the eighteenth century, started to refrain from doing so from the early nineteenth century.[19]

An account of one who visited Beijing in 1804 said that Koreans visiting Beijing following the Catholic Persecution of 1801 in Korea never dared to call at such places as Catholic churches.[20] This attitude is clear in the account of Kim Gyeong-seon (1788–1853) who went to Beijing in 1832 as a third-ranked envoy. As for Catholic churches, Kim Gyeong-seon quoted accounts of Kim Chang-eop, Hong Dae-yong, and Bak Ji-won at length and remarked that now that the Western practices were not only banned in both countries but were extremely sinister, no one would even see them. His attitude was such that, although he wanted to

17. Seo Ho-su, Dairies of July 18, Aug. 25, and Sept. 2, 1790, *Yeonhaenggi* (Beijing Travelogue), in *Yeonhaengnok seonjip*, vol. 3.

18. Yu Deuk-gong, *Nagyangnok* (Luoyang Travelogue).

19. Yu Deuk-gong, *Yeondae jaeyurok*, in *Yeonhaengnok seonjip*, vol. 1, pp. 613-650, 651-668.

20. Anonymous, Diary of Jan. 26, 1804, *Gyesan gijong* 3; Anonymous, Diary of June 25, 1828, *Buyeon ilgi*. These two accounts are included in *Yeonhaengnok seonjip*, vols. 1-2.

see the painting techniques of the West and examining elaborate utensils or instruments, his curiosity had to be satisfied instead by reading detailed accounts by Kim Chang-eop, Hong Dae-yong and Bak Ji-won.[21]

The Beijing travelogues by Korean envoys can be characterized as reflecting various levels of real interest in Western science. First, of the many Koreans who had been to China from the end of Ming and the beginning of Qing through the nineteenth century, those who were keenly interested in the learning of the West, or particularly, in the science of the West, formed a minority. Second, though some scholars (such as Hong Dae-yong and Seo Ho-su) were deeply interested in the science of the West, this interest was not a main concern of the time. Travelogues by Silhak scholars show not much interest in science in general while merely few exhibited deep interest. Third, interest in science by Korean visitors to Beijing declined somewhat following the Catholic persecution of 1801, when contact with Western learning was officially banned.

Korean attitudes toward Western science as revealed in their Beijing travelogues did not necessarily match those of scholars at home, particularly Silhak scholars, who inherited an interest in the science of the West from their seniors. This enthusiasm was confined to a small number of Korean scholars centering on Silhak. Therefore, in order to see how the science of the West was accommodated in modern Korea, individual studies of some representative scholars should follow a review of Beijing travelogues.

Yi Ik, Hong Dae-yong, and Western Science

The influence of Western science and technology can be found in the thought of many Silhak scholars since Yi Su-gwang (1563–1629) to such a large extent that it would be safe to characterize an interest in the science and technology of the West as an important characteristic of Silhak. Among early Silhak scholars, the one who was most influenced by the West was Yi Ik (1682–1764). One may claim that the image of the science of the West first took shape, in the science history of Korea, in Yi Ik's *Seongho saseol* (Collected Works of Seongho).

---

21. Kim Gyeong-seon, *Yeonwon jikji*, in *Yeonhaengnok seonjip*, vol. 3.

Yi Ik seems to have been ahead of anyone in reading a number of translated versions of Western books. The books he must have read include the following:[22]

Tianzhu shiyi	by Matteo Ricci
Gangun tiyi	by Matteo Ricci
Taixi shuifa	by Sabbathin de Ursis
Tianwenlue	by Emanuel Diaz
Zhuzai qunzheng	by Adam Schall
Zhifang waiji	by J. Alleni
Qike	by Didacus de Pantoja
Fangxing tujie	by Philippus Maria Grimaldi
Zhili yuanchi	by Nicholas Longobardi
Jihe yuanben	by Matteo Ricci
Jianping yizhi	by Sabbathin de Ursis

He is also known to have read astronomical charts or maps. Seven of the 11 titles in the list above are included in *Tianxue chuhan* (First Collection of Heavenly Studies) compiled by Li Zhizao in 1628. Yi Ik might have read all nineteen titles of Western books comprising *Tianxue chuhan.*

Yi Ik recognized the superiority of the science of the West on account of its precision in astronomy and in calendric calculation. He praised the *Shixian* calendar (*Siheonnyeok*) compiled by Adam Schall as "an apex in calendar-making" with no error in forecasting solar eclipses, saying that even Confucius would abide by the calendar if he was to be born again.[23] In introducing Matteo Ricci's theory of the "12-fold heavens," he regretted being unable to observe the sky for himself with a Western telescope.[24] Even with a telescope in his hands, he would have been

---

22. The first nine books have already been known. For instance, refer to Yi Won-sun, "Joseon hugi silhakja-ui seoyang uisik" (Consciousness of Western Studies by Silhak Scholars in the Latter Period of Joseon), *Yeoksa gyoyuk* (Korean History Education Review) 17 (1975): p. 173; and "Seoyang munmul hanyeok haksulseo-ui jeollye" (Introduction of Translated Books of Learning in Chinese about the Civilization of the West), *Hanguksa* (History of Korea), vol. 14 (Gwacheon: National Institute of Korean History, 1973), p. 70. The last two in the list were added by this writer from Yi Ik's *Seongho saseol* (Collected Works of Seongho Yi Ik).

23. Yi Ik, *Seongho saseol.*

24. *Ibid.*

unable to see multi-layered heavens (nine- or twelve-fold heavens), since the theory of multi-layered heavens was a misconceived view of the universe handed down among Westerners from the days of Greece through medieval times. However, many important discoveries with the telescope of Galileo after 1609 had been introduced in *Tianwenlue* (Astronomical Documents) and it was natural for Yi Ik to have wanted to confirm them for himself with a telescope.

What most influenced Yi Ik was the theory of the earth. It was not that no one in the traditional views of the universe in the orient conceived the earth as round, based on the phrase, "heaven is round, the earth square."[25] Yi Ik maintains that the concept that man can live on the every side of the earth if the earth were round was first advocated by Westerners. Then, how can one explain how man can live on every side of the earth? Yi Ik explains this with his theory of "the center of the earth," that everything is drawn towards the center of the earth from all directions.[26] However, Yi Ik does not explain "what" converges to the center of the earth. He merely had a vague notion that everything is drawn towards the center of the earth, since the center of the earth is the center of the universe. The West traditionally explained the phenomenon with the notion of "gravity." Yi Ik's theory of the center of the earth seems not to differ greatly from that of the West in medieval days. Yet, it is not clear whether Yi Ik's view was influenced by Western notions.

A question that inevitably emerges from the theory of the center of the earth was whether the center of the world should be necessarily China. A century before Yi Ik, a translator named Yi Yeong-hu accompanied Jeong Du-won to Beijing and asked the Western missionary John Rodrigues about astronomy and the calendar. He obtained an important answer from Rodrigues, who answered as follows:

> Though all the world maps place China in the center, this is for the convenience of viewing. This means that any nation can be placed in the center if one takes a view that the earth is round.[27]

---

25. The view of the universe is well explained in Jeon Sang-un, *Hanguk gwahak gisulsa* (Scientific and Technological History of Korea) (Seoul: Gwahak Segyesa, 1966), pp. 36-39. As for its philosophical meaning, refer to Hwang Won-gu, *op. cit.*, pp. 2-8.
26. Yi Ik, *op. cit.*
27. Hong I-seop, *op. cit.*, p. 243. The same account is found in Pasquale de Elia, *Galileo in China* (Cambridge: Harvard University Press, 1960), pp. 42-44.

Based on the theory of the earth, Yi Ik points out that people living on a round earth may regard the place where they live as the highest spot.[28] Thus, he came to think that China, after all, was nothing but a part of earth in the world.[29]

The reality of the time was that Qing took the place of Ming, occupying the center of China. The prevailing thought of the Korean intelligentsia came to ponder the question of what defined the center of civilization in the world. The lesson in history that control over the center of China does not necessarily mean control over the center of the world was a precious one to them. Through this lesson, some men of learning, particularly Silhak scholars, were able to turn their attention to their own country. The sense of keen interest (namely, concern for national studies) that surfaced in Silhak as an interest in one's own self was thus induced by the influence of the Western theory of the earth.

Yi Ik also talks about the possibility that the round earth may rotate on its own axis, a point that Zhuangzi of China already had already vaguely remarked about 2,000 years before. The book of Zhuangzi voices a question, "Does heaven move or is the earth static?"[30] This is merely a part of a consistently agnostic attitude and one can read between the lines that Zhuangzi intended to voice the possibility that the earth may move. At any rate, this attitude was also voiced by Zhu Xi. Yi Ik quotes the remarks of Zhu Xi, "How can one dare to say that the earth does not rotate itself around heaven which moves afar?"[31] It was under the influence of Western astronomy that Yi Ik came to seriously doubt the rotation of the earth. He says that according to the calendar of the West, a permanent star has a circumference of more than 500,000,000 *ri* and according to the calendar of China, one degree of heaven corresponds to 2,932 *ri* of earth. Conceding that he does not know which astronomy is more accurate in measuring the size of heaven, he says that it is clear that the circumference of heaven is too big for heaven to rotate once a day, thus he is led to the notion that earth may rotate.[32] Again, he recognizes the partial truth of the theory of the rotation, quoting a remark frequently resorted to be Western astronomers as a metaphor in late Ming

---

28. Yi Ik, *op. cit.*
29. *Ibid.*
30. Zhuangzi, "On the Movement of Stars," *Zhuangzi.*
31. Yi Ik, *op. cit.*
32. *Ibid.*

and in early Qing: "If a boat moves around on me same spot of water, the shore looks like it is moving around the boat."[33]

However, his question about the rotation of the earth merely ended up as a curious footnote. He made some attempts to explain why the earth would not fall even though it exists in the middle of the cosmos. But he ultimately denies the theory of the rotation of the earth, basically relying on the sayings of the sages (*Yijing*) that heaven constantly moves. His reasoning was that since the sages knew everything, the theory of the movement of heaven must be reliable.[34] Since Yi Ik was deeply charmed by Western astronomy, he would not have been obsessed with the theory of the movement of heaven if Western missionaries told him about the truth of the theory of the rotation of the earth. However, books in those days written by Western missionaries ruled the theory of the earth's rotation erroneous, even with that fact that there were some Western scholars who advanced other theories, as exemplified with the metaphor of the rotating boats off the shore.[35]

Hong Dae-yong (1731–1783) was a Silhak scholar who inherited the tradition of Yi Ik; he also showed keen interest in Western science. As for his theory on the rotating earth, a number of Korean scholars such as Cheon Gwan-u, Jeon Sang-un, and Yi Yong-beom published their views while Min Yeong-gyu attributes the merit for the discovery of the theory to Kim Seok-mun (1685–1735), a man of a generation before. Hong Dae-yong's theory attracted the attention not only of Korean scholars but also of many scholars from Japan and China.[36] Those

---

33. *Ibid.*

34. *Ibid.*

35. About the detail of Yi Ik's view on the rotating earth, refer to Yi Yong-beom, "Yi Ik-ui jidongnon-gwa geu non-geo" (Yi Ik's Theory of the Rotating Earth and Its Basis), *Jindan hakbo* (Review of Jindan Association) 39 (1972).

36. Most of the articles by Korean scholars are contained in Bak Seong-rae, "Hong Dae-yong jijeonseol-ui tteut" (Hong Dae-yong's Idea of the Rotating Earth), *Hanguk gwahak sahakhoe ji* (Journal of the Society of the Korean Scientific History) 1.1 (1979): pp. 39-49. In that paper, Kokawa Haruhisa's "Hong Dae-yong's Theory on the Infinity of the Universe" (in Japanese) (The Institute of Comparative Cultural Research, Tokyo Women's University, vol. 38, 1975) is missing. Jeon Sang-un published a paper again on this subject and that paper is also missing there. Jeon Sang-un, "Damheon Hong Dae-yong-ui gwahak sasang" (Scientific Thought of Damheon Hong Dae-yong), in *Yi Eul-ho baksa euntoe ginyeom silhak nonmunjip* (Collected Monographs on Silhak in Commemoration of the Retirement of Dr. Yi Eul-ho) (1975).

scholars, who initially highly praised the inventiveness of Hong Dae-yong's theory, now show a relatively cautious attitude.

Hong Dae-yong showed keen interest in Western science. His interest was well revealed in his Beijing travelogue of 1765–1766.[37] During more than 60 days in Beijing he called at the South Cathedral four times and met Hallerstein and Gogeisl three times. The account of these meetings, described at length in a chapter "Questions and Answers with Hallerstein and Gogeisl" in his travelogue, must be the most detailed account of conversations with Western missionaries in the history of Silhak. By that time, Western missionaries were reluctant to receive visits from Koreans, since Koreans did not return the courtesy. They merely accepted gifts from the Westerners, were rude, and smoked or even spat inside the cathedral, as they played with and stained sacred utensils. Thus, Hong Dae-yong took a very courteous approach, sending his servant with gifts and with his greetings, to ask for a meeting beforehand. As a result, he met them three times on January 8, January 19, and February 2, 1766, talking at length and observing many things.

It is not clear what talk he exchanged with them. In his visit of February 2, he asked many questions about astronomy in the presence of the rituals officer Yi Deok-seong, but the account is not given in his travelogue. Some other conversations were concerned mainly with Catholic catechism. What he was more interested in was observing some items of interest. In his first visit, he saw an organ, which he tried to play, as well as a large clock on the top of a tower. During his second visit, he saw a telescope and chime bells. The clock Hong Dae-yong saw at the time was a large automatic clock—what we now call an "alarm clock"—which Hong Dae-yong calls chime bells. In those days, Hong Dae-yong himself was making a small clock, but the other things he was seeing for the first time. Hong also saw a telescope for the first time, something Yi Ik was not able to see, despite his great curiosity. Seeing the sun through a meter-long telescope, he was caught by surprise, since he saw a vertical line running through the sun. Upon inquiry Hallerstein explained, smiling, that the line was not on the sun but on the telescope to keep it horizontal.

---

37. Hong Dae-yong's *Damheon yeon-gi* is found in extra works of *Damheonseo* and in vol. 1 of *Yeonhaengnok seonjip* of Daedong Cultural Institute at Sungkyunkwan University. A paper written in Korean *Eulbyeong yeonhaengnok* is in the collection of the Library of Sungjun University and recently a translated version of *Damheonseo* in Korean has been published.

Though he wanted to buy a telescope while in Beijing, he seems not to have been able to do so.[38] One curious thing about Eastern astronomy was that a telescope was not used in astronomical observation. Jeong Du-won was said to have looked through a telescope for the first time, but Yi Ik was unable even to see one, and Hong Dae-yong was able to see it only after he went to Beijing. There is no record that a telescope was ever employed in astronomical observation prior to the twentieth century. This is explained by Rufus as "routine standardization of observation procedure."[39] In other words, the need for a new mode of experiment and observation had not been felt.

Against this background, Hong Dae-yong's notions of Western science were surprisingly far advanced. He was aware that Western science was ahead of that of the Orient, since the West was far advanced in mathematics and in observation. Conceding that the astronomy of the West was far superior, Hong Dae-yong attributes this to its observation of every shape and phenomenon with the use of instruments based on arithmetic.[40]

Aware that mathematics and instruments of observation were the bases of astronomy, he published *Juhae suyong* (Explanation of Arithmetic) and he equipped himself with astronomical instruments, setting up in his courtyard at an astronomical observatory called Nongsugak.

In his book on mathematics—*Juhae suyong*—he introduced Matteo Ricci's *Hungai tungxian* (Explanation of the Celestial Sphere) as well as a Western book of mathematics called *Shuli jingyun* (Elementary Principles of Mathematics,), of the Emperor Kangxi edition. In addition, *Shufa chuan shuo* (by Jiang Shucheng) of Qing, *Sangmyeong sugyeol* (by Kyeong Seon-jing) and *Suwon* were both published in Korea, as well as *Yullyeok yeonwon*, a book of unknown origin, which introduced some aspects of mathematics from the West.[41]

Hong Dae-yong had his astronomical instruments set up in his courtyard even before his visit to Beijing. In his observatory Nongsugak,

---

38. Hong Dae-yong, "City of Longfu" (in Korean), in *Damheon yeon-gi*.
39. Carl W. Rufus, "Astronomy in Korea," *Journal of Royal Asiatic Society, Korea Branch* 26 (1936): p. 46.
40. Hong Dae-yong, "Yupo mundap" (Questions and Answers of Hallerstein and Gogeisl), in *Damheon yeon-gi*.
41. Hong Dae-yong, "Bibliography" (in Korean), *Juhae suyong* (Explanation of Arithmetic).

which he had named after a phrase from Tu Fu, he had an armillary sphere and a Western clock (a kind of an alarm clock).[42] Hong Dae-yong made the clock and the armillary sphere, employing the astronomical knowledge and craft of Na Gyeong-jeok and An Cho-in. Also present was another armillary sphere called *tongcheonui* at the Nongsugak and some other observation instruments called the *cheukgwanui* and *gugoui*.[43] In 1759, Hong Dae-yong met the old man Na Gyeong-jeok (pen name Seokdang), who was already over 70. A hermit at Geumseong, the old man had his own clock made, modeled after a Western clock. Hong Dae-yong found that the old man Na was well versed in the operation of such instruments, including the astronomical ones. Knowing that the old man regretted the lack of money to make such instruments, Hong offered him his financial assistance. Na Gyeong-jeok managed to make an armillary sphere with the aid of his student An Cheon-in in three years. Lest the precious instrument be stained, Hong Dae-yong dug a small pond in his courtyard in the south and made a small artificial island in it and kept the instruments in a small shelter built on the island. Then, he named the shelter Nongsugak, picking up two characters from a poetic phrase of Tu fu which meant "The sun and the moon are like birds in a cage (*nong*) and the cosmos is like floating grass on the water (*su*)."[44]

Hong Dae-yong endeavored to expose himself to Western science, so availed himself of the opportunity to go to Beijing. Though he looked keenly at Western science, he could not operationalize his insight and knowledge in action. Though his propensity to introduce the science of the West led him to write *Juhae suyong*, his efforts seem to not deserve high claim.[45] The astronomical instruments of Hong Dae-yong well illustrate his limits. Records on the Nongsugak tell that he was not

---

42. Hong Dae-yong, "Hangjeon cheokdok," in *Damheonseo*, 2:11a-b.
43. Hong Dae-yong, "Nongsugak uigiji" (On Instruments at Nongsugak), in *Juhae suyong*.
44. Hong Dae-yong, "Hangjeon cheokdok," in *Damheonseo*, 3:12b-14a. During his stay in Beijing, Lu Fei who befriended him wrote him "An Account on Nongsugak" and Kim I-an also wrote a script to his book. Hong Dae-yong, *Damheonseo*, annex 7b-9a; "Jemun" (Ritual Odes).
45. Kim Yong-un says the introduction of new mathematics ended in failure, evaluating the mathematical thought of Hong Dae-yong as nothing new. Kim Yong-un and Kim Yong-guk, *Hanguk suhaksa* (Mathematical History of Korea) (Seoul: Gwahak-gwa Inseong Sa, 1977), p. 260.

directly involved in the making of the instruments. Instruments made in Geumseong were brought to his house but were not used for astronomical observation. He made them mere items of appreciation, keeping them in custody on the artificial island in his courtyard lest they be stained. The mental attitude of the Orient regarding the non-use of telescopes for astronomical observation also shows up in the case of Hong Dae-yong.

Seen in this way, Hong Dae-yong was a man of scientific thought, rather than a scientist proper. What best reveals this aspect is his work *Uisan mundap* (Dialogue on Mount Yishan). In this 12,000-word book, Hong Dae-yong talks about the theory of the earth, revealing the influence of Western science, and negates the theories of *yin-yang* and the five elements, saying that the mistake of the Confucianists of old lay in their failure to know the way of heaven. Obsessed with *yin-yang* and other reasoning,[46] he maintains that the truths of the universe were not necessarily defined by and confined to the five elements. Recalling the Six Matters, the Eight Phenomena of Hexagrams, the Five Elements and the Four Elements in Buddhism, he says that wood and metal cannot be elements since they are born out of the sun and the earth.[47] Again, he says that heaven is nothing but *gi* (the energizing element), the sun nothing but fire, the earth nothing but water and soil.[48] Here, what Hong Dae-yong refers to may be explained either in terms of three-heaven, earth and sun, or in terms of four-*gi*, water, earth, and fire. On this score, he seems to have been influenced by the Western theory of four elements (earth, water, wind, and fire) as was imparted by Western missionaries; but we have no way of knowing that for certain.

Aristotle's theory of three souls can be found in the writings of Hong Dae-yong. Aristotle classified life into three-plants, animals, and man, each governed by a vegetative soul, sensitive soul, and rational soul, and this view had been introduced to the orient in the books of Western missionaries including Ricci's *True Principles of Catholicism*. Hong Dae-yong also classified life into three-man, beasts, and vegetable, each governed by *hye* (wisdom), *gak* (sensation), and *ji* (knowing).[49]

---

46. Hong Dae-yong, "Uisan mundap," in *Damheonseo*, 4:27b.
47. Ibid., 4:30b.
48. Ibid.
49. Ibid., 4:18a-b.

The refraction of light, which Hong Dae-yong noticed, also seems to have been influenced by the field of optics, which began to rise in the late medieval period in the West. He explains that when one recedes from a bathtub so far that one can see just the tip of a coin on the bottom of the tub, the whole coin can be seen when the tub is filled with water; in this lies the power of water to refract light. Hong goes further, explaining that the energizing element from water and soil goes above, covering the surface of the ground, makes low appear high and small appear larger. He says that this phenomenon was studied by Westerners, calling it *cheongmong*. When the sun and the moon are just above the head, *cheongmong* is not thick enough, so that the sun and the moon appear to be small. When the sun and the moon are on the horizon, *cheongmong* is thick, so they appear to be larger.[50]

In that the earth is surrounded by the energizing element of the soil (the earth here refers to water-soil), *cheongmong* was defined as a kind of *gi*. However Hong Dae-yong acknowledges a more fundamental *gi* that fills up the cosmos and calls it the ultimate—the beginning of everything.[51] Western philosophers since Greece have posited "pneuma"as the archetyped matter filling the cosmos. The concept of *gi* referred to by Hong Dae-yong could have come, if not from pneuma, from scholars of the *Yijing* (Book of Changes) from Song China (Zhang Zai, Shao Yung). At any rate, Hong Dae-yong believed that *gi* was compressed by the rapid rotation of the earth, creating the "force of above and below,"[52] and that things fall through this force. Far from the earth, there is no "force of above and below."

The scientific thought of Hong Dae-yong was influenced by Western science and he was led to view cosmos as infinite. He developed his characteristic thought of viewing even sociological phenomena in relative terms. His view that there was no "force of above and below" far from the earth seems to have derived from his reasoning that there was no center of the cosmos since the cosmos is infinite. Yi Ik was led to believe that China could never be in the center of the world since the earth is round.

Hong Dae-yong claimed that there was no difference between China and barbarians and that if Confucius had lived outside China, his *Chun-*

---

50. Ibid., 4:28b-29a.
51. Ibid., 4:19a.
52. Ibid., 4:20b.

qiu (Spring and Autumn Annals) would have been written for whichever country outside China he had called home. This view may be seen as a mere extension of the thought of Yi Ik that any nation of the world can be in the center of the world. However, Hong Dae-yong went further by saying that the earth could not have been in the center of an infinite cosmos and that earth was nothing but one of the stars in the cosmos.[53] Hong Dae-yong's relativistic view of man as an intellectual being who could exist around any other star in an infinite cosmos is well exemplified by Bak Ji-won. In his Beijing travelogue, Bak Ji-won says that men on the moon may watch the changing phases of the earth or that there may be some other creatures like men who live in the air, such as those living in fire or in water.[54]

That Hong Dae-yong outgrew the man-centered view, which went a step further than that of Yi Ik, was possible through his characteristic view of cosmos. His theorizing about the possible existence of many worlds with intellectual beings in an infinite cosmos was similar to the view of the infinity of the universe and a plurality of worlds that caused Giordano Bruno to be put to the stake in 1600. From Bruno through Johannes Kepler and B. de Fontenelle, a number of seventeenth century scholars developed the idea that there could be a world of stars with intellectual beings outside of the world of human kind. And this led to the new world of science fiction which has developed since the eighteenth century.

Then, what relationship does the thought of Hong Dae-yong share with the science of the West from Bruno on? Officially, Bruno's view of an infinite universe and a plurality of worlds was a heresy. Thus, Western missionaries abandoned the traditional cosmic view of China (such as *huntian* or *xuanye*) that was similar to Bruno's, and instead preached the more outmoded, Middle Ages view of a finite universe. On this score, Joseph Needham remarked that it was ironic that while Westerners were being liberated from the finite view of the universe of Aristotle, Western missionaries kept the Chinese people from the view of Copernicus, charming them with an outmoded view of a finite cosmos.[55] However, it is not yet clear whether Western thought, ranging from Bruno's

---

53. Ibid., 4:22b.
54. Bak Ji-won, *Yeolha ilgi* (Jehol Diary).
55. Joseph Needham, *Science and Civilization in China*, vol. 3 (Cambridge: Cambridge University Press, 1959), p. 438.

through Fontenelle's, was known to the Chinese by the middle of the eighteenth century. However, it is quite probable the writings of Western missionaries must have been introduced the view of an infinite universe and a plurality of worlds with the note "heretical" in the same manner that the view of a rotating earth was explained away as "erroneous thinking." Hong Dae-yong might have arrived at his view of an infinite universe and a plurality of worlds at least under the indirect influence of the astronomy of the West.

At any rate, it was a surprising intellectual effort for Hong Dae-yong alone to outgrow the bounds of a finite universe, even as almost all people were seized with the view of nine or twelve heavens. No matter what weight the influence from the West might have had, this would not have been possible to a man without creativity. Nevertheless, his reasoning remained squarely in the realm of intellectual curiosity, failing to bear the fruit of social importance. Christianity bestowed upon man the prerogative to live in the center of an infinite universe as the supreme creature; assertions by Copernicus, Bruno and Galileo shook medieval society, built upon these medieval, theological assumptions, to its foundations. In China and Korea, the Confucian system of society would not be affected, whether the earth rotated itself or it was at the center of the universe. Thus, views about the rotating earth, the infinity of the universe or a plurality of the worlds had no social importance.

Jeong Yak-yong and Western Science

The writings of Dasan Jeong Yak-yong (1762–1836) are more voluminous than those of Hong Dae-yong. However, it is difficult for us to trace the scientific thought of Dasan systematically in his writings, because he has left no scientific work comparable to Hong Dae-yong's *Uisan mundap*. We have to grope in his voluminous writings for traces of his scientific thought and only then can we trace the influence of Western science on him.[56]

---

56. As for the scientific thought of Jeong Yak-yong, the writer once attempted a general survey, though in a rude form. Bak Seong-rae, "Jeong Yak-yong-ui gwahak sasang" (Scientific Thought of Jeong Yak-yong), *Dasan hakbo* (Journal of Dasan) 1 (1978): pp. 151-176.

Five Elements

Like Hong Dae-yong, Dasan did not think that the ultimate of the universe could be reduced to five things only. To him, many scholars had their own concepts of the basic elements. Hong claimed that the basic elements could be four, five, six, or eight in number and that there is not much deep reasoning in the number.[57]

What did Dasan think of instead of the five elements? The answer is not clear but it is certain that he must have been under the influence of a Western version of a four elements system. At a special state examination in 1790, his elder brother, Jeong Yak-jeon answered a question about the five elements, quoting from the Western theory of four elements; his answer sheet was given a top honor by the examiner Yi Ga-hwan. In 1795, five years later, a military official Bak Jang-seol took issue with the answer sheet. Accusing Yi Ga-hwan of taking an erroneous view of *cheongmong* and Jeong Yak-jeon of explaining the five elements with the Western version of four elements, he appealed to the King for due punishment. To the accusation, Yi Ga-hwan, Minister of Public Works defended himself, saying that the theory of *cheongmong* had already been advanced by Shu Xi, a scribe of Qing China, thus it was not an invention of the West. In addition, he asserted that Yi had not been the sole examiner at the time.[58]

Cheongmong was mentioned in the optics of Hong Dae-yong and its notion corresponds to the air or the atmosphere of today. As was clearly indicated by Hong Dae-yong, the notion of *cheongmong* had been merely employed to explain the refraction of light in the atmosphere, borrowing from Western science. The excuse that the word was already coined in the days of Qing China was nothing but a pretext with which to mount a defense. Again, the four elements in the West denoted a medieval concept of four elements from the days of Aristotle: namely, those of fire, air, water, and earth. The theory of the four elements was a basic approach of Western science from the publication of Matteo Ricci's *True Principles of Catholicism* in 1603.[59]

---

57. Jeong Yak-yong, *Dasan munjip* (Collected Works of Jeong Dasan), II-25:31a-b.
58. Dasan also wrote a full account of the incident. See *Dasan munjip*, I-15:20a-21b.
59. Matteo Ricci, *True Principles of Catholicism*, vol. 1 (Seoul: Institute of the History of the Korean Church, 1972), 6a, 32a-b, 48b.

In letters addressed to his two sons, after release from exile following the Catholic persecution of 1801, Dasan wrote as if he was taking the Four Phases of the *Yijing* (heaven, earth, water, and fire) as the basic elements. In the same letter, he also says that heaven is *gi*.[60] In fact, he talks about the Western theory of four elements (*gi*-air or wind, earth or soil, water and fire) by replacing heaven with *gi* in explaining the Four Phases of *Yijing*. He also says that "water, fire, dry, wet" are what make the nature of things equal as "benevolence, righteousness, courtesy, wisdom" make human nature equal.[61] In a pathological view, Dasan says that illness occurs when the harmony among the four affections (cold, hot, dry, wet) is broken.[62] The four affections here are similar to the Western theory of four elements. In the concept of basic elements, Dasan had the same Western view of the four elements as his elder brother. But he may have camouflaged his view in the guise of the authority of the *Yijing* at a time when Catholic followers were being persecuted.

Optics

In the Jeong Yak-jeon incident at the state examination, the question given at the test included the theory of *cheongmong-gi* in addition to that of the four elements. The notion of *cheongmong-gi* was the one Hong Dae-yong borrowed from the Western concept of the atmosphere in order to explain the phenomenon of the sun and the moon looking bigger when they rise above the horizon. This he explained as the refraction of light, but he explained the phenomenon by saying that the image of the sun or the moon is heaved up by the force of *jeokgi* (namely "accumulated air"). By the same reasoning, he also explained the phenomenon of a coin being visible on the bottom of a tub from afar when water fills the tub. In this case, what pushes the image up is the force of "water."[63] "Accumulated air" and water can refract light and this explanation could be found already in the account or Hong Dae-yong.

However, Dasan left behind more writings about optical science than

---

60. Jeong Yak-yong, *Dasan munjip*, I-21:19a.
61. *Ibid.*, I-11:29a.
62. *Ibid.*, VII-6:27a.
63. *Ibid.*, I-10:8a.

Hong Dae-yong. Drawing the functions of convex and concave lenses in pictures, he explains that one can start a fire with a convex lens.[64] Knowing that human eyes are similar to these lenses, he explains the mechanics of short- and far-sightedness.[65] He also explains that a beam of light through a hole in a closed room projects the image of the outside in color upside down when the beam goes through the lens.[66]

Rotation of the Earth

After Kim Man-jung and Yi Ik, most Korean scholars did not dissent to the theory of a round earth. Dasan also explains the shape of the earth by drawing a picture.[67] However, a hint of a rotating earth, in the pattern of Hong Dae-yong, cannot be found in his writings. His elder brother Jeong Yak-jeon, in exile on Heuksando island following the Catholic persecution of 1801, seems to have believed in a rotating earth. According to the letter addressed by Dasan to his elder brother, Jeong Yak-jeon seems to have written to his younger brother, after he observed a comet in 1811, that the comet is a sign that "verifies the theory of the rotating earth." Jeong Yak-jeon could have perceived not only the rotation but the revolution of the earth, since he used the word "the moving earth" instead of "the rotating earth." For, the Copernican theory had been openly propagated in China for some decades. However, in his answer to the letter, Dasan says he also observed the comet in July and August of the year, and says that it did not explain the movement of the earth. According to him, the earth is made up of the accumulated elements of soil, and the earth sticks to something else, not rotating itself or revolving around.[68]

Nevertheless, this does not mean that Dasan had any definite view about the movement of the earth. Koreans had used the Reformed Calendar (*Siheonnyeok*), based on medieval Western astronomy, since the middle of the seventeenth century and they had naturally conceived heaven as multi-layered and isolated celestial globes. An important defect in the theory of a multilayered heaven was, as the non-acceptance

---

64. *Ibid.*, I-10:5b-7a.
65. *Ibid.*, VII-6:29b-30a.
66. *Ibid.*, I-10:7b.
67. *Ibid.*, I-10:9a-11a.
68. *Ibid.*, I-20:24b (a letter in the winter of 1811).

of the view of the rotating earth, postulating that celestial globes each had to circle around the earth once a day and that the outermost globe had to move around at an incredibly rapid speed. We have seen above that Yi Ik was inclined to the theory of a rotating earth because of this question, but he stopped halfway at this snag of phrase in the *Yijing*, "Heaven moves around." Dasan also faced the same question. But Dasan was a little bolder than Yi Ik and denied the existence of the outermost sphere, the "Primum Mobile." Even so, he did not hold to his view on the infinity of the universe, and consequently he remains more conservative than Hong Dae-yong. Ultimately his attitude was rather agnostic, reminiscent of Yi Ik. Dasan's conclusion was as follows:

> This is what we cannot know. We cannot discuss what we cannot know. Didn't Zhuangzi say—Does heaven move or is the earth really standing still? The working of heaven and the earth we cannot know fully. And we don't merely have to believe what we cannot know by ourselves.[69]

Vaccination

As was discussed above in relation to the theory of four elements, Dasan explains that disharmony among the four affections (cold, hot, dry, wet) caused illness. This is similar to Aristotle's theory, reminiscent of the Hippocratic theory of pathology based on four body fluids.

One reason for Dasan's fame was that he first introduced to Korea vaccine inoculation which Edward Jenner devised in 1798. At the end of his book *Magwa hoetong* (Comprehensive Treaties on Smallpox) introducing the so-called *indu* (human smallpox) method, a traditional Oriental cure, he wrote a brief account of Jenner's vaccination. In this account, he did not give his own opinion at all, but merely copied from a book published in 1828 in Qing, thus omitting the name of the original author, Pearson. According to the record of Yi Gyu-gyeong, Dasan seems to have administered vaccinations himself.[70] However, he seems to have done so secretly, since it was a time of persecution against

---

69. *Ibid.*, I-12:15a-16a.
70. Kim Du-jong, "Uri nara-ui duchang-ui yuhaeng-gwa jongdubeop-ui silsi" (Practice of Vaccination and Occurrence of Smallpox in Korea), *Nonmunjip* (Collected Papers) (Seoul National University) 4 (1956): p. 52.

Catholics. At any rate, his introduction of Western vaccination was not handed down and vaccination had to be imported again after 1880 by Ji Seok-yeong.

Technology

Dasan was known to have assisted in the construction of a pontoon bridge on the Hangang river in 1789, as well as in the construction of a castle in Suwon in 1792, by utilizing cranes and other construction tools. In devising such techniques, he not only referred to various books on traditional techniques, but also the book lent to him for reference by King Jeongjo, entitled *Qjgi tushuo* (Illustrated Tools and Instruments). This was a representative book introducing dynamics and new technology of the West since the seventeenth century, written by the Western missionary Jean Terrenz (1576–1630). Based on such materials, Dasan devised cranes and was commended by the King for saving about 40,000 *ryang* (unit of currency) in construction expenses.[71] He did not show much inventiveness in accommodating the technology of the West and as a result some minor defects were detected.[72]

Dasan's understanding of Western technology was not deep but following Bak Je-ga, he was insistent that Western technology should be brought in as quickly as possible. Conceding that he was much impressed by reading *Qigi tushuo* and *Bukhakui* (Discourse on Northern Learning) by Bak Je-ga and *Yeolha ilgi* by Bak Ji-won, he recommended the creation of a new government post to be called *iyonggam* (official of utility and utilization), saying that "the urgent task of the times is northern studies." He proposed to man the office with senior officials well versed in mathematics, clerks adroit in craft, and four researchers for rapid introduction of Western and Chinese technology. He urged a positive introduction of Western and Chinese technology even at big expense by selecting and sending to China two officials well versed in mathematics and in the Chinese language from the Office of Translation and the Office of Observatories.[73] He again recommended that those who would carry out this mission successfully be appointed to govern-

---

71. Jeong Yak-yong, *op. cit.*, I-16:4a-b.
72. His error in the use of pulley has been recently pointed out. Kim Yong-un and Kim Yong-guk, *op. cit.*, pp. 221-222.
73. Jeong Yak-yong, *op. cit.*, V-2:28a-29b.

ment posts in the countryside so as to bring down the barriers dividing professionals (*jungin*) and nobility (*yangban*).

According to Dasan, endeavors for "Northern Learning" (Bukhak, namely Chinese studies) with the creation of the Office of Utility and Utilization were necessary for the sake of the "wealth of the nation and the national defense."[74] Possibly due to the fact that he lived during the Catholic persecution, Dasan seems not to have shown a positive attitude toward Western science. However, in comparison to Hong Dae-yong, he was keenly interested in the high level of the Chinese and Western technologies of the time and was for their rapid introduction into Korea.

Accommodation of Western Science by Choe Han-gi

While Yi Ik, Hong Dae-yong and Dasan have been studied relatively widely, the case of Choe Han-gi (1803–1877 or 1879) is almost unknown, with the exception of a summary treatment by Bak Jong-hong.[75] However, as even a cursory glance through his writings would immediately indicate, his main concern was science, and Western science in particular. In order to evaluate his position in history, one has to see the content and characteristics of his many scientific concepts. Since no evaluation of him has been made from the aspect of the history of scientific thought, I will identify the Western scientific concepts in some of his representative works and compare them with those of other scholars surveyed so far.

The most suitable of his works for this purpose are the *Sin-gitong* (Interactions between the Spirit and the Creative) and the *Chucheungnok* (Speculations on the Movement of the Spirit) of 1836, later collected as one book and called *Gicheuk cheui* (Analysis of Human Body for the

---

74. *Ibid.*, I-12:42a or V-1:4a.
75. Bak Jong-hong, "Choe Han-gi-ui gwahakjeogin cheolhak sasang" (Scientific Philosophy of Choe Han-gi), *Asea yeongu* (Asian Studies) 8.4 (1965): pp. 1-34. In addition, Yi Don-nyeong's paper on the philosophical thought of Choe Han-gi for a periodical *Changjak-gwa bipyeong* (Creation and Criticism) was reprinted in The Korean Historical Association, ed., *Silhak yeongu immun* (Introduction to the Study of Silhak) (Seoul: Ilchokak Publishing Co., 1973). Yi U-seong introduced his life and his thought in *Myeongnamnu chongseo* (Collected Works of Choe Han-gi), vol. 1. Both Bak and Yi made a partial introduction of him, not much mention on his scientific thought.

Comprehension of the Objects), and *Jigu jeonyo* (Descriptions of the Nations of the World) of 1857. His *Seonggi unhwa* (Dynamic Changes of Stellar Chi), written in 1867, was the final scientific work, but is recently published as *Myeongnamnu chongseo* (Collected Works of Choe Han-gi). However, this collected works does not contain the *Seonggi unhwa*, and the original text is difficult to obtain.[76] The *Sin-gi cheonheom* (Medical Experiments of the Spirit), written in 1866, is a good source with which to examine Choe's interest in medicine, but medicine will not be surveyed in this paper. Also, *Ujuchaek* (A Book on the Universe; twelve volumes in six books, works before 1857) seems to explain his view of the universe, but its whereabouts are unknown.

Optics

Water makes the image of an object appear to float above its actual position. Choe Han-gi thus explains that a fisherman has to aim his harpoon a little below the fish. Likewise, he explains that the sun or the stars appear to float a little higher over the horizon than their actual positions since the *monggi* of the air functions like water.[77] This is his account of the refraction of light. He changed the term *cheongmonggi* to *monggi*.

He also explains about lenses. Strangely enough, he seemed to understand the function of convex and concave lenses in reverse. He says that in a telescope comprised of of an empty pipe with crystal mirrors attached at both ends, a convex lens at the front converges the image of an object and a concave lens at the rear scatters the image. In other words, he claimed that a concave lens to makes an image appear larger and a convex lens smaller.[78] Here, the "mirrors" referred to are not convex or concave ones, since he was clearly referring to lenses at both ends of a telescope. In this way, he also explained the function of eyes. Human eyes are the same as convex mirrors, making objects appear smaller than actual size when they are refracted through the eyes,[79] since its angle against the eyes becomes small. And in the same manner,

---

76. *Seonggi unhwa* in two books of 12 volumes is now preserved in the Library of the Asiatic Research Center of Korea University.

77. Choe Han-gi, *Chucheungnok*, 2:19a-b; reprinted in *Myeongnamnu chongseo*, vol. 1, p. 124.

78. *Ibid.*, 6:32b; reprinted in *Myeongnamnu chongseo*, vol. 1, p. 198.

79. Choe Han-gi, *Sin-gitong* 2:2b; reprinted in *Myeongnamnu chongseo*, vol. 1, p. 37.

a small object near the eyes appears bigger since its angle against the eyes becomes large. This optical knowledge of Choe Han-gi suggests that Korea was accommodating Western science more widely in his time.

Wave Motion

Choe Han-gi explained that sound occurs in objects and diffuses in all directions by vibrating *gi*. He drew concentric circles to depict the process of sound diffusion, likening the waves to ripples in the water.[80] He called this wave motion *hun*. According to this theory, if the noise were loud, the sound *hun* would likewise be large as well but when were a noise soft, the sound *hun* would be accordingly small. If there were no wind blowing, the *hun* would form concentric circles. In case the wind blows, *un* is formed in a long oval form in the direction of the wind. He explains that not only sounds, but color and smell also diffuse in the same manner.[81]

Though the original source of this view is not identified, Choe Han-gi's theory of wave-motion is certain to have been obtained from Western books of science.

Thermometer and Hygrometer

We discussed how Dasan's "four affections" (*sa jeong*: cold, hot, wet, and dry) correspond to the theory of Aristotle. Claiming that these four properties can be measured with instruments, Choe Han-gi claimed that there is nothing in this world that cannot be measured in a mathematical manner. As one who holds *gi* as the prevailing element, he maintains that every *gi* has *i* (logos) and every has a hexagrammic phase, and every hexagrammic phase carries its own number.[82]

This view was expressed in terms of hexagrammic phases and numbers by Shao Yung and Zhang Zai of Northern Song. Choe Han-gi explains the traditional way of thinking in terms of the modern science of the West. Here, he introduces the thermometer and hygrometer as instruments with which to measure cold, hot, wet, and dry. The *eum-*

---

80. *Ibid.*, 1:17a; reprinted in *Myeongnamnu chongseo*, vol. 1, p. 16.
81. *Ibid.*, 1:13a-14a; reprinted in *Myeongnamnu chongseo*, vol. 1, p. 13.
82. *Ibid.*, 1;49a-b; reprinted in *Myeongnamnu chongseo*, vol. 1, p. 33.

cheongui is a hygrometer of today, used to measure the humidity, while the *naengnyeolgi* is what we would now call a thermometer. In Choe's view, this thermometer functions in this manner: under a glass bulb filled with compressed air is a U-shaped glass pipe with water inside; the temperature is measured by the balance of heights of water on both sides.[83] Of course, water will not work so in this manner. It is quite possible that either Choe Han-gi was mistaken, or a typesetter made the mistake of omitting the proper Chinese character in the process of type-setting, since water is *su* and mercury is *sueun*.

In an account of the hygrometer, he did not give an illustration, saying merely that illustrations of the thermometer and hygrometer are already printed in Yixiangzhi, making it clear that these were all Western instruments. *Yixiangzhi* here refers to *Lingtai yixiangzhi* (in 16 volumes including two volumes of illustration) written by a Jesuit missionary F. Verbiest (?–1687) in early Qing.

The View of the Universe

Choe Han-gi's view of the universe underwent a drastic change between 1836–1857. In his *Sin-gitong* and *Chucheungnok*, both written in 1836, he maintained a geocentric view of the rotating earth in the fashion of Hong Dae-yong, with the addition of Kepler's elliptical orbit. However, in his *Jigu jeonyo* of 1857, he talks about the rotation and the revolution of the earth, accommodating the view of Copernicus. First, we should examine the state of his thinking in 1836, at a time when he claimed that the earth, moon, sun, and the stars constantly revolve,[84] with the speed of revolution becoming faster the more inner the position of the planet.[85] When the Western theory of the earth was first introduced to China in early Ming, people did not accept this at first but they gradually accepted the theory and became convinced of its truth. On the other hand, some people in the West had long believed in the theory of a rotating earth, and there were some people in China who accepted this view. On this point Choe Han-gi explained that since there was not much differ-

---

83. *Ibid.*, 2:18a-19a, 6:67b-68b; reprinted in *Myeongnamnu chongseo*, vol. 1, pp. 123-124, 216.

84. *Ibid.*, 6:70a; reprinted in *Myeongnamnu chongseo*, vol. 1, p. 217.

85. Choe Han-gi, "Jiche geup jeyo," in *Sin-gitong*, 1:24a; reprinted in *Myeongnamnu chongseo*, vol. 1, p. 20.

ence in the outcome of observation between the two, the theory of the rotating earth had not become the dominant one. But he says that any reasoning had to be explored, and since planets rotate more slowly the further they are positioned from the earth, the theory holding that the earth rotates once a day is quite reasonable.[86]

The theory of the earth's rotation and revolution began to spread gradually in China from the end of the eighteenth century, but it is not clear from where Choe Han-gi obtained this theory or whether it had been a tradition since the days of Hong Dae-yong. It is important to note here that Choe Han-gi pointed out that the orbits of the sun and stars are elliptical, clarifying that this is what he learned from the observation data of Cassini and Flamsteed, contained in *Lixiang kaocheng houbian*. He noted that thus, it is clear that the earth was not the center of the universe.[87] The book, *Lixiang kaocheng houbian* was completed by Andreas Pereyra and Ming An-tu in 1724, under the aegis of Ignatius Koegler, and introduced new knowledge that followed the earlier introduction of Western astronomy at the end of Ming and the beginning of Qing.[88] A note to be added here is that Hong Dae-yong seemed not to have known of the elliptical orbits and that this new book did not discuss the theory of Copernicus or the earth's rotation around its axis, though the book computed the movement of planets based on the theory of elliptical orbits.

However, Choe's attitude changed a great deal in 1857, when he held, for the first time, that the theory of Copernicus was true. In his *Jigu jeonyo*, four models of the universe were illustrated in order. His understanding is that each illustration has its own protagonist.

There may seem no difference between Figures 1 and 2. But, according to his explanation, Figure 2 is of a static earth and Figure 3 is of a rotating earth. The concept of Figure 3 is similar to that of Hong Dae-yong and this was the view of Choe Han-gi in 1836.[89]

Though no historical claim can be absolutely certain, this must have been the first time the Copernican theory of the earth's rotation and rev-

---

86. Choe Han-gi, "Jigu useon," in *Chucheungnok*; reprinted in *Myeongnamnu chongseo*, vol. 1, p. 117.

87. *Ibid.*, 2:7b-8a; reprinted in *Myeongnamnu chongseo*, vol. 1, p. 118.

88. Yabuuchi Kiyoshi, *Astronomy and Calendar of China* (in Japanese) (Tokyo, 1969), pp. 165-166.

89. Choe Han-gi, *Jigu jeonyo*, 1:12a-16a; reprinted in *Myeongnamnu chongseo*, vol. 4, pp. 9-11.

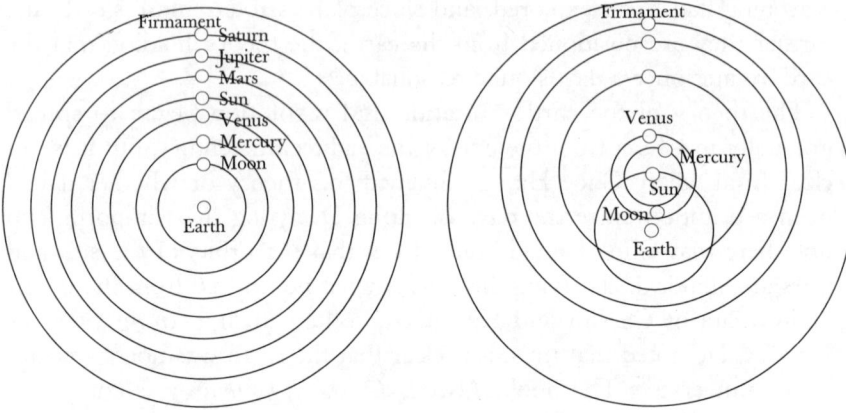

Figure 1. Ptolemy   Figure 2. Tycho Brahe

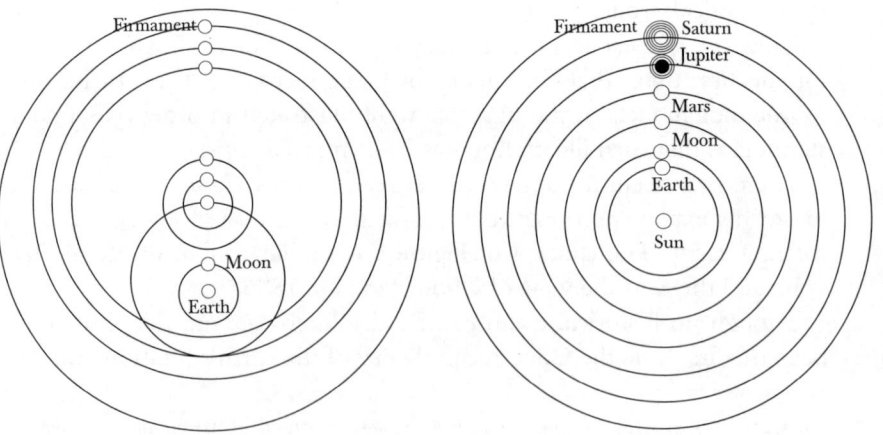

Figure 3. Mersenne   Figure 4. Copernicus

olution was ever recorded in Korea. Choe Han-gi claimed, in his introductory remarks to *Jigu Jeonyo*, that this view was borrowed from
Haiguo tuzhi (Wei Yuan, 1842) and *Yinghuan Zhilue* (Xu Ji-she, 1848),
and that his book *Jigu jeonyo* was "edited."[90]

However, Figure 4 still contains the *gyeongseongcheon* (heaven of 28
star constellations), indicating that he was still thinking of a finite universe. In comparison to Hong Dae-yong, who was thinking of an infinite
universe 80 years prior to him, Choe Han-gi's view of the universe
seems not to have progressed much beyond that. It will be necessary to
closely study the view of the universe of other scholars between 1836
and 1857.

From Jugiron *to* Gihwa

The name of *gi* varies, depending on its function. In one context, it is
called *cheon* (heaven), its presiding function *je* (emperor) and its prevailing function *do* (way). When *gi* is given to mankind, it is called *myeong*
(life). *Gi* can be nature or the mind, giving birth to *sin* (spirit), *gwi*
(demon), *eum* (*yin*), *yang* (*yang*), *dong* (dynamics) or *jeong* (stasis).[91]
Choe Han-gi's *jugiron* (theory viewing *gi* as the prevailing element) was
clearly based on the traditional philosophy of China. For instance, *gi* is
the same as water on the land.[92] Or, man lives in *gi* as fish live in
water.[93] Such sayings of Choe Han-gi are based on the traditional view
of Nature and are reminiscent of a saying of Dong Zhongshu a thousand
years ago. According to Dong, in the universe man is always wrapped in
the *gi* of *yin* and *yang*, just as fish live in the water.[94]

Choe Han-gi's theory of *gi*, based on traditional thought, immediately
associates itself with that of Western science. As was seen in the case of
Hong Dae-yong, the concept of a universe filled with *gi* is seems to have
been enhanced by influence from Western science. Western science since
Aristotle did not recognize the influence of the vacuum, and Choe Han-
gi claimed that there was no vacuum between heaven and the earth, and

90. *Ibid.*; reprinted in *Myeongnamnu chongseo*, vol. 4, p. 57.
91. Choe Han-gi, *Chucheungnok*, 2:12b; reprinted in *Myeongnamnu chongseo*, vol. 1, p. 120.
92. *Ibid.*, 2:17b; reprinted in *Myeongnamnu chongseo*, vol. 1, p. 123.
93. *Ibid.*, 2:8b; reprinted in *Myeongnamnu chongseo*, vol. 1, p. 118.
94. Feng Youlan, *Philosophical History of China* (in Chinese) (Hong Kong, 1970), p. 504.

likewise, that there was no place without *gi* anywhere in the universe.[95]

A concept in agreement with that of *gi*, albeit just a bit different, is that of *monggi*. Though Hong Dae-yong already called it *cheongmonggi*, Choe Han-gi explained that the very big defect in astronomy and the calendar of China centered around this point and that this defect was rectified by the accommodation of Western science.[96] *Monggi* means air or atmosphere. However, according to Choe Han-gi, the wandering *gi* within the earth goes upward around the earth in a condensed form, in the same way that even a minor creature has its own odor. Because of this, the moon and stars appear to be larger than they are, while light and round shapes appear to be elliptical.[97]

Clearly, *monggi* is different from the *gi* that wraps up everything in the universe. But Choe Han-gi does not explain why and how they differ from one another. In attempting to explain tidal ebb and flow, he explains the phenomenon not in terms of *monggi* but in terms of *gi*. Saying that *gi* around a planet moves in pace with the movement of the planet itself, he explains that the ebb and flow of the tide takes place in an encounter of the vortex of *gi* thus produced.[98] This thought of 1836 surfaces again in the same form in *Jigu jeongyo* of 1857. The only difference this time was that he provided illustrations of the phenomenon in his book of 1857.[99]

In *Jigu jeongyo*, this concept is again explained in terms of *gihwa* (changing nature of *gi*). According to the account here, planets revolve along their orbits as debris churning in a vortex travels around a bowl. Put a bit differently, a boat floats on the water with a varying degree of drift depending on its weight and shape.[100] Clearly, this is an attempt to explain the ebb and flow of the tide, or the orbital movement of the planets, with the vortex theory of Rene Descartes, without resorting to the gravity theory of Newton. When and how the Newtonian theory of gravity came to Korea will be another subject of study to be made in the future.

---

95. Choe Han-gi, *Chucheungnok*, 2:18a; reprinted in *Myeongnamnu chongseo*, vol. 1, p. 123; *Gisu mugan* 2:28; reprinted in *Myeongnamnu chongseo*, vol. 1, p. 128.

96. *Ibid.*, 6:58b; reprinted in *Myeongnamnu chongseo*, vol. 1, p. 211.

97. *Ibid.*, 2:6a-b; reprinted in *Myeongnamnu chongseo*, vol. 1, p. 117.

98. *Ibid.*, 2:7a; reprinted in *Myeongnamnu chongseo*, vol. 1, p. 118.

99. Choe Han-gi, *Jigu jeonyo*, 1:24a-b; reprinted in *Myeongnamnu chongseo*, vol. 4, p. 15.

100. *Ibid.*, 1:24b-26a; reprinted in *Myeongnamnu chongseo*, vol. 4, pp. 15-16.

Conclusions

Indirect contact with Western science, starting in the seventeenth century, had been steadily maintained for hundreds of years prior to the opening of Korean ports to the outside world. And some Korean scholars, particularly of Silhak, endeavored hard to accommodate it, having been impressed with its precision. Yi Ik, Hong Dae-yong, Dasan and Choe Han-gi represented this group of Korean scholars.

In this process, some of them exhibited bold creativity, and Hong Dae-yong was a pioneering example. He juxtaposed various concepts from Western science with the traditional scientific thought of the Orient, building up his own system of thought with his own critical consciousness. This sort of secondary creativity was shown more in the generation of Choe Han-gi, who had accommodated himself to Western science more than Hong Dae-yong, to the point of blind devotion. This may be due to the weighted novelty and importance of Western science, as well as because he was somewhat stupefied by the onslaught of Western scientific knowledge, to the point of uncritical, complete accommodation.

Bak Jong-hong highly praised the creativity of Choe Han-gi in his study of him. Having read the preface to his *Seonggi unhwa* of 1867, Bak Jong-hong surmised that the scientific thought of Choe Han-gi seemed to have exerted more influence on the thought of Chinese scholars, since his views became more popular and more known in China than in Korea. He wrote about this as follows:

> What draws our attention in the preface to *Seonggi unhwa*, a book written by Choe Han-gi in 1867 when he was 65 years old, is that he was introducing and discussing *cheukheom*, *sin-gi* or *unhwa* which are discussed in a book, *Tantian* written by Hou Shihle in China. *Tantian* is said to have been published in the eighth year of Emperor Xianfeng, 1858, 22 years after the publication of Choe Han-gi's book, *Gicheuk cheui* in 1836. In other words, Choe's writing preceded that of *Tantian* by 22 years. Since *Gicheuk cheui* was published by Inhwadang Publishing House in Beijing, it may be that Hou Shihle had been influenced by the book of Choe Han-gi.[101]

---

101. Bak Jong-hong, "*Gicheuk cheui*," in Hyonam Publishing Co., comp. *Hanguk-ui myeongjeo* (Great Books of Korea) (Seoul: Hyonam Publishing Co., 1969), p. 1096.

However, this is an overblown estimate emanating from a minor misunderstanding. The *Tantian* (Outlines of Astronomy) was not written by a Chinese but was a translation in Chinese of an astronomical book by Britain's representative astronomer William Hershell (1738–1822). Thus, Hershell, who died in 1822, could not have read Choe Han-gi's book, *Gicheuk cheui,* written in 1836. Such terms as *seonggi* or *unhwa* had long been in use in China since Western astronomy was introduced; they were not new words coined by Choe Han-gi. *Tantian* by W. Hershell was translated and published by British missionary Alexander Wylie (1815–1887) in cooperation with a Chinese mathematician Li Shanlan in 1858,[102] and Choe Han-gi's *Seonggi unhwa* was written under the influence of this book.[103] In the end, the estimation of Choe Han-gi will be that of a pioneering scholar in the systematic accommodation of Western science prior to the opening of the Korean ports to the outside world, rather than a man possessed of original scientific thought. Though not touched upon in this paper, Choe Han-gi also compiled medical books from the West written between 1851–1858 by a British missionary doctor Benjamin Hobson (1816–1873), such as *New General Introduction, Summary of Western Medicine, New Theories of Internal Medicine* and he wrote *Sin-gi cheonheom* in 1866.[104] The book shows that he was very quick in introducing Korea to the version of scientific thought circulating in China. Choe Han-gi, in proposing the creation of the Office of Utility and Utilization, further promoted the notions of technological and historical progress exhibited by Dasan. He claimed that if the people of ancient times were born again, they would be flexible enough to avail themselves of the new experiences of their posterity.[105] While advocating the accommodation of Western science and recognizing the brilliant progress made by science and technology, Choe Han-gi says, after all, that the ultimate aim of such endeavors lay in clarifying Confucian virtues and Confucian sayings.[106] He admonishes that since the

102. W. Hershell, *Tantian,* translation in cooperation with Li Shanlan (Beijing, 1958).
103. For instance, some words indicating "Herschel William" are seen in *Seonggi unhwa,* vol. 8.
104. W. Hershell, *op. cit.*
105. See Choe Han-gi, *Sin-gitong,* 1:23a; reprinted in *Myeongnamnu chongseo,* vol. 1, p. 20, and *Chucheungnok,* 6:2a; reprinted in *Myeongnamnu chongseo,* vol. 1, p. 183.
106. Choe Han-gi, *Chucheungnok,* 1:25b-26a; reprinted in *Myeongnamnu chongseo,* vol. 1, p. 97.

ways of Confucianists, Buddhists and the West have a merit of their own, a way for universal education should emerge from the combination of ethics from Confucianism, calendric computation, as well as from the West, with the realistic approaches replacing the vague teachings of Buddhism.[107] *Dongdo seogi* (Eastern Way and Western Technology) was already the mental attitude of Silhak scholars in efforts to accommodate Western science and technology even before the opening of Korean ports to the outside world. Nevertheless, enthusiasm for the accommodation of Western science in the absence of any particular crisis consciousness, and the subsequent attitude of "Eastern Way and Western Technology," were unable to find translation from theory into practice on a large scale. As was seen in the survey of Korean travelogues to Beijing, most of the ruling class did not show much interest in Western science. Enthusiasm for it remained solely in the hearts of the intelligentsia until a national crisis took more definite form and presented itself on Korean shores in the days to come.

---

107. Choe Han-gi, *Sin-gitong*, 1:15b; reprinted in *Myeongnamnu chongseo*, vol. 1, p. 16.

Dasan's Thought on Western Learning and Confucianism

Keum Jang-tae

Preface

Dasan, or Jeong Yak-yong (1762–1836) was active at the end of the eighteenth and the beginning of the nineteenth century, at a time when the Confucian system of the Dohak (Learning of the Way) school, which had represented orthodoxy for hundreds of years, was being seriously challenged. This was the period of the "Western powers' Eastern advance," when the Korean peninsula was being besieged by "Western Learning" (the Catholic faith and Western scientific techniques). The intellectual activities spurred by this learning caused a great stir in the orthodox Confucian society. It is impossible to state that this "Western intellectualism" indicated the collapse of tradition and the beginning of modernization. However, traditional absolute authority and order came into conflict with philosophy of a different nature, and this confrontation limited conservative power. This provided the opportunity for the critical reformation movement to come into being.

This period can be connected to the rise of the enlightenment movement and modernization at the end of the nineteenth century. The introduction of Western social thought marked the transition from the tradi-

* Originally published in the *Korea Journal*, vol. 26, no. 2 (Feb. 1986).

Keum Jang-tae is Professor of Religious Studies at Seoul National University. His doctoral dissertation is entitled "A Study of the Modern Korean Thoughts during the Interaction between East and West." His publications include *Joseon jeon-gi-ui yuhak sasang* (Confucian Thoughts in the Early Joseon Dynasty) (1997), *Toegye-ui sam-gwa cheolhak* (The Life and Philosophy of Yi Toegye) (1998), and *Hyeondae hanguk yugyo-wa jeontong* (The Legacy of Confucianism in Contemporary Korean Society) (2003). E-mail: keumjt@snu.ac.kr.

tional period to the modern age. Dasan was the representative of this age in that he best expressed the conditions of his time. He devoted himself completely to the task of finding solutions to the problems of his age.

This paper examines how Dasan received Western learning, especially Catholic thought, and the influence Western thought had on his Confucian thought. Research into these problems can provide useful material to help us understand the reaction to, as well as the development that arose from, contact between traditional thought and Western learning in recent Korean historical thought.

Dasan's Age and Intellectual Background

The Intellectual Environment of Dasan's Time

The latter period of Joseon saw the Dohak school, which had been growing and developing since the beginning of the Joseon period and which considered Neo-Confucianism to be orthodox, solidify its position as society's orthodox ideology. The anti-Qing sentiment, which appeared after the Manchu war of 1636, resulted in restraints on the import of the Qing dynasty's culture and adherence to the Neo-Confucianism of the Song and Ming period. Accordingly, Dohak Neo-Confucianism of early Joseon lost its novelty and becoming immersed in formalism and pedantic theory, and enslaved by conservative authoritarianism, fell into stagnation. The failure that became apparent in this later Joseon period was due to factional conflicts, power struggles that arose from adverse criticism of the complex judicial system, the decay of the bureaucracy and general social disorder. Since the beginning of Joseon Daoism, Buddhism and the doctrine of Wang Yangming were criticized as heretical and Dohak was examined more deeply. Internally, Neo-Confucianism was unable to maintain its orthodoxy and authoritarian attitude while externally, interest in the realities of life and criticism and doubt of traditional systems, which were aroused by the objective freedom of the intellect, began to appear.

With Ban-gye Yu Hyeong-won (1622–1673) as forerunner, then Seong-ho Yi Ik (1681–1763), Dasan and several other scholars[1] formed a new

---

1. Cheon Gwan-u said, "With the appearance of Yu Hyeong-won, Silhak confirmed its existence as a school of thought, and it is not an exaggeration to say that with the

school which insisted on reform of the system and the growth of industry. They tried to relate many of the problems that arose from research in the Chinese classics to the actual reality and needs of the time. They advocated experience and the search for evidence to establish true facts. Generally speaking, they exhibited a critical objective attitude towards the already existing authoritarian system, creating what is called today Silhak (Practical Learning). It is impossible to ignore that one of the main reasons for its development was the impetus given by the introduction of the Chinese positive inquiry school and by Western civilization. Internally, of course, the negative attitude of the Silhak thinkers towards the Neo-Confucian school was also a reason. Through the comings and goings of the envoys to China, Silhak thinkers Seo Myeong-eung, Hong Yang-ho, Hong Dae-yong, Bak Ji-won, Yi Deok-mu, Yu Deuk-gong and Bak Je-ga actively tried to import Chinese culture and formed the Northern Learning school. Their particular characteristic was that they adopted an active posture in seeking new knowledge and the direction necessary to solve the problems of the time. Silhak furnished the foundation for the development of the culture during the reigns of King Yeongjo and Jeongjo due to policies encouraging scholasticism. A great number of scholars became preoccupied not only in problems concerning the classics and history, but with adopting the Silhak position and ardently researching politics, economics, education, military history, and science. They extended this to all fields and in so doing presented themselves as authors of a new critical theoretical system. It cannot be stated, however, that Silhak, as a new trend of thought, generally took the lead in this era's scholarship or that it posed a fatal disruption of Dohak's traditional character and authority which had been established since the beginning of the Joseon period. In reality it was in the Seoul area amongst the Namin (Southerners) scholars that the Silhak academic tradition began to deepen its roots.[2] It was also in this group that the Catholic faith caught fire. Dasan and the Southern Silhak thinkers encountered great

---

appearance of Yi Ik, Silhak affirmed its existence as a school of learning." See Cheon Gwan-u, "The Silhak Vanguard—Yu Hyeong-won" (in Korean), in *Joseon silhak-ui gaecheokja 10 in* (The Ten Pioneers of Joseon Silhak) (Seoul: Shin Gu Publishing Co., 1974), p. 15. In this he shows the genealogy of academic tradition.

2. Hong I-Seop, "Silhak-e isseo namin hakpa-ui sasangjeok gyebo" (The Genealogy of the Thought of the Namin Faction in Practical Learning), *Inmun gwahak* (Review of Cultural Sciences) 10 (1963): pp. 191-204.

opposition when they tried to adapt the Catholic faith to the orthodox Silhak learning and were therefore unable to continue.

Even though the Dohak school brought about a differentiation of schools through deep research into Neo-Confucian philosophy, it was active in accumulating works. Consequently Dohak maintained its authority and was the leading ideology until the end of the Joseon dynasty. Despite King Jeongjo's policy of tolerance, the general atmosphere of authoritarianism and orthodoxy became the foundation for the realization of an anti-Western movement and severe suppression of the Catholic faith. After King Jeongjo and until King Gojong, *cheoksaron* ("rejection heterodoxy" argument) and *saok* (Catholic persecution) were the base for what can be called Dohak's "rebuttal of the heterodox approach."[3] This conservative orthodox attitude adopted a position rejecting not just Western learning but even Qing China's civilization.

Accordingly, the time before and after Dasan can be summarized by saying that although orthodox Dohak Neo-Confucianism continued to be the thought that dominated society, people began to become deeply conscious of its abuses and critical of its conservative and rigid atmosphere. Intellectual unrest rose up in many quarters of society, bringing about the formation of a reformation theory together with a movement to accept Qing China's new civilization. At this time, factional powers appeared to reject not just metaphysics but even Confucian concepts. The conflict between orthodox Confucianism, which considered metaphysical theory as its basic principle, and the new Western learning became one of the problems of that time. It is necessary to examine carefully how the scholars of both schools tried to bring about harmony by groping for ways to harmonize the direction of their own academic traditions. It is essential to examine Dasan's thought in this light.

The Introduction of Catholicism to the Joseon Dynasty

Knowledge of the Catholicism was first introduced to Korea by Yi Su-gwang at the beginning of the seventeenth century, and it gradually became more widely known after Yi Su-gwang introduced Matteo Ricci's *Tianzhu shiyi* (True Principles of Catholicism). It was at this time that

---

3. Keum Jang-tae, "The Joseon Period's Orthodox Confucian Ideology and Criticism of Heresy" (in Korean), in *Yugyo-wa hanguk sasang* (Confucianism and Korean Thought) (Seoul: Sunggyungwan University Press, 1980), pp. 55-92.

Heo Gyun was said to have converted to Catholicism. From the seventeenth century until the end of the eighteenth century, knowledge of Western culture was accumulated and interest in Western culture grew. The indigenous appearance of the Catholic movement on the Korean peninsula, therefore, was not something that happened suddenly.

During the seventeenth and eighteenth centuries the Catholic faith and scientific knowledge were effective in attracting the interest of the Chinese intelligentsia. Because the Catholic missionaries were able to cater to Chinese needs by offering rational and efficient Western knowledge about astronomy and calendric science, they were treated well. This meant that they were able to introduce and spread the Catholic faith easily. At the same time, Joseon society became increasingly interested in Western culture, especially in astronomy, calendric science, world maps, and utensils. The use of the Current Standard Calendar (*siheonnyeok*) during the fouth year of the reign of King Hyojong (1653) is proof of these changing times.

Aside from their interest in Western scientific technology, the Silhak thinkers in the latter part of the Joseon period actively displayed diverse interest in Western science. While the important Silhak scholars acknowledged the Dohak schools of metaphysics, they turned away from those beliefs and adopted an attitude of respect for practicality. They attached importance to concrete experience, seeking facts grounded on solid evidence. This new attitude enhanced an active interest and positive evaluation of Western scientific techniques. It is noteworthy that the process of the development of the Silhak school's learning, which advanced with the discovery of Catholic teaching, took place when the positive interest in Western science led to an effort to also understand the cultural background of scientific knowledge.

The Seongho school, with Seongho (Yi Ik) as its leader, displayed a greater interest in Western science and the Catholic faith than any other schools at that time. Their acceptance of the Catholic faith had an important influence on the direction of the thought of other schools in the latter Joseon period.

Yi Ik inherited Yi Su-gwang's erudition and open-mindedness to Western culture and Yu Hyeong-won's critical reform theory. This, together with his already deep interest in Western culture, led to the forming of the Seongho school within the Silhak school. Yi Ik himself was fascinated by Western science, and agreed with Adam Schall's Reformed Calendar and calculations of solar and lunar eclipses. He proclaimed that this calendar was the zenith of calendric science and praised Adam Schall, saying that even if a saint were to be born again, he could not but agree with him. He confessed that Chinese astronomy was inferior to its Western counterpart and that the West was first in this field, followed by Arabia. He understood Western astronomy, the calendar system and the map of the world and praised Western scientific technology. He therefore showed a great interest in Catholicism. His interests ranged from science books such as Diaz's *Astronomy*, Aleni's *Zhifang waij*, Verbiest's *Kunyu tushuo*, and Ursis's *Jianping yishuo*, to books on Catholic doctrine such as Ricci's *Tianzhu shiyi*, Pantoja's *Qiji*, Ricci's *Doctrine of Friendship*, and Adam Schall's *Zhuzai qunzheng*. He said that the concept of the Lord of Heaven corresponded with the Confucian "Ultimate Being" (*sangje*), thus accepting the Christian idea of the existence of an absolute being. However, he made a distinction between the fear, hope, and faith shown to the Lord of Heaven in the Catholic faith and the Ultimate Being in Confucianism, comparing this to the attitude shown towards Buddha in Buddhism. While recognizing Western superiority in the field of astronomy and the calendar and the concurrence of Catholicism and Confucianism on ethical matters, Yi Ik rejected the idea of Heaven and Hell, upholding, rather, the Confucian position on the subject.

Yi Ik's attitude of open acceptance of Western learning greatly shocked his followers and brought two factions against each other. One faction called the Gongseopa (Anti-Western Faction), which identified itself with the Orthodox Dohak Neo-Confucian position, strongly criticized and rejected these attitudes. The other, Sinseopa (Pro-Western Faction), were positively inclined towards Western learning and the Catholic faith. Some people in this group even advocated increased research in the Catholic faith and the starting of a faith movement. Two of Yi Ik's disciples, Sin Hu-dam (1702–1761) and An Jeong-bok (1712–1791), were instrumental in instituting the former faction by spreading a theory critical of Catholic doctrine. At the age of 23, Sin Hu-dam wrote a book called *Seohakbyeon* (Comments on Western Learning), in which he established a system critical of Catholic faith. In this book, he systematically criticized Sambiaso's *Lingyan lixi*, Ricci's *Tianzhu shiyi* and Aleni's *Zhifang waiji* and accused Catholicism of being bloodthirsty and valuing death egoistically. He criticized *Lingyan lixi*, saying that the concept of the soul is the basic problem of the Catholic faith. This concept comes directly in conflict with philosophical issues clarified by essential themes of Neo-Confucianism, which discuss man's mind, nature and feeling. In this way his activities ranged from criticizing the Catholic faith to investigating the original Neo-Confucian standards. An Jeong-bok also carefully criticized the Catholic doctrine of Heaven and Hell and the concept of the soul in a letter to Yi Ik in 1757. In 1784, An Jeong-bok directly criticized the Catholic movement which had sprung within the Sinseopa faction, and he wrote *Cheonhak mundap* (Questions and Answers to Catholicism) and *Cheonhakgo* (On Catholic Doctrine), in which he set up his critical theory.

Sin Hu-dam, An Jeong-bok and other figures in the Gongseopa faction inherited only one part of Yi Ik's thought. The Sinseopa faction (Kwon Cheol-sin, Kwon Il-sin, Yi Ga-hwan, Yi Byeok, Yi Seung-hun, Jeong Yak-jeon, Jeong Yak-jong, Jeong Yak-yong), on the other hand, inherited Yi Ik's positive attitude towards Western learning. This faction, a part of the Seongho school, consisted of Yi Ik's direct disciples, his disciples' disciples, and people who admired his learning. They cultivated an interest in Catholic doctrine in the process of researching astronomy, calendric science, mathematics and Western science. Catholicism became a subject of their public scholarly discussions. From 1777 to 1779 they held study meetings (*ganghakhoe*) centered on Kwon Cheol-sin at Cheonjinam and Ju-eosa temples in Gwangju-gun county, Gyeonggi-do province. These meetings became the impetus for the growth of the Catholic faith. Yi Byeok is understood to have played an important role in these meetings.[4] Dasan's second brother, Jeong Yak-jeon, also attended these meetings. After Yi Byeok and Dasan's brothers joined in around 1784, Dasan himself researched the teachings of the Sinseopa faction and actively participated in the Catholic movement. In 1784–1785, the leaders of the Seongho school's Sinseopa faction took advantage of Yi Seung-hun's arrival from Beijing after he had been baptized, and began to perform Catholic rituals. These meetings, however, were exposed by the Justice department and a great amount of social criticism ensued. Thus, the Catholic faith movement became a social problem.

---

4. Kim Ok-hui, "Jonggyohakjeok-euro bon Gwangam Yi Byeok-ui seonggyo yoji gujo-e gwanhan yeongu" (The Symbolical Meaning of Thought of Yi Byeok in *Seonggyo yoji:* The Chief Truth of Holy Church), *Jonggyohak yeongu* (Review of Religious Studies) 2 (1979): pp. 49-60.

Dasan and His Catholic Faith

Dasan married at the age of fifteen, and moved to Seoul. In 1777, when he 16, he read Yi Ik's works, and, following Yi Ga-hwan (1742–1801) and Yi Seung-hun (1756–1801), he began to concern himself with the scholarship of the Seongho school. At the time, 36-year-old Yi Ga-hwan, the grandson of Yi Ik, inherited the leadership of the Seongho school. Dasan and 22-year-old Yi Seung-hun, Yi Ga-hwan's nephew and Dasan's brother-in-law established themselves as young Confucian scholars. Dasan writes that between 1777–1779, Kim Won-seong, Kwon Sang-hak, Yi Chong-ok, Yi Seung-hun, Yi Byeok and Jeong Yak-jeon held study meetings led by 42-year-old Kwon Cheol-sin (1736–1801), Yi Ik's disciple, at Cheonjinam and Ju-eosa temples. It is not sure whether or not 18-year-old Dasan attended these meetings. However, his second brother, Jeong Yak-jeon, did attend these meetings. Dasan himself already had a relationship with the Seongho school, and the more contact he had with it, the greater the opportunities he had to come into contact with Western science and the Catholic doctrine. Moreover, because Yi Byeok (1754–1786) was the brother-in-law of Jeong Yak-jeon (Dasan's elder brother), Dasan and Yi Byeok, despite an eight-year age difference, developed a close relationship between them.

Dasan himself attests to learning about the Catholic faith from Yi Byeok in 1784:

> On the 15th day of the 4th month of the year of the dragon (1784) after my eldest brother's wife's memorial service, my brothers and I got in the same boat as Yi Byeok and came down river. In the boat, I heard about the origin of creation, the body and the spirit and the reason for life and death, and I was surprised and doubtful. It reminded me of the infiniteness of the Milky way. Arriving in Seoul I followed Yi Byeok and looked through *Tianzhu shiyi* and a few other books, and for the first time I was joyful and grew curious.[5]

In this passage, Dasan explains how he became a Catholic. As a 23-year-old Confucian scholar, he was very moved and fascinated by the Catholic explanation of the problems of man and the universe. He was

---

5. Jeong Yak-yong. "The Epitaph to Seonjung" (in Korean), *Yeoyudang jeonseo* (Complete Works of Jeong Yak-yong), bk. I-15.

greatly shocked upon hearing the Catholic doctrine for the first time and this experience undermined his fixed Neo-Confucian ideas of the universe. The Catholic doctrine became a bridge for him to cross as well as an impetus for the development of his ideas regarding Neo-Confucianism. His brother, Jeong Yak-jeon, studied mathematics and calendric science from Yi Byeok. He researched the *Jihe yuanben* (Original Geometry Text), and, according to Dasan, he was very joyful when he first heard the Catholic teachings. His writings reveal that Catholicism was introduced to him and his brother through Yi Byeok. The fact that Yi Byeok also introduced the Catholic faith to Kwon Cheol-sin and Kwon Il-sin and to Yi Ga-hwan and Yi Seung-hun proves that Yi Byeok was the forerunner and motivating force behind the introduction of Catholicism to the Seongho school. The unification between Yi Ik's scholarship and Yi Byeok's followings (Yi Ik's learning and Yi Byeok's faith movement) formed the basis for the development of the Sinseopa faction.

Dasan's own writings attest that he first came into contact with Catholic teachings in 1784 when he was 23 years old, and that he began studying at the Seonggyungwan (National Confucian Academy) in the previous year. In the summer of 1784 King Jeongjo presented the university with questions about the Doctrine of the Mean. In order to find answers to all 70 questions, he found Yi Byeok at Seoul's Supyo-gyo bridge. After discussing the matters with Yi Byeok, he wrote *Jungyong daechaek* (Countermeasures to the Doctrine of the Mean) and *Jungyong gangui* (Lectures on the Doctrine of the Mean). Dasan and Yi Byeok met frequently during that year. In 1783 Yi Seung-hun followed the envoy to Beijing and was baptized there. In the following March, he returned and vigorously organized and spread the faith movement. Before Yi Seung-hun was baptized, he had received abundant and detailed knowledge about Catholic doctrine and ceremony. After his return, a concerted faith movement began.

In 1784, Yi Byeok returned from his hometown in the same boat as Dasan and his brothers. With the picturesque Hangang river in the background, he taught them about the Catholic faith. This deliverance, along with Yi Seung-hun's news of the Beijing church and his persuasive explanation of the vision of the New World were very inspiring. Yi Byeok continued to be very active and made every effort to spread the Gospel. These efforts developed into organizing faith meetings. In the spring of 1785 the authorities found out that these meetings were being held in Myeongnye-dong at the house of Kim Beom-u. The day they were discovered, Yi Byeok was leading the meeting with Yi Seung-hun, Kwon Il-sin and the three brothers Jeong Yak-jeon, Jeong yak-jong, and Dasan in attendance. Later, Kwon Il-sin and a few others went to the authorities and demanded the return of the icon they had confiscated. When this incident became known, those children of noble birth were severely reprimanded by their families. Yi Seung-hun rejected his faith, writing *Cheoksamun* (A Writing Rejecting the Catholic Faith), and the situation Seonggyungwan students handed out leaflets demanding the exile of Sinseopa faction leaders worsened.

The Catholic faith movement was stopped after its exposure in 1785, but it started again in the spring of the following year, this time as an underground movement. In the winter of 1787, Yi Seung-hun, Dasan and Kang I-won were discovered while they were researching Catholic doctrine in a private house near Seonggyun-gwan and publicly denounced by two fellow students, Yi Gi-gyeong and Hong Nak-an. In 1790, the Beijing Church sent directions to the underground Catholic church forbidding the practice of ancestor worship. In the following year in Jinsan, Jeolla-do province, Yun Ji-chung and Kwon Sang-yeon failed to prepare an ancestral tablet for their parents. This event caused a great stir all the way up to the central government. At this time Dasan held a position of the Office of Royal Decrees (Yemungwan), but with the conflict between the Catholic faith and ancestor rites he left for ten days to Haemi in Seosan district (1790). He writes that from 1787 to 1791 when the Jinsan event broke out, he was deeply involved in the Catholic faith, but he cut off all his relationships after the event.

After 1785, the government put accelerated efforts to repress the Catholic faith. In spite of this, the faith movement went beyond the limits of several young intellectuals of the Sinseopa faction and spread to the people. There were a few others who, like Yi Seung-hun, Dasan, and Kwon Il-sin, participated in the faith movement at first, but rejected their faith with social pressure. At the time, Dasan not only openly reject his faith, but also kept his brother Jeong Yak-jong, who still remained a believer, at a distance. By doing so, he managed to escape suspicion. Together with the Noron (Old Docrtine) faction, Yi Gi-gyeong, Hong Nak-an, and figures of the Party of Principle (Byeokpa) of Namin (Southerners), attacked King Jeongjo's supporters, Prime Minister Chae Je-gong, and his close advisors Yi Ga-hwan and Dasan. And yet the activities of the Qing Chinese priest Zhou Wenmo who secretly entered Korea in 1795 brought about many new converts. This led to the banishment of Yi Seung-hun to Yesan. Yi Ga-hwan was demoted from Minister of Punishments to Magistrate of Chungju county, and Dasan was demoted from the royal right-secretary to the inspector of the Geum-jeongyeok. The town of Geumjeongyeok was in an area in which the Catholic faith had deeply infiltrated. Dasan was responsible for recon-verting those of the Catholic faith back to Confucianism. He carried out his duties faithfully and through the Cheoksagye (a ceremony to cast off evil spirits) he managed to persuade many Catholic believers to return to Confucianism. In Dallet's *Histoire de l' Eglise de Corée* (History of the Korean Catholic Church), he condemns Jeong Yak-yong, saying "In order to compensate for his sin of being in the Catholic church, he tor-mented his fellow believers." Dasan resigned in 1797 to defend himself from criticism aimed at him while he was serving in the post of royal vice-secretary, and he submitted his resignation from the post of royal vice-secretary, taking instead a new post as Goksan's local administrator. Despite continuous attack and slander at the time, he was kept safe due to the confidence of King Jeongjo.

But when King Jeongio died and Sunjo became king, a cruel suppres-sion of Catholicism immediately ensued, known as the Catholic persecu-tion of 1801. It was during this period that Dasan asserted his rejection of the Catholic church. Nevertheless, he only barely escaped death and was banished to Janggi on the coast of Gyeongsang-do province. The same year, the Chinese priest Zhou Wenmo was executed and Hwang Sa-yeong was discovered when he secretly attempted to send his famous "Silk Letter" to the Catholic Bishop in Beijing. His letter explained the situation and hardships of the Catholic Church and appealed to Western nations to dispatch naval and land forces to compel the Korean govern-ment to grant religious freedom. After this event Dasan was again inter-rogated and was banished to Gangjin on the farthest southern tip of the coast of Jeolla-do province. He remained there for 18 years until he turned 57. In his "Silk Letter," Hwang Sa-yeong wrote that although Yi Ga-hwan, Dasan, Yi Seung-hun, and Hong Nak-min publicly rejected and denounced the Catholic church, they still held to their beliefs. Dasan mentioned how lonely he felt at the time, when even believers were few. Even though Dasan rejected his faith, he was still the brother of Jeong Yak-jong, the brother-in-law of Yi Seung-hun and uncle to Hwang Sa-yeong, all of whom had been executed, endangering his own life. He was also unable to deny the fact that he had a political position in the Party of Expediency (Sipa) of Namin and had the complete trust of King Jeongjo together with Yi Ga-hwan. During his 18 years of banishment in Gangjin, he devoted all his energy to the study of the Chinese Classics: *The Book of Changes, The Book of Odes, The Spring and Autumn Annals*, the Four Books and to the writing of literature. While in banishment, he wrote many works in which he analyzed and criticized the conditions of society based on his personal experiences and investigations. In *Gyeongse yupyo* (Design for Good Government) he put forward his views on government structure; in *Mongmin simseo* (Admonitions on Governing the People) he proposed reforms in the local administration. While it is difficult to find any trace of Catholic activity during this period of banishment, Dasan's research and writings about the Confucian classics and the methods of realization of Confucian political concepts resulted in bringing Korean Confucianism to a new level, proving him as a true Confucian scholar. Dallet, however, offers another opinion that conflicts with his above-mentioned condemnation of Dasan, noting that he never lost his faith. He states that Dasan "became weak and rejected his faith because of persecution, but in fact he was truly remorseful and devoted himself to the public affairs using all his energy in trying to atone for his sins."

From the age of 57 in 1818 until his death in 1836, Dasan went to his hometown Majae, where he devoted himself to writing. His works include *Sangseo gohun, Maessi sangseopyeong* about the Chinese classics, *Gukjo jeollyego* (The National Five Rites) and *Heumheum sinseo* (Toward a New Jurisprudence) about his theory of government. While it is difficult to find any trace of the Catholic faith in his literary writings, Dallet stresses that Dasan was a firm believer from the time he came out of banishment until his death:

> After his return from exile, John Jeong (Dasan) began to earnestly keep all church duties even more than he had before. Deeply repentant of his rejection of faith in Jesus Christ in 1801, he separated himself from the rest of the world. He almost always sat in his room, meeting no one except a few of his friends. He often fasted and performed other kinds of ascetic rituals. He turned a metal chain into his belt and never took it off. He often meditated for long periods of time, and wrote voraciously. He wrote partly about his meditations, or refuted the superstition of people outside the church. He also wrote various books for teaching new believers about the Catholic faith. During the persecution, he had hidden many of his books in the ground, where they rotted away as insects scratched and ate them. But many of his writings

were kept safe. Even after John Jeong was rehabilitated, he did not change his lifestyle the least. With time, his earnest beliefs moved and brought joy to all believers, thus repairing the negative image attached to him in the past with his rejection of the church. In 1835 he received the last sacraments from the hands of Father Liu Fangji, a Chinese priest who had recently entered Korea, and then departed from this world."[6]

Dallet adds that Dasan's eldest son Jeong Hak-yeon (pen name, Yusan) was baptized a few years before his father's death. Dallet also notes that after Dasan's release from exile he wrote many religious books, including a memoir about the entrance of the Gospel to Joseon.[7] This memoir was called the *Hanguk bogeum jeollaesa* and it was this work on which Dallet based his *History of the Korean Catholic Church*. Dallet also credits Dasan with writing the postscript to Yi Seung-hun's collection of works *Mancheon yugo*.[8] Dasan's own writings and official documents about his rejection of the Catholic church are extremely contradictory. Although it may be true that after 1791 and especially after 1801 the unanswered question about his life of faith may be an important condition for understanding his thought, the lack or uncertainty of historical material makes this discernment difficult. A better approach would be to try to investigate the influence that the Catholic faith had on Dasan's thought, especially his Confucian philosophy.

Dasan was born and died in Majae village, Neugnae-ri, Wabu-myeon, Yangiu-gun, on the east side of the lake of Paldang Dam, not far from Seoul, the meeting place between the north and south parts of the Han-gang river intersect. Dasan liked the riverside, and he enjoyed calling himself by the pen name "Yeolsu" (the old name for the Hangang river) or "Yeolsang Noin" (the old man of the Hangang). It can be said that the several small tributaries gathering into two forks, the "Yeolsu" and

---

6. Dallet, Charles, *Hanguk cheonju gyohoesa* (History of Korean Catholic Church), trans. An Eung-nyeol and Choe Seok-u, vol. 2 (Seoul: The Research Foundation of Korean Church History, 1980), p. 17; originally published as *Histoire de l'Eglise de Corée*, 2 vols. (Paris: Librairie Victor Palme, 1874).

7. *Ibid.*, pp. 185-186.

8. Choe Seok-u, "Dallet's Quotation of Jeong Yak-yong's History of the Spread of the Korean Gospel" (in Korean), in *Yi Hae-nam baksa hwan-gap ginyeom sahak nonchong* (Collected Papers in Commemoration of Yi Hae-nam's Sixth Birthday) (Seoul: Ilchokak Publishing Co., 1970), pp. 205-216.

"Yeolsang," deeply influenced Dasan's thought. Living in the latter Joseon period under the influence of Confucian Dohak Neo-Confucian orthodoxy, he accepted the philosophy of Wang Yangming, the Chinese Classics and Western learning, and his thought were realized into a new "big river" of knowledge.

Dasan's Confucianism and Western Thought

The first book Dasan wrote about Chinese studies was *Jungyong gangui* (Discourse on the Doctrine of the Mean). He completed the first draft in 1784 when he was a 23-year-old university student. The first manuscript of *Jungyong daechaek* was concerned with answers to King Jeongjo's questions and was written following discussions with Yi Byeok. We find in this book that he was strongly influenced by Yi Byeok. His *Jungyong gangui* draft was corrected and finally completed in 1814 as *Jungyong ganguibo* during his exile in Gangjin, 30 years after he started it. Even then, it is clear from his reminiscing about Yi Byeok's wisdom and virtue that he still held on to much of his original thought. In his book *Jungyong gangui*, there was a creative reconciliation between Confucian and Western thought. Let us examine the harmonious meeting of Confucianism and Western Learning in Dasan's thought.

Firstly, in his preface to *Jungyong ganguibo* he criticizes the Neo-Confucian concept of *yin* and *yang*. He says that "*yin* and *yang*" or light and shade have reciprocal form but do not have physical substance or property. He starts by rejecting the basic Neo-Confucian concept and agreeing with Matteo Ricci's concept of *taegeuk* (the Great Ultimate), in that it adopts the form of odd and even, it has no concrete existence as the *yin* and *yang* in *taegeuk*, but is form only.

Secondly, he challenged the cosmic role of the Five Elements (*ohaeng*). He said that the Five Elements have no special qualities and that it was unreasonable to think of them as able to produce a myriad of other things. He rejected the understanding that the Five Elements were the basic elements. He said that it was possible for any number of elements to produce basic matter. Rather, he spoke about the "Four Main Hexagrams" in the *Book of Changes* (heaven, earth, water, fire) as being the basic entities. *Geon* (heaven, *gi*), *gon* (earth, *to*), *gam* (water, *su*), *ri* (fire, *hwa*), *gi*, *to*, *su*, *hwa*, all indicate matter. This is compatible with the Western natural philosophy's explanation of the "Four Sources." The

Sinseopa faction used the explanation of the "Four Sources" to overcome the Neo-Confucian "Five Elements Doctrine." His second older brother Jeong Yak-jeon, in an answer to an exam question, denied the "Five Elements" and discussed the "Four Sources," arousing a certain amount of public criticism. Dasan himself, in rejecting the Doctrine of the "Five Elements," turned away from the basic structure of the Neo-Confucian view of nature thereby showing that he was closely involved with Catholic doctrine.

Thirdly, he made a distinction between *cheon* (heaven) as a transcendental being and as a natural being. The transcendental Heaven is spiritual, bright, and is the governing power of creation. The natural Heaven is blue and has vast spherical features. This kind of classification of the nature of Heaven can be understood from the intention to explain the concept of *cheon* as the object of faith. The existence of *cheon* as spiritual and bright being means that there exists a transcendental form that has the ability to perceive at the same time. Dasan also emphasized that this *cheon* was the governing power. This concept of *cheon* is similar to the one that Ricci indicated in his *Tianzhu shiyi*. This concept departs from the Neo-Confucian concept of Heaven, which sees Heaven as dwelling within man's original nature, being at one with it and having no power of perception. Dasan distinguished between the two concepts of *cheon*, saying that one was bright and spiritual, could become the object of faith, and could be found in the Heaven which governs creation, while the other Heaven was blue, had large spherical features, had a physical form and was limited.

Fourthly, he rejected the Neo-Confucian position of *mura ilche ron* (the theory that objects and self are one body) or *inmul seongdong ron* (the theory that man and objects have the same nature), and insisted that there was a fundamental difference between creation and man. He claimed that the plants, birds and beasts follow the principle of infinite production. They live to maintain their species. Mankind, on the other hand, is endowed with a spirit and with bright virtue. Man is superior to creation, and the fact that he can enjoy and take advantage of creation makes a fundamental difference. He understood that man and creation as the position of lord and servant. By introducing the idea that the basic character of man was spiritual and bright, he explained that this was the point in which man shared qualities with Heaven. There is a significant connection between the Catholic doctrines' concept of man's inherent soul and Dasan's concept of man as having a bright spiritual nature.

Dasan used the word *cheon* or *sangje* (Ultimate Being) in relation with the orthodox Confucian terminology. Even though he did not use the term *yeonghon* (soul), he used the term *yeongmyeong* (an enlightened spirit) which contains the concept of *yeonghon*. He rejected the idea that the "Four Virtues" of humanity, righteousness, propriety and wisdom were the principles of man's nature. He said that the "Four Virtues" were not profound perceptions within the mind, but were gained through the actions of man. Heaven endowed man with *yeongmyeong*, but did not bestow virtue. Dasan said that if one saw virtue as being inside mentality, given innately, then men's duty would be to sit in meditating in front of a wall (*hyangbyeok gwansim*). He criticized this saying that it would lapse into Zen Buddhism.

Fifthly, Dasan notes in the first chapter of the *Doctrine of the Mean* that "The superior man is cautious about what he does not see and apprehensive about what he does not hear." Here he differs from the customary interpretation which claims that what a man does not see or hear is the condition before conscious action arises. He claims that this was a spirit descending from Heaven and seeing everything. So the original, being cautious and apprehensive, was not connected with man's internal mind, but rather connected with a spirit (God or Ultimate Being) that comes down and surveys the activities of man. In the *Book of Rites* there were three forms of the Divine: the Divine of Heaven, the energy of the Earth and the spirit of man. In this regard, Dasan stresses that even though there were three different forms in the order of sacrificial offerings only the Divine of Heaven and the spirit of man actually exist. He rejects the traditional view that man has to serve Heaven and Earth. He holds that man absorbs the earth and that man and the earth (creation) are in a position below Heaven. In the Neo-Confucian explanation of spirit, the spirit is *yin* and the Divine is *yang*. Dasan says that the spirit of man and the Divine of Heaven are fundamentally different and because of this they could not be confused. According to him the "Divine" of Heaven and the "spirit" of man are treated equally and things not seen and not heard are the spirit descending from Heaven. Dasan regards man as having a pious posture sitting face to face with the governing God of Heaven. Man has to respect Heaven as the Lord. His ideas are based on the same structure of the Catholic Lord of Heaven who endows man with his soul and rules over both man and creation. Dasan's Confucian system, apparent in his commentary on the *Doctrine of the Mean*, was is essence an effort to grope for union between Catholic doctrine and Confucian concepts. His position reflects the basic thought and character that Yi Byeok, Yi Seung-hun, and Dasan held in the beginning.

Dasan's rejection of the *yin-yang* and the five elements in the Confucian natural philosophical system and acceptance of the *Book of Changes'* structure of nature does not indicate that he was ignorant of Western learning's view of nature. To the idea of a transcendental Heaven he added the character of spirituality and governorship. Man, being endowed with an illustrious spirit from Heaven, is similar to the Western idea of being endowed with a soul, while Heavenly attributes or governorship is not transferred. Dasan shows a surprising harmony between the Catholic doctrine and old Confucian concepts in terms of the relationship between Heaven and man. Here, understanding of heaven as a part of the world of the Divine, or the concept that the Divine and man as spirit are not interchangeable, is transplanted from orthodox Confucianism to Catholicism. At the same time we can say that Confucianism has received Catholicism, thus forming a new Confucian thought.

Dasan's thought as expressed in his interpretation of the *Doctrine of the Mean* is diffused within his Confucian system. In the general principles of the *Book of Great Learning*, "illustrious virtue" is not bestowed on man by Heaven; it is something that comes about by being virtuous, acting with perfect virtue. He structured the illustrious virtue as being the three virtues of filial piety, brotherly affection and compassion. Filial piety, brotherly affection, and compassion qualify the relationships of man to those above, to his neighbors and to those below. He understood *in* (perfect virtue) to refer always to two people. *In* preaches filial piety, brotherly affection, and compassion in human relationships. He understood the virtue of man not as something that man pursued internally but as something realized through the relationships with other people. This is directly related to the idea of Christian love: love that is received from heaven, and the love of man for Heaven and other people.

Also in his *Maengja yo-ui* (Summary of Mencius), he reconfirmed that the Four Cardinal Virtues, humanity, righteousness, propriety and wisdom were realized after action. If we follow the Neo-Confucian idea that humanity, righteousness, propriety, and wisdom are perfected within the original mind, then this would be, as mentioned above, *hyangbyeok gwansim*, or sitting in meditating in front of a wall. Dasan rejected Zhengzi's idea that mind, original nature and Heaven are one principle is the same as the Master Choju's theory that all myriad phenomena are one. Here he was analyzing and criticizing the Buddhist logic influencing Neo-Confucian thought, that is, the strict division of the relationship between the mind of man and the transcendental Heaven. He compared the King of a country to the governing Lord of Heaven. And he indicated that Heaven that was blue, vast, spherical, had a form signified nothing more than a house or tent for us, human beings; its class was on a par with that of soil, water, or fire. To him Heaven was essentially the governing Lord and, accordingly, one can find Heaven's original character within the name *sangje* (The Ultimate Being). He stresses the concept of a governing power that cannot be seen as a material natural phenomenon or a conceptual principle.

In the beginning of his exile in Gangjin, Jeong Yak-yong returned to the appreciation of the science of divination. In the *Book of Changes*, the ethical goal is to correct one's weak points and follow the path of goodness. This can be seen as having the character of faith, derived from the attitude of waiting for the heavenly order and following its dictates. Fortune telling is a way to accept Heaven's decree, and one should accept and obey this order. One cannot do as one pleases. Dasan recognized the significance of fortune telling as the Divine decree of Heaven.

Dasan's work *Chunchu gojing* is not limited only to moral theory but can be understood as proof of the practice of various kinds of ceremonies found during the Spring and Autumn period. Here he brought to light the ceremonial form of *gyo* (sacrificial rites for heaven), *sa* (sacrificial rites for the state), *che* (sacrificial rites for royal family's ancestors), *sihyang* (seasonal ancestral rites), *myoje* (shrine system for Confucius), and he exposed the mistaken system, the misunderstood meaning and the improper form in the funeral rites. His detailed arrangement of the ceremonies of coming of age, marriage, funeral and ancestral worship shows his extraordinary interest in Confucian ceremonies, thus leading to the doubt of the depth of his religious beliefs. In reality, the Catholic movement entered a period of trials in 1791 during which believers failed to prepare ancestral tablets after the papal decree saying that ancestor worship and the Catholic faith were incompatible. This frontal attack on the Confucian ceremonies spread, causing the decisive criticism to arise. However, nowhere does it refer to the fact that Jeong Yak-yong argued to abolish ancestor worship, even when he was a fervent believer. His knowledge of the Catholic doctrine came from the Jesuit missionaries' *boyuron* (the position that Catholicism can supplement Confucianism). And when he recognized the relative importance of ceremony within the Catholic doctrine, it is likely that he found new interest in the Confucian ceremony.

Conclusion

To understand the relationship of Jeong Yak-yong and the Catholic faith, a question regarding whether he really was a Catholic must first be addressed. On this point, Dallet's *History of the Korean Catholic Church* and Jeong Yak-yong's own writings give contradicting answers. In some ways, the severe suppression of the Catholic faith during Dasan's time, and the life-threatening danger he was in might have forced him to lead a double life in which outwardly he had to hide his religious beliefs. To give a final answer to this question, however, we have to wait for more definite proof to be found. The more important question requiring clarification is the relationship between the basic character of Jeong Yak-yong's thought and his Catholic faith.

It is significant to note that after the age of 23, when he wrote *Jungyong gangui*, until the age of 73, when he wrote *Maessi seopyeong*, he did not reject but rather maintained his position with regard to the problems presented in *Jungyong gangui*. Even though he wrote *Jungyong gangui* when he was leading a deeply religious life, the work is not concerned with Catholic doctrine, but is rather a systematic interpretation of the logic of the Confucian sacred books. Accordingly we can say that the basic position of Jeong Yak-yong is a reinterpretation of the Confucian concepts together with the Catholic doctrine. In the same way that he criticized Neo-Confucianism as being too Buddhist, the Christian transmutation of his Confucian thought can also be criticized. Even though Neo-Confucianism was largely influenced by Buddhism, it did not appear to be Buddhist. In the same way, even though his Confucian thought was formed within the Catholic doctrine, it was not Christian. The absorption of the Catholic doctrine into his Confucian thought opened up a new domain for Confucian thought in general. It is in this that we can discover the unique character and value of Dasan's thought. Rather than inquiring into his individual religious beliefs, we must recognize the significance of his thought from the point of view of the history of Korean philosophy and what it means for Korean thought of this present day.

PART IV

MODERN PERIOD

Was Korea Really a "Hermit Nation"?

Yi Tae-Jin

Introduction

Early modern Korea is often categorized as having been a "hermit nation." This designation is admittedly accurate in describing Korea during the reign of the Daewongun (1863–1873). As a result of his isolationist policy, Korea experienced several outside intrusions including the "Foreign Disturbance of 1866" (France) and the "Foreign Disturbance of 1871" (U.S.). However, even beyond this period Korea is unable to rid itself of the "hermit" label. Even though it had signed the Treaty of Ganghwa with Japan in 1876 and similar treaties with the U.S. (1882) and England (1883) and thereby initiated friendly trade, Korea at that time was still considered to be a "hermit nation." In fact, some even feel that Korea's forcible annexation by Japan in 1910 was the natural result of Korea's reclusive and isolationist nature. With this understanding, scholars have concluded that Korea failed at modernization based on its own strength.

Even today, whenever Koreans face some major international trial or problem, scholars point to Korea's "failed modernization." They tend to single out Korea's early modern history to ascribe the blame to others or to awaken themselves to their circumstances. It was not different during the early stages of the IMF bailout. There is nothing wrong with look-

* Originally published in the *Korea Journal*, vol. 38, no. 4 (Winter 1998).

Yi Tae-Jin (Yi, Tae-jin) is Professor of Korean History at Seoul National University. He has published many books, including *Joseon yugyo sahoesa ron* (Discussion on the History of the Neo-Confucianist Society in the Joseon Period) (1989) and *Joseon hugi-ui jeongchi-wa gunyeongje baldal* (Politics and the System of Central Army Garrisons during the Late Joseon Dynasty) (1985). E-mail: tjyi@plaza.snu.ac.kr.

ing back at history and reflecting on past mistakes to learn a lesson.[1] However, it is self-destructive to try to learn lessons from a historical past which is incorrectly understood. Countless Korean people today talk about reflecting on Korea's failed modernization, but in the end such reflection seems to have no effect. For all the supposed self-reflection, Korean people today do not seem to have improved at all in terms of their ability to deal with the outside world or their diplomatic sensitivity. It would not be wrong to say that the ultimate causes for Korea's recent economic crisis were Korea's ignorance of international society and its inability to properly respond to international circumstances. Could it be that singling out Korea's failed modernization has been not so much an act of self-reflection as an act of self-contempt?

It is a solemn fact that Korea's early modern history ended in a bleak ruin. However, it is important to closely evaluate whether or not this ruin was generally caused by the Korean people's lack of ability to do otherwise as some people insist. For the purpose of proper self-reflection on a certain historical period, such a preconception that Korea lacked ability should be avoided, and at the minimum it is required to analyze what efforts were made and what was lacking. Historians who lay the blame on the "isolationist" policy do not recognize the efforts and progress made by Koreans during that period. Could it be that one of the reasons why Koreans have not refined their ability to respond to international events is this flawed perception of history? Korean people today are lacking a systematic or detailed understanding of this period of "failed modernization" they are trying to reflect upon. Given this superficial understanding of this period, it is hard to expect such self-reflection to be effective. This paper will examine how Korea came to be categorized as a "hermit nation," which led to this perception of Korea's failed modernization. The objective, of course, is to help Koreans to refine their adaptability and responsiveness to the outside world.

Griffis' *Corea, The Hermit Nation*

Perhaps the biggest reason why people considered Korea to be a hermit

---

1. Korean people have a strong tendency to look back on history and reflect on past mistakes, almost as a form of punishment or penance, in the belief that recognizing past mistakes will straighten things in the future.

nation was the book by William Eliot Griffis called *Corea, The Hermit Nation*. Calling Korea a "hermit nation" in his title could not help but leave this impression. The book was first published in October 1882 by AMS Press in New York and proved so popular that eighth (1906) and ninth (1911) editions were printed. In the preface to the eighth edition, the author comments on the popularity of the book and writes, "for twenty-four years, this book, besides enjoying popular favor, has been made good use of by writers and students, in Europe and America, and has served even in Corea itself as the first book of general information to be read by missionaries and other new comers." However, as of yet no one has really examined how accurately this book examines Korea's situation at the time.

The author, William Eliot Griffis (1843–1928) was born in Philadelphia and graduated from Rutgers University in 1869 with a degree in the natural sciences. In December of 1870, he traveled to Fukui, Japan as an American Reformed missionary to teach at Hanko Meishinkan.[2] While at Rutgers, he had met Saheita and Taihei Shonan, the nephews of Yokoi Shonan, who was the teacher of Matsudaira Shungaku, the *daimyo* of Echizen. While there, he taught the natural sciences, chemistry, and biology. However, with the reform of the provincial system (*haikan shiken*) on July 18, 1871, he finished teaching in Fukui and in 1872, he was hired by the Meiji government and went to Tokyo to teach the natural sciences and chemistry at Nanko, the predecessor to today's Tokyo University. From February to July of 1874, he worked as chemistry professor at the Kaisei-gakko and helped to set up the chemistry department. During this time, he had several opportunities to meet with the Meiji Emperor. After almost four years of living in Japan, he returned to the United States in July 1874 and entered the Union Seminary in New York. Afterwards, he was active as a pastor and wrote often on Japan, while occasionally writing also about Korea.

In the preface to the first edition of Griffis' *Corea, The Hermit Nation*, he describes his motivation for writing the book as follows:

---

2. A more detailed description of Griffis' background can be found in the Showa Women's University's *Kindai bungaku kenkyu sosho* (Modern Cultural Studies Series), no. 28 on William Eliot Griffis, and also the postscript of Professor Kamei Shunsuke's *Mikado* (Tokyo: Iwanami Bunko, 1995), which was originally published as William Eliot Griffis, *Mikado Institution and Person* (New Jersey: Princeton University Press, 1915).

In the year 1871, while living at Fukui, in the province of Echizen, Japan, I spent a few days at Tsuruga and Mikuni, by the seas which separates Japan and Corea. The thought often came to me as I walked within the moss-grown feudal castle walls—old in story, but then newly given up to schools of Western science and languages—why should Corea be sealed and mysterious, when Japan, once a hermit, had opened her doors and come cut into the world's market-place? When would Korea's awakening come? As one diamond cuts another, why should not Cho ka (Japan) open Chosen (Corea)?[3]

According to the above passage, when he was in Fukui in 1871 he had already become interested in Korea. While spending a few days in Tsuruga and Mikuni, the regions facing Korea across the sea, he asked himself, "Why should Corea be sealed and mysterious?" and "When would Corea's awakening come?" It would be eleven years before he published what would be one of the first Western books on Korea. Without ever having directly visited Korea, he managed to produce a 520-page work on the country.

However, the main focus of his interest in and work on Korea was its relationship with Japan and a relative comparison. Regarding this, he wrote in his preface, "Turning with delight and fascination to the study of Japanese history and antiquities, I found much that reflected light upon the neighbor country. On my return home, I continued to search for materials for the story of the last of the hermit nations." In 1876, Griffis published his major work on Japanese history and culture, *Mikado's Empire*. It was after this he began writing *Corea, The Hermit Nation*. In his preface, he notes that the bulk of *Corea* was written between 1877 and 1880.

As he was writing this book, he was greatly aided by John Ross' *Corea, its History, Manners, and Customes* (1880) and Charles Dallet's *Histoire d'Eglise de Corée*, which he admits to in his preface. In fact, he borrowed heavily from Dallet's work, particularly in the chapters on folklore, social life, and Christianity. As he published this book about a country never visited, he defended himself by pointing out the difference between a "traveller" and a "compiler." While a traveller only sees a part of the country at one time, he bragged that a compiler could produce a handbook of information more valuable to the general reader. The prob-

---

lem is that Griffis chose to compare Korea—again a place he had never visited—with Japan, which he naturally praised, in an effort to explain Japan's success.

To find out more about Griffis' view of Japan, it is instructive to look at a critical view by Professor Kamei Shunsuke, who translated Griffis' other work, *The Mikado: Institution and Person* into Japanese. In his translator's notes, Professor Kamei writes that Griffis measured the Japanese people or their mentality according to Western rationalism and welcomed their Westernization and modernization. Griffis thought that Mikadoism was most important to Japan's successful modernization, the central pivot around which Japan's modernization progressed. However, he thought that the Japanese people's belief in unbroken lineage of the Imperial Dynasty was a political fabrication, and he criticized the fact that such a false institution was still valid in spite of Japan's remarkable modernization and that Japan was unable to outgrow its intellectual and moral primitiveness. He highly regarded Mikadoism as the manifestation of the collective spirit of the Japanese people to join together to create a dynamically developing unified country, as evidenced during the rule of the then Emperor Meiji.

Griffis, with his broad trust in Western civilization, his Christian faith, his respect for individuality, and his confidence in democracy, was trying to help Japan's modernization and came to love the modernized Japan. Griffis was a firm believer in modernism, which was in vogue among Western intellectuals of the time. When he saw how the Meiji government was actively embracing Westernization, he praised Japan from a modernist viewpoint. To him, any country refusing or slow to adopt Western civilization was a "hermit nation." He believed that Japan, which was originally also a hermit nation, had begun walking on the "road to civilization" with its opening by Commodore Matthew Perry, whereas China and Korea were still hermit nations which lacked this positiveness.

The book is divided into three parts entitled "Ancient and Medieval History," "Political and Social Corea," and "Modern and Recent History." In the first part, there are 22 chapters: one on geography, six on ancient history, one on ancient Korea-Japan relations, one on Goryeo or united Corea, one on Goryeo's outside relations, one on the founding of the Joseon Dynasty, nine on Japan's invasions of Korea, and two on the coming of the West. As can be seen, most of this section is devoted to Korea's relationship with Japan and outside nations. As regards China, he emphasizes the early Han Chinese commanderies and the tributary relationship, and he also writes about the supposed Japanese colony Mimana as postulated by the Japanese, which shows that he was heavily influenced by the ultranationalist historical views of contemporary Japanese intellectuals. In fact, he spelled the names of the Korean kingdoms of Goguryeo, Baekje, and Silla according to their Japanese pronunciation—*korai, hyakusai,* and *shinra.*

The second part consists of eighteen chapters: an introduction to the eight provinces, four chapters on the political system, and thirteen chapters on social life and customs, religion, and education. Since much of this section was borrowed from Dallet's *Histoire d'Eglise de Corée,* his viewpoints reflected in this section need to be analyzed in detail. In the section on politics, he focuses on despotism and factional strife, and in the section on traditional culture and beliefs, he describes Korea as a "land of paganism, bigotry, superstition, which reveals his strong modernist views. In part three of the first edition, he starts with the introduction of Catholicism in 1784, followed by chapters on the Catholic persecution, the resulting French naval expedition, Korea-U.S. relations and the U.S. naval expedition, Korea's opening by Japan, and the initiation of commerce with Western nations in the early 1880s.[4]

In Chapter 48, the last chapter of the first edition, he writes about the chain of events which occurred in 1882 and makes some future predictions. In 1882, Korea signed a treaty of amity and commerce with the U.S.; a military mutiny broke out in June and troops from Qing China intervened; and the Treaty of Jemulpo was signed to compensate Japan for damages incurred during the mutiny. Therefore, Griffis decides to entitle this chapter, "The Year of the Treaties." However, even though there were numerous indications that Korea's hermit-like ways were ending, his view of Korea at the time was still not positive. While acknowledging that Korea was ending its isolation and becoming the focus of the world's attention, he paints a dark picture of Korea as the future battleground of China, Japan and Russia. Furthermore, he avoids mentioning Japan's aggressive intent toward Korea, but instead predicts that the Korean valleys will be the site of collision between the "hoary empire"

---

4. In the preface of the first edition, he writes, "For lack of space, the original manuscript of 'Recent and Modern History," part III, has been greatly abridged, and many topics of interest have been left untouched," which shows he was unable to write about everything he wanted to.

(China) and the "young northern giant" (Russia), and a war between "the dragon and the bear" is a possibility. Regarding the outcome of this battle, his outlook for Korea is cold and bleak. While trusting that the integrity of the "little kingdom" Joseon is preserved, he hopes that "paganism, bigotry and superstition in Corea, and in all Asia, may disappear; and that in their place, the religion of Jesus, science, education, and human brotherhood may find an abiding dwelling place."[5]

In publishing the eighth edition in 1906, he adds five chapters to describe the events which occurred after 1882 ("The Economic Condition of Corea, Internal Politics"; "Chinese and Japanese, The War of 1894"; "Corea an Empire"; "Japan and Russia in Conflict"; "Corea a Japanese Protectorate"). With Japan making Korea a protectorate in November 1905, he could not help but add this new material. At that time he recognized that the "center of the world's politics has shifted from the Atlantic and the Mediterranean to the waters surrounding Corea" and also praised Japan's rapid rise as follows:

> The rise of Japan, within half a century of immediate contact with the West, to the position of a modern state, able first to humiliate China and then to grapple successfully with Russia, has vitally affected Corea, on behalf whose independence Japan a second time went to war with a Power vastly greater in natural resources than herself. The present or eighth edition shows in both text and map, not only the swift, logical results both of Japan's military and naval success in Manchuria and on the sea of Japan and of her signal diplomatic victory at Portsmouth, but more. It makes clear the reasons why Corea, as to her foreign relations, has lost her sovereignty (Preface to the eighth edition).

For Griffis, Korea's loss of sovereignty due to Japan's rapid growth to become a modern nation and its' successive victories over China and Russia, who were trying to expand their influence over Korea, were not just a diplomatic victory, but the logical conclusion of Japan's having shed its isolationism early. Furthermore, he clearly states his belief as to

---

5. This same attitude is found in the dedication of *Corea, The Hermit Nation:* "To all Corean Patriots: who seek by the aid of science, truth, and pure religion, To Enlighten themselves and their fellow-countrymen, To rid their land of superstition, bigotry, despotism, and priestcraft—both native and foreign—and To preserve the integrity, independence, and honor, of their country; This unworthy sketch of their past history and present condition is dedicated."

the reason why Korea lost its sovereignty: the leaders of the kingdom were pursuing "intrigue" instead of "education" and "class interests" instead of "national welfare." He puts forth the harsh judgment that Korea's loss of sovereignty was directly the result of the "final failure of intriguing *Yangban*ism" and also the "moral trial before the world."

In the ninth edition, he adds a chapter on Japan's annexation of Korea entitled "Chosen: A Providence of Japan." He rationalizes Japan's takeover of Korea, writing "I doubt not that the hopes of twelve millions of people will be increasingly fulfilled under the new arrangement." Whether it was because of his staunch modernist beliefs or his pleasure in seeing his predictions fulfilled, he came to praise Japan's aggressions.

After returning back to the U.S. in July 1874, he continued his theology studies and then worked as a pastor. In 1884, he received his D.D. from Union Seminary, and in 1900, he was awarded a L.H.D. from his alma mater, Rutgers. In 1903, he left the clergy and continued with his writing, completing a total of 178 works by the time of his death in 1928 at the age of 85. Most of his works were on Japan, but nine were on Korea.[6]

In 1908, he was awarded the Asahi Order of the Fourth Degree Merit by the Japanese government, in gratitude for his lifelong efforts to positively help and evaluate Japan's modernization. In December of 1926, at the age of 83, he returned to Japan for a visit, at the urging of his son, working at a New York bank, and also with the invitation of Shibuya Eiichi, a famous banker. During the visit, he was awarded the Asahi Order of the Third Degree Merit and allowed to stay six months at the Imperial Hotel. It was in the course of this extended stay in Japan that he finally visited Korea for the first time in 1927. Afterwards he returned to Fukui and Tsuruga in April and traveled in Japan. He passed away on February 5, 1928, at the age of 85 in Winter Park, Florida. He was at

---

6. According to *Kindai bungaku kenkyu sosho* (Modern Cultural Studies Series) (Showa University) 28, William Eliot Griffith wrote *Corea, Without and Within* (Philadelphia: Presbyterian Board of Publication, 1885); "Jack and the Giant in Korea," *Outlook* (1894); "China and Japan at War in Korea," *Chatanquan* (1894); "Korea and Koreans: In the Mirror of Their Language and History," *Bulletin of the American Geographical* (1895); "Korea, the Pigmy Empire," *New England Magazine* (1902); "Japan's Absorption of Korea," *North American Review* (1910); *A Modern Pioneer in Korea* (New York: Flemming II. Revell Company, 1912), "The Opening of Korea," *The Korea Magazine* (1917); "Women of Chosen," *Missionary Review of the World* (1918); and "Japan's Debt to Korea," *Asia* (1919).

work writing an imperial biography of the Meiji Emperor and a work on "the newly-born Japan."

The view of Korea expressed in *Corea, The Hermit Nation* was not unique to Griffis. In the bibliography of his book, there are references to two articles with a similar title: "Corea, the Last of the Hermit Nations" (*Sunday Magazine*, New York, May 1878), and "Corea, the Hermit Nation" (*Bulletin of the American Geographical Society*, no. 3, New York, 1881). One can easily guess that Griffis took his title from these articles. These similar titles also suggest that the idea of Korea as the last of the hermit nations was common among Westerners at the time. He writes in the preface that many people think of Korea as "no more than a sea-shell" or they ask, "What's in Corea?" and "Is Corea of any importance in the history of the world?" In many ways, Griffis' book best represents this Western view.

The Hermit Image Promoted by Japan

The perception of early modern Korea as a hermit nation was also promoted by the Japanese. No one has really examined how much of an influence Griffis' works had on the Japanese, but judging from the fact that his major work on Japan, *The Mikado's Empire*, was in its 13th edition by 1913, it would appear that his influence was hardly insignificant. Furthermore, the fact that the Japanese government bestowed on him the Asahi Order of the Third Degree and Fourth Degree Merit medals indicates how much they appreciated his views on Japan and East Asia. There are also several direct records that the Japanese were also interested in Griffis' *Corea, The Hermit Nation*.

In January 1895, the Suikosha Society in Tokyo published a work entitled *Chosen kaika no kigen* (The Origin of Korean Civilization), which was a summarized translation of Part Three of Griffis' book.[7] In the preface, the editor writes that this book was printed for the members to read because "it contains many interesting events and precious stories

---

7. The chapters of Part Three translated were: "The Beginning of Christianity 1784–1794"; "Persecution and Martyrdom 1801–1834"; "The Entrance of the French Missionaries 1835–1845"; "The Walls of Isolation Sapped"; "The French Expedition"; "American Relations with Corea"; "A Body-Snatching Expedition"; and "Our Little War with the Heathen."

we have never heard before, and we believe this is a valuable source in trying to discover the truth behind the origins of Joseon's modernization." Six years later, there is also a reference to Griffis' book in Shinobu Junpei's *Kanhando* (The Korean Peninsula) (Tokyodo-shoten, 1901). In one of the reviews of the book, there is a mention that Griffis' book is one of the major Western books on Korea. In his own preface, Shinobu writes, "In their studies on the Korean peninsula, the Westerners sometimes look down on the Koreans. Even though I may not be totally qualified, I have written this partly under their influence," which implies that he referred to Griffis' book. In fact, there are many places within his book where he quotes from Griffis.

As was just described, Griffis' *Corea, The Hermit Nation* had a direct influence on Japanese intellectuals, whom he obviously liked. At the same time, his book was also influenced considerably by Japanese intellectuals, particularly the section on history in Part One and the section on politics and customs in Part Two. Since he did not have any sources of information— especially in these areas—outside those in Japan, the influence of Japanese intellectuals inevitably must have been strong. Thus his relationship with Japanese intellectuals was of a give-and-take nature.

The Japanese view of Korea started to show an aggressive inclination starting from the Japanese history studies of the Edo period (1603–1867).[8] Perhaps because the Hideyoshi Invasions (1592, 1598) failed to produce the desired results, a feeling of antagonism toward Joseon became widespread in Japanese society during the Edo period, even among common people. Intellectuals at first tended to admire and respect Joseon civilization, but by the eighteenth century, a strong ultra-nationalist slant had emerged in historical studies, and Japan's sense of superiority over Joseon began to grow and strengthen. Japanese historians regarded foundation myths or legends in which ancient Japanese emperors ruled over Joseon as being historically true and fostered Japan's sense of superiority over Joseon, which was at that time being spread among the Japanese populace. Articles stating that the Japanese

---

8. The following section is mainly based on Hatada Takahashi "Chosen kanno tendo," in *Nihonjinno chosen kan* (Takakusa, 1969); Bak Yeong-jae, "Geundae ilbon-ui chimnyakjuuijeok daeoeron-gwa hanguk ron" (Modern Japan's Aggressive Foreign Policies and Its Korea Policy), *Hanguksa simin gangjwa* (Public Lectures on the History of Korea) 19 (August 1996).

gods or emperors controlled Joseon or that the Joseon kings and nobility submitted to Japan were printed as historical truths without any criticism, which fanned the sense of antagonism against Joseon growing in Japanese common society.

This sense of superiority over Joseon fostered by Japanese historians developed into various forms of expansionism after the opening of Japan. In Hayashi Shihei's *Sankoku tsuran zusetsu,* written in 1785, he writes that Joseon, along with the Ryukyu and Emish (Ainu) islands, had close ties to Japan's defense, and emphasized the urgent need to study Joseon. After Japan's opening, those worrying about the West might expand this analysis and argue that Japan should preempt the Western powers and take over Korea and other Asian countries for the sake of Japan's overall defense. After the Meiji Restoration, this position that Japan must invade Joseon in order to survive or the "Seikanron" (the theory of conquering Korea) became Japanese intellectuals' basic position toward Korea. In fact, in 1873, one faction of leaders officially discussed subjugating Joseon to the Imperial Court. This faction was defeated by an opposing faction; however, the opponents were not against the idea of conquering Joseon but instead had different opinions on the timing, method, and the question of leadership.

By the early Meiji Restoration period, all Japanese intellectuals and social leaders espoused the "Conquer Korea" school of thought. The proponents can be called the Greater "Conquer Korea" school, while the more aggressive faction who proposed conquering Korea in 1873 can be classified as the Lesser "Conquer Korea" school. In truth, this distinction remained valid through the early 1900s.[9] The annexation of Korea in 1910 was the complete realization of the Greater "Conquer Korea" school's vision; with this event, there was no need for this term. Afterwards, Japanese leaders were absorbed in trying to legitimize its colonization of Korea, based on the "Giving Blessing" theory, and the Greater School concealed itself behind this school, leaving the Lesser School as only a remnant in history books.

The "Conquer Korea" school of the 1860s and 1870s opened Joseon's doors by bringing about the Ganghwa island incident in 1875. However, with the Imo Gullan (Military Mutiny of 1882) and the advance of Qing

---

9. Kemiyama Sentaro, *Seikanron jisso* (The Real State of the Conquer Korea School) (Waseda University, 1907), p. 3. He calls the "Conquer Korea" proponents who were defeated at the Imperial Court in 1873 the Lesser "Conquer Korea" school.

troops into Korea, the situation became unfavorable for Japan in various ways. As a result, those in Japan advocating invading Korea were forced to retreat from their position and changed their emphasis to "solidarity." The new position claimed that the various Asian nations were all possible targets of invasion by the Western powers and that solidarity among them was needed for them to survive. However, this was based on the precondition that Japan was to be the leader. They regarded Qing China as a "rigidly ignorant, ultraconservative country" and Joseon as the "most inflexibly bigoted country in East Asia." Accordingly, for their "enlightenment," Japan needed to intervene in their domestic affairs and, if necessary, be prepared to invade them.

A "Greater East Asia Unification" school also arose, advocating that Japan unify with Korea. This was one of the more indirect forms of the "Conquer Korea" school which emerged when it became clear it would be difficult to overcome Qing China's superiority. This school argued that Japan and Korea, as equals, should form a unified country and maintain close ties with China to withstand Western advances into Asia, particularly that of Russia. The proponents of this school even produced a book in Chinese characters expounding this view for Korean and Chinese intellectuals. However, this position too could not hide Japan's aggressive self-complacency. They believed that Korea showed symptoms of lagging behind: the Korean people, having maintained *sadae* (serving the great) relations with China for so long, were lacking in terms of autonomous spirit, their politics were in disarray being a autocratic nation, and the people had lost their vitality. On the other hand, they naturally argued that Japan possessed a unique imperial state structure, superior natural beauty, a fully autonomous populace, wealth and power, enlightenment, etc.—all in all, a nation of which one could be truly proud. They argued that as Joseon came closer to Japan, it would become infused with Japan's *ki* or spirit and develop considerably; therefore, merging with Japan would benefit Joseon greatly and produce substantial rewards. After Japan's victory in the Sino-Japanese War (1894), this self-righteousness developed into the logic that Japan must become the leader of Asia.

Prior to the Sino-Japanese War, Japanese intellectuals did not write any worthwhile introductory books or writings on Korea in spite of their strong belief in conquering Korea. When major events occurred such as the battle between Korean shore batteries and a Japanese ship (*Unyang* Incident, 1875), the Treaty of Gangwha (1876), the Military Mutiny of

1882, they printed and distributed many leaflets and booklets describing the event. With names like *Chosen kunki, Chosen jiken,* and *Chosen shobun sanron,* these booklets were very demagogic in nature, even though they were published by private groups. Full-fledged writings on Korea began appearing in Japan in the 1890s, and until the Sino-Japanese War in 1894, these too were limited to writings of Korea's ancient history.[10] It was only in 1896 that books which examined the contemporary period finally started to appear. The three most representative works were: (1) Kikuchi Genjo's *Chosen okoku* (1896, Minyusha); (2) Tsuneya Seifuku's *Chosen kaikashi* (Toa tobun kai, 1901); and (3) Shinobu Junpei's *Kan hando* (Tokyodo shoten, 1901).[11] The first book introduces Korea in three parts—geography (158 pages), society (120 pages, from a historical perspective), and history (279 pages). The history section affirms the existence of Gija Joseon, a Chinese sub-state and the Japanese colony Mimana. In the early modern history part, it deals with the major developments relating to Japan, including the Daewongun's isolationist policy, the Gapsin Jeongbyeon (Coup d'Etat of 1884), the Sino-Japanese War, and the assassination of Queen Min. He also emphasizes Joseon's liberation from Qing China with Japan's victory in the Sino-Japanese War. In the society section, he writes that Joseon was on the verge of decline due to corruption and depravity. Furthermore, he blasts Joseon, going so far as to say that the thousand years starting from the Goryeo dynasty (918–1392), was an immoral period. The geography part of the second book also affirms Korea's supposed past colonialist history through examples such as Mimana and Gija Joseon. In the ethnography section, he writes that the Japanese and the Koreans have similar ancestors. In the cultural section, he criticizes the Korean people, saying that they have no customs worthy of maintaining; their hearts are filled with jealousy, suspicion, and lies; they all try to cheat each other; they have no sense of aggressiveness or independence, and they frequently have to depend on others. Furthermore, he emphasized that Joseon was fortunate in being able to become an independent

---

10. Hayashi Taisuke's *Chosen shi* (1892), Yoshida Shogo's *Nikkan koshi dan* (1893), Nishimura Yukata's *Chosen shiko* (1895), etc.
11. For more about these books, please refer to Jo Dong-geol, "Singmin sahak-ui seongnip gwajeong-gwa geundaesa seosul" (The Establishment of Colonial Historical Studies and the Description of Modern History), *Yeoksa gyoyuk nonjip* (Treaties on History Education) 13-14 (1993).

nation through the help of the Japanese (316) and that Japan's objective in the Sino-Japanese War was to give Joseon its independence. This idea that Joseon finally gained its independence through Japan's opening and victory in the Sino-Japanese War came to be the established theory on early modern Korean history by Japanese historians, which first appeared in a book by Tsuneya Seifuku. He also wrote, "Why has acceptance of the new civilization been so different in Japan and Korea? This has been the difference between accepting it naturally and accepting it forcefully." This view is exactly same as Griffis'.

The third book is mainly about human geography, economics, and international relations. He begins by writing about the major cities, palaces, and the financial status and organizational structure of the Korean government and covers topics pertinent to the time of his writing. He also writes about Korea's relations with Japan, China, Russia, and other Western countries again up to the time of writing, but he does apologize for not knowing more about the internal situation of the Korean government and for writing more about Korea's relations with the West than those with Japan and China. Nonetheless, he also expresses the same distinctive perspective as the Japanese intellectuals of the time. When writing about the close ties between Japan and Korea dating back to ancient times, he uses Griffis' exact words: "It is as nearly impossible to write the history of Corea and exclude Japan, as to tell the story of medieval England and leave out France" (Griffis 51, Shinobu 382). He then refers in succession to the supposed Mimana colony, the theory that Empress Jinko conquered Korea, the Hideyoshi invasions, and ends up with the Convention of Tianjin, coming to the conclusion that "The Korean peninsula in general has developed as a tributary of Japan." In other words, looking back at the relationship from ancient times, he concludes that Korea was basically a vassal of Japan which sometimes paid tribute and sometimes did not.

Korea's relationship with China, he describes, as a rising and falling relationship of dependency divided into four periods. During the first period (from the reign of King Injo (1623–1649) to 1866), Korea was truly dependent on the Qing, but in the second period (1866–1876), even though Korea was nominally a vassal, Qing China acknowledged Joseon's independence in its domestic and foreign affairs to the Western powers. In the third period (1876–1882), Japan regarded Joseon as an independent nation, and the same period saw China's influence declining. But in the fourth period (1882–1894), after the Military Mutiny of

1882 and intervention of Qing troops, China's control strengthened once again, and Korea was once again dependent. Korea's dependent relationship with China was the biggest problem for the Japanese, who wanted to conquer Korea. They feared that if they tried to invade Korea, China would intervene and come to the aid of its vassal. The book deals with this problem in order to show that Japan wiped out the dependent relationship by defeating China in the Sino-Japanese War.

Through its examination of Korea's outside relations, the book places a distinct emphasis on Japan's preemptive rights over Korea in an effort to legitimate Japan's rule of Korea. In the section on Korea's trade relations, he first writes, "Between the nineteenth and twentieth centuries, a new trend has developed among the Western powers. Their primary ambition toward primitive or partially modernized nations is to increase their room for profit by expanding their markets, while controlling the territory is secondary." He adds, "Given the special relationship Japan shares with Korea not only in terms of geography and history, but future diplomacy, Japan has the natural right and natural responsibility of expanding its room for profit by including this market" (662).

The views on Korea appearing in the above-mentioned three books share the "Conquer Korea" perspective. As of 1902, when the third book came out, Korea was not yet occupied by Japan. Korea was inevitably to be a target for conquest as the "Conquer Korea" school insisted. This is why Japanese historians emphasized Japan's preemptive rights over Korea since ancient times, and why they showed inordinate interest in Korea's independence in order to eliminate China's existing preemptive rights. After Japan's victory in the Russo-Japanese War of 1904, this "Conquer Korea" view on Korea changed considerably. Against the background of its military victory, Japan was finally able to forcibly annex Korea and the historical accounts of Japan's relationship with Korea took on the form of a "victor's" history. As if to celebrate the annexation of Korea, countless books appeared at the time, the first of which was Ikeda Tsunetaro's *Nikkan gappo shoshi* (A Bibliographical Work on Japan-Korea Relations).[12] The book had the following chapter titles:

---

12. Ikeda Tsunetaro, *Nikkan gappo shoshi* (A Bibliographical Work on Japan-Korea Relations) (Tokyo: Yomiuri shinbun Nisshusha, 1910).

Chapter 1: Period of Tribute and Isolation
Chapter 2: Sino-Japanese War Period
Chapter 3: Negotiation and Maneuvering between Russia and Japan
Chapter 4: Russo-Japanese War Period
Chapter 5: Period of Advisory Politics
Chapter 6: Period of Protective Politics
Chapter 7: Korea's Annexation

The chapter outline is based on the "Conquer Korea" view of Korea and misleadingly suggests to the reader to believe that Japan fought for Korea's independence and protection. What should be taken notice of here is the attitude of Korea, the target of protection and annexation, in this process. In Chapter 1, the author writes that the reason why Japan began to actively intervene in Korean affairs was the fault of Korea to some extent. After the Meiji Restoration, Japan wanted to initiate a new diplomatic relationship with Korea, but "arrogant Joseon" "refused Japan's diplomatic message," and so there was no choice but to develop the plan to conquer Korea, which is why the *Unyang* (Unyo) Incident and the subsequent Treaty of Gangwha were used to first open Korea. With the "Conquer Korea" plan now having been realized, Japan sought to legitimize and prettify its conquest process by categorizing Korea's isolationism as the "most inflexibly bigoted country in East Asia" and as a historical mistake which needed to be remedied at the heavy cost of "annexation." Many of the books which appeared after Tsunetaro's *Nikkan gappo shoshi* have similar structure and content.

Buried History of Korea's Open-Door Policy

Griffis and Japanese intellectuals established the belief or school of thought that in the latter half of the 1800s, Korea resisted the global trend toward openness, and that the direct result of which was Korea's annexation by Japan in 1910. This historical perspective was greatly reinforced by the harsh reality of Korea's loss of sovereignty. Furthermore, as the circumstances did not permit Koreans to study the true nature of Korea's modern history, it became difficult to offer up an academic challenge to this perspective. As a result, the concept of "the hermit nation Korea" came to be accepted as the truth. However, as was shown before, the writings which gave birth to this school of thought were either biased from the start, had multiple intentions, or were not backed up by primary historical records or sources. As a result, it is urgent that efforts be made to examine the issue closely based on primary sources. Regardless of the outcome, it is intolerable that such an important issue remains untouched.

A noteworthy research on Korea's opening of its ports was presented in the 1970s.[13] This study covers the time span from the Treaty of Friendship signed with Japan at Ganghwa (1876) to the Treaty of Amity and Commerce signed with the U.S. (1882). This study showed that after much effort by Korean diplomats to ensure international equality, mainly focusing on tariffs duties on Japanese and U.S. goods, Korea became the first country in Asia to obtain the right to determine its own customs duties in the Treaty of Amity and Commerce. The study also showed that the successful negotiations were the result of the king's leadership and the determined efforts of a few enlightened bureaucrats. However, because of the longstanding, unfair bias towards Korea's early modern history, the results of this study did not receive much attention. This research study could have washed away traditional misconceptions, but instead the early modern period has been smothered by the heavy, mud-like bias toward the early modern period. There are countless other issues like this one where the sources are readily available to test questionable assumptions about the past and possibly come up with entirely different explanations from a different perspective. Here I will discuss a couple of examples where new interpretations may be in order.

First, let us look at the reign of the Daewongun. As everyone knows, Korea's foreign policy during Daewongun's rule (1864–1873) is generally categorized as *swaeguk* or a "seclusionist" policy. The term *swaeguk* was first used by the Japanese historian Shitsuki Tadao in translating *Geschichte und Beschreibung von Japan* by the German naturalist Engelber Kaempfer in the section heading describing how Japan would not let its citizens leave or foreigners enter the country. The first time it was applied to Korea was in the previously mentioned *Chosen okoku* by Kikuchi Kenjo.[14] In the section on the Daewongun's second reign,

---

13. Kim Gyeong-tae, "Gaehang jikhu-ui gwansegwon hoebok munje" (The Question of Tariff Compensation after the Opening of Korea), *Hanguksa yeongu* (Journal of Korean History) 8 (1972); "Bulpyeongdeung joyak gaejeong gyoseop-ui jeon-gae" (The Development of Negotiations over the Revision of the Unequal Treaty), *Hanguksa yeongu* 11 (1975).

14. Yeon Gap-su, "Daewongun jipgwon-gi (1863–1873) seoyang seryeok-e daehan dae-

Kikuchi writes that the Daewongun strengthened the nation's defenses, fought with intruding French warships, clashed with American warships, and severed diplomatic relations with Japan after a demonstration by a mob of Japanese at the *waegwan* (the Japanese residence area) in Busan in 1872. In this manner, Kikuchi shifted all the blame on Joseon and described the period as an "age of seclusion" (*swaeguk sidae*). After the term *swaeguk* first appeared in Kikuchi's book, later books including *Chosen-kaikashi* and *Kan hanto* also used the term in a similar manner. In other words, they felt that the Daewongun had strengthened the national defense to reject the advancing tide of Westerners and labelled this as a *swaeguk* or isolationist policy.

As is well known, the French navy attacked Ganghwado island because of Joseon's suppression of Catholicism. In response to Joseon's official persecution of French missionaries and their believers, a French *division navale* captured Ganghwa Island. From a foreigner's perspective, Joseon's prohibition of Catholicism in itself could be regarded as an isolationist policy. However, there are many ways in which Joseon was not fully responsible for the diplomatic clash with Japan which occurred shortly after this. It is common knowledge that toward the end of 1867, the Japanese Emperor regained power from the Tokugawa Bakufu, and Imperial rule was restored. On January 15, 1868, the new government informed the various ministers from other countries of this change and accepted their diplomatic credentials. However, an exception was made in the case of Joseon. As in the past, the Lord of Tsushima was invested with the full authority for foreign affairs and to act as a proxy for the new government. On June 28, a delegation called the Daishu-daisashi was organized to inform the Joseon government of the Imperial restoration. The delegation arrived at Dongnae on December 19, and copies of the diplomatic documents were sent to the Joseon side. The Joseon government did not receive the delegation because of problems such as Japan's unilateral changing of the head and the official name of the delegation, the usage of a seal newly made by the Japanese government instead of the official seal given to them by Joseon, and also the usage of the term *hwangje* (emperor).[15] As is commonly known, this was a pend-

---

eung-gwa gunbi jeunggang" (Regarding Countermeasures and Military Expansion of Western Powers on the Daewongun's Seizure of Power) (Ph.D. dissertation, Seoul National University, 1998), pp. 2-3.

15. Until then, documents between Japan and Korea came in the name of the Japanese Shogun translated as *daegun* or "great prince."

ing diplomatic issue between Korea and Japan for the next six years. Japan foisted the blame entirely on Joseon and began to call Joseon "isolationist" or a "hermit" nation.

It is true that the Daewongun government initially rejected Japan's request to establish new diplomatic relations, but there was sufficient reason for this. First, Japan's diplomatic actions were overly unilateral and arbitrary. Normally, if a major political change such as the Imperial Restoration occurred, the appropriate sequence of action would have been to take steps to properly inform the other party of the news, and then to enter into consultations on how the diplomatic style and procedures would be affected by the changes in the form of the state. However, Japan chose its own method of informing Joseon of the Imperial Restoration and its own diplomatic procedures to reflect the changed polity, and expected Joseon to accept them. Expecting Joseon to calmly accept such actions as a whole, of course, is entirely one-sided. Second, an incident occurred a year or two before Japan sent its delegation, which could not help but make Joseon weary of Japan. On December 12, 1866, one year before the Meiji Restoration, a Japanese self-claimed Confucianist named Hachinoe Junshuku wrote the following in the Chinese newspaper *Zhongwi xianbo* in Guangdong: at the call of the shogun, 260 Japanese feudal lords gathered in Edo concluded that there was no choice but to take up arms and enhance Japan's national prestige by launching a major military undertaking to conquer Joseon since Joseon refused to pay tribute every five years. In an article in a different newspaper, he also claimed that from the Silla period, the Samhan Three Han States in Korea had paid tribute to Japan, and that from the time of the Hideyoshi invasion, the Joseon king would send an envoy to Edo every five years to have an audience with the shogun. This was a direct manifestation of the "Conquer Korea" view flourishing among the samurai society in Japan at the time, and cannot be explained as a mere rumor like the Japanese later claimed. The Chinese government sent word of this article to Joseon, who took this matter seriously and sent a notice to the Japanese government through Tsushima which demanded an explanation under the name of the Chief of Staff of the Ceremonies Board.[16] In light of this, Joseon's rigid stance one year later, when Japan arbitrarily changed the form and style of its delegation, and suddenly started

---

16. Tabohashi Kiyoshi, *Kindai nissen kankei no kenkyu* (Studies on the Relations Between Japan and Chosen During the Modern Period), part 1, pp. 121-124.

using the term *hwangje* without warning, seems only appropriate. To put it simply, Japan must also bear a large part of the blame for the diplomatic stalemate after the Meiji Restoration. The reason why Joseon has shouldered all of the blame until now is that the historical analysis has always been from the Japanese perspective. Faced with enormous pressure from China and Japan in its early modern history, Korea had no opportunity to set the record straight at the time.

It cannot be denied that the Daewongun government's response to Japan's request was extremely problematic. According to a detailed account of the progression of events,[17] Joseon sent the *hundo* (the first-line diplomat for relations with Japan) and the Dongnae county magistrate to negotiate. After they pointed out the problems with the Japanese documents, they did not really attempt any sort of compromise. Because of this, negotiations stood at a standstill for three years. Finally, since Joseon would not budge from its rigid stance, the delegation withdrew from Korea in January 1872. In late May of that year, the Tsushima-born head of the *waegwan* announced that he wished to meet with the Dongnae county magistrate, and left the Japanese permitted area to enter Dongnae, which caused a disturbance lasting five days. This event did not benefit Japan in any way and only served to worsen the bilateral relations. Japan's unilateral actions did not end there. Japan's Foreign Ministry took this incident as evidence that the people of Tsushima were no longer capable of conducting diplomacy with Joseon. They used this event to assume direct control over foreign relations with Joseon, and they secretly took measures to overtake the *waegwan*. The *waegwan* was originally built by the Joseon government, and Japanese only possessed the right to use the facilities, not own them. Therefore, it is only natural that any changes in the situation needed to be discussed with the Joseon government. However, the Japanese started in May and completed the following February the unilateral measures to take over the *waegwan*, even going so far as to rename it Dai nippon kokan ("The Official Residence of Great Japan" or the "Japanese Residence" hereafter).

The Japanese Foreign Ministry's occupation of the *waegwan* was just another manifestation of their aggressive "Conquer Korea" mentality.

---

17. The following account is taken from the above-mentioned Tabohashi Kiyoshi's book. While there may be some problems in terms of viewpoint or bias, overall his account seems accurate and well-detailed in describing the progress of events which took place at that time.

The so-called Lesser "Conquer Korea" school's proposal at the court in late May 1873 was a more active expression of the same attitude. In light of these events, it is improper to say that all the blame should be placed on Joseon for being isolationist or seclusionist.

The confrontation stemming from the issue of establishing bilateral diplomatic relations which had dragged on for some five years since June 1868 finally took its toll and led to changes in the power structure of both governments. However, the original situation, represented by Japan's offensive stance and Joseon's defensive stance remained unchanged. In Japan, the Lesser "Conquer Korea" school fell out of grace in October, while in Korea, it was the Daewongun who fell from power in late December, directly showing how much of a burden this diplomatic clash was. One common denominator in the power shift of each country was that it was the hard-liners or "hawks" which lost power. In the case of Japan, the faction which replaced the Lesser "Conquer Korea" school did not relinquish the idea of conquering Korea; rather, their views differed in terms of timing and leadership. On the other hand, the monarch who deposed Daewongun, King Gojong, adopted a policy of complete openness. He firmly believed that the only way to save the declining Joseon was through openness, and by establishing diplomatic relations with foreign countries.

In late December 1873, the Joseon monarch appointed a close, trust-worthy official as a special investigator and sent him down to Dongnae to examine why diplomatic relations had become deadlocked. In addition, he rotated all of the officials, including the Dongnae county magistrate, who had been involved in diplomatic matters with Japan. From this point onward, the attitude of the Joseon king and government toward Japan was almost the complete opposite of the previous stance. In April of 1874, Japan launched a military expedition against Taiwan. The Joseon government found out about this from the Chinese Ministry of Rites on August 4. But unlike in the past, the Joseon government did not tighten its attitude toward Japan. They came to the conclusion that too much reliance had been placed on the words of the *hundo* to the point where bilateral relations were in danger. Therefore, in the middle of August, the relevant officials were all punished, and a negotiator was sent to the Japanese Residence in Busan to discuss the basic direction of future bilateral relations. The Japanese side suggested a direct exchange system where the Joseon Minister of Rites would interact with the Foreign Minister, the Joseon Vice Minister of Rites would interact with the

Japanese Vice Foreign Minister, and so on, to which the Joseon side agreed. In addition, it was also agreed that Joseon would not raise any issue if Japan used the term *hwangje* in its diplomatic documents, but had the right not to use the term in its responses according to the circumstances. The preliminary agreement was formally proposed on September 3, and on September 19, the Joseon government convened a ministerial meeting. At the meeting, they accepted the proposal, saying that the Japanese government clearly had "friendly and amiable intentions," and received the king's approval. The Joseon government demonstrated without a doubt its commitment to openness. Now, everything was up to the Japanese.

That October, the head of the Japanese Residence in Busan, Moriyama Shigeru, went back to Tokyo to report on the latest developments. His actual mission had been only to report on the state of affairs, but because events had transpired so quickly he also signed the agreement. The Japanese Foreign Ministry took steps to promote him and make him the official head of the Residence. On December 28, he was promoted to the vice-ministerial rank and dispatched as the *isagwan* or "executive director" of the Japanese Residence in Busan. However, because the Foreign Ministry was preoccupied with the military expedition in Taiwan, the foreign affairs matters with Korea were pushed to the back, and Moriyama did not arrive at his new post until the following year on February 24, 1875.

Starting from March 2, the Dongnae country magistrate began preparations to formally welcome the Japanese Residence Executive Director as an official diplomat. He asked for copies of the diplomatic papers and also diplomatic passage authorization. Upon receiving the copies, he noted that the original diplomatic papers were written in Japanese (instead of Chinese), carried the stamp of the Foreign Ministry (instead of the head of state), and used terms such as "Great Japan" and "the present Emperor," and therefore asked the central government to make the final decision. On March 12, King Gojong held a meeting with his three High State Councillors, who advised that the documents should be returned for correction. But the king said that "it is clear there is nothing suspicious about Japan's intentions," and since the Japanese had brought the diplomatic papers as was agreed upon, "it would not be in good faith if we did not accept them." He also said that if there were any problems after receiving the documents, it would not be too late to reject them. The fact that the Japanese official had arrived in Busan on a steamship had prompted some concerns in relation to the "anti-Western" school of the past, but the king rejected this, saying that Qing China was also using steam ships because of their speed and convenience and so there was no problem with the Japanese doing the same. Since the king showed such a progressive attitude, no one could argue and the procedures were quickly implemented. Future obstacles to rapid progress in bilateral relations came from the Japanese side.

On March 27, working-level officials entered into detailed discussions on the protocol measures for the meeting between the Dongnae county magistrate and the Japanese executive director. At this time, the Japanese side announced that Moriyama would be arriving at a banquet ceremony for guests of state through the central front gate wearing a Western evening coat.[18] The flustered Joseon officials reported this to the county magistrate, who then asked the court to deal with the matter. On April 9, the court decided that in terms of this matter alone, the traditional ways should be observed and informed the Japanese Residence as such on May 9. Moriyama's attempt to impede the smooth progress in resuming diplomatic relations over such a trifling matter was guided by an ulterior motive. On April 15, he sent the assistant executive director to Tokyo to report that judging from various incidents, the current Joseon political situation was unstable and that the most effective method of diplomatic relations would be to threaten Joseon by dispatching a warship to the waters off its coast, and asked for instructions from Tokyo to proceed in this direction. This clearly shows that Japan's attempts to initiate foreign relations with Joseon were from the beginning based on the "Conquer Korea" proposition. Their true intent was to establish new diplomatic relations with Joseon to their advantage through a demonstration of military might. Judging from the attitude of the Japanese diplomats, it was no accident that the *Unyang* Incident off Ganghwado island occurred only four months later.

While recognizing the validity of Moriyama's request, the Japanese Foreign Ministry ordered that diplomatic means be tried to achieve their earlier objective. On May 15, the Dongnae county magistrate again tried to persuade the director, saying that Joseon wanted to hold a banquet in the traditional style since the director and his subordinates had traveled from a far, and wanted a special celebration of the resumption of rela-

---

18. Until then, diplomats would enter through one of the front gates to the side of the central front gate in traditional attire.

tions after some ten years of stalemate. However, Moriyama criticized the move as a mere stalling tactic, and even detained the Korean officials within the Japanese Residence. On May 17, the Japanese executive director issued a public statement saying that Joseon was trying to intervene in another country's internal affairs, even going so far as to say that this was a matter of national disgrace. Given his status as a diplomat, this was akin to issuing a final ultimatum. The Dongnae county magistrate criticized the statement as a damaging insult to the Joseon state, to which Moriyama issued another counter-attack in writing on May 19. On May 21, the Korean magistrate ended negotiations with the Japanese diplomat and asked the court for help.

At the meeting of ministers of the second rank and higher held on June 9 (10th day of the 5th lunar month), the moderate camp prevailed. Those advocating compromise, saying that a break in relations with Japan should be avoided, and those emphasizing accommodation, saying that neighboring countries had no right to resist changes in Japan's polity, were the predominant views. The king also said the first priority should be to avoid a head-to-head collision. But at the meeting of the High State Councillors, the hard-line view won out once again. On August 6 (9th day of 7th lunar month), the High State Council announced that as long as the Japanese executive director insisted on entering through the central front gate wearing Western attire, the ceremony could not be held. The king, searching for a way out, replaced the Dongnae magistrate and ordered the new magistrate to make the Japanese understand Joseon's situation and ensure the ceremony would be held. However, on September 20, Moriyama received an order from the Japanese government to return home and left that very day. September 20 was the exact day when the *Unyang* Incident occurred off Ganghwado island.

Conclusion

Until now, the basic position on early modern Korea's foreign relations has been that Korea was "hermit-like" or "exclusionist." This paper first examined the origins of this attitude and then the accuracy of this perception. In particular, this paper examined the period starting from 1868, right after the Meiji Restoration when Japan sent a delegation to Korea to request the initiation of new diplomatic relations, and up to

1875, right before the *Unyang* Incident occurred. This examination showed that Joseon's rejection of Japan's proposal to initiate new diplomatic relations was not because of Joseon's overall exclusionary attitude but because of Japan's aggressive intentions toward Korea. The paper also proved that Joseon's attitude shifted rapidly toward openness after the restoration of King Gojong and to call Joseon "hermit-like" or "seclusionist" at the time is not appropriate at all. In fact, the Joseon government was even more active than the Japanese government in trying to establish diplomatic relations. This was probably done in an effort to recover from the decline caused by Joseon's late opening of its ports.

The Japanese were perplexed by the Joseon government's stance, and so when they requested the reestablishment of new diplomatic relations, they did so in a manner which the Joseon government could not accept. They expected Joseon to reject their proposal, and that is what they wanted. Their actual aim was to create an opportunity to use military force or pressure and eventually conquer Korea. The reason why Japan decided to end the negotiations over the state dress issue in the final stage of setting up diplomatic relations was that the negotiations were not going the way they desired because of Korea's open stance. Normal negotiations were thrown aside and, using that fact as a pretense, the *Unyang* Incident occurred, a threat of military force. In truth, early modern Korea was not seclusionist but rather a nation which was spontaneously opening itself. Japan was not a "messiah" trying to save a "hermit" nation but instead an aggressor. In categorizing early modern Korea as a hermit nation, Griffis was only acting as the spokesperson for Japan's aggressionists.

The Joseon government maintained its open stance after the *Unyang* incident when it signed the Treaty of Friendship with Japan in 1876. At this time as well, the Japanese had made plans to respond by force in the event the talks broke down, but these plans were made useless by Joseon's voluntary attitude.[19] After signing the treaty of friendship with Japan, Joseon gathered many materials to conduct preparations and research for signing a treaty of amity and commerce with the United States. When it did so in April 1882, Joseon became the first country in

---

19. Please refer to "Kuroda benridaishi chosen shikosimatsu" (Minister Kuroda's Reports on Activities in Joseon) and "Kuroda benridaishi chosen shikonikki" (Minister Kuroda's Diary on Activities in Joseon) in *Nihongaikoubunshyo*, vol. 9, document 26, p. 139. The author is currently preparing a study on this topic.

Asia with the right to determine its own customs duties.[20] However, Korea was then hampered by China, which was trying to reassert its authority over Korea.

The Daewongun, who fell out of power with the restoration of King Gojong, rallied the forces opposing the policy of openness and caused the Military Mutiny of 1882 or the Imo Gullan in an effort to regain power. This event gave Qing China an opportunity to regain control over Joseon, which seemed to have escaped from its sphere of influence through its treaty with the United States. China, after confirming that the military mutiny was indeed against the king, used the pretext that it was the protector country of the Joseon dynasty to send troops into Joseon. While the Qing troops captured the Daewongun and sent him by force to China, they remained in Joseon and began to directly intervene in Joseon's domestic affairs. Among the progressive-minded bureaucrats appointed by the king, a faction of them tried to capitalize on the strength of Japan and initiated the Gapsin Jeongbyeon or Coup d'Etat of 1884, but in the end, this only further weakened the monarch's influence.

China unilaterally imposed an agreement on trade and commerce which guaranteed Chinese merchants the unlimited right to do business on the Korean peninsula and placed the Joseon Tax Office directly under the Chinese Tax Office in Shanghai. As a result, the Joseon government could not help slipping into financial poverty. Under the king's guidance, intermittent progress was made in pursuing an open-door policy, but in the end, the efforts proved ineffective because of the lack of finances. In his book *China and Korea* (1888), Owen N. Denny, an American who was an advisor to the Joseon King and Director of Foreign Affairs, wrote that Korea's determination to open itself was clearly proven, as evidenced by its conclusion of treaties with various Western nations and its firm declaration of being an independent nation. While having been appointed as an advisor to the Joseon monarch on the recommendation of the powerful Chinese official, Li Hongzhang, he became a firm admirer of King Gojong once he came to understand more about the situation in Joseon. Even though he and William Eliot Griffis were both Americans, they had entirely different attitudes toward

---

20. Kim Gyeong-tae, "Bulpyeongdeung joyak gaejeong gyoseop-ui jeon-gae," *Hanguksa yeongu* 11 (1975): pp. 198-199.

Korea. Having actually been to Korea during that period, Denny was able to witness Korea's efforts to open itself to the West.

The failure of Korea's modernization was not necessarily its own fault, as is generally believed. On the contrary, Korea was actively trying to enter into the international society, albeit late, but was impeded by the selfish interests of its neighbors, aggressive Japan and egoistic China. It is true that Joseon had weak national defenses and could not overcome their dilemma, but it is not historically accurate to say that Joseon lacked the will to modernize. Korean historians should move quickly to rectify these mistaken historical perceptions by attempting or refining their research efforts from new angles.

Not only has this flawed understanding or awareness of Korea's early modern history caused a great loss of pride among most Koreans today, but it has also made it difficult for them to reflect back and learn from history. This greatly hampers the ability of Korean people today in all areas, particularly in their international activities and engagements. Faulty knowledge and shallow thinking preclude effective judgment and analytical ability. Trying to expand one's international activities and raise one's international competitiveness without a proper understanding and recognition of one's own history is truly a futile effort.

The Peasant War in 1894 and the Growth of the Peasant Society

Lee Young-ho

Foreword

The Peasant War of 1894 was an anti-feudal and anti-imperialistic movement aimed at establishing a modern nation-state by overcoming feudal and national crises. The Peasant War unified on a national scale the various peasant uprisings that had been taking place in the late Joseon period at the local level, with the goal of eradicating problems related to feudalism. At the same time, it attempted to protect the nation against invasions by imperialist powers following the opening of ports. However, the anti-feudal reform aspirations that had erupted from below through the Peasant War were only partly accommodated by the Reform of 1894 (Gabo Gyeongjang). Moreover, the Sino-Japanese War, which broke out as the Peasant War unfolded, strengthened Japan's imperialistic invasion and subsequent rule of Korea.

If the initiation of a "modern" Korea is understood as being related to the overthrow of the feudal system and the start of the anti-imperialist

* Originally published in the *Korea Journal*, vol. 34, no. 4 (winter 1994).

Lee Young-ho (Yi, Yeong-ho) is Professor of Korean History at Inha University. He received his Ph.D. from Seoul National University in 1992, with a dissertation entitled "1984 nyeon-eseo 1910 nyeon-kkaji jise jedo yeongu" (A Study on the Land Taxation System of Korea in 1894–1910). His publications include "Gabo nongmin jeonjaeng ihu donghak nongmin-ui donghyang-gwa minjok undong" (The Movement of the Peasant Army and National Movement after the Peasant War of 1894) (1990), "Gaehwapa jeongbu-ui nongmin jeonjaeng suseup daechaek" (Korean Government's Response to the Peasant War in 1894) (2000), and *Hanguk geundae jise jedo-wa nongmin undong* (Land Tax System and Peasant Movement in Early Modern Korea) (2001). E-mail: yholee@inha.ac.kr.

movement, 1894 can be seen as the starting point. The Peasant War of 1894 was the first-ever revolutionary movement aimed at solving national problems and class conflicts in Korea. Hence, it provides a historical lesson in overcoming these same problems today.

Although there is no lack of research on the Peasant War, efforts to understand the historical context of national crisis and class conflict have not been overwhelming. Since 1980, the historical significance of the Peasant War has been emphasized as a result of a new attitude toward this revolutionary movement.

In this paper, I will examine the socioeconomic background of the Peasant War of 1894 and the growth of the revolutionary force, and divide the background largely into the failure of the feudal system and the encroachment of imperialism. I will focus on two types of mutual relationships found in the feudal system: the landlord-tenant relationship based on rents, and the state-peasant relationship based on taxes. I will then examine the encroachment of imperialism in terms of the economic threat it posed. Finally, this paper will explore aspects of the formation of the leading force of the Peasant War, taking feudal exploitation and imperialistic economic invasion as the backdrop against which to frame my analysis.

Present State of Research on the Peasant War and Its Tasks

Research on the Peasant War of 1894 performed under Japanese imperial rule was dominated by the view that it was an uprising by Donghak adherents. In the 1950s, scholars brought its anti-feudal and anti-invasion nature to prominence and highlighted its historical significance as a peasant war. During the 1960s, research based on intrinsic development theory became active and much attention was given to the study of the Peasant War. Research based on this theory dealt mainly with the socioeconomic history of the late Joseon period and thus greatly expanded understanding of this aspect of the Peasant War. Since the 1980s, with the advent of a heighten interest in popular movements, emphasis has been placed on the significance of the Peasant War of 1894 as the historical core of modern popular movements.[1]

---

1. The following are some of the references on the history of research on the Peasant

Socioeconomic background, the leading force, organization, ideology, and goals can be cited as important research topics for the study of the Peasant War. Among these, this paper will examine socioeconomic background and the main leading force of the war.

Recognizing how interpretations of these topics are contingent on their assessments of the Donghak movement, researchers have actively debated the relationship between the movement and the Peasant War. There are three major positions: the Donghak movement theory, the Peasant War theory, and a combination of the two theories. The Donghak movement theory proposes that the Donghak ideology, organization, and members led the Peasant War. The Peasant War theory either sees the Peasant War as a union of all the revolutionary movements

---

War of 1894. Jeong Chang-nyeol, "Donghak-gwa donghangnan" (Donghak and the Donghak Rebellion), in *Hangukhak yeongu immun* (Introduction to Research on Korean Studies) (Seoul: Jisik Sanupsa, 1981); "Gabo nongmin jeonjaeng-gwa gabo gaehyeok" (The Peasant War of 1894 and Gabo Reform), in *Hanguksa yeongu immun* (Introduction to Research on Korean History), 2nd ed. (Seoul: Jisik Sanupsa, 1987); Han U-geun, "Donghak-gwa donghangnan" (Donghak and the Donghak Rebellion), in *Hangukhak immun* (Introduction to Korean Studies) (Seoul: The National Academy of Sciences, 1983); An Byeong-uk, "Gabo nongmin jeonjaeng-ui seonggyeok-gwa yeongu hyeonhwang" (Nature of the Peasant War of 1894 and the Present State of Research), in *Hanguk geunhyeondae yeongu immun* (Introdution to Research on Modern and Contemporary Korea) (Seoul: Yuk Sa Bi Pyoung Sa, 1988); Yang Sang-hyeon, "1894 nyeon nongmin jeonjaeng-gwa hangil uibyeong jeonjaeng" (The Peasant War of 1894 and Anti-Japanese Righteoug Army War), in *Nambukhan yeoksa insik bigyo gangui* (Comparative Lecture on the South and North Korean Perceptions of History) (Seoul: Ilsongjeong, 1989); Ko Dong-hwan, "Gaehang ihu arae-robuteoui byeonhyeok undong" (Reform Movement from Below after the Opening of Ports), in *Minjok haebang undongsa* (History of National Liberation Movement) (Seoul: Yuk Sa Bi Pyoung Sa, 1990); Ha Won-ho, "Bureujua minjok undong-ui balsaeng, baljeon" (Origin and Development of Bourgeois Nationalist Movement), in *Bukhan-ui hanguksa insik* (North Korea's Perception of Korean History), vol. 2 (Seoul: Hangilsa Publishing Co., 1990); Lee Young-ho (Yi, Yeong-ho), "Hanguk geundae minjung undong yeongu-ui donghyang-gwa guksa gyogwaseo-ui seosul" (The Trend in the Research of Modern Korean Popular Movement and Its Description in Korean History Textbook), *Yeoksa gyoyuk* (Korean History Education Review) 47 (1990); Bak Maeng-su, "Donghak-gwa donghak nongmin jeonjaeng yeongu donghyang-gwa gwaje" (The Trend and Tasks of Research into Donghak and the Peasant War of 1894), in *Hanguk dongnip undongsa-ui insik: Baeksan Bak Seong-su gyosu hwagap ginyeom nonchong* (Perception of the History of the Korean Independence Movement: A Collection of Treaties in Commemoration of the 60th Birthday of Professor Baeksan Bak Seong-su) (1991).

from below that had been taking place during the late Joseon period, or regards the Southern Assembly of Donghak (Namjeop) as a main force for social reform. This theory takes care to distinguish the Southern Assembly of Donghak from the Northern Assembly of Donghak (Bukjeop) in ideological, organizational and compositional aspects. The position of the combined theory posits an integration of the Peasant War and Donghak that formed out of their mutually intrinsic relationship. Among historians, the Peasant War theory is generally regarded as more valid.

Examinations of the socioeconomic background of the Peasant War are tasked with elucidating the directions for constructing a new society, to which the Peasant War ultimately aspired. By examining the problems related to feudalism, which had intensified in the late Joseon period, along with national problems that had worsened following the opening of Korean ports, it would be possible to confirm in detail the historical nature of the war as an anti-feudal and anti-imperialistic movement. The former was connected with land, taxation, and finances, while the latter was related to the changes in the commodity distribution economy following the opening of ports. While socioeconomic background is directly related to the aims of the Peasant War, this paper, although working from within this perspective, will focus on the driving force behind the movement that developed as the leadership body of the war.

This leading force can be divided into the participant group and the leadership group. There is no question that the former group included the direct victims of feudal and national conflicts such as the lower class, poor peasants, petty craftsman, and petty merchants. On the other hand, opinions differ as to which group of people formed the leadership group: the *janban* (ruined *yangban*), wealthy peasants, or poor peasants.

The *janban* leadership theory holds that *janban*, the lowest level of the *yangban* class whose status was not significantly higher than that of commoners, had taken sides with the peasants and became the leaders of the peasant army as *jeopju* (head of a local unit of Donghak, called *jeop*). The process by which the *janban* established themselves as the main body of the peasant uprising is outlined as follows:[2]

poor *yangban* → become peasants → taxpayers → rebels

---

2. Han U-geun, "Donghak-ui rideosip" (The Donghak Leadership), *Baeksan hakbo* 8 (1970).

The "wealthy peasant leadership theory" argues that the wealthy peasants demonstrated their bourgeois aspirations for popular and revolutionary modernization from below through the Peasant War.[3] According to this theory, although they had accumulated wealth through frugality and improved agricultural methods, they were exploited by the local authorities and the *yangban*. Hence, they joined the Donghak movement, which took up the cause of the peasants and acted as their leaders during the Peasant War.[4] The "poor peasant leadership theory" argues that the leadership consisted of, in terms of social status, the commoners and the lower class that was centered around the slaves, and, in terms of social class, consisted of the poor peasants. Under their leadership, tenant farmers, as well as petty merchants, petty hand-craftsmen laborers and the unemployed all participated in the movement.

On the issue of the main leading force of the Peasant War, the poor peasant leadership theory is considered to be a more convincing interpretation. This paper examines the issue of the main body from the perspective of class and of social forces. In particular, this paper attempts to generally examine the social status of both the wealthy and poor peasants following the opening of the ports.

Socioeconomic Background of the Peasant War

This section undertakes a general inquiry of the socioeconomic background of the peasant war with attention centered on the worsening conflicts of feudalism and the nation. First, we will examine the demands of the peasant army in order to obtain a clear picture of the nature of feudal and national problems.

The demands of the peasant army are represented in the Program for the Reform of Misgovernment, which contained 12 articles that were to be carried out by the Jipgangso (Local Directorates) established in Jeolla-

---

3. Kim Yong-seop, "Geundaehwa gwajeong-eseoui nongeop gaehyeok-ui du bang-hyang" (Two Directions in the Process of Modernization and Agricultural Reform), in *Hanguk jabonjuui seonggyeok nonjaeng* (Controversy over the Character of Korean Capitalism) (Seoul: Dae Wang Sa, 1988).

4. Sin Yeong-u, "1894 nyeon yeongnam seobukbu jibang nongmin jidoja-ui sahoe sin-bun" (The Social Status of the Leaders of the Peasant Army in the Northwestern Part of Yeongnam Area in 1894), *Hangnim* 10 (1988).

do province as a result of the First Peasant Uprising. However, these 12 articles in the *Donghaksa* (The History of Donghak), written by O Ji-yeong, were a recollection of the author's own experiences. Therefore, a minute textual analysis of the articles would be profitless. Furthermore, three of the twelve articles in the edition published in 1940 differed from the original edition of the *Donghaksa* written in 1924.[5] Hence, it is inadequate to generalize the demands of the peasant army based on this reform program. Since the peasant army presented manifestos and reform plans according to its needs, it would be more appropriate to reconstruct the demands for the reform of misgovernment by comparing the Four-Point Manifestos and the 13 articles of the *Daehan gyenyeonsa* (The Last Years of Korea), the 6 articles of the *Hanguk tongsa* (The Tragic History of Korea), 9 articles of the *Juhan ilbon gongsagwan girok* (Record of the Japanese Legation in Joseon), 14 of the 27 articles of the "Judgement of Jeon Bong-jun," the 14 articles and additional articles of the *Sok eumcheongsa* (Supplement to the Diary of Kim Yun-sik), as well as other declarations and appeals.[6] In fact, the activities of the peasant army were far more diverse than those summarized in the above reform plans, as not all the demands were recorded. The activities of the peasant army should be seen as directly reflecting their demands, and accordingly, a record of their activities and practices should supplement the written demands of the peasant army.

Based on the above, the reform plans of the peasant army can be divided into those that called for the eradication of the feudal conflict and those criticizing the economic exploitation of the imperialist distrib-

---

5. Sin Yong-ha, "Gabo nongmin jeonjaeng-gwa dure-wa jipgangso-ui pyejeong gae-hyeok" (The Peasant War of 1894 and the Dure in the Reform of Misgovernment by Local Directorates), in *Hanguk sahoesa yeonguhoe nonmun jip* (Collection of Treaties of Korean Social History), vol. 8 (Seoul: Moonhak Kwa Jisung Sa, 1987); I I-hwa, "O Ji-yeong donghaksa-ui naeyong geomto; juro 1894 nyeon donghak nongmin jeon-jaeng-gwa gwallyeon hayeo" (An Investigation of the *History of the Donghak* by O Ji-yeong: With Analysis of Events Related to the Donghak Peasant War of 1894), *Minjok munhwa* 12 (1989).

6. Han U-geun, "Donghakgun-ui pyejeong gaehyeogan geomto" (A Preliminary Investigation of the Donghak Army's Reform of Misgovernment), *Yeoksa hakbo* (Journal of History) 23 (1964); Jeong Chang-nyeol, "Hanmal byeonhyeok undong-ui jeongchi, gyeongjejeok seonggyeok" (The Political and Economic Characteristics of Revolutionary Movements of the Late Joseon Period), in *Hanguk minjokjuui ron* (Theory of Korean Nationalism), vol. 1 (Seoul: Changbi Publishers Inc., 1982).

ution system. The former can be further divided into criticism of the state of anarchy in political discipline, demands for the abolition of social classes, demands for the eradication of the disorder of the taxation system, and the call for land reform. The latter centers on the rejection of both foreign merchant infiltration and the collusion between foreign merchants and domestic distribution organizations.

In reality, the feudal and national problems appear to be interrelated in the historical context of the opening of the ports. However, I will attempt to summarize them separately and discuss their mutual relationship with respect to the development of the reform body in the next section.

Korean medieval society had a unique trait, that being the combination of a centralized power system and a landlord-based economic system. The king, the central figure in the power system, bureaucratized the nobility and the *yangban* through the civil service examination and included them in the centralized power system. As a reward, the king guaranteed their economic benefit. The representative economic gain of the nobility and the *yangban* was ownership of land and slaves. However, central rule over the land and ownership of slaves by the nobility and the *yangban* (i.e. the geographical concentration of land possession and the collective nature of the possession of slaves) threatened the centralized power system. Hence, their rule over the land and ownership of slaves was guaranteed based on the premise of decentralization.

The ruling class, based on the landlord system that was composed of the king, the nobility, and the *yangban*, controlled the ruled class, which was composed of owner farmers as well as tenant farmers. The economic reality of this relationship was manifested in taxes and rent. In other words, a tax relationship between the state and the peasants, and a rent relationship between the landlord and the tenant was established. Of the two, the basic production relationship was that of the landlord-tenant, while the state-peasant relationship had secondary significance. Therefore, the substance of feudal problems could not but be manifest in the landlord-tenant relationship. However, as the king, the nobility, and the *yangban* formed the landlord class, whereas the peasants were mostly owner-farmers and tenant farmers, feudal conflicts were in actuality also found in the state-peasant relationship based on taxation. Furthermore, as land taxes came to constitute most of the taxation at the end of the Joseon feudal society, they worked to strengthen the power of the landlord. Hence, the conflicts of the state-peasant relationship were concealed in the landlord-tenant relationship and therefore made the conflicts of the latter more prominent.

The fundamental nature of the feudal conflict lay in the landlord-tenant relationship, and as the peasants' situation progressively worsened, conflicts in the landlord-tenant relationship intensified. The so-called "struggle against taxation" became fiercer. Tenant farmers postponed, lowered, and rejected the payment of rents and came to recognize through experience the conflicts inherent in the landlord-tenant relationship. However, in reality, even though the struggle against taxation became more widespread, the possibility of organizing any struggle was minimal. The external cause which hindered tenant farmers' collective efforts was the isolation of these farmers due to the dispersal of land possessed by their landlords. The internal cause was the undeveloped class consciousness of the tenant farmers. Conversely, allocation of the total amount of taxes at the local level and the practice of joint payment of taxes by peasants were the objective conditions that made the concentration of peasants' struggles at local levels possible. For this reason, the peasants in the nineteenth century began the peasant struggle as an anti-rent struggle rather than as an antitax struggle and in the process laid bare the conflicts of landlord-tenant system, along with the taxation issue of the "three administrations" (land allocation, military service, and grain loan system). The Peasant War of 1894, as the culmination of the nineteenth century peasant uprisings, initially demanded rectification of problems related to tax collection and the social status system, but then progressed to include demands for land reform as well.

Peasant uprisings at local levels called for the reform of the disorder of the three administrations (land allocation, military service, and grain loan system) which was the primary cause of the uprising. Upon seizing local government offices, the peasants burnt the tax receipt records related to the three administrations and attacked the petty functionaries in charge of tax collection. The rich peasants, who by colluding with the authorities had appropriated much profit in the tax collection process, were also attacked. As the struggles became severe, the peasants came to realize that the inequality of land ownership was the basic cause of economic inequality and thus began to attack the local gentry and large landlords of the rural districts, demanding a resolution of the inequality. As seen above, with the increased severity of the peasant uprisings, the issue of land ownership became a more serious problem.

Therefore, progressive intellectuals who were conscious of this aspect of the peasant struggles proposed the reform of the land ownership system in the process of preparing a reform plan for the three administrations. Traditional land reform theories—such as those based upon on "land allocated to male adults" (*jeongjeon*), "equal possession of land" (*gyunjeon*), and "limitation of land possession" (*hanjeon*)—were reinterpreted and theories on "equal tenant farming (*gyunjak*)" and "rent reduction (*gamjo*)" were put forward.[7] In particular, the theory of "rent reduction" was connected to the anti-tax struggles; it may have also been a practical and incremental plan aimed at land reform by helping peasants realize the inherent conflict in the land ownership system. Ultimately, the land reform theory took the direction towards the actualization of land ownership by peasants according to the rule that "Those who cultivate the land have the right to possess it." The land reform principle of the Peasant War seems to have reflected the tradition of such land reform proposal.

The demand for land reform proposed during the Peasant War is most clearly embodied in the demand for "distributing land equally to the farmers" among the 12 articles of the Program for the Reform of Misgovernment. It was also demonstrated in the demand for the punishment of the *gyunjeonsa* (land surveyor general) and the burning of the land register and tax records. Interpretations of the demand for "distributing land equally to the farmers" may vary because it was a reflection of the peasants' demands and intentions at a stage when its detailed enforcement regulations were not yet established. However, it seems clear that the peasants aspired to own land. That is, they called for the abolition of the landlord-tenant system and the realization of the peasant ownership of land, and stated their intention to become petty commodity producers. Therefore, the Confucian scholars who belonged mostly to the landlord class could not support the reform of the peasant army, and while both took an anti-imperialist position, they could not but oppose each other in the face of the forceful imperialistic invasion.

The "inherent contradictions of feudalism" became more grave following the opening of the ports. The financial burden arising from the feudal crisis and the process of modernization increased, bringing about a crisis in state finances. This, in turn, was transferred to the peasants whose decline was accelerated as the landlord system, which had been

---

7. Kim Yong-seop, "Hanmal gojonggi-ui toji gaehyeok ron" (A Study on Land Reform during the Reign of King Gojong), *Dongbang hakji* (The Journal of Korean Stdies) 41 (1984).

in decline as a result of the weakening enforcement of noneconomic measures, was strengthened again by the export of rice following the opening of the ports. In addition, the exploitation by the middle class of the commodity-monetary economy became more severe. The peasant was thus exposed to various types of exploitation, including rent and tax exploitation. This situation provoked the peasant uprisings at the local levels in the nineteenth century, which in turn, escalated into the Peasant War of 1894. This "war" was thus an anti-feudal movement that attempted to abolish the feudal system and to promote revolutionary reform from below. It aimed at overcoming all the contradictions inherent in feudalism, from the issue of taxation to that of land ownership.

After the opening of the ports, such feudal contradictions overlapped with the national problems that arose from imperialist economic invasion. This is because the imperialist power had either colluded with the domestic feudal class or had fostered *comprador* power, who were collaborationists acting as an intermediary in business affairs with foreign forces.

The imperialist invasion subsequent to the opening of the ports can be divided into three phases between 1876 and 1905. The period from 1876 to 1894 was a period of intense hegemonic struggle between China and Japan, in an international context of the division of the world by imperialist powers. As a result, the Sino-Japanese War broke out in 1894. One outcome of the war was that China dropped its imperialist aspirations and instead became a target of other imperialist powers; another was that Japan joined the ranks of the imperialist powers and Korea became a semi-colony. However, in the ensuing power struggle among the Western powers, the Japanese monopoly over Korea was rejected, but Korea became obliged to accommodate the transfer of various concessions to Western powers. The Russo-Japanese war of 1904 was the last barrier to Japan's gaining control over Korea. Japan won the war and signed The Protectorate Treaty of 1905 (between Korea and Japan), thus making Korea its colony.

This paper engages this first phase of hegemonic struggle between China and Japan. During this period, along with the emergence of the Western powers, these two Asian nations entered into an intense rivalry. China considered Korea to be its subordinate while Japan rejected this idea. China was attempting modernization through the Yangmu movement, while Japan, following the Meiji Restoration, carried out a primitive accumulation of capital in order to exploit the agricultural industry and foster a close interrelationship between business and politics. Japan desperately needed trade with Korea in order to facilitate its capital accumulation. Although Japan at that point did not possess imperialistic characteristics, with the emergence of pro-Russian powers following the signing of the Joseon-Russia Treaty of Protection and Commerce (1884), the Gapsin Jeongbyeon (Coup d'Etat of 1884) and following the British occupation of Geomundo island in 1885–1887, it began to demonstrate traits of imperialistic aggression towards Korea to counter such measures. Korea was the main target of a power struggle between Japan and China, which had not yet reached the level of imperialism.

The imperialistic economic invasion first penetrated the distribution sector, as its objective was to gain access to markets to sell industrial goods from advanced capitalist countries and to drain agricultural and mineral products from Korea. In particular, Japan, which had not yet industrialized and was playing the role of middleman in trading the manufactured goods of the advanced countries, demanded raw materials and agricultural products such as rice for the development of Japanese industries. Korea possessed all the right conditions for such a market.

After penetrating the distribution sector, the imperialist forces reorganized the distribution system around the open ports. For inland distribution, they formed a *comprador* substructure comprised of Koreans; however, with increased colonization this middleman function gradually came under the control of foreign merchants. Accordingly, the many people who had colluded with the imperialists for distribution at an early stage slowly became more nationalistic. However, prior to the Peasant War, the imperialistic economic invasion had not spread inland and the *comprador* role of merchants was still of utility. Thus, their activities became subject to peasant criticism and attack.

Specifically, the outflow of grain directly affected the peasants. When the Japanese drained Korea of its grain to develop their industries, it disturbed the domestic grain supply system, raised prices, and invited opposition from poor farmers as well as wage laborers in cities and in rural areas. As grain became a commodity due to the outflow to Japan, the desire of the peasants to accumulate a surplus became greater. However, merchant organizations, which included Japanese merchants, as well as the feudal ruling class exploited not only the peasants' surplus products but their personal consumption as well. In addition, the feudal government over-issued worthless currency in order to secure finance which, along with the grain export to Japan, caused inflation in the price of grain and other goods.

Imperialist economic plunder thus brought about the decline of poor peasants, urban and rural wage laborers, and small merchants. Furthermore, the extortion of the imperialist forces combined with feudal exploitations aggravated social conflicts. Monetary tax payments further victimized peasants as Japan seized the financial sector, the outflow of grain to Japan strengthened the landlord system, and the privileged feudal merchants functioned as *compradors* for the imperialist power.

The Growth of Reform Forces

Only those who directly suffered the feudal and national crises were able to become the reform forces that had the potential to overcome these crises. Among the political powers after the opening of the ports—the "Enlightenment group" (*gaehwapa*), the "defending orthodoxy and rejecting heterodoxy" (*wijeong cheoksa*) faction, and the common people (*minjung*)—, the *minjung* were the most willing to overcome feudal and national problems. Because the *minjung* was exploited through both rent and taxes, the people whom it comprised sought anti-feudal modernization. But unlike the Enlightenment group, the *minjung* attempted to carry out modernization autonomously from below. In addition, they had been exposed to imperialist economic invasion and had thus suffered more than any other group. This acute iniquity and exploitation motivated them to emerge as the clearest leadership force of the reform movement.

The process by which the subject of reform, the *minjung*'s power, emerged can be discussed from two perspectives. One is from that of class structure and the other is that of social forces. The development of capitalistic production in the late Joseon period quickened the dissolution of the land ownership system that was defined by non-economic "*yangban*/landlord-commoner, slave/tenant" bonds. As a result, classes, which were defined in terms of an economic relationship, and social forces, which assigned social status at birth, became entangled, causing a transitional maldistribution of power.

In terms of class structure, the landlords were divided based on the size of their land holdings into large, medium, and small landlords. Owner-farmers and tenant-farmers were divided, according to their management ability, into wealthy farmers, medium farmers, poor farmers and wage laborers. Other groups included merchants who were divided according to the size of their capital, and the urban poor. In terms of social forces, the local landed gentry and the wealthy (*yoho bumin*) occupied the upper level of the status system, and the poor, made up of commoners or lowborn, occupied the bottom. The local landed gentry strata was constituted by large landlords, and the wealthy strata was made up of small-and-medium landlords, wealthy peasants, and merchants; the poor strata was composed of poor peasants and wage laborers.

In the course of the Peasant War of 1894, the local landed gentry organized their own private militia to oppose the peasant army. It was the wealthy, those small-and-medium landlords, wealthy peasants and merchants, and the poor, those poor farmers and wage laborers, who were problematic as the leaders of the Peasant War.

The wealthy (*yoho bumin*) secured economic power through the development of the commodity-monetary economy during the late Joseon period. Based on this, they climbed the social ladder from commoners to *yangban* status and gained local power as well. The economic base of the *yoho bumin* lay in agricultural production, commercial activities, and contracts for tax collection. However, among this group were those who accumulated wealth by increasing productivity and reforming production methods, as well as those who colluded with government authorities and used privileges to accumulate wealth. The former tended to oppose the feudal authorities, while the latter benefited from the feudal power structure. In other words, there was a distinction between progressive and conservative tendencies in regard to their relationship with the feudal powers. The progressive *yoho bumin* could not escape feudal exploitation and thus stepped forward as leaders in the anti-feudal uprisings. The conservative *yoho bumin* colluded with the feudal authorities and, having joined the exploiters, were as a result attacked by the peasant army. The collaboration between the conservative *yoho bumin* and the local magistrates, whose power grew as local societies collapsed, was central to feudal exploitation.

As seen above, prior to the opening of the ports, the wealthy were confused about their relationship with the feudal authorities. Even after the opening of ports, they continued to be agitated by this issue and once again fluctuated over their position on the imperialist economic invasion. The imperialist power, first of all, demanded a market for its commodities and as commercial activities outside the open ports were forbidden, the distribution of imported commodities had to be entrusted to native merchants. Merchants were given the opportunity to earn a profit by importing both cheap and high quality goods. As Japan needed cheap food for the development of capitalism, it instituted the import of Korean grain, and Korean merchants took the middleman role in the collection of it. The export of grain strengthened the landlord system that had weakened somewhat during the struggles against rent and peasant uprisings. The landlords and merchants of the wealthy strata, following the opening of ports, had the opportunity to accumulate more wealth through their contacts with the imperialist economic powers, and this led to a *comprador* economy. Before 1894, the effects of the imperialistic economic invasion had not extended to the production structure, including land management and the sub-structures of commodity distribution. Therefore, the domestic landlords and merchants were not directly affected. The conservative *yoho bumin* took this opportunity to accumulate wealth. However, the progressive *yoho bumin*, who had been growing rich through increased productivity and improved production methods, were in danger of decline. The imported industrial goods dealt a blow to the national handicraft manufacturing business, and the export of grain made landlords more powerful, limiting the growth of wealthy peasants.

As such, the possibility that the *yoho bumin* could take leading roles in reform was weakened in the face of feudal and national crises. As they faced economic ruin and as the landlords' power grew, some of the *yoho bumin* came to participate in the Peasant War. But the *yoho bumin* class as a whole was unable to establish themselves as leaders of the Peasant War and were even attacked by the peasant army. Thus, the leading forces of the Peasant War were found among poor peasants, wage laborers, petty handicraft men, petty merchants, and some wealthy peasants, all of whom suffered from feudal iniquity and imperialist aggression. Collectively, these people can be called the *minjung*.

Concluding Remarks

This paper centered its discussion of the socioeconomic background of the Peasant War of 1894 on feudal and national problems and offered a general summary of the formation of the reform body that positively participated in the revolutionary movement. Although it was not possible submit a definitive study of the Peasant War, hopefully the research presented here will help in the general understanding of the socioeconomic background of the Peasant War.

When the Peasant War of 1894 is evaluated as an event with historical significance as a revolutionary movement instigated from below to establish a modern society, the need for more theoretical and substantial investigation becomes more apparent. The task of carrying out active research on the socioeconomic background of the Peasant War, the detailed course of the war and its principal organizations and ideologies, as well as clarifying what kind of war it was remains unfulfilled. The position of the progressives and the conservatives in relation to the Peasant War after the opening the ports should also be explicated. In addition, the place of the Peasant War in the history of the Korean people's movement should be examined, namely, the development stages and the nature of the peasant uprisings that culminated in the Peasant War of 1894, and the growth of the people's movement thereafter. Both of these topics should be brought together in a coherent, thorough study. Such discussions will reaffirm the importance of the Peasant War in world history and will lead to a better historical understanding of popular movements in general.

A Comparision of the 1894 Peasant Army Revolution and the French Revolution

Shin Yong-Ha

I

One of the most important research subjects in the modern history of the nations of the world must be on how the medieval *ancien régime* was dismantled, allowing a new modern system to be established in its place.

According to the orthodox interpretation of the French Revolution which celebrates its bicentennial this year, the bourgeoisie of France brought down the *ancien régime* by revolutionary means and established a new modern system, which opened the door to republicanism, civil society and capitalism. In other words, the French Revolution was a bourgeois revolution led by the bourgeoisie (in alliance with other classes of farmers and laborers).[1]

* Originally published in the *Korea Journal*, vol. 29, no. 10 (October 1989).

Shin Yong-Ha (Sin Yong-ha) is Professor Emeritus of Sociology at Seoul National University. He received his Ph.D. in Sociology from Seoul National University in 1975. He has authored a number of books, including *Hanguk geundae sahoe sasangsa yeongu* (Studies on the History of Modern Korean Social Thought) (1987), *Hanguk hyeondaesa-wa minjok munje* (Modern History and the National Question) (1990), and *Hanguk geundae-ui minjok undong-gwa sahoe undong* (National Movement and Social Change in Modern Korea) (2001).

1. See Sin Yong-ha (Shin, Yong-Ha), "Gabo nongmin jeonjaeng-ui juche seryeok-gwa sahoe sinbun" (The Identity of the Driving Forces and Its Social Status in the Revolutionary Movement of the Peasant War), *Hanguksa yeongu* (Journal of Korean History) nos. 50/51 (December 1985); "Gabo nongmin jeonjaeng sigi-ui nongmin jipgangso-ui seolchi" (Establishment of Local Directorates in Donghak Peasant Revolutionary Movement of 1894), *Hanguk hakbo* (Journal of Korean Studies) 41 (December 1985).

My view of the modern history of Korea, however, is that Korea's medieval *ancien régime* was brought down by farmers through the revolutionary movement of the Donghak peasant army in 1894. In its wake, the Enlightenment faction (Gaehwapa) undertook bourgeois reforms. In other words, these two forces played their own distinctive roles in bringing down the *ancien régime* in 1894 and establishing a new system. Farmers undertook revolutionary action to bring down the medieval *ancien régime* and from there, the Enlightenment faction carried out the bourgeois Gabo Reform of 1894 (Gabo Gyeongjang). The collaboration of the two forces led to the establishment of a new, modern system in Korea.

In this article, I will set forth a theory describing the relationship between the revolutionary movement—the so-called "peasant army"—and bourgeois reform, all in relation to the issue of modernization in modern Korean history. I also assert that although the Donghak peasant movement resembled a peasant war when examined superficially, it was actually a revolutionary peasant movement, both in terms of its content and its relevance to the writing of Korean history. I oppose the interpretation that the character and historical nature significance of the Donghak peasant movement was simply that of a peasant war.

II

The revolutionary movement of the Donghak peasant army in 1894 proceeded in four stages.

The first stage was that of the "peasant uprising at Gobu." About 1,000 peasants at Gobu, Jeollanam-do province, stormed the county office at Gobu under the leadership of Jeon Bong-jun in protest against extortion and exaction by corrupt county officials. Punishing the dishonest functionaries, they distributed rice illegally collected by the county magistrate Jo Byeong-gap in the guise of an irrigation tax to the original taxpayers. As a result, the magistrate was replaced by Bak Won-myeong, who, as a new magistrate, managed to persuade the peasants to disperse. This stage of unrest among the peasants had not yet reached that of a revolutionary peasant movement; it was rather a prelude in a stage of a small-scale disturbance or uprising. The period from January 11 to March 3, 1894 according to the lunar calendar (February 17–April 8 on the solar calendar) corresponds to the first stage.

The second stage was the "first phase of the revolutionary peasant movement." In this stage, peasants from throughout the Honam region set up a command post at Mujang in preparation for a rebellion, under the leadership of Jeon Bong-jun, Son Hwa-jung and Kim Gae-nam. Organizing a Donghak peasant army of about 4,000, centered around the followers of Donghak (Eastern Learning), they occupied several towns and counties starting from Gobu and entered the city of Jeonju and defeated the government army. The revolutionary peasant movement started full scale in earnest from this stage. The second stage can be dated on the lunar calendar from March 20 to May 7 (April 25–June 10 solar calendar) of the same year.

The third stage concerns the establishment of Local Directorates (Jipgangso) for the Donghak revolutionary movement. This occurred when a peace agreement was signed at Jeonju between the Donghak peasant army and the government in order to expedite the withdrawal of the Chinese and Japanese armies that had entered Korea on the pretext of putting down the Donghak revolutionary movement. The Donghak peasant army voluntarily disbanded *pro forma* in order to create a condition for the withdrawal of foreign armies. Local Directorates were established in 53 counties in Jeolla-do province to conduct the rule by peasants. The period corresponds from May 8 to September 12 according to the lunar calendar (June 11–October 10 on the solar calendar).

The fourth stage concerns the "second phase in the revolutionary peasant movement." The Japanese army, far from moving out, provoked the Sino-Japanese War in Korea. Japanese soldiers stormed the royal palace of Korea, disarmed the honor guards of the Korean Kingdom at will and interfered with the domestic affairs of Korea by manipulating the power relations in the royal court. This happened in response to the Donghak peasant army's bloody attempt, under the leadership of Jeon Bong-jun, to drive the Japanese army out of the Korean peninsula. This period lasted from September 13 on the lunar calendar (October 11, solar) through to the end of the year.

The signs of "revolutionary peasant movement" became more prominent in the second stage.

III

The Four Great Causes proclaimed at Baeksan on around March 25 in the "first phase" of the second stage contained as its third item, "Drive out the barbarous Japanese and clean up the ruling circles around the King." This was a proclamation for an anti-imperial struggle to drive out the Japanese imperial influences that had penetrated into Korea following the opening of Korean ports. The fourth item read, "March into the capital with the army and crush all those in influence and *yangban*." This is interpreted as a proclamation for anti-feudal peasant revolution to bring down the *ancien régime* centered around Queen Min and the *yangban* class on the top of society.

Again, the call to arms circulated in Jeolla-do province and throughout the nation on around March 27 by the Donghak peasant army manifested the anti-imperial and anti-feudal nature of its revolutionary peasant movement as follows:

> We rise up in the cause of righteousness not for anything else but to save the multitudes from agony and to place the state on the firm rock-like foundation. Internally, we are to behead the corrupt and wicked officials and externally to drive out the arrogant hordes of our fearsome foes. People at large persecuted by the *yangban* and by the wealthy and rich, and petty government functionaries tramped down by magistrates and governors all share the same grievances as we do. They should not hesitate but rise up at this moment with us. If we should let this opportunity pass, it will be too late for us to regret . . . .
>
> By the General for the cause of Righteousness
> at Baeksan in Jeolla-do province

The call to arms pinpoints the target of struggle as "*yangban* vs. people," thus manifesting itself as an anti-feudal struggle. In its reference to "driving out the arrogant hordes of our fearsome foes" the call also shows its anti-imperial nature, embodied in the national revolutionary movement by the peasants.

The Donghak peasant army occupied more than 20 counties before it succeeded in entering the fortress of the city of Jeonju. In the occupied areas, the administrative order of the *ancien régime* by the *yangban* bureaucrats was crushed to pieces and the Donghak peasant army rapidly undertook emergency measures for rebuilding the lives of the people.

Rule by peasants through Local Directorates in the third stage further exemplified the revolutionary nature of the Donghak peasant army that put an end to the *ancien régime*. The essentials of the reform program proposed by the Local Directorates included the abolition of the social class system and enfranchisement of serfs in five areas, provisions for the punishment of corrupt officials, the wealthy, and pro-Japanese elements, the annulment of high interest loans, and reform of the land-owning system. Some reforms implemented by the Local Directorates in merely three months of peasant rule included: (1) stern punishment of the wealthy who owed their fortunes to highhanded extortionist practices, (2) emancipation from the yoke of the social class system, (3) punishment of venal and corrupt officials and confiscation of their wealth (4) a ban on the collection of all arbitrary and irregular taxes, (5) cancellation of all outstanding debts, whether owed to government agencies or to private individuals, (6) annulment of high interest loans, (7) a ban on the export of rice to Japan, (8) attempted annulment of the landlord system, (9) disposition of complaints from people, (10) inspection and review of official documents, (11) propagation of Donghak study and strengthening of the peasant army, (12) distribution of arms and horses among the peasant army, and (13) the stockpiling of money and rice as preparation for war.

Of these, items 1, 2, 3, 4, 5, 6, 8, 9 and 10 were mainly concerned with anti-feudal struggle, while items 7, 11, 12, and 13 were motivated by the anti-imperial struggle. It is worth noting here that peasant rule through Local Directorates was intent upon bringing down the conservative *ancien régime* of Queen Min. For this purpose, it aimed at abolishing the social class system, emancipating the lower class, and abolishing the feudal landlord system and the feudal taxation system, which ranged over the entire social landscape of the *ancien régime*. In short, the revolutionary self-rule by peasants through Local Directorates aimed at abolishing the feudalistic *ancien régime* and establishing a new regime of peasants as land-tilling farmers. During the fourth stage of the "second phase of the peasant army revolutionary movement," the movement spread out throughout the country spilling over from the Jeolla-do region to Chung-cheong-do, Gyeongsang-do, Gyeonggi-do, Gangwon-do, Hwanghae-do, and part of the Hamgyeong-do and Pyeongan-do provincial regions. The second phase ended in failure with the defeat of the Donghak peasant army by the Japanese at the battle at Ugeumchi of Gongju. The original goal of the movement was to drive the Japanese army from the Korean peninsula, as well as to eradicate the *ancien régime* and implement peasant rule through the Local Directorates of the

Donghak movement. According to an estimate made by Bak Eun-sik, the casualties inflicted upon the peasants of the Donghak movement in the series of two phases of the peasant army revolutionary movement reached about 300,000 lives.

The revolutionary movement of the Donghak peasant army of 1894 was a representative revolutionary movement in modern Korean history. Though the anti-feudal and anti-imperial aspects were combined in the "first phase of the peasant revolutionary movement," the anti-feudal aspect was more conspicuous than the anti-imperial element. In the "second phase," both anti-feudal and anti-imperial elements were present but the anti-imperial character was much more marked than anti-feudal inclinations.[2]

IV

On account of the weak sense of class consciousness among Korean peasants in 1894, some views have downplayed the importance of the movement, claiming that the Donghak revolutionary movement of 1894 can not be seen as a "peasant revolution" or "peasant revolutionary movement," but merely as a "peasant war." Such arguments ignore the basic difference between the class structures of different societies, namely, the class structure in nineteenth-century Korea and that of France prior to the outbreak of the French Revolution.

The class hierarchy of the West prior to the French Revolution was, in short, a descending order of aristocrats, bourgeois and farmers (and laborers); in the Orient, this would be understood in terms of the social order of "scholar, farmer, artisan, and merchant." In the West, the bourgeois achieved rapid growth right beneath the aristocrats, while farmers existed mostly in a state of serfdom, living in ignorance and illiteracy. Quite unlike that found in the West, the class hierarchy in Korea toward the end of the nineteenth century was a descending order of "scholar, farmer, artisan, and merchant" where peasants (or farmers) were situated right under the *yangban* (scholar class); artisans and merchants, who corresponded to the bourgeois of the West, were treated as belonging to

---

2. See Min Seok-hong, ed., *Peurangseu hyeongmyeongsa ron* (Views on the History of the French Revolution) (Seoul: Kachi Publishing Co., 1988).

despicable occupations with a social status much less respectable than the peasants and farmers. Farmers in Korea in the nineteenth century were economically poor, but in terms of social status were mostly *yangin* (commoners). In the latter part of the Joseon dynasty, lecture halls spread out rapidly even in the countryside, markedly raising literacy among farmers, producing a sizable book-reading population in the farming communities, along with a subsequent rise in the level of their political consciousness. Therefore, the social status of Korean farmers was far better than that of medieval serfs in the West. Therefore, it is a mistake to apply the case of Europe to Korea, claiming that farmers were an underdeveloped class incapable of mounting a revolutionary movement and that only the bourgeois class could be the driving force of such a movement. Such a contention would be in error in that it neglects particular elements in the modern history of Korea.

In the modern history of Korea, the bourgeois was underdeveloped. Therefore, there is nothing strange about the historical development that the *yangban* aristocracy—the supporters of the *ancien régime*—became the target of attack in a revolutionary movement led by the farming class, which had been relatively mature, having existed immediately beneath the aristocrats or *yangban*. Even though the Donghak revolutionary movement could not afford to negate the monarchy itself in the light of the prevailing conditions of the time, the shifting trend from autocratic monarchy to constitutional monarchy was inevitable. The Enlightenment faction took a similar political stand, and had been the driving force behind bourgeois reform. The latter, too, did not advocate republicanism in 1894 but was claiming for a constitutional monarchy.

Nevertheless, the revolutionary movement of the Donghak peasant army managed to bring down the conservative regime of Queen Min, the last stronghold of the *ancien régime*. It also achieved the emancipation of people from the yoke of low social status by completely abolishing the system of social hierarchy, the social backbone of the medieval *ancien régime*. It pursued a new modern system by resolutely negating the feudal landlord system and its exploitative system of extortion, which had defined the medieval system's economic backbone. The Donghak revolutionary movement of 1894 failed to establish its regime in the capital. On this score, the event may be conceptualized as a "revolutionary movement" though it may fall short of being categorized as a "revolution." Though the Donghak revolutionary movement of 1894 failed to establish a new system, it succeeded in bringing down the medieval *ancien régime* in Korea through a revolutionary means.

The process of collapsing the *ancien régime* and establishing a new order in the modern chapter of Korean history shows that peasants who were the followers of the Donghak discipline initiated a revolutionary peasant movement in March 1894. They brought down the conservative regime of Queen Min, the feudal landlord system and the exploitative feudal economic system, in pursuit of a new system of peasant rule. Within three months the Enlightenment faction seized power and intiated bourgeois reform. Without the revolutionary movement by the Donghak peasant army, the Enlightenment faction would have been incapable of seizing power from the *ancien régime*. In addition, without the radical reforms implemented by peasants through Local Directorates, the legal reform undertaken by the Enlightenment faction in 1894 would have been mere "paper reform." In fact, this radical change led by the Enlightenment faction shortly following its grab for power was patterned after the mode of reform taken by peasants in the Donghak revolutionary movement, with some addition and revision that suited the Enlightenment faction's style.

The Enlightenment faction's 1894 reform was basically a bourgeois one in the eyes of Westerners, as most from the Enlightenment faction were from the *yangban* class. At the time, the Enlightenment faction had no potentiality or no aspiration to pursue "bourgeois revolution." What they pursued in actuality was not bourgeois revolution, but bourgeois reform. The Enlightenment faction, which undertook the reform of 1894, proceeded resolutely with bourgeois reform while the revolutionary movement of the Donghak peasant army was underway. Following the defeat of the Donghak peasant army at the battle of Ugeumchi, however, the speed of reform was notably slackened down.

From the point of view of a historical methodology that constructs history merely as a chronicle of events, the Donghak peasant movement may seem to be an event separate and independent from the bourgeois reform that was the Gabo Reforms undertaken by the Enlightenment faction. However, if adopting a methodology that focuses on structure, totality and depth in the study of social history, we could easily see that the *ancien régime* was brought down in 1894 by the revolutionary movement of the Donghak peasant army and a new modern system was established on that foundation. The Enlightenment faction's bourgeois reform instituted such process. Thus we can see that the modern social system of Korea toward the end of the nineteenth century was established by a combination of the peasant army's Donghak revolutionary movement and bourgeois reform. These must be the characteristic elements in the modern history and the modernization process in Korea in contrast to the French Revolution.

Copyright © Some Rights Reserved.

Korea's Responses to Social Darwinism

Lee Kwang-rin

Preface

In the Korean society of the late Joseon dynasty, the patriotic enlightenment movement was launched on a grand scale. This movement was
aimed, in short, at raising national strength. It was due to her lack of
national strength that Korea had to face the crisis of national ruin. The
Korean people realized that in order to build national strength, it was
imperative to establish social organizations and develop education and
industry. As the influence of this movement increased, many political
organizations, academic institutes, and private schools came into being.

One characteristic of this movement was that it was based on the
masses of people who possessed modern consciousness. Be that as it
may, it was while the people were strongly engrossed in a crisis consciousness, as they had been before, that the movement was launched.
The movement reached its peak during the period from the last days of
1905, when the treaty had already been concluded to degrade Korea
into a protectorate of Japan, to 1908. Although a crisis consciousness
was an outcome of the tense political situation that drove Korea to the
verge of downfall, another cause might have been the influence of
Darwinism on Korean society. One example supporting this assertion

* Originally published in the *Korea Journal*, vol. 18, nos. 4-5 (April/May 1978).

Lee Kwang-rin (Yi, Gwang-rin) is Professor Emeritus of Sogang University. He also
presently serves as a member of the National Institute of Korean History. He is the
author of many books, including *Gaehwadang yeongu* (A Study of the Joseon Progressive
Party) (1973), *Gaehwapa-wa gaehwa sasang yeongu* (A Study of Enlightenment Group and
Its Thought) (1989), and *Hanguk gaehwasa yeongu* (A Study of the Korean History of
Modernization) (1999).

lies in a festive song composed by a student of the Gwanghwa School, founded in Gwanghwa-myeon, Yongcheon-bu, Pyeongan-do province in November 1906. The actual lyrics paint the picture quite vividly:

> Ahem! We students should
> Think of our great duty.
> In what era is the world situated?
> Powers are confronting each other.
> Apparent is triumph for the stronger and
> defeat for the weaker.
> Why should each of us not strive to advance?
> Without giving ourselves up to despair
> But by mobilizing our national identity,
> Let us pursue our purpose of enlightenment
> and development
> Through education and industry.[1]

Another example can be found in the statement of the purpose for the Seou Hakhoe (Western Friends Academic Association) founded in October 1906, which reads as follows:

> Everything faces danger when it is isolated; it grows stronger when it is grouped with others; it thrives when it is united with others; it is defeated when it parts from others. This is a natural rule. Struggle for existence is omnipresent in the world today and an evident precedent is that the stronger became triumphant and the weaker were defeated. For this reason, we can foretell the future of a country by examining how strongly the constituents of its society are united. Devising means of protecting our families and our country, developing our youths' education, training able persons, and illuminating popular wisdom by keeping in mind the current trend of fierce competition will doubtless lay the groundwork for restoring our national rights and expanding our human rights.[2]

What was stressed in the statement was that the Koreans should collectively strive to improve themselves as much as possible and nimbly

---

1. "The Present Situation at Gwanghwa School" (in Korean), miscellaneous reports, *Daehan maeil sinbo*, (Korea Daily News) 15 December 1906.
2. The Korean Historical Association, comp., *Hanguksa saryo seonjip* (Sourcebook of Korean Civlization) (Seoul: Ilchokak Publishing Co., 1973), p. 222.

adapt to changing trends, for this was a time of struggle for existence, of triumph for the strong and defeat for the weak. The terms "triumph for the stronger and defeat for the weaker" (*useung yeolpae*) and "struggle for existence" (*saengjon gyeongjaeng*) were both concepts borrowed from Social Darwinism.

As is widely known, the Theory of Evolution was given a firm basis with the publication of *The Origin of Species* in 1859 by Charles Darwin (1809–1882). It tried to demonstrate natural selection and evolution on the basis of facts observable in the world of plants and animals, showing that the struggle for existence is constant, and that the stronger wins and the weaker loses in the struggle. Soon after Darwin's *The Origin of Species* was published, philosophers such as Herbert Spencer (1820–1903) and Thomas Huxley (1825–1895) applied the theory to human society and asserted that man evolved from apes, and that a relentless struggle for existence was taking place in human society, too. This assertion, called Social Darwinism, exerted profound influence on thinkers in general and attracted a greater interest from the general public than Darwin's theory of biological evolution.

When Social Darwinism was first introduced to China, the Chinese translated "survival of the fittest" as *wujing tianze* (物鏡天擇) and "struggle for existence" as *yousheng liebai* (優勝劣敗). The Japanese translated the former as *tekisha seizon* (適者生存) and the latter as *seizon kyoso* (生存競爭).[3] Both translations were introduced to Korea and used widely.

This paper is aimed at clarifying when and how the Theory of Evolution was introduced to Korean society in the late Joseon dynasty, as well as what influence it exerted. It seems that no notable academic study has been made on this subject in our country, so a brief introductory note is in order. In a sense, this will be tantamount to a project of examining one trend of thought prevalent in that period.

Acceptance of Darwinism

It was during the 1900s that Darwinism was accepted in earnest in Korea. However, some people began to absorb it as early as the 1880s. Representative was Yu Gil-jun (1856–1914). He was Korea's first student

---

3. Liang Qichao, "Tanzong," in *Yinbingshi wenji* (The Collected Works of Liang Qichao), vol. 10 (Shanghai: Kuangchih Publishing Company, 1907).

sent to Japan and the United States. In Japan, he was taught by Fukuzawa Yukichi (1835–1901), one of Japan's leading proponents of enlightenment at that time. In America, he had been taught directly by Edward
Sylvester Morse (1838–1925), a fervent supporter of Darwinism. Yu Gil-
jun studied in Japan for a year and a half, from 1881 to 1882. By that
time, books on Darwinism had already been published in Japan.[4] Especially noteworthy is the fact that Morse had been invited to Japan to lecture soon after the founding of Tokyo University in 1877, and his enthusiastic introduction of Darwinism contributed much to its wide diffusion
among the Japanese.[5]

At the time of Yu's return from Japan and arrival in the United States
in 1883, Morse had been serving as curator at the Peabody Museum in
Salem, Massachusetts. Having been acquainted with Morse in Japan, Yu
called on him. Before his enrollment at high school, Yu received private
instructions from Morse for nine months.[6] This naturally provided him
with an opportunity to come into contact with ideas of Darwinism.

In "On Competition," which he wrote immediately after his return
from study in Japan, Yu said:

> There is nothing among human affairs, which does not rely on compe-
> tition, ranging from trivial affairs affecting individuals to significant
> state affairs. Everything can advance through competition. If there is
> no competition in human life, how could any one among us cultivate
> wisdom and virtue in himself and promote his happiness? If there is no
> competition in relations among states, how could any one of them ele-
> vate its prestige and promote its wealth?[7]

---

4. For instance, Huxley's *Lectures on Origin of Species* was translated by Shuji Ito under
   the title, *Seishu genshiron* (1876) and Darwin's *The Descent of Man* (1874) by Sen-
   saburo Kamizu under the title, *Jinsoron* (1881). Concerning this point, refer to Masao
   Watanabe, *Nihonjin to kindai kagaku: seiyo eno taio to kadai* (Tokyo: Iwanami
   Shoten, 1976), p. 110.
5. His lectures were rearranged in Japanese and published in 1883 under the title *Dobu-
   tsu shinkaron*. It was Chiyomatsu Ishikawa who actually dictated and rearranged the
   lectures. Concerning this point, refer to *ibid.*, p. 110.
6. Lee Gwang-rin (Yi Gwang-rin), "Yu Gil-jun during His Study in the United States"
   (in Korean), *Hanguk gwahaksa yeongu* (A Study of the History of Korean Science)
   (Seoul: Ilchokak Publishing Co., 1969).
7. Compilation Committee of the Complete Works of Yu Gil-jun, comp., *Yu Gil-jun
   jeonseo* (Complete Works of Yu Gil-jun), vol. 4 (Seoul: Ilchokak Publishing Co.,
   1971).

What he stressed here was that human society can progress through competition. The excerpts were doubtless written with the logic of Social Darwinism. Whereas Darwin's theory of evolution dealt with competition among individuals of the same species, the theory of social evolution or Social Darwinism expanded the scope of its interpretation to cover competition among different societies and different states. In addition, Social Darwinism was connected with the idea of progress in society. In other words, it made people believe that everything progressed, thereby infusing in them a bright outlook toward the future and a sense of collective self-confidence.

After his study in the United States, Yu Gil-jun wrote *Seoyu gyeonmun* (Observations on a Journey to the West). Consisting of 20 chapters, this book dealt extensively with various subjects such as geography, history, politics, economy, science, education, and society of the world. Recognizing social development in the Western world, the book is filled with a progressive consciousness advocating the introduction of modern civilization. The book was aimed at helping the Korean people recognize the reality facing their country: that it lagged behind others in its degree of civilization. The text also helped to introduce the Korean populace to the new knowledge of the West.

Chapter 14 of this book, entitled "Grades of Civilization," sets forth his view of civilization. It was his assertion that mankind progresses from the uncivilized (barbarous) stage to a half-civilized one, before finally moving on to a final state of civilization. This view too was undoubtedly based on Social Darwinism. Therefore, it can be said that Yu wrote in terms of what he had absorbed from Social Darwinism, though he did not publish writings that directly introduced it.

To absorb Darwinism correctly requires knowledge of such basic fields of biology as taxology, morphology, ecology, comparative anatomy, and paleontology. However, such branches of science did not exist at that time not only in Korea, but even in Japan. Under these circumstances, Koreans naively tried to apply Darwinism to their society rather than accepting its natural science components.[8]

Even though Yu Gil-jun was taught directly by Morse, an eminent zoologist and Darwinian, his scholarly preparation had centered mainly on the English language for the purpose of admission to an American

---

8. Masao Watanabe, *op. cit.*, pp. 108-109.

high school. When Yu studied in Japan , he had learned such subjects as politics and economics; and at no time did he receive formal training in the natural sciences. Therefore, he had no academic basis on which to absorb knowledge from Morse, nor was it possible for him to learn such knowledge in such a short span of time. This was the more so because he gave up schooling four months after his admission to high school.

Naturally he learned something about Social Darwinism, which was easier to understand. This trend, in fact, was observable not only in Yu, but persisted even in the 1900s when other Koreans began to absorb Darwin's theories in earnest.

During the decade of the 1890s—ten years after Yu Gil-jun had come to understand Darwinism—Korea's government crumbled and the country plunged into internal chaos in the wake of the Donghak rebellion and the Gabo Reform in 1894. Externally, Qing China, which had prided itself upon its prestige as the Middle Kingdom, was defeated by Japan in a war, became an arena for competition among imperial powers, and faced the crisis of territorial partition by the encroaching powers.

It was rather natural under these circumstances that Social Darwinism, which taught the principle of survival of the fittest, would have a strong appeal to the general public.

In the first place, Darwinism met strong opposition and gave rise to disputes in the Western world because it was regarded as a denial of the Christian doctrine of creation. It was assailed especially because it grouped men in the same rank as other living things, which professes that men and beasts shared the same progenitor. This was antithetical of the belief that men had been created by God by his extraordinary favor.

In the East, where people had a view of God and an outlook on the world which were different from those of the West, Darwinism did not arouse any opposition. Rather it was accepted readily as being based on the principle of struggle for existence and survival of the fittest. This interpretation of Darwinism expanded its scope to be understood as a theory that would justify efforts to make one's country wealthier and its military stronger, and to rally the people to support notions of nationalism.

As we have seen, Koreans accepted Darwinism through Japanese translations and books in the 1880s; but after the 1890s and especially in the 1900s, they accepted it through Chinese writings. It was after the Sino-Japanese War (1894–1895) that Darwinism was first introduced to China. The introduction was through *Tianyanlun* (On Evolution), which was a translation of Huxley's *Evolution and Ethics and Other*

Essays[9] by Yan Fu (1853–1921), a Chinese thinker.

This book is a free translation of the original; one characteristic of the translated version is that it added a commentary at the end of each or several clauses, which the author called "*an*" (案), in which he stated what he thought of each section's contents. In some of them, he deplored the actualities existing in China; in other postscripts he passed his own judgment upon what Huxley asserted, with the help of theories advanced by other scholars, notably Spencer. While *Tianyanlun* was a translation of Huxley's work, it also introduced Spencer's theories which the translator apparently supported. In addition, Yan Fu translated and published Spencer's *The Study of Sociology* under the title *Qunxue yiyan* in 1903.

It can be presumed that Yan Fu's *Tianyanlun* found its way to Korea. However, Korean intellectuals were influenced more by the writings of Liang Qichao (1873–1929), who had incorporated Darwinian principles after having read *Tianyanlun*. Having exiled himself to Japan after the abortive political coup of 1898, Liang published magazines in Yokohama. His first magazine was *Qingyibao* (Topics of the Day; published from November 1898 to January 1901), and from 1902 he published *Xinmin congbao* (New Citizen's Journal; from January 1902 to October 1907). With an easy and fluent style, he assailed his corrupt home government, while endeavoring to destroy the old mode of thought and propagate modern ideas. His radical writings won wide readership.[10] Although he lived in Japan, his reputation and influence in China were enormous.

Liang's activities in Japan were widely known in Korea. The *Hwangseong sinmun* (Imperial Capital News) reported in its 13 January 1899 issue:

> The *Qingyibao* inaugurated by a Chinese residing in Yokohama turned out its first issue on the third day of the last month of last year according to the lunar calendar, and the publisher is Liang Qichao. He previ-

---

9. The translation was completed in 1986 and was printed in *Guowenbao*, a magazine published in Tianjin, the following year. Later in 1898 it was published in book form.

10. Though Liang Qichao receded from his drastic theory of revolution to moderate progressivism in 1906, he could not retract the strong influence he had already exerted on young people. Concerning this point, refer to Hidemi Onogawa, *Shinmatsu seiji shiso kenkyu* (Tokyo: Sato Shinji, 1969), pp. 276-277.

ously wrote for *Shiwubao* (China Progress) published in Shanghai. In the inaugural issue, he published two papers, one on a new proposal for Chinese philosophy and the other on the beginning and end of the Chinese political coup. The *Qingyibao* bitterly criticized the current state of affairs, warning millions of Chinese people against their idle slumber and expressing his earnest desire to see oriental scholars providing teachings.

With this report, a newspaper in Seoul introduced in detail the publication of the *Qingyibao* in Yokohama. As the Chinese periodical had sales and circulation offices in Seoul and Incheon,[11] it could reach Korea as soon as a new issue was sent out. Liang Qichao had left for the United States in November 1899 and returned to Japan in April 1901 after a stay of a year and a half. In January of the following year, he inaugurated a new magazine, the *Xinmin congbao*.[12] It was after the fall of the Qing dynasty and the establishment of the Republic of China that Liang returned home in 1912. This means that he spent 14 years in exile in Japan and the United States. During this period he left many writings.

His writings entered Korea and influenced her people as soon as they left the hands of the author. *Mouxu zhengbianji* (A Note on the 1898 Political Upheaval), which Liang wrote immediately after his flight to Japan, was translated and published in Korean as soon as it was brought to Korea. Hyeon Chae (1856–1925) translated it and the Ministry of Education published it. The fact that this material was published by a branch of the government charged with education suggests that the publication was aimed primarily at students; but it was read by the general public as well.[13]

Other writings of Liang Qichao (penname: Yinbingshi) were translated and published in Korea. For example, the *Yuenan wangguoshi* was

---

11. According to a treatise by Zhong Mingyuan, "Liang Qichao and the Late Qing Revolution," *Academia Sinica* (Modern History Research Institute) 2 (1966), the 32 circulation offices of *Qingyibao* included two in Korea, one in Seoul and the other in Incheon.

12. According to the above treatise, one circulation office of *Xinmin congbao* was located in Incheon.

13. For instance, in *Sok eumcheongsa*, vols. 1-10, November 8, fifth year of Gwangmu (1901), Kim Yun-sik wrote, "Advent of winter, clear. I read the two-volume *Mouxu zhengbianji* . . . ." It is clear that Kim Yun-sik, who was exiled to Jejudo island, read the book the year after it was translated.

also translated by Hyeon Chae. However, it was *Yinbingshi wenji* (The Collected Works of Liang Qichao), among all the writings of Liang Qichao, that was read most widely and exerted the most earnest influence on the people in Korea. This collection of Liang's essays was published in 18 volumes by the Kuangchih Publishing Company in Shanghai in February 1903;[14] it contained the writings he made public during the seven-year period in which he began participating in the publication of the *Shiwubao*, which was inaugurated in Shanghai in July 1896 and lasted until he inaugurated the *Xinmin congbao* in Yokohama in 1902. Immediately after its publication, the collection of Liang's works was brought to Seoul;[15] the *Yinbingshi ziyoushu* was published in Korean by Jeon Hang-gi in April 1908 under the title *Eumbingsil jayuseo* on the basis of his translation of "Tanzong," which is contained in the collection of Liang's essays.[16] The *Yidali jianguo sanjie chuan* (Biographies of Three Great Men in the Founding of Italy) was translated into Korean by Sin Chae-ho (1880–1936) and published in October 1907.

In addition, the writings contained in his collection were either reprinted or translated in various magazines published in Korea. For example, the *Joyangbo* carried a translation of "Gesudu xiongyali aiguochuan" (A Sketch of the Hungarian Patriot) in its ninth issue (published in 1906), the *Daehan jaganghoe wolbo* (Korea Self-Strengthening Society Monthly) carried "Jiaoyu zhengze siyi" (A Private Opinion on Education Policies) translated by Jang Ji-yeon (1864–1921) in its third issue (published on September 25, 1906) and fourth issue (published on October 25), and "Lizaishuo" (A Discourse on Financial Management) translated by Kim Seong-hui in its tenth issue (published on April 25, 1907). In its seventh issue (published on January 25, 1907) and eighth issue (published on February 25), the latter bulletin reprinted "Lunbao guanyouyi yuguoshi" (On the Profitability of the Press to State Administration).

---

14. This book was published again in August 1904 by the Kuangchih Publishing Company after it was first published the year before.
15. Extant copies of this book bear the seal of either the Hoedong Seogwan or the Gwanghak Sopo. Therefore it seems that these book stores imported and sold them. They were carried in the new book advertisement column of the *Daehan maeil sinbo* dated 17 October 1907.
16. The translated book, consisting of 240 pages in octavo, was published by the Tabinsa Company. It selected eight items of the 71 items of "Tanzong" and added two items from other sources. It consisted of 65 items.

The *Honam hakbo* (Bulletin of the Jeolla Academic Association) reprinted "Zhengzhixue xieli zhiyan" (Remarks on the Principles of Political
Science) in its eighth issue (January 25, 1909) and ninth issue (March
25). In addition, many newspapers, especially the *Daehan maeil sinbo*
(Korea Daily News), frequently referred to *Yinbingshi wenji* for their editorials. Liang's writings were even used as Chinese composition textbooks.[17]

The modern thought that Liang introduced easily won supporters in
Korea. His work named above was regarded by Korean intellectuals of
the time as being on a par with their own. Concerning this point, a letter
to the editor carried in the September 6, 1907 issue of the *Korea Daily
News* said:

> On his way from a tour of an agricultural experimentation station in
> Suwon last spring, Yu Won-pyo (Miraja) called on a government min-
> ister he was well acquainted with. . . . Miraja advised him to buy and
> read carefully the 18-volume *Yinbingshi wenji* by Liang Qichao because
> the book would naturally show how the world was situated as well as
> the right direction for government and the right guideline for humani-
> ty. He said, "Once these are shown it would not be difficult for us to
> save the nation from collapse, no matter how weak it has grown and
> even though the nation is on the verge of ruin." . . . As *Yinbingshi wenji*
> is the most wonderful remedy, Miraja told the minister that he should
> buy it and read it carefully, for a bitter medicine is efficacious for dis-
> ease, and unwelcome advice promotes good conduct.

Among some of the assertions made by Liang Qichao were ideas from
The Social Contract of Jean Jacques Rousseau (1712–1778). Nevertheless,
Darwinism constituted its main theme. Liang was so much interested in
and sympathized so much with Darwinism that he borrowed the draft of
Tianyanlun from the translator before its publication and copied it.
"Lunjinbu" (A Discussion of Progress) contained in "Xinminshuo" (A
Discourse on Modern People) stated:

> Progress on the whole is the general rule of the world. It can be likened
> to water which invariably flows downward, or to throwing a thing

---

17. It is said that Daeseong Hakgyo in Pyeongyang used his writings as a textbook.
    Refer to Ju Yo-seop, comp., *An Dosan jeonseo* (Complete Works of An Dosan)
    (Seoul: Samjungdang, 1971), p. 87.

which always flies to its target . . . . Nevertheless, China now shows phenomena or stagnation and we should find out their cause through discussions and remove them.[18]

In explaining the outstanding features of his *Qingyibao*,[19] Liang enumerated the following: First, advocacy of civil rights; second, promotion of modern ideas; third, clarification of the transitions in politics; and fourth, exposure of national shame.

Lastly, Liang reiterated that the basic tenets of Darwinism—"survival of the fittest" and "struggle for existence"—and the essential purposes of his *Qingyibao* were, in short, to broaden the people's wisdom and to stir up their spirit. The two examples amply show how strongly Darwinism influenced Liang Qichao.[20]

As Liang's writings won wide readership in Korea, Darwinism also naturally gained wide acceptance. The terms "struggle for existence" and "survival of the fittest" came into vogue and were frequently talked about in daily conversations among ordinary people. Korean intellectuals, too, published many essays introducing Darwinism. Those published in magazines include the following:

Jang Eung-jin. "The Law of Struggle for Existence in Darwinism." *Taegeuk hakbo* 4 (November 1906).

Jo Jong-gwan. "Theory of Evolution in Animals." *Gongsu hakbo* 1 (January 1907).

Bak Yu-byeong. "Darwinism." *Gongsu hakbo* 2 (April 1907).

Ku Ja-hak. "Struggle for Existence." *Gongsu hakbo* 5 (March 1908).

Yun Tae-yeong. "An Outline of Darwinism." *Yaroe*, no. 5 (June 1907); no. 6 (July 1907).

Yun Hyo-jeong. "Struggle for Existence." *Daehan jaganghoe wolbo* 11 (May 1907).

Won Yeong-ui. "Evolution in Politics." *Daehan hyeophoe hoebo* 1.5 (July 1908); 1.7 (October 1908); 1.8 (November 1908); 1.9 (December

---

18. Contained in the first volume of *Yuenan wangguoshi*.
19. Liang Qichao, *Qingyibao*.
20. Also contained were writings which directly introduced Darwinism. They were "A Discussion on the General Trend of Competition Among Nations" carried in the second, third, fourth, and fifth issues of the *Xinmin congbao*, "The Scholarship and Biography of Darwin, the Founder of the Theory of Evolution" in the third issue, and "Benjamin Ridd Who Revolutionized the Theory of Evolution" carried in the 18th issue. These treatises are contained in the last volume of *Yinbingshi wenji*.

1908); 1.10 (January 1909); 2.1 (February 1909); 2.2 (March 1909).

Kim Yeong-gil. "Survival of the Fittest." *Daehan heunghakbo* 1 (March 1909).

Na Hong-seok. "Let Us Encourage Our Compatriots by Elucidating the Principle of Social Evolution." *Daehan heunghakbo* 1 (March 1909).

Kang Ha-hyeong. "Causes of Evolution." *Gyonam gyoyukhoe japji* 2.10 (February 1910); 2.11 (March 1910).

Yi Su-sam. "An Outline of Evolution in Animals." *Bojung chinmokhoe hoebo* 1 (June 1910).[21]

Of the magazines listed above, the *Taegeuk hakbo* (Bulletin of the Taegeuk Association) and the *Gongsu hakbo* (Bulletin of the Joint Learning Association) were published by Korean students studying in Japan. All the rest were published at home. This fact is a clear reminder that Korean intellectuals were interested in Darwinism both at home and abroad. The qualitative level of these papers was generally low without exceeding the stage of enlightenment. Some of them dealt with aspects of natural science; but most were concerned with social science, namely so-called Social Darwinism.

Many writings introducing Darwinism were made public in media other than magazines, and not only in Seoul but in the provinces. One example is *Jinhwa jipseol* (An Explanation on Evolution)[22] written by Yi Sang-ryong (1858–1932), a scholar of the Andong district in Gyeongsang-do province.

When a branch of the Daehan Hyeophoe (Korea Association) was organized in Andong in 1907, Yi Sang-nyeong was named its chairman, and the group held a lecture meeting on the current situation once every month in order to enlighten the local people. It is presumed that *An Explanation on Evolution* was written around that time.

Besides these works, essays directly introducing Darwinism were published in book form. These books included *In-gan jinhwaron* (Evolution of Man), *Segye jinhwasa* (History of World Evolution), *Jokje jinhwaron* (On Evolution of the System of Relationship),[23] *Munmyeong jinhwaron* (On Evolution in Civilization),[24] *Sipgu segi guju munmyeong jinhwaron*

---

21. These writings are written in Korean.
22. Yi Sang-ryong, *Seokju yugo* (Collection of Manuscripts of Yi Sang-ryong) (Seoul: Korea University Press, 1973).
23. Refer to advertisements of the *Daehan maeil sinbo*, 30 January 1907.
24. *Daehan maeil sinbo*, 3 December 1908.

(On Evolution in European Civilization in the Nineteenth Century), and *Jinmyeong hwiron* (A Note on Progress). Of the books, the first four were advertised in the newly published book section of the *Korea Daily News*, in the advertisement column. Even though this writer has not seen any of the books in person, it is presumed that they were translations of books already published in Japan or China.[25] *On Evolution in European Civilization in the Nineteenth Century* was a translation of a book written by Chen Kuoyung, a Chinese scholar; and the translator was Yi Chae-u, who completed the work in April 1908. This book explained the process of evolution in European civilization in the nineteenth century. *A Note on Progress* was written and published by Yi Jong-tae in October 1906. In the preface to his book, the author admitted that he had referred to several books compiled by the Chinese and had discussions with his friend Kim Sang-cheon in order to publish this book. The books he referred to included the *Yinbingshi wenji* by Liang Qichao. Yi's book, divided into two parts, was written purely in Chinese characters; its contents enumerated such headings as races, geography, states, politics, law, religions, sciences, military affairs, and industry. It explained progress in each of these fields. This book can be considered as one that deals with social history. In the beginning of the first chapter, the author states that the reason why man is precious is that he is able to reform and evolve. As this statement shows, the contents of this book were based generally on Darwinism. The writer further introduced some of the treatises and books concerned with Darwinism; they were read widely and influenced Korean intellectuals in the last years of the Joseon dynasty.

As pointed out earlier, Darwinism was regarded as a challenge to the Christian doctrine and aroused public censure in the Western world because it was thought that Darwinism placed men, long believed to be God's creatures existing under his special grace, on a par with animals in terms of their origin. For this reason many tried to criticize and totally repudiate Darwinism.

In Korea, however, the situation was different. Even Christian followers did not criticize it. As they witnessed cases of encroachment by impe-

---

25. According to Masao Watanabe, *op. cit.*, p. 120, Japanese scholar Nagao Ariga wrote *Shakai shinkaron* (1883), *Shukyo shinkaron* (1883), and *Zokusei shinkaron* (1884). As the book with the same title of *Zokusei shinkaron* was published in Seoul in the last years of the Great Han Empire period, this writer advanced the presumption.

rial states that preyed upon weaker nations, Koreans came to accept Darwinism as a legitimate form of political thought. In an editorial on the subject, "Strengthening Ourselves with Spiritual Belief," the *Korea Daily News* said in its 1 December 1905 issue:

> Hundreds of millions of people live under heaven and on the globe, and they compete with each other on the basis of their power. For this reason, states as well as people can at no time avoid the law of survival of the fittest. Those nations in today's world which are not strong enough to protect themselves cannot enjoy due treatment and are apt to become servile to others, as well as being destined to ruin. Examples of this law are evident in our world; how can we aptly describe the horrible situation? There are visible self-strength and invisible self-strength. The former consists of financial and military power, while the latter is formed by spiritual belief . . . .

What the editorial asserted was that the Koreans should promote their invisible self-strength, namely, they should develop their religious life, if they were resolved to retain their national sovereignty. This assertion can be regarded as an effort to make Darwinism compatible with Christianity.

Exaltation of Political Consciousness

Tianyanlun, a translation by Yan Fu, observed that human society progresses in proportion to the degree of the man's conquest of nature and that because of the man's conquest of nature, Europe was able to achieve formidable wealth in the past 100 years. It went on to say that whereas the law of survival of the fittest has been applied to the natural world through struggle for existence, the human world is able to overcome it. This observation attests to the fact that Darwinism is connected with the concept of progress; and, in fact, Darwinism was understood in that manner in Korea. For instance, the *Korea Daily News* said in an editorial entitled, "Evolution and Downfall," carried on February 8, 1908:

> Darwinism can stimulate human minds, make people strive toward the goal of civilization with hope, and enable them to construct a golden country. On the other hand, the theory of the advent of the devil degenerates human minds, promotes despair in people and plunges

them into darkness and hell.

On August 1, 1909, the same newspaper said in an editorial, "An Outline of the *Theory of Evolution through Competition*":

> Generally observed, world civilization has suddenly accelerated the speed or its own progress since the nineteenth century. Progress achieved in one year now is greater than progress achieved in thousands of years in the past. Its force is like the onrushing flow of the Yellow River. With great rapidity, Europe has created a new world unprecedented in man's history. Who should be credited for this achievement? It is Darwin. Why should Darwin be credited for this achievement? It is because of his theory of evolution through competition. All scholars of the West and East before the emergence of Darwin judged human history with the word retrogression, preaching that modern people are inferior to ancient people and the contemporary world to the ancient world. This expresses the hope that the modern people would abide by the rules set forth by the ancients and strive to become servile to men of bygone days. With the emergence of Darwin, however, it was made clear that man is not retrogressing but progressing after research on the truth of the universe and historical precedents . . . .

In the above excerpts, the editorial stated that Darwin wrote the *Theory of Evolution through Competition*; but this was a mistake and the correct reference should be *The Origin of Species*. As Darwin's theory of evolution was based on struggles among individuals of the same species, the editorial made the mistake of citing his main work as the *Theory of Evolution through Competition* as a result of its overemphasis on struggle. As Darwinism was so closely connected with the concept of progress, it was believed that spreading his theory among the people would help to discard their old-fashioned fixed ideas and harbor a bright outlook on the future. However, as the social state of affairs that existed in Korea in the 1900s already had grown very critical, Darwinism failed to help the Korean people harbor a bright outlook on the future; instead, it aroused a strong political consciousness devoted to national salvation.

In the latter half of the 1890s, Philip Jaisohn (Seo Jae-pil) inaugurated the *Dongnip sinmun* (The Independent) and established the Dongnip Hyeophoe (Independence Club), for the purpose of awakening his compatriots to notions of independence and civil rights, and helping them understand, albeit inadequately, what conditions they were situated in, how their officials ran the country, and what rights the people were entitled to, as well as what duties they were obliged to discharge. Gradually the people became interested in politics. One notable result was that, when the Independence Club held a mass meeting of people to discuss problems facing the nation, they expressed their positive support of what was asserted by the association.

However, the support lasted but a short time and the people's concern with politics vanished after the Independence Club, after operating for two and a half years, was ordered by the government to close under a forcible measure in December 1898. An editorial by Jang Ji-yeon on the subject "The Situation of the Past," carried in the 11th issue of the *Korea Self-Strengthening Society Monthly* (published on May 25, 1907) lamented that the Korean people had remained reluctant to use the word "independence" for the past five or six years, with the result that their national spirit withered and their national rights were reduced to nothing, as Korea became an arena for competition between Russia and Japan.

The outbreak of the Russo-Japanese War in February 1904 subjected Korea to a more serious crisis. Some leaders who were concerned with politics came to the fore with the resolve to overcome the national crisis by rallying public opinion. Nevertheless, the number of people who were sufficiently awakened to the impending national peril was small at that time. Under these circumstances, intellectuals found it imperative for themselves to lead the vanguard of an enlightenment movement. Explaining the particular situation of the time, intellectuals asserted that the people should realize their time was one characterized by a struggle for existence. In a speech on the subject, "Struggle for Existence," Yun Hyo-jeong said:

> Every one of us should sense how severe the struggle for existence is as the current trends of the world have recently penetrated our country and the number of foreigners encroaching upon our country is increasing day by day in the wake of opening our ports. . . . The rule that the stronger wins and the weaker loses is observed in our daily life and it is an acknowledged practice in our time that the stronger preys upon the weaker. Observing the situation of our country, however, we cannot but feel regret. . . . If one does not know the rule of struggle for existence, one is apt to fall victim to the stronger. It should be asserted that our compatriots who live in the twentieth century should delve into the

essence of the law of struggle for existence.[26]

The intellectuals also explained to the people that their time was an imperialistic era. For instance, the *Korea Daily News* carried a series of editorials on the subject, "Modern People of the Twentieth Century," from February 22 to 27, 1910, one of which, titled "The Trend of the World," said:

> This is an imperialist world. The stronger victimizes the weaker and the bigger annexes the smaller; this was a practice prevalent in the primitive age. This trend has recently become fiercer, and we see an imperialist drama envelop the whole world. European powers with long whips are overrunning the world, invading Asia to the east, dividing Africa to the south, and occupying the Pacific. Wherever the Europeans make inroads, all the mountains and rivers tremble; wherever their flags flutter, heaven and earth change . . . .

In this manner, the intellectuals understood imperialism as an "-ism" dedicated to enlarging territory and national rights.[27] Imperialism was, in fact, rampant in the world in their time.

It was with such dismal terms as "triumph of the stronger and defeat of the weaker" and "survival of the fittest" that Darwinism explained the reality in which all nations competed with each other for survival and imperialism was rampant. It was natural, therefore, that those who were influenced by Darwinism seriously pondered over means of preserving their national sovereignty and safeguarding their nation. Under these circumstances, Bak Seong-heum wrote in an editorial, "On Patriotism," which was carried in the inaugural issue of the *Seou hakhoe wolbo* (Monthly of the Western Friends Academic Association) (published in December 1, 1906):

> Eventful is the world today. Some nations engulf others in a competition for civilization. The degree of civilization differs from one month to another and the situation is undergoing a rapid change. . . . In ancient times, the fall of a country merely resulted in a change of the ruler and the name of the country. Nowadays, however, it results in

---

26. Contained in the 11th issue of the *Daehan jaganghoe wolbo*, 25 May 1907.
27. Refer to the editorial on "Imperialism and Nationalism" (in Korean), *Daehan maeil sinbo*, 28 May 1907.

enslavement of its whole people and their persecution continues until all of them perish. If our people should incur such a disaster how horrible it would be . . .

Another editorial on "A Plan for Preserving Our Race," which appeared in the 31 July 1907 issue of the *Korea Daily News* said:

Alas! The national sovereignty of the Great Han Empire has been totally destroyed; there is no room for doing anything to remedy the situation. Left behind in the deprivation are our 20 million compatriots. Historical precedents show that, when a country is erased, its people cease to exist. Many words are not necessary to explain our present situation. Generally speaking, the rise and fall of a country depends on its entire people. Our 20 million compatriots cannot evade the responsibility for the loss of their national sovereignty . . . .

How did the Korean people try to overcome the national crisis? Intellectuals asserted that all the people should stick to nationalism. An editorial, in the same newspaper said in the May 28, 1909 issue, entitled "Imperialism and Nationalism":

What is the method for us to adopt in order to oppose imperialism? It is to display nationalism (which refuses intervention by other nations). Nationalism is the only way to safeguard our nation. . . . If our nationalism arms our people with heroic fortitude, imperialism will not encroach upon them no matter how fierce and sinister it might be, for it infiltrates only countries where nationalism is weak . . .

"Nationalism" as referred to here can be replaced with the concept of "national spirit." What the editorial asserted was that the Korean nation could survive only if its people were formidably armed with nationalism. Other intellectuals expressed nationalism as the spirit of Joseon or Great Han.[28] In order to uphold such a spirit, they found it necessary to assail individualism.[29]

---

28. Refer to Jang Ung-jin, "Discussing the Social Ego" (in Korean), carried in the seventh issue of the *Taegeuk hakbo*, 24 February 1907, and Bak Eun-sik, "A Writing of the Daehan Spirit in Blood" (in Korean), carried in the column of miscellaneous reports, *Daehan maeil sinbo*, 25 September 1907.
29. It was rejected thoroughly in an editorial on the subject, "Do Not Seek Your Life with Individualism" (in Korean), *Daehan maeil sinbo*, 21 November 1907.

Nevertheless, the crisis could not be overcome with national spirit alone. In an age of triumph for the stronger and defeat for the weaker, real ability counted most. In other words, the Korean people needed a movement to cultivate and amass their national ability on the basis of their national spirit. First of all, they needed to form organizations. Jang Ji-yeon said in an editorial, "Safeguarding the Nation Will Be Possible after Forming Organizations," which was carried in the *Korea Self-Strengthening Society Monthly*:

> Alas! Our sacred nation is now deprived of any hope for its own protection for the first time in its 4,000-year history. Foreseeable is its downfall and disappearance. That the stronger wins and the weaker loses is a self-evident truth of the world. That the inferior, the ignorant, the isolated, and the weaker are destined to be defeated and experience downfall, succumbing to the superior, the united, and the stronger is the law of natural selection. . . . If our people exert themselves further while reflecting on their being fettered and enslaved, then discard all their chronic mental disease, cease their indulgence in jealousy, remove their habit of relying on others in idleness, and, instead, rise up with patriotism and unite themselves with the resolve to serve the common good, they will surely achieve the task of strengthening. This is the only way of strengthening and safeguarding themselves. Cooperation in unity will protect our human rights from encroachment and our nation from bondage. This will also insure our independent national sovereignty safe from any foreign intervention. One effect of forming organizations is to keep our nation intact. . . .[30]

In response to the call, many organizations were formed. The following is a list of such political organizations:

1. Boanhoe (Korea Preservation Society) formed in July 1904 by Song Su-man, formerly a member of the Privy Council
2. Gungminhoe (Korean National Association) in September, with Yi Jung-jin as its leader
3. Hyeopdonghoe (Cooperative Association) in the same month, with Yi Jun, Yi Sang-jae, and Yi Dong-hui as its leaders
4. Gongjinhoe (Society of Common Progress) in December, led by Yi Jun, Na Yu-seok, and Yun Hyo-jeong

---

30. Contained in the fifth issue of the *Daehan janganghoe wolbo*, 25 November 1908.

5. Heonjeong Yeonguhoe (Constitutional Government Research Society) formed in May 1905, with Yi Jun as its chairman
6. Daehan Jaganghoe (Korea Self-Strengthening Society) in April 1906 by Jang Ji-yeon
7. Daehan Hyeophoe (Korea Association) in November 1907 by O Se-chang
8. Sinminhoe (New People's Association), a secret organization, in 1907 by Yang Gi-tak, An Chang-ho, Yi Dong-hwi, Yi Seung-hun, and Sin Chae-ho.

Many of these political organizations were, needless to say, subjected to suppression by imperial Japan and forced to disband some months after their formation. However, they could win popular support on a broad scale beyond any comparison with that given to the Independence Association (Dongniphoe); and they could exert far greater influence on the people.

Moreover, a number of academic circles were formed in order to promote education. Concerned with the necessity of education, Bak Sang-yong wrote an editorial (carried in the 10th issue of the *Bulletin of the Taegeuk Association* dated May 25, 1907) on the subject, entitled "No National Survival with Obscure Education":

> Western scholars say that struggle for existence is the self-evident truth on earth and it is the law of the world that the superior wins and the inferior loses. Their science is just like the above saying. Like their science, the Western powers are omnipresent around the world today, boasting of their skills, sharpening their claws, their activities overrunning the five oceans and the six continents, rushing to the east and to the west without restraint, engulfing the weaker . . . . The twentieth century was born out of competition and forces every nation to choose between death or life. Now we must ponder. In what condition is Korea situated and what treatment is she receiving? If we do not learn and ask, our old custom will repeat itself and we shall not be able to preserve our national independence. If our nation is to prosper, we must discard our easy-going attitude and go to the West for study. The prosperity of our 4,000-year-old fatherland and the destiny of our 20 million people rest on the shoulders of our youth. Without postponing until tomorrow, our young men should do anything they are resolved to do today . . .

In September 1905, Gungmin Gyoyukhoe (Society of National Education) was organized, followed by the Western Friends Academic Association in October 1906, with Bak Eun-sik (1859–1926) and others as the promoters. Hanbuk Heunghakhoe (Hanbuk Association for the Promotion of Education) in the same month on the initiative of Yi Jun and Yi Dong-hwi, the latter two integrating themselves into Seobuk Hakhoe (Northwestern Academic Association) on August 1st of that year. In July 1907, Honam Hakhoe (Jeolla Academic Association) and Hoseo Hakhoe (Chungcheong Academic Association) came into being, followed by Giho Heunghakhoe (Seoul Association for the Promotion of Education) in January 1908, Gwandong Hakhoe (Gwandong Academic Association) in March, and Gyonam Hakhoe (Southeastern Academic Association) at around that time. Besides these provincial educational organizations, pan-national ones were organized, such as Heungsadan (Young Korean Academy) established by An Chang-ho and Yeoja Gyoyukhoe (Association for Women's Education) by Jin Hak-sin. In addition, Korean students studying in Japan also organized their own academic associations. The representative organizations being the Taegeuk Hakhoe (Taegeuk Association), the Gongsu Hakhoe (Joint Learning Association), and the Dongin Hakhoe (Comrades' Academic Association). These educational organizations, on the one hand, operated schools, and on the other, published educational journals, thereby promoting the people's zeal for education and knowledge. According to official statistics, more than 3,000 private schools were established at that time, reaping a great result in education.

At the same time, the development of industry was considered essential if the nation was to be able to cultivate its real ability. This necessity was well emphasized in a statement explaining the purpose of the Korea Self-Strengthening Society organized by Jang Ji-yeon and Yun Hyo-jeong in 1906:

> Whether this country can preserve its sovereignty or not depends on how strong it becomes. Because it did not devise means of strengthening itself and its people remained ignorant . . . our country has finally faced this adversity and crisis of becoming a protectorate of a foreign nation . . . . If we make our country wealthy and strong, we shall be able to restore our national sovereignty. Now is the time for us to strive further. A means of strengthening ourselves is nothing but to promote education and industry. Without developing education, our people will remain in the state of being unenlightened; without developing industry, we shall not be able to make our country wealthy.

There is no other way to enlighten the people's wisdom and cultivate our national strength than to promote education and industry . . . .[31]

Factories were established in accordance with the call for industrial development. One example was a porcelain company set up by the New People's Association in Masan-dong, Pyeongyang. Observed generally, however, the reality was that industry could not be promoted as much as education. Industry can be developed only with a sufficient amount of capital, technology, and facilities. However, Korea lacked all of these at that time. Be that as it may, this movement (often called the patriotic enlightenment movement) developed with a positive response from the people who cultivated modern political consciousness in themselves.

Advocacy of the Ideology of New People

Another result of their acceptance of Darwinism was their advocacy of the "ideology of new people." The ideology was dedicated to the aim of renewing our people's spirit and stance. The intellectuals believed that in order to overcome the national crisis of their time, it was imperative above all to renew the people's spirit. What they advocated, in a sense, was a spiritual or moral reform.

Liang Qichao had direct influence on the intellectuals in this movement as well. As explained earlier, Liang, who exiled himself to Japan in 1898, went to the United States and returned to Japan in 1902. In Japan, he published the *Xinmin congbao*. In this magazine, he made public his discourse on a new people under the serial title "Xinminshuo," advocating his ideology of a new people. He preached that the most urgent task for China of his time was to discuss what a new people should be like. He also believed that the law of survival of the fittest could benefit the Chinese if they promoted the ideology of a new people. He emphasized the concept of "new people" in the course of discussing public morality, nationalist thought, progressiveness, adventurism, rights, liberty, self-rule, development, and self-esteem.[32]

His theory of the "new people" came to be widely known among Korean intellectuals and won their response after the *Xinmin congbao*

---

31. Contained in the inaugural issue of the *Daehan jaganghoe wolbo*, 31 July 1906.
32. Liang Qichao, "Xinminshuo," in *Yinbingshi wenji*, vol. 1.

and *Yinbingshi wenji* found their way to Korea. The *Korea Daily News* was the first to carry an editorial on the subject, "Korea Urgently Needs New People," in the 5 July 1910 issue, which asserted:

Our 20 million compatriots, throwing blame on each other, are heading toward self-destruction. On whom can our country rely to insure its survival? What we intend to achieve with the new people is to renew ourselves. Our government is called on to renew politics and our people to renew their knowledge. We must renew ourselves by our own efforts without waiting for others to come to help us renew ourselves. . . . If we renew ourselves, we can expect a new system and new politics. After observing the peoples of England, America, France, and Germany at their capitals, especially their relations with their governments, Liang Qichao once said that their manner of running their cities and hamlets, their manner of managing their parties and schools, and their manner of governing themselves as individuals were as orderly as that which one could find in the government of a well-run country. And that their peoples being so, the governments of the countries in Europe and America could rely on them and they, in return, could rely on their governments. Because the people of Korea, to the contrary, relied on others, they were thrown into this national crisis. If, however, they discard their attitude of reliance and are infused with modern thought, they will be able to create a new world.

Advocating the ideology of a new people, the Korean intellectuals began to open a barrage of criticism against old learning and old thought. They stressed that as long as the Koreans were infatuated with old learning and old thought, they would never become a new people. An essay on the subject, "Distinction between New and Old Learning," said it succinctly:

All civilized nations of the world have become as powerful as they are due to new learning. Despite the fact that the effect of the old learning is naught, some obstinate people still do not wake up from their long slumber and hold fast to the old learning. With this attitude, they try to maintain their existence in this age of competition. This can be likened to an attitude of wanting to pluck morning dew but waiting until the midday. Our young men and women should exert themselves and make progress in absorbing new learning now.[33]

---

33. Seou Hakhoe, *Seou* (Western Friends) 1.8 (1 January 1909).

At the same time, the intellectuals assailed conservatives who adhered to the old learning and old ways of thinking. In an essay on the subject, "An Educational Method Employed by a Country Corresponds to the Degree of Its Civilization," Kim Won-guk said:

> . . . people who adhere to things old ask what the relation is between the new learning and the old order and how we can utilize the new learning. It is as if summer worms talk about ice and toads confined to a well talk about the sea . . . . Such persons can hardly imagine how the world is changing, not knowing the current of the times that the six continents are exchanging with each other, people of all races are intermingling with each other. The Western influence is making an inroad into the East, the stronger prey on the weaker, and everything is being renewed.[34]

In other words, the monthly magazine urged the conservatives to open their eyes to the currents of the time. The progressives attacked the conservatives mainly because they held blind obedience to the teachings of Confucian sages and to the Confucian scriptures. In an editorial, "Science Can Progress Only after the Servile Spirit Is Removed," dated August 4, 1909, the *Korea Daily News* said:

> Holding fast to the teachings of old sages, the conservatives regard them as true as the Ten Commandments, refusing to add one word to them or strike out even one word. This attitude constitutes one evil practice we find among oriental scholars. Some say that it reflects the broad-mindedness of gentlemen; but it poses the most serious obstacle to the progress of human knowledge . . . .

The same newspaper editorialized further on the subject, in a piece called "A Warning to Conservatives," carried in the 26 July 1910 issue:

> Although more than 30 years have passed since the modern trend reached this country, the manners and customs of our people are still corrupt and our people's knowledge is still far from being enlightened. A group of conservatives emerged out of this situation. . . . The world has entered an age of struggle for existence and no one can devise a means of checking the change or the times and blocking the progress of human knowledge with his queer vision and his limited imagination.

---

34. *Ibid.* 1.1 (1 June 1908).

Propriety and art are of no use in this world and trying to cultivate good manners is also of no use. What is essential for us is to nurture our real strength and not to concede our rights to others. We must wake up from an obstinate slumber and foresee the eventuality that lightning and sleet befall us . . . .

In short, the editorial censured unreserved reverence of Confucian sages and scriptures, as such things would pose the greatest obstacle to progress. Since such reverence sprang from a servile spirit, the editorial warned, learning alone could enable progress to be made and a new people to be created only after servitude was removed.

Confronted with the criticism against the old learning and conservatism, the older faction resisted. Disputes arose between the two, which lasted for some time. The conservatives asserted that no one could erase the old learning at will, as the progressives were trying to do. In a monthly published through their academic institute, Daedong Hakhoe (Great Unity Association), the conservatives maintained that there was neither new nor old in learning if one aspired to learn the new learning.[35] They even went so far as to claim that trying to create new people actually was part of a plot to undermine the gallant spirit of the people and make them docile. The progressive intellectuals responded that this was groundless slander. For instance, the *Korea Daily News* editorialized about the subject in "New People of Korea," on June 4, 1909:

It is repeatedly urged that we must create new people. What kind of people can be called new people? Are they docile people? No. Docility leads to cowardice, cowardice to retrogression, retrogression to defeat, and defeat to extinction. To try to create a docile people at this time when the East and the West are soaked in bloody rain can be likened to setting sheep free among a herd of ravenous tigers. Are they serene people? No. Serenity leads to conservatism, conservatism to effeteness, effeteness to defeat, and defeat to extinction. To try to create serene people can be likened to leaving a sleeping person in a pool of gushing water. What should our new people be like? They should be serious and forward-moving people. Why? Because without being serious no

---

35. Sin Gi-son published "There Is Neither New Nor Old in Learning" and Song Nak-hyeon "If One Wants New Learning, One Must First Study Old Learning" in *Daedong hakhoe wolbo* (25 June 1908). The dispute between old and new learning found its way even to classroom compositions. Pertaining to this point, refer to *Janghak wolbo* 1.3 (March 1908).

people can fight gallantly in order to safeguard their survival in this age of rampaging swords and devils. These days, vicious persons dazzle the minds of our people and frustrate their spirit by advocating their slogan to create docile and serene people. How dangerous the effect of their deed will be! It is their delusion, and they are determined to lead Korea to extinction. What they aim at is to create people who are destined to perish . . .

Some intellectuals were not satisfied with this kind of poignant criticism against the old learning and the conservatives. Taking one step further, they came to assert that all the traditions and old thoughts should be destroyed. If the Korean people were truly eager for progress, they asserted, they had to first thoroughly destroy these outdated thoughts and traditions, for a mere partial revision would not help them realize their objective. Especially at this moment, they said, destruction was inevitable. The sooner the destruction, the earlier bliss would come. In an editorial on "The Age of Destruction," the above-cited newspaper commented on July 30, 1910:

Here is a large house whose thousand-year-old roof-tiles are eroded by the wear and tear of time, whose windows are broken, and whose fences are mined, hard for anyone to live in. If a new building is ever to be constructed on the site, we must first destroy the old edifice with a giant axe. Korea is a 4,000-year-old country. Even though the manners and customs of our people are not impure and our politics is not turbid, it is likely that evils will ensue if customs and politics get old. Old institutions have degraded our people and weakened their national strength to such an extent that people now do not behave like people and the country does not act true to its mission. Is it right for a great hero, if he emerges among us and aspires to govern the country by resorting to extraordinary means, to follow the old order and adopt temporary measures? No. If we do not perform an operation on the diseased part but try to infuse vigor into the patient with the tonic herb of ginseng, the disease will further develop and become incurable. There is no civilized nation that did not experience an age of destruction . . . .[36]

The progressive intellectuals organized the New People's Association in

---

36. Liang Qichao published an article "Destructionism." He asserted that Japan's progress after the Meiji Restoration was due to destruction. Refer to Liang Qichao, "Tanzong," in *Yinbingshi wenji*, vol. 2.

secret. The group was organized by An Chang-ho, who returned home from the United States in 1907, and his colleagues who included Yang Gi-tak, Yi Gap, Yi Dong-hwi, An Tae-guk, and Im Chi-jeong. In 1908 and 1909, the New People's Association established the Daeseong School, Taegeuk Publishing House, and Cheongnyeon Haguhoe (The Youth Academic Fraternity) as sister organizations. What is immediately noticeable here is the connection between the prospectuses of the New People's Association and the Youth Academic Fraternity. As the New People's Association was organized in secret, its prospectus was not made public. However, we can presume what it was like by referring to An Chang-ho's appeal to the nation at that time. He told the people:

1. Independence cannot be won with the help of others; it can be realized only when we cultivate ourselves to possess the requirements for it. An independence that we win by ourselves will last forever.
2. We can display our abilities when we become honest and true through moral training, and when each of us learns one skill in technical or academic fields.
3. We should fortify our national unity by dedicating ourselves to fidelity and cooperation.[37] Similar contents can be found in the prospectus of the Youth Academic Fraternity.[38]

It seems that An Chang-ho also sympathized with what was asserted by Liang Qichao. In other words, An Chang-ho may have believed that what Liang advocated for China could be applied to Korea. Such an assertion can be supported by the fact that An Chang-ho adopted Liang's *Yinbingshi wenji* as a textbook for his Daeseong School. The following episode also offers support for this:

An aspirant from a southern district visited An Chang-ho and asked him what he should do first for the nation. An Chang-ho replied: "It is not that only great achievements can benefit the country. I advise you to acquire several copies of Liang Qichao's *Yinbingshi wenji* and give them to famous scholars in your district. By doing so, you will contribute to the country.[39]

It also seems that, among writings contained in the *Yinbingshi wenji*, An

37. *An Dosan jeonseo*, p. 71.
38. The prospectus was printed in *Daehan maeil sinbo*, 17 August 1909.
39. *An Dosan jeonseo*, p. 87.

liked Liang's theory of "new people" most. This assumption is founded on the fact that An Chang-ho named his association New People's Association. In other words, he founded the society in order to promote the ideology of the new people among his brethren and encourage them to practice it.

Immediately after the annexation of Korea in 1910, the Japanese Empire fabricated the so-called Case of the One Hundred Five (Baegoin Sageon) to arrest and suppress members of the New People's Association. The association was disbanded and all the projects it had been undertaking were permanently suspended. In 1913 An Chang-ho organized Heungsadan (Young Korean Academy) and adopted the slogan of "putting into practice what is essential" for the new society that inherited the spirit of the New People's Association. The Young Korean Academy continues to exist to this date.

Establishment of a Nationalistic View of History

By assimilating Darwinism, and through the process of discussing means of overcoming the national crisis, Korean people's historical consciousness reached a greater height, as the people were not allowed to take the reality of their crisis-stricken existence lightly.

In this way, we should not overlook efforts made by historians to heightening our people's consciousness of history. The historians taught the people how precious national history was to them and stressed that they should learn about it. In this way, Sin Chae-ho expounded on the subject in the article, "Relations between History and Patriotism," carried in the third issue of the *Daehan hyeophoe wolbo* (Korea Association Monthly) (published on June 25, 1908):

> What is history? Why is it regarded as sacred? History is an actual record of all happenings in the process of a nation's rise and fall. A nation that has a brilliant history is certain to prosper . . . . There are many nations and so there are many histories. To read the history of a foreign country may help us understand it and compete with it, but it merely provides subsidiary assistance in stirring up patriotism in our hearts, short of playing a leading role in it. What I mean when I talk about history is our national history. History is as complicated as phenomena; and so mere is history of religion, history of literature, and so on. Knowledge of this kind of history that deals with specific aspects

may contribute to the country and promote patriotism, but it is unable to conceive patriotism. What I mean by history is, therefore, the history of our country's politics. Being sacred, it is able to help our people build a grand pavilion of politics through self-awakening . . . .[40]

Sin Chae-ho also encouraged the people to read avidly in order to know about Korean history. Historians of that period besought the people to cultivate burning patriotism in their hearts because they believed that patriotism would surely enable them to firmly preserve their national sovereignty. They recommended that people read books of national history in order to nurture patriotism. The historians who took the lead in this manner in promoting patriotism or consciousness of national identity among our people are called nationalist historians by our present standard of classification. Their view of history had distinct characteristics. Their predecessors, namely, scholars of the School of Practical Learning (Silhakpa), who were active in the eighteenth century, arranged their encyclopedic knowledge centering around dynasties in describing history. They were also swayed by a moralist view of history, even though they too endeavored to overcome the heavily China-centered view and write a history of Korea in a right manner. The nationalist historians, unlike their predecessors, described national history with a nationalist view springing from the desire to help the nation overcome the adversity it faced. Sin said in another work:

> If someone asks where, with what books, and how we should study our history, the answer must be a hard one. Be that as it may, I will tell my own experience. Indignant at the national shame of 16 years ago, I read *Dongguk tonggam* (Comprehensive Mirror of the Eastern Kingdom) thoroughly for the first time and undertook to write *Daedong sacheonnyeonsa* (Four-Thousand-Year History of Korea) in the style of evaluation at the request of scores of students. I wrote it in the pattern of Chinese story telling as a compromise between a book of history and a novel. An accident, however, suspended it.[41]

The term "national shame" was referring to the conclusion of a protec-

---

40. Compilation Committee of the Complete Works of Sin Chae-ho, comp., *Danjae Sin Chae-ho jeonjip* (Complete Works of Sin Chae-ho), vol. 2 (Seoul: Eul Yoo Publishing Co., 1972).

41. Sin Chae-ho, *Joseon sanggosa* (Early History of Korea), vol. 1 (Seoul: Samsung Foundation of Culture, 1977).

torate treaty with Japan in November 1905. In his case, too, a historical study began with the desire to help the nation overcome the adversity it faced. The fact that he began to write the history of Korea in the style of evaluation meant that his primary aim was to interpret historical events rather than simply sequentially arrange them. This again meant that Sin studied history, even as he remained realistically conscious of the issues of his time.

As is widely known, besides Sin, both Bak Eun-sik and Jang Ji-yeon were representative nationalist historians as well. Early in their careers both Bak and Jang launched their activities in journalism. While writing newspaper columns, they also wrote papers on history. Both entered the *Hwangseong sinmun* as editors-in-chief in 1898 and Sin followed them in 1905. Bak and Sin moved to the *Yuenan wangguoshi* (Fall of Vietnam) in 1906. They were also active in academic and social organizations. For instance, when leaders hailing from the Pyeongan district organized the Western Friends Academic Association, Bak was invited to the post of editor-in-chief for its *Monthly of the Western Friends Academic Association*. When the Western Friends Academic Association and the Gwanbuk Association for the Promotion of Education (Gwanbuk Heunghakhoe) merged into the Northwestern Academic Association, he was again named editor-in-chief for the *Monthly of the Western Friends Academic Association*, for which he wrote many articles. Jang was named editor-in-chief at the *Sisa jeongbo* (Information on Current Topics) in 1899. Subsequently, he was a member of the editorial staff of the *Joyangbo* in 1906, editor-in-chief at the *Haejo sinmun* (Mainstream) in 1908 after his self-exile to Siberia, as well as being the editor-in-chief at the *Gyeongnam ilbo* upon his return in 1909.

They believed that history and journalism had deep mutual relations. Jang looked on newspapers as *sillok* (veritable records) of the past, while he saw newspapermen as government historians of the past. Concerning this point, he wrote:

> Today's newspaper company holds the position of yesterday's chief historian; therefore, its responsibility is very heavy. Newspapermen should be prudent and fair when they write commentaries in order to meet the expectation of the public.[42]

---

42. The National Institute of Korean History, comp., *Wiam mun-go*, vol. 7 (Seoul: The National Institute of Korean History, 1956).

They in fact wrote editorials with this very posture, establishing their nationalist view of history in the course of their editorials. Even though the major works of Bak Eun-sik and Sin Chae-ho, who launched their activities in earnest as historians, were made public after they exiled themselves abroad following Korea's annexation by Japan in 1910, their views of history were shaped during the years when they wrote editorials for the *Imperial Capital News* and *Korea Daily News*. They did not confine themselves to their home libraries for static research into historical data but engaged in historical studies in close connection with practice. While serving the *Korea Daily News* as editor-in-chief, Sin wrote articles on history such as "Yi Sun-sin silgi" (A Biography of Admiral Yi Sun-sin), "Dongguk gogeol Choe Do-tong jeon" (A Biography of Choe Do-tong, Great Man of Korea), and *Doksa sillon* (A New Reading of History).

These nationalist historians were as greatly influenced by Liang Qichao as ordinary Korean intellectuals of that time. They utilized *Yinbingshi wenji* as if it were a reference book when they wrote editorials and translated Liang's works into Korean.

Together with Darwinism,[43] Korean intellectuals naturally introduced Liang's theory of new history, which tried to explain historical happenings and realities on the basis of Darwinism. Liang once defined history as a science whose task was to seek out a set of principles that governs phenomena of evolution in human organizations.[44] He believed that the science of history should be concerned more with evolution of human organizations and with evolution of human individuals. Judging from these facts, it can be said that Liang's theory of new history attached importance to evolution and organizations.[45]

Liang's greatest concern was with the question of how to reform Chinese government and society. According to Liang, Chinese history could be dated as follows: The period before Huangdi was an age of barbaric liberty, while the period from Huangdi to Shi Huangdi could be characterized as an age of aristocratic imperial rule. The period from Shi

---

43. Nationalist historians wrote many articles on the influence of Darwinism. One example is Bak Eun-sik, "Without Rise in Education, Existence Cannot Be Insured" (in Korean), in the inaugural issue of *Seou hakhoe wolbo*.

44. Liang Qichao, "Shixue zhixue shuo," in *Yinbingshi wenji*, vol. 2.

45. This is pointed out in Hidemi Onogawa, *op. cit.*, p. 269.

Huangdi to Emperor Qianlong was an age in which royal powers had reached its peak prosperity, and the period after Emperor Qianlong was an age of civilized liberty.[46] This dating suggests that Liang believed that China should enter an age of civilized liberty. The greatest concern of Korea's nationalist historians was the reality facing their country that its sovereignty was on the verge of extinction in the whirlpool of aggression by imperialist powers. From Liang's concept of "human organizations," the nationalist historians of Korea extracted the concept of "nation"; from Liang's concept of "evolution," they extracted the concept of "struggle for existence." The Korean historians were concerned first with the task of examining how the Korean nation developed itself in the course of struggle against other nations.

In short, "nation" and "struggle" occupied the central position in the nationalist view of history. They believed that without nation or struggle no history could be made. On relations between nation and history, Sin Chae-ho had the following to say in *A New Reading of History*:

> The history of a nation describes how it underwent vicissitudes, which led it either to prosperity or to downfall. Without a nation there is no history. Without history no nation can stay faithful to the state. How heavy the responsibility of historians is. . . .

On competition, Bak Eun-sik said in an editorial titled, "Our Business Develops through Competition," carried in *Seobuk hakhoe wolbo* (Monthly of the Northwestern Academic Association, vol. 3, no. 16):

> Our business is based on motive force and its result is measured primarily by rebounding force. A competitive spirit is the springboard for the rebounding force. If one is not sufficiently armed with a competitive spirit in case one's products are similar to those produced by others and one has to contend with others, one is destined to succumb to others, not to speak of the eventuality that one's business will wither. Various European businesses far surpass the scope of Oriental businesses because there are many countries in the Occidental world and they compete together furiously. If one concedes even a little to others in business, one cannot insure one's existence according to the law of survival of the fittest. Each of the European nations strives to steal a march upon others in invention by scientists and in production by

---

46. Liang Qichao, *Yinbingshi wenji*, vol. 1.

businessmen, with the result that the Europeans have developed wealthy civilization. This is truly an age of struggle for existence . . . .[47]

As they advocated "nation," it was natural for the nationalist historians to become concerned with the spiritual aspect. This is because they believed that the nation would become almost dead if its people were not alive spiritually. One typical writing on this subject was Bak Eun-sik's "The Daehan Spirit." In connection with the national spirit, the historians turned their attention to heroes and advocated hero-worship. This is because they believed that only heroes could embody the national spirit. In an article on the subject, "I Read a Rubbed Copy of the Monument of Goguryeo King Yeongnak," carried in the *Monthly of the Northwestern Academic Association* (vol. 1, no. 9), Bak Eun-sik said:

> History embodies the spirit of a nation and heroes are its vigor. I observe that all nations in the world, if they do not consist of barbaric villages but are founded on institutions and their people are well qualified, respect their history and worship their heroes. To respect the national history and worship national heroes lead to love of the country.[48]

In the preface to "Eulji Mundeok," Sin Chae-ho said:

> The land of a country was made solemn by the self-sacrifice of its heroes and its people were protected by their bloodshed. Their spirit is as lofty as mountains and their contribution to the nation is as bottomless as the sea. If the people do not recognize their heroes, it would be hard for them to safeguard their national sovereignty. . . . Heroes should emerge among our people.[49]

In the conclusion of the book, he disclosed his earnest desire to see heroes appear in our country. Sin wrote biographies of heroes such as Eulji Mundeok, Choe Yeong, and Yi Sun-sin, who fought invaders to defend their country.

Either immediately before or just after Japan annexed Korea, Bak Eun-sik and Sin Chae-ho exiled themselves abroad. Wandering from

---

47. Institute of Oriental Studies, Dankook University, comp., *Bak Eun-sik jeonseo* (Complete Works of Bak Eun-sik), vol. 2 (Seoul: Dankook University Press, 1975).
48. *Ibid.*
49. *Danjae Sin Chae-ho jeonjip*, vol. 2.

one place to another, they devoted themselves wholeheartedly to the struggle for independence while continuing their historical studies with great zeal. Bak specialized mainly in modern history and Sin studied ancient history. Results of their studies were *Hanguk tongsa* (The Tragic History of Korea) and *Hanguk dongnip undong-ji hyeolsa* (The Bloody History of the Korean Independence Movement), published in Shanghai by Bak, the former in 1915 and the latter in 1920. The *Joseonsa yeongu cho* (Exploratory Studies in Korean History) and *Joseon sanggosa* (Early History of Korea) were authored and published by Sin, the former in 1925 and the latter in 1931. Their manuscripts were sent to the home country and published in Korea through the *Dong-a Ilbo* and *Chosun Ilbo*.

Their view of history had become far more refined, for, as a result or their arduous research of much data they had collected, it had integrated not only the modern methodology of the Western science of history, but also Western sociological thought. We can find how refined it was if we make a comparison, in the case of Sin, between *A New Reading of History* written before the annexation and *Early History of Korea* written after the annexation.

They clung to their principle that one should view history with "nation" and "competition (or struggle)" as the main themes. The view of history that they molded into shape while writing editorials at the *Imperial Capital News* and *Korea Daily News* was observed strictly in their subsequent historical studies, or, to put it more exactly, had even developed in them.

Conclusion

It was mainly in its sociological aspect—the Social Darwinist aspect— that Darwinism was introduced to Korean intellectuals in the last years of the Joseon dynasty, entering Korea mainly through Liang Qichao's *Yinbingshi wenji*. It was in the 1900s that Koreans began to accept the theory in earnest, when an age of imperialism had been sweeping across the world. As Korea was about to fall, her intellectuals could readily accept Darwinism, which taught the rule that the weaker fall prey to the stronger and only the fittest could survive. In the West, on the other hand, Darwinism was understood as denying the Christian doctrine of creation and gave rise to fierce controversy. In Korea, on the contrary, even Christians accepted it as a legitimate and new strain of political thought, and tried to seek coexistence between Christianity and Darwinism.

We may cite a strong political consciousness dedicated to national salvation, as one influence of Darwinism in Korea. The political consciousness spurred Koreans to form various political organizations, academic societies, and private schools, as well as to launch patriotic enlightenment movements.

Among some Korean intellectuals, there arose the ideology of the new people. They asserted that to renew the national spirit and stance was essential for saving the nation from the dire crisis it confronted. They fired a barrage of criticism at old learning, old thought, and the conservative faction that they thought would be a barrier to the spread of the ideology of new people. Ideological disputes ensued when the conservatives counterattacked.

Darwinism also stirred up historical consciousness among the Korean people, leading to a new view of history with which nationalist historians tried to help the nation overcome the adversity it was experiencing. In short, Darwinism helped these scholars establish a nationalist view of history having "nation" and "competition (or struggle)" as main themes.

Japanese Challenge and Korean Response, 1876–1910:
A Brief Historical Survey

Lew Young Ick

Introduction

For more than two and a half centuries following the traumatic Japanese invasion of Korea in 1592–1598, Joseon Korea (1392–1910) and Tokugawa Japan (1600–1868) maintained harmonious bilateral relations. This long concord in Korean-Japanese relations was disrupted and broken by the rise of expansionism in Japan following the Meiji Restoration of 1868. During the ensuing forty years, Japan's new leaders forced an unequal treaty upon Korea, intervened in Korean domestic affairs, exploited the Korean market for economic gain, fought two major wars with continental powers to wrest away and retain control over the Korean peninsula, which finally culminated in an outright annexation.

The history of Korean-Japanese relations from 1870 through 1910 was characterized by an aggressive Japanese challenge and a feeble Korean response. This essay is intended as a brief survey of Korean-Japanese

* Originally published in the *Korea Journal*, vol. 25, no. 12 (December 1985).

Lew Young Ick (Yu, Yeong-ik) is Chair of Korean Studies at the Graduate School of International Studies, Yonsei University. He obtained his Ph.D. in History and East Asian Languages from Harvard University in 1972. He is the author of a number of books and articles, including *Gabo gyeongjang yeongu* (A Study on the Reforms of 1894) (1990), *Korea Old and New: A History* (1990, coauthored), *Donghak nongmin bonggi-wa gabo gyeongjang* (Donghak Peasant Uprising and the Reforms of 1894) (1998), and *Jeolmun nal-ui Yi Seungman* (Youthful Syngman Rhee) (2002). E-mail: yilew@yonsei.ac.kr.

interaction during this period, in the framework of challenge and response, with emphasis on such key events as the signing of the Korean-Japanese Treaty of Ganghwa in 1876, the abortive pro-Japanese coup of 1884, the Sino-Japanese War of 1894–1895, the Russo-Japanese War of 1904–1905, and the Japanese annexation of Korea in 1910.

The Opening of Korea by Japan, 1876

Joseon Korea and Tokugawa Japan enjoyed peaceful relations with each other from the early 1600s to the 1870s, each party adhering to a policy of restricted contact with the other. Korea sent a total of eleven diplomatic-cultural missions, styled the *tongsinsa*, literally "communication embassy," to the shogunal capital of Edo (modern Tokyo) from 1609 to 1764. It permitted only a specified number of Japanese officials and merchants from Tsushima to visit Busan for diplomacy and trade at a trading compound called the *waegwan* (Japanese office). No Japanese imperial or shogunal envoy was allowed access to the Korean capital. Since the restriction of state-to-state contacts was the norm in premodern East Asia, neither Joseon Korea nor Tokugawa Japan had legitimate cause for complaint about this bilateral arrangement.

Japan took the initiative to alter this time-honored traditional arrangement immediately after the Meiji Restoration. Since Japan had already signed modern treaties with the United States, Great Britain, France, Russia, and Holland in the 1850s, leaders of the Meiji government wished to place Japanese-Korean relations on a similar footing. They adopted an aggressive stance toward Korea for a variety of other reasons: fear of Russian encroachment upon the Korean peninsula, the desire for enough profit to make up for losses Japan was certain to sustain in trade with Western nations, the political necessity of finding an outlet for the newly disenfranchised samurai, and the chauvinistic impulse to spread Japan's "imperial glory" abroad. Accordingly, the Meiji government sought negotiations with the Korean government by sending a stream of envoys to Korea for the purpose of establishing new, modern relations with that country.

Korea, under the rule of the xenophobic Daewongun ("the Prince of the Great Court": Yi Ha-eung, 1820–1898), father of the reigning boy king, Gojong (1852–1919; r. 1864–1907), consistently rejected the Japanese overtures, as it had done to the French and American overtures in

1866 and 1871. This unyielding attitude on the part of the Korean government eventually led to a series of policy debates on Korea in the high council of the Japanese government, which culminated in the so-called Seikanron ("the conquer Korea proposal") in the fall of 1873. Although the proponents of Seikanron failed to carry the day, the Meiji oligarchs by no means abandoned their aggressive design toward Korea. Under the leadership of Okubo Toshimichi (1830–1878), the Japanese government adopted a policy of forcing the "benighted" Korean leadership to accept Japanese demands, resorting to gunboat diplomacy, in emulation of the humiliating example set by the Americans in exacting the Treaty of Kanagawa from Japan in 1854. It sent a naval vessel, the *Unyo*, to a heavily guarded area on the Korean coast in the fall of 1875 for the purpose of provocation. Using the resultant hostile Korean reaction as pretext, it dispatched a formidable squadron of six warships and 800 men in the following February escorting Lieutenant General Kuroda Kiyotaka (1840–1900), the chief Japanese negotiator whose mission was to dictate a Western-style treaty to Korea. This set the stage for the conclusion of the Treaty of Ganghwa on February 26, 1876.

The Daewongun was no longer at the helm of the Korean government when the Kuroda mission reached Ganghwa Island. Instead, his weak-willed son, King Gojong, had to decide whether or not Korea should accept the Japanese demand. After a series of conferences with his confused councilors, the king yielded to Japanese pressure and ordered his plenipotentiary at Ganghwa, Sin Heon (1810–1888), to sign the Japanese drafted treaty. The timely advice of a Chinese (Qing's) imperial envoy, who arrived in Seoul in mid-February, "not to go to extremes with Japan" to the king seems to have influenced the royal decision to sign the treaty with Japan. Needless to say, the Daewongun and conservative officials opposed the treaty and launched an eleventh-hour campaign to block it, but to no avail.

The twelve-article Treaty of Ganghwa was a modern, unequal treaty modeled after the American-Japanese Treaty of 1854. Article I proclaimed that "Korea, being an independent state, enjoys the same sovereign rights as does Japan." This was obviously intended by Japan as a repudiation of the traditional Chinese claim of suzerainty over Korea. The remaining eleven articles granted Japan a set of unilateral privileges, which included the right to trade at designated Korean ports, extraterritoriality for Japanese nationals in Korea, the right to survey Korean coastal waters, and the exchange of envoys between the two countries.

By a supplementary treaty and an accompanying memorandum signed six months later, Japan gained additional privileges, including the right to use Japanese currency at Korean ports and exemption from tariffs on Japanese imports into Korea. As a result, Japanese merchants traded in Korea duty-free until 1883, when a Korean-Japanese trade agreement established tariffs on Japanese goods imported into Korea for the first time.

The Treaty of Ganghwa opened the "Hermit Kingdom" to the outside world, which in turn brought about manifold changes in Korean-Japanese relations. In addition to Busan, two more ports, Wonsan and Incheon, were opened to Japanese trade, in 1880 and 1883, respectively. Hanabusa Yoshitada (1842–1917), the first Japanese minister accredited to the Korean court, opened his legation in Seoul in 1880. A large volume of Japanese merchandise, including British-manufactured fabrics, began flooding the Korean market, in exchange for an increasing amount of Korean products exported to Japan, including grain (i.e., rice and soybean) and gold (see Table 1). Changes in Korean-Japanese diplomatic and economic relations inevitably had repercussions in domestic conditions in Korea.

Table 1. Volume of Korean-Japanese Trade, 1872–1882

Year	Exports Korea to Japan	Imports Korea from Japan	Total
1872	52,382 *yen*	59,664 *yen*	112,048 *yen*
1873	55,935	57,522	113,457
1874	59,787	68,930	128,717
1875	82,572	81,374	163,946
1876	——————————————— (no figures) ———————————————		
1 July 1877 to 30 June 1878	119, 538	228,554	348,092
1 July to 21 Dec. 1878	154,707	142,618	297,325
1879	677,061	566,953	1,244,014
1880	1,373,671	978,013	2,351,684
1881	1,882,657	1,944,731	3,827,394 (*sic*)
1 Jan. 1881 to 30 June 1882	897,657	742,562	1,639,787

Source: Adapted from a table in Hilary Conroy, *The Japanese Seizure of Korea, 1868–1910* (Philadelphia: University of Pennsylvania Press, 1960), p. 457.

The Korean "Enlightenment" Movement and the Coup of 1884

One of the major consequences of the opening of Korea was the rise of the so-called "enlightenment" (*gaehwa*), also called "self-strengthening" (*jagang*), movement in Korea. Prompted by a desire to learn about Japan's modernization program, King Gojong dispatched a seventy-five-man mission to Japan in the fall of 1876, in the name of a "trust cultivating embassy" (*susinsa*), led by Kim Gi-su (1832–1893). This was the first mission of this kind since 1764, when the last communication embassy had visited Edo. Its purpose was to study changes taking place in new Japan. Upon his return home, Kim made a generally favorable report. The Korean government, however, did not immediately take any measure to emulate the Japanese. It was after the second mission to Japan, led by Kim Hong-jip (1842–1896), had returned in October 1880 that the king and a coterie of his officials launched a moderate reform movement for enlightenment, spurred on by the mission's report that Korea needed to strengthen itself and cultivate friendly ties with the United States if it was to survive the threat from Russia. This was what the prominent contemporary Chinese statesman, Li Hongzhang (1823–1901), who was then the "governor-general of the metropolitan province and the imperial commissioner for the northern [Chinese] ports," had been urging on Korea since 1879.

Under this reform program, the Korean government created a proto-modern foreign office called the Office for Extraordinary State Affairs (Tongni Gimu Amun) and organized a modern military unit called the Special Skills Force (Byeolgigun) in 1881. Meanwhile, the task of negotiating a Korean-American treaty with the American plenipotentiary, Commodore Robert W. Shufeldt (1822–1895), was more or less left to the discretion of Li Hongzhang in Tianjin. In addition, the Korean government dispatched a large fact-finding mission composed of twelve high-ranking courtiers and twenty-six attendants, collectively dubbed the Courtiers' Observation Mission (Josa Sichaldan), to Japan in 1881. Its purpose was to study Japan's new Western-style governmental institutions, military system, and customs service. The report of this mission to the king prompted a flurry of enlightenment activities in the country in the early 1880s.

The opening of Korea by Japan in 1876 and the Japanese-inspired enlightenment movement in the early 1880s provoked a strong anti-

Japanese and anti-Western movement among the conservatives in the country, which included followers of the Daewongun and Neo-Confucian scholar-officials and literati. The conservatives regarded "barbarian" Japanese and Western cultures as incompatible with Eastern culture and tradition. In 1881, they launched a campaign to "defend the [Confucian] orthodoxy in repudiation of the [Christian] heterodoxy" (*wijeong cheoksa*), with the intent of stymieing the government's enlightenment program. After some initial setbacks, the campaign eventually became responsible for a violent riot by disgruntled soldiers, popularly referred to as the Soldiers' Riot (Imo Gullan), in the summer of 1882. The rioters were soldiers from the old army units, who felt that they had been discriminated against after the creation of the Special Skills Force. They murdered Lieutenant Horimoto Reizo, the Japanese drillmaster for the Special Skills Force, and set fire to the Japanese legation. Their hero, the Daewongun, was reinstalled in power. During his brief, month-long tenure of power, the Daewongun undid all the institutional innovations introduced since 1881.

Upon hearing the news of the riot, both China and Japan dispatched troops to Korea. The Chinese expeditionary force rounded up and punished the rioters and abducted the Daewongun to China for his involvement in the incident. China thus began its intervention in Korean domestic affairs. It restored King Gojong and Queen Min (1851–1895; q. 1866–1895) to power and appointed a number of Chinese and foreign advisers to the Korean government, including Paul G. von Möllendorff (1848–1901), a German who became the vice-minister of Korean foreign office and the inspector-general of the newly created Korean customs service. Meanwhile, the 3,000-man Chinese expeditionary force stayed on in Seoul. Under the Sino-Korean Maritime and Overland Trade Regulations signed in October 1882, China began breaking up the Japanese monopoly of Korean foreign trade by extending special protection to Chinese merchants.

Japan also sent troops to Korea to demand compensation for the loss of Japanese lives and property. Under duress, the Korean plenipotentiary Kim Hong-jip signed the Treaty of Jemulpo with Hanabusa on August 30, 1882. Under this treaty, Japan obtained Korea's pledge to send an apology mission to Japan and to pay a 500,000-*yen* indemnity to cover the damage and military operations cost caused by the incident. It also obtained the right to station "a small number" of troops in Seoul to guard its legation in Seoul. By a supplementary agreement, Japan forced

Korea to open Yanghwajin, a river port southwest of Seoul, to Japanese trade and to ease travel restrictions for Japanese residents in the three Korean trade ports. In addition, Japan obtained the right of free travel within Korea for its officials and their families. At the behest of the Japanese envoy, in late 1882 the Korean government also destroyed the "anti-appeasement stele"(*cheokhwabi*), which had been erected by the order of the Daewongun in all major cities throughout the country in 1871 as a symbol of Korean determination to resist foreign intruders.

Diplomatic and cultural exchanges increased between Korea and Japan following the settlement of the 1882 incident. Many Korean officials and students visited Japan during 1882-1884 for the purpose of studying Japan's modernization. Notable among them, Bak Yeong-hyo (1861–1939), who led the Korean apology mission to Japan in 1882, established contacts with many prominent Japanese leaders, both in and out of the government, including Inoue Kaoru (1835–1915), Fukuzawa Yukichi (1835–1901), and Goto Shojiro (1838–1897). Bak's friend, Kim Ok-gyun, made similar visits to Japan, traveling there three times during 1882–1884 on various royal missions. More than fifty Korean students, including Yu Gil-jun (1856–1914) and Yun Chi-ho (1864–1946), were enrolled in modern schools in Tokyo in 1882. Fukuzawa, the leading advocate of "civilization and enlightenment" (*bummei kaika*) in Japan, tried to promote enlightenment in Korea by accepting Korean students in his private school, Keio Gijuku, and by sending his disciples, such as Inoue Kakugoro (1860–1938), to Seoul to help the Korean government inaugurate the first modern Korean newspaper, *Hanseong sunbo* (Seoul Thrice Monthly) in 1883.

In the meantime, Korea concluded its first treaty with the United States in May 1882. The first American minister, Lucius H. Foote (1826 – ?), arrived in Seoul a year later to establish an American legation. In order to strengthen the newly formed ties with the United States, King Gojong dispatched an eight-man roving mission to the United States in the fall of 1883. When the mission returned home in October 1884, a pro-Japanese radical group known as the Progressive Party (Gaehwadang) was plotting to overthrow the government, which was dominated by the pro-Chinese conservative faction. After seizing power, the conspirators planned to institute reforms modeled after those of Meiji Japan. Their leaders were Kim Ok-gyun, Bak Yeong-hyo, Hong Yeong-sik (1855–1884), Seo Gwang-beom (1859–1896), and Seo Jae-pil (Philip Jaisohn, 1863–1951)—all individuals who had been to Japan or the

United States in various capacities between 1881 and 1884. Their goal was to make Korea the "France of Asia." On December 4, 1884, they staged a coup d'état with the support of the Japanese minister in Seoul, Takezoe Shinichiro (1842–1917). Without any specific instruction or authorization from his home government, Takezoe mobilized his legation personnel and 200-man legation guard for the operation. Fukuzawa, too, helped the coup by providing the conspirators with weapons and bravos (*soshi*). Both the conspirators and their Japanese supporters apparently believed that the Chinese troops in Seoul would remain inactive because China was involved at this time in a major armed conflict with France over Vietnam.

This coup is known in history as the Coup d'Etat of 1884 (Gapsin Jeongbyeon). The Progressives held power for three days from December 4 through 6. During this period, they murdered six leading conservative officials and proclaimed a fourteen-point reform edict, calling for, among other things, Korean independence from China, the concentration of power in a "cabinet," and the abolition of the *yangban* class. But the coup was crushed by the armed intervention of the Chinese troops in Seoul controlled by Yuan Shikai (1860–1916), a staff officer in the Chinese garrison army in Seoul holding the title of a "director-general of the military secretariat and the concurrent associate director of the Korean military affairs"—a man destined to play a major role subsequently. Upon receiving specific instructions not to support the Korean coup from his government in the midst of the melee, Takezoe decided to withdraw his support from the coup on the third day and flee from Seoul with his legation staff and the Japanese residents. Forty Japanese lost their lives during the three-day coup and the Japanese legation was again burned down by a Korean mob. Eight leaders of the coup, including Kim Ok-gyun, Bak Yeong-hyo, Seo Gwang-beom, and Seo Jae-pil, managed to flee to Japan, while many of their relatives and friends were arrested and put to death by the pro-Chinese regime after the collapse of the coup. The failure of the 1884 Coup was a mortal blow not only to the Progressives, but also to the incipient enlightenment movement of the early 1880s.

The Japanese government dispatched its foreign minister, Inoue Kaoru, to Seoul to deal with the crisis in Korean-Japanese relations created by the abortive coup. Inoue hastened the conclusion of the Treaty of Hanseong (Seoul) with the Korean plenipotentiary, Kim Hong-jip, on January 9, 1885, knowing full well that Takezoe had been deeply involved in the plotting and execution of the coup. By this treaty Japan obtained an indemnity of 150,000 *yen* and a Korean pledge to pay for the construction of military barracks in Seoul capable of accommodating 1,000 Japanese troops. Inoue referred the settlement of more fundamental issues relevant to the incident to a Sino-Japanese parley to be convened later in Tianjin. Subsequently, Li Hongzhang and Ito Hirobumi (1841–1909) met in Tianjin in the following April and signed the so-called Li-Ito Convention of Tianjin. Under this convention, the two contracting parties agreed to withdraw their troops from Korea simultaneously, to advise the Korean king to organize a modern military force by engaging military advisers from a third country, and to notify each other should either of the contracting powers decide to send troops to Korea in the future. In short, Japan became a joint guarantor of Korean security on a par with China by signing this convention.

The Sino-Japanese War and Japanese Involvement in the Gabo Reforms, 1894–1896

A decade of peace followed in Korea after the signing of the Li-Ito Convention. During this period, however, Korea was reduced to a Chinese protectorate under the Qing policy of strengthening its suzerain hold on Korea. Yuan Shikai, who served as China's "director-general of diplomatic and consular affairs resident in Korea"—"resident" in short— from 1885 to 1894, suppressed the Korean government's enlightenment program and interfered in Korea's foreign relations. Although Korea had concluded treaties with Japan, the United States, Great Britain, Germany, Italy, Russia, and France by 1886, Yuan prevented it from establishing its legations in these countries, with the exception of Japan and the United States. Korea opened its legation in Tokyo in July 1887 under its first minister to Japan, Min Yeong-jun (1852–1935), and its legation in Washington D. C. in January 1888 under its first minister to the United States, Bak Jeong-yang (1841–1904).

During this period, Japan followed a policy of acquiescing to Chinese intervention in Korean affairs because it feared Russian encroachment on the Korean peninsula. Even as it cooperated with China regarding Korea, Japan kept hearing recurrent rumors in early 1885 and mid-1886 of the Korean court's attempt to seek Russian protection. In order to prevent the pro-Western and particularly pro-Russian king and queen from signing a secret pact with Russia, Japan urged China to repatriate the anti-Western Daewongun from China and bring American advisers into the Korean foreign office and customs service. They would replace von Möllendorff, who had become increasingly pro-Russian since 1884. While the Japanese government was pursuing a policy of cooperation with China, Japanese merchants were competing fiercely against Chinese merchants in Korea, in order to retain their commercial lead. They found it increasingly difficult to best their Chinese competitors in the Sino-Japanese trade rivalry in Korea (see Table 2). Japan even resorted to litigation against the Koreans. In 1892, the Korean government settled the so-called "grain embargo dispute" by paying "compensations" to Japanese merchants for the losses they had allegedly suffered as a result of the "unlawful" measures taken by Korean local officials to stop the export of rice to Japan in the Wonsan area in 1889. On its part, the Korean government sought to control rampant Japanese fishing activities along the southern coast of Korea by negotiating a fishery agreement with Japan in November 1889.

Korean-Japanese relations became suddenly strained in the spring of 1894, following the assassination of the ill-fated pro-Japanese reformer Kim Ok-gyun in Shanghai and the outbreak of the Donghak Peasant Uprising in southern Korean provinces. When the Japanese government learned that China had decided to dispatch troops to Korea to quell the

Table 2. Volume of Japanese and Chinese Trade at Korean Ports, 1885–1893

Year	Trade with Japan	Trade with China	Percentage	
			Japan	China
1885	$1,747,546	$ 310,468	85%	15%
1886	2,508,671	455,337	85	15
1887	2,855,472	751,599	79	21
1888	2,963,844	919,805	76	24
1889	3,406,904	1,195,554	74	26
1890	6,545,876	1,722,738	79	21
1891	6,424,172	2,180,913	75	25
1892	4,814,414	2,200,715	69	31
1893	3,492,157	2,039,783	63	37

Source: Adapted from a table in Ito Hirobumi, comp., *Hisho ruisan: Chosen kosho shiryo*, vol. III (Tokyo: Hisho Ruisan Kankokai, 1936), pp. 522-523.

peasant uprising, it also decided to send troops to Korea, with an eye to fishing in troubled waters. The Japanese decision to intervene in Korean domestic affairs in mid-1894 was prompted by several factors. First of all, Prime Minister Ito Hirobumi and his cabinet were facing a major political crisis in mid-1894 because of the repeated moves to impeach him in the Diet. They, therefore, were tempted to divert public attention abroad by undertaking a foreign military adventure. Second, leaders of the Japanese military, including General Yamagata Aritomo (1838–1922), were concerned with the growing possibility of Russian encroachment on the Korean Peninsula since 1891, when the Czarist government launched the Trans-Siberian Railway project. They wished to consolidate the Japanese position in Korea before the Russians took the initiative. Third, the Japanese business community was concerned over the rising influence of Chinese merchants in Korea under Yuan Shikai's residency. Its leaders were urging their government to take some drastic measures to stem the tide. A combination of these political, strategic, and economic factors led the Ito cabinet to adopt an aggressive stance toward Korea and China in 1894.

In early June 1894, Japanese Foreign Minister Mutsu Minemitsu (1844–1897) instructed Otori Keisuke (1833–1911), Japanese minister in Seoul, to look for a *casus belli* with China after 8,000-strong Japanese expeditionary forces reached the Korean capital, outnumbering the 3,000-strong Chinese forces which arrived at Asanman bay. In the meantime, the Donghak insurgents, under the leadership of Jeon Bong-jun (1853–1895), voluntarily disbanded themselves on June 11 when they learned of the dispatch of Chinese and Japanese troops to Korea. Otori, therefore, contrived an argument that the Japanese troops could not be withdrawn from Korea unless and until the Korean government carried out satisfactory reforms according to his reform formula. On July 23, Japanese troops forcibly occupied the royal Gyeongbokgung palace in Seoul under the flimsy excuse that the Korean government had neglected taking action against the Chinese expeditionary troops who proclaimed that Korea was China's "vassal country." With the help of pro-Japanese Korean reformer-officials the Japanese minister then established a pro-Japanese puppet regime headed by Kim Hong-jip, ostensibly for the purpose of promoting the requisite reforms. At the same time, Otori and his Korean collaborators succeeded in persuading the Daewongun, the political enemy of the all-powerful and pro-Western Queen Min, to accept the regency for the henpecked king, in order to carry out the

Japanese-sponsored reforms. Japan declared war on China on August 1, that is, after disarming the Korean troops in Seoul, sinking the Chinese naval transport, *Kaoshing*, in the vicinity of Pung Island, and dealing a crippling blow to the Chinese expeditionary forces in Korea in the Battle of Seonghwan.

Otori pursued a Janus-faced policy toward the pro-Japanese Korean puppet regime in the opening phase of the Sino-Japanese War. He pretended to help a group of pro-Japanese Korean reformer-officials undertake a major institutional reform, known in history as the Reforms of 1894, through the so-called Deliberative Council (Gun-guk Gimucheo). At the same time, he was busy exacting from the regime special privileges for the Japanese, including the right to appoint Japanese advisers to the Korean government and army, build and operate railroads and telegraph lines in Korea, and open additional ports to Japanese trade. He secured these privileges by the so-called Provisional [Korean-Japanese] Agreement signed on August 20, 1894. In addition, he forced the Korean government to help the Japanese war effort against China by signing the Korean-Japanese Treaty of Alliance on August 26, which, among other things, obligated the Korean "ally" to supply free labor for Japanese war activities. In the meantime, on August 17, the Japanese cabinet adopted, on a tentative basis, a policy guideline to convert the Korean kingdom to a Japanese protectorate.

After Japanese forces scored victories in the Battle of Pyeongyang on September 15 and the Battle of the Yellow Sea on September 17, the Tokyo government replaced Otori with the more powerful Inoue Kaoru as its minister in Seoul, in order to more vigorously promote its plan for converting Korea to a Japanese protectorate. By the time Inoue reached Seoul in late October, a large-scale anti-Japanese "righteous armies" (*uibyeong*) had been organized by the Donghak followers in the southern provinces, under the leadership of Jeon Bong-jun. The Daewongun, who had turned against his Japanese sponsors in mid-September because of his displeasure with Japanese activity in Korea, was secretly supporting the Donghak army. Acting with dispatch, Inoue stripped him of power and conducted a military campaign against the Donghak by mobilizing a special Japanese task force and Korean government troops. The Donghak forces were defeated in a series of battles near Gongju; their leaders, including Jeon Bong-jun, were captured in late December and put to death after a trial by a mixed Korean-Japanese court in May 1895.

Having destroyed the Donghak righteous armies in December 1894,

Inoue began pushing a major reform program aimed at transforming Korea into a Japanese protectorate. For this purpose, he reshuffled the Korean government in order to bring in Bak Yeong-hyo and Seo Gwang-beom, who had been living in Japan and the United States in exile after the miscarriage of the Coup of 1884. In the so-called Second Kim Hong-jip cabinet, Bak was appointed as home minister and Seo, minister of justice. As the all-powerful home minister, Bak was the moving spirit behind the reform movement from December 1894 to July 1895. Inoue forced the Korean king to proclaim a fourteen-point reform program in January 1895, which, among other things, affirmed Korea's determination to gain independence from China and called for the separation of the royal household and the government, while concentrating power in the cabinet. He appointed some forty Japanese advisers and assistant advisers to key posts in the Korean government. He also arranged a three-million-*yen* Japanese loan for the Korean government in March 1895. He was ready to sign a full-fledged protectorate treaty with the Korean government when the war ended with the signing of the Treaty of Shimonoseki on April 17, 1895. The Japanese government, however, was compelled to give up its ambitious plan by the Triple Intervention of Russia, Germany and France on April 23, 1895.

The Triple Intervention boosted the morale of the pro-Russian and pro-American factions in the Seoul political arena. The king and queen began reasserting their authority. First, they expelled Bak Yeong-hyo, forcing him to seek political asylum again in Japan in July 1895. In the following October, they tried to disband the Japanese-controlled palace guard, the Hullyeondae (Kunrentai in Japanese), as a preliminary step toward toppling the Kim Hong-jip cabinet. Faced with the possibility of the imminent collapse of the Japanese position in Korea, which had been carefully crafted during the war, Miura Goro (1846–1926), who had replaced Inoue as Japanese minister in Seoul in September, decided to eliminate Queen Min, the leader of the pro-Russian party in Seoul. Miura engineered the murder of the queen on October 8 using a large band of Japanese legation personnel, troops, and bravos with the support of the Daewongun and Hullyeondae soldiers.

The Japanese government recalled Miura and forty other Japanese implicated in the incident. After perfunctory trials in Hiroshima, however, they were acquitted in February 1896 for "lack of definitive evidence." In Seoul, pro-Japanese members of the Kim Hong-jip cabinet regained their power after the death of Queen Min and continued to push the Japanese-oriented reforms. But their position became increasingly precarious as a result of the rise of anti-Japanese righteous armies throughout the country, this time led by Confucian literati. On February 11, 1896, after the pro-Japanese government troops had been sent out to the countryside to fight these righteous armies, a group of pro-Russian and pro-American politicians in Seoul, including Yi Beom-jin (1852–1910), succeeded in smuggling the king out of his palace and into the Russian legation. With the flight of the Korean monarch, the Japanese position in Korea suffered serious damage. With the sudden decline of Japanese influence, the leading pro-Japanese Korean politicians, including Kim Hong-jip, Eo Yun-jung (1848–1896), and Jeong Byeong-ha (1849–1896)—all ministers of the pro-Japanese cabinet—were murdered either by policemen or mobs in Seoul and its vicinity. Others, including Yu Gil-jun, Jo Hui-yeon (1856–1915), Kwon Hyeong-jin (1858–1900), and U Beom-seon (?–1901)—all cabinet ministers or high-ranking police or army officials—fled to Japan.

The Russo-Japanese War and the Japanese Annexation of Korea, 1910

Korean-Japanese relations became relatively tranquil after the flight of the Korean king to the Russian legation. The king stayed at the Russian legation for more than a year, until March 1897. Following his return to his own Gyeongungung palace, his official title was elevated from king to "emperor"; the official name of the country was changed from Joseon to Daehan ("Great Han"). Behind the facade of these pretentious but seemingly progressive changes, Korean politics was reverting to its old habits and practices of the pre-1894 days. It was against this background that a group of reform-minded officials and intellectuals organized the Independence Club (Dongnip Hyeophoe) in July 1896, under the leadership of Seo Jae-pil. Seo was a former progressive leader, who had returned home from the United States at the end of 1895 after obtaining a medical degree and American citizenship. Members of the Independence Club, including Yun Chi-ho, Yi Sang-jae (1850–1927), and Yi Seung-man (Syngman Rhee, 1875–1965), championed political reform geared to a constitutional monarchy based on democratic principles. In addition, they campaigned for the protection of Korean natural resources from foreign concession-seekers. The Club, however, was forcibly disbanded in December 1898 by Emperor Gojong and his conservative ministers, who suspected that the Club's ulterior aim was to establish a republican government by overthrowing the Joseon monarchy. The Japanese minister in Seoul, Kato Masuo, recommended the emperor to use force in disbanding the Club.

The Japanese government pursued two major policy goals in Korea between 1896 and 1904. One was the maintenance of a superior diplomatic and strategic position in Korea vis-à-vis Russia, and the other was that of taking the lead over the United States, Great Britain, Russia, and China in obtaining concessions and other economic advantages in Korea. Japan's efforts to secure a superior position vis-à-vis Russia resulted in a series of Russo-Japanese agreements between 1896 and 1898, namely, the Lobanov-Yamagata Protocol, signed in Moscow on June 9, 1896, and the Nishi-Rosen Convention, signed in Tokyo on April 25, 1898. After Russia decided, in 1898, to build Port Arthur as its

Table 3. Volume of Trade between Korea and Foreign Countries, 1894–1910

Year	Japan	China	Russia	Great Britain	United States	Others
1984	5,691,632	2,226,573	218,572			
1895	8,202,166	2,211,324	153,526			
1896	8,690,351	2,423,005	146,668			
1897	14,522,099	4,272,235	247,075			
1898	11,300,134	6,059,453	167,464			
1899	10,863,582	4,156,772	204,831			
1900	15,473,712	4,550,354	356,261			
1901	16,453,997	6,417,833	286,589			
1902	15,238,866	6,368,422	251,191			
1902	19,154,593	5,907,806	455,749	780,265	398,377	
1904	24,703,658	6,286,264	91,041	767,806	1,813,115	76,000
1905	28,951,813	7,447,129	113,999	364,117	1,978,812	8,013
1906	29,831,002	4,804,680	538,293	47,762	2,557,736	7,769
1907	40,013,139	7,645,541	657,629	5,517,596	3,295,558	805,242
1908	35,003,818	7,129,705	818,006	6,787,461	4,239,635	1,160,209
1909	22,933,983	7,676,670	828,932	6,528,350	2,465,953	1,463,770
1910	40,726,728	6,871,110	1,173,327	6,251,243	3,509,535	1,164,656

Source: Adapted from the tables in Eugene C. I. Kim and Han-gyo Kim, *Korea and the Politics of Imperialism, 1876–1910* (Berkeley and Los Angeles: University of California Press, 1968), pp. 229-230.

principal naval base in East Asia, Japan tried to secure Russian recognition of Japan's predominant position in Korea in exchange for Japanese recognition of a similar position for Russia in Manchuria. In the meantime, Japan was doing well in the "scramble for concessions" in Korea against the United States and other powers. It had Mokpo and Jinnampo opened to Japanese trade in 1898, obtained franchises to build the Seoul-Incheon railroad in 1899 and the Seoul-Busan railroad in 1902, and secured the right to use Japanese currency in Korea in 1902. Consequently, after 1896 the annual volume of Korean-Japanese trade more than doubled from that of 1894 (see Table 3).

Japanese-Russian relations became strained after Russia had dispatched large military forces to Manchuria in the wake of the 1901 Boxer Uprising in northern China. The Japanese government demanded that Russia withdraw its forces from Manchuria and agree with Japan on a formula for "exchanging Manchuria for Korea" in determining each other's sphere of influence. Meanwhile, Japan concluded an alliance with Great Britain in 1902, mainly in order to improve its bargaining position vis-à-vis Russia. Finally, the Japanese cabinet of Prime Minister Katsura Taro (1847–1913) and Foreign Minister Komura Jutaro (1855–1911) decided to go to war with Russia in February 1904 after a series of Japanese-Russian negotiations had reached an impasse. Japan declared war on Russia on February 10, 1904 after staging a surprise attack on Port Arthur and sinking a Russian man-of-war in the Incheon harbor.

The Japanese army quickly overran the Korean peninsula after the outbreak of hostilities, ignoring the Korean declaration of neutrality in January 1904. On February 23, Hayashi Gonsuke (1860–1939), Japanese minister in Seoul, forced the Korean government to sign a protocol obligating Korea to collaborate with Japan in conducting the war and "accept Japanese advice for the improvement of administration." Thus began the wartime Japanese intervention in Korean internal affairs that ultimately led to the Japanese seizure of the Korean kingdom, first as a protectorate and then later as a full-fledged colony. By another agreement signed on August 22, 1904, Japan established firm control over the Korean government by bringing in a number of Japanese and Japanese-recommended American advisers, including Megata Tanetaro as financial adviser and Durham W. Stevens (1851–1908) as adviser on foreign affairs. Japan then secured international acquiescence for its ambition to convert Korea to a protectorate by signing the secret Katsura-Taft Agreement on July 27, 1905 and the second Anglo-Japanese Alliance on

August 12, 1905. Japan crowned this effort by obtaining from Russia the right to "direct, protect, and supervise" Korea under the Russo-Japanese Peace Treaty consummated in Portsmouth, New Hampshire on September 5, 1905.

The Japanese government selected one of its oligarchs, Ito Hirobumi, for the mission of dictating a protectorate treaty to the Korean government. Ambassador Ito succeeded in forcing the protectorate treaty upon a reluctant but divided Korean cabinet on November 17, 1905 by threatening Korean ministers with the Japanese gendarmerie. Ito became the first Japanese resident-general (*tonggam*; *tokan* in Japanese) in Korea in February 1906. Remaining in that post until 1909, he carried out the reform of Korean internal administration while supervising Korean external relations. Among other things, he began organizing a gendarmerie-police system (*heonbyeong gyeongchal jedo* in Korean; *kempei keisatsu seido* in Japanese) as an instrument of suppression against Korean resistance and promulgated laws designed to suppress Korean political and educational activities. He facilitated Japanese control over finance, banking, mining, fisheries, forestry, transportation, and communication in Korea. He also arranged Japanese loans totaling forty-five million *yen* for the Korean government and sponsored the establishment of the Oriental Development Company in March 1908 for the purpose of promoting Japanese economic exploitation of Korea. In short, Ito prepared the ground for the Japanese colonial rule of Korea, which was to last thirty-five years, from 1910 until 1945.

Resident-General Ito reduced Korea to a Japanese colony all but in name in mid-1907, when he forced Emperor Gojong to abdicate in favor of his retarded son, Emperor Sunjong. He then disbanded the 8,000-strong Korean army after learning that Gojong had secretly dispatched emissaries to The Hague Peace Conference to plead for Korean independence. Under an agreement signed on July 23, 1907, he forced the Korean government to accept Japanese as vice-ministers in all government ministries. The Japanese decision to annex Korea was made by the Katsura cabinet in July 1909, after Ito had resigned from his Korean post under pressure from the Japanese military as well as such ultra-nationalist organizations as the Amur River Society (Kokuryukai). Japanese leaders' increasing fear that Japan might lose its grip on Korea in the face of growing Korean resistance and foreign criticism must have led them to this fateful decision. In May 1910, the Japanese government appointed General Terauchi Masatake (1852–1919) as resident-general of Korea, charged with the mission of carrying out the annexation. Terauchi forced Prime Minister Yi Wan-yong's (1858–1926) pro-Japanese Korean cabinet to sign the Treaty of Annexation on August 22, 1910, while Japanese troops and gendarmerie held Seoul under firm control. With this treaty, the Empire of Japan brought an end to the 518-year old Joseon Kingdom, also known as the Daehan Empire from 1897, by seizing it as a colony.

From 1904 to 1910, the Korean people and their leaders struggled against Japanese encroachment upon their country with increasing alarm and hostility. Except for a small number of pro-Japanese officials and members of the Japanese-sponsored Iljinhoe (Advancement Society), they were united in opposing Japanese aggression. Emperor Gojong made a series of unsuccessful diplomatic moves to restore Korea's independence. For example, he made his government send Syngman Rhee as a secret emissary to President Theodore Roosevelt of the United States to plead for Roosevelt's good offices on behalf of Korea during the Portsmouth Peace Conference. Roosevelt, however, refused to grant the Korean wishes, believing that the Koreans "could not strike a blow in their own defense" against Japanese aggression. Gojong also dispatched a secret mission to Hague in June 1907, only to meet Ito's retaliation, as mentioned above. His effort to mobilize world public opinion against Japan through a bilingual Korean-English newspaper, the *Daehan maeil sinbo* (Korea Daily News), with the help of a British journalist, Ernest T. Bethell (1872–1909), produced little tangible results.

The Korean people tried to preserve their national independence from 1905 to 1910 in three different ways: joining the righteous armies, participation in various "patriotic enlightenment movements" (*aeguk gyemong undong*), and engaging in individual acts of heroism. First, many patriotic Koreans joined the righteous armies in the tradition of Korean resistance against the Japanese invasion in the late sixteenth century. The first of the major righteous armies was organized by Min Jong-sik, a former government official, and by Choe Ik-hyeon (1833–1906), a Neo-Confucian scholar-official, in early 1906, after the Japanese had imposed the protectorate treaty on Korea. The righteous army movement gained strength following the disbanding of the Korean army in August 1907, as many former Korean army officers and soldiers joined the ranks of the righteous armies with modern weapons in hand. Leaders of the righteous armies were drawn from various social backgrounds, including Confucian *yangban* literati, former officers of the defunct Korean army, and commoners with martial talent. The majority of the rank and file of the righteous armies was, however, of peasant background. The righteous armies attained their peak strength in 1908, when some 70,000 men fought a total of 1,451 engagements against Japanese troops. In the course of protracted guerrilla-style warfare from 1905 until 1912, the righteous army casualties totaled 17,779 deaths and 3,707 wounded, while inflicting only 136 deaths and 2,777 wounded on the Japanese side. The movement lost momentum after 1910 as a result of a systematic mopping-up campaign launched against it by the Japanese army and police. The survivors of the righteous armies eventually moved their bases to southern Manchuria and the Russian Maritime Province and continued their fight against the Japanese throughout the Japanese colonial period.

Second, patriotic Koreans organized quasi-political organizations, built private schools, or joined Christian churches as a means of "enlightening" their fellow countrymen, for the purpose of arousing their patriotism and building national strength. One such organization, the Sinminhoe (New People's Association), organized by An Chang-ho (1878-1938), who had returned from the United States in 1907, set up or sponsored a dozen modern schools, published numerous books, pioneered modern industries, and developed a political program for regaining national independence. Leaders of the society included former members of the Independence Club and converts to Protestantism. More than 2,000 private schools were established during 1905–1910, with the goal of imbuing patriotism in Korean youth and increasing their knowledge of the modern world. Approximately one third of the private schools that mushroomed at that time were affiliated with Protestant Christian churches, which had developed rapidly under the influence of American missionaries. It was also during 1905–1910 that a number of prominent journalist-historians, such as Jang Ji-yeon (1864–1921), Bak Eun-sik (1859–1926) and Sin Chae-ho (1880–1936), began publishing their writings, with the aim of inculcating national pride and a sense of national awakening in their compatriots through modern newspapers and magazines.

Third, many patriots performed individual acts, including protest by suicide. Some resorted to terrorism. At least a dozen scholars and officials loyal to the Joseon dynasty, including the noted historian, Hwang Hyeon (1855–1905), and a high-ranking government official, Min Yeong-hwan (1861–1905), took their own lives in the ultimate act of protest upon hearing the news of the protectorate treaty in late 1905. Many others chose exile in China, Russia or the United States, in order to carry on the fight for the restoration of national independence. In 1907, Jang In-hwan (1877–1930) and Jeon Myeong-un (1884–1947), two young Korean expatriates living in California, assassinated Durham W. Stevens, the Japanese-sponsored American adviser to the Korean foreign office, who was on a speaking tour designed to bolster support of Japanese policy toward Korea, in San Francisco. Yi Jae-myeong (1890– 1910), another Korean youth who had returned from the United States, made an unsuccessful attempt on Yi Wan-yong's life in Seoul in 1909. Above all, An Jung-geun (1879–1910), a self-styled righteous army commander in Manchuria and devout Catholic, assassinated Ito Hirobumi in Harbin, Manchuria, in October 1909.

Conclusion

During the Tokugawa period, the Japanese people treated their Korean neighbor with cordial deference, if not sincere respect, out of their traditional reverence for East Asian culture. After Japan opened its doors to the West and began introducing Western culture in the middle of the nineteenth century, however, its attitude toward Korea underwent a drastic change. Japanese leaders looked down on China-oriented Korean culture with contempt. Having learned the logic and tactics of Western imperialism as a victim, they now tried to victimize their closest neighbor using the very same logic and tactics. They pursued a policy of intermittent encroachment on Korea's sovereignty with the arrogant and hypocritical conviction that they could promote the happiness of the Korean people by spreading the "benefit" of their new, modern culture. In fact, however, Japan was motivated by selfish considerations, including its strategic need to secure the Korean peninsula as a sphere of Japanese influence to ward off the Russian threat, its economic desire to utilize the Korean market and resources for the development of capitalism at home, its political impulse to use Korea as a panacea for solving domestic political problems, and its chauvinistic wish to spread Japan's "imperial glory" abroad.

At first, they sought a vaguely defined goal of rejecting China's traditional claim of suzerainty over Korea and of establishing Japanese control over the peninsula. After the Sino-Japanese War, they redefined their policy goal in Korea and attempted to convert the peninsular kingdom to a Japanese protectorate or colony. In pursuing this goal, they employed a variety of methods and means developed by modern imperialism, such as gunboat diplomacy, diplomatic deception, the extension of loans in exchange for economic concessions, and the use of violent means, including political assassination and murder. Their policy culminated in the annexation of Korea into the Japanese Empire in 1910. By these means they did fulfill the ancient Japanese dream of conquering Korea, which Toyotomi Hideyoshi had implanted in the minds of the Japanese people with his devastating but ultimately unsuccessful invasion of Korea in the late sixteenth century. By annexing Korea as a colony, Japan attained the status of a first-rate imperialist power in the council of world power politics. Yet, the Japanese achieved these and many other such "successes" at the expense of Korean goodwill. Furthermore, the machine of conquest that they put into motion in Korea was destined to continue rolling over other parts of East Asia until it was stopped in August 1945—traversing a process in which the Japanese empire itself was destroyed.

The Korean people, leaders and followers alike, were poorly equipped to meet modern Japan's challenge in the latter half of the nineteenth century. Among other things, they were slow in recognizing the superior aspects of Western civilization and, consequently, failed to learn the ways of modern international diplomacy or the method of attaining national wealth and power in time. In the face of relentless Japanese aggression, the rulers of Joseon Korea employed the stratagem of "playing one barbarian off against another" and tried to gain time by delaying tactics, hoping in the meantime to achieve national enlightenment and self-strengthening. They failed to reform their institutions in time partly because of lack of unity among themselves and partly because of foreign intervention. While their incompetent rulers were yielding time and again to the avaricious demands of the Japanese, the Korean people struggled to preserve their national honor, dignity, and independence. Some organized volunteer forces to fight the Japanese in the time-honored tradition of the righteous armies. Others undertook the more time-consuming but fundamental task of educating their compatriots, in order to nurture the national strength necessary to preserve independence. Still others resorted to individual acts in protest and revenge against aggression. But, in the end, all this failed to block the Japanese seizure of their country. Through this tortuous and painful process of trial and error, the

Koreans learned how to cope with reality in the modern world and how to attain national wealth and power. In short, they were slowly, though belatedly, acquiring the prerequisites of modern nationhood, but were learning it the hard way. The lessons of modern nationalism, which they learned through their struggle against the Japanese from 1876 to 1910, helped them survive the Japanese colonial rule that would last for thirty-five years, and make a successful new start in building an independent nation after Liberation in 1945.

REFERENCES

Chandra, Vipan. 1974. "An Outline of the Ilchin-hoe (Advancement Society) of Korea." *Occasional Papers on Korea* 2 (March 1974).

Chay, Jongsuk. 1968. "The Taft-Katsura Memorandum Reconsidered." *Pacific Historical Review* 37.

Chien, Frederick Foo. 1967. *The Opening of Korea: A Study of Chinese Diplomacy, 1876–1885.* Hamden, Conn.: Shoe String Press.

Choe, Ching Young. 1972. *The Rule of the Taewŏngun, 1864–1873: Restoration in Yi Korea.* Cambridge, Mass.: East Asian Research Center, Harvard University.

Ch'oe, Yong-ho. 1982. "The Kapsin Coup of 1884: A Reassessment." *Korean Studies* 6: 105-124.

Conroy, Hilary. 1960. *The Japanese Seizure of Korea, 1868–1910: A Study of Realism and Idealism in International Relations.* Philadelphia, Pa.: University of Pennsylvania Press.

Cook, Harold F. 1972. *Korea's 1884 Incident: Its Background and Kim Ok-kyun's Elusive Dream.* Royal Asiatic Society Korea Branch Monograph Series, no. 4. Seoul: Seoul Computer Press.

Deuchler, Martina. 1977. *Confucian Gentlemen and Barbarian Envoys: The Opening of Korea, 1875–1885.* Seattle and London: University of Washington Press.

Duus, Peter. 1995. *The Abacus and the Sword: The Japanese Penetration of Korea, 1895–1910.* Berkeley, Los Angeles and London: University of California Press.

Esthus, Raymond A. 1966. *Theodore Roosevelt and Japan.* Seattle and London: University of Washington Press.

Harrington, Fred Harvey. 1944. *God, Mammon, and the Japanese: Dr. Horace N. Allen and Korean-American Relations, 1884–1905.* Madison, Wis.: University of Wisconsin Press.

Hulbert, Homer B. 1906. *The Passing of Korea.* New York: Doubleday Page.

Hwang, In K. 1978. *The Korean Reform Movement of the 1880s: A Study of Transition in Intra-Asian Relations.* Cambridge, Mass.: Schenckman Publishing Company.

Kim, Eugene C. I., and Han-kyo Kim. 1967. *Korea and the Politics of Imperialism, 1876–1910.* Berkeley and Los Angeles: University of California Press.

Kim, Key-Hiuk. 1980. *The Last Phase of the East Asian World Order: Korea, Japan, and the Chinese Empire, 1860–1882.* Berkeley and Los Angeles: University of California Press.

Lee, Bae Yong. 1972. "Competitive Mining Surveys by Foreign Powers in Korea—with Emphasis on the 1880s." *Journal of Social Sciences and Humanities* 36 (June 1972).

Lee, Sun-keun. 1963. "Historical Reflections of Korean-Japanese Relations." *Journal of Social Sciences and Humanities* 19 (December 1963).

Lensen, George Alexander. 1982. *Balance of Intrigue: International Rivalry in Korea and Manchuria, 1884–1899.* 2 vols. Tallahassee, Fla.: University Press of Florida.

Lew, Young Ick (Yu, Yeong-ik). 1977. "The Reform Efforts and Ideas of Pak Yong-hyo, 1894–1895." *Korean Studies* 1 (1977): 21-61.

———. 1981. "Korean-Japanese Politics behind the Kabo-Ŭlmi Reform Movement, 1894–1896." *The Journal of Korean Studies* 3 (1981): 39-82.

———. 1983. "Japan in the Evolution of Korean-American Relations." In *Reflections on a Century of United States-Korean Relations,* edited by Academy of Korean Studies and the Wilson Center. Lanham, Md.: University Press of America, 1983.

———. 1984. "Minister Inoue Kaoru and the Japanese Reform Attempts in Korea During the Sino-Japanese War, 1894–1895." *Asea yeongu* (The Journal of Asiatic Studies) 27.2 (July 1984): 145-186.

———. 1984. "Yüan Shih-kai's Residency and the Korean Enlightenment Movement, 1885–94." *The Journal of Korean Studies* 5 (1984): 63-108.

———. 1990. "The Conservative Character of the 1894 Tonghak Peasant Uprising: A Reappraisal with Emphasis on Chŏn Pong-jun's Background and Motivation." *The Journal of Korean Studies* 7 (1990): 149-180.

Malozemoff, Andrew. 1958. *Russian Far Eastern Policy, 1881–1904: With Special Emphasis on the Causes of the Russo-Japanese War.* Berkeley, Calif.: University of California Press.

Mayo, Marlene J. 1972. "The Korean Crisis of 1873 and Early Meiji Foreign Policy." *Journal of Asian Studies* 31.4 (August 1972).

McCune, George M. 1946. "The Exchange of Envoys between Korea and Japan during the Tokugawa Period." *Far Eastern Quarterly* 5.3 (May 1946).

McGrane, George A. 1973. *Korea's Tragic Hours: The Closing Years of the Yi*

Dynasty. Seoul: Taewon.

McKenzie, Frederick A. 1908. *The Tragedy of Korea*. London: Hodder and Strongton.

Mutsu, Munemitsu. 1982. *Kenkenroku: a Diplomatic Record of the Sino-Japanese War, 1894–95*. Tokyo: University of Tokyo Press.

Nahm, Andrew C. 1979. "Durham White Stevens and the Japanese Annexation of Korea." In *The United States and Korea: American-Korean Relations, 1866–1976*, edited by Andrew C. Nahm. Kalamazoo, Mich.: The Center for Korean Studies, Western Michigan University.

—————. 1982. "U.S. Policy and the Japanese Annexation of Korea." In *U.S.-Korean Relations, 1882–1892*, edited by Tae-hwan Kwak et al. Seoul: Kyungnam University Press.

Palais, James B. 1975. *Politics and Policy in Traditional Korea*. Cambridge, Mass.: Harvard University Press.

Park, M. N., and Wayne Patterson. 1984. "Russian Policy toward Korea before and During the Sino-Japanese War of 1894–95." *The Journal of Korean Studies* 5.

Park, Seong-Rae. 1977. "Fukuzawa Yukichi on Korea." *Journal of Social Sciences and Humanities* 45 (June 1977).

Swartout, Robert R. Jr. 1908. *Mandarins, Gunboats, and Power Politics: Owen Nickerson Denny and the International Rivalries in Korea*. Honolulu, Hawaii: The University Press of Hawaii.

Synn, Seung Kwon. 1981. *The Russo-Japanese Rivalry over Korea, 1876–1904*. Seoul: Yuk Phub Sa.

Tsiang, T. F. 1933–34. "Sino-Japanese Diplomatic Relations, 1870–1894." *Chinese Social and Political Science Review* 17.

Korea and Tsarist Russia:
Russian Interests, Policy, and Involvement in Korea, 1884–1904

Andrew C. Nahm

Russia emerged as one of the main participants in the politics of imperialism in the Far East as a result of the policy of territorial expansionism pursued by Nicholas Muraviev and others like him, following his appointment as governor-general of eastern Siberia in 1847. The conclusion of two treaties with Japan in 1854 and 1858, respectively, permitted Russia to expand her interests in the Far East. The three treaties[1] that Russian expansionists had forced upon China, in addition, not only added a large amount of territory to the Russian empire,[2] but also made Russia increasingly ambitious in that region.

The Treaty of Friendship and Commerce, which was signed between Korea and Russia on July 7, 1884, marked the beginning of Russia's active involvement in Korea's internal and external affairs. Until Japan successfully eliminated Russia from Korea with her victory in the Russo-Japanese War of 1904–1905, Russia had been one of the most persistent contenders for power on the peninsula.

The purpose of this paper is to examine the major aspects of interests, policy, and involvement of Tsarist Russia in Korea from 1884 to 1904.

* Originally published in the *Korea Journal*, vol. 22, no. 6 (June 1982).

Andrew C. Nahm, who was born in Korea and educated in the United States, is Professor of Asian History and Director of the Center for Korean Studies, Western Michigan University, U.S.A.

1. The Treaty of Aigun of 1858 signed by Nicholas Muraviev, the Treaty of Tianjin of 1858 signed by Admiral Evfimii V. Putiatin, and the Treaty of Beijing signed by N. P. Ignatiev in 1860.
2. The Amur and the Ussuri (Maritime Province) districts.

Although Russia showed interest in establishing trade relations with Korea from 1864,[3] being economically backward, Russia was more interested in capturing markets in the Far East for the future. However, it seems that the Russians were driven by a thirst for power to be a dominant political and military force in the Far East. The pattern of national behavior of the Soviet Union in the recent past is not different from that of Tsarist Russia. The difference is found in the methods of achieving their aims.[4]

Many Russians, including Prince E. E. Ukhtomsky, expressed the romantic aims of Russia. For example, in 1881 Feodor Dostoievsky championed a Russian version of "the white man's burden." He asserted that Russia was not only in Europe but also in Asia, and the Russians were as much "Asians" as other Asians.[5] "Asia," he argued, "holds out greater promise to us than Europe. . . . In our future, Asia is, perhaps, our main outlet."[6]

Dostoievsky insisted that Russia helped the Europeans, particularly the Germans, but they in turn rejected the Russians as equal. He claimed that "In Europe, we are hangers-on and slaves, whereas we shall go to Asia as masters . . . . Our civilizing mission in Asia will bribe our spirit and drive us thither. It is only necessary that the movement should start."[7] He believed that "Asia . . . will forthwith become Russian land. A new Russia will arise which in due time will regenerate and resurrect the old one and will show the latter the road which she has to follow."[8] While insisting that "Asia . . . has to be not only refreshed out, resurrected, and transformed," Dostoievsky was certain that Asia was "our future outlet, that our riches are there, that there is our ocean . . . Asia holds

---

3. The Russians made numerous attempts to establish trade relations with Korea in the Korean region adjacent to the Maritime Province (the Ussuri district) of Russia between 1864 and 1884. *Gojong sunjong sillok* (Veritable Records of Gojong and Sunjong), *gwon* 2 (Seoul: Tamgudang, 1970), pp. 139, 159, 202, 261, 292, 322, and 613.

4. Michael Karpovich, "Russian Imperialism or Communist Aggression?" in *Readings in Russian Foreign Policy*, ed. Robert A. Goldwin et al. (New York: Oxford University Press, 1959), p. 662.

5. "Goek-Tepe. What is Asia to Us?" from Feodor Dostoievsky, *The Diary of a Writer*, vol. II, translated and annotated by Boris Brasol (New York: Scribner's, 1949); in Goldwin, *op. cit.*, p. 270.

6. *Ibid.*, p. 273.

7. *Ibid.*, p. 274.

8. *Ibid.*, p. 276.

out to us many a promise, many an opportunity, the full scale of which we here cannot clearly conceive. . . ."[9]

Not many Russian intellectuals preached such a romantic Russian *mission civilisatrice*, but Nicholas II was "always willing to listen to loose talk about Russian *mission civilitrice* in Asia" without any realistic assessment of the situation in the Far East or her own capabilities to become involved successfully in that region.[10] But it was a group of Russian expansionists, not romantics, who persuaded the Tsar to adopt an aggressive policy in the Far East. Foreign Minister A. M. Gorchakov had expressed his opinion in 1856 that "the future of Russia was in Asia," and S. Ia Witte, finance minister under Nicholas II, insisted that "From the shores of the Pacific and the heights of the Himalayas, Russia would dominate not only the affairs of Asia but those of Europe as well."[11]

If Russia had such a self-appointed civilizing mission in Asia, the Russians failed to demonstrate their desire to "refresh, resurrect and transform" Korea. It was their thirst for power that constituted their main objective. In general, Russia's Korea policy lacked coherence, her actions were often indecisive and uncoordinated, and her tactics were ineffective and often blundering. The policymakers were inexperienced men, who had no knowledge about Korea and the Koreans, or about their main opponent, Japan. As a result, Russia caused international crises in Korea rather than either gaining benefits or helping it.

There were many problems associated with Russia's failure in the Far East during the period studied in this paper. The overall problem was Russia's ineffectiveness in foreign affairs during the periods of Alexander III (1881–1894) and Nicholas II (1894–1917), due to the general difficulties encountered by Russia in making the transition from traditional to modern ideas and institutions.[12] The backwardness of Russia and the absence of experienced and capable ministers to conduct foreign affairs constituted two particular problems. "If Nicholas II had been associated with a statesman of the caliber of Bismarck . . ." Russia's foreign policy

---

9. *Ibid.*
10. Donald W. Treadgold, "Russia and the Far East," in *Russian Foreign Policy: Essays in Historical Perspective*, ed. Ivo J. Lederer (New Haven and London: Yale University Press, 1962), p. 545.
11. Gorchakov's statement was quoted in Soviet Commissar of Foreign Affairs G. V. Chicherin's speech. *Ibid.*, p. 554.
12. Cyril E. Black, "The Pattern of Russian Objectives," in Leaderer, *op. cit.*, p. 29.

might have been effective and successful in promoting long-lasting Russian influence in the Far East and their efforts would have been successful in Korea.[13] Nicholas II had no such ministers.[14]

Be that as it may, Nicholas Muraviev, Admiral Evfimii V. Putiatin, and many other expansionists not only sought to establish a strong Russian position in the Far East, but also nurtured the ambition that "Russia should rule the East."[15] Such an ambition on the part of Russia only aroused Japanese apprehension and suspicion, as well as their determination to stop Russian expansionism in Korea, since they viewed the peninsula as "a dagger pointed at the heart of Japan."

A combination of those factors, together with Korean domestic factors and Japanese persistence in opposition to Russian penetration, did not allow Russia to be successful in her involvement in Korea. Moreover, various ineffective and ambiguous steps taken by the Russians in dealing with the Korean question eventually brought about Russia's downfall in Korea and a drastic curtailment of her influence in the Far East.

The Establishment of Relations with Korea and the Ascendance of Russian Influence, 1884–1897

Efforts made by the Russians from 1864 to establish trade relations with Korea at Gyeongheung near the Tumen river in Hamgyeong-do province did not bear any fruit. It was only after Korea concluded the Jemulpo Treaty with the United States in May 1882 that the Russians were able to establish diplomatic and commercial relations with Korea, which they did on July 7, 1884.[16]

---

13. Barbara Jellavich, *St. Petersburg and Moscow: Tsarist and Soviet Foreign Policy, 1814–1974* (Bloomington: Indiana University Press, 1974), p. 223.

14. Foreign Minister A. B. Lobanov-Rostovsky was an experienced and able statesman, but he died in 1896, and M. N. Muraviev, who succeeded Lobanov, was a man of much less ability and served the Tsar until 1900. V. N. Lamsdorff, who succeeded Muraviev, was a "sober, hard-working" man, but he lacked experience in service abroad and diplomatic vision and tactics.

15. Treadgold, op. cit., pp. 540-541.

16. For the Korean text of the treaty and commercial agreements, see *Gojong sunjong sillok, gwon* 2, pp. 153-157; Sin Gi-seok, *Dongyang oegyosa* (The Diplomatic History of the Far East) (Seoul: Dongguk Munhwasa, 1959), p. 249. Russia gained extraterritorial rights under the treaty.

The 1884 treaty allowed the Russians to trade at four Korean open ports, including Jemulpo (now Incheon) and Wonsan, which helped them establish a foothold in the Korean peninsula. Russia's voluntary and involuntary involvement in Korean affairs began with the arrival of Carl Waeber as Russian minister and consul-general to Korea. Waeber received much help from Paul G. von Möllendorff, a German who was sent to Korea in 1883 by Li Hongzhang to protect Chinese interests and become an adviser on foreign affairs as the superintendent of maritime customs service of Korea. Waeber's own "outstanding skill and knowledge" also enabled him to establish cordial relations with the Korean court and nurture the Korean court's favorable attitude toward Russia.[17]

Russia's Initial Political and Military Involvement in Korea, 1885–1887

The Tsarist government had no concrete plans for Korea in 1884 and 1885 other than to increase trade with Korea, and if possible, to incorporate the Hoeryeong area in the northeastern-most corner of Korea into the Russian sphere of influence.[18] The opportunity for Russia to be involved in Korean affairs was provided by both King Gojong and Möllendorff in 1885.

Following the Chinese military intervention, which overthrew the reform government of the Progressives in December 1884, Gojong desperately sought ways and means to protect the sovereignty and independence of his kingdom, however inept or unrealistic he might have been. At the same time, in view of the new situation in Korea, Möllendorff, who was sent to Korea to look after Chinese interests but developed distaste for them, sought Russian military assistance and protection for Korea. In his opinion, China was backward and detrimental to Korea while Japan could not be trusted.[19] American assistance was sought by Gojong, but the United States was unwilling.[20]

---

17. Sugimoto Masasuke and Oda Shogo, *Chosen sai kinse shi* (The Most Recent History of Korea) (Keijo, n.d.), p. 110.
18. *Ibid.*, p. 111.
19. "Baron von Möllendorff," *The Korea Review* 1 (1901): p. 252.
20. Lucius H. Foote, American minister to Korea, wrote to the Secretary of State on September 3, 1884 that "It would be particularly desirable that that influence of the United States should be felt in the regeneration of Corea, and that that influence should become a permanent factor in her progress." On May 15, 1885, George C. Faulk,

Möllendorff, who believed that foreign military assistance was urgently needed by Korea in order to protect her own independence, sought Russian help. The temptation was too strong for the Russians to resist, and in the end, Russia became entangled in the international affairs of Korea for the first time in 1885.

Möllendorff and the king's envoy, Seo Sang-u, were in Japan in late 1884 and early 1885, negotiating with Alexis de Speyer, secretary of the Russian legation in Tokyo, in order to secure Russian assistance. Meanwhile, the Korean king sent Kim Yong-won as his secret agent to Vladivostok for the same purpose without any knowledge or consent of his ministers.[21] The Russians were favorably inclined to the Korean proposal, and Speyer went to Seoul in January 1885 to negotiate with the Koreans for an agreement.

The secret Russo-Korean agreement was approved by the Tsar,[22] and Speyer went to Korea again in June in order to ratify the agreement as "Agent Provisoire." Since he had no credentials, he had to wait for the arrival of the Russian minister in Seoul. Meanwhile, he discovered that

who became acting charge in February 1885, wrote to the Secretary of State that "His majesty of Korea always and frequently expresses in strong terms his preference for Americans to fill the positions (military instructors)" and that he was embarrassed by the inaction on the pan of his government. See Foote to Secretary of State, No. 105, 3 September 1884 and Faulk to Secretary of State, No. 171, 15 May 1885 in *The Initial Period: 1883–1886*, vol. 1 of *Korean-American Relations: Documents Pertaining to Far Eastern Diplomacy of the United States*, ed. George M. McCune and John A. Harrison (Berkeley and Los Angeles: University of California Press, 1951), pp. 54-55, 57-88. Many other similar requests were made by Foote and Faulk that the United States should help Korea. But the United States remained disinterested in Korean affairs because her interest was mainly commercial rather than political. Acting Secretary of State, James D. Porter wrote to Faulk that the United States policy was not to interfere in internal politics of Korea officially. See Porter to Faulk, No. 70, 22 September 1885 in *The Initial Period: 1883–1886*, p. 124.

21. C. I. Eugene Kim and Han-kyo Kim, *Korea: Politics of Imperialism, 1876–1910* (Berkeley and Los Angeles: University of California Press, 1961), p. 62; Sugimoto and Oda, *op. cit.*, p. 110; McCune and Harrison, *op. cit.*, p. 14; Sin, op. cit., p. 251. For a detailed study on this subject, see Shigeyoshi Manji, "Sen-Ro hogo mitsuyaku teiketsu no kuwatate ni tsuite-1884 nen yori 1886 nen ni itaru" (Concerning the Attempts Made for the Conclusion of a Secret Protectorate Treaty between Korea and Russia), in *Inaba hakushi kanreki kinen man-sen-shi ronshu* (Collection of Essays in Histories of Manchuria and Korea in Commemoration of Dr. Inaba's 60th Birthday) (Tokyo: Inaba Hakushi Kanreki Kinen Ronshu Hensankai, 1937), pp. 319-352.

22. Faulk to Secretary of State, No. 191, 3 July 1885 and No. 192, 5 July 1885 in McCune and Harrison, *op. cit.*, pp. 80-83.

the secret agreement was made without the consent of Gojong's ministers, and it was negotiated solely on the initiatives of the king and Möllendorff without the knowledge of the government ministers. The Korean ministers, particularly Foreign Minister Kim Yun-sik, not only opposed such an agreement between Korea and Russia, but also bitterly criticized the actions taken by the king and Möllendorff.[23] Understandably, they rejected the agreement. Afterwards, Möllendorff was dismissed and recalled by Li Hongzhang, and with the departure of Mölendorff from Korea in November 1885, the Russians lost a valuable ally.

Although the attempts made by Gojong and Möllendorff failed, it was known that Korea entered into a secret agreement by which the Russians promised "to protect the integrity of Korea against all attacks by whomsoever made," as well as to send military instructors and give financial assistance to Korea in return for Russia's lease of Wonsan (Port Lazaroff).[24] Following his talks with Speyer, the American charge in Korea "guessed that the whole tenor of the Russian negotiations was to establish Korea as a protectorate of Russia . . ."[25] if not, "to establish complete Russian suzerainty over the peninsula."[26]

Needless to say, Speyer was not only disappointed, but also embarrassed by the entire affair. After dealing arrogantly with the Koreans, Speyer returned to Japan.

In the midst of the confusing state of affairs developed in the course of forging the Russo-Korean secret agreement, Great Britain ordered the occupation of a Korean island off the southern coast by British troops, while British naval forces took over Geomundo island (which they called Port Hamilton) on April 15, 1885, extending Anglo-Russian rivalries to the Far East. Obviously, it was "a hostile action against Russia," one aimed at the prevention of the establishment of Russian naval strength in the Far East,[27] as it was rumored that Russia had leased Wonsan and she was going to make it a Russian naval port.

---

23. Kim and Kim, *op. cit.*, p. 62; Sin, *op. cit.*, p. 215.
24. Tyler Dennett, *Americans in Eastern Asia: A Critical Study of United States Policy in the Far East in the Nineteenth Century* (New York: MacMillan, 1922), p. 480.
25. McCune and Harrison, *op. cit.*, p. 14. See Faulk to Secretary of State, No. 192, 5 July 1885 in McCune and Harrison, *op. cit.*, pp. 81-82.
26. Dennett, *op. cit.*, p. 480.
27. Faulk to Secretary of State, No. 180, 16 June 1885 in McCune and Harrison, *op. cit.*, pp. 77-78; Sin, *op. cit.*, p. 252.

When Speyer, who was in Korea at the time, learned about the British occupation of Geomundo, he bluntly stated to the American charge that he was instructed by his government to acquire "ten times as much territory for Russia" in Korea,[28] and he seemed ready to take some steps to counter British expansionism in Korea. Although the British insisted that the occupation of Geomundo was "a temporary measure," the construction of a fortress and other works carried out by the British troops on the island increased tension on the peninsula. The Korean government made a series of protests against the British and requested the immediate withdrawal of British troops from the island, but its efforts were not successful. Only when Li Hongzhang intervened and secured British assurances that they would withdraw from the island, and only after the actual withdrawal of British troops from the island in November 1886, along with the understanding that Russians would not occupy any points in Korea, was the threat of an Anglo-Russian clash removed. The Geomundo affair clearly showed that Russia was not only interested in establishing its influence in Korea, but also checking the growth of British strength, or that of other powers, in Korea.

In November 1885, Yuan Shikai, armed with stern instructions given by Li Hongzhang, arrived in Seoul as China's Minister Resident of Political and Commercial Affairs. He acted more like a Chinese viceroy rather than a Chinese minister, however, antagonizing not only the Koreans but also foreign diplomats. He showed his determination to root out any and all pro-Russianism in Korea; he felt that if Russian interest in Korea grew, it would be "a dire calamity."[29] In order to deal with Gojong, who was regarded as pro-Russian, and other pro-Russian Koreans, the Chinese allowed the Daewongun (ex-Regent and father of Gojong who had been taken captive by the Chinese in the summer of 1882 to China) to return to Korea in 1885. It was Yuan's secret plan to make him Regent one way or another in order to protect Chinese interests in Korea.

Yuan, who interfered in Korea's internal and external affairs in a high-handed manner, antagonized the Korean king and his ministers. Mean-

---

28. McCune and Harrison, *op. cit.*, p. 13. See Faulk to Secretary of State, No. 180, 16 July 1885 in McCune and Harrison, *op. cit.*, pp. 77-78.
29. Fred H. Harrington, *God, Mammon and the Japanese; Dr. Horace N. Allen and Korean-American Relations, 1884–1905* (Madison: The University of Wisconsin Press, 1944), p. 213.

while, Yuan found Min Yeong-ik, Queen Min's nephew, to be his ally. Gojong made vain efforts to counteract Yuan. Witnessing the helplessness of the king, some pro-Russian ministers sent a secret request to Carl Waeber, Russian minister to Korea, in the name of Prime Minister Sim Sun-taek. The note sent to Waeber had the king's seal and was dated August 1885.[30]

Yuan, who sensed the anti-Chinese and pro-Russian attitude of the king, was determined to dethrone Gojong by taking advantage of the new situation, although both Gojong and Prime Minister Sim denied any connection with the secret request sent to the Russian minister. Waeber also denied that there had been any bid for protection from the Korean king.[31] But denials made by the king and Waeber did not matter to Yuan. The report regarding the arrival of "a fleet of four Russian war vessels" (actually only one Russian warship) in Wonsan made the situation worse. A rumor that a secret agreement had been signed between Korea and Russia and that it had included an agreement "to transfer to Russia the sovereignty over Korea" persisted.[32]

Yuan's plot to dethrone Gojong failed when his plot was detected and exposed by American and British diplomats,[33] and thanks to Li Hongzhang's sober decision not to send Chinese troops to Korea in 1886 by reacting to Yuan's claims, the crisis was ended.[34]

After the 1885–1886 affairs, Waeber maintained a low profile, conducting a quiet diplomacy to promote Russian interests in Korea. He cultivated cordial relations with the Korean court and won the confi-

---

30. The royal seal had evidently been stolen and used by the plotters, Sin, *op. cit.*, p. 252.
31. Harrington, *op. cit.*, p. 14.
32. Dennett, *op. cit.*, p. 483. The secret agreement was said to have included the following items: (1) Korea's concession of the northern-most corner of Hamgyeong-do province to Russia; (2) Korea's recognition of Russian right to station troops there; (3) Korea's opening of Yeongheungman bay to Russia for trade; and (4) Korea's recognition of the right of Russian naval vessels to anchor in the port of Bukcheong in Hamgyeong-do province. See Watanabe Shujiro, *Toho kankei* (Eastern Relations) (Hamamatsu: Hokokai, 1894), p. 344 and details in Shigeyoshi, op. cit., pp. 229-341.
33. Dennett, *op. cit.*, p. 483. For details of Yuan's actions and Li Hongzhang's response, see Harrington, *op. cit.*, pp. 214-215; Sin, *op. cit.*, pp. 253-254; Hilary Conroy, *The Japanese Seizure of Korea, 1868-1910: A Study of Realism and Idealism in International Relations* (Philadelphia: University of Pennsylvania Press, 1960), pp. 204-205; Shigeyoshi, op. cit., pp. 337-352.
34. Among other things, Yuan requested Li to send a large number of troops and war vessels to Korea.

dence of many Koreans, including Queen Min. The Russians wanted to establish naval coaling stations at Wonsan and on Jeoryeongdo (Deer) island near Busan, but when the Chinese objected strongly they suspended their negotiations with the Korean government.[35] However, Waeber was able to open Gyeongheung, a town in Hamgyeong-do province near the Korean-Russian boarder, for trade in August 1888. It was suspected that the Russian plan was to make Gyeongheung an forward base of Russia from which to penetrate into Korea.[36]

When the Sino-Japanese War seemed inevitable, the Russian minister in Tokyo, Mikhail Hitrovo, attempted to find out what Japan's real intentions in Korea were.[37] Meanwhile, Waeber, presently in Seoul, under instructions from his government, sought to ally with Western nations in order to intervene in the Sino-Japanese conflict, while expressing Russian concerns for Korea's security directly to the Japanese.[38] Joint efforts made by the Russians, British, and Americans failed to prevent the war between China and Japan over Korea.

The Rise of Russian Influence, 1895–1897

The Triple Intervention of Russia, France, and Germany, which forced Japan to cancel the Liaotung lease in the Shimonoseki Treaty of April 1895, the assassination of Queen Min by the Japanese and their Korean collaborators in October 1895, and the Korean king's establishment of his residence in the Russian legation on February 11, 1896 brought about a sudden rise of Russian influence in Korea.

Whereas the Triple Intervention led the Koreans to overestimate Russian power and capability, the assassination of the Korean queen by the Japanese aroused strong anti-Japanese sentiment in Korea.

In October 1895, an alliance was formed between Waeber and politically ambitious Koreans, such as Yi Beom-jin, Yi Wan-yong, and Yi Yun-yong, who hated the Japanese. It was this group of Koreans which attempted to "kidnap" the king and put him under their protective cus-

---

35. Han Woo Keun, *History of Korea*, trans. Kyung-Shik Lee and ed. Grafton K. Mintz (Honolulu: University of Hawaii Press, 1970), p. 398.
36. Sin, *op. cit.*, p. 250; Tabohashi Kiyoshi, *Kindai nishisen kankei no kenkyu* (A Study of Recent Sino-Korean-Japanese Relations) (Keijo: Chusui-in, 1940), pp. 200-203.
37. Sin, *op. cit.*, p. 274.
38. Tabohashi, *op. cit.*, pp. 208-209.

tody on November 29, 1895.[39] Meanwhile, Speyer arrived in Seoul to be a successor to Waeber. Yi Beom-jin and his men drew up a careful plan in cooperation with the Russians to strike a coup.[40] Some one hundred Russian troops were brought to Seoul on November 20, 1895,[41] and on February 9, 1896 about two hundred additional Russian troops arrived in Seoul and the security of the Russian legation was strengthened.[42] Early morning in February 11, King Gojong and the crown prince moved their residence from the Gyeongungung palace (now Deoksugung palace) to the nearby Russian legation, escorted by a large number of Russian soldiers.[43] The Russians and pro-Russian Koreans at the Russian legation welcomed them. Immediately after this, pro-Japanese Prime Minister Kim Hong-jip, Finance Minister Eo Yun-jung, and Minister of Agriculture-Commerce-Industry Jeong Byeong-ha were killed, while other ministers fled to Japan.

Dr. Horace N. Allen, American legation secretary in Korea, disclosed that on February 10, the day before the king moved to the Russian legation, the Korean king asked him if it would be wise to seek the aid of Russia. Allen had "wished" it and he "hastened to endorse the king's suggestion and personally assisted in perfecting plans."[44] Allen and Waeber met a Korean officer that night in order to carry out the plan that had been drawn up and readied by Waeber and the Koreans for some time.

During King Gojong's stay at the Russian legation, which lasted a little over a year, the Russians gained an indisputable political advantage over other foreign powers in Korea. Soon after the king moved to the Russian legation, a new cabinet was formed and it included such ministers as Bak Jeong-yang, Yi Beom-jin, Yi Yun-yong, and Yun Yong-seon, all of whom were regarded as either pro-Russian or pro-American. During that period, the Korean government was "completely manipulated by the Russians,"[45] and "Russia assumed as complete a control over

39. Sugimoto and Oda, *op. cit.*, p. 143; Kikuchi Kanejo, *Kindai chosenshi* (The Modern History of Korea), vol. 2 (Keijo: Keimei-sha, 1939), p. 450. There were attempts made by some Koreans to dethrone Gojong or poison him in November 1895.
40. Yi Byeong-do, *Guksa daegwan* (A Survey of Korean History) (Seoul: Bomungak, 1957), p. 545.
41. Kikuchi, *op. cit.*, p. 451.
42. *Ibid.*, pp. 451-452.
43. *Ibid.*, p. 453.
44. Harrington, *op. cit.*, p. 288.
45. Sugimoto and Oda, *op. cit.*, p. 148.

Korean affairs as China and Japan, respectively, had tried out yet failed to acquire."[46] The Russians were pleased, and Russian control over Korea seemed permanent.

Russian influence in Korea was at its zenith. But Waeber played cautious diplomatic games. First of all, he concluded an agreement with Komura Jutaro, Japanese minister to Korea, in May 1896 and secured Japanese consent to a new Russian right to station troops in Korea to protect the Russian legation and consulates.[47] In view of the new situation developed in Korea, the Japanese formally acknowledged, for the first time, that Russia had as much right as Japan to be interested in Korean by signing the Komura-Waeber Agreement. In return for a vague Russian promise to advise the Korean king to return to his palace, the Japanese agreed to reduce its troops in Korea, acknowledged its past wrongdoings (the murder of Queen Min) by Japanese nationals, and agreed to accept the recently formed anti-Japanese cabinet as being "liberal and moderate."[48] Meanwhile, General Charles LeGendre, an American who had cordial relations with Waeber, was made adviser to the Korean court.[49]

In the late spring of 1896, the Russian government struck a diplomatic coup when representatives of many foreign governments were in St. Petersburg to attend the coronation ceremony of Tsar Nicholas II. Rus-

---

46. Dennett, *op. cit.*, p. 504.
47. The Komura-Waeber agreement of May 14, 1896 included the following items: (1) the Korean king was to return to the palace at his own discretion, (2) control of Japanese in Korea was guaranteed by the Japanese government, (3) the present members of the Korean cabinet were to be recognized and accepted by Russia and Japan, (4) Japan was to continue to have troops in Korea to guard the Japanese telegraph line between Seoul and Busan, and (5) Japanese troops were to be temporarily stationed in Seoul, Busan, and Wonsan for the protection of Japanese settlements. Russia was entitled to keep an equal number of troops at those places for the protection of Russian properties. It was agreed that the number of Japanese troops to be stationed in Korea to protect telegraph line should not be more than 200, and the number of Japanese troops in Seoul and other places should not exceed four battalions of 200 men each. For the English text, see Frederick A. Mckenzie, *Tragedy of Korea* (London: Hodder and Stoughton, 1908), pp. 299-300. See also, Carnegie Endowment for International Peace, *Korea: Treaties and Agreements* (Washington, 1921), pp. 21-22; NGB, XXIX, p. 682; Sin, *op. cit.*, pp. 324-325; Han, *op. cit.*, p. 343; Conroy, *op. cit.*, p. 323; Kikuchi, *op. cit.*, pp. 500-502.
48. Kim and Kim, *op. cit.*, pp. 90-91.
49. Sugimoto and Oda, *op. cit.*, p. 148.

sia concluded a secret treaty (the Li-Lobanov Treaty) signed by Li Hongzhang of China and Foreign Minister A. B. Lobanov Rostovsky in June,[50] and the protocol of Moscow dated June 9, 1898[51] was signed between Yamagata Aritomo of Japan and Foreign Minister Lobanov. In the Li-Lobanov Treaty, Russia made a promise to protect Korea and Manchuria from Japanese encroachments, and in the Lobanov-Yamagata Protocol, Russia gained Japan's consent to build a telegraph line between Seoul and Vladivostok, as well as the right to advise the Korean government in financial affairs and make loans to Korea. In addition, both Russia and Japan agreed to assist the Korean government in maintaining its own internal security without outside assistance, and they agreed to send troops to Korea only when absolutely necessary, only with the knowledge and consent of the other. In such a way, Russia established many equal rights in Korea that Japan had previously enjoyed almost exclusively. At the same time, Russia rejected a Japanese proposal to divide Korea into two spheres of influence along the 38th parallel, with North Korea as a Russian sphere and south Korea as a Japanese one.[52]

A secret agreement, which was as important as that of the Li-Lobanov, was signed between Korea and Russia in June 1896. It was signed by Russian Foreign Minister Lobanov and a Korean envoy, Min Yeong-hwan, who attended the coronation ceremony of Tsar Nicholas II. During this audience with the Tsar, Min asked that his country "be taken under the protection of Russia." The Tsar accepted the Korean request on the spot, but was later persuaded by Lobanov that that was not possible.[53] But the Min-Lobanov agreement assured Russian protection for the Korean king, as well as military and financial aid.[54] In return, Russia gained the right to station Russian warships on Jeoryeongdo island near

---

50. For details of the Sino-Russian agreement, see Immanuel C. Y. Hsu, *The Rise of Modern China* (New York, London and Toronto: Oxford University Press, 1970), pp. 413-415.

51. For details, see Kim and Kim, *op. cit.*, p. 91; Sugimoto and Oda, *op. cit.*, pp. 154-155; Sin, *op. cit.*, p. 325; Dennett, *op. cit.*, p. 504. For the English text, see *Korea: Treaties and Agreements*, pp. 23-24.

52. Treadgold, op. cit., p. 543; Sin, *op. cit.*, p. 325.

53. Hugh Seton-Watson, *The Decline of Imperial Russia, 1885–1914* (New York: Praeger, 1912), p. 205.

54. For details, see Sin, *op. cit.*, pp. 327, 332; Kim and Kim, *op. cit.*, pp. 92-93; Kikuchi, *op. cit.*, pp. 500-502.

Busan and protect the island from foreign (Japanese) fishermen, train Korean troops, employ Korean workers in Siberia, form an alliance between Russia, China, and Korea, mine in Hamgyeong-do province, establish timber industries in Hamgyeong-do and Gangwon-do provinces, and enjoy freedom of movement of Russian warships off the coasts of Hamgyeong-do and Pyeongan-do provinces.[55] In addition, Russia gained the right to station troops in those two provinces. Korea agreed in a separate memorandum to send Korean students to Russia to study and employ Russian advisers in the government. Thus the stage was set for a greater Russian involvement in Korea.

In July 1896, Russia obtained mining and railway rights in Gyeongheung and Jongseong areas in Hamgyeong-do province, and sent two representatives of the Russo-Chinese Bank to Seoul, together with a small group of Russian military personnel, 400 rifles and ammunition in violation of the Lobanov-Yamagata Protocol. In October, Colonel Potiata, three other officers, and twenty military instructors arrived from Russia in Seoul. At the same time, a secret three-million-yen loan agreement was signed between Korea and Russia.

In 1896, the ascendancy of the Russian influence was conspicuous, and Russian control over the Korean government was firm. A Russian, Jules Bryner, had gained a timber concession along the Yalu river in August 1896, and Waeber was able to make the Korean government rescind its earlier concession made to the Japanese to construct the Seoul-Busan railway line. Through Waeber's help, an American, James R. Morse, received a concession from Korea to build the Seoul-Incheon railway line, and a French syndicate received the right to construct the Seoul-Uiju railway line in July.[56]

In March 1897, a branch of the Russo-Chinese Bank was opened in Seoul, and in October a Russian, K. A. Alexiev replaced the British McLeavy Brown as superintendent of the maritime customs service and financial adviser to the Korean government.

So confident was the Russian minister regarding the Russian position in Korea, and in view of the growing nationalistic sentiment among Korean reform advocates, that the Russian minister did not raise any

---

55. Ministry of Foreign Affairs, Japan, *Komura gaiko-shi* (History of Komura Jutaro's Diplomacy), vol. 1 (Tokyo, 1953), p. 95 (hereafter cited as *Komura Diplomacy*).
56. For concession made by the Korean government to Western powers, see Sin, *op. cit.*, pp. 330-332; Kikuchi, *op. cit.*, pp. 542-543.

objections when the king decided to leave the Russian legation and return to his palace in February 1897. Be that as it may, Japan was "alarmed by Russian penetration" in Korea as well as in the Far East, and the Japanese became more apprehensive of Russian domination, although Russia had no Far Eastern plan as such, except to block Japanese domination over Korea.[57]

The Decline of Russian Influence and the End of Russian Intervention in Korea, 1898–1904

In 1893, D. A. Dmitrevsky, a Russian representative in Seoul, told American minister to Korea, Augustine Heard, that the Japanese were "mad with dread and hatred to Russia."[58] The Japanese felt that they had to do something to curb Russian influence in Korea in 1897. In order to discredit the Russians and weaken the confidence of the Koreans in Russia, Japanese Foreign Minister Okuma Shigenobu made public in March 1897 the Komura-Waeber Agreement and the open articles of the Lobanov-Yamagata Protocol. Following that, some Korean officials displayed their resentment against the Russians for their double-dealings, as well as the signing of agreements with Japan without the knowledge of the Koreans, but these concerns were raised only in private.[59] Such criticism and resentment did only little damage to Russian influence.

The Eclipse of Russian Influence

It was the rising nationalism and the new spirit of independence among the reform advocates in Korea, particularly those of the Dongnip Hyeophoe (Independence Club), which motivated the Korean govern-

---

57. Treadgold, op. cit., pp. 542-543.
58. Spencer J. Palmer, ed. with an introduction, *The Period of Growing Influence, 1887–1895*, vol. 3 of *Korean-American Relations: Documents Pertaining to the Far Eastern Diplomacy of the United States* (Berkeley and Los Angeles: University of California Press, 1963), pp. 251-252.
59. Andrew Malozemoff, *Russian Far Eastern Policy, 1881–1902* (Berkeley and Los Angeles: University of California Press, 1958), p. 91; Japan, Ministry of Foreign Affairs, *Nihon gaiko bunsho* (Japanese Diplomatic Documents) (Tokyo: Nihon Kokusai Rengo Kyokai, 1945–), XXX, pp. 385-386 (hereafter cited as *NGB*); *Komura Diplomacy*, vol. 1, pp. 91-92.

ment to adopt a new foreign policy and promote self-strength. It was this group of reform advocates that urged the Korean king to return to his palace from the Russian legation and not rely on foreign powers for Korea's safety and independence. They also openly criticized the agreements made in 1896 between Korea and Russia.[60]

The rise of Korean nationalistic reform advocates, and the hesitance of the Korean government to employ some 160 Russian military personnel for the Korean army signaled the beginnings of the eclipse of Russian influence in Korea. However, the Russian minister failed to understand the nationalistic Koreans or form an alliance with them in order to preserve Russian interests in Korea. The replacement of Waeber by Speyer in January 1898 was one of the most important factors associated with the decline of Russian influence in Korea. Waeber's diplomatic tact had won him the royal favor and the goodwill of many foreign diplomats in Seoul, but Alexis de Speyer was "an overly aggressive man who had dealt arrogantly with the Koreans."[61]

Speyer was determined to strengthen the control that Russia had over the Korean government. In 1897, he said to Horace N. Allen, secretary of the American legation in Korea, that he did not approve of what Waeber had done, and that he was "a true Russian" while "Mr. Waeber was not."[62] Speyer's words and actions made "it look as though the Russians were about to absorb Joseon," and Allen himself believed that "the jig is up for Korea."[63] Speyer acted "in a bad way,"[64] and his "haughty and self-righteous attitudes" won the enmity of many Korean ministers and foreign diplomats.[65] The way in which Speyer forced Min Jong-muk, acting minister of foreign affairs, to sign an agreement with Russia granting a lease for a coaling station on Jeoryeongdo island near Busan in February 1898 aroused Korean hostility.[66] Not only that, the pressure he exerted upon the Korean government to appoint Min, who had been

---

60. For details of their activities, see Han, op. cit., pp. 439-442; Chong-sik Lee, *The Politics of Korean Nationalism* (Berkeley and Los Angeles: University of California Press, 1963), pp. 55-69.
61. Malozemoff, *op. cit.,* pp. 89-90.
62. Horace N. Allen, Diary, 14 and 16 October 1897, quoted in Harrington, *op. cit.,* p. 299.
63. Harrington, *op. cit.,* p. 300.
64. *Ibid.,* p. 301.
65. Lee, *op. cit.,* p. 63.
66. Harrington, *op. cit.,* p. 301.

dismissed a short while ago, to the position of Foreign Minister created strong anti-Russian feelings in Korea.[67]

The most intemperate and damaging action taken by Speyer was his demand for the unequivocal declaration of the Korean government for its pro-Russian stand, the punishment of anti-Russian Korean officials, and the seeking of a greater Russian assistance.[68] Speyer had been extremely annoyed by those Koreans who were against any alliance between Korea and Russia and Korean reliance on Russia for Korea's own safety. He was bitterly critical of anti-Russian Korean officials whom he regarded as "idlers . . . claiming to be the gifted politicians."[69] He accused the Korean government of ingratitude and delivered an ultimatum that the Korean government make a decision for further Russian assistance within twenty-four hours.[70] When Speyer had an audience with the Korean emperor (the Korean king changed his title from king to emperor in 1898) in March 1898, he stipulated that unless a number of anti-Russian officials were dismissed and the hostile demonstrations of the nationalists against Russia suppressed, his government would withdraw its financial and military instructors from Korea.[71]

Speyer's tactics backfired, and when the Korean government, irritated by the tactless Speyer, refused to comply, he fell into his own trap and was forced to withdraw all Russian employees of the Korean government. The Russo-Korean Bank, which was established in Seoul less than a month before, was closed, and a Briton, McLeavy Brown, replaced Alexiev as Superintendent of the Maritime Customs Service and financial adviser to the Korean government. Speyer himself was transferred to Brazil in April. Thus, the Russian influence in Seoul that had been skillfully and patiently cultivated by Waeber was destroyed overnight,[72] and the Russian tide had begun to recede rapidly from its high watermark of 1896–1897.[73] At the same time, to the Russians Korea seemed of

---

67. *Ibid.*, p. 300.
68. Lee, *op. cit.*, p. 63; Kim and Kim, *op. cit.*, p. 95.
69. Quoted in Harrington, *op. cit.*, p. 301.
70. Lee, *op. cit.*, p. 63.
71. Quoted from Lee, *op. cit.*, p. 63. It was Speyer's opinion that "the Korean royal court could not be saved without resorting to some radical measure . . . [and that] Korea could never be independent and hence it was necessary for Japan and Russia to divide Korea and protect it." *Komura Diplomacy*, vol. 1, p. 97.
72. Kim and Kim, *op. cit.*, p. 95.
73. *Ibid.*, p. 96.

"secondary importance" even as Japanese interests in Korea grew. It looked as though Russia might "make a political retreat from Korea altogether."[74] However, although the Russians made a blunder and Russian influence was reduced drastically, no one in Korea thought that Russia withdrew from Korea permanently. As Allen said, Russia would "come for good and all."[75]

Both Japan and Russia desired to find an acceptable solution for the Korean question in 1898. However, when the Japanese sought an understanding with Russia regarding Korea in that year, the Russians refused to relinquish its interests on the peninsula. R. R. Rosen, Russian minister to Japan, said: "We cannot admit the exclusion as a matter of principle of all influence of Russia who cannot divest herself of all concern in the destinies of a state adjacent to her frontier."[76] Be that as it may, in view of the new situation that developed in Korea, as well as a new Russo-Chinese agreement concluded in March 1898 regarding the Liaotung lease, the Russians became a little more conciliatory and concluded the Nishi-Rosen Convention of April 25, 1898.[77]

Although Russia concluded the 1898 agreement with Japan she never abandoned her interests in Korea, and it was quite clear that she was waiting for an opportunity to revive her influence in the Korean peninsula one way or another. Her desire to establish Russian naval stations in warm-water ports of Korea remained strong. For this reason, Russia refused Japan's proposal to make Manchuria a Russian sphere of influence and recognize Korea as a Japanese sphere of influence.[78]

Nicholas Matunin, the new Russian minister to Korea, who succeeded Speyer in 1898, was personally associated with the lumber enterprises of

---

74. *Ibid.*, p. 99.
75. Quoted in Harrington, *op. cit.*, p. 301.
76. Quoted in Kim and Kim, *op. cit.*, pp. 95-96. See also, *NGB*, XXXI, pp. 163-164; Seton-Watson, *op. cit.*, p. 206.
77. It was concluded between Russian Minister to Japan Rosen and Japanese Foreign Minister Nishi Tokujiro. In it, both parties agreed: (1) to recognize Korea's independence and sovereignty, (2) to refrain from nominating military and financial advisers to Korea without a prior understanding between them, and that (3) Russia would not interfere with Japanese commercial and industrial interests in Korea. For the English text, see *Korea: Treaties and Agreements*, pp. 23-24.
78. *Komura Diplomacy*, vol. 1, p. 98. Japan's plan was known as that of "Man-Kan Kokan" or "Manchuria-for-Korea." The "Manchuria-for-Korea" idea of the Japanese persisted, and the Japanese suggestion was also made in 1902 and 1903 to the Russians.

Alexander M. Bezobrazov, and A. I. Pavlov who succeeded Matunin in January 1899 was "an out-and-out expansionist."[79] Both were instructed by their government to be cautious and avoid any rash actions. Meanwhile, Finance Minister S. Ia Witte restricted the activities of Russian businessmen in Korea. However, Russian ministers to Korea worked in close cooperation with other Russians in Seoul, such as Antoinette Sontag, a relative of Mrs. Waeber and Baron Gunzburg, Seoul representative of Russian lumber interests, as well as pro-Russian Koreans such as Yi Yong-ik, in order to revive Russian influence.

Following the occupation of Manchuria by a large number of Russian troops in the aftermath of the Boxer Rebellion, Russian actions became increasingly reckless and irresponsible.[80] Finance Minister Witte had advocated "a policy of gradual economic penetration" but he came into conflict with those who wished to strengthen Russian power in the Far East "quickly and with military means."[81] In addition, the tactics employed by Russian ministers in Korea only aroused stronger antagonism and apprehension on the part of the Japanese.

In 1899, the Russians seemed to have become resolved to secure the Korea Strait, which they probably considered an Asian Dardanelles. If the Japanese established one or more naval bases on the south coast of Korea, the movement of Russian ships, whether they were military or commercial, would surely be severely restricted, and Vladivostok would be useless in time of crisis. In as much as the Russians considered the south coast of Korea between Busan and Jinhae a strategic area, the Japanese also regarded that region as a critical point, and they had been concerned over possible Russian occupation of the area.

Shortly after the Russians gained whaling rights off Ulsan and Jangjin in the southeast coast of Korea in March 1899, Pavlov went to Masan—located between Busan and Jinhae—in order to buy a strip of land there. Soon after his arrival in Masan, a small Russian fleet arrived in April, and Pavlov began his negotiations with the Koreans. The intentions of the Russians were clear, as they were to establish a naval base in Masan and secure the Korea Strait for their strategic advantage.

---

79. Harrington, *op. cit.*, p. 303.
80. Charles and Barbara Jelavich, *The Establishment of the Balkan National States, 1804–1920*, vol. 8 of *History of East Central Europe* (Seattle: University of Washington Press), p. 242.
81. *Ibid.*, p. 236.

When it became known to the Japanese that the Russians were attempting to build a naval base in Masan, a Japanese colonel told Hayashi Gonsuke, who was designated as a new Japanese minister to Korea, that "If this point is occupied by the Russians the future of Japan would be done with."[82] The Russian plan was frustrated by quick action taken by Minister Hayashi in July, who preempted the choice pieces of land in Masan.[83]

In October 1899, the Russians made another attempt to lease a piece of land in Mokpo, a seaport on the southwest coast of Korea, but that plan also met with Japanese opposition and failed.[84] In 1900, however, the Russians were able to lease Yulgumi, a small port near Masan, but they abandoned their plans at Yulgumi because of its defects and cancelled the lease. Repeated Japanese interference irritated the Russians, who by now were becoming desperate. Meanwhile, efforts made by the Russians in Korea led Japanese Prime Minister Katsura Taro to suspect that Russia would attempt to seize Korea after Manchuria.[85] With such a suspicion, Katsura authorized the negotiations for an alliance between Japan and Great Britain.

In January 1901, the Russian minister to Japan failed to receive Japanese consent to neutralize Korea under an international guarantee.[86] Meanwhile, in 1902 Russia again rejected a Japanese request for Russian recognition of Korea as Japan's exclusive sphere of interest in exchange for Japanese recognition of Manchuria as Russia's exclusive sphere of interest.[87]

The End of Russian Intervention in Korea

Nicholas II, who vacillated until 1901 between two opposing groups in his court, fell in 1903 under the influence of an expansionist, Alexander M. Bezobrazov, who had visited the Far East in 1902 under the Tsar's request. Bezobrazov had received a sum of two million rubles from the

---

82. Quoted in Hayashi Gonsuke, *Waga sichijunen o kataru* (Speaking of My Seventy Years) (Tokyo: Daiichi Shobo, 1936), p. 120.
83. *Ibid.*, pp. 124-126. The land in question was purchased by Japanese merchants.
84. Sugimoto and Oda, *op. cit.*, p. 163.
85. *Komura Diplomacy*, vol. 1, pp. 257-259.
86. *NGB*, XXXIV, p. 521; Hayashi, *op. cit.*, pp. 206-211.
87. *NGB*, XXXV, pp. 292-294.

Russo-Chinese Bank under instructions of the Tsar, and in 1903 he formed a company for the exploitation of the timber resources of the Yalu river valley under the timber concession given by Korea to Russia in 1896.

Meanwhile, War Minister General A. N. Kuropatkin expressed his wish to annex north Manchuria and his belief that agreement could be reached with Japan to make south Korea a Japanese sphere and establish a neutral zone comprising south Manchuria and north Korea.[88]

Nicholas II had been brainwashed by William II of Germany, who told the Tsar not to yield Korea to Japan. Korea, William II said, was "a tongue of land which may—in an adversary's hand—become a new son of Dardanelles.[89] Not only that, William II led the Tsar as early as 1895 to believe that "Russia's destiny was to cultivate the Asian continent and to defend Europe from the inroad of the Great Yellow Race."[90] "Twenty to thirty million Chinese," said William II to the Tsar, "trained and helped by half a dozen Japanese divisions and led by five hundred Christian-hating Japanese officers" were threatening the Western world.[91] Therefore, William II insisted that it was the duty of the Tsar to "defend the Cross and the Old Christian European culture against the inroads of the Mongols and Buddhism. . . ."[92] The German emperor promised the Tsar that "In this you will always find me on your side ready to help you as best I can."[93] In 1903, William II told Nicholas II that "It is evident to every unbiased mind that Korea must and will be Russian."[94] Interior Minister Viacheslav K. Plehve declared in 1903 that "We must decide the question at issue with China and Japan with bayonets and not with diplomatic Pen."[95]

Whatever his plans for Korea may have been, Nicholas II was supported by such aggressive expansionists as Interior Minister Plehve, Bezobrazov who was appointed as Imperial Secretary in May 1903, and

---

88. Seton-Watson, *op. cit.*, pp. 210-211.
89. Quoted in *ibid.*, p. 212.
90. Quoted in *ibid.*, p. 202; Jelavich, *op. cit.*, p. 242.
91. Seton-Watson, *op. cit.*, p. 202.
92. Quoted in Jelavich, *op., cit.*, p. 243.
93. *Ibid.*, p. 242.
94. *Ibid.*, p. 243; Seton-Watson, *op. cit.*, p. 212.
95. Jelavich, *op. cit.*, p. 243; Komatsu Midori, *Meiji shijitsu gaiko hiwa* (Secret Tales Related to Diplomatic Affairs of the Meiji Period) (Tokyo: Chugai Sangyo Shimposha, 1927), p. 266.

Admiral Alexeev who became regent of the Far East in August. General Kuropatkin complained to Witte in February 1903 that the Tsar "wants Manchuria, hopes to unite Korea with Russia."[96] Finance Minister Witte and Foreign Minister V. M. Lamsdorff favored gradual and peaceful penetration in the Far East and the avoidance of any entanglement with Japan over Korea. However, with the dismissal of Witte in 1903, an outspoken critic of the policy of the Tsar and his supporters, the voice of the moderates in the Russian court was silenced. In September, Bezobrazov became secretary of the newly created Far Eastern Committee.

While disputing with Japan and other powers over the Manchurian issue in 1903, the Russians made a final blunder in Korea. In April, some sixty Russians and about forty Chinese workers came to Yongampo, a small town located at the mouth of the Yalu River, near Uiju and occupied a large amount of land to build barracks for "lumbermen." Following this, the Russians proceeded to construct the cable line between Yongampo and Andong, a Manchurian town across the Yalu river, and to build a military base in the town.[97] It was Bezobrazov's intention to use his enterprise to penetrate and seize Korea.[98]

The Russians told the Koreans that those Russians in Yongampo were lumbermen of the company formed by Bezobrazov. But they were Russian soldiers in disguise. The Korean government, as well as the British and the Japanese, protested against Russian action. Russian Minister Pavlov not only ignored the protest, but proceeded to lease a piece of land in Yongampo.

Such an action taken by the Russians led Prime Minister Katsura Taro and other Japanese leaders to conclude that Russia was about to seize Korea.[99] In June 1903, the Japanese leaders agreed at an Imperial conference not to make any concessions to Russia regarding Korean territory.[100] However, the Japanese showed their willingness to negotiate with Russia regarding Korea and presented a proposal dated July 28 to Russia in which they indicated their willingness to recognize Manchuria as

96. Quoted in Seton-Watson, *op. cit.*, p. 212.

97. Japan, Ministry of Foreign Affairs, *Nihon gaiko hyakunenshi* (One Hundred Years of Diplomatic History of Japan) (Tokyo: Yamada Shoin, 1958), p. 56; Sugimoto and Oda, *op. cit.*, pp. 170-171; Kikuchi, *op. cit.*, pp. 571-576. Kikuchi has a lengthy discussion on Russian lumber interest in Korea and on the case of Yongampo.

98. Seton-Watson, *op. cit.*, p. 211; Treadgold, op. cit., p. 545.

99. *Komura Diplomacy*, vol. 1, pp. 257-259.

100. *Nihon gaiko hyakunenshi*, p. 56.

Russia's exclusive sphere of interest if Russia recognize Korea as Japan's exclusive sphere of interest. In as much as the Japanese proposal was unacceptable to the Russians, the Russian counterproposal of October 3 regarding Manchuria and Korea was unacceptable to Japan.[101] The Japanese rejected the Russian proposal to establish a neutral zone in the area north of the 38th parallel in Korea, and insisted that Japan have rights in Korea equal to those of Russia in Manchuria.

All subsequent negotiations between Japan and Russia carried out from December 1903 to February 1904 failed to settle the Korean question, leading to the outbreak of the Russo-Japanese War.[102] Both Russia and Japan ignored the Korean government's declaration of neutrality, signed on January 21, 1904.[103] The Japanese victory over Russia in 1905 put an end to Tsarist Russia's influence and her ambitions in Korea, and whatever she had accomplished was undone by the Japanese.

Conclusion

Tsarist Russia became involved in a variety of ways in Korea's internal and external affairs from 1884. However, this study shows that various efforts made by the Russians during the period failed to achieve their objectives.

Evidence shows that Russia had no coherent Korea policy as such, and her intervention in Korea was prompted by her desire to establish political and military hegemony in Korea and to check British and Japanese expansionism in the Far East. Having no modern industrial

---

101. In the counterproposal, Russia wanted a free hand in Manchuria, but refused to allow Japan to have the same rights in Korea. Moreover, the Russians insisted that no part of Korea was to be used for strategic purpose by Japan and there were to be no Japanese military installations on the Korean coast. More importantly, the Russians proposed to make the 38th parallel a demarcation line, and the area north of that line to be a neutral zone, and that Japan may have economic interests in the southern part of Korea, but regard Manchuria and its coastline as outside the Japanese sphere of interest. See, Seton-Watson, *op. cit.*, pp. 213-214; Malozemoff, *op. cit.*, pp. 239-240; *Komura Diplomacy*, vol. 1, pp. 334-335; and Kim and Kim, *op. cit.*, pp. 100-101.

102. See details in *Komura Diplomacy*, vol. 1, pp. 335-360; Malozemoff, *op. cit.*, pp. 241-249.

103. For the Korean text of neutrality declaration, see *NGB*, XXXVII, pt. 1, pp. 310-311.

economy, Russia's commercial interest was insignificant, whereas her desires to have warm-water ports in Korea were strong. If she had any sense of *mission civilisatrice* she failed to show any signs, and if it was Russia's design to seize and unite Korea with Russia, her efforts were as utterly inadequate as they were ineffective.

With certain minor exceptions, Russian aims in Korea were not realized for various reasons. First of all, Russia lacked historical experience in the art of diplomacy. The Russians were able to conquer and subjugate others with military power, but they were unable to achieve their goals diplomatically. Secondly, Russia had only a few experienced and capable men in the field of foreign affairs, and strategies and tactics employed by the Russian diplomats in Korea were not only ineffective, but also counter-productive in terms of making Russian intervention viable and profitable. If Russia had any economic interest in Korea, she failed to establish a sound foundation to make her economic penetration into Korea possible, certain economic concessions gained from the Korean government notwithstanding. While Russian ministers in Korea were committing many errors, they had no support from Russian merchants and politically astute people in Korea, as was the case with Japan. As a matter of fact, there were virtually no Russian merchants or nonofficial political figures in Korea.

Now and then, the Russians gained favorable positions in Korea and exercised a certain degree of influence over the Korean government, but this was due more to the willingness of others to compromise and wait for a better opportunity to achieve their aims in Korea, or to the anti-Japanese (pro-Russian) activities of Koreans themselves, rather than to the result of Russian power or skillful diplomatic maneuvering in Korea.

Russian influence grew much in Korea when Japan grudgingly accepted the demand made by the Triple Intervention in 1895 and suspended her aggressiveness in Korea temporarily. When the Russians gained influence in Korea and control over the Korean government in 1896, it was due to what anti-Japanese Koreans had done. In a sense, Japan was often an involuntary ally to Russia and contributed to the rise of Russian influence in Korea, for the more anti-Japanese Koreans became, the greater was Russian influence.

In Korea, Russia encountered the persistent opposition of Japan, which had identical, if not greater and more extensive, aims in Korea. The Japanese had already established considerable economic strength and a certain political advantage in Korea after 1876. As a result, from the beginning of Russian involvement in Korea, Japan stood in Russia's way, utilizing more effective diplomatic strategies coming from a stronger economic position and more skillful diplomats and businessmen. In addition to Japanese opposition, the Chinese, at least up to 1894, opposed any increase of Russian influence or expansion in Korea.

It was inevitable that Russian intervention in Korea would fail because Russia failed to win any support from a meaningful number of influential Koreans. It would not be unfair to say that Russian intervention in Korea only made Japan more aggressive in Korea and brought about the demise of the Korean nation.

The Road to Colonization:
Korea under Imperialism

Kim Ki-Jung

Introduction

Like many weak powers, Korea's fate has been significantly influenced and easily distorted by external powers' aggressive behavior, or external pressure. One of the most vivid examples can be seen during the period from the late nineteenth century to 1910, when the course of unbearable, drastically intensifying external pressure on Korea finally resulted in its colonization by Japan. This era was one of the most critical phases in the entire modern history of Korea. Therefore, this article aims to explain how the international environment of East Asian regional politics from 1897 to 1910 drove Korea into colonization, by focusing on structural transformations and the subsequent international instability.

Korea, mainly because of its geopolitical location, became an important target among competing powers. The first confrontation over the control of the Korean peninsula appeared when the tension between China and Japan escalated. Japan, a newly risen regional military power,

* Originally published in the *Korea Journal*, vol. 38, no. 4 (winter 1998).

Kim Ki-Jung (Kim, Gi-jeong) is Professor of Political Science at Yonsei University. He received his Ph.D. in Political Science from the University of Connecticut in 1989. He published many books and articles, including *Fifty Years after the Korean War* (2001; co-edit), "Teaching International Studies from a Regional Perspective" (2002), and *Miguk-ui dongasia gaeip-ui yeoksajeok wonhyeong-gwa 20 segi cho hanmi gwan-gye yeongu* (The Historical Roots of U.S. Intervention in East Asia and the U.S.-Korea Relations in the Early 20th Century) (2003). His fields of specialization are East Asian international history. He is currently working on a topic concerning the historical transformation of East Asian regional order. E-mail: kimkij@yonsei.ac.kr.

defeated an already weakened China and set a new beginning for the structural transformation of turbulent East Asian international politics.

First, the Sino-Japanese War (1894–1895) symbolized a contest between China and Japan, both of whom had endeavored to establish a modern nation-state mainly by strengthening their military policies. Seen in this perspective, Japan's victory meant that its hasty drive toward a military power was relatively more successful compared to China's attempt. The militant nature of the two regional powers' path to a modern state directly affected Korea. Korea's external activities, as well as its internal autonomy for development, were completely constrained by the hostile and militant actions of the two powers. Tension over Korea did not diminish after the war. Rather, it was intensified, which later led to the outbreak of the Russo-Japanese War (1904–1905).

Second, the result of the Sino-Japanese War brought about a new pattern of imperialist powers' intrusion toward China: metaphorically known as the "slicing of the Chinese melon." The major powers' (Japan, Germany, Russia, and France) attempts to partition Chinese territory displayed more explicitly the aggressive behaviors of imperialism. The major powers' moves toward territorial acquisition within the Chinese territory made international politics in the region more hostile and unstable. In particular Russia, who wanted to strengthen its position in the area, emerged as a new rival against Japan after the war especially with regard to the Korean and Manchurian issues. Russia's emergence began with the Triple Intervention (1895), which formed an alliance with Germany and France against Japan. This new type of regional confrontation and hence a new pattern of power struggle in East Asia eventually forced Korea toward an unwanted road to colonization.

All of these new features in the East Asian political arena after the Sino-Japanese War did not appear by accident. Transformations of power structures were direct reflections of a changing world order. Thus, this article begins with a discussion of the changing features of the world-system, in order to explain the ways in which external pressures led to Korea's colonization.

Structural Features of the World-System at the Turn of the Century

Throughout the nineteenth century, East Asia was not isolated from the whole world-system but was increasingly becoming an integrated part of it. The evolution of the modern world-system, according to both the "long-cycle perspective" of global leadership and the "world-economy perspective," has shown cyclical patterns of structural changes.[1] One of the patterns is often identified as the cyclical change of the rise and fall of hegemonic powers. While the first half of the nineteenth century was the heyday of British hegemony, the 1870s marked the beginning of its deterioration, as affirmed by both perspectives.

Viewed from a structural perspective, the decline of British hegemony was accompanied by a structural transformation of the world-system: from unicentric to multicentric structure. Multicentricity meant a distribution of power among several powers. Whereas a unicentric structure of the world-system under a single hegemon assumes a relative stable order, multicentricity calls for increasing competition, rivalry, conflict, and hence, an unstable environment of international politics. World politics of the late nineteenth century was not an exception, but a perfect example of the increasing instability in international politics along with the decline of British hegemony.

The structural transformation of the world-system also paralleled the changes in the character of the world economy in those days. During the mid-nineteenth century, fundamental changes occurred in the industrial sectors of major Western industrial countries. The most striking was the greatly expanded role of science and technology.[2] In the era of the "Second Industrial Revolution," Western industry shifted from "a base of coal and iron to one of steel, oil, chemicals, and electricity."[3] Such new base depended on "a continuing supply of materials and sources of energy from the non-Western world."[4] Competition among the core

---

1. Despite the differences in theoretical notions between the "long-cycle perspective" of global leadership and the "world-economy perspective," these two are categorized as a world-system perspective based on several common assumptions. See William Thompson, "Introduction: World-System Analysis With and Without the Hyphen," in *Contending Approaches to World-System Analysis*, ed. William Thompson (Beverly Hills: Sage Publications, 1983), pp. 7-11.
2. E. J. Hobsbawm, *Industry and Empire* (London: Weiden & Nicolson, 1968; Penguin books, 1983), p. 172.
3. Frances Moulder, *Japan, China, and the World Economy* (Cambridge: Cambridge University Press, 1977), p. 93; Hobsbawm, *op. cit.*, pp. 172-174.
4. *Ibid.*, p. 93.

powers was inevitable and in fact became severe, particularly in the non-Western parts of the world. Their efforts focused mainly on eliminating other potential supplies in order to provide secured markets for their own surplus capital.[5] Competition, therefore, was not confined to diplomatic matters. The most effective method for securing markets outside the West was to acquire non-Western territories as monopolized markets. As Paul Kennedy succinctly observed, "the Great Powers struggle" in the intensified situation of that period was "no longer merely over European issues . . . but over markets and territories that ranged across the globe."[6] In this context, most of the peripheral countries in the world-system were powerlessly reduced to a colony or a protectorate.

For weak peripheral countries like Korea, increasing competition among core powers under the multicentric structure added further external pressure. More coercive measures were applied to the periphery to integrate them into the world-system. For the core powers, securing their colonies and simultaneously excluding them from other core powers' influence became the ultimate foreign policy goal. Also, the conflicting behaviors were concentrated in their determination to enforce a hierarchical structure upon the periphery. (This kind of conflicting behaviors were employed to enforce a hierarchical structure between the core and periphery.) For peripheral countries, these decades were marked as an era of "suppressive system."[7] These countries were penetrated by capital exploitation, divided according to the core's need for markets, and integrated within separate sphere of influence. In this process, hostilities intensified and the hierarchical relationship between the center and periphery was strictly enforced. These situations, becoming more explicit in East Asia at the turn of the century, show how Korea became a focus of a major international confrontation and subsequently lost its autonomy.

---

5. *Ibid.*
6. Paul Kennedy, *The Rise and Fall of the Great Power: Economic Change and Military Conflict from 1500 to 2000* (New York: Random House, 1987), p. 195.
7. Shoyuki Kotani, "Asia-eseoui jegukjuui-ui seongnip" (Establishment of Imperialism in Asia), in *Hanguk geundae jeongchisa yeongu* (Studies on Political History of Modern Korea), ed. and trans. Yang Sang-hyeon (Seoul: Sagyejul Publishing Co., 1985), p. 15.

Russo-Japanese Confrontation over Korea and China Factor

After Russia entered into the power struggle under the multicentric structure by successfully curbing Japan's ambition in 1895, its position was drastically enhanced in Korea. Russia's stronghold was mainly due to Korea's anti-Japanese attitude, inasmuch as the Koreans disliked Japan's bold and reckless activities on the Korean soil. Anti-Japanese sentiment intensified when it was publicized that Japan was directly involved in murdering Queen Min of Korea in 1896. Furthermore, Korean King Gojong fled to the Russian legation for his physical safety. Under this situation, Japan's position in Korea diminished in comparison to that of Russia. The Korean ruling class trusted Russia, and King Gojong perceived Russia as a possible ally in securing Korea's independence against Japan's aggression.

The atmosphere, however, was changing. Japan's continuing efforts to enhance its political position in Korea gained partial success at the Nishi-Rosen Convention in 1898. At the Convention, Russia agreed not to hinder the development of Japanese commercial and industrial interests in Korea. In other words, Russia acknowledged Japan's paramount interests in economic, though nonpolitical, realm in Korea. The outcome of the Convention showed a noticeable change in the contest of power between Japan and Russia, particularly in comparison to Japan's relative weak position two years before.

The question raised is why Russia conceded to Japan despite its relatively stronger position in Korea. It represented the complexity of regional politics under the multicentric world-system. At least two factors could be offered to explain the situation: one, international, the other, domestic. First, the modification of Russia's Far Eastern policy was caused by its strategic motives regarding the Chinese situation. Under the multicentric structure of the world-system of the late 1890s, Western imperialists' intrusion in East Asia heightened after China's defeat in the Sino-Japanese War. The central focus of the imperialistic design aimed to partition Chinese territory. Initiated by the German lease of the Jiaozhou (Kow Chow) Bay in 1898, major powers followed the same direction within several months. Russia was also an active participant in the "carving" of Chinese territory. Russia intended to lease Port Arthur and Port Dailian (Dairen), two strategically and commercially important ports located on the Liaodong peninsula. Considering Japan's possible antagonism against Russian moves in Manchuria, Russia did not want to provoke Japan for pursuing their prior Manchurian policy. Russia was very careful not to aggravate Japan in Korea where Japan's foreign policy was fully concentrated. This was the international political background of the Nishi-Rosen Convention. Thus, the Korean problem was, and was believed to be, linked with the political situation in China.

Another factor behind Russia's concession to Japan in 1898 was domestic. The year 1897 marked the beginning of Korea's struggle toward the formation of a modern state. On the one hand, the name of the country was changed from Joseon to the Empire of Great Han (Dae-han Jeguk), and, accordingly, the royal title was elevated from King to Emperor. But reform tendency was still constrained and regressive. On the other hand, nationalistic calls for reforms were raised outside the ruling circle. The establishment of the Dongnip Hyeophoe (Independence Club) was a good example. This organization served as an active political pressure group which successfully mobilized the people for anti-Russian rallies. Accordingly, the Korea-Russia relationship deteriorated as Russia withdrew its advisor and military instructors from Korea and closed the Korean-Russian Bank in response to the rise of anti-Russian sentiment in Korea. It was such domestic determinants, along with the changing circumstances in China, that formed the background of Russia's diplomatic compromise with Japan in 1898.

Noteworthy is that Japan's strategy toward Russia was applied in relation to the Korean and Manchurian problems: namely, the "ManKan Kokan" formula. The "ManKan Kokan" formula meant, literally, an exchange of Manchuria and Korea. That formula, a quid pro quo, was derived from an agelong Japanese desire to acquire political control of Korea by purposely separating the Korean problem from affairs in other areas of East Asia, particularly Manchuria. It aimed at mutual recognition of separate spheres of influence, that is, if Russia would entrust Korea to Japan, Japan would in return recognize Manchuria as being outside of its sphere of influence.[8] The formula clearly revealed Japan's foreign policy priority and their desperate efforts to gain control of Korea. This "ManKan Kokan" was widely adopted by most Japanese leaders and, in 1898, proposed to Russia by Nishi Tokujiro, the then Japanese foreign minister. At least until 1900, in fact, the Manchurian

---

8. Ian Hill Nish, *The Anglo-Japanese Alliance: the Diplomacy of Two Island Empires, 1894–1907* (London: Athlone Press, 1966), pp. 57-58.

problem did not attract much attention from the Japanese. Instead, Japan was overwhelmingly preoccupied with gaining control over Korea. Still, Russia did not need to abandon its privileged position in Korea voluntarily, though its central priority was Manchuria. When Russia refused to accept a diplomatic settlement over Korea in 1898, insisting that Russian power will not be completely removed from Korea,[9] Japan had to be satisfied with the Russian decision. The year 1898 was, therefore, opened a new chapter in the bilateral power relationship between Russia and Japan with regard to Korea and Manchuria. In addition, Korea's international position became more explicitly entwined with the Chinese problem, which eventually determined Korea's course to colonization during the next decade.

The Manchurian Crisis and Korea

The attempted partitioning of China by the major powers in 1898 was a direct result of Chinese vulnerability, as proven by China's defeat in its war with Japan. Nonetheless, it also illustrated the fact that the ongoing global rearrangement process between the center and the periphery was reaching its final stage. It was the year 1898 when Germany occupied the Shandong peninsula, Russia had its base in the Liaodong peninsula, Great Britain obtained Weihaiwei and Jiulong (Kowloon), and France leased Guangzhou (Kwangchou) Bay. The same year, the United States acquired the Philippines as a trophy from its war with Spain. Even though the acquisition of the Philippines meant that the United States was ready to emerge as a world power and forge a "new empire,"[10] the United States did not participate in the competitive game of partitioning China. Instead, the U.S. opted for the acquisition of the Philippines, to translate its political victory into economic consideration for the benefit of American foreign policy.[11]

---

9. Japan, Ministry of Foreign Affairs, *Nihon gaiko bunsho* (Japan Diplomatic Documents), vol. 31-1 (Tokyo: Nihon Kokusai Rengo Kyokai, 1945–), p. 141 (hereafter cited as *NGB*).
10. Robert D. Schulzinger, *American Diplomacy in the Twentieth Century* (Oxford: Oxford University Press, 1984), pp. 16-20.
11. Many political and military leaders of the United States saw the new colony as a region "nearest to the great centres of trade in the Far East [China] and strategically located on the trade routes from the United States and Honolulu to these centres."

By the end of the nineteenth century, American businessmen too were attracted by the Chinese market, which was perceived to be a perfect outlet for American manufacturing surplus. The Chinese market at the same time was a political matter. One of the American leading politicians of the day, Senator Albert J. Beveridge claimed that "We must dispose of our surplus abroad. Upon the sale of our surplus abroad depends the prosperous conditions of all our commerce . . . . The most populous portion . . . of the earth's surface is Asia, and especially the Empire of China with its 400,000,000 of consumers."[12] In fact, American cotton textile exports to China grew dramatically in the late 1890s.[13] It was, therefore, inevitable that an Open Door Policy was proclaimed, which called for securing equal opportunities in China under threatening situations when other major powers began to establish exclusive spheres of influence within the Chinese territory.

The American suggestion of the Open Door Policy in China was not welcomed by all major powers involved. Taking into consideration that economic factors were one of the most profound motives for foreign policymaking during the age of imperialism, and that all the core powers did not achieve the same stage of capitalistic development, it soon became clear that some of the core powers would not want commercial competition in an open market. On the contrary, expanding spheres of influence and securing and even strengthening control over a certain periphery might be perceived to be more vital to the national interests of less commercially efficient nations. Such considerations were particularly critical for "latecomers" to industrialization like Japan and Russia. Those nations, pursuing rapid industrialization, despite immature capitalistic development within their domestic economy, needed to acquire foreign markets in the periphery where their economic interests would not be blocked by other powers. Without secured markets, the economic vul-

---

This particular statement was made by Admiral George Dewey, the "Hero of Manila." Peter Karsten, *The Naval Aristocracy: The Golden Age of Annapolis and the Emergence of Modern American Navalism* (New York: Free Press, 1972), pp. 149-150.

12. Quoted in Jerry Israel, *Progressivism and the Open Door: America and China, 1905–1921* (Pittsburgh: University of Pittsburgh Press, 1971), p. 12.

13. By 1905, American cotton textile exports commanded thirty-five percent of the total Chinese market for foreign cotton goods. Michael H. Hunt, "Americans in the China Market: Economic Opportunities and Economics Nationalism, 1890s–1931," *Business History Review* 51 (autumn 1977): p. 286.

nerability of those nations would be exposed to the competitive world economy. For such nations, colonization or annexation was the best way to overcome this vulnerability. This essentially worked as the source of conflict among the major powers which eventually led to the instability in the East Asian region.

Under these circumstances, the Open Door Policy could not achieve international cooperation and stability in East Asia. Immediately following America's promulgation of the Open Door Policy, Russia's occupation of Manchuria in 1900 and the ensuing struggles among the powers all revealed the naked contradictions in East Asia.

The Boxer Rebellion, a symbolic manifestation of the Chinese people's struggle against foreign imperialism, provided a significant step toward the development of Far Eastern international politics. This incident drew even more interest towards China among the major powers. Russia sent its forces so as to maintain its firm military control over Manchuria. Indeed, the Boxer Rebellion provided Russia with a perfect opportunity for invading Manchuria through the so-called "New Policy."[14] Russian War Minister Aleksei Nikolaevich Kuropakin declared, "I am very glad. This [The Boxer Rebellion] will give us an excuse for seizing Manchuria . . . . We will turn Manchuria into a second Bokhara."[15] When Russia ended the "conquest of Manchuria" by occupying Mukden and establishing Russian control along all the railroad lines of the Chinese Eastern Railway,[16] other powers including Japan, Great Britain, and the United States, began monitoring Russian actions in Manchuria. Although Sergei Witte, the Russian minister of finance and an architect of Russian Far Eastern policy, claimed that Russian occupation was "only temporary and due solely to the desire of the Russian Government to restore order in the territories of the Chinese Empire,"[17] and the other powers believed that the Alekseiev-Tseng Agreement of November 1900 amounted to a virtual Russian protec-

---

14. Andrew Malozemoff, *Russian Far Eastern Policy, 1881–1904: With Special Emphasis on the Course of the Russo-Japanese War* (Berkeley: University of California Press, 1958), pp. 120-123.
15. Quoted in Edward H. Zabriskie, *American-Russian Rivalry in the Far East: A Study in Diplomacy and Power Politics, 1895–1914* (Philadelphia: University of Pennsylvania Press, 1946), p. 66.
16. Malozemoff, *op. cit.*, p. 143.
17. Quoted in *ibid.*, p. 146.

torate over South Manchuria.

The reaction of Japan was the most decisive. For Japan, Russia's domination of Manchuria was regarded as a serious menace to Japanese stakes in Korea. Though the peninsula remained an influence-overlapped area between Japan and Russia at the turn of the century, Korea had always been a greater concern for Japan. Since the 1870s, the issue of "Seikanron" (Conquest of Korea) had been an unresolved problem for Japanese political leaders, even after defeating China in the Sino-Japanese War of 1894–1895. As Hayashi Tadasu, a Japanese Minister to Great Britain, remarked in 1901, control of Korea was deemed "a matter of national survival for Japan."[18] Simply put, the Russian occupation of Manchuria thus produced unstable circumstances in Far Eastern international politics, which served as an impetus for the Russo-Japanese War (1904–1905).

The Manchurian Crisis and Russo-Japanese Antagonism

Among the nations harboring an anti-Russian sentiment, Japan was most forcible. Thus, it played a leading role in organizing explicit protests against Russian policy in East Asia by infusing anti-Russian sentiments into other powers, like Great Britain and the United States. The Russo-Japanese confrontation became intensified during the Manchurian crisis. And Japan's taking a leading role in responding to the crisis afforded Japan with an opportunity to solve the Korean problem by initiating structural changes in regional politics. This was the key factor in Korea's road to colonization.

Japan responded in a decisive manner to the unstable situation created by the Russia's military occupation of Manchuria. The alternatives given to the Japanese leaders were to either take an antagonistic attitude toward, or compromise with Russia. If the option of an antagonistic relationship were to be chosen, Japan needed other powers' cooperation, particularly that of Great Britain. Cooperation with other powers necessitated the creation of a collective bloc against Russia. Japanese policy-

---

18. In a conversation between Hayashi Tadasu and British Official James Whitehead in negotiating the Anglo-Japanese Alliance, Hayashi described the concern of the Japanese government regarding the Korean problem as such. Great Britain, Public Record Office, Whitehead's Draft, 16 August 1901, F.O. 46, Japan (microfilm, 303).

makers had to determine their course to either deal with Russia or with Great Britain. Japan believed that the Korean problem could be solved either by an agreement with Russia by a quid pro quo in terms of "Man-Kan Kokan" or by obtaining British acknowledgement of Japan's full control of Korea.

Japanese policymakers began to perceive that the Japanese stake in Korea was seriously imperiled by Russia's vigorous Far Eastern policies, already exemplified by the construction of the Trans-Siberian Railroad, the lease of Port Arthur and Dailian, and the occupation of Manchuria. Japan believed Russia's next step would be a full control of Korea. As far as the Korean problem was concerned, Russian occupation of Manchuria was perceived to be a serious enough menace to elicit a prompt reaction from Japanese leaders.

In fact, Korea posed a "security dilemma" for both powers. Policymakers on both sides perceived that if the peninsula were to go under either power's military control, it would directly affect the other's security. This concern was a more serious matter to the Japanese. Japan's leading politician, Yamagata Aritomo's memorandum of 1900 well illustrated the point. He noted:

> Korea is only separated from our outlying island-possession, Tsushima, by a mere girdle of water and is really closely connected with us; if Korea were to fall under occupation by someone else, our people no longer sleep undisturbed. . . . If Korea passes into someone else's possession, it would be a serious menace to the safety of our country. So Korea cannot be allowed to fall into the hands of others.[19]

Even though Russia had relatively fewer political and economic stakes in Korea, Russian leaders also believed that the Korean peninsula should be, at least, a buffer zone, insofar as they sought autonomy over Manchuria. In this sense, Russia did not want Korea to be fortified by Japan. As the Tsar himself remarked: "Russia did not like Korea to become a foothold for Japan, though Russia had no ambition in Korea. And if Japan attempted to establish a foothold in Korea, that would constitute a cause for war to Russia."[20]

---

19. *NGB*, vol. 33-3, no. 2370; Reproduced in Ian H. Nish, *op. cit.*, Appendix A, pp. 378-379.

20. Quoted in Shunoske Kazima, *Nihon gaikou seisaku no shiteki kousatsu* (Japan's Foreign Policy in Historical Perspective) (Tokyo: Kajima Kenkyujyo, 1959), p. 619.

Japan's Road to Alliance and Changing Structures in East Asia

In response to the crisis of 1901, significant changes were made in Japan's foreign policy. One was a shift in Japan's strategy from "Man-Kan Kokan" to "ManKan Fukan." The latter literally means "no exchange of Korea and Manchuria."[21] It implied that Japanese leaders now perceived power rearrangement in the two peripheral areas, Korea and Manchuria, as a single issue; the term thus meant "inseparability between Korean and Mauchurian issues," or "linkage between the two issues." The new *démarche* began to replace the old formula of "Man-Kan Kokan."

Perceiving a real menace in Korea, Japan now decided that the Korean problem should not be separated from Manchuria. With the absence of strong reactions from other powers regarding the Manchurian situation in 1901, the main concern of Japan shifted once again to the future status of Manchuria. As a consequence, Japan increased its maneuvers against Russia. By the same token, the transition from the "ManKan Kokan" to the "ManKan Fukan" indicated that Japan's position in East Asia had improved from its previous position when Japan held a more disadvantageous position *vis-à-vis* Russia, concerning the Korean problem between 1895 and 1900.

The first indication of the change in their relationship appeared when Japan responded to a Russian proposal of neutralization of Korea in January 1901. Because the Russian proposal of neutralization aimed to acquire freedom of action in Manchuria, the Japanese did not consider the proposal negotiable. Accordingly, Japan responded to the Russian proposal in a firm manner. Komura Jutaro, then Japanese minister to China, advised Tokyo, stating:

> Since it is clear that Russia's proposal is derived from its desire to have freedom of action in Manchuria, solution to the Korean problem will not be satisfying if it is not related to the Manchurian problem. Therefore, although Russia agreed with neutralization of Manchuria, it is important for the Japanese government not to approve the Russian proposal for that reason.[22]

---

21. Masuda Hiroshi and Kimura Masato, *Nihon gakoushi handbook* (A Handbook of Japanese Diplomatic History) (Tokyo: Yushindo, 1994), p. 30.
22. *NGB*, vol. 34, p. 524.

Here was a concrete and detailed expression of the new Japanese policy toward Russia regarding Korea and Manchuria. Japanese leaders demanded a simultaneous neutralization of Manchuria. This marked a significant breakthrough in Japanese Far Eastern policy.

The Japanese now approached the other powers with this "ManKan Fukan" formula. In other words, Korea, over which Japan and Russia had struggled, was linked with the partition of China, which concerned all the other powers. Since the Sino-Japanese War of 1894–1895, the Korean problem had remained exclusively a bilateral issue between Japan and Russia. By 1901, however, the Japanese decided to solve the Korean problem by cooperating with other powers and refused to negotiate with Russia alone. Therefore, Japan sought support from a third power, Britain. An alliance with Great Britain was the final goal that Japanese leaders had envisaged during the period of Far Eastern crisis of 1901. This marked another significant shift in Japanese Far Eastern policy during that period.

Since Japan regarded the two peripheral areas as a single issue and intended to solve the problem with the other powers, Japanese leaders decided that Japan would not act alone on the matter related to the Manchurian affair because Japan could not allow any changes in the Manchurian situation in favor of Russia by negotiating a settlement of this problem only with Russia.[23] Such determination was evident in the Japanese Prime Minister Katsura Taro's statement. He asserted that "If Japan were to conclude a treaty with Russia in order to obtain Russian concessions in Korea, Japan could only do so by concluding an agreement which was inconsistent with its former attitude over Manchuria."[24] Instead, as Katsura stressed, Japan should "follow the larger principle [Open Door Policy] that prohibited any agreement to impair Chinese sovereignty."[25]

Therefore, Japan sought diplomatic support from Great Britain and the United States to enhance its position *vis-à-vis* Russia. In order to

---

23. Kazuki Yoshida, "Yeongil dongmaeng-gwa ilbon-ui joseon chimnyak" (Anglo-Japanese Alliance and Japan's Encroachment of Korea), in *Hanguk geundae jeongchisa yeongu*, pp. 118-119.

24. Hiratsuka Atsushi, comp., "Katsura to Ito, Dec. 21, 1901" (in Japanese), in *Ito Hirobumi hiroku* (Private Writings of Ito Hirobumi), no. 58 (Tokyo, 1928–1930); Reproduced in Nish, *op. cit.*, appendix E, pp. 387-388.

25. Quoted in Yoshida, op. cit., pp. 118-119.

obtain this alliance, Japan reiterated its support for the Open Door Policy in China, in which the two powers were pursuing commercial activities. The British government saw that Japan would "desire, as far as China was concerned, to maintain the policy of the 'open door' and the integrity of the Chinese Empire."[26] Japan also tried to convince Britain that concerning China, "the policy of Japan is identical with that of Great Britain."[27] This new course in Japanese foreign policy led to the creation of the Anglo-Japanese Alliance of 1902.

While Great Britain was at first reluctant, the crucial turning point for the alliance occurred in July 1901. Russia unofficially proposed the neutralization policy again, which seemed more acceptable to the Japanese then than it was in January. Russia would, Witte proposed, agree to making Korea a neutral area but giving Japan the right to supply the Korean government with administrative and financial advisers as well as with a chief of police. In turn, Japan should officially recognize Russia's influence in Manchuria.[28] This proposal was more disturbing to London than Tokyo. The British began to fear a possible Russian-Japanese rapprochement, which would constitute the worst case for the British in East Asia, for Britain would then be isolated in the imperialistic competition.

Accordingly, Lansdowne declared on July 31, 1901, "the time has come to discuss seriously the question of making a permanent treaty with Japan."[29] In short, the British now agreed to Japan's formula of arrangement in East Asia by recognizing Japan as a power that would not only monopolize foreign influence in Korea but have equal influence over Chinese affairs. A section of Article 1 of the treaty reads as follows:

> [T]heir special interests, of which those of Great Britain relate principally to China, while Japan, in addition to the interests which she possesses in China, is interested in a particular degree politically as well as commercially and industrially in Corea, the High Contracting Parties

---

26. Whitehead to Solisbury and Balfour, 14 August 1901, F.O. 46, Japan (microfilm, 303).
27. Whitehead's Draft, 16 August 1901, F.O. 46, Japan (microfilm, 303).
28. William Langer, *The Diplomacy of Imperialism, 1890–1902*, vol. 2 (New York: Alfred A. Knopf, 1935), pp. 748-749; John White, *Diplomacy of the Russo-Japanese War* (Princeton: Princeton University Press, 1964), p. 84.
29. *NGB*, vol. 34, pp. 25-26; Lansdowne to Whitehead, 31 July 1901, F.O. 46, Japan, vol. 563 (microfilm, 302).

recognize that it will be admissible for either of them to take such measures as may be indispensable in order to safeguard those interests if threatened either by the aggressive action of any other Power, or by disturbances arising in China or Corea, and necessitating the intervention of either of . . . [30]

In East Asia, Japan led the campaign promoting joint actions for the control of Korea. In as much as these two powers mutually acknowledged their rights of intervention in China and Korea, the Anglo-Japanese Alliance, as a Japanese scholar succinctly described, was a typical "alliance of imperialists."[31]

The formal declaration of the Anglo-Japanese Alliance on January 31, 1902 astounded Russia. Failing to conciliate Japan through the modified proposal of Korean neutralization, the Russians, instead, faced more aggressive reactions from Tokyo, backed by British support. Russia now had to checkmate the Anglo-Japanese Alliance. Foreign Minister Lamsdorf instructed the Russian ambassador in Paris, Count Urusov, to begin negotiations for a Franco-Russian agreement which would formally extend the Franco-Russian Entente to East Asia.[32] Lamsdorf also hoped to bring Germany into further alignment with Russian interests, but the Germans declined to move in that direction. Berlin maintained its "free hand" policy toward the other powers, particularly between London and St. Petersburg.[33]

When the Franco-Russian proclamation was issued on March 16, 1902, there stood ostensibly two blocs confronting each other in East Asia. But the counterpart to the Anglo-Japanese Alliance, in reality, did not extend the Franco-Russian Entente to East Asia. It is important to note, however, that as a response to the creation of the Anglo-Japanese Alliance, the Russian counteraction appeared to follow the same pattern taken by Britain and Japan.

By and large, East Asian international politics in the early twentieth century witnessed the emergence of blocs. The behavioral pattern of the powers implied the possible use of military force. In this sense, the

---

30. Department of State, Papers Relating to the Foreign Relations of the United States, 1902 (Washington, D.C.: GPO, 1903), pp. 514-515 (hereafter cited as FRUS).
31. Yoshida, op. cit., p. 121.
32. Malozemoff, *op. cit.*, p. 174.
33. Paul Kennedy, *The Rise of the Anglo-German Antagonism, 1864–1914* (Boston: George Allen and Unwin, 1980), pp. 234, 243.

Anglo-Japanese Alliance led to the emergence of a central structure, which gradually reshaped the fragmented nature of multicentric structures dominating East Asian politics. Such phenomena also implied that the competition among the major powers regarding their autonomy within separate spheres in the East Asian periphery became critical enough to call for joint actions among the major center powers.

In East Asian world politics, the formation of the Anglo-Japanese Alliance of 1902 triggered an overall structural transformation. With the creation of this alliance, East Asian international politics entered into a new era, in which competition in the periphery of East Asia intensified so that cooperative and overt diplomatic maneuvers replaced independent and covert actions. Simply stated, the Anglo-Japanese Alliance was a cooperative acknowledgement established between two key core powers who wanted to secure their common interests in East Asia.

For the United States, the emergence of the Anglo-Japanese Alliance and the counter-alliance by Russia and France posed new problems. American Far Eastern policy had to be modified to compete with the emerging bicentric structure in East Asia. The modification of American policy turned out to be the establishment of diplomatic solidarity with Britain and Japan. The course of strengthening ties with the Anglo-Japanese Alliance was determined by America's concern for maintaining the "open door" in China. As long as policymakers in Washington believed in nonmilitary commitment, independent and firm action for securing economic interests in China seemed out of the question, because it would require the use of military power in an entangled competition. Instead, the two allied powers pursued the same goals and interests in East Asia as with those of the United States. American policymakers knew of these identical interests, particularly with the case of Britain. As Howard K. Beale noted, President Theodore Roosevelt believed in the "oneness of the American and British interest" and "in combination, the Americans and the British could dominate the world."[34] "England's interest," Roosevelt later confirmed, "is exactly ours as regards to this Oriental complication, and is likely to remain so . . . ."[35]

---

34. Howard K. Beale, *Theodore Roosevelt and the Rise of America to World Power* (Baltimore: The Johns Hopkins Press, 1956), p. 81.

35. Roosevelt to George von Meyer, 6 February 1905; Roosevelt to Cecil Spring-Rice, 27 December 1904, Library of Congress, Papers of Theodore Roosevelt (hereafter cited as TR MSS).

Japanese efforts to encourage Japanese-American cooperation became open and direct. Playing a leading role in the anti-Russian coalition since 1901 because of its vital interests in Korea, Japan persuaded the United States to establish a united front with the Anglo-Japanese Alliance by frequently reiterating Japanese diplomatic support of the Open Door Policy in Manchuria.

Responding to the changing diplomatic atmosphere within Japan, Britain, and the United States, Russia hastily concluded the Russo-Chinese convention calling for evacuation from Manchuria on April 8, 1902. According to the Russo-Chinese convention, Russia was supposed to evacuate its troops from Manchuria in three years beginning with the date of the convention. To an extent, Russia's agreement to evacuate eased the strained situation in East Asia, as Japan, Britain, and the United States continued to monitor Russian compliance.

Renewed Crisis in 1903

In the next six months, Russian troops evacuated west of the Liao River ahead of schedule.[36] In the second period of evacuation, however, Russian attitudes changed. Even though Russia, in response to the Anglo-Japanese Alliance, was forced to evacuate its troops from Manchuria, it by no means meant that Russia would completely abandon advancing into the periphery. For Russia, avoiding a war with Japan during the crisis of 1901, at least temporarily, became an immediate goal. Witte, who had dominated Russian Far Eastern policy,[37] decided that the best means of solving the Manchurian problem was to renounce political intentions in Manchuria and limit Russian interests there to the protection of the Chinese Eastern Railroad as a private enterprise.[38] For securing the Chinese Eastern Railroad, Witte's strategy toward Japan regarding Korea was that Russia should be ready to concede Korea to Japan and "even if Japan seized Korea, Russia should not consider it a *casus*

---

36. According to Malozemoff, there was little strategic value in the presence of Russian troops west of Liao, so they were immediately withdrawn. Malozemoff, *op. cit.*, p. 175.
37. David S. Crist, "Russia's Far Eastern Policy in the Making," *Journal of Modern History 14* (September 1942): p. 318.
38. Malozemoff, *op. cit.*, pp. 167-168.

belli."[39] Witte thus sought conciliation with Japan in East Asia by agreeing to evacuate.

Not all of the political leaders in St. Petersburg, however, shared Witte's view. A group, called the "Koreans," or the "Bezobrazov circle," worked at influencing the Tsar to adopt an immediate and aggressive policy of political and economic pressure in Manchuria and to challenge Japan's position in Korea, rather than a policy of a gradual economic penetration of Manchuria as advised by Witte. These men were preoccupied with a vision, which they had pressed on the Tsar as early as in 1898, maintaining that the attainment of a vast Far Eastern empire depended upon absolute dominance in Korea and Manchuria.[40] For the Bezobrazovs, it was necessary to reinforce troops in Manchuria rather than to evacuate. This time, the Bezobrazovs won the political game against Witte.

The new "Forward" policy was thus implemented, the aim of which was to establish complete Russian dominance in Manchuria as well as in Korea.[41] Thus, in April 1903, Russia not only resisted the second evacuation of troops but reinforced its troops in southern Mukden and on the Korean border. With regard to Korea, the Bezobrazovs tried to reverse Witte's compromise, in which Russia had been willing to concede the peninsula to Japan for the sake of Manchurian interests. In February, the Russian government asked the Korean government to grant a concession for the construction of a railway from Seoul to Uiju to a Russian entrepreneur.[42] Military support followed with the deployment of troops in Yongampo and several other sites in Korea in May 1903.[43]

Aggressive Russian action with regard to Manchuria and Korea under the new Forward policy alarmed other powers, who considered it as a revival of the crisis of 1901. For Japan and Britain, the Forward policy was seen as an open challenge to their joint attempts to counter Russia's

---

39. Quoted in Molozemoff, *op. cit.*, p. 168.

40. White, *op. cit.*, pp. 36-37.

41. *Ibid.*, p. 328. It was based on two fundamental plans of action: (1) to promote a wide range of politico-economic activities in those regions important to Russia, so that all foreign interests be barred from those areas; and (2) for the establishment, in the least amount of time and at any cost, of full "military preparedness" for the protection of Russia's political and economic interests.

42. See Ian H. Nish, *The Origins of the Russo-Japaense War* (New York: Longman, 1985), p. 155.

43. Zabriskie, *op. cit.*, p. 85.

ambitions. The Japanese apprehension was particularly evident. It was, however, Japanese fortune insofar as it quickly became evidenced that the United States was on their side during the crisis. Throughout this period, American policy evidently shifted towards curbing Russian monopolization of the Manchurian market, showing diplomatic alignment with the Anglo-Japanese Alliance. While avoiding military commitment, American diplomatic action signaled a noticeable change—from a policy of vacillation to a clear alliance with the anti-Russian coalition; from limited engagement in commerce to limited political commitment regarding the periphery issue; and most importantly, to end political intervention concerning Japan in East Asian international politics. In response to the escalating crisis in the region, the United States shifted its larger policy framework to strengthen Japanese-American cooperation. Considering the fact that confrontations between Japan and Russia over Korea and Manchuria became more hostile, the situation called for a clearer United States policy opposing Russia. At the same time, American policy toward Korea backed the Anglo-Japan Alliance. The result was America's support of Japan's scheme for determining the status of Korea.[44]

Japanese leaders immediately put forward several propositions to guide Japanese foreign policy. The main objective, as before stated, was to take advantage of the unstable situation in East Asia to obtain Korea: to get firm recognition of Japan's full control of the peninsula. If Russia did not concede this time, Japanese leaders, especially Katsura and Komura, would initiate war with Russia. Faced with renewed Russian threat, Japanese leaders faced the alternative of either surrendering to Russia's requirements or pressing Russia to the brink of war. As long as Japan did not consider conceding its position in Korea, the Japanese decision to reopen negotiations was recognized as nearly tantamount to a decision for war.[45]

In terms of structural conditions, reinforcement of Russian troops in

---

44. President Roosevelt's perception played a critical role in determining America's recognition of Japan's control over Korea. For more explanation, see Kim Ki-Jung, "Theodore Roosevelt's Image of the World and United States Foreign Policy Toward Korea, 1901–1905," *Korea Journal* 35.4 (winter 1995): pp. 39-53; "Theodore Roosevelt and Korea: His Personal Diplomacy and American Foreign Policy Toward Korea, 1904–1905," *Korea Observer* 21.2 (summer 1990): pp. 179-198.

45. White, *op. cit.*, p. 101.

Manchuria and on the border of Korea provided maximal instability. As Japan pressed its adversaries to the brink of war, negotiations became deadlocked. One point of difference, which Russia could not accept, was Japan's "ManKan Fukan." Russia rejected this proposal and demanded instead that Japan declare Manchuria as outside its sphere of influence.[46] A serious cause for dispute was the arrangement of Korea. Russia dismissed Japan's demand for complete freedom of action and proposed that the Korean territory north of the 39th parallel be preserved as a neutral zone.[47] To an even greater extent than the Russian monopolization of Manchuria, this was an issue with which Japan could not compromise.[48] Under such circumstances, both sides' unnegotiable positions on the arrangement of the periphery only intensified the highly unstable condition of the East Asian international system through the second half of 1903. The instability in East Asia was the central cause for the Russo-Japanese War of 1904–1905.

The War and International Recognition of Japan's Control of Korea

The Russo-Japanese War was a direct result of the intensified crisis of 1903 during which the position of the two powers remained irreconcilable and spiraled toward a military clash. The struggle over the arrangement of the periphery in East Asia under the unstable multicentric structure ended inevitably in violence. With the outbreak of the war, Korea's autonomy was even more strictly constrained.

An episode that clearly illustrated the pressure on Korea was Korea's declaration of neutrality. The Korean Emperor openly expressed his desire for Korean neutrality immediately after the emergence of the two alliances in East Asia. The formation of the alliances "caused some degree of alarm" and he wanted "the long desired guarantee of neutrality" by "playing off" Russia against Japan, both of whom had "equally divided influence in Korea."[49]

---

46. Paul A. Clyde, *International Rivalries in Manchuria, 1689–1922*, rev. 2d ed. (New York: Octagon Books, 1966), pp. 124-127; White, *op. cit.*, p. 108.

47. *NGB*, vol. 36-1, pp. 22-23.

48. White, *op. cit.*, p. 108.

49. Allen cynically described the Emperor's desire for neutrality by stating, "Koreans

In January 1904, realizing the imminence of a war, the Korean Emperor declared neutrality to Japan three weeks before the outbreak of the war and also notified the other powers, including the United States.[50] Koreans believed such a proclamation of neutrality safeguarded Korean independence, at least diplomatically. Immediately after outbreak of the war, Yi Yong-ik, the Minister of the Imperial Household Treasury of Korea, told Frederick A. McKenzie, a British journalist, that he believed that Korea would not be tangled in the Russo-Japanese conflict. "Let Russia and Japan fight," he said, "Korea will take no share in their fighting. Our Emperor has issued a declaration of neutrality, and by that we will abide. If our neutrality is broken, the Powers will act without being asked, and will protect us."[51]

Despite these visions, the declaration of Korean neutrality was simply ignored by the major powers. Contrastingly, many of the major powers, particularly the United States, were willing to express that the neutrality and administrative integrity of China should be respected.[52] When issuing the revised version of its neutrality proclamation for China to the other powers, the United States excluded Korea from the neutral zone so as to assist Japan's advance into Korea. For Americans, whose policy depended on cooperation with Japan, Korea's effort to secure neutrality for its independence was a mere fiction.[53] In opposition, Russia complained to the U.S. about biased American intentions regarding the neutrality of China and Korea, inquiring "Why the United States in her eagerness to deprive Russia of Manchuria had made no mention of the Japanese in Korea?"[54] But the Russian protest did not work: the United

---

were very far from ready for [self-government], and the present chaotic state will sooner or later end in interference from the outside, which will probably give to Korea the guiding hand she so greatly needs." Allen to Hay, 31 May 1902, Dispatches, Korea (M-134).

50. Cho to Hay, 22 January 1904, Notes, Korea (M-166); Yi to Komura, 21 January 1904, *NGB*, vol. 37-1, pp. 310-311.

51. F. A. McKenzie, *The Tragedy of Korea* (New York: E. P. Dutton & Co., 1908; reprint, *A Series of Reprints of Western Books on Korea*, no. 2 (Seoul: Yonsei University Press, 1969), p. 109.

52. Hay to All Diplomatic Representatives of the United States, 20 February 1904, FRUS (1904), p. 2.

53. Allen to Hay, 10 May 1904, Despatches, Korea (M-134).

54. Quoted in Tyler Dennett, *Roosevelt and the Russo-Japanese War* (New York: Doubleday, Page and Company, 1925), pp. 69-70; A. Whitney Griswold, *The Far Eastern Policy of the United Sates* (New York: Harcourt, 1938), pp. 96-97.

States openly expressed sympathy with Japan following the guidelines of Japanese-American cooperation pact.

The situation in Korea during the war worsened. At the onset of the war, Japan took quick action concerning Korea in obtaining two protocols. The Protocol of February 1904 provided a legal basis for Japan's political intervention, which forced Korea to adopt the advice of Japan as well as for the use of the Korean territory for military purposes.[55] Another Japanese measure for complete control of Korea followed the February protocol. In August, Japan forced the Korean government to agree to another agreement[56] for the appointment of advisers to the Korean finance and foreign affairs departments. Japan appointed Tanetaro Metega as the financial adviser and Durham Stevens, an American, as the adviser for foreign affairs.[57] Then, Japan took control over the Seoul police force, as well as the postal, telegraph, and telephone services in Korea by another protocol of April 1905,[58] before finally imposing the Protectorate Agreement on the Korean government

---

55. Already regarding the Protocol as a protectorate, Washington did not even consider the Korean-Japanese agreement significant enough to acknowledge. As a result, Hay told Allen that sending the text of the agreement was unnecessary. Simultaneously, the State Department prepared a memo that due to this "Protectorate Treaty," the United States did not need to carry out the legal duties of the Korean-American Treaty of 1882. In the memo submitted from Alvey Adee (the second Assistant Secretary) to Hay, the text read: "The United States can have no concern in the proposed arrangement which necessarily would exclude consideration of Article one of our Korea treaty." This text was not telegramed to Allen. FRUS (1904), p. 437; Hay to Allen, 23 February 1904, Telegram, Instructions, Korea (M-77).

56. FRUS (1904), p. 439. What should be noted is that the bilateral negotiation was conducted in the format of a "Memorandum" which, unlike Protocol, Agreement, or Treaty, does not enforce legal obligations for contracting parties. But the Japanese distorted it to "Agreement" when they proclaimed the conclusion of the negotiation to other foreign powers. Yi Tae-jin, "Joyak-ui myeongching-eul buchiji mothan 'Eulsa boho joyak'" (The Unnamed Eulsa Protectorate Treaty), in *Ilbon-ui daehan jeguk gangjeom* (Japan's Coercive Occupation of Korea), ed. Yi Tae-jin (Seoul: Kachi, 1995), pp. 78-90.

57. Stevens was later assassinated by a Korean in San Francisco in 1907. For an explanation of the Stevens' contributing role in Japan's colonization of Korea, see Andrew C. Nahm, "Durham White Stevens and the Japanese Annexation of Korea," in *The United States and Korea: American-Korean Relations, 1866–1976*, ed. Andrew C. Nahm (Kalamazoo: Center for Korean Studies, Western Michigan University, 1979), pp. 110-136.

58. See FRUS (1905), pp. 625-626.

in November of the same year.

As Japan was nearing victory in war against Russia, a series of international arrangements were set forth for the recognition of Japan's full control of Korea. The first signal came from Washington, D.C. in July 1905—the Katsura-Taft Agreement. In July 1905, Roosevelt sent William H. Taft, the Secretary of War, to Japan for the approval of Japan's control over Korea. Roosevelt earlier informed Taft of his intentions regarding the Korean problem. "I heartily agree with the Japanese terms of peace, insofar as they include Japan having the control over Korea."[59] Taft affirmed the U.S.'s acknowledgement of Japan's control of Korea during his visit to Japan. Japanese Prime Minister Katsura called for a definitive solution to the Korean problem, for Japan was "constrained to take some definite step" to prevent Korea from reverting to her former condition. Taft admitted "the establishment by Japanese troops of a suzerainty over Korea to the extent of requiring that Korea enter into no foreign treaties without the consent of Japan was the logical result of the present war and would directly contribute to permanent peace in the east."[60] Taft's view was firmly supported by Roosevelt.[61]

The Katsura-Taft Agreement was the first and most desirable signal for Japan, who was now forming an amicable international environment to solve the Korean problem once and for all. Katsura welcomed the American gesture describing Japan's relations with the United States as "an alliance in practice is not in name . . . insofar as respects the affairs of the Far East."[62] Likewise, Britain also acknowledged Japan's dominant position in Korea by signing the second Anglo-Japanese Alliance in August 1905. And, finally, through the Portsmouth Peace Treaty, Japan also received an official approval of Japan's control of Korea from Russia. Indeed, the Korean issue never became a serious obstacle during negotiations between the two countries. Instead, indemnity and territori-

---

59. Roosevelt to Taft, 20 April 1905, TR MSS.
60. Ibid.
61. To Roosevelt, the implication of the Katsura-Taft Agreement was as equally as important as the second Anglo-Japanese Alliance and as the Portsmouth Peace Treaty in terms of international arrangements regarding Korea. He "approved" of Japan's complete control over Korea, as the Russians and British did in their treaties. Jongsuk Chay, "The Taft-Katsura Memorandum Reconsidered," *Pacific Historical Review* 37 (August 1968): p. 325.
62. Roosevelt to Spring-Rice, 1 November 1905, TR MSS.

al issues were more serious problems in the aftermath of the war.[63] As a result Russia recognized Japan's paramount position in Korea and agreed not to obstruct Japan's way of establishing full control over Korea.

The Japanese government sent Ito Hirobumi to Korea to finalize the matter. Against a backdrop of Japan's military demonstration inside the Palace in Seoul, he forcibly urged the Korean Emperor to endorse the agreement, but Emperor Gojong strongly refused. As a consequence, Ito threatened the ministers of the Korean Government to conclude the process. Five Korean ministers out of the eight signed the agreement out of terror. Ito then proclaimed the negotiation to be officially resolved between the two governments on November 17, 1905. With this agreement, Korea's diplomatic sovereignty was nullified by Japan. Strictly speaking, however, it was a legally invalid agreement, since the Korean Emperor never officially authorized the proceedings of the negotiation. Moreover, there was no ratification process in the diplomatic settlement. This was why the document lacked a title when they concluded the coercive process, and why the Japanese later referred to the document with a dual title: "Agreement" and "Convention."[64]

The Korean Emperor resisted to the bitter end according to an emissary to the United States, as described by Article 1 of the Korean-American Treaty of 1882.[65] One of those missions was carried out by Homer Hulbert, who took the Korean Emperor's secret letter to Washington, D.C. The Korean Emperor pleaded for help from the United States, and even requested, in a telegram sent to his emissary in Washington, D.C., that, if necessary, Korea would allow the joint control of Korea by Japan and the United States.[66] But his mission never succeeded because the

---

63. Raymond Esthus, *Double Eagle and Rising Sun: The Russians and the Japanese at Portmouth in 1905* (Durham: Duke University Press, 1988), chs. 10, 12.

64. Yi Tae-jin, op. cit., pp. 91-108. According to Yi, Japan had originally planned to settle the Korean problem with an official "treaty" at that time. After November 20, 1905, however, the Japanese Foreign Office entitled the diplomatic settlement as "agreement." Along with the fact that there was no title on the original document, this means that Japanese officials were clearly aware of the fact that the negotiation with the Korean Government was legally incomplete.

65. According to historian Jongsuk Chay, the Korean Emperor sent four missions to Washington in the fall and winter of 1905. One was carried out by Syngman Rhee. Jongsuk Chay, *Diplomacy of Asymmetry: Korean-American Relations to 1910* (Honolulu: University of Hawaii Press, 1990), pp. 151-154.

66. In the telegram, Emperor Gojong declared "the agreement [the Protectorate Agreement] was cancelled because it was under duress." And he seriously considered the

United States recognized Japan's full control of Korea under already established diplomatic conditions. As historian John Wilz argues, in many ways the United States "betrayed" Korea.[67] Thus, these international actions in 1905 led to the later colonization of Korea.

Despite nationwide anti-Japanese uprisings after 1905, Japan gradually maneuvered diplomatic as well as domestic affairs in Korea to proceed toward the eventual annexation. The Korean Emperor organized another secret mission to the Hague Conference in 1907, but Korea's painful attempt to nullify the Korean-Japanese Protectorate Agreement of 1905 was not recognized. Instead, this incident gave Japan a chance to accelerate towards annexation by stressing the forceful resignation of Emperor Gojong. While the British government began to concentrate on European affairs after 1905, the United States checked Japan's further advance into the Asian continent. Even though the United States experienced temporary tension with Japan in 1907 due to immigration issues and realized the tactical falsity of Japan's diplomatic support for the Open Door Policy, the Korean issue was never recognized as being important enough to intervene in Japan's efforts to annex Korea. The United States had little strategic interests in Korea during that time. During this period of power transition following the Russo-Japanese War, Russia formed a cooperative relationship with Japan in the face of United States threat, a new competitor in Manchuria. As a result, Japan and Russia collaboratively divided Manchuria into two spheres of influence. The annexation of Korea, therefore, meant a sort of "institutionalization" of power structures so that no power ever questioned Korea's international position.[68]

Throughout the period from 1897 to 1910, few other powers had serious and vital interests in Korea in comparison to Japan. Even Russia, who had confronted Japan after the Sino-Japanese War, placed greater emphasis on Manchuria than Korea. Korea perceived Russia to be a vehicle for checking Japan's aggression toward its sovereignty. But it

---

alternative of a joint-control of Korea by Japan and the United States in order to terminate the agreement. The Korean Emperor to Homer B. Hulbert, 11 December 1905, Note from the Korean Legation (M-166).

67. John Wilz, "Did the United States Betray Korea in 1905?" *Pacific Historical Review* 54 (August 1985): pp. 243-270.

68. Ku Dae-yeol, *Hanguk gukje gwan-gyesa yeongu* (History of Korean International Relations) 1 (Seoul: Yeoksa Bipyeongsa, 1995), p. 141

remained only as a wishful thinking. Koreans' expectation of good office from the United States was likewise illusive. In sum, the Korean strategy of balancing competing powers was immature and ineffective. It was mainly due to the aggressive nature of international politics during the era of imperialism. Korea's road to colonization, therefore, was a direct result of the ethos of imperialism shared by the major powers, and a product of the structural transformation of the world-system toward multicentricity where aggression prevailed as an imperative of the age.

## PART V

COLONIAL PERIOD AND POST-LIBERATION PERIOD

Korean Resistance to Imperial Japanese Aggression and the Development of the Independence Movement

Yun Pyong Suk

Introduction

It may be said that the modern history of Korea, from the opening of the country to the outside world to the liberation from Japanese rule at the end of World War II in 1945, is marked by two important characteristics: national resistance to imperial Japanese aggression and the growth of nationalist movements to transform the country from a traditional aristocratic society to a modern one.

In Korea, it appears, nationalism in the modern sense was born and developed in the course of anti-Japanese movements, including the activities of the *uibyeong* (righteous armies), which waged armed struggle against the Japanese. These movements spread across the country from 1876, when Japan imposed a treaty of commerce on Korea with her warships off Ganghwado island, to 1905, when Japan, on the strength of her victory in the Russo-Japanese War, forced Korea to sign a so-called pro-

* Originally published in the *Korea Journal*, vol. 24, no. 3 (March 1984).

Yun Pyong Suk (Yun, Byeong-seok) is Emeritus Professor of Korean History at Inha University. He received his B.A. in Korean History from Seoul National University in 1957 and an honorary doctor's degree from Soongsil University in 1995. He published a number of books and articles, including *Samil undongsa* (History of the March First Independence Movement) (1976), *Hanguk dongnip undongsa* (Korean History of Independence Movement) (1987), and "Miju hanin sahoe-ui seongnip-gwa minjok undong" (Establishment of Korean Community in the U.S. and National Movement) (1989).

tectorate treaty, depriving the Korean government of the right to diplomatic relations. Korean nationalism intensified between the 1905 Eulsa
Treaty and the March First Independent Movement, when anti-Japanese
armed struggle was still small in scale and narrow in scope. Furthermore, nationalist ideology was strengthened in the course of the patriotic
enlightenment movement that intended to awaken the people to the
need for restoration of the nation's sovereign power. Korean nationalism, in a modern sense, was established in this movement. The March
First Independence Movement in 1919 provided a momentum for a big
stride forward in the development of Korean nationalism, to the extent
that independence movements were vigorous both in and outside the
country until liberation in 1945. In this paper I will discuss the resistance movements against imperialist aggression, while focusing on stressing the ideologies of the anti-Japanese independence movements.

Anti-Japanese Thought of Conservatives, Donghak, Righteous Armies, and Progressives

The anti-Japanese movements that arose during the formative period of
Korean nationalism can be roughly divided into four types. One was a
conservative movement rejecting everything foreign. This movement
was prevalent in the period from 1876 through 1894, which saw such
political strife in the country as the Military Revolt of 1882, the Coup
d'Etat of 1884, the Sino-Japanese War and the Reform of 1894.[1] It was
initiated by the conservative gentry, which favored the traditional values
based on the Neo-Confucian thought of conservative Confucian scholars. Among the leaders were Kim Pyeong-muk, Choe Ik-hyeon, Yu In-
seok, Yi Man-son, and Hong Jae-hak, who all were protégés of Yi Hang-
no, a strong opponent to any talks with any foreigners when Western
powers invaded Korea.[2]

They considered Japan to be no better than the "Western barbarian"
because Japan had adopted Western culture and institutions. In addition,
this conservative group held an anachronistic view that diplomatic and

---

1. Yun Pyong Suk, *Uibyeong-gwa dongnipgun* (Righteous Armies and Independence
   Army), (Seou: King Sejong the Great Memorial Society, 1977), pp. 21-38.
2. The lineage of those who argued for the expulsion of everything foreign and preservation of everything Korean after Yi Hang-no is shown on the next page.

commercial relations with Japan would result in the propagation of Catholicism in such a manner as to destroy the traditional values and order based on Neo-Confucianism.[3]

But the government disregarded this conservative anti-Japanese movement and opened three ports—in Busan, Incheon, and Wonsan—to Japan under the Ganghwa Treaty in 1876. As a result, Japan encroached upon the Korean economy, especially the rural economy, to the extent of driving it to almost total failure. Under these circumstances, the conservative anti-Japanese movement found its supporters not only in the political circles, but in the peasantry, and became the mainstay of the nationwide anti-Japanese movements launched throughout the period of the government's open-door policy. The conservatives strongly criticized Japan's encroachment policy after the signing of the Ganghwa Treaty and reproved the Chinese councillor Huang Zunxian's *Zhaoxian zhanlue* (Korea Stratagem) in which he called for "Korea's keeping friendship with China, connecting herself with Japan, and allying herself with the United States" as a means to defend the country from Russian aggression. He had also favorably discussed Western culture and institutions, including Christianity. The conservatives held that if relations with Japan should be continued, strict restrictions must be imposed on the number of envoys and ships coming and going between the two countries, as well as trade issues that included the number of items to be traded between Korea and Japan. They even argued for the burning of Japanese and Western books imported from Japan.[4]

However, the conservative ideology of the time did not remain so. The conservatives had insight into Japan's aggressive intention, and their anti-Japanese movement was based on a strong patriotic sense of national independence that would keep the country from becoming a victim of Japanese aggression.[5] They believed that the onrush of West-

---

3. The view that identifies the "Japanese barbarian" with the "Western barbarian" is well discussed in a paper written by Kim Pyeong-muk on behalf of Confucian scholars in Gyeonggi-do and Gangwon-do provinces in January 1876. *Jungam munjip* (Collected Works of Jungam Kim Pyeong-muk), *gwon* 5.

4. The theory and contents of the antiforeign movement are relatively well presented in a paper submitted by Confucian scholars of Gyeongsang-do area, led by Yi Man-son, to King Gojong on January 26 in the 18th year of his reign. *Gojong sillok* (Annals of King Gojong), *gwon* 18.

5. Choe Chang-gyu, *Geundae hanguk jeongchi sasang sa* (The History of Modern Korean Political Thought) (Seoul: Ilchokak Publishing, 1972).

ern culture and institutions from Japan would entail the fall of the country and the nation's economic subordination to Japan.[6] Symbolically speaking, their ideology played a major role in heightening the sense of nationalism among the people by awakening them to the principle of national independence, which argued that a national history not based on self-will and self-determination would only mean national suffering and ordeal. By advocating a check on the political forces of foreign powers, which was emerging through a reckless open-door policy, this ideology provided some theoretical ground for resistance to imperialist aggression.[7]

The second type of anti-Japanese resistance movement was that of the peasant army that was born of the 1894 Donghak Revolution. This revolution was caused by three factors: economic encroachment on the country by foreign powers, including Japan, after the open-door policy; the failure of the rural economy due to the extortion of heavy taxes from peasants; and the ever intensifying contradictions of traditional society that had been declining since the day when the relatives of the royal family exerted authority on the court and the government. Especially noteworthy was Japan's imperialist advancement into Korea after the Ganghwa Treaty. Because the Japanese imperialists were turning Korea into a market for both their manufactured goods and raw materials in an attempt to develop capitalism in Japan, the rural society of Korea fell victim to this imperialist policy. Japan brought to Korea consumer goods manufactured in either Japan or ordered from Chinese ports including Shanghai, and took from Korea raw materials such as rice, beans, gold, silver, and hides.

The introduction of Japanese capital into Korea devastated Korean farmers, as they had to buy Japanese-made goods at high prices and sell their rice, beans, gold, and silver at very low prices. They sometimes had to sell unripe rice still standing in paddy fields and even take out loans at usurious interest rates. As a result, the rural economy entered

---

6. This view of anti-alien movement leaders can be found in various papers, but Choe Ik-hyeon discussed in detail in his writing, "Gi ilbon jeongbu" (Strange Japanese Government), in *Myeonam jip* (Collected Works of Myeonam Choe Ik-hyeon), *gwon* 16. He referred to every change in Korea-Japan relations after the Ganghwa Treaty.

7. Han U-geun, "Donghangnan giin-e gwanhan yeongu" (A Study of the Causes of the Donghak Peasant Revolution), *Asea yeongu* (Journal of Asian Studies) 7, nos. 3, 4 (1964).

into a great depression.

The Donghak peasant army that rose up against the order of traditional aristocratic society was dispersed when China and Japan sent their troops into Korea at the request of King Gojong. But it resisted Japan when Japan forced the court to establish a pro-Japanese cabinet and waged a war against China in an attempt to annex politically Korea.[8] During the first uprising, the Donghak peasant army failed to launch a joint operation by its Northern and Southern forces because of conflict of opinion among its members. But in the second uprising against the aggressive policy of imperialist Japan, Northern and Southern forces launched joint operations to advance into Gongju, where a bloody fight took place at Ugeumchi between the Donghak forces and the joint Japanese-Korean government forces.[9] The Southern force of the Donghak peasant army was led by Jeon Bong-jun and the Northern force by Son Byeong-hui. The total strength of the Donghak peasant army at its apex numbered in the hundreds of thousands.[10]

The Donghak peasant army suffered a severe defeat against the well-equipped and well-trained Japanese troops and Korean government troops. Jeon Bong-jun, Son Hwa-jung, Kim Gae-nam and many other leaders were captured and executed. Even after the total defeat of the Donghak peasant army, the Japanese and Korean government jointly searched across the country for members of Donghak peasant army who were either in hiding or had gone underground, and killed them whenever and wherever they were found.[11]

In spite of such suppression, the Donghak peasant army extended its influence throughout the country, establishing its base not only in the south, but in central and northern provinces such as Gyeonggi-do, Gangwon-do, Hwanghae-do, Pyeongan-do, and Hamgyeong-do. Operat-

---

8. This fact is well presented in the court's death sentence paper on Jeon Bong-jun who led the army's anti-Japanese resistance.

9. Han U-geun, "Donghak-ui seonggyeok-gwa donghak gyodo-ui undong" (The Characteristics of the Donghak and the Movement of Donghak Believers), in *Hanguksa* (History of Korea), vol. 17 (Gwacheon: National Institute of Korean History, 1973), pp. 147-166.

10. Veterans Administration, Independence Movement History Compilation Committee, "Anti-Japanese Resistance of Donghak Peasant Army" (in Korean), chap. 2 in *Dongnip undongsa* (History of Independence Movement), vol. 1 (Seoul: Independence Movement History Compilation Committee, 1966), pp. 107-118.

11. Ibid.

ing out of these bases, the army persistently, albeit vainly, resisted Japanese imperialism. The resistance movement was finally put under control by the government, with Japanese assistance.[12] But the peasant army's anti-Japanese movement helped deepen their hostile feelings against Japan, while heightening their sense of need for national independence. It may be thus said that the Donghak peasant army's anti-Japanese resistance significantly contributed to the establishing of a grass-roots base of national resistance to Japanese imperialism.

The third form of resistance to the Japanese was that waged by the righteous armies in 1896 against both the government and Japan. This resistance movement was directly caused by the Japanese assassination of Queen Min and the Hair-Cut Decree in 1895. The righteous armies was led by provincial Confucianists who had led the conservative anti-alien movement after the opening of three ports to Japan. These Confucianists found supporters in the masses as they appealed to them to save the country by taking revenge on the Japanese for the slaying of Queen Min, and driving them out of the country. The "nation-saving" spirit underlying this anti-Japanese movement found its source in the 1882 Military Revolt. And it can be said that the righteous armies' armed struggle in the 1890s was a more developed form of the conservative anti-alien movement in the 1870s. First organized in such central provinces as Gyeonggi-do, Gangwon-do, and Chungcheong-do, the resistance forces extended their influence to all the southern provinces, in which anti-Japanese movements swept across the country.[13] Among the leaders of this armed resistance were Yi So-eung of Chuncheon, Yi Chun-yeong of Jipyeong, Yu In-seok of Jecheon, Kim Ha-rak of Icheon, Kim Bok-han of Hongju, Heo Wi of Seonsan, No Eung-gyu of Jinju, Ki Sam-yeon of Jangseong, and Kwon Se-yeon of Andong. In particular, Yu In-seok of Jecheon led thousands of righteous armies and at one point occupied Chungju,[14] a strategic point linking Gyeonggi-do to the south-

---

12. Han U-geun, op. cit., pp. 166-202.
13. Yun Pyong Suk, *Uibyeong-gwa dongnipgun*, pp. 39-76.
14. Reference documents on the activities of the righteous armies after the assassination of Queen Min in 1895 include *So-ui sinpyeon* compiled by Kim Hwa-sik et al., which also dealt with the anti-alien movement of Yu In-seok and others. See also Yi Jeong-gyu's *Jongui rok*, *Changui gyeonmun rok* and *Yuk uisa yeoljeon*, Bak Jeong-su's *Un-gang seonsaeng changui illok*, and *Hasa an-gong eulmi changui sasil*, Won Yong-jeong's *Uiam yuseonsaeng daeryak*, Jeong Un-gyeong's *Dongyu rok*, Kim Ha-rak's *Jeongto illok*, Cheo Ik-hyeon's *Myeonam jip*, Yu In-seok's *Uiam jip*, Im Byeong-chan's

ern provinces, and No Eung-gyu had put all Jinju area under his control.[15] Kim Ha-rak of Icheon had advanced as far as the Namhansanseong walled fortress that defended the capital city, and contemplated an offensive against Seoul.[16] The armed resistance subsided when King Gojong moved to the Russian legation as the pro-Russian faction gained power in the court and the government. The pro-Russian government drove the pro-Japanese forces out of the government, and on the strength of this anti-Japanese policy it succeeded in bringing armed resistance under control with an appeasement policy. As a result, the Confucian-led righteous armies of the 1890s had been dispersed and disorganized for the time being.[17] But the armed resistance infused a strong sense of nationalism into the masses, thus providing a spiritual base for the revival of anti-Japanese resistance movements after the 1905 Eulsa Treaty. It is significant that the anti-Japanese armed struggle in the 1890s helped enhance the sense of independence in the formation of nationalism in Korea at the turn of the century.

The fourth and last type of anti-Japanese movement was the patriotic enlightenment movement launched by the Dongnip Hyeophoe (Independence Club), and other civil organizations between 1896 and 1899. The Independence Club can be regarded as a progressive organization aimed at awakening the people to the need for modernization and saving the country from imperialist foreign powers.[18] It called for progressive reforms to promote national independence based on civil rights and enlightenment and instilled a modern and self-reliant sense of nationalism into the minds of the masses, which was to form the core of Korean nationalism.[19] The Independence Club comprised of two schools of pro-

Dunheon mundap gi, Heo Bok's *Wangsan Heo Wi seonsaeng changui jeonmal,* Im Hanju's *Hongyang gisa,* Ki U-man's *Honam changui rok* and *Songsa jip,* Yi So-eung's *Seupjae changui gi,* No Eung-gyu's *Sinam changui seo* and *Musul ilgi,* and Kwon Jong-hae's *So-eun yugo.*

15. Posthumous papers of No Eung-gyu, entitled *Changui seo,* and his biography are good reference materials.

16. Kim Ha-rak, *Jeongto illok.*

17. Yun Pyong Suk, *Uibyeong-gwa dongnipgun,* pp. 116-124.

18. Studies of the Independence Club include Sin Yong-ha's *Dongnip hyeophoe yeongu* (A Study of the Independence Club) (Seoul: Ilchokak Publishing, 1976), and Yu Yeong-ryeol's "Donghip hyeophoe-ui minjok sasang yeongu" (A Study of the Independence Club's Democratic Thoughts), *Sahak yeongu* (Journal of Historical Studies), no. 22 (1973).

19. Sin Yong-ha, *op. cit.,* pp. 247-49.

gressives: one included Seo Jae-pil and Yun Chi-ho, who argued for the introduction of Western democratic principles, and the other included more progressive Confucian scholars such as Namgung Eok and Jeong Gyo, who demanded progressive reforms on the basis of the Confucian tradition.[20] The third group led by Yi Sang-jae amalgamated the thoughts of these two schools to contribute to the strengthening of the Independence Club and its progressive movements. Criticizing that the enlightenment and independence measures taken by the pro-Japanese political circles were too dependent on foreign forces, the Independence Club insisted that foreign imperialist pressures needed to be rejected in order to build a modern nation-state based on political, economic, and military self-reliance. The government had once attempted to adopt "nation-saving" and strengthening measures the people demanded through the Independence Club's civil rights and progressive reforms.[21]

However, the government soon started to suppress the Independence Club at the recommendation of the Japanese imperialists, labeling it an anti-state group. Manipulated by the Japanese imperialists, the government mobilized *bobusang* (pack and back paddlers) to organize the reactionary Hwangguk Hyeophoe (Imperial Association) to attack the Independence Club and Manmin Gongdonghoe (Convocation of Ten Thousand People), an organization that often developed into bloody fights. The Imperial Association misled King Gojong into believing that the Independence Club had as its goal a constitutional republic government, instead of the then existing absolute monarchy, which resulted in the king ordering the dissolution of the Independence Club and imprisoning its leaders. Thus the club was dissolved and its activities came to a halt, at least on the surface, in 1899.[22] It can be pointed out, however, that the people's sense of modernization and nationalist consciousness cultivated through the Independence Club's nation-saving enlightenment movement formed the ideological nucleus of Korean nationalism.

---

20. *Ibid.*, pp. 103-106.
21. Yun Pyong Suk, "Dongnip hyeophoe-ui seongnip, sasang, hwaldong" (The Establishment of the Independence Club and Its Ideology and Activities), in *Hanguksa,* vol. 18, (Gwacheon: National Institute of Korean History, 1973), pp. 188-223.
22. Bak Yong-ok, "Manmin gongdonghoe" (Convocation of Ten Thousand People), in *Hanguksa,* vol. 18 (Gwacheon: National Institute of Korean History, 1973), pp. 223-280.

Direction and Ideology of Anti-Japanese Struggle of the Righteous Armies and Patriotic Enlightenment Movements

The nationalist independence movements that were under way between the Protectorate Treaty of 1905 and the March First Independence Movement in 1919 can be divided into armed struggle of the righteous armies and the so-called patriotic enlightenment movement. It may be said that Korean nationalism established its direction and ideology along these two types of resistance. In fact, Korean nationalism made big strides forward after its formative period in the 1870s and 1880s. The armed resistance was led by provincial Confucian scholars, who had led similar anti-Japanese resistance in 1896 after Queen Min's assassination by the Japanese in 1895, as well as former government officials and Confucian students.[23] In the face of the nation's fall to Japanese imperialists, they waged final resistance against Japan with the support of the peasantry who had already been instilled with a strong anti-Japanese sentiment. Noteworthy leaders of the armed struggle were Min Jong-sik, who fought Japanese troops in Hongju, Choe Ik-hyeon and Im Byeong-chan, who organized their troops in Taein and deactivated these troops in Sunchang, Sin Dol-seok, who was known for his successful leadership as a military commander in Gyeongsangbuk-do province in spite of his commoner family lineage, Yu In-seok, who led soldiers of the Gangwon-do and Chungcheong-do areas, and No Eung-gyu, who fought the Japanese in the Chupungnyeong pass area. Encouraged by the armed struggles of these leaders, people from other areas also organized military units to fight the Japanese, and armed resistance spread almost throughout the country.[24]

Anti-Japanese armed resistance continued desperately from 1907 to 1910, when the country was formally annexed to Japan, and to 1914 when the anti-Japanese independence armies were organized in Manchuria and

---

23. Yun Pyong Suk, *Uibyeong-gwa dongnipgun*, pp. 79-96.
24. Reference documents on the armed resistance of righteous armies include Bak Jeong-su's *Maedang jip*, Jeong Un-gyeong's *Bugyu gonyeon*, Im Han-ju's *Hongyang gisa*, Choe Ik-hyeon's *Myeonam jip*, Im Byeong-chan's *Donheon munjip*, Hwang Hyeon's *Maecheon yarok*, Bak Eun-sik's *Hanguk dongnip undong-ji hyeolsa* (The Bloody History of Korean Independence Movement), Im Byeong-chan's *Ddnheon munjip*, etc.

Siberia.[25] This armed resistance can be considered an extension of the righteous armies' resistance following the assassination of Queen Min, and was the last "nation-saving" movement that expressed the Korean people's spirit of national independence.

The anti-Japanese military units were greatly strengthened in 1907 when the Korean government disbanded its army. The capital garrison troops rose against the deactivation order, and garrison troops in Wonju and Ganghwado island followed suit. Furthermore, many demobilized garrison soldiers in the country joined the righteous armies units to replenish their weapons and introduce better battle formations for the armed resistance.[26] The reinforced resistance units operated not only in the central provinces of Gyeonggi-do, Gangwon-do, Hwanghae-do, and Chungcheong-do but in the southern and northern provinces of Gyeongsang-do, Jeolla-do, Hamgyeong-do, and Pyeongan-do. In fact, armed resistance was found in every province, every county and every township of the country.[27] Even in southeastern Manchuria and Siberia, where many Korean immigrants lived, anti-Japanese resistance units were organized, and they crossed the Tumen river to fight the Japanese garrisons in the border area. In an attempt to form a joint front, righteous armies in provinces held a meeting in Yangju to organize a combined 13-Province Righteous Army for an offensive operation against Seoul. However, worsening logistical problems kept the righteous armies from initiating a large-scale operation, whereas Japan was able to greatly strengthen her combat capabilities against the Korean righteous armies. Accordingly, the righteous armies was forced to break itself into small units based in remote mountainous areas and resort to small-scale guerilla operations. But the intensified Japanese suppressive operations caused the righteous armies to move its base to Manchuria and Siberia, where a combined 13-Province Righteous Army was once again organized for

---

25. It is considered that the righteous armies were reorganized into the Independence Army around 1914 when the Korean Restoration Army Command was established. Yun Pyong Suk, "1910 nyeondae-ui hanguk dongnip undong siron" (A Study of Korean Independence Movement in the 1910s), *Sahak yeongu*, no. 27 (1977).

26. Yun Pyong Suk, *Uibyeong-gwa dongnipgun*, pp. 96-108.

27. Yun Pyong Suk, *Uibyeong-gwa dongnipgun*, pp. 109-127. The Independence Movement History Compilation Committee, "Forced Dissolution of the Korean Government Army and the Armed Anti-Japanese Resistance" (in Korean), chap. 4 in *Dongnip undongsa*, vol. 1 (History of Independence Movement).

invasion of the home country.[28] But the anti-Japanese resistance movement of righteous armies came to a stop around 1914 both in and outside the country, and many of these soldiers became members of the independence armies organized in Manchuria and Siberia.

The armed resistance to Japan after the Protectorate Treaty of 1905 and the Korea-Japanese New Agreements of 1907 (which deactivated the government army) failed because of intensified Japanese suppressive operations, but the armed resistance movement possessed a significant spiritual aspect. Above all, it laid the spiritual foundation of the "independence war theory." According to the theory, all national problems of the time, such as a self-reliant development of the nation through the preservation of national culture and the restoration of sovereign power as a nation, can be dissolved only when Japan is defeated by force, whether it be called the righteous armies, the independence armies or the liberation armies.[29]

There were many varieties of nationalist movements in this period. These movements, often referred to as patriotic enlightenment movement, focused on political activities intended for saving the nation. The movement used the press, meetings and associations to heighten the nationalist consciousness of the people. It also included campaigns to develop the national economy and education, with a view to building strong national power. In addition, there were cultural movements to preserve the nation's traditional culture through the study of Korean history and the Korean language, and to selectively introduce foreign cultures suitable to the country's cultural environment.

The ideology of the patriotic enlightenment movement was developed first of all through nationalist education.[30] The nationalists who led the movement considered the education on nationalism as the starting point in constructing the foundation or the essence of nationalist movements. From the 1905 Treaty with Japan, they had thus attempted to establish as many schools as possible throughout the country, and insisted on the implementation of nationalist education at meetings and associations, including the Seobuk Hakhoe (Northwestern Academic Association). As a result, by the time the country was annexed by Japan in 1910, there

---

28. Yun Pyong Suk, "Sipsamdo uigun-ui pyeonseong" (Organization of the Combined I3-Province Righteous Army), *Sahak yeongu*, no. 36 (1983): pp. 241-245.
29. Yun Pyong Suk, *Uibyeong-gwa dongnipgun*, pp. 76-124.
30. Yun Pyong Suk, "1910 nyeondae-ui hanguk dongnip undong siron" (1977).

were some 2,300 schools in the country and over 180 schools in southern Manchuria.[31] Included among these schools were those established before 1905 and those not considered institutions of nationalist education, but these numbered less than 100.

What was important to these educational institutions was the educational goal or ideology. It may be said that these institutions stressed the development of nationalist manpower needed in building national power. The curricula of these schools thus included not only Western learning but cultivation of nationalist consciousness and military training. The military training was designed to educate youthful leaders capable of putting into practice the "independence war theory." National independence was an ideological goal of the nationalist movements in those days. To achieve this goal, it was necessary to educate young people who could lead a war of independence should it ever needed to be waged on Japan.[32] However, under the colonial educational system designed to liquidate the national characteristics and culture of the Korean people with an educational ideology stressing "the honor of the glorious imperial subject of Japan," no military training was allowed for Korean students. Rather, schools emphasized gymnastic exercises throughout the country.[33]

But in Korean schools in southern Manchuria, military training drew great attention because the Japanese colonial authorities could not keep an eye on these schools. The education that included military training in those days was quite nationalist, and this was well expressed in the following remarks on the educational program of the Sinminhoe (New people's Association) by An Chang-ho, a leading figure of the association and the patriotic enlightenment movement.

> How should we promote the education of young people? The comrades of our association must infuse the education spirit into the minds of people in their assigned areas of responsibility so as to encourage them to build schools for their children. In key places throughout the

31. Korean Provisional Government, *Records on Korea-Japan Relations* (in Korean), vol. 3 (Shanghai: Provisional Government of Korea, 1919); available from National Institute of Korean History, *Hanguk dongnip undong mullyu* (Reference Documents on Independence Movement History), vol. 1 (Gwacheon: National Institute of Korean History, 1974).
32. Yun Pyong Suk, "1910 nyeondae-ui hanguk dongnip undong siron" (1977).
33. Ibid.

country, secondary schools must be established for teaching students not only general subjects but also the military arts so as to qualify them as leaders of the civil army in the frontline, if occasion demands. In other words, we want to make secondary schools a spiritual base for the organization of the civil army.[34]

Among the schools teaching students on the basis of such educational ideology in the country were the Osan School in Seoncheon, the Dae-seong School of the Sinminhoe, the Youth School in Seoul and the Hyeopdong School in Andong. In addition, the Seojeon School was established by Yi Sang-seol, the Myeongdong School was built by Kim Yak-yeon, the Sinheung School by Yi Si-yeong and the Daejeon School, all in Manchuria. And the Gyedong School in Siberia had the same educational ideology.

The second ideology advocated by the enlightenment movement was the "independence war theory," which called for the establishment of independence movement bases abroad to wage an independence war against Japan.[35] According to this theory, the right and sure way to win national independence from the militarist Japan was to force war on Japan during an opportune time. For such a war, it was necessary that the people organize an independence army or a liberation army, providing it with money for the procurement of weapons and equipment. This army had to defeat the Japanese at any cost. The opportune time to wage such a war, it was thought, was the day the Korean nation's political, economic and cultural powers were sufficiently built up on the one hand, while the power of Japanese imperialism was spread thin in an expanded fight with China, Russia or the United States for world hegemony on the other.

To put this theory into practice, the nationalist leaders of the time actively promoted campaigns for establishing the independence movement's bases abroad. The areas selected for such base were southern Manchuria and the Soviet Maritime Province because they are contiguous to Korea just across the Yalu and the Tumen rivers, thus having easy access to the country. The nationalists, as the first step, built Korean communities armed with a strong sense of nationalism in these areas for

---

34. An Chang-ho's memorial paper in honor of the late An Tae-guk contributed to *Dongnip sinmun* (The Independent), 21 April 1921.
35. See Note 32.

making them bases of the future independence war on Japan. Their immediate objectives in these communities were developing industry for providing an economic foundation for their nationalist activities, and instituting modern military education for the training of future leaders of independence movements and the independence armies. They also had plans to use these bases as campaign sites for awakening the consciousness of the people at home to nationalism, while organizing and arming overseas Koreans in preparation for an independence war.

The Korean community in Sanyuanbao, in southern Manchuria just across the Yalu, was made into such a base by Yi Hoe-yeong, Yi Si-yeong, Yi Dong-nyeong, and Yi Sang-yong. Other Korean communities used as bases for independence movements were in Longjing of southeastern Manchuria across the Tumen river and in Hanxingdong on the Manchu-Siberian border.[36] To teach the military arts and general subjects to children from these Korean communities, the Sinheung School and the Daejeon School were built in Manchuria. In 1914 Yi Sang-seol, Yi Dong-hwi, Yi Dong-nyeong, and Jeong Jae-gwan set up the Korean Liberation Army Command in Vladivostok to lay the foundation of the independence armies' armed resistance against Japan, succeeding the anti-Japanese armed resistance of the righteous armies.[37]

---

36. See Note 32.

37. In his travel accounts to Russia carried by *the Independent* from the 20 February to the 12 April 1920, Dwibabo (phonetic) wrote about the establishment of the Korean Liberation Army Command as follows:

> In 1914 Russia marked the 10th anniversary of the Russo-Japanese War in ceremonies held across the country, and the Russians desired to revenge the defeat they suffered 10 years ago. As a result, the signs of a new Russo-Japanese war could be seen across Russia. Observing this situation, Yi Sang-seol, Yi Dong-hwi, Yi Dong-nyeong, Yi Jong-ho and Jeong Jae-gwan established the Korean Liberation Army Command in cooperation with their comrades in Manchuria and Siberia. Yi Sang-seol was elected as the commander of the Army and Yi Dong-hwi as the vice commander.
>
> In addition, they secretly organized military units and even established a military academy in Louzigou, China. They also planned to hold a ceremony of marking the 50th anniversary of Korean immigration to Siberia, with a view to using it for collecting war funds. For this ceremony they received approval from the Russian authorities. But World War I broke out in August 1914, and this intensified Japanese surveillance of the Korean communities in Siberia. Accordingly, the Korean Commerce Association in Siberia was dissolved, and the Korean newspaper was closed down with the 126th issue. Moreover, Yi

The following passages from a Japanese court paper regarding the Sinminhoe incident involving the patriotic enlightenment movement in 1912 attest to the development of independence movements in Manchuria.

> The Sinminhoe attempted to emigrate a large number of Koreans to southern Manchuria for the purpose of having them, especially the rich, buy land and build Korean villages there. It also recruited many comrades and educated youths and sent them to these Korean villages for organizing associations of Koreans in Manchuria and building schools and churches. The Sinminhoe then established a military academy in Manchuria for the training of Korean youths recruited from Korea as well as from Korean villages in Manchuria in preparation for an independence war to regain Korea's sovereign power.[38]

The independence war theory was put into practice chiefly in Manchuria and Siberia, but it should be noted that its basic foundation was in the home country. Although there were many restrictions and suppressions under Japanese colonial rule, every possible effort was made to develop a nationalist education system and industry, and promote the ideology of Korean nationalism through the preservation and study of national culture, which would provide the motive power for subsequent independence movements.[39]

Meaning and Thought of the Anti-Japanese Independence Movement

The nationwide uprising against Japanese rule on March 1, 1919 can be considered "a big current of thought into which all the previous nationalist movements converged and from which all the following nationalist movements branched out."[40] It was in fact an expression in action of the

---

Jong-ho was given the order to leave Vladivostok within 24 hours, and many other leaders of the independence movement had to leave the city for hideouts scattered in various areas.

38. Japanese Government-General of Korea, *Korea Court Records* (in Japanese), Meiji 44 II.
39. See note 32.
40. Cheon Gwan-u, "Samil undongsa gaegwan" (An Overview of the March First Movement History), in *Dongnip undongsa*, vol. 2 (Seoul: Independence Movement History Compilation Committee, 1966), pp. 59-93.

consensual will to win independence for the whole Korean people, irrespective of social status, occupation, area, religion, property, and sex.
This March First Movement can also be regarded as having provided an
opportunity for Korean nationalism to develop in harmony with democratic principles.[41]

The nationalist movement—or the independence movement after the
March First Movement—is considered to have followed the following
four streams of thought. The first was the "independence war theory,"
which had already been set as the main ideology of nationalism after the
Treaty of 1905. According to this theory, the nation needed to be well
prepared for war with Japan if it was to regain national independence by
force. To this end, all the people needed to be determined to shed their
blood in war with Japan.[42] That is why all funds donated to independence movements were labelled as "war funds," not as "independence
movement funds."

The second was the "cultural principle theory" that was promoted
chiefly after the March First Movement. As in the case of the independence war theory, this cultural principle posited that building up nation-

---

41. Yun Pyong Suk, *Samil undongsa* (The History of the March First Movement),
    (Seoul: Jeongeumsa, 1975), pp. 11-13.
42. The Korean Provisional Government declared war on Japan in its State Council
    Decree No. 1 and Military Affairs Decree No. 1 issued in April 1919.

    State Council Decree No. 1:
    The Provisional Government of Korea on the occasion of the second year of
    the government era and the first year of the Great Independence War which
    the 20 million Korean people must fight to a man for freedom or death, here-
    by declares war on Japan before the two million Korean people in Manchuria
    and Siberia as they form the main force to fight this war. It is firmly believed
    that you will fight a heroic and bloody battle to win freedom, otherwise, death
    would await us. Because the situation is very critical and serious, we should
    not hesitate or worry about fighting this war. we can determine the future of
    our country only in the last bloody battle which the 20 million Korean people
    must fight to a man.

    Military Affairs Decree No.1:
    The time has come for the brave Korean men and women to win freedom in a
    bloody war. We must march toward justice, freedom, and national indepen-
    dence. We must continue this march until we save the country with blood and
    iron will. Don't hesitate and don't worry. Let's all become the soldiers of the
    government. We the 20 million Korean people must pledge our loyalty to the
    Liberation Army and fight with it to the last man and woman.

al power to match that of Japan's was the only way to gain national liberation and independence; it shunned the view that national independence could come through foreign help or the generosity of Japan. But because the realities of Japanese colonial rule did not allow the Korean people to train an army for war with Japan, the cultural movement had as its objective the promotion of a particularly Korean politics, economy, education, press, and civic groups as the means to bolster national power.[43]

The third was the "diplomatic principle theory." Seeing that the building of a modern nation-state on the principles of world peace and coprosperity was possible, this movement sought international support for Korea's independence movement. This movement's advocates publicized the cultural tradition of Korea and the a priori need for Korea's political independence in foreign countries and international meetings. They also argued that the Japanese imperialists' repressive colonial rule not only inflicted suffering on the Korean people but also posed a great threat to peace in Asia. In short, they wanted world powers to check the Japanese imperialists, who were impeding Koreans from building a modern nation-state.[44]

The fourth and last was the "theory of struggle of the masses." According to this theory, the only way to national independence under the militarist rule of Japan was through the participation of all people in an anti-Japanese struggle, so as to make Japanese colonial rule impossible. As this theory goes, mass participation would lead to national liberation and independence.[45]

One or two of these theories found their sources in the nationalist movement after the Protectorate Treaty of 1905. In particular, the independence war theory had been the main underlying thought of the nationalist movement between the Treaty of 1905 and the March First

---

43. Yu Hong-yeol, "National Movements in the Country after the March First Movement" (in Korean), in *Samil undong osip junyeon ginyeom nonchong* (Collection of Essays Commemorating the 50th Anniversary of the March First Movement) (Seoul: Donga Ilbosa, 1969), pp. 679-700.

44. Kim Sang-gi, "National Movements outside the Country after March First Movement" (in Korean), in *Samil undong osip junyeon ginyeom nonchong*, pp. 701-718.

45. Sin Chae-ho discussed anti-Japanese struggles of the masses in his "Joseon hyeongmyeong seoneon" (Declaration of Korean Revolution), in *Danjae Sin Chae-ho jeonjip* (Collection of Sin Chae-ho's Writings), vol. 2, edited by Sin Chae-ho Memorial Society (Seoul: Eul Yoo Publishing Co., 1972).

Movement in 1919, though it did not clearly present its outlines until the March First Movement. And until the advent of this nationwide independence movement, there had been few relationships established between the different nationalist factions because of a lack of communication. However, the March First Movement provided an opportunity for these ideologies to establish effective relationships to the extent that they generated the driving force in the social development of Korea and furthermore the development of Korean nationalism in resistance to imperialism.

The declaration of independence at various rallies and demonstrations in the country expressed the Korean people's strong desire for independence, but it also came with the high price of human sacrifice, for many Koreans were massacred by Japanese policemen and soldiers. As a result, a more fundamental and effective independence movement was sought. Thus emphasis was put on a movement designed to enlighten the people to the importance of becoming a modernized nation. The people's enthusiasm for education, therefore, swept across the country, and was marked by a sharp rise in applicants for secondary and higher education. They wanted to be educated in the modern sciences and arts, even in Japanese schools, with the determination not to lose their national consciousness as a Korean. Many private schools, institutes and night schools were established throughout the country. These efforts greatly helped to develop the national education system, even to the extent of launching a movement to establish a private university with Korean funds and organizing the Joseon Gyoyukhoe (Korean Education Society).[46]

With the publication of the two daily newspapers, *The Dong-a Ilbo* and *The Chosun Ilbo*, and many magazines in the 1920s and the 1930s, modern journalism matured in the country, and the press advanced the people's modern historical consciousness. This modernization trend was evident in the various artistic circles in which Western literature and arts were imported for application to the development of modern Korean thought.[47]

---

46. O Cheon-seok, "National Education after the March First Movement" (in Korean), *Samil undong osip junyeon ginyeom nonchong*, pp. 741-750.

47. Choe Yeong-sik, "National Journalism after the March First Movement" (in Korean), in *Samil undong osip junyeon ginyeom nonchong*, pp. 719-728; Kim Geun-su, "The Press and Press Policy in the 1920s" (in Korean), in *Samil undong osip junyeon ginyeom nonchong*, pp. 729-740.

With the view that the modernization of a nation rested, in part, on the development of the economy through its national industries, a campaign was launched to encourage the use of Korean products, and the Mulsan Jangnyeohoe (Society for the Encouragement of Native Products) was organized. The Society called on the people to practice frugality, austerity and self-sustenance and to use domestic products and abstain from drinking and smoking, thus creating a self-sustaining trend in daily necessities, such as food, clothes and shelter in the country. Stressing this trend, some nationalists went so far as to say that the course of action for Korean nationalism to gain independence could be found in economic nationalism.[48]

In Manchuria and Siberia, where over one million Koreans were living, the bases for the independence movements had been set since the Protectorate Treaty of 1905 and the 1910 Treaty of Annexation. When Koreans waged the March First Movement against Japan in 1919, the Korean residents there organized independence armies equipped with small arms to start armed struggle against the Japanese troops deployed along the Yalu and the Tumen river.[49] In southern Manchuria alone, several independence armies, with a total strength of some 100,000, were organized. They were comprised of the People's Association Army, the Northern Route Military Command, the Korean Independence Army, the Western Route Military Command, the Korean Independence Group Volunteer Army, and the Restoration Army. In battles at Fengwudong and Qingshanli in 1920, they dealt a decisive blow to Japanese garrison units. Apart from these battles, the armed struggle against Japan along the Korean-Manchurian border continued tenaciously until 1930. In Rongjing in 1940, the Korean Provisional Government organized the Gwangbokgun (Restoration Army), with the assistance of the Chinese Guomindang government, to join the allied forces in the Pacific War against Japan, succeeding the armed resistance of independence armies in southern Manchuria in the 1920s.[50] Diplomatic activities, including a petition in support of independence movements submitted to the Versailles Conference after World War I, were chiefly the responsi-

---

48. Jo Gi-jun, "Joseon mulsan jangnyeo undong-ui jeon-gae gwajeong-gwa geu yeoksajeok seonggyeok" (A Study of the nature of the Korean Industry Promotion Movement), *Yeoksa hakbo* (Journal of History) 41 (1969).
49. Yun Pyong Suk, *Uibyeong-gwa dongnipgun*, pp. 129-143.
50. *Ibid.*, pp. 145-228.

bility of the Korean Provisional Government in China. It had Euro-American Department and sent a mission in Paris in order to launch a diplomatic offensive against the Japanese occupation. Other organizations of Koreans in Europe and America also supported such diplomatic activities. At the meeting of the League of Nations, the Pacific Conference, and other international forums, the representatives of the Provisional Government of Korea not only called for the liberation of the Korean people from the fetters of Japanese colonial rule, but for the sake of Asia. Contributing articles to Western newspapers and magazines, and conducting myriad lectures, overseas Koreans publicized the self-reliant characteristics of the Korean people and the indigenousness of Korea's traditional culture, and highlighted their unjust oppression.[51]

Furthermore, covert anti-Japanese societies, such as the Aegukdan (Patriots Corps) and the Uiyeoldan (Righteous Brotherhood), were organized after the March First Movement to terrorize ranking officials of the Japanese government and the Japanese colonial authorities in Korea."[52] Moreover, labor disputes and peasant revolts began to take on an anti-Japanese character as they developed into a movement of the masses.[53] The March First Movement in 1919 was followed by similar movements, such as the June 10 Independence Demonstration in 1926, the Gwangju Student Movement in 1929 and many other demonstrations and rallies. These all contributed to making the independence movement a movement of the masses.[54]

Externally, these movements appeared to be independent from each other. But internally they were closely related to one another through the Korean Provisional Government in China, various anti-Japanese organizations in and outside the country, and the efforts of nationalist leaders. Moreover, their supreme goal was always the same—the liberation and independence of the nation. Depending on their social, economic, and geographic position, the movement decided on its own style,

---

51. Korean Provisional Government, Paris Mission, "Our Programs in Europe" (in Korean); available from *Sindonga* (August 1967).

52. Kim Chang-su, "Activities of the Uiyeoldan as a National Movement" (in Korean), *Samil undong osip junyeon ginyeom nonchong*, pp. 809-820.

53. Kang Dong-jin, "Labor Movements after the March First Movement" (in Korean), *Samil undong osip junyeon ginyeom nonchong*, pp. 783-794; Jo Dong-geol, *Ilje ha hanguk nongmin undongsa* (A History of Korean Peasant Movements under Japanese Rule) (Seoul: Hangilsa Publishing Co., 1979), pp. 92-96.

54. See note 43.

and every participant in the movement engaged in activities that would best suit his or her situation for the cultivation of Korean nationalism.

Concluding Remarks

The Korean anti-Japanese movements took on various forms, depending on the historical condition and period. The ideological positions of these movements all differed, just as the methods for achieving their goals varied. The anti-alien movement intended to re-establish the traditional Neo-Confucian order, and the armed resistance developed from this movement was based on the theory of rejecting any talks with foreigners on any matters, which could be considered an anachronistic, conservative and reactionary way of thinking. The peasantry's anti-Japanese and anti-Establishment struggle was based not on any modern ideology but was derived from ordinary peasants and the followers of Donghak thought who believed that Neo-Confucian thought and aristocratic mores should be discarded to defend the country from foreign aggression and ensure social reforms on behalf of the people. Anti-Japanese and anti-Western sentiments also served as an impetus for peasant movements. The patriotic enlightenment movement of the Independence Club and other civil organizations touted a progressive ideology that aimed for political and social reforms which would expel aggressive foreign powers from the country.

In spite of such differences in thinking and methods of these anti-Japanese movements, their ultimate goals were always the same—the preservation of national independence and sovereign power and expulsion of imperialist foreign powers. These anti-Japanese movements instilled a sense of national consciousness and a concept of modern history in the Korean people; on the basis of this new found awareness, Korean nationalism developed to a point where it marks the beginning of modern Korean history. Thus, Korean nationalism set its direction and ideology through the armed anti-Japanese resistance movement and the patriotic enlightenment movement after the Treaty of 1905, and also developed the strategy of anti-Japanese resistance calling for the build-up of national capabilities in political, economic, military, and cultural fields in the course of these movements.

Korean nationalism which provided the driving force for the independence movements after the March First Movement overcame three

574 COLONIAL PERIOD AND POST-LIBERATION PERIOD

obstacles to maintain its nationalistic component.

First, the Japanese imperialists mounted a "cultural politics" in Korea after the March First Movement in an attempt to suppress the Korean people's nationalist movements at the root.[55] The switch from "police-state politics" to a "cultural politics" was couched in the guise that it would contribute to the cultural development of Korea, but its real objective was the liquidation of Korea's national culture and even its national identity by Japanizing the Korean people. Through cultural politics, Japan attempted to check and distort every nationalist and independence movement, and denounced the diplomatic activities and the independence war theory of the independence movement.

Second, world politics after World War I posed an obstacle for Korean nationalism by protecting the interests of imperialist powers. This order, set in the Versailles Peace Treaty, moved in the opposite direction of Korean nationalism. As a result, Korea's independence movement was checked by world politics, though it drew some moral sympathy from a few countries.[56] In spite of the persistent diplomatic activities of the Korean Provisional Government and Korean organizations in Europe and America, no country recognized the provisional government that existed between 1919 to 1945, except the Sun Wen government of China. This was typical of how world powers regarded Korea's independence movement before World War II.

The third obstacle was the communist Revolution in Russia in 1917. The Russian Communists approached the Korean independence movement with a policy that supported the liberation and independence movements of weak nations. But this problem should be dealt with in a separate study.

---

55. Yun Pyong Suk, "The Japanese Government's Policy toward the March First Movement" (in Korean), *Samil undong osip junyeon ginyeom nonchong*, pp. 415-442.
56. Yun Byeong-seok, *Hanguk geundae saryo ron* (A Bibliography of Modern Korean History) (Seoul: Ilchokak Publishing Co., 1979), pp. 291-292.

The Nature and Process of the Korean National Liberation Movement during the Japanese Colonial Period

Kang Man-gil

Introduction

As with the history of humankind and any national history, the history of a particular period or area, as it is commonly said, is impossible to realize or recreate "as it was." Ultimately, history is always recreated from a particular point of view. Recreating the national liberation movement as a part of the contemporary and modern history of Korea is no different.

When the history of the colonial period is examined from a perspective based on the notion that Korea degenerated into a colony before having achieved the establishment of a modern bourgeois nation-state, the national liberation movement of the period can be viewed as both a liberation movement and a movement to establish a modem nation-state. As a movement to establish a modern nation-state, however, the national liberation movement was unfortunately not promoted independently by a single sociopolitical force or policy.

From a perspective of modem class distinction, to borrow from West-

*Originally published in the *Korea Journal*, vol. 36, no. 1 (spring 1996).

Kang Man-gil now serves as the president of Sangji University. He received his Ph.D. in Korean history from Korea University in 1975. He is the author of many books, including *Bundan sidae-ui yeoksa insik* (Historical Perceptions of the National Division Period) (1978), *Hanguk hyeondaesa* (Contemporary History of Korea) (1994), and *Tongil jihyang uri minjok haebang undongsa* (History of Korea's National Liberation Movements toward Unification) (2000). E-mail: bbdbej@korea.com.

ern theory, a sufficient development of bourgeoisie and proletariat classes necessary to independently carry out a national liberation movement was retarded. The necessary ideological perspective embodied in a socialist-oriented national liberation movement followed the March First Independence Movement of 1919. But it must first be stated that the conditions of Korea's national history and the immaturity of capitalism during the Japanese colonial period hardly allowed for the growth of the kind of class structures that were necessary to support such a movement. Korean national liberation movement pursued under the conditions of colonialism was destined from its inception to develop into a movement constituted of leftist and rightist forces, driven by anti-Japanese and anti-imperialist policies, and united by the necessity for cooperation (and eventually unifying) among all these forces.

Throughout the entire process of national liberation movement, it was true that there was a division between rightist and leftist forces. From a perspective of a system of division that took root following national liberation, the aspects of conflict and confrontation between rightist and leftist lines may have been highlighted, leading to see only the "history of national independence movement" by the rightists as the history of the national liberation movement, whereby relegating the leftist line not as a history of national liberation movement but only as a "history of the Korean communist movement." Similarly, a converse perspective may regard only the leftist line as comprising the history of the national liberation movement, or regard both left and right as legitimate, but only as separate sects within them, and not as part of the national liberation movement.

If, on the other hand, assertions that the national liberation movement during the colonial period was divided into rightist and leftist lines are rejected, and the movement is viewed as having been led by one line, it leads to a dangerous historical perspective that assigns fundamental causes of the national division following liberation to external powers. In this instance, even without discussing the issue of historical independent consciousness, although recognizing that the influence of external powers was strong in the division of the country, it is dangerous in that it diminishes the objectivity of history by reducing the causes of a particular historical reality.

If the national liberation movement of the colonial period is seen as a process of establishing a modern nation-state, and if it is acknowledged that in the process not a single line, but both rightist and leftist lines coexisted, then the process of this movement can be understood as a process of establishing a "unified" nation-state. It is important, then, to consider how closely the rightists and leftists came to establish a unified nation-state. According to this argument, the national liberation movement of the colonial era worked towards establishing a unified nation-state. Given the realities of national division and the direction of national history, this perspective is related to the historical consciousness that insists upon a unified nation-state being established in a peaceful and autonomous manner.

Any study of the history of national liberation movement needs to clarify the nature of the relationship between rightist and leftist lines. For example, was it one of confrontation and conflict only, or the reverse in which it attempted to form cooperative or unified relations in order to increase the potency of the national liberation movement fronts? It is dangerous to presume a division system, asserting that the rightists and leftists, or their orientations, could only be confrontational or conflicting. It is also an unscholarly attitude to presume the contrary, even if there were efforts to form cooperative or unified relations or there were several instances of such successful efforts, for such presumption could blind the other.

To put it roughly, in a division-system view, the awareness and the study of the history of the national liberation movement may have been undertaken mostly from a perspective that does not acknowledge the existence of the leftist line, or conversely, the rightist line. This is not a problem within academia, but rather is a result of nonacademic conditions. However, as it is commonly said, the value of scholarly pursuit lies in its ability to stay above the fray of common knowledge and one of its function criticizing it. It is ardently hoped that a study of the history of a divided nation will overcome the tendency in academia to be constrained by conditions of the system, or to support the system's conditions. The same applies to understanding the history of the national liberation movement in the colonial period. It is with these thoughts in mind that we summarize the process of the national liberation movement of the colonial period as we know it, based on studies conducted on it to date.

The National United Front Movement of the 1920s

The First Half of the 1920s

The national movement, just before colonization, was divided between an armed struggle of the righteous armies (*uibyeong*) and the nonmilitary movement of patriotic enlightenment. Once the country entered the colonial period, the national movement inevitably underwent a certain degree of transformation. As in the case of the Sinminhoe (New People's Association), which had been destroyed by the arrests associated with the alleged Baegoin Sageon (Case of the One Hundred Five) conspiracy in 1912, the nonmilitary movement transcended its nature as patriotic enlightenment movement, established an independence movement base overseas and fostered the Dongnipgun (Independence Army) while the armed struggle of the righteous armies continued.

It is true that the March First Independence Movement, which exploded against the backdrop of the national independence movement after colonization, was limited to the nonviolent methods of the upper-class national bourgeois, represented by thirty-three people who signed the Declaration of Independence. However, it is also true that a significant number of youths, students, laborers, and peasants actually spread the independence movement nationally, thus facing armed suppression by the Japanese police, crossing over the line of nonresistance and nonviolence.

The March First Independence Movement, as a nationwide struggle, served to ignite changes in the national liberation front thereafter. First, although the March First Independence Movement began with a declaration of nonviolence, the futility of nonviolence in the face of Japanese forceful suppression was soon realized. However, it was soon recognized that national liberation would not be possible without an all-out armed struggle, and this recognition prompted the armed resistance in the Manchurian region in the early 1920s.

Second, although there was some shift toward republicanism in the national movement ranks before colonization, the national liberation front became an all-out republican movement with the March First Independence Movement. Politically, the March First Independence Movement itself had several characteristics of a movement to establish a republican form of government. As a result, the provisional governments in exile, both within the country and abroad, all proclaimed republicanism. The Korean Provisional Government in Shanghai, a federation of all the provisional governments in exile, styled in the republican fashion, demonstrates the politico-historical milieu of the March First Independence Movement.

Third, although much of the March First Independence Movement itself was part of a bourgeois nationalist movement before the colonial period, a socialist character needed to be added to the national liberation front after the March First Independence Movement began. And this socialist character breathed new wind into the front. In particular, some of the national bourgeoisie turned to a policy of gradual improvement, therefore assuring those uncompromising bourgeois factions and socialist factions to take the helm of the national liberation movement.

The explosion of the March First Independence Movement set off the national liberation movement that was afoot in the first half of the 1920s. It also jointly promoted, albeit temporarily, both a nonviolent movement as well as one of armed struggle, which had both been taking place before the colonial period. The outcome manifested itself as armed resistance in the Manchurian region, at a time when no liberated area (*haebanggu*) was allowed, as the whole country had been completely colonized. Also, while a socialist line appeared in the national liberation movement in this period, the conditions were not such that it could take root domestically. Accordingly, even though there was an era of the Goryeo Gongsandang (Goryeo Communist Party), its activity was limited to abroad.

At the time of the Korean Provisional Government's establishment, it was hoped that it would become the headquarters of the national liberation movement by embracing the various groups, even if only temporarily. The movements that developed as the result of the March First Independence Movement were divided according to three regions: the provisional government movement centered around Shanghai, armed resistance in the Manchurian region, and the Goryeo Communist Party movement covering the Maritime Province of Siberia and the Shanghai region. The national liberation movement of the first half of the 1920s was, for the most part, associated with the provisional government movement. Although the military branch of the Korean Provisional Government could not directly control and lead an active armed resistance in the Manchurian region, a significant number of armed resistance groups had some sort of connection with the Korean Provisional Government through the Western Route Military Command and the Northern Route Military Command. In the case of the Goryeo Communist Party movement, although it quickly parted ways, its central powers approved and participated in the establishment of the Korean Provisional Government, making it a type of allied government. This allied Korean Provisional Government formed secret treaties with the Soviet government for fostering the Independence Army, carrying out activities it would not be able to engage in as a rightist government.

In summary, the nationalist movement during the first half of the 1920s was promoted under the leadership of the Korean Provisional Government, which was established with the hope that it would act as the headquarters for the national movement. However, the government could not be maintained as a unified government or allied government to accommodate several different movement philosophies and political camps. The leftist front separated first and then the active resistance front followed. In an effort to make the Korean Provisional Government a united front government, a rally of national representatives convened with the financial aid of the Comintern, but it was not successful. Thus the curtain fell on the national liberation movement with the Korean Provisional Government acting as its leader.

The Second Half of the 1920s

The national liberation movement of the latter half of the 1920s followed the failure of the Korean Provisional Government-centered movement, but it was unique in that it was markedly an all-out realization of the national united front movement. This movement was developed when some of the national bourgeois compromised with the Japanese after the March First Independence Movement. In some respects, the establishment of the Joseon Communist Party in 1925 also served as a momentum for such movement. The formation of the Joseon Communist Party in the country aimed to eradicate the incessant factional struggles and divisions in the overseas socialist Goryeo Communist Party movement. On the other hand, throughout the first half of the 1920s, the domestic socialist movement saw some progress, with other popular movements having developed with great success. Both events made possible the beginning of a communist movement in the country, forming an important part of the background of the national liberation movement. Needless to say, it was the formation of the Joseon Communist Party that made possible the national united front movement.

In the latter half of the 1920s, the Joseon Communist Party movement underwent four dissolutions, followed by reorganizations, and continued to be beset by an inherent factional struggle within the overseas Goryeo Communist Party. Still, efforts to unify all of the communist powers and to form a united front with the noncompromising national bourgeoisie continued. The decision by the Central Executive Committee of the Joseon Communist Party to organize a nationalist party in alliance with Cheondogyo (Religion of the Heavenly Way) members at its national convention was a concrete example of this attempt at unification.

Compared to the First and Second Joseon Communist Parties, which basically centered around the Hwayohoe (Tuesday Society) faction, the Third Joseon Communist Party (the leftist Marxist-Leninist Party) initially attempted to include all factions, although in the end the party itself became a faction. The ML Party also argued, through its "Jeonguhoe (Righteous Fraternity Society) Declaration," for a united front with the noncompromising national bourgeoisie. It also accommodated the united front line of the Comintern, actively participating in the Singanhoe movement as a national united front.

The national united front movement, which was a unique part of the national liberation movement from the latter half of the 1920s, first emerged overseas in 1926. With the formation of the National Society for Rapid Realization of a Korean Independent Single Party (Hanguk Dongnip Yuildang Chokseonghoe) in Beijing in 1926, this movement rapidly spread to Shanghai, Nanjing, Wuhan and Guangdong. The next year, the Singanhoe was formed in Korea as a part of that movement. The following year, the rightist groups from Jeonguibu (Righteous Government) and Chamuibu (General Staff Headquarters) and the leftist groups from the North-Manchu Labor Youth League (Bungman Noryeok Cheongnyeon Dongmaeng) and the South-Manchu Labor Youth League (Namman Noryeok Cheongnyeon Dongmaeng) formed the Council for the Establishment of a Pan-National Single Party (Jeon Minjok Yuildang Jojik Hyeobuihoe) in an effort to unify the various movements.

The single national party movement ultimately did not succeed overseas. But on the domestic front, the non-compromising rightists, along with the Joseon Communist Party, succeeded in forming the Singanhoe as a countermove to the compromising powers' formation of the Yeonjeonghoe (Political Research Society). The Singanhoe, which was active for the next five years, was viewed in later historiography as a transitional movement that transformed from a rightist-led national liberation movement to a leftist-led one. It was also viewed as a petit-bourgeois movement. However, it has finally come to be seen as a national united front movement.

Though the Singanhoe represented the national liberation movement, especially in the latter half of the 1920s, it was dissolved by the leftists. There were several reasons for this. There was, as the 1930s unfolded, continuous suppression by Japan and limits placed on the activities of all organized movements under the fascist system that emerged in full force after the invasion of Manchuria. Other factors were the reformist line adopted by the Singanhoe's leadership, the strengthened leftist front in the 1920s that led to a parting of ways from the national bourgeoisie, and the leftist leanings of the Comintern line taken after the Sixth Conference in 1928.

When the Singanhoe dissolved in the 1930s, the non-compromising rightists on the domestic front lost their ground, either disintegrating or degenerating into reformists. However, the Singanhoe proved to be a valuable experience and asset to the national unification movement front. In particular, the Singanhoe movement was highly valued as a "surface" organization movement that functioned openly but served as a prop for the various underground movements.

The National United Front Movement since the 1930s

China

The national liberation movement of the 1920s developed in an attempt to achieve an allied front of leftists and rightists through the left-right coalition, provisional government movement of the first half of the decade, as well as through the establishment of a single national party in the latter half of the decade. From the 1930s on, political parties and organizations equipped with concrete party platforms and party policies were organized in response to Japan's imperialist invasion and growing fascism.

The national liberation movement pursued the establishment of a politically and militarily united front as a means to construct a unified nation-state after liberation. It predicted that the continental invasion by the Japanese imperialists would develop from the Manchurian invasion into a Sino-Japanese War, and escalate further into a Russo-Japanese War, and eventually the Pacific War. During this period, the national liberation movement consistently focused on creating a national united front, aimed at defeating Japan and liberating Korea. Because of Japan's occupation of Manchuria and the Sino-Japanese War, it was difficult for all the dispersed fronts to connect with each other. Because of this, the national united front movement had to be divided into movements in China, Manchuria and Korea, according to the geographical location in which the movement developed.

The Korean Provisional Government in Shanghai, even if weakened, continued to exist, and a significant part of the national liberation movement forces in Manchuria moved to China when Japan occupied Manchuria. Accordingly, changes occurred in the national liberation movement front in China as it acted to confront Japan's full-scale invasive penetration into the Chinese continent. The Hanguk Dongnipdang (Korean Independence Party), formed by the core powers of a rightist front a year before the Manchurian Incident, along with the Uiyeoldan (Righteous Brotherhood), became the central powers. The Righteous Brotherhood, which was formerly limited to violence-oriented and private movement groups, came to display characteristics of a political party around 1927; it possessed a clear party platform and policies, and changed itself into a socialist organization with a defined relationship to the Comintern. The Joseon Hyeongmyeongdang (Korean Revolutionary Party) joined the Korean Independence Party and the Righteous Brotherhood, along with the Association of Comrades for Korean National Restoration (Hanguk Gwangbok Dongjihoe). Together they formed an anti-Japanese unification league in 1932 as a united front organization.

A loose united front formed by an alliance of groups generally yielded difficult and ineffective struggles. Realizing this, the Korea-based anti-Japanese front unification league reformed as the Joseon Minjok Hyeong-myeongdang (Korean National Revolutionary Party), with added participation from the New Korean Independence Party (Sinhan Dongnip-dang) and the General Association of Korean in the United States (Jaemi Gungmin Chonghoe) in 1935. The Korean Provisional Government defenders, who centered around Kim Gu, did not participate in this party because at the time its predecessor argued for the dissolution of the Korean Provisional Government. However, it was still a strong united front party in which most of the national liberation movement front in China participated. Its party platform and party principles had the characteristics of a united front and it acted as a political party in which the properties of all the participating political parties and organizations were combined.

Even so, at that point, the path of the Korean National Revolutionary Party as a united front political party was not smooth. Since the Korean Provisional Government continued to operate, despite having supposed to be disbanded, the two entered into a confrontational relationship. Furthermore, some groups abandoned the party right after this government's establishment. However, the united front line was accomplished, and, in 1937, when Japan began the Sino-Japanese War, the united front was joined by the socialist Korean National Liberators' League (Joseon Minjok Haebang Undongja Dongmaeng), and the anarchist Korean Revolutionists' Alliance (Joseon Hyeongmyeongja Yeonmaeng), to form the Joseon Minjok Jeonseon Yeonmaeng (Korean National Front Alliance). As a part of its military arm, it organized the Joseon Uiyong-dae (Korean Righteous Volunteers Corps). The Joseon Cheongnyeon Jeonwi Dongmaeng Young Korean Vanguards' Alliance, formed by young radical socialists who had bolted from the Korean National Revolutionary Party, joined the Korean Righteous Volunteers Corps, further strengthening the united front of the Korean National Fronts' Alliance.

On the other hand, the rightists in China achieved a united front in 1937 with the establishment of the Union of Korean National Liberation Movement Organizations (Hanguk Gwangbok Undong Danche Yeon-haphoe). This was a joint-council formed by the Korean Independence Party and the Korean Revolutionary Party, which had been organized by those who had seceded from the Korean National Revolutionary Party, as well as the Korean Nationalist Party (Hanguk Gungmindang), which had been organized after the formation of the Korean National Revolutionary Party. Even after this, the national united front movement in China continued. In 1939 the Korean National Fronts Alliance and the Union of the Korean National Liberation Movement Organizations combined to form the National Association of Allied Fronts (Jeon-guk Yeonhap Jeonseon Hyeophoe) and announced a common party platform, but the party failed.

Around 1941, a significant portion of the Korean Righteous Volunteers Corps left the Chinese Guomindang government army zone and moved to the one occupied by the Chinese Communists. Following this move, the unification movement of the Guomindang army zone front shifted its direction more in line with the Korean Provisional Government. In 1942, the Korean National Fronts Alliance participated in the Korean Provisional Government's parliament and those members of the Korean Righteous Volunteers Corps, which had not moved to the communist area, joined the Restoration Army of the Korean Provisional Government. In 1944, the Nationalist Revolutionary Party and the anarchist organization joined the Korean Provisional Government, thus making the Korean Provisional Government the united front government.

In another development, the Union of the Young Koreans' Association in Huabei (Hwabuk Joseon Cheongnyeon Yeonhaphoe), formed in 1941 by Koreans who had participated in the Red Army's Long March, the central powers of the Young Korean Vanguards' Alliance, who had moved to the Red Army area after withdrawing from the National Revolutionary Party, as well as its successor, the Korean Independence Alliance in Huabei (Hwabuk Joseon Dongnip Dongmaeng). These organizations all agreed in 1945 to join the Korean Provisional Government. However, with the defeat of Japan in the same year, each group returned to the north and south of the 38th parallel.

Both the rightist and leftist national liberation movement fronts in China made efforts to form a united front around the Korean Provisional Government right up until the defeat of Japan. The important goals of their efforts were to form a united front of political and military powers, with the approval of the Allied Forces, and to participate in the war against Japan. However, Japan was defeated before the two goals could be achieved. Thus, the decision regarding the Korean peninsula was left to the foreign ministers of the U.S., Great Britain, and the Soviet Union at the Moscow Conference, in which no faction of the national liberation movement front participated.

Manchuria

After the failure of the single national party movement, which was promoted in the latter half of the 1920s, the national liberation movement front of the Manchurian region was formed by the Korean Revolutionary and Korean Independence Parties. Their military carried out armed resistance against Japan's invasion of Manchuria but this did not continue for long. The leader of this movement either died in the war or moved to China. Most of the socialist leaders who had been active in this region joined the Manchuria Province Committee of the Chinese Communist Party upon the dissolution of the Joseon Communist Party, following the issuing of the "December Theses" and the promulgation of the principle of "one country, one party."

It was under such conditions that around 1933 the revolutionary committees of the local soviet were formed, under the strategy of the Manchuria Province Committee of the Chinese Communist Party in the Manchurian region. Particularly in the Yanji, Heilongjiang, Wangqing, and Xunchun counties in eastern Manchuria that had soviets as the base, anti-Japanese guerrilla units were organized. A great number of Koreans lived in this region, and accordingly most of the leaders of the guerrilla units were Korean, as were the guerrillas themselves. The situation was similar in the southern Manchurian guerrilla units.

In 1933, the central bureau of the Chinese Communist Party decreed the "January Note" to the Manchuria Province Committee to strengthen the anti-Japanese national unted front in the Manchurian region. The "January Note" included the guarantee of the basic rights and interests of the minority population, the reformation of the guerrilla units into the People's Revolutionary Army, and the replacement of the Soviets with the People's Revolutionary Government. Accordingly the guerrilla units in the Manchurian region were formed into the First, Second, Third, and Fourth Armies of the Northeast People's Revolutionary Army (Dongbuk Inmin Hyeongmyeonggun). The First and Second Independent Units of the Second Army had many Korean members. In the case of the Second Independent Unit, most of the officers, with the exception of the head of the unit, were Koreans.

Around this time, the anti-Minsaengdan (People's Welfare Corps) struggle, which arose from the Japanese imperialists' strategy of attempting to increase pro-Japanese anti-communism in Manchuria as well from the so-called leftist adventurist line of the Chinese Communist Party, dealt a great blow to the region's anti-Japanese national united front. However, the change in line during the seventh conference of the Comintern and the "August First Declaration" by the Chinese Communist Party, which ratified the changes, brought about a new phase in the Manchurian region's anti-Japanese national united front. All of the region's anti-Japanese military powers, including the Northeast People's Revolutionary Army and the Dongbuk Banil Yeonhapgun (Northeast Anti-Japanese United Army), were organized into the Dongbuk Hangil Yeon-gun (Northeast Anti-Japanese Alliance Army).

From 1936 to 1937, the Northeast Anti-Japanese Alliance Army was formed with a total of eleven armies. Of these, more than half the soldiers of the Second Army were Koreans. The First Route Military Command of the Northeast Anti-Japanese Alliance Army, made up of the First and Second Armies, established a guerrilla base in the Baekdusan mountain area, and this area became the center of Korean armed resistance against the Japanese. Following this, the Korean unit of the First Route Command carried out domestic struggles, centering around Hamgyeongbuk-do province as its strategic point.

After the Seventh Conference of the Comintern, the Chinese Communist Party's minority national policy underwent change. The Manchuria Province Committee, in its "Platform of Northeast People's Revolutionary Provisional Government," recognized the autonomy of minority nations in 1935. Subsequently, in 1936, the Fatherland Restoration Association (Joguk Gwangbokhoe) of the Korean people in Manchuria was formed, declaring that it would "fight the Japanese enemy in solidarity to liberate the mother country, regardless of differences in class, gender, position, party, age or religion."

After this, the Changbai County Operation Committee of the Fatherland Restoration Association formed three *guhoe*, 11 *jihoe*, 41 *bunhoe*, 10 *ban* and four production units under it. Domestically, it organized 3 jihoe, 3 bunjo and one Korean national liberation alliance, one Jeonguhoe (Righteous Fraternity Society), one anti-Japanese society, and 14 anti-Japanese groups. In the Gapsan region, the existing operation committee was transformed to an anti-Japanese national liberation league, a national united front organization. At the same time, to form a united front with Cheondogyo, the league won the leaders of Cheondogyo, such as the chief rector (*dojeong*) and the chief of the Jongniwon, representatives of the youth groups in the Hamgyeong-do province and China's Changbai county. At one time, it sent an operating officer to Seoul to form a liaison with the Cheondogyo central body.

Near the end of 1940, the main troops of the Northeast Anti-Japanese Alliance Army moved to the Soviet Union region, leaving only small troops to continue their activities in Manchuria. From research conducted so far, even when the Northeast Anti-Japanese Alliance Army was active in the Manchurian region, neither the Korean unit nor the Fatherland Restoration Association seemed to have had ties with the Korean Independence Alliance (Joseon Dongnip Dongmaeng) that would have led to the formation of a national united front. However, the Manchurian region front of the national liberation movement also predicted liberation of the motherland in the near future, and the efforts to form a national united front by communists and anticommunists were apparent, indicating that the political power of Koreans within the Northeast Anti-Japanese Alliance Army was taking on an individual and separate character.

Korea

It would be no exaggeration to say that the activities of the national liberation movement front in Korea in the 1930s are represented by the movement to rebuild the Joseon Communist Party, which dissolved under the Comintern's instructions. At the Sixth Conference of the Comintern in 1928, regarded as the moment the international communist movement adopted its leftist line, the approval of the Joseon Communist Party was revoked, and the Korean revolution was defined as a bourgeois democratic revolution. The Comintern ordered a revolutionary solution to the issue of land ownership and the establishment of the revolutionary democratic dictatorship of the proletariat and peasants, claiming that such power could be established only through the Soviet form.

After the dissolution of the Joseon Communist Party, many Korean communist movement activists joined either the Chinese Communist Party or the Japanese Communist Party, following the "one country, one party" principle of the Comintern. Thus, its ability to rebuild itself was reduced. The movement to rebuild the Joseon Communist Party, taking place under such conditions, was initiated by a call to end factionalism, arising from the past intelligentsia- and petit bourgeoisie-centered movement. The movement also called for the rebuilding of a united Bolshevik-type party centered around laborers and peasants. However, the early stage of the reconstruction movement was again carried out competitively among those factions formed in the 1920s, including the Tuesday Society faction, Seoul-Shanghai faction, and Marxist-Leninist faction.

The early stage of the faction-centered party reconstruction movement acquired its cell organization in industrial centers and agricultural areas under the leadership of the preparatory committee for party reconstruction, which was organized nationally. Labor and peasant unions were to be established with cell organizations serving as the base. However, from about 1931, this method was changed to one in which revolutionary labor and peasant unions would be established first and regional units of communist groups were to be formed based on those unions. The reconstruction effort from the top was transformed to a reconstruction from the bottom. It was also a way to solve the problem of factions. The "September Theses" and the "October Note" were instructions for such reconstruction.

Legal labor unions and peasant unions in cities and agricultural areas were reorganized into illegal and revolutionary labor and peasant unions. As a result, the revolutionary labor and peasant union movements infiltrated factories and agricultural areas throughout the country. The labor movement formed factory chapters and organized regional and industrial branches or local committees. Based on these, provincial committees and the central bureau were to be formed. In the case of the peasant movement, unions were formed in various parts of the country, including Hamgyeong-do, Gyeongsang-do, and Jeolla-do provinces. As a result, despite the desperate suppression by the Japanese fascist regime, there were 902 cases of major strikes between 1931 and 1935, in which over 70,000 laborers participated. Strikes by tenant farmers numbered 351 cases during the same period, and 17,000 farmers participated.

Regional communist groups with several types of organization were formed and operated nationwide under various names. They led and encouraged revolutionary labor and peasant movements. Among them were the Gyeongseong Communist Group, the Andong Communist Group, the Jinju Regional Association of the Korean Communists, Yeongam Communist Association, the Jeonju Regional Association for Reconstruction of Joseon Communist Party, the Buyeo Communist Association, the Yeongdong Anti-Rightist Alliance, the Onseong Labor Alliance, the Wonsan Labor Vanguard Leader Group, the Gyeongju Comrades Association, the Yi Jae-yu Group, and the Kwon Yeong-tae Group. There were also many communist groups whose names were unrevealed.

The national liberation movement front of the 1930s in Korea centered itself around the Joseon Communist Party reconstruction movement and adopted the united front line of the Seventh Conference of the Comintern. The Soviet power oriented line through the "nationalist dictatorship of the proletariat and the peasants" was negated. Instead, the need to adopt a national united front line with the anti-imperialist bourgeois nationalists was confirmed. Kim Ha-il participating in the seventh conference of the Comintern gave a speech in which he said that in the anti-war struggle, the contradictions between the Korean bourgeoisie and Japanese imperialism needed to be used to the fullest extent. The Comintern sent operatives to Korea and instructed them in strategies and tactics for the anti-Japanese unified front movement.

However, in the case of the reconstruction movement for the Joseon Communist Party in Korea, the united front line of the Comintern was not uniformly accepted. Some communists, while recognizing the inevitability of the formation of an anti-Japanese united front, look a position that the revolutionary labor and peasant union movements needed to be undertaken concurrently to achieve the goal of proletariat hegemony. Others defined the view of a revolutionary labor and peasant union movement line as a "leftist sectarian policy," arguing that such a movement had to be dissolved and a mass anti-Japanese organization formed in its stead.

As we have seen, even in the process of the communist party reconstruction movement, despite arguments by some that a national united front line should be accepted, conditions were not such that a united front could be formed in Korea between the communist party reconstruction movement leadership and anti-Japanese groups until the defeat of Japan. However, some of the anti-Japanese political camps, though not connected with the communist party reconstruction movement powers, organized a united front organization, albeit belatedly, and attempted to connect with overseas fronts with some success. For example, activities of the Geon-guk Dongmaeng (National Foundation League) were formed secretly during the last phase of the colonial period.

The National Foundation League was formed in 1944 by domestic anti-Japanese forces, including Yeo Un-hyeong and communist forces who were not directly linked to the party reconstruction movement. This league was an organization oriented toward a united front, "a grand union of all persons and all factions, encompassing anyone with national conscience, strictly excluding pro-Japanese elements and national traitors." The league secretly sent people to the Chinese front to form a united front with the Korean Independence League in Yenan and the Korean Provisional Government in Zhongjing. It was able to form ties with the Korean Independence League, and they agreed to convene a pan-national rally at Yenan. However, Japan was defeated before this plan could materialize.

At the start of the 1930s, the national liberation movement in Korea followed the leftist objective of the communist party reconstruction movement. Still, after the seventh conference of the Comintern, it accepted the national united front objectives and aims to some extent. But it was never able to establish a wide-ranging, anti-Japanese national united front, due largely to two factors: the debilitating and constantly aggressive suppressive measures taken by the Japanese fascist regime, coupled with the discord within the party reconstruction movement itself. It should be noted here that the anti-Japanese political forces, which at the time sensed and predicted the imminent defeat of Japanese imperialism, managed to suffer less suppression than the communist party reconstruction. These forces were therefore at least partially able to form a national united front in preparation for national liberation.

Conclusion

Korean scholars have yet to arrange the many threads of the national liberation movement's process during the 35 years of the Japanese colonial period in a meaningful historical sequence. It is the only way in which the nature and the historicity of the movement can be understood. As Bak Eun-sik argues in *Hanguk dongnip undong-ji hyeolsa* (The Bloody History of the Korean Independence Movement), some scholars have placed the heart of the movement within the national liberation movement front in the colonial period. Doing so, however, they are merely dealing with the movement's early stages. The lack of complexity and wholeness in this scholarship is understandable, especially because in the period immediately following the national liberation, Korean scholars had neither the freedom nor the opportunity to study the movement in depth.

It was not until the 1960s that scholars began to study various episodes of the national liberation movement's history and historically assess its achievements. Yet it remains true that no scholarship attempted to systematically delineate the trends of the whole movement, nor did any work explain the historical position and the very nature of the movement in a consistent manner. Most works published under the rubric of "A History of the Korean Independence Movement" have dealt only with the history of the rightist front.

The leftist front of the national liberation movement, formed in the early 1920s, had continued its course until liberation, yet scholars have always treated it as a part of the history of the communist movement. An important reason for the exclusion of the leftist front activities from

histories of Korea's independence movement has been the nearly palpa-
ble national historical consciousness nurtured by the division system
born from anti-communism that continued from the moment of national
liberation to the present. From such a perspective, the leftist front was
not viewed as having played a significant role in the history of the Korean independence movement.

However, since the late 1980s, democratization has worked in tandem
with a movement toward peaceful national unification, and academic
and scholarly freedom has finally become a fact of life. This freedom has
encouraged studies dealing with various topics on the leftist fronts of the
colonial period. As a result, our consciousness of the leftist movements
has become relatively free of bias, and we are now able to accord the
leftist factions of the liberation movement their rightful place in history.

From the perspective of the Japanese colonial policy, the Japanese
colonial period can be divided into the following phases: 1) the military
rule of the 1910s, 2) the national dissension policy period that followed
the March First Independence Movement, often expressed as a time of
"cultural rule" during the 1920s, and 3) the fascist regime and war period that began in the 1930s. But if we look at the same period of time
from the perspective of the national liberation movement's attempts to
establish a unified nation-state, we can conceivably come up with quite a
different set of categories. The following three are an example: 1) the
March First Independence Movement preparatory period in the 1910s,
2) the national united front movement period of the 1920s, and 3) the
period of the national united front movement, or the national allied front
movement period, which existed from the 1930s.

After the March First Independence Movement, when the division
within the national liberation movement front along the leftist and rightist lines became clear, the national liberation movement developed into a
movement aimed at establishing a provisional government through the
cooperation between the Left and the Right, the national alliance front
movement against national reformism, and the national united front
movement against the fascist nature of the colonial regime. Arranging
the history of the national liberation movement from such a perspective
connects it to the history of the national unification movement after
national liberation, thus forming a vein in the history of all modern and
contemporary national movements.

Admittedly the delineation set forth in this article is labyrinthine and
complex, but four crucial points emerge. First, many movements

emerged to establish a single independence front in the 1910s, but it was only following the March First Independence Movement that the main national liberation movement emerged in full force. Based on this argument, the national liberation movement of 1920s can be considered as the national united front movement. The national liberation movement during the first half of the 1920s centered around the Korean Provisional Government, which was made possible by the cooperation between leftists and rightists. But the Korean Provisional Government was finally dissolved due to the failure of the national representatives rally, which was convened as a united front movement.

Second, the national united front movement of the 1920s can now be viewed as fully active in the latter part of the 1920s. The single national party on the foreign front and the Singanhoe movement on the domestic front should be seen as movements in the same category. The Singanhoe movement, which was successful at one point only as part of the former, expressed both the weakness and the significance of the national alliance movement. But it must be noted that the single national party movement was able to recover the failures of the Korean Provisional Government during the first half of the 1920s and aimed to integrate the national liberation movement front.

Third, the difference between the national liberation movement of the 1920s and 1930s is that the latter continued as a movement for the formation of a national united front aimed at establishing a unified nation-state. The movement, under the influence of the united front line of the international communist movement, led to the formation of political parties and organizations with party platforms and policies that could confront fascist Japanese imperialism. The national liberation movement since the 1930s can be seen in terms of the process and development of a national united front movement.

Fourth, the movement of the l930s was divided into the China front, the Manchurian region front and the domestic front as a result of Japan's invasion of Manchuria and China. There was considerable difficulty in unifying the different fronts. However, on the China front, leftist and rightist camps and the whole anti-Japanese anti-fascist front were becoming united. On the Manchurian and the domestic leftist fronts, the movements were overcoming their leftist orientation and transforming into a national united front, following the Comintern policy. And the National Foundation League on the domestic front not only unified the Left and the Right, but also formed ties with overseas fronts.

In general, the argument presented here views the national liberation movement during the colonial period as part of a process located on a continuum, moving through the national alliance movement of the 1920s to the national united front movement which took hold in the 1930s. Such a view does not detract from the importance of any particular movement during the periods noted. Rather it seeks to integrate all the movements by exposing the depth of each movement's relationship to one another and its significance to our present situation and future.

Inauguration of the Singanhoe Society and the Establishment of Its Chapters

Yi Kyun Young

National Cooperative Front Movement prior to Inauguration

The anti-Japanese movement in the 1920s can be divided into two main streams: nationalism and socialism. These two streams can again be divided into many depending on methods used, objectives pursued and leading figures in control. The fact that there existed over 300 socialist organizations in Korea at the end of 1926, just prior to the inauguration of the Singanhoe ("New Trunk Society"), indicates how complicated the anti-Japanese movement was at that time. The Singanhoe society was inaugurated as a national united front with a view to overcoming such fragmentation and attaining the nation's liberation from Japan. The Society can be described as a body incorporating many streams of the anti-Japanese movement in the 1920s. A study of the Singanhoe, therefore,

* Originally published in the *Korea Journal*, vol. 27, no. 9 (September 1987).

The late Yi Kyun Young (Yi, Gyun-yeong) had served as Professor of Korean History at Dongduk Women's University from 1985 to 1996. He received his Ph.D. in History from Hanyang University in 1985. He is the author of many books and articles in the field of Korean history, including "Iljeha jeongchi, sahoe seryeok-gwa geu undong" (Political and Social Forces and Their Movements under Japanese Imperialism) (1988), "Joseon gongsanjuui undong-gwa komintereun" (Joseon's Communist Movement and the Comintern) (1991), and *Singanhoe yeongu* (A Study of the Singanhoe) (1993). He is also well known as a novelist as he published several novels, including *Tteodoneun geotdeul-ui yeongwon* (Eternity of Wandering Beings) and *Noja-wa jangja-ui nara* (The Land of Laozi and Zhuangzi). He received the Yi Sang Literary Award in 1984 with "Eodu-un gieok-ui jeo pyeon" (Beyond Dark Memories).

will not only reveal the methods, objectives, nature, and leading forces of the anti-Japanese movement in the 1920s, but also serve as the window into various anti-Japanese movements that continued until Korea's liberation in 1945.

Studies to date have grasped the general outline of the Singanhoe, but there remain many problems still to be examined. For example, there are three perspectives on what influenced the "Jeonguhoe (Righteous Fraternity Society) Declaration," which provided an ideological background for socialists' participation in the inauguration of the Singanhoe. One is the ideology of Fukumoto and another is that of Yamakawa, and the other is the anti-imperialistic united front theory. In addition to these, there is the theory of anti-autonomy and national united front theory, which holds the belief that the Society was formed to meet the national and class needs of the Korean society. These three theories will be reviewed in this paper. Regardless of whether the "Jeonguhoe Declaration" was influenced by the theory of Fukumoto or the anti-imperialistic united front, had the need for a united front lacked popular support to such an extent as to make it the "consensus of an era," the Society would not have become a national united front, nor seen an active formation of its chapters. For this reason, importance should be attached to the "anti-limited autonomy" and national united front theories, which were debated among Korean nationalists and socialists prior to the emergence of Singanhoe.

I first look into the nationalist and socialist camps' attitudes toward the nation and class structure and how such attitudes were related to the national united front theory. To do so, I, in particular, note the Campaign for the Encouragement of Native Products (a "movement to buy Korean products").

The campaign's slogan was: "Let us Koreans eat, wear, and use products made by Koreans." This campaign apparently spawned a debate between nationalists and socialists. An article published in the January 2, 1923 edition of the *Dong-a Ilbo* also set off arguments for and against the movement. It should be noted that both sides involved in the controversy based their arguments on Marxist theory. Accordingly, their attitudes toward Marxism neither differentiated them, nor was it their theoretical distinction over defining class. The two camps rather differed from each other as to identifying the beneficiaries of the campaign. The movement failed in the end because the majority of the masses thought it was not beneficial to them. As a matter of fact, land capital constituted the predominant material basis of the nationalist camp in the country, and it was in turn based on parasitic landowner system, which came into being during the Japanese land survey projects. Accordingly, high farm rents provided the main financial resources for the establishment of national enterprises, which would specifically nurture and strengthen the nation, and the establishment of modern educational institutions. Such a structure gave rise to contradictions in which relationships between landowners and tenants were reinforced behind the promotion of nationalism. It can thus be said to be a natural historical stage in the national liberation movement in which the national movement at the time shifted from the nationalist camp to an anti-imperialist, anti-feudalistic movement by way of labor and farmer movements. Korea's initial socialist movement furthermore played a central role in such labor, farmer, and youth movements.

"The Fraternity Declaration" issued in February 1922 by the Joseon Gohaksaeng Donguhoe (Korean Self-Supporting Students Fraternity), a socialist organization formed by Korean students in Japan, appears to be the first statement to articulate class struggle in Korea. It stated in essence: "The Fraternity shall wage a labor movement and launch class struggle." In March 1923, the Jeon Joseon Cheongnyeondang Daehoe (Pan-Korean Youth Party Convention), under the leadership of the Seoul Cheongnyeonhoe (Seoul Youth Society, SYS), discussed these themes: "Those who share the same principles and ideologies should be regarded as having the identical nationality"; "National liberation is of no use today. Urgent is class liberation"; and "Let us exert ourselves in eliminating national discrimination and removing class distinctions." Judging from such rhetoric, it would appear that the socialist camp did not consider the possible formation of a united front with the nationalist camp, and saw itself as preparing for a proletariat dictatorship.

In fact, however, the socialist camp never gave up the idea of a united front in its national liberation struggles. Han Sin-gyo, a key figure of the SYS that led the Pan-Korean Youth Party Convention, asserted in an article he contributed to the *Dong-a Ilbo* at about the same time as the Convention: "A united front with the nationalist camp is necessary to a certain extent and until a certain time." In an extraordinary convention in April 1924, the Joseon Cheongnyeon Chongdongmaeng (General Youth League of Korea), also led by the SYS, adopted a resolution stating, "We absolutely reject a compromising national movement but support a revolutionary national movement." These two statements indicate that the socialists underwent a major change in just one year.

Bukpunghoe (Northern Wind Society), which enjoyed as much support as the SYS in the socialist camp, also displayed the same attitude toward a united front as the SYS. The platform of the Northern Wind Society, announced in April 1924, contains this passage:

> We repudiate a national movement that neglects class relations. Since a national movement is indispensable under the present Korean situation, we seek, for the time being, cooperation toward a parallel execution of socialist and national movements.

Thus the Northern Wind Society was also considering the possibility of forming a united front with the nationalist camp.

The inclusion of class liberation in the declarations and platforms of such prominent socialist organizations cannot be regarded as merely theoretical exposition of materialism. Rather the concept implied liberation not only from Japanese imperialism, but also from land and industrial capital of the exploitative landowners and from a feudalistic caste system.

Meanwhile, it was in early 1924 that the nationalist camp outlined plans to cope with socialist activities. In January 1924, these plans appeared in an article Yi Gwang-su contributed to the *Dong-a Ilbo*, entitled "Minjokjeok gyeongnyun" (National Steering), which proposed the formation of the Yeonjeonghoe (Political Research Society). The article sparked the "compromise" camp into action, and precipitated the confrontation between the "compromise" and "intransigent" camps among the nationalists. Having given up on the notion of Korea's regaining her autonomy anytime in the near future, and advocating working inside the Japanese Imperial system for the gradual independence of Korea, the "compromise" camp supported the "limited autonomy doctrine" (*jachiron*) offered by the Japanese. The "intransigent" camp, which was composed of leftist nationalists, led the nationalist movement to the formation of the Singanhoe. They also thought it necessary to accommodate, for the time being, the socialists' united front that considered national liberation to be only one part of a longer process of realizing a proletariat dictatorship. They also recognized the need for labor, peasant, and student movements, although they dissociated themselves from class motives.

The nationalists began to reveal their position regarding the united front. This demonstrates that the socialist camp had grown sufficiently as a political force. What actually prompted both camps to openly discuss the united front, however, was the intensified Japanese imperial control. Typical was the 1925 enforcement of the Security Maintenance Law. The June 1925 edition of *Gaebyeok* (Creation) carried responses by thirteen leaders of socialist organizations, lawyers and representative commentators of the *Dong-a Ilbo*, *Chosun Ilbo*, and *Sidae Ilbo* to queries about "future relations between socialist and nationalist movements." They were unanimous in recognizing an urgent need for forming a united front.

With the enforcement of the Security Maintenance Law serving as a momentum, the Joseon Communist Party (JCP) was organized underground, and nationalist and socialist camps launched systematic moves to form a legal united front. The Northern Wind Society, the Hwayohoe (Tuesday Society), the Joseon Nodongdang (Korea Labor Party) and the Musanja Dongmaeng (Proletariat League), all of which were socialist, formed the four organizations' joint committee in April 1925. In a joint meeting held in January 1926, they decided to promote a united front with the "intransigent" nationalists. The committee was later reorganized into the Jeonguhoe which announced in November 1926 the "Jeonguhoe Declaration" under the leadership of the Irwolhoe (January Society), a socialist organization composed of Korean students in Japan. Numerous socialist organizations merged into two groups early in 1926: the Jeonguhoe and the Jeonjinhoe (Advance Society), an ideological body affiliated with the SYS. Leftist nationalists, meanwhile, made a similar move by launching the Joseon Sajeong Yeonguhoe (Korean Affairs Research Society) in September 1925.

The JCP' attitude toward the united front must be examined. But before doing so, we need to determine if it is possible to distinguish between socialists and communists of that time? Such a distinction is indeed meaningless, as most socialist leaders were also affiliated with the JCP, and the socialist organizations were nothing but a front for the JCP. A certain distinction, however, is necessary since the extent of response to the Comintern instructions and the degree of popular support varied. There were cases in which popular support for socialist movements did not provide the basis of identical popular support for decisions made by the JCP's Central Executive Committee.

Immediately following its inauguration in April 1925, the JCP adopted these slogans: "Down with Japanese imperialism and complete independence for Korea," "Exposure of deceptions by national revisionists and adventurists" and "Korea for Koreans." To achieve these ends, they believed it necessary to "form a single national party front." Thus, the JCP during the second period (November 1925–June 1926) placed emphasis on the formation of a national united front. The Thirteenth Central Executive Committee meeting on February 26, 1926 discussed in detail the ways and means of forming a national united front. (This will be discussed in more detail later in the paper.) This plan, however, vanished in the wake of the second wave of arrests following the June 10 Independence Demonstration. The JCP, therefore, could put into practice the national united front theory until the third period.

The nationalist and socialist camps in Korea and the national united front theory discussed by the JCP have been reviewed thus far. What came into being as a national united front prior to the formation of the Singanhoe is the Joseon Minheunghoe (Korean People's Prosperity Society, KPPS).

Joseon Minheunghoe (Korean People's Prosperity Society)

Joseon Minheunghoe was proposed on July 8, 1926 as the first national united front. Confined to a limited number of persons, the Minheunghoe selected preparatory and standing committee members, but was banned from holding its inaugural convention. Hence it could not engage in specific activities. Its objectives and a large portion of its accumulated experience in the course of organization were inherited by the Singanhoe. Understanding of the Minheunghoe, therefore, is a prerequisite to reviewing the background of the Singanhoe and the various arguments surrounding it. The Minheunghoe's relationship with the National Party Preparatory Committee (Minjokdang Jubihoe, hereafter NPPC) and the Comintern's policy toward Korea, and specific contents in the promotion of the Minheunghoe will be reviewed.

As mentioned above, the socialist camp in Korea early in 1926 consisted of two (streams): Jeonguhoe (the front for the JCP) and Jeonjinhoe (ideological organization of the SYS). Jeonjinhoe took part in the NPPC formed in Vladivostok in March 1926. The NPPC was aligned with the Creation faction of the Provisional Government in Shanghai, the Irkutsk faction, and with certain circles of the Shanghai faction, and the Sinminbu (New People's Government)[1] and independent forces (represented by Kim Gyeong-cheon). Promoters of the NPPC tried to form an alliance with movements at home as well, and as a result Jeonjinhoe permitted Kim Yong-man and Choe Chang-ik to participate in the formation of the NPPC. I believe this constituted the beginning of the single national party movement (*minjok yuildang undong*).

During the same period, JCP promoted the formation of the Nationalist Party (Gungmindang), identical in nature with the NPPC. The plan, which called for party headquarters in Manchuria, discussed financial resources and methods of organization in detail. A resolution adopted at the JCP's Third Central Executive Committee held on February 26, 1926 envisaged forming its organization at home based on the structure of Cheondogyo (The Religion of the Heavenly Way) and establishing overseas organizational ties with the Yi Dong-hwi faction in Vladivostok. As a result of such efforts, Yi Dong-hwi, Kye Bong-u, and Baek Chu, eliminating ill-feelings from the past, dispatched Bak Eung-chil to the JCP in the name of promoting mutual understanding. The Yi Donghwi faction later affiliated itself with the JCP and also took part in the JCP's Manchurian General Bureau formed in May of the same year. With a goal of forming the Nationalist Party, JCP contacted the Shanghai faction. A consensus was reached as to the need for forming a united front. The formation, however, was withheld on grounds that the leader of Cheondogyo's new faction, Choe Rin, and others would make use of it for their own purposes. The second wave of arrests took place three months after that meeting, and it is presumed that the Nationalist Party's inauguration plan accordingly came to naught. It is not known, however, why members of the nationalist camp discussed the possibility of a united front not with the SYS but with the JCP. Around May 1926, two camps in the country, namely the SYS and the JCP, respectively maintained contacts with overseas forces through the formation of the NPPC and the Nationalist Party, and they attempted to reinforce their domestic foothold at the same time. The SYS launched the Minheunghoe and the JCP later inaugurated the Singanhoe. The Minheunghoe had organizational relationship with the NPPC while the latter came into being with the Comintern's approval. It is necessary, therefore, to review the Korean policy toward the Comintern at the time in order to study the promotion of Minheunghoe.

---

1. An anti-Japanese organization established in Manchuria by Kim Jwa-jin in 1925.

"Theses of the Fourth Congress of the Communist International on the Eastern Problem" adopted at the Fourth Comintern Congress, held from November 5 - December 5, 1922 set up an anti-imperialist allied front for the first time. But it demanded both the execution of a national revolution and the maintenance of class interests while maintaining their independent line. Therefore, the formation of the Minheunghoe can be seen as a mere application of the theoretical model suggested by the above thesis. Additionally, the SYS recognized that the Minheunghoe "would become an organization containing the nature of the national movement camp." On the other hand, the Comintern authorities underwent a change in their understanding of the oriental issue between the Fourth and Fifth congresses. "The Protocol concerning the Korean Issue," adopted at the Fifth Comintern Congress, called for "the formation of a national revolutionary party identical with China's Guomindang." It stressed that "the task needs to be carried out not under the name of a communist party but under the slogan of the struggle for Korea's independence." It can be assumed therefore that the inauguration of both the Minheunghoe and the Singanhoe, which will be reviewed later, was influenced by the anti-imperialist allied front theory. It is safe to assume that the call for forming "a national revolutionary party identical with China's Guomindang," as referred to in "The Protocol Concerning the Korean Issue," conforms to the national united front. Thus, we may safely conclude that this line of the Comintern influenced, to a certain extent, the launching of the Minheunghoe, the single national party movement overseas, and the inauguration of the Singanhoe. It should be observed that three factors influenced the proposition of the Minheunghoe in 1926: aspirations and movement in the country for the formation of a united front; the single national party movement overseas; and change in policy line of the Comintern.

The Minheunghoe was formally proposed on July 8, 1926, and twenty-nine preparatory and standing committee members were chosen in November of that year. The SYS and the Society for the Encouragement of Native Products constituted the two main groups of the Minheunghoe, and other nationalists in religion, military, and education participated.

The leftist faction of the nationalists supported the proposition of the Minheunghoe but did not take part in it. No exact reasons for this course of action are known, but it may be because they had been discussing the formation of a separate united front with the JCP since March 1926.

The JCP did not consider the Minheunghoe too seriously at the out-set. However, as it was wanting to promote a national united front, the JCP schemed to divide the SYS, absorb the Minheunghoe and have it affiliate with the Singanhoe. The scheme succeeded as the SYS began to divide into new and old factions after September 1926, and as a result, the Minheunghoe unconditionally joined the Singanhoe in February 1927. This does not mean however that the SYS also merged with the JCP, giving up its previous position. The SYS maintained its position as stated by the "Review of the Jeonjinhoe," which served as the ideological basis of the Singanhoe movement that adopted the "theory objecting the dissolution of ideological organizations," "two-party theory," and "liqui-dation theory."

Inauguration of the Singanhoe

The anti-autonomy theory provided the direct momentum for the inau-guration of the Singanhoe. In the latter half of 1926, Choe Rin, Kim Seong-su, Song Jin-u, and Choe Nam-seon attempted to organize an "limited autonomy" movement organization, theoretically based on the afore-mentioned idea expounded in Yi Gwang-su's "National Steering." They, however, encountered strong objections from figures who they expected would join in their efforts, particularly those belonging to the *Chosun Ilbo* faction. For example, An Jae-hong and Kim Jun-yeon opposed the "limited autonomy" movement and reported their plan secretly to the Minheunghoe.

It was Hong Myeong-hui who played the major role for the promo-tion of the Singanhoe. Judging from his actions to that time, it is appro-priate to regard him as a leftist nationalist. Hong, then an instructor at Osan School located in Jeongju, Pyeonganbuk-do province, called on Choe Nam-seon in Seoul to learn about the motion to form a body designed to promote Korea's autonomy in consultation with the Japan-ese Government-General. The very next day he started working on the promotion of the Singanhoe. Based on the term "winter vacation" appearing in the record, it can be assumed that the preparation for the Singanhoe's inauguration began after mid-December 1926. However, since Hong started to make preparations the day after his meeting with Choe, it would be more correct to assume that preparations began earli-er than December 26. The *Chosun Ilbo* at the time contributed to an atmosphere conducive to the establishment of the Singanhoe by publishing editorials and commentaries, criticizing the "limited autonomy" drive and calling for a grand unity of uncompromising nationalists.

Preparatory work for the Singanhoe made rapid progress in 1927. Early in January, Kwon Dong-jin, Hong Myeong-hui, Yi Gap-song, Bak Dong-wan, Baek Gwan-su, An Jae-hong, Sin Seok-u, and Han Gi-ak in a meeting held at the *Chosun Ilbo* office agreed to promote the Singanhoe and drafted the platform.

As the formation was launched in an open and legal manner from the beginning, they had to obtain approval from the Japanese Government-General on a number of matters. The name of the organization, originally proposed as "Sinhanhoe" (New Korea Society), had to be changed to Singanhoe, which is said to have been coined by Hong Myeong-hui who wanted to capture the sense of new stems growing out of an old tree (*gomok sin-gan*). Their platform had to be revised as well.

The original platforms included the following points: 1) We shall seek an eventual political and economic solution as a nation; 2) We shall solidify our national unity; and 3) We shall deny the compromising line. These were changed to read: 1) We shall promote political and economic awakening; 2) We shall solidify our unity; and 3) We shall deny all opportunism. As to who drafted the platforms, there are two theories. One has it that they were drafted by Sin Seok-u, An Jae-hong and Baek Gwan-su of the *Chosun Ilbo*, and the other claims they were written by Hong Gi-mun, the son of Hong Myeon-hui, and Yi Seung-bok, the business manager of the *Chosun Ilbo*, under the direction of Hong Myeong-hui. But it is safe to assume that they were most likely drafted by senior members of the *Chosun Ilbo* and Hong Myeong-hui.

The Singanhoe was inaugurated on January 19, 1927. The inaugural congress of the Singanhoe took place at the YMCA Auditorium on Jongno street at 7:15 p.m. on February 15, 1927. The number of members attending the congress varied according to different sources. The *Chosun Ilbo* said it was over 200, the *Dong-a Ilbo* reported 202, the *Chosun Mungwang* said over 250 and still another source reported 500. Those who attended the gathering, including the general public, totaled over 1,000. Through balloting Yi Sang-jae was elected chairman, Hong Myeong-hui vice chairman and 35 persons secretaries. The inaugural congress came to an end at 4:30 a.m. on February 16, about 10 hours after its opening. Hong Myeong-hui adamantly declined to accept the post of vice chairman immediately following the ballot and was replaced by Kwon Dong-jin. No exact reason for Hong's resignation is available although some assert that it was to keep a balance in strength between the nationalist and socialist camps.

Among the 51 founders and secretaries of the Singanhoe, a majority are those who were involved in the March First Independence Movement, including five (Bak Dong-wan, Yi Gap-seong, Bak Hui-do, O Hwa-yeong, and Jeong Chun-su) of the thirty three national representatives who signed the "Declaration of Independence." In addition, Sin Seok-u, An Jae-hong, Han Wi-geon, Hong Myeong-hui, Kwon Tae-seok, and Cheo Ik-hwan participated in the independence movement. Yi Sang-jae, Kwon Dong-jin, and Sin Chae-ho were figures of the enlightenment movement, while Kim Jun-yeon, An Jae-hong, Baek Gwan-su, Sin Seok-u, and Han Wi-geon all played important roles in the national drive for independence while studying in Japan.

By occupation, those who were affiliated with newspapers numbered fifteen forming the biggest group (twelve from the *Chosun Ilbo*, two from the *Dong-a Ilbo* and one from the *Chungoe Ilbo*). They were followed by seven educators, three Cheondogyo members, three Christian clergymen and one Buddhist. Three were Confucianists, and Jang Gil-sang and Hong Sun-pil were capitalist-landowners.

Members of those closely related to the JCP were Kim Jun-yeon, Han Wi-geon, Yi Seok-hun, Kwon Tae-seok, Song Nae-ho, and Choe Ik-hwan. Japanese official records have it that Hong Myeong-hui was a member of the JCP, but it is not clear if that was the case. It is unlikely that the JCP permitted its members take key posts in the Singanhoe. It is not clear if Kim Jun-yeon, Han Wi-geon, and Yi Seok-hun joined the Singanhoe individually or as members of the JCP. Kwon Tae-seok, Song Nae-ho, and Choe Ik-hwan were members of the Seoul Youth Society who involved themselves actively with the Minheunghoe.

Regulations, provisional regulations, congress rules and chapter rules, all of which were discussed at the inaugural congress, were banned from publication, but the originals still remain today.

Arguments prior to and following Inauguration

This section discusses the relationship between "The Jeonguhoe Declaration" (hereafter "Declaration") and "Review of the Jeonjinhoe" (hereafter "Review"), along with the theory of "objection to dissolution of ideological organizations," "two-party theory" and "liquidation theory." The "Declaration," issued on November 15, 1926, served as the theoretical basis upon which the nation's socialist and communists joined the Singanhoe. On the other hand, the "Review" provided the SYS with a theoretical basis upon which it opposed the dissolution of ideological organizations and issued the so-called "two-party theory" and "liquidation theory." A review of "Declaration" and "Review" will reveal the backgrounds, contents and influences of those arguments. Also to be discussed here is whether the Fukumoto-ism or an anti-imperialistic united front theory provided a theoretical basis for the "Declaration."

Some previous studies allege that the Jeonjinhoe in its "Review" opposed arguments in the "Declaration." Various documents prove, however, that the Jeonjinhoe positively supported the formation of a national united front, which in the "Declaration" is called the "shift in direction theory," and to that end contacted the Four Organizations' Joint Committee and the Jeonguhoe.

The "Declaration" contained the following problems. First, what will become of the proletariat's independence and initiative when a united front is formed? The declaration failed to give a clear-cut answer to this question. This problem provided a basis upon which the Jeonjinhoe set out the so-called "two-party theory." Second, the "Declaration" called for collaboration with the nationalist forces "by recognizing their nature as only a temporary alliance." It did not specify how long the "temporary alliance" should last. It was not possible to provide an exact duration or length for this alliance. The Comintern too could not offer a precise answer. Third, the "Declaration" asserted that "economic struggles should be developed into political struggles with the participation of more class consciousness and more masses." What form such political struggles should take was also left unanswered in the "Declaration." Political struggles denote "a struggle of going into a general fight by means of forming a political party" and "party to party struggle." Such a struggle was impossible to wage under Korea's circumstances at that time, and hence the meaning of political struggles was unclear in the "Declaration."

These problems provided clues to arguments concerning Fukumoto-ism or Yamakawaism, which took place until early in 1928 in the form of an anti-imperialistic united front theory.

Yamakawa Hitoshi, Japan's socialist leader in the earlier stage, in an article printed in the *Zanei* (Vanguard) journal in August 1922, advocated that economic struggles should be shifted to political struggles. He defined economic struggles as those fought for specific interests in each proletarian element, and political struggles as those fought for the interests of the whole proletariat which consolidate economic struggles. To cite key points of his theory, Yamakawa held first that shift in direction should be executed based on pending requirements of the proletariat. The slogan of "Into the Masses" emerges from here. Second, in order to wage a positive struggle for the sake of the proletarian interests, he asserted that the nature of political struggles should be combined with economic struggles. Third, political struggles waged in the process of achieving such a shift in direction means an expansion in the economic front. In other words, trade specific forms of economic and political struggles are not separated from each other.

The principles of Fukumoto Kazuo, which swept Japan's ideological circles in 1926 and the first half of 1927, were different from those of Yamakawa. Fukumoto-ism believed that first political and economic struggles, i.e. the trade union and the communist party movement, have to eventually become a general and unified movement (a political struggle). The forms of the two struggles, according to them, are not separate but led by the communist party. An economic struggle, thus, have to be the peripheral or subordinate movement. What then are the political struggles of the communist party as referred to by Fukumoto Kazuo? They call for forming a proletarian party and advancing it to the parliament. The Fukumoto principle also separated the united front from party organization. They called for "a clean separation before alliance" and the formation of a communist party by its vanguard. This party should exercise proletarian dictatorship even in a united front, according to Fukumoto-ism.

Neither Yamakawa's nor Fukumoto's theories could be transferred to Korea as is, for Korea's political and economic conditions were very different from those of Japan, which at the time permitted trade unions and communist party movements. The "Declaration," however, borrowed much terminology from Japan's socialist movement, and in this respect it is easy to note that its authors were encouraged by Fukumoto's theories in many respects. In addition, Fukumoto asserted that the bourgeoisie should be rejected from party organizations. Those scholars who understand that Fukumoto prevented the bourgeoisie from joining the united front appear to have mistaken his party organization policy for his united front policy.

The anti-imperialistic united front was already discussed in connection with the Minheunghoe and the Comintern. Relations between the united front and the Minheunghoe can be applied to the case of the Singanhoe as well, though it is not without problems. These problems arise from the fact that Comintern's theses are not consistent. Typical are the issues of proletarian hegemony and land revolution as a united front in various struggles. For this reason, importance should be attached to persistent moves in Korea for the formation of a united front. Relations between official these adopted at the Comintern and its executive committee, and papers and articles written by individuals involved in the Comintern also constitute an important issue to be examined.

There are pros and cons to the dissolution of ideological organizations. The Jeonguhoe and the JCP, prior to and following the announcement of the "Declaration," attempted to dissolve an ideological organizations as a major means of launching the Singanhoe. Ideological organizations at the end of 1926, as announced by the Japanese Government-General's Police Bureau, totaled 338.

Arguments regarding the dissolution of ideological organizations first emerged in November 1926 when the "Declaration" was issued. In an article printed in the journal titled *Joseon-ji gwang* (The Light of Korea), Sun Ang, who is believed to have belonged to the SYS, opposed the dissolution of ideological bodies.

Citing that ideological organizations distanced the proletariat from nationalism and transformed various mass organizations instead into the proletariat, he asserted that despite many problems such as confrontation and internal strife between organizations, they should not be dissolved, given the realities in which the proletariat are not allowed participation in political activities. Hidden in his assertion is an idea that class independence and the rise of the proletariat would be threatened, should a national united front be formed in accordance with the "Declaration." As a means of resolving this issue, Sun Ang proposed the formation of "a single ideological organization." This leads to the "two-party theory" which requires attention and will be discussed shortly. Members of the January Society faction, who played a leading role in the preparation of the "Declaration" on the other hand, contended the necessity of dissolving ideological organizations. They argued that now that the ideological organizations' mission to promote a primitive and quantitative development of the proletariat was accomplished, they had arrived at the stage of objective-conscious and pan-class movement. They insisted on a need to form a single control body and considered too many ideological organizations as an obstacle to its formation and dubbing the organizations the hotbed of factional strife.

Theories opposing dissolution are summarized as follows: first, a single control organ ultimately means a class party, the formation of which is realistically impossible, and the Singanhoe is not a class party; second, ideological organizations, although they are supposed to develop class movements, have a more important goal of refining the quality of such movements; third, if ideological organizations are the hotbed of factional strife, organizations of laborers, peasants, youths and women would also have to be dissolved. All in all, they argued, "To go into a nationalist party, recognizing its platforms, has a basic motive of further promoting and realizing class spirit, rather than being dissolved in it. Therefore, there is no reason why ideological organizations should be dissolved in order to join a nationalist party."

Central to those theories opposing the dissolution of ideological organizations, as was the case with the "Declaration," was the issue of class independence and initiative on the part of the proletariat. The Jeonguhoe (actually then led by members of the January Society) and the JCP, however, carried out the dissolution of ideological organizations without providing any theoretical explanations. Ideological organizations, including even those in which the Jeonjinhoe wielded great influence, dissolved following the Irwolhoe's dissolution. This could be ascribed partially to the JCP's successful strategy, but mainly to the fact that the "Declaration," which presented a national united front, won the support of the masses. Even members of the JCP were surprised at the successful dissolution of ideological organizations.

Arguments about ideological organizations came to an end in April 1927. Issues raised in objection to their dissolution and the written review issued by the Jeonjinhoe, however, remained unsolved and led to the "two-party theory."

The "two-party theory" came to the fore at the inaugural convention of the Joseon Sahoe Danche Jungang Hyeobuihoe (Korea Social Organizations Central Council) in May 1926. The SYS conceived of a two party theory even before the inaugural convention. The Jeonjinhoe intended to make the KSOCC a standing body, but was forced to make it a non-standing organization due to an organizational confrontation with members affiliated with the JCP. This, in fact, put an end to the argument.

The "two-party theory" was coined unilaterally by the leftist ML (Marxist-Leninist) Party factions who defined the KSOCC as a proletariat party, and the Singanhoe as a single national party. As the JCP was already recognized as the Korean branch of the Comintern, the KSOCC, were it to be defined as a political party, would lose justification and theoretical foundation to exist as a body in the proletariat class struggle. Accordingly, members affiliated with the JCP attempted to prove that the KSOCC was an organization aspiring to develop into a political organization, while the Jeonjinhoe tried to convince others that the KSOCC, although not a political party, was a body worthy of existence.

What was then the basis upon which the Jeonjinhoe attempted to make the KSOCC a standing body? It was the need of having "a preparatory body of a proletariat party" in anticipation of a separation between the bourgeoisie and proletariat. As a political party incorporates itself into various organizations, they contended, its preparatory body also should exist in the form of a council to perform "parliamentary" functions, promote class consciousness on the part of various organizations and struggle to gain realistic interests of the proletariat, all of which can hardly be achieved by an underground party.

The JCP, on the other hand, regarded the KSOCC as an organization that could challenge the Singanhoe and eventually the JCP. The Jeonjinhoe countered that cooperation and confrontation characterize the relationship between the two organizations. "Cooperation" indicated the deployment of a common front in the struggle against imperialism, and "confrontation" referred to the different ways in which each sought class independence and initiative. Class independence and initiative on the part of the proletariat, coupled by factional consciousness, provided the basic motive for the two-party theory. That the two-party theory came to an end while the issue still remained unsolved indicates that the JCP prevailed over the SYS in terms of organization, but the seed of dispute and organizational division remained. Thus, the "liquidation theory" must be understood under such a premise.

The liquidation theory had it that since the proletarian movement was "an element" and "a trend" in the nationalist movement, it is inevitable that the organization abandon the proletarian class independence for the participation in the Singanhoe. Advocates of this liquidation theory, members of the SYS faction, mostly affiliated themselves with Chungyeongwondang party[2] which was formed in December 1929 with the support of overseas socialists of the Yi Dong-hwi faction. Liquidation theory was therefore advanced by the SYS for the purpose of challenging the JCP as a superficial strategy of the Chun-gyeongwondang party. The Chun-gyeongwondang party published its party organ in Tokyo called *Joseon undong* (Joseon Movement) as a means of expanding its influence overseas. The party organ provided an important forum for propaganda and this is clearly telling of the relationship between the Chun-gyeongwondang party and the liquidation theory. This provides an answer to a question as to why the SYS, which persistently advocated for a proletarian class independence and initiative in the "Review" and opposed the dissolution of ideological organizations and two-party theory, took an entirely opposite position in the liquidation theory. Namely, the liquidation theory was Chun-gyeongwondang's strategy against the JCP.

The liquidation theory was first advanced as a dissent against An Gwang-cheon's call for proletarian hegemony in the Singanhoe. An drafted the "Declaration" and served as a senior secretary of the JCP. An's assertion was his personal one, as it was denied by the JCP. An's call appears to have been designed to cope with the class commotion in the Singanhoe, which would occur as a repercussion of the cancellation of Fukumoto-ism at the Comintern and the continuing increase of nationalist and pro-Japanese forces.

In addition, the liquidation theory was stimulated by the expulsion of the SYS faction members from the JCP, which was touched off by internal friction within the party in the wake of the "Yeongnam Fraternity Society Incident" (Yeongnam Chinmokhoe Sageon). The Chun-gyeongwondang was organized to cope with the expulsion (the organization is believed to have been conceived in advance) and members of the Chun-gyeongwondang constituted the bulk of the advocates of liquidation theory. The JCP had to take measures to cope with the series of incessant arguments that have been discussed thus far. Moreover, the Singanhoe was unable to carry out their intended activities even though a number of branches were formed. This raised further problems.

---

2. Chun-gyeongwon is a name of a restaurant located in Seoul in the 1920s.

Changes in Organization Pattern Arising from Establishment of Chapters

Prior to and following the inauguration of the Singanhoe, various ideological organizations were dissolved. Organizations of similar nature formed a single body following their dissolution, while established organizations held the so-called "reform meetings" in an attempt to reform their organizations and activities. Most of these organizations supported the Singanhoe and formed its chapters in their respective areas. In other words, the formation of "a leftist national front" for a national liberation struggle represented a spirit of that era.

In the socialist camp, however, such issues as proletarian class independence and initiative, and until when the cooperation with the nationalist camp should last remained unresolved. But these issues did not emerge as major obstacles to the expansion of the Singanhoe movement until October 1927. This indicates a possibility that formation of the Singanhoe chapters was encouraged more by a call for a national liberation struggle than by class contradictions within the nation.

In fact, it was after the inauguration of the KSOCC on May 15, 1927 that various organizations were able to take a clear position on the Singanhoe. Even those organizations that were associated with the Jeonjinhoe could join the Singanhoe without any conflict.

By the end of February 1928, preparatory meetings for the Singanhoe chapters were held at 224 locations across the country. Most such preparations were made by organizations already active in specific areas or by alliance of such organizations. This indicates that youth, labor, peasant, and equality movements were also active. Such a phenomenon was conspicuous particularly in Hamgyeongnam-do and Gyeongsangnam-do provinces. Constituents of organizations might be affiliated with a number of similar organizations in one area at the same time. Youth organizations were greater in number than other organizations and played a leading role in the formation of the Singanhoe chapters.

In spite of such expansion of its chapters, the Singanhoe did not have specific guidelines for their activities until the end of 1927. Accordingly, activities executed by the Singanhoe chapters could not but be virtually identical with those conducted previously by other social organizations. This gave rise to a considerable conflict among the Singanhoe leaders. They attempted to define the "organization pattern" of the Singanhoe on a stage-by-stage basis.

From its inauguration to the first half of 1927, the Singanhoe was defined as "an intermediary to a single national party." Following its expansion, due to chapter formation and emergence of the "liquidation theory" in late 1927, the Singanhoe was re-defined as "an intermediary to a national united front." A problem emerged in that both were of a party organization which was centralized, and hence laborers and peasants could not form the core of the organization and could not conduct substantive activities within their chapters. Such an organizational weakness was even more blatant to the socialist camp, for no proletarian class independence and initiative could be guaranteed under such an organization. Moves to reform the Singanhoe thus emerged within individual chapters, the socialist camp and in the Comintern.

The Yeongil Chapter on December 10, 1927 and the Gilju Chapter in February 1928 called for reforming the structure of the Singanhoe. These chapters asserted that the arrangement of president, vice-presidents, secretary-general and standing secretary, which they said symbolized centralization, should be replaced by a committee system. To them, the president system meant classical, conservative, and undemocratic, while the committee system was regarded as democratic.

Unggi, Gilju, Gimje, and Miryang Chapters demanded that district chapters be allowed to form allied bodies in respective provinces with the goal of gaining some degree of autonomy away from central control. Some chapters centered around the Miryang Chapter demanded that the Singanhoe's organizational structure be established in order to more actively promote communication between regional chapters and the central chapter.

Headquarters and members of the SYS faction, in particular, also called for organizational affiliation at the same time. Even the JCP in 1927 considered the idea of having the Singanhoe implement organizational affiliation. The JCP defined the Singanhoe's organizational structure differently as "an intermediary to a national party," "an intermediary to a national united front party," and "an intermediary to a national united front."

This may have been influenced by the Comitern. In January 1928 Yi Jeong-yun visited Seoul carrying with him the "Comintern Decision" addressed to the JCP by the Comintern body in Shanghai. The seven-point decision criticized the JCP and presented policy for the future. It stressed class independence of the party and used the slogan "To the factory." The Comintern also instructed the Singanhoe to use military means for reformation and called for the formation of a mass party and organization affiliation.

The JCP took advantage of the decision to rectify organizational defects and errors the party had committed. The slogan "To the Factory" was utilized in attacking the "liquidation theory" and presenting a strategy for the Singanhoe. The "Principles concerning National Liberation Movement" and the JCP's reply to the Comintern's decision both called for replacing the individual affiliation system of the Singanhoe with organizational affiliation. The Singanhoe thus would have been obliged to reformulate its organizational structure and change the line of its activities in 1928.

REFERENCES

In Korean

Chosun Ilbo, 4 February 1922–16 February 1927.

Dong-a Ilbo, 1 December 1922–23 February 1927.

Gaebyeok (The Creation) 60 (June 1925) & 66 (February 1926).

Glenn, Paige. 1960. "Korea and the Communism, 1919-1935." *Journal of Social Science and Humanities*.

Gyeongsangbuk-do Province Police Bureau, *Godeung gyeongchal yosa* (A Short History of the Political Police Department) (n.p., 1967).

Hyeondae pyeongnon (Modern Criticism) 3 (April 1927).

Jo, Gi-jun. 1969. "Joseon mulsan jangnyeo undong-ui jeon-gae gwajeong-gwa geu yeoksajeok seonggyeok" (Unfolding of Movement for the Encouragement of Native Products and Its Historical Characteristics). *Yeoksa hakbo* 41.

Joseon ji gwang (The Light of Korea) 73 (November 1927).

Kang, Dong-jin. *Ilje-ui hanguk chimnyak jeongchaeksa* (Imperialist Japan's Policy of Aggression against Korea). Seoul: Hangilsa Publishing Co.

Kim, Gi-rim. 1931. "Singanhoe jeonche daehoe bangcheonggi" (Record of Attendance for the General Assembly of the Singanhoe). *Samcheolli* 11 (January).

Kim, Jun-yeop, and Kim Chang-sun. 1973. *Hanguk gongsanjujui undongsa* (History of the Korean Communist Movement). 3 vols. Seoul: Korea University Press.

Kim, Yun-hwan, and Kim Nak-jung. 1970. *Hanguk nodong undongsa* (History of the Korean Labor Movement). Seoul: Ilchokak Publishing Co.

Sin, Il-cheol. 1978. "Hanguk dongnip undong-ui sasangsajeok seonggyeok" (Characteristics of the Ideological History of the Korean Independence Movement). *Asea yeongu* 21.1.

Yi, Byeong-heon. 1969. "Singanhoe undong" (Singanhoe Movement). *Sin donga* (August).

Yi, Seok-tae. 1948. *Sahoe gwahak dae sajeon* (Dictionary of the Social Sciences). Seoul: Munuin Seogwan.

In Japanese

金正明. 編. 1967.『朝鮮獨立運動』(Korean Independent Movement). 東京.

飯沼二郎. 姜在彦. 共編. 1981.『近代朝鮮の社會と思想』(Society and Thought of Modern Korea). 東京: 未來社.

北條一雄. 1927.『理論鬪爭』(Struggle in the Realm of Theory). 東京: 白楊社.

Crisis and Discord in Colonial Korean Agricultural Society during the Great Depression

Chung Youn-Tae

Preface

The period from the end of the 1920s to the beginning of the 1930s was a great turning point from world, East Asian or national historical perspectives. The Great Depression, began in October of 1929. With the outbreak of the Great Depression, many nations tried to introduce various "beggar-my-neighbor-policies" such as protective tariffs, reduction in exchange rates, creation of economic blocs, and export dumping. As a result, uncertainty and tension escalated within the world capitalist structure, which had been experiencing a period of relative stability since the close of World War I; the consequence of this was World War II.

Japanese capitalism, which had been languishing under chronic depression following the 1920s, also received a blow due to the Depression. In order to avoid the political and economic crises brought about

* Originally published in the *Korea Journal*, vol. 38, no. 4 (winter 1998).

Chung Youn-Tae (Jeong, Yeon-tae) is Associate Professor of Korean History at the Catholic University of Korea. He graduated from Seoul National University with a Ph.D. in History in 1994. He has written many publications on the modern history of Korea including "The Changes in the Course of Japanese Policy for Faiming-Based Colonization Before and After the Annexation of Korea" (1996), "19 segi huban 20 segi cho seoyangin-ui hangukgwan" (Westerners' Observation on Korea in the Late 19th and Early 20th Centuries) (1999), and "How Korean Local Gentry Had Endeavored to Grow during the Early 20th Century: A Case Study of the Commercial Port Ganggyeong" (in Korean) (2003). E-mail: ytchung@catholic.ac.kr.

by world economic decline, Imperial Japan provoked the Manchurian Incident and increased its exploitation of colonial Korea. Although the Japanese economy was able to come out of the crisis earlier than Western countries, the rapid militarization of Japanese society and its economy started the country down the road towards war. In this way, the front line of conflict in East Asia expanded from "Imperial Japan versus the Korean people" to "Imperial Japan versus the people of East Asia."

Korea was also unable to avoid the negative impact of the Great Depression. Such factors as Korea's inability to devise an independent policy to fight the crisis due to its colonial status, coupled with its function as an outlet for the inconsistencies of Japanese capitalism, helped exacerbate the impact of the Great Depression on the Korean people. Furthermore, as the landowners and capitalists in Korea passed the economic hardships of the depression on to the farmers, laborers, tradesmen and small handicraft manufacturers, those working in these sectors were hit especially hard. Thus the increase in mass movements to protect the right to survival was unprecedented.

The economic failure and increase in mass movements led to the escalation of confrontations between imperialist Japan and the national liberation movement camps. In addition, conflict unfolded between socialist and nationalist factions over the grasp of the hegemony of the national liberation movement. In this respect, the Great Depression served as the impetus to change the nature of national and class contradiction in colonial Korea.

At that time, the principal source of disagreement and confrontation in Korean society was the rural community. The Korean society in the 1930s was a typical agrarian society, with agricultural products representing 66 percent of total production, and the agrarian community representing 80 percent of the total population. The agricultural crisis that followed the worldwide depression drove the economy of the agricultural community to ruins, and thus the peasant movement intensified. With the agricultural community as a backdrop, a fierce battle unfolded between socialists and nationalists, who attempted to strengthen their movements by drawing more peasants to their side; there was also conflict between these influences and the Japanese Government-General of Korea, who attempted to stabilize the colonial system.

This paper will explain the following two points while keeping in mind the above-mentioned social tensions brought about by the Great Depression. First, I will offer a concrete analysis of the crises and disagreements brought about in Korea by the Great Depression. Special attention will be given to how the Great Depression not only increased national antagonism between Imperial Japan and Korea, but also how it amplified class discord within the Korean society. Second, the paper will investigate how the triangular axes of the Japanese Government-General, the socialists and the nationalists regarded the Great Depression and the reality of the Korean agricultural community, and how they dealt with the situation. In this process, special attention will be paid to the influence of the socialists' understanding of the state of things and their methods of struggle.

The Great Depression and the Crisis in Agricultural Society

The Great Depression and the Change in the Basis of Japan's Colonial Policy

Japanese capitalism, which had experienced a period of unprecedented prosperity during World War I, entered a period of chronic depression after 1920. Japan attempted to avoid the situation by implementing an inflationary financial policy. However, the worldwide depression that began in the early 1930s, as well as the ensuing agricultural crisis it caused, struck a severe blow to Japanese capitalism; in the end Japan resorted to the invasion of Manchuria in order to find a breakthrough that would help its economy recover.

There is always a conspicuous difference between agriculture and industry's ability to confront chronic depression because the price elasticity of agricultural products is less than that of industrial goods. A close look at the price fluctuations of Japan's two main agricultural products, namely those of rice and silkworm cocoons, shows that their price indices fell from 100 in 1926 to 49 and 33, respectively, by 1931. As the price index of industrial goods purchased by farm households was 59 in the same year, one can conclude that the price differences had expanded.[1] The prices of agricultural products could not stem the downward trend even after 1932, when the industrial sector came out of the world-

---

1. 楫西光速 (Kajinishi Mitsuhaya) et al., "農村不況の深化とその救濟策" (The Deepening of the Agricultural Crisis and its Relief Measures), chap. 2 in 『日本資本主義の沒落』 (The Downfall of Japanese Capitalism) (Tokyo: Tokyo University Press, 1970).

wide crisis, and only in 1934–1935 were prices able to recover to general price levels.

The fall in the prices of agricultural products implied a marked decline in agricultural income. Despite this, Japanese farmers had to pay fixed taxes regardless of the Great Depression, and as income from sources other than agriculture declined rapidly due to the Depression, the agrarian economy was faced with great pressure. In addition, the urban unemployed, who were originally from rural areas, returned home, thereby exacerbating the economic situation in the rural communities as well. This led to a rapid increase in the debt among farmers.

The slump in rice prices and the arrearage of tenant rents resulting from the worsening of the agricultural economy also struck a blow to the landowners. As large landlords also invested other than agricultural products, such as in industry, finance, securities, etc., they were affected by the Great Depression from both the agrarian and non-agrarian fronts. On the other hand, though the small landlords in the villages were relatively resilient to the effects of the Great Depression due to the confiscation of tenant land and the expansion of direct cultivation, such measures led to the aggravation of disputes with their tenant farmers, thereby worsening the overall crisis situation in the agrarian sector.[2]

The crisis in the agricultural community, which had been the foundation for the supply of the food and labor force, as well as the human and spiritual foundation of the Japanese military, heavily impacted imperial Japan. Therefore, the Japanese government rapidly introduced various countermeasures in farming, prices, finance, land and immigration policies from the early 1930s.

Among these, the policy related to Korean agriculture was the rice price support policy. This policy was introduced to relieve the landlord and the farmers in general, in particular middle-class farmers and above. The rice price support policy, which began in 1931 as an import license for East Asian rice, expanded to regulate the bringing in of Korean and Taiwanese rice. In particular, as Korean rice closely resembled Japanese rice in terms of taste and quality, and could be distributed at a relatively low price, it threatened the stability of the price of Japanese rice. Prior to the Great Depression, the total amount of Korean rice carried out to

2. 暉峻衆三 (Teruoka Shujo), "昭和恐慌期の農業問題" (Agricultural Problems of the Showa Depression Era), chap. 5 in 『日本農業問題の展開』 (Development of Japanese Agricultural Problems) (Tokyo: Tokyo University Press, 1984).

Japan ranged from 5 million to 9 million *seok*, representing 60-70 percent of the total amount of rice brought in to Japan, and approached 10 percent of total Japanese consumption. Thus the Japanese rice price support policy could not be successful without controlling the inflow of Korean rice.[3]

For these reasons, the prevailing view within Japan was that the import of Korean rice had to be restricted. As a result, beginning with the import limitation decree on foreign rice in 1928, to the rice management autonomy law of 1936, numerous measures were taken. The main substance of these measures was related to the purchase of Korean rice, the expansion of rice storage facilities within Korea, the application of import licenses for the import of rice to Korea, the import limitation of hulled millet from Manchuria, etc. The selection of such a policy implied a revision in the basis of the colonial policy that had been followed up to that point, with the development of Korea as Japan's food provision area.

The revision of the colonial policy was further accelerated by the invasion of Manchuria and its inclusion in Japan's yen-bloc economic structure. The Japanese Governor-General of Korea, Ugaki,[4] stated that "from now on, the imperial industry needs the common control of Japan, Korea and Manchuria," and claimed that a course of industrialization should be followed, using Korea's abundant electric power and labor force and Manchuria's plentiful natural resources rather than pushing the development of Korea's agriculture. That is, Imperial Japan attempted to restructure an industrial system with Japan as the base for precision machinery industry, Manchuria as an agricultural area, and Korea as the link between the two and the locus of the manufacturing industry. This was how Korea partially handed over to Manchuria the role it had played till now as a food supply zone and began to drive the colonial industrialization process according to the division structure of Japanese capitalism. This policy served to enhance agriculture and industry side by side.

Japan formally ended its policy of increasing rice production, or its so-called food provision policy in 1934, and shifted to a policy of transforming Korea into a raw material and labor force base for the industri-

---

3. Ibid., pp. 166-168.
4. 『宇垣一成日記』 (Ugaki Gazushige Diary) 2, p. 847 (14 May 1932), p. 834 (17 March 1932), p. 880 (3 January 1933).

alization of its colonies. The projects of development in the northern regions of Korea (1932), the Northern cotton-Southern sheep production policy (1934) and the migration stimulation policy to the Northern region and Manchuria are symbolic of this measure.

The Failure of the Agrarian Economy and the Rapid Increase in Tenancy Disputes

The chronic depression of the Japanese economy, followed by the world-wide Great Depression and the agricultural crisis, aggravated the decline within the Korean rural communities. As Korea's agricultural community had already been incorporated as a food provision area for Japan, and the agricultural system of single-crop production (rice) had been developed to the extreme,[5] the impact of the agricultural crisis could not help but be more serious than that experienced by the Japanese farming communities.

First, it will be useful to examine the impact on the slump in the farming economy in terms of the prices of agricultural products.

In terms of agricultural goods, if the prices of rice and silkworm cocoons (which can be considered to have been the backbone of the Korean farming economy) were at 100 in 1926, the price indices fell to 43 and 22, respectively, by 1931. Such a decline was more severe than that experienced in Japan. On the other hand, the ratio of income from rice to total farm income increased rapidly due to the promotion of the single-crop policy. Rice cultivation, according to a 1930 survey, represented 50 and 60 percent, respectively, of the income for Jeollanam-do and Gyeongsangnam-do provinces, and by 1935, accounted for 70 percent of farm income for all of southern Korea. Compared to 38 percent in 1910, one can see that the farm economy's reliance on rice increased rapidly over this period.[6] Accordingly, the negative impact of the fall in

---

5. Chung Youn-Tae, "1910 nyeondae ilje-ui nongeop jeongchaek-gwa singminji jijuje" (Imperial Japan's Agricultural Policy and Colonial Landlord System in the 1910s), *Hanguksa ron* (Treatises on Korean History) (Seoul National University) 20 (1988).

6. 朝鮮農會 (Korean Agricultural Society), 『農家經濟調查—全羅南道ノ分, 慶尙南道ノ分』 (Economic Survey of Agricultural Families—Jeollanam-do, Gyeongsangnam-do) (1932); 小早川九郎 (Kobayagawa Kuro), ed., 『補訂 朝鮮農業發達史—發達篇』 (Revised Edition of Developmental History of Korean Agriculture: On Development) (1960), pp. 574-575.

rice prices was especially severe for the farm economy.

As an aftermath of the lengthy agricultural crisis, price differences were magnified and this led to a further deterioration of the farming economy. With 1926 as the base year, the prices of industrial products such as cotton cloth, petroleum and matches, which represented the primary expenditures of the farming community, fell to 79, 81 and 80, respectively, by 1931. This reveals that the breadth of price differences had increased substantially, relative to the price indices for rice and cocoons.[7]

Despite the slump in agricultural prices, the Government-General increased taxes. Taxes were especially heavily imposed on the lower-class farmers. Although the amount of taxes per 2 *danbo* (990m^2 per 1 *danbo*) was 11.798 won in 1920, this increased to 16.795-17.795 won by 1932. Furthermore, a farm association charge, a forest association charge, a livestock association charge and various other burdens of payment were either newly established or increased.[8] There were successive occurrences of levying of irrigation association charges in excess of the conversion amount related to the actual harvest increase. This not only affected the common farmers, but also the landowners as well.[9] Such increases in taxes and various kinds of other public charges helped to worsen Korea's farming economy.

However, the impact of the crisis, which was primarily represented by the slump in agricultural prices, brought about varying results along the lines of class and nationality. The landlord class attempted to supplement the loss suffered from the depression by strengthening the management of its holdings. They began to intervene more in the production process to extract the maximum labor force from the tenant farmers. In addition, using the forfeiture of tenant rights as a weapon, the landowners frequently increased tenant rents. Those farmers who refused to pay the increase in tenant rents or fell into arrears in their payment were dealt harshly by being stripped of their tenant rights.

---

7. Government-General of Korea, 『朝鮮總督府統計年報』 (Annual Statistical Report of Government-General) (1935 edition).

8. Bureau of Colonial Production, Government-General, 『朝鮮の農業事情』 (The Agricultural Condition of Korea) (1921 edition), p. 47; (1932 edition), pp. 168-170.

9. Jeon Gang-su, "Iljeha suri johap sa-eop-i jijuje jeon-gae-e michin yeonghyang" (Influence of Irrigation Association Project on the Development of the Landlord System during Japanese Colonial Rule), *Gyeongje sahak* (Review of Economic History) 8 (1984): pp. 148-159.

That the landowners could exploit the peasants to this extent partly lies in the fact that premodern tenancy practices were so firmly entrenched. The customary practice during this period was that the peasants had to rely on the geniality of the landowners, possessing no political rights. They were also required to pay high proportions of their harvest as rent, and subject to the arbitrary exploitation by landowners or the supervisors of tenant farms. Furthermore, the introduction of modern civil law, which made the landowner's right of ownership absolute and the implementation of capitalist management principles that considered the pursuit of profit as most important, spurred on the landowner's pursuit for more land rent.[10]

Another cause contributing to the landowner's exploitation was the intense competition among tenant farmers to borrow land. Population pressure for farmland increased due to the rising overpopulation in rural communities as a result of insufficient urban industrialization, coupled with the return of people to farms due to the depression. This destabilized the position of the tenant farmer. As a result, the transfer of tenant rights occurred more frequently. The number of transfers between October 1929 and September 1930 totaled 237,238 cases. If one farmer forfeited one tenant right, then approximately 11 percent of the tenant farmers and owner-tenants would forfeit their tenant right during this one-year period. Thus the factional rivalry among the old and new tenants rose as a serious societal issue during the early 1930s.

In 1930, 48 percent of all landowners passed a land tax on to tenant farmers, despite the already proclaimed land tax law encouraged by the imperial Japanese government. Especially in the Gyeongsangnam-do, Gyeongsangbuk-do, Chungcheongbuk-do, and Jeollabuk-do provinces, 60-80 percent of the landowners transferred a land tax to tenant farmers. In addition, a considerable number of landowners passed on a farm association charge, an irrigation association charge and a water charge. In particular, the landowners in the irrigation regions, under the condition that they assume these charges, raised tenant rents in excess of these amounts.[11]

---

10. Kim Yong-seop, "Ilje gangjeomgi-ui nongeop munje-wa geu tagae bangan" (Farm Issues during Imperial Japan's Forced Occupation and Plans for Their Resolution), in *Hanguk geunhyeondae nongeopsa yeongu* (Studies on the Agrarian History of Modern Korea) (Seoul: Ilchokak Publishing Co., 1992).

11. Government-General of Korea, 『朝鮮ノ小作慣行』 (Practice of Tenancy in Korea), vol. 1 (1932), pp. 560-561.

The exploitation of the farmers by large Japanese landlords became increasingly widespread as a way to handle the economic crisis. The symbol was the dissemination of a new manner of farm management called the "consignment farming system." Consignment farming refers to the system in which the landowner provides the land and management capital, while the farmer provides the labor and a set amount of produce is later supplied as remuneration for that labor.[12] Although this system had been introduced around 1914, it did not spread to many regions until the period of panic. During this time, as stable guarantees of tenant rents became difficult, large Japanese landlords introduced this system, which had been popular in Japan. In 1930, centering in Jeollabuk-do, around 20 landlords consigned 6,000 farmers to work on some 4,500 *jeongbo* (1 *jeongbo* = 2.45 acres) of cultivated land and this gradually spread nationwide like wildfire among landowners.

Japanese landlords who had relatively sufficient funds and a portion of large Korean landlords utilized the panic and pursued the purchase of additional land with fervor. They used the rapid fall in land prices to acquire farmland at depressed prices. A middle-class rice-field, which had been 141 won in 1928, had fallen to 81 won by 1931, representing a 43 percent decline in only three years.[13] Accordingly, there was a rapid increase in the number of Japanese landlords and the scale in their land-holdings during the period of the great panic. According to Jang Si-won's estimate, Japanese landlords with large holdings of over 50 *jeong-bo* increased in number from 330 in 1926 to 552 by 1930. In the case of the Korean landlords, the number decreased from 2,451 to 2,238. Additionally, even in the case of very large landlords with holdings of over 100 *jeongbo*, Japanese landlords increased steadily in number from 201 in 1926 to 301 in 1930, to 321 in 1936, while Korean landlords declined from 968 to 800, and then to 659 over the same period.[14]

As the number of Japanese landowners increased, their landholdings also increased. With the exception of the Oriental Development Compa-

---

12. Jang Si-won, "Iljeha daejiju-ui jonjae hyeongtae-e gwanhan yeongu" (A Study on the Mode of Existence of the Large Landlords during Colonial Period in Korea) (Ph.D. diss., Seoul National University, 1989).
13. 角木傳一・加藤清吾, "朝鮮の耕地價格と其の變遷に就いて" (On Price of Farmland in Korea and its Changes), 『殖銀調査月報』 (Monthly Report of Shokusan Bank) 6 (1938): p. 8.
14. Jang Si-won, op. cit., pp. 57-63.

ny, the landholdings of Japanese landlords increased rapidly from 223,000 *jeongbo* in 1928 to 393,538 *jeongbo* by 1932, with rice paddy fields increasing from 145,000 *jeongbo* to 264,742 *jeongbo*. That is, Japanese landholdings increased by 170,538 *jeongbo* within a mere four-year period, and much of this increase was rice paddies.[15] Overall, Japanese landholdings increased rapidly during the Great Depression.

Conversely, landholdings by Koreans, regardless of whether landowner or farmers, generally declined during this period. Although Korean landlords with small and medium-sized landholding tried to overcome the panic through an intensified exploitation of the peasants, a large number of them could not avoid the decrease in land management. However, only a small number of Korean landlords with large holdings prospered under the great panic. They purchased the forfeited holdings of small or medium landlords at depressed prices in order to enhance their own holdings.

Most farm households went deep into debt during this period. Even the surveys of the rich farmers showed that most of them in Gyeonggi-do, Jeollanam-do, and Gyeongsangnam-do in 1930 were in a deficit. In 1931 farm debts amounted to approximately 500 million won, and mortgaged land was calculated to be 40 percent of total cultivated land. In particular, the debts of tenant farmers were so severe as to reach 87 percent of total assets. In addition, a large number of farmers had borrowed from landowners or usurers and could not avoid the exploitative practice of having to pay the usurious interest rates of 4-5 percent per month. Nor could many of them avoid the fate of going hungry, as roughly 70 percent of tenant farm households suffered from the "spring famine" problem.[16]

The economic situation brought about by a slump in agricultural prices, the magnification of negotiated price margins, an increase in the

---

15. Agriculture and Forestry Bureau, Government-General of Korea, 『朝鮮の農業』 (Argiculture in Korea) (1932); 中谷技官. 『朝鮮における日本人農業植民』 (Japanese Agricultural Colonization in Korea) (unpublished manuscript) (Section of Planned Development Economy, Bureau of Development, Ministry of Agriculture, 1949).

16. *Dong-a Ilbo*, 7 September 1931, "Nongchon buchae 5 eogwon" (Agricultural Debts of 500,000,000 Won); 7 September 1932, "Toji gyeombyeong-gwa sojangnong-ui jeung-ga" (Annexation of Land and Increase in Tenant Farmers); Government-General in Korea,『朝鮮ノ小作慣行』, vol. 2 (1932), pp. 112-113, 145-146; No Dong-gyu, "Joseon nongga gyeongje silsang josa haebu" (Analysis of the State of the Korean Agricultural Economy), *Dongbang pyeongnon* 3 (1932).

tax burden, and an increase in debts accelerated the collapse of the peasant class. Of the total farm households that included landowners, the percentage of owner-farmer and owner-tenants fell from 51.6 percent in 1926 to 41.6 percent by 1932. On the other hand, the percentage of tenant farmers increased from 43.4 percent to 52.8 percent over the same time period. As a result, the percentage of owner-farmers' farmland relative to total cultivated land declined from 57.3 to 50.2.[17]

The general economic situation of Korean rural communities was in a state of extreme collapse as a result of the Great Depression and the agricultural crisis. A great number of farmers went bankrupt and the extent of damage was even more severe for tenant farmers. Of the bankrupt farmers, there was a large increase in the number of emigrations to Japan, Manchuria, and other countries.

As discussed above, the Great Depression and the agricultural crisis brought about different results along class and nation. This served as an impetus for aggravating class discord and national dispute within Korean agricultural society. As the landowners tried to strengthen their methods of exploitation to escape the great panic, the tenant farmers attempted to protect their foundation through the rejection of unilateral exploitation. This, in turn, led to a rapid increase in the number of tenancy disputes.

Of all the causes of tenancy disputes, those having to do with the protection of tenant rights continued to be the most prevalent. However, a conspicuous change in this era was that the number of disputes arising from the opposition to the raising of tenant rent or the imposing of various taxes and miscellaneous charges began to increase. This primarily resulted from the process of the landowner attempting to pass on the losses related to the slump in rice prices to the tenant farmer.

The number of tenancy disputes increased both in scale and frequency. Setting aside the rapid increase in small-scale tenancy disputes of 1928, which resulted from the great crop failure, dispute cases increased from 275 in 1927 to 726 in 1930, and to 1,975 by 1933. Of these disputes, over 90 percent represented small-scale disputes involving fewer than 10 individuals, emerging from the general economic struggle to maintain the foundation of the management of small farms.[18]

---

17. 小早川九郎 (Kobayagawa Kuro), *op. cit.*, p. 93, table 3; p. 99, table 9.
18. Agriculture and Forestry Bureau, Government-General in Korea, 『朝鮮小作年報』 (Annual Report of Tenancy in Korea) (1938), pp. 34-35.

The number of large-scale tenancy disputes also increased at the beginning of the 1930s. These disputes originated in areas where there was a high concentration of tenant farms. The newspapers of that time stated that "the great plantations of Gyeongsangnam-do, Gyeongsang-buk-do, Jeollanam-do, Jeollabuk-do, Hwanghae-do, Pyeonganbuk-do provinces, etc. were in the vortex of disputes." Most of these disputes occurred in Japanese farms.[19] This proves that Japanese landlords who possessed the large tenant farms increased their exploitation of farmers as a method of breaking out of the panic. Utilizing the peasant movement organizations as a background, these were systematic and collective disputes representing a violent and continuous struggle.

Perceptions of Political Influences in the 1930s

The crisis and tension in agricultural society that followed the Great Depression heavily influenced the socialists, nationalists, and the authorities of imperial Japan's Government-General. Even so, the socialists which stood with a social revolutionary viewpoint, the nationalists which wanted to enhance the mass foundation of its movement, and the Government-General, who tried to stabilize its colonial system all confronted the great panic with the view towards turning the situation to their own advantage.

The Socialist Influence

The socialist movement of the 1930s discarded the policy of struggle that advocated a national united front movement in association with the nationalists, and rapidly turned to the left to plan for a social revolution. Such a change was greatly influenced by the course of the international communist revolutionary organ and its direction, such as the international communist party Comintern's "December Theses" (1928), the international communist trade union Profintern's "September Theses" (1930), the pan-Pacific labor union "October Note" (1931). They advocated a left-leaning course that discarded the united front with the

---

19. Police Bureau, Government-General in Korea, 『最近に於ける朝鮮治安状況』 (The Recent Security Situation in Korea) (1933), pp. 154-156.

nationalists. Their strategies involved seizing the proletariat's hegemony, creating a land revolution, and establishing a labor-peasant alliance as well as a Soviet-style government centered around laborers and peasants. In order to realize such a course, a communist party centering on intellectuals was dissolved, and a revolutionary Bolshevik-type party centered on laborers and peasants, as well as revolutionary labor and peasant unions, were to be established.[20]

The Korean socialists began to seriously implement such directives from the end of 1929 to early 1930. This coincided with the outbreak of the great panic and the spread of the Gwangju Student Movement (November 1929) nationwide. The socialist influence regarded the world capitalist structure as being on the verge of collapse, and Japanese capitalism to be near extinction. They diagnosed that world revolution movements were escalating internationally, whereas the domestic state was finally entering a revolutionary period because the Gwangju Student Movement was spreading throughout the nation while strikes and tenancy disputes worsened. Such an "era of revolution" argument showed a Copernican shift from the early 1929 view that "Proletarian movement of Korea today is in a state of stagnation" and therefore a "progressive assault should be avoided and that a retrogressive stance must be taken."[21]

Hence, the socialists dismantled the Singanhoe in 1931 and adopted a hostile stance against the nationalists. Furthermore, they concentrated their efforts on the establishment of illegal movement structures such as revolutionary labor and peasant unions. At this time, the foundation of the revolutionary peasant unions was the legal peasant unions led by the socialists, who were actually the reorganization of a socialist-leaning segment of the tenant farmer groups that had been at the heart of the peasant movements in the early 1920s. These included not only tenants, but

---

20. Yi Gyun-yeong, *Singanhoe yeongu* (A Study of the Singanhoe) (Seoul: Hangilsa Publishing, 1993); The Organization of Korean Historians, *Iljeha sahoejuui undongsa* (History of Socialist Movement under Imperialist Japan) (Seoul: Hangilsa Publishing Co., 1991); Yi Ae-suk, "Segye daegonghwanggi sahoejuui jinyeong-ui jeonsul jeonhwan-gwa Singanhoe haeso munje" (Change of Tactics of Socialist Camp during the Period of the Great Depression and the Cancellation of Singanhoe), *Yeoksa-wa hyeonsil* (Quarterly Review of Korean History) 11 (1994).

21. Im Gyeong-seok, "Segye daegonghwanggi sahoejuui/minjokjuui seryeok-ui jeongse insik" (The Socialist/Nationalist Powers and their Recognition of the Situation during the Era of the Great Depression), *Yeoksa-wa hyeonsil* 11 (1994).

also general farmers, thereby expanding the base of the movement. According to Ji Su-geol's survey of the period between the late 1920s and the mid-1930s, approximately 92 legal peasant unions were organized throughout the nation by county or subcounty. These unions generally dealt with tenancy-related struggles for improvement, struggles against colonial farm policies such as irrigation associations and labor services. They campaigned for the enlightenment of farmers through night schools, fostered educational activities such as reading clubs and lectures, and issued statements related to various popular movements, and May Day commemorative events.[22]

Although revolutionary peasant unions inherited the basic business of the legal peasant unions, they experienced important changes in the aspects of structure, course and struggle. The most important change was the realization of the principle of "putting the poor farmer first." It was to be in the management of the organization, or in the campaign process itself, that the interests of the poor farmer would be thoroughly reflected. Furthermore, the revolutionary peasant unions selected members following strict procedures, demanding a high degree of discipline from them.

The organizing principle for such a revolutionary peasant union was the reflection of the leftist course of struggle. Political struggle and social revolution were selected as the new course of struggle, with the essential points including an anticolonial farm policy, land revolution, the defeat of Japanese imperialism, and the establishment of a Soviet government centered around laborers and peasants. For this, a close union between economic and political struggle was stressed to transform spontaneous mass movements into anti-Japanese political uprisings. As a result, the struggles began to appear more aggressive in nature. Representative examples included attacking or setting fire to landlords' homes, farms, and offices of irrigation associations, as well as punishing their employees, even to the point of assaulting the petty clerks of Japan's colonial administrative or town offices.[23] These methods of struggle were con-

---

22. Ji Su-geol, *Iljeha nongmin johap undong yeongu* (A Study on Farmers Union Movements under Imperial Japan) (Seoul: Yuk Sa Bi Pyoung Sa, 1993), pp. 98-103.

23. 竝木眞人 (Namiki Masahito), "植民地下朝鮮地方民衆運動の展開―咸鏡南道 ホンウオン郡の事例を中心に" (Development of Regional Nationalist Movement in Colonial Korea—Using Example of Hongwon-gun, Hamgyeongnam-do), 『朝鮮史研究會論文集』 (Bulletin of Society for Study on Korean History) 20 (1983).

spicuously different in appearance from previous ones, such as those that had simply demanded tenant rights, the improvement of colonial farm policy, or the stabilizing of small farmers.

Of course, the idea of giving priority to poor farmers and undertaking major land reform measures clashed with the interests of small and medium landowners, as well as those of the land-holding peasant class, which had been near ruin due to economic panic and the Japanese farm policy. There also existed a large scope of contradiction within the interests of the wealthy farmers. But in reality, these groups were excluded from the movement. As illegal methods of struggle were used, there were fewer opportunities to come into contact with the masses and recruit them into the movement. Therefore, the mass foundation of the peasant movement became more limited and the revolutionary peasant movement became more isolated from the general farm population. This led to the exclusion of a majority of the farmers who were active in the legal arena relegating them to the realms of the bourgeois nationalist movement, or to the domain of those advocating Imperial Japan's land reform policies. This resulted in the decline of peasant movement organizations and also of peasant movements that included tenancy disputes.

The Nationalist Influence

The nationalists' attention was also drawn to the economic crisis that defined the Great Depression. However, unlike the socialists, the nationalists regarded the Great Depression as part of the cyclical panic caused by imbalances in economic supply and demand and believed that the economy would recover sooner or later. In actuality, as the economy of Japanese imperialism began to recover after the Manchurian Incident, and as a Manchurian boom was created in 1932, the Korean bourgeoisie competed with the Japanese imperialists to open the Manchurian market and hence entered a course of development through economic dependency.[24] On the other hand, after the creation of the Singanhoe, as intransigent movements reached their limit due to their suppression by Imperial Japan, the issue of autonomy surfaced and an atmosphere of

---

24. Im Gyeong-seok, op. cit.; Ji Su-geol, "1930 nyeondae jeonban-gi bourgeois min-jokjueuija-eui minjok gyeongje geonseol jeollyak" (The Bourgeois Nationalists Construction Tactics for the National Economy during the First Half of the 1930s), *Guk-sagwan nonchong* (Treaties on Korean History) 51 (1994).

instability began to spread. Furthermore, from the latter half of the 1920s, as the socialist movement became revitalized and societal tensions escalated with the outbreak of the Great Depression, the nationalists attempted to expand their power base in order to recruit the masses into their own sphere in an attempt to prevent people from shifting toward the socialist camp.

The nationalists also called for "rural development," and turned it into a popular slogan; they believed that "if the farming community is res-cued, Korea could be sustained, but if it cannot be rescued, then Korea would disappear."[25] Thus the nationalists aided the farm economy, while at the same time helped develop the peasant movement, which would help them pull the farmers into their camp.

The nationalists petitioned the Government-General to carry out poli-cies that would reflect the interests of the farmers. They demanded that the Government-General execute projects to create owner-farmers, implement public works projects for the relief of the poor, undertake high-interest debt adjustment, enact tenancy legislation, etc. As part of the countermeasure against the Great Depression, the Government-Gen-eral had also been examining such areas and the nationalists proposed that the farmers' interests be reflected and carried out. For example, in criticizing Imperial Japan's conservative tenancy legislation, which pro-tected tenant rights for a period of only three years, the nationalists demanded the enactment of tenant legislation fully reflecting the scope of farmers' interests: the recognition of tenant rights for 10-20 years, the establishment of a system limiting the amount of crop yields given to the landowner to 40 percent of the gross yield, the levying of taxes at the landowner's expense, and the establishment of the right of organizing and collective bargaining.[26] In addition, it should be noted that in criti-cizing Japan's project to create owner-farmers on a small scale, as well as a model business level of five *danbo* (one *danbo* is equivalent to 300 *pyeong*) per family for 24,000 families over a period of 10 years, the

25. *Dong-a Ilbo*, 7 November 1930, "Nongchon jinheung-ui uiui-wa nongchon gyeongje-ui gwan-gye" (Significance of the Promotion of Agriculture and Relationship with Agrarian Economy); 3 July 1932, "Gungmin gujechaek jisang gandamhoe" (Confer-ence on Relief Measures for Poverty-Stricken People), part 1.
26. Chung Youn-Tae, "1930 nyeondae joseon nongjiryeong-gwa ilje-ui nongchon tongje" (Korean Agricultural Land Law of the 1930s and the Control of Agricultural Com-munity by Imperialist Japan), *Yeoksa-wa hyeonsil* 4 (1990).

nationalists introduced a scheme to create 10,000 farms annually, allotting one *jeongbo* to each family. The nationalists also granted long-term loans at the extremely low interest rate of one or two percent per year, to be repaid over a 10 to 30-year period, and gave priority to the extremely poor when selecting those who would be eligible for such schemes. These and other plans, they hoped, would fully reflect the farmers' interests.[27]

Moreover, the nationalist influence developed the movements for the improvement and enlightenment of agricultural communities. Some representative movements included: movements to reform the rural economy such as reform of farming methods, improvements in living conditions, reduction in irrigation association charges, adjustment of high-interest debt, formation of cooperative sales, etc.; the enlightenment movement through education and literacy programs for farmers, lectures and publication of magazines; and movements to found agricultural cooperative associations. These movements unfolded through various diverse organizations. The representative groups were, in the Pyeongan-do region, the Joseon Nongminsa (Korean Farmers Group) led by Cheondogyo, and the Jeon Joseon Nongminsa (Korean General Farmers Group) led by non-Cheondogyo members. There were also projects for rural development, deployed by YMCA/Presbyterian/Methodist and other Christian groups for missionary purposes from the late 1920s. Incidentally, the Hyeopdong Johap Undongsa (Cooperative Movement Group), the *Chosun Ilbo*, and the *Dong-a Ilbo* fostered a movement for the propagation of Hangeul.[28]

However, the nationalist-backed peasant movements were too conservative relative to the dire crisis in which the agricultural community found itself. These movements merely urged the awakening of the farm-

---

27. Chung Youn-Tae, "1930 nyeondae jajak nongji siseoljeong sa-eop-e gwanhan yeongu" (Research on Establishment of Self-Owned Farmland Project in the 1930s), *Hanguksa ron* (Treaties on Korean History) 26 (1991).

28. Yi Man-yeol, "Hanmal iljeha gidokgyo sahoe undong-ui maengnak" (The Christian Social Movement at the End of the Pre-colonial Period through the Colonial Period), *Gidokgyo sasang* (Christian Ideology) 8 (1984); Kim Hyeon-suk, "Iljeha-ui sahoe undong" (Social Movement under the Japanese Imperialism), in *Hanguk sahoesa yeonguhoe nonmunjip* (Papers from the Research Group on Korean Social History), no. 9 (Seoul: Munhak gwa Jisung Sa, 1987); 飛田雄一 (Hita Uichi), 「朝鮮農民史」 (History of Korean Peasants), in 『日帝下朝鮮農民運動』 (Korean Farmers Movement under Japanese Imperialism) (Tokyo: 未來社, 1991).

ers or relied on the Government-General's reform policy. As a result, not only were the nationalists unsuccessful in attracting more peasants into their camp, they also failed to utilize the economic crisis and political tension that had spread throughout the rural society as an opportunity to elevate their movement.

Imperial Japanese Government-General Authorities

With the increase in the peasant movement and national liberation movement camps' attempts at structural reform, imperialist Japan developed a crisis consciousness. It especially regarded as a threat the dissemination of the revolutionary peasant movements, whose purpose was the "reform of the national polity" and the "negation of the private property system." Accordingly, it dealt with the socialist peasant movements encompassing revolutionary peasant ones by beginning a "thorough and strict crackdown," to suppress them.[29] Japan tried 2,609 cases involving 19,374 individuals over the 1929–1933 period for violating the Security Maintenance Law, "the law related to punishment for violent actions," and the crime of sedition under criminal law. Between 1930–1931, when the peasant union movement was especially active, the number of cases and persons increased tremendously.[30] According to other statistical data, of the 3,319 violators of the Security Maintenance Law during the 1929–1933 period, 1,077 were farmers.[31] Therefore, it appears that among these, the number of people who were oppressed for being involved in peasant movements was not inconsequential.

Seeing that there was room for improvement in terms of the nationalist agenda for rural reform, enlightenment, and tenancy disputes involving the protection of the right to survival, Japan adopted a policy of oppression on one hand and of appeasement on the other. The cooperative projects of the Joseon Nongminsa (Korean Farmers Group) were legally regulated and night classes intended to increase literacy were suppressed. On the other hand, as they appeased the leaders and broke

---

29. Government-General of Korea, 『道警察部長會議諮問事項答申書』 (Response to Advisory Items to Conference of Provincial Police Chiefs) (1931); Police Bureau, Government-General, *op. cit.*, p. 48.
30. Police Bureau, Government-General, *op. cit.*, pp. 62-63.
31. Ji Su-geol, op. cit., table 1-12, p. 76.

up the group, they absorbed it into the Rural Development Association, which was an official organ of imperialist Japan, to carry out rural development.[32] Thus Japan did not permit the existence of even the moderate peasant movement of the nationalists who recognized the colonial system.

However, Japan recognized that such suppression and appeasement policies would not be sufficient to fundamentally impede the development of the peasant movement. In 1931, at the conference of provincial police chiefs, a plan to absorb the peasant population into the colonial system was proposed. It provided for the protection of moderate organizations, the formation of exemplary youth groups and enlightenment groups, facilities to enforce social policy on unemployment and relief of poverty, the establishment of government-made industries and consumption associations, reform of tenancy system, and the enactment of tenancy law and tenancy disputes regulation law.[33]

Although they all differed in terms of degree, the need for such countermeasures was fully recognized by the Governor-General and agricultural administration officials. The Governor-General Ugaki believed that Korea's economy, on the whole, had been becoming more capitalistic, whether through natural development or through concrete policies, following the industrialization of cities and the capitalization of rural areas. Therefore, he believed that class conflict between laborer and capitalist, landlord and tenant, would unfold in a serious manner. Furthermore, it was considered that through the machinations of the socialists, the struggle among classes would take the appearance of a confrontation between Korea and Imperial Japan. As a result, in order to prevent the intensification in the class conflict among the rural communities stemming from the inflow of capitalism, as well as the danger from the spread of communism, serious measures were thought to be needed. On the one hand, fascist measures of suppression were instituted, while on the other social reform measures involving an appeasement approach between landlord and tenant were considered necessary.[34]

The relevance of such concerns were verified by Shioda Masahiro,

---

32. Police Bureau, Government-General of Korea, *op. cit.*, pp. 175-176.
33. Government-General of Korea, 『道警察部長會議諮問事項答申書』 (Response to Advisory Items to Conference of Provincial Police Chiefs) (1931), references.
34. 『宇垣一成日記』 (Ugaki Kazushige Diary), p. 806 (10 August 1931); p. 909 (24 July 1933); p. 911 (30 July 1933); p. 913 (20 August 1933); p. 919 (7 October 1933).

who was Chief of the Agricultural Division of the Government-General, as well as by Asagura Noboru, who was Chief of the Industrial Division in Gyeongsangnam-do province. Shioda Masahiro stated that "unless a plan is devised, the rural communities will become a land of bloodshed and chaos" and that "Korean rural communities . . . will cause an enormous problem in ruling Korea." He also emphasized that there was a pressing need to secure the peace of the rural community through "pledging a far-reaching reform of tenancy law."[35] In addition, Asagura Noboru believed that not only the tenancy mediation law, which had been enacted in Japan as a countermeasure to the tenancy problem, but also a tenant union law promising the rationalization of the tenancy system had to be utilized. This law, at the same time, would bolster the policy of creating owner-farmers.[36]

Thus, imperialist Japan established system-stabilization policies whose primary target was the peasant class. It was implemented primarily by amending farm policy, which had aimed at food production increase and had been centered on the landowner. The Rural Development Movement, that is, the self-help program for the agrarian sector, the project of creating farmland, as well as the farmland decree of the early 1930s, all represented new measures that arose from the above intentions.

These measures were meant to (1) promote farm productivity and the stabilization of the farm economy through the forcible demand of a life of privation and greater exertion of labor force, (2) absorb a portion of the farmers into the structure by giving economic and administrative support and guidance and used them as publicity models for the "self-help" ideology, and (3) stabilize rural communities and farmers through the cooperation and reconciliation between the landlord and peasant and through the systemic regulation on tenancy.[37]

These measures were somewhat successful after 1935, as the agricul-

---

35. 鹽田正洪 (Shioda Masahiro), 「自作農創定策における苦干の考察」 (A Little Thought on Initiating the Land-owner System), 『朝鮮農會報』 (Report of Korean Agricultural Society) 1: p. 45; 2, p. 21.

36. 朝倉昇 (Asagura Noboru), 「朝鮮の小作問題とその對策」 (Tenancy Problems and Measures for Them in Korea), in 『農業經濟研究』 (Research on Agricultural Economics), pp. 7-22.

37. Kim Yong-seop, op. cit.; Chung Youn-Tae, "1930 nyeondae ilje-ui singmin nong-jeong-e daehan jaegeomto" (Reexamination of Colonial Agricultural Policy of Imperial Japan in the 1930s), Yeoksa bipyeong (Critical Review of History) (spring 1995).

tural depression ended and the farming economy entered an era of prosperity. The industrial sector began to recover in 1932 through the opening up of new markets with the Japanese invasion of Mancuria. Rice prices gradually recovered from their low point in 1931 such that by 1935 that country had entered a high-priced rice era, which surpassed the prices prior to the depression, and the economy, in general, took a turn for the better.

Conclusion

Due to the aftermath of the Great Depression and the agricultural panic, Korean society experienced economic crises and increased political tension. The primary arena for such crisis and tension was the agricultural society that had occupied a dominant position in terms of industry and population. The crisis in agriculture had its origin in the impoverished state of its the economy, which was the result of the severe slump in the prices of agricultural products. However, two factors worked to make the crisis environment more severe for the Korean agricultural sector than others. One had to do with the excessive progress of the single-crop policy instituted by Japan as part of its food provision policy, the fall in rice prices that had a greater negative impact. Another was that the damage caused by the panic was passed on to and concentrated among the tenant farmers, due to the strong and entrenched premodern tenancy practices. Accordingly, social tensions accelerated in the agricultural sector, resulting in such things as the explosion in the number of tenancy disputes.

The crisis and tension in agricultural society that followed the Great Depression increased discord between the Government-General and the national liberation movement camps—the socialist and nationalist influences. The socialists attempted to develop the crisis and tension in the agricultural society into a social revolution, on the basis of which would be built being the "opportunity for revolution," while the nationalists used reform methods to stem the collapse of the farm economy and tried to take control of the national movements through the grasp of farmers. On the other hand, Imperial Japan tried to stabilize the ruling system, through food production increases and structural stability and separated the peasant class from the national liberation movement camp while absorbing them into the colonial system. Thus during the time of the

Great Depression, there was a heightened level of discord and confrontation among socialists, nationalists, and Japan's Government-General over the recruitment of farmers.

The reality of the Great Depression was that it was an encouraging environment for socialists for inciting movements. The Great Depression had been interpreted as a sign of the collapse of the capitalist system and the escalating tension in the agricultural society was regarded as the harbinger of a revolutionary era. Needless to say, the left-oriented revolutionary course taken by the international communist party greatly influenced the view that the Great Depression was a revolutionary era. Therefore, the socialists power used prioritizing the poor farmer as a foundation for land revolution and the establishment of the Soviet-style government centered around laborers and peasants, and went down the road of social revolution and political struggle.

The leftist revolutionary course taken by the socialist power helped to increase the advance of the peasant masses. However, it did not function to develop the anti-Japanese nationalist movement through the collection of the vast range of discontent and crisis mentality felt by the various classes, that is, by the small and medium landlords as well as the peasant, except for some large landholders. By taking an antagonistic stance against the nationalists reform and improvement movements of farming community, it brought about the limit of a wide ranging legal mass movement and the national united front. From the perspective of the national liberation movement, one can conclude that they made a mistake of turning to the leftist. On the one hand, this is attributable to the socialists' reliance on the authority of the international socialist revolutionary organ and to their automatic application of the left-oriented revolutionary course. On the other hand, this is also the result of the underestimation of Japan's ability to overcome the Great Depression through the Manchurian Incident and the lack of objective judgement on the inferior capacity of their movement relative to the power of the ruling imperialist Japan.

Finally, the national liberation movement camp failed to turn the economic crisis and political tension brought about by the Great Depression to their advantage to develop the anti-Japanese national movement. The mistake of the nationalist influence of taking advantage of imperialist Japan's structure stabilization policy and remaining in compromising movements such as farm improvement and enlightenment movements cannot be ignored. And the responsibility of the socialist influence who misjudged the situation as the arrival of a revolutionary era, regarded the nationalists with hostility and followed the course of social revolution is also not inconsequential.

Deduction of the National Division and the Premise of Reunification of the Korean Peninsula

Doh Jin Soon

Introduction

Last year in Korea we experienced the onslaught of the IMF crisis, which brought about rapid political and economic upheaval to our lives. There have been various diagnoses for the crisis,[1] but one thing we should not fail to note is the conspicuous "absence of the intellect" in dealing with the crisis. After the collapse of the former Soviet Union and the East European bloc in 1989, we should have concentrated our energy in drawing up a blueprint for the nation's future in the post-Cold War era, with a determination to accomplish a "second nation-building." Instead, caught up in the illusion of the victory of capitalism and South Korea, we spent the past 10 years provoked away critical time.

---

* Originally published in the *Korea Journal*, vol. 38, no. 4 (winter 1998).

Doh Jin Soon (Do, Jin-sun) is currently a visiting scholar at the Korean Institute at Harvard University. He is Professor of History at Changwon National University. He received his B.A., M.A., and Ph.D. in History from Seoul National University. He has authored *Juhae Baekbeom ilji* (An Annotated Diary of Kim Gu) (1997), and *Hanguk minjokjuui-wa nambuk gwan-gye* (Korean Nationalism and the North-South Relationship) (1997). E-mail: dodemy@sarim.changwon.ac.kr.

1. The fact that the region now experiencing the "Asian crisis" (and previously the "Asian Miracle") corresponds to the region covered in the U.S. crescent defense line in East Asia, leads us to presume that it has a close relationship with the Cold War order and its disintegration. See Doh Jin Soon, "Neo-Liberal Globalization, East Asia, and the Korean Peninsula," *Korea Journal* 38.2 (summer 1998); Benedict Anderson, "From Miracle to Crash," *London Review of Books* 20.8 (March 1998).

The "lost time" stems from our inaccurate conceptions about the reality of national division and how it is now changing. After the end of the Cold War, we were completely caught up in the issue of national division by looking at the two Koreas as fixed systems, adhering to the optimistic view that the South can reunify the nation by absorbing the North.[2] The gusto with which we embellished the victory of the "Korean" (and, by extension, the Oriental or the Asian) value while the center of power still lies in the West (the United States) reveals our lack of any clear understanding of our reality.[3] Besides, we have persisted in a one-sided view that national division is an intra-Korean problem in the post-Cold War period.[4] Unless we correct these misconceptions, we will keep making the same intellectual mistake.

Even now we can see the same kind of mistake being repeated with the handling of the artificial satellite launched by the North. The absence of intellectual leadership in preventing the IMF crisis was followed by a display of intellectual panic in the excessive production of reckless patch-up measures, and now, in the face of the satellite incident things have reached a virtual stalemate. As I will discuss later in the paper, the IMF crisis and the satellite incident are closely related to the division of the Korean peninsula and its changing reality.

The great bulk of discourse on national division since the armistice has not made any linear progress, and it has been the same with other aspects of national history. Though it is true that the discourse from the 1970s contributed to raising consciousness about the issue among broader segments of the public, it has somewhat drifted away from the central

---

2. The absorption theory of Korean reunification is closely related to the U.S. hard-line policy towards North Korea, which will be discussed later in the paper. Even after the U.S. shifted its policy to the "soft landing of the North," there still remains a difference of opinion between the U.S. and South Korea.

3. Discussions on "East Asian discourse" and "Asian values" have somewhat contributed to fostering a self-reliant spirit, but there were generally "intellectual bubbles" derived from the absence of a clear understanding of the reality of national division.

4. Kim Dong-chun, "Gukjehwa-wa hanguk-ui minjujuui" (Internationalization and Korean Nationalism), *Yeoksa bipyeong* (Critical Review of History) 27 (fall 1994); Jeong Hae-gu, "Nambukhan bundan-ui jeon-gae gwajeong: bundan-gwa tongil-ui byeonjeungbeop" (The Process of Korea's Division: The Dialectics of Division and Reunification), in *Bundan gukga 50 nyeon, geu baeban-ui yeoksa-wa tongil-ui gil* (The Divided Nation's 50 Years: The History of Betrayal and the Path to Reunification) (Seoul: Korean Council of Academic Groups, 1998).

issue.[5] From the perspective that "one's consciousness is determined by one's existence," we can say that there is probably nothing more constrained by the reality of the division than discourse itself.

Currently, diverse and broad research and discussion are being conducted, mostly in the United States, on the topic of Korea's division and reunification, the 1953 Armistice Agreement and alternative measures for these issues. This signals that North-South relations, which have been characterized by hostility, have entered a new stage. Yet the intellectuals' approach inside Korea remains at the level of relying mostly on "hunch" rather than on cool judgements of the situation.

The Problems of the View of a Division System

Division is Not a System

Nowadays the phrase "division system" contains diverse meanings.[6] It may be acceptable, though not desirable, if it is stressed that the South and the North have different systems, such as capitalism vs. socialism, or democracy vs. totalitarianism.

But the phrase distorts reality if it is used to mean that "the system will not or could not collapse, because it possesses considerable self-reproductive capability on the basis of the existence of a hostile symbio-

---

5. Although most of the discourses on the issue of national division have taken shape after the "division system" view appeared in the 1970s, there had been considerable discussion on the issue prior to that, and in a sense, even more essential arguments on the issue formed before the 1970s. Just as in order to understand the "first human," one would have to begin by examining the primitive ages, to understand the nature of national division, we must give attention to the historical period that witnessed national division between South and the North, as well as the respective occupations by the U.S. and the Soviet Union, the establishment of two governments, the Korean War, and the Armistice Agreement.

6. Researchers use the word "system" in discussing national division for no particular reason, simply to emphasize that the South and the North are in hostile confrontation or that the division has a system, regime, or some systematic principles of operation. See Baek Nak-cheong, *Bundan cheje byeonhyeok-ui gongbu gil* (How to Transform the Division System) (Seoul: Changbi Publishers, 1994); Baek Nak-cheong, *Heundeullineun bundan cheje* (The Division System in Change) (Seoul: Changbi Publishers, 1998).

sis or interdependence between the conservative forces in the South and the North," or that it is "a system with its own life force."[7] As the nation has remained divided over half a century, it is understandable that some consider it "a system with a self-generating ability." However, the context of the division is far from being so simple. It is true that the South and the North have been in a state of hostile confrontation for a long time and that each side has consolidated its own self-reproducing structure, but this cannot be viewed as the dominant principle of the division.

In this paper, I will not discuss the process of the national division such as the partitioned occupation by the United States and the former Soviet Union and the subsequent establishment of two separate governments. Rather, I wish to focus on the Korean War Armistice Agreement, which still remains as the basis for the division. The Armistice Agreement has 5 articles and 63 paragraphs, which can be grouped into three categories.[8] The first group includes paragraphs that are no longer viable because they were enforced at the time of the armistice; examples are Article 2 "Concrete Arrangements for Cease-Fire and Armistice," Paragraphs 12, 14-17 and Article 3 "Arrangement Relating to Prisoners of War," Paragraphs 51-59.

The second group includes clauses which are important to the maintenance of peace after the truce, but which have been practically nullified and currently have no effect. Examples are Article 2 "Concrete Arrangements for Cease Fire and Armistice," Paragraphs 13-d and 13-g on the ban on bringing arms from overseas; Paragraph 19-35 on the Military Armistice Commission; Paragraph 36-50 on the Neutral Nations Supervisory Commission; Paragraph 60 on the amendments and additions to

---

7. See Baek Nak-cheong (1998). The concept of "hostile symbiosis between the South and the North," which became popular in the wake of the "North Wind" during the 1997 presidential election, is a variant of this view.

8. For the entire text of the Armistice Agreement, in Korean, refer to O So-baek et al., *Haebang 20 nyeon: jaryopyeon* (Twenty Years after the Liberation: Materials and Data) (Seoul: Semun Publishers, 1965), pp. 222-269. For studies on the Armistice Agreement, see Patrick M. Norton, "Ending the Korean Armistice Agreement: The Legal Issues" (1997); Kim Myong Chol, "DPRK Perspective on a Post-Armistice Regional Order" (1997); Kim Myong Chol, "Kim Jong-il's Peace Policy" (1998); and Pak Chol Ku, "Replacement of the Korean Armistice Agreement: Prerequisite to a Lasting Peace on the Korean Peninsula" (1997). These four papers were received through Internet. The copyright and e-mail address are as follows: Copyright ? 1998 Nautilus of America/The Nautilus Institute; Web: http://nautilus.org/napsnrt.

the peaceful settlement of the Korean question; and Paragraph 61 on the amendments and additions to the Armistice Agreement. Some of them are listed below.

> 13-(d). Cease the introduction into Korea of reinforcing combat aircraft, armored vehicles, weapons, and ammunition . . .
>
> 13-(g). Afford full protection and all possible assistance and cooperation to the Military Armistice Commission, its Joint Observer Teams, the Neutral Nations Supervisory Commission, and its Neutral Nations Inspection Teams, in the carrying out of their functions and responsibilities hereinafter assigned . . .
>
> 60. In order to insure the peaceful settlement of the Korean question, the military Commanders of both sides hereby recommend to the governments of the countries concerned on both sides that, within three months after the Armistice Agreement is signed and becomes effective, a political conference of a higher level of both sides be held by representatives appointed respectively to settle through negotiation the questions of the withdrawal of all foreign forces from Korea, the peaceful settlement of the Korean question, etc.
>
> 61. Amendments and additions to this Armistice Agreement must be mutually agreed to by the Commanders of the opposing sides.

The ban on bringing arms into the peninsula from overseas was nullified right after the armistice.[9] The replacement of the Armistice Agreement with a peace agreement through dialogue was cancelled at the Geneva Conference, and the political conference, initially planned to be held "within three months," has been delayed to this day. Of course, the revision and nullification of individual clauses of the Armistice Agreement occurred not by mutual agreement but by unilateral decisions.

Excluding these two groups, Article 1 "Military Demarcation Line and Demilitarized Zone" remains effective. As we know, the Military Demarcation Line is still observed, and the so-called Demilitarized Zone is the most heavily armed area in the world.

---

9. At a hearing of the U.S. House Appropriation Committee on 27 February 1960, Gen. Remnichi, who had served as the Chief of Staff of the U.S. Army during the Korean War, said, "Through years-long efforts, we were successful in nullifying Paragraph 13-(d) of the Armistice Agreement and introducing the latest-type equipment there (into South Korea)."

In short, of the many clauses in the Armistice Agreement, only the Military Demarcation Line is still observed, while the nature of the Demilitarized Zone has been transmuted, and clauses important to securing a stable state of peace have become eventually either ineffectual or nullified. A total system of management or an institution governing Korea's division does not exist on the Korea peninsula. Therefore, Korea's division is characterized primarily by instability without any institutional arrangements for the establishment of peace.

Due to the fragile nature of peace, political developments surrounding the Korean peninsula may at any time develop into a crisis of imminent war. Between 1993 and 1994, when the nation was swept up by anxiety over the North's nuclear capability, a Second Korean War Plan (OpPlan 50-27-16), which the U.S. Forces in Korea (USFK) prepared, was submitted to President Clinton in a special strategy meeting. Through a multi-year review process, the emphasis changed from a defensive stance against North Korea to an offensive one. In particular, OpPlan 50-27-16, laid out by Gary Luck in 1994, chief in command of USFK, prepared for a real war, not for an operational exercise. According to Don Oberdorfer, "As North Korea began defueling its reactor and storm clouds darkened, Luck flew to Washington to join an extraordinary military meeting to prepare to fight in Korea. Secretary of Defense Perry and Joint Chiefs of Staff Chairman General John Shalikashvili summoned every active four-star general and admiral in the U.S. military, including several brought from commands across the world, to a Pentagon conference room on May 18 [1994]. The subject was how the entire U.S. military would support Luck's war plan for Korea. . . . The following day Perry, Shalikashvili, and Luck took the results of the meeting to the ultimate commander-in-chief at the White House."[10]

The seriousness of the situation at the time is exemplified in an episode following the adoption of the OpPlan 50-27; when U.S. Ambassador Laney and General Gary Luck agreed to proceed with plans for an immediate evacuation of American civilians from the country, Laney "told his daughter and his three grandchildren, who were visiting at the time, that they should leave Korea by Sunday, 3 days thence."[11]

OpPlan 50-27 predicted that the U.S. would ultimately win the war

---

10. Don Oberdorfer, *The Two Koreas: A Contemporary History* (Reading, Mass.: Addison-Wesley, 1997), pp. 314-315.

11. *Ibid.*, p. 326.

with 545,000 U.S. troops engaging in a high-intensity war for 82 to 112 days or four months, at the cost of about 1 million human lives, including 80,000 to 90,000 U.S. troops. It also entailed the possible release of radioactivity over the Korean peninsula, Japan and Hawaii,[12] a sea of fire across Seoul and the vicinities where 40 percent of the Korean population reside, complete destruction of the South Korean economy and trade, and war expenses of more than $100 billion for the U.S. alone, with $1,000 billion in total for all allied countries combined.[13] In short, should the U.S. choose the war option, it would have to bear an astronomical amount of damage and loss even with one-half of its military capabilities mobilized.

If the U.S. resorted to war, the Clinton administration would have to delay numerous domestic agendas he had promised to his people. Furthermore the CIA and the DIA, which have taken the strongest stand against North Korean nuclear proliferation, opposed the war scenario because of the likelihood of heavy casualties.[14] Eventually, President Clinton had to make a swift turn to a diplomatic resolution and proposed to hold a third round of high-level talks with North Korea. The war line, which was pushed by U.S. Joint Chiefs of Staff Chairman General Colin Powell, who said "I am down to Castro and Kim Il Sung" after the completion of the Gulf War, also switched to diplomatic negotiation. Soon after, Jimmy Carter visited the North and obtained a pledge from the North to hold a summit meeting with the South.

OpPlan 50-27 has some important implications. First, it reaffirmed that the division is essentially unstable especially without any institutional peace mechanisms in place. Koreans are accustomed to living in a state of national division, but war may break out suddenly at any time. It is easy to overlook the danger, because it becomes apparent only in moments of crisis. In short, the most important forces that have created and maintained the division are external forces rather than internal, controlling rather than self-generated, non-institutional rather than institu-

---

12. Unlike during the Korean War, the range of the North Korean operation may expand outside the Korean peninsula, and if so, nuclear power plants along the seashores (11 in South Korea and 53 in Japan) and U.S. warships carrying nuclear weapons can be the target of North Korean offense (Kim Myong Chol, "DPRK Perspective . . . ").
13. Don Oberdorfer, *op. cit.*, pp. 311-316.
14. Leon V. Sigal, *Disarming Stranger: Nuclear Diplomacy with North Korea* (Princeton, New Jersey: Princeton Univ. Press, 1998), p. 155.

tional, and unstable rather than stable. This is how the division has been systematically internalized in both the South and the North.

What has allowed the division of the peninsula to exist for more than half a century, despite its structural weakness and instability? As demonstrated by the cancellation of OpPlan 50-27, the division has not been maintained by a concrete system but through confrontations of the so-called "naked powers."[15] The U.S. pointed at Kim Il Sung as "the next villain to go after Hussein" and prepared a war scenario, to which North Korea reacted with a "preemptive offensive to another's preemptive offensive to it."[16] But ironically in this kind of intense confrontation, war and dialogue for peace are interdependent. This irony still holds true. I will examine these aspects again when I discuss the structure of the division.

The Division is Not a Division

The "phenomenon" and the "essence" of the division are in a peculiar functional relation in which the former distorts the latter. The national division is often approached as a regional issue, or understood as a conflict between social classes or social forces.[17] In the former view, contemporary division is compared to historical divisions: the establishment of the Three Kingdoms, of the Southern and Northern Kingdoms (Unified Silla and Balhae), and of the Later Three Kingdoms period.[18] In the lat-

---

15. North Korea is not subsumed as a subsystem of the global capitalist system, but in direct confrontation with it. The two Koreas' contact with the world can be defined better in terms of their relations with the U.S.—whether hostile or friendly—rather than in terms of the general concept of the world capitalist system.

16. North Korea studied the desert [Operation Desert Storm against Iraq] more than the U.S. did and assessed that Hussein lost the Gulf War because it allowed the U.S. to build up a large military in the Gulf region. Based on this, the North declared that it would not just watch the U.S. build up its forces in the Northeast Asia region (Don Oberdorfer, *op. cit.*, p. 325).

17. Korean scholars' view of recognizing the division as a system, which is represented by Kang Man-gil's *Bundan sidae-ui yeoksa insik* (Historical Consciousness of the Era of Division) (Seoul: Changbi Publishers, 1978), contributed to shedding light on the division as an epochal issue. However, it was defined as a regional problem, and there was a failure to examine its relationship with foreign forces based on scientific methods. Hence, his study can be categorized as a kind of sentimental nationalism.

18. As Kim Yong-ok advocates in *Samguk tongil-gwa hanguk tongil* (Unification of the Three Kingdoms and Unification of Korea) (Seoul: Tongnamu, 1994), this view is more widespread than we would expect.

ter view, the origin of the division is traced back to the conflicts between nationalist and socialist forces during the 1920s,[19] which in essence translates into the left-right conflict. Of course, regional differences between the northern and southern parts of the peninsula and conflicts between socialism and liberalism played a role in the division of the peninsula, but such differences are not primary, but rather secondary. Korea's division was in nature a result of its contact with superpowers and with the world.

If we are reminded of similar cases in other nations, we can understand the defect of the fragmented view that ideological confrontation between left and right during the 1920s caused internal splits. There are many cases in history where nations were ideologically divided, such as the split that occurred between Western modernizationists and Greek Orthodox nationalists in modern Russia, between Westernizationists/modernizationists and Islamic fundamentalists in Turkey, and between globalizationists and Zapatistas in Mexico.[20]

Historically, left-right conflicts have swept across Europe, Russia, Asia, Latin America, the United States, along with many other countries. It may well be exceptional to find a nation where left and right did not engage in conflict. History develops through conflict and confrontation between center and periphery, generations old and new, as well as between different ideologies, as evidenced in the history of Korea and other nations throughout the world. So this view does not provide an answer as to why left-right conflicts resulted in a repressive division in Korea.

The same logic can be applied to the perspective that treats national division as a regional issue. Here let us compare the contemporary national division and that of the ancient Three Kingdoms period.

As shown in the above Table, the contemporary national division and the establishment of the Three Kingdoms have fundamental differences besides the obvious temporal one. In the latter case, various small kingdoms integrated into three regional kingdoms over a period of time. It was primarily part of the historical development process of the peninsu-

---

19. Those who claim that national division was caused by internal factors share this view.
20. In *The Clash of Civilizations and the Remaking of World Order* (New York: Simon & Schuster, 1996), Samuel Huntington defines these as divided nations and cites several examples.

Table 1. Comparison between the Contemporary National Division
and that of the Three Kingdoms Period

Classification		Historical Process	Factor
The Three Kingdoms	Establishment	From various small kingdoms to three regional kingdoms	Primary factor: Internal forces
	Unification	Silla unified them through alliance with Tang China	Combined with external forces in the process
North-South Division		From one nation to two nations	Primary factor: External forces

la, in which the intervention of external forces was secondary and procedural.[21]

Historically, the replacement of dynasties resulted in a temporary division of nations. In China, the Ming dynasty emerged after seceding from the Yuan dynasty, and in Korea, the Later Goguryeo Kingdom and the Later Baekje Kingdom seceded from the Unified Silla. But no one calls these instances of national division into question, because such divisions were primarily due to internal factors. In other words, they were part of the natural process of historical development. If the North-South division of the peninsula were something of this sort, it would not be so serious a problem. The main problem with the contemporary division is that it is not a regional division but a repressive one, caused by Cold War regimes. Normal development of Korea after the liberation was hindered and distorted by the superpowers engaged in the Cold War.

Though foreign forces caused the division, it was neither an accident nor an anomaly. To the contrary, it is a modern manifestation of the

---

21. The cause of the South-North division is more similar to that of the unification of the Three Kingdoms than to that of the establishment of the Three Kingdoms. By saying this, I do not intend to slight Silla's unification or to speak highly of the destroyed Goguryeo. I just want to point out that as the unification of the Three Kingdoms took place as part of the process of maintaining contact with China-centered Northeast Asia, the contemporary division also occurred in the process of its contact with the modern world. The two cases are quite similar in this sense.

perennial problem in Korean history. Surrounded by world superpowers, Korea has enjoyed the advantage of importing advanced foreign culture and materials, but at the same time, frequent foreign pressure and interference have plagued it incessantly. In this context, one of the persisting problems Korea has faced is the question of how to open up to the outside world while at the same time retaining national sovereignty. But the reality is that development tends to lean in one or the other direction, with national tragedy occurring at the polar extremes. When Korea sought openness and advancement, it tended to fall into subordination, colonialization, and division; and when it stressed sovereignty and self-reliance, it underwent retreat and took the risk of national ruin.

The history of Korea's contact with the outside world can be divided into four stages. The first stage covers the period from its foundation to the Three Kingdoms period, during which Korea achieved prosperity in relatively equal and pluralist relations with other nations in Northeast Asia. In the second stage, Korea was incorporated into the Chinese cultural sphere around the Unified Silla period, during which it offered tribute to China and accepted investitures from it, but retained its sovereignty based on the principle of "serving the great and maintaining amicable ties with neighboring states" (*sadae gyorin*). In the third period, during the tumultuous time from the late Joseon dynasty to the period of opening up its ports to the outside world, Korea was incorporated into the modern world and finally became a colony of Japan, the then leading maritime power in Asia. In the final stage, Korea experienced national division in the Cold War regime, as a result of having come into contact with foreign nations. In this sense, the underlying context of the current national division is exactly the same as that of the other three periods.[22]

It is not uncommon that seemingly contradictory phenomena such as secession and independence vs. integration and unification manifest in the same dimension. For example, "reunification" is an epochal issue to the Korean people, but "secession" was momentous for the former Soviet Union countries around 1990. Under colonial rule, Korea sought secession from imperialist Japan. These two opposite phenomena of secession and unification actually strive for the same thing—national

---

22. This is a rough classification, but it is a broad topic involving many issues. Refer to my paper, "Bundan cheje-ui yeonyeok-gwa yeoksajeok yuchu" (Deduction of the Division System and Historical Inference) (paper presented at the Decennial Meeting of the Organization of Korean Historians).

self-reliance. In sum, though there is a great difference between minorities in the Soviet Union and people of the two Koreas, and although the nature and intensity of the foreign forces are different in the case of the colonial period and contemporary Korea, they are identical in the sense that both seek to achieve freedom, whether by secession or integration.

With the introduction to Korea of the so-called dependence theory during the 1980s, in which researchers emphasized the importance of a nation's contact with the advanced world and the resolution of ethnic problems in analyzing political outcomes in a nation, Korea encountered a new analytical approach to dealing with division. But lacking concrete understanding of national division and the foreign forces involved in it, most analyses made the error of overgeneralization by treating the Korean case as identical to other Third World nations in Asia and Africa.

There is a clear difference in the geopolitics of the Cold War between Korea and Africa or Latin America (which do not have any superpower of either socialist or capitalist bloc in their respective region). Another important difference arises when the state is the primary unit of analysis. Though Third World nations are dependent on foreign nations, they are basically individual nation-states. But in the case of Korea, both the South and the North are member nations of the United Nations. One is in armistice with the world's most powerful nation, the U.S., and has been described as a "besieged state,"[23] while the other is in close alliance with the U.S. Each defines and is defined by the other. For this reason, although there are two states on the Korean peninsula—or perhaps it might be more accurate to say, precisely because there are two states— they are not recognized as national governments by the United Nations.[24] Any simplistic method of detaching South or North Korea from their triangular relationship with the U.S. and comparing either one with other nation-states, a means which is frequently employed in case study analy-

---

23. North Korea is described in various ways such as "guerilla Korea," "totalitarian state," etc., but its efforts to militarize its territory and unify its people to cope with the quasi-state of war with the U.S. reminds us of a nation striving to protect its castle.
24. The U.S-dominated United Nations did not recognize North Korea as a legitimate nation until 1991, and indeed even South Korea was not registered as such. In January 1948, U.S. Secretary of State Marshall ordered to review establishing a "definite government" in the South, and the United Nations document approving the South Korean government in December 1948 did not use the term "National State." This became the grounds by which the South could not have jurisdiction over the northern territory during the Korean War.

sis in the social sciences, is bound to make a serious error.

Considering this, we must start with a concrete analysis of the "here and now" and move on to the general, instead of trying to force the reality of national division on "Procrustes' bed" in the name of a generalized theory. Though the problem of superpowers and foreign forces is common for third-world nations including Korea, we should note that each case is inherently different, depending on time and place. In short, because the Korean case differs from other nations in Asia, Africa, and Latin America, and because its contemporary division is different from its past subordination to China and colonialization by Japan, we must achieve concrete analysis of the here and now in order to fully understand the division. Deduction from generalization and inference from history are possible only with a concrete scrutinization of the particular.

The Structure of the Division: The Unbalanced Triangular Relations among South Korea, North Korea, and the U.S.

Korea's division resulted from the relationship between Korea and the world; more specifically, the triangular relationship among South and North Korea and the U.S., which is maintained not by an agreement or an institution but by power. The following section examines this triangular relationship, which is the physical basis of Korea's division.

Three Sides: North-South, North-U.S., and South-U.S.

So far, discussions of national division have revolved around a regional perspective of North-South relations. This is the same stance both Seoul and Washington take with regard to four-party talks. Looking back on past experiences, North-South relations were not continuous but rather discrete, though who is ultimately responsible for the division is debatable.

The reason that the relationship between the two Koreas is discrete and devoid of vitality is because of their connection to the U.S.[25] The

---

25. Of course the linkage does not necessarily make the relationship between the two Koreas discrete, but the problem is that the three parties concerned seek fundamentally different things from each other.

following evidence attests to this. The armistice talk went ahead despite the Syngman Rhee regime's strong objection, and the historic Basic Agreement of 1991 and the Joint Declaration of the Denuclearization of the Korean Peninsula of 1992 were achieved less to promote reconciliation between the two Koreas than to fulfill the Bush administration's Northeast Asia agenda.[26] Also, the North-South summit talks were suddenly proposed in 1995 by the U.S. with Jimmy Carter's mediation. Besides, despite the Kim Young-sam administration's protest, the Clinton administration provided $6.2 million of aid in the form of food to the North, and conducted colonel-level talks at Panmunjeom to discuss the submarine infiltration incident in 1996. These are only a few such examples. Viewing the North-South relationship as self-sufficient overlooks its linkage to North Korea-U.S. relations. Unfortunately, this kind of one-sided view persists even to the present day.

The North Korea-U.S. relationship can be characterized as a "state of hostility in truce" that plays out in two ways: "hostile confrontation on the verge of war" and "negotiation for the normalization of relations." The two facets are not separate but interdependent. After the armistice, hostility dominated North Korea-U.S. relations, as revealed in the Pueblo Incident in January 1968, the American plane EC 121 Incident on April 15, 1969, and the poplar tree-cutting incident at the DMZ on August 17, 1976. But the U.S. resorted to talks, rather than hard-line military sanctions, in stark contrast to its policy toward Libya and Iraq.

This "tendency of conversion" is evident in both the Republican Bush administration and the Democratic Clinton administration. Right after the Gulf War, the Bush administration pointed at Kim Il Sung as "the next villain to go after Hussein." However, that same administration decided to pull nuclear weapons out of the Korean peninsula in mid-1991. This led to talks between North Korea and the International Atomic Energy Agency (IAEA) and eventually, to the signing of the Basic Agreement between the South and the North in 1991 and the Joint Declaration of the Denuclearization of the Korean Peninsula in January 1992. The contact between North Korea and the U.S. was upgraded to a higher level, so North Korean official Kim Yong-sun met with Arnold Kanter, the undersecretary of state for political affairs in Washington.

During the early days of the Clinton administration, Clinton endorsed

---

26. Documents recently unsealed by the U.S. Pacific Command Headquarters support this. Refer to *JoongAng Ilbo*, 24 June 1998.

a hard-line policy against North Korea, even preparing a war scenario (OpPlan 50-27-16), to which North Korea responded with a threat to withdraw from the Nuclear Non-Proliferation Treaty (NPT). Then suddenly the U.S. switched to dialogue and signed the Basic Agreement with North Korea in Geneva on October 21, 1994. Article 2 of the Agreement specifies the three-stage process of normalizing U.S.-North Korea relations.

> II. The two sides will move toward full normalization of political and economic relations.
> 1) Within three months of the date of this Document, both sides will reduce barriers to trade and investment, including restrictions on telecommunications services and financial transactions.
> 2) Each side will open a liaison office in the other's capital following resolution of consular and other technical issues through expert level discussions.
> 3) As progress is made on issues of concern to each side, the U.S. and DPRK will upgrade bilateral relations to the ambassadorial level.

Though the diplomatic relationship between the U.S. and North Korea is being delayed for several reasons, the prediction is that they will make progress by 2003, when the light-water reactor construction project will be completed. Under the basic framework, which proposes to transform the present state of the hostile Armistice Agreement into a normal peace agreement, North Korea considers normalization of its relations with the U.S. as a task that should follow the Basic Agreement. Meanwhile, the U.S. is delaying its effort to improve relations with North Korea, and urging the North to put into action the Basic Agreement with the South first.

South-North relations cannot substantially improve, without a progress in North Korea-U.S. relations. Actually, it is highly probable that the latter will improve somehow to make up for the nullified Armistice Agreement and the absence of the truce monitoring system on the peninsula. The 30th Session of the UN General Assembly held on 18 November 1975 adopted the U.S.' and South Korea's Joint Resolution 3390A and North Korea's Resolution 3390B simultaneously. The latter (3390B) called for dissolving the "UN Forces Command" as a measure to achieve a durable peace on the Korean peninsula. The former (3390A) also made a reference saying that it would enter into negotiations for making a new arrangement to replace the armistice agreement and dissolve the "UN Forces Command" if there were an alternative. Talks about measures to stem the absence of a truce monitoring system are nothing new. As the Neutral Nations Supervisory Commission, a truce-monitoring system, has collapsed, the North Korean troops are in direct confrontation with the U.S. troops along the DMZ. Thus, the two parties are compelled to come to the negotiation table.

The presence of U.S. troops in Korea is an important factor in the peace agreement process. As a way to improve its relations with the U.S., North Korea has retracted its call for the withdrawal of U.S. troops from the South; instead, it is demanding that hostility be eliminated by forming "a transitional peace agreement," an important element of which is the legitimization[27] and neutralization of the USFK. According to this, the USFK would remain in Korea until after the unification of the commonwealth by "creating a Democratic Confederation of Goryeo"[28] on the condition that the USFK no longer target North Korea for military aggression and that their status in Korea be similar to that in Germany.

Meanwhile, during the Cold War period after the Korean War, South Korea-U.S. relations formed a special brand of alliance, which worked both as a constraint and an advantage in many aspects. However, after the collapse of the former Soviet Union and East Europe, the nature of the alliance changed drastically. South Korea's political and military importance as a base camp to confront the socialist block has radically decreased. Now the Korean capitalist system will no longer be protected solely for its politico-military value for the U.S., and it will be subject to the general capitalist market principles. The IMF crisis currently sweeping Korea and other Asian nations may be understood in this context.

Nonetheless, with South Korea's large economic scale and its close economic relationship with Japan, a major economic ally of the U.S., its geopolitical importance still remains intact. Here "geopolitical importance" means that the U.S. has many strategic interests in South Korea

---

27. The Resolution 84 (1950) of the UNSC, adopted on 7 July 1950, only recommended that all members providing military forces make such forces available to a "unified command under the USA." Therefore, North Korea does not interpret the UN Command troops in Korea as a UN-affiliated organization, such as the UN peacekeeping forces. North Korea argues that the USFK contingency is illegitimate because it exists in violation of the Armistice Agreement.

28. It provides that the South Korean government and the U.S. Command will decide the size of the U.S. troops to remain in the South.

as it still has unsettled problems with North Korea, and it will need Korea as a buffer state between itself and the newly-emerging China. Thus, it is unlikely that capitalist market relations will thoroughly dominate South Korea. In his first speech as the new U.S. Ambassador to South Korea on January 23, 1998, Stephen W. Bosworth declared three main U.S. interests in Korea: security, economy, and democracy.[29] Security is still above economy, though the gap between them has been much reduced. It is certain that the U.S. will apply market principles and seek economic interests in South Korea, but it still has to consider security first and cannot let the South Korean economy roll into calamity.

Three Angles: South Korea, North Korea, and the United States

In the previous section, I discussed the unbalanced triangular relations among South Korea, North Korea, and the U.S. Here I will briefly mention their three "angles." Generally, a given nation, society, or culture has diverse aspects within it. The United States, the world's foremost superpower, is a symbol of the West, advancement, and imperialism all in one. Koreans have often confused the "advanced" U.S. with imperialism, and have accepted its "Western" or imperialist qualities as advancement. I mention this to point out that both the South and the North must achieve a more accurate understanding of the U.S. and apply a comprehensive and pragmatic approach to dealing with that country.

Here is a case in point. When the economic crisis struck Korea and other Asian nations in 1997, the media in advanced nations reported that Asia was responsible for its own calamity, an assertion that is not entirely supportable. However, the contention that "the Asian model is not backward" seems to be a mere quibble resulting from confusion between the concepts of self-reliance and advancement. I do not intend to engage in a detailed discussion of this topic, but want to note two things: 1) adherence to the Cold War order in the changed environment is backward; and 2) Asia's crisis must be viewed as a global problem because it is a by-product of an inadequate and hasty mixture of backwardness and advancement.[30]

---

29. "Transcript: 1/23, Remark by Amb. Stephen W. Bosworth on U.S.-ROK Relations" (http://nautilus.org/napsnrt/specialreps.html).
30. Doh Jin Soon, op. cit.; Linda Lim, "Asian Values' Idea: Is It Out?," *Straits Times,* 29 March 1998.

We must open up to the world although we should be wary of foreign oppression. It is true that aggression and exploitation are lurking in international relations, but diverse exchanges between nations and peoples contribute to their advancement. Of course, Fascism, Nazism, and military nationalism did emerge in the 1930s and Stalinism after World War II, but these have been, more or less, anomalies.

The role of the U.S. remains a determinant variable for the identities of South and North Korea. North Korea detached from the Soviet Union or China is imaginable, but detachment from the U.S. is unimaginable. In order to understand North Korea, we need to understand its unique characteristic, namely, its truce relations vis-à-vis the U.S., as well as its socialist principles. The North's pursuit of economic policy is different from that of China's, and its adherence to an excessive military policy—as revealed in Kim Jong Il's statement that what he regrets the most is that he proposed to Kim Il Sung to reduce military expenditure[31]—can be attributed to the special circumstances originating in its truce relations vis-à-vis the U.S. The North's stance will not change until its relations with the U.S. moves in a new turn.

While the U.S. is perceived to be a foreign force hostile to North Korea, the U.S. (and its troops) is considered to be an integral benefactor to South Korea. But the U.S. influence on South Korea is often oversimplified. The U.S. is much more than an external variable to South Korea, as witnessed in the replacements of South Korean regimes, the economic development drive launched by Park Chung-hee, and the globalization campaign after the Cold War.

The same logic governing this triangular relationship governs the four-party talks. It would be very superficial if the structure of the four parties were to be viewed as a bipolar opposition with South Korea and the U.S. on one side and North Korea and China on the other. The China and North Korea alliance relationship is pretty accurate. But in the former, the U.S. is more than South Korea's ally; it exercises immense influence on South Korea and in turn, on North Korea as well, due to its truce relationship with North Korea vis-à-vis the United Nations.

We can think of two possibilities with regard to the future of the four-party talks. On the one hand, the four-party talks may be delayed with-

---

31. Kim Myong Chol, op. cit., 1998.

out substantial development or dissolve due to the existing triangular relationship. On the other hand, the four-party talks may embrace the tripartite relationship. It is highly possible that such a convergence would develop in two parallel ways. First, the U.S. and North Korea will negotiate to end the state of war and replace the Armistice Agreement with a (transitional) peace agreement. Along with this, North-South relations will improve, resulting in the enforcement of the Basic Agreement and the conducting of summit talks. Meanwhile, the fourth party, China, will be given the role of an intermediary or a facilitator to improve tripartite relations. It should be noted that the four-party talks or any other multilateral approach to the problem of the peninsula will not succeed if they fail to comprehend the particularity of the triangular relations.

The Future of Division is Unification. Or Is It?

The Korean people whole-heartedly endorse the premise that the future of division is unification. South Koreans talk about two kinds of approaches to reunification. The first one is "reunification through absorption," which is predicated on the collapse of North Korea. This approach gained popularity amid the North's severe food shortage, along with the hard talk that came with the U.S. hard-line policy against the North, and the Kim Young-sam regime's anti-North policy.

However, the empirical basis of this view is too weak. Famine has never been a direct cause of dissolution of a nation in history. Systematic opposition forces are virtually nonexistent in the North, and furthermore, the leader and the masses have a "pseudo-parent-child" relationship within a cooperative society, based upon a synthesis of traditional Confucian culture and socialism. But the weakest point in the "unification through absorption" view is not its understanding of the North, but of the superpowers and South Korea. Looking back on the past experience that the North was put under the jurisdiction of the United Nations during the Korean War, there is no guarantee by the international community that the South will take over the North should it dissolve.

Over time, the U.S. cast doubt on the possibility of a sudden collapse of the North, and with this, the "soft landing theory of North Korea," the second approach, emerged. Joseph S. Nye, who drew up the Nye Initiative for U.S. policy in East Asia, laid out a three-stage process for North Korea's soft landing. According to this, North Korea will first resolve the food shortage problem, then adopt a market economy and finally, undergo a political transformation to a pluralist system.[32] Nye considers the Basic Agreement between the South and the North as the starting point of this transformation process.

In the wake of a series of developments after the launch of the Kim Dae-jung regime, including a renewed emphasis on the Basic Agreement, the so-called "sunshine" policy towards North Korea, the transportation of 500 cattle to the North, and the Geumgangsan tour project, many of us dream that the day of national reunion may arrive soon. Although we must keep our hopes alive, we should understand the reality of the situation more clearly. Here let us examine our historical experiences in similar situations and the policy directives of the surrounding superpowers—especially the U.S.—to figure out what will come following "the Cold War-style hostile division maintained by force."

When the UN forces occupied the North during the Korean War, it was not the South Korean government but the UN that had jurisdiction over the region. This was not by accident, but by predetermined organization. It confirmed once again the UN's "Document on the Approval of the Republic of Korea," which stipulated that the sovereign power of the Republic of Korea is limited within the South Korea region. Besides, it carried an additional important implication that the same rule will be applied if something of a similar nature occurs in the future. On October 31, 1997, the U.S. Naval Research Laboratory conducted a simulation of possible developments in Northeast Asia in preparation for a possible collapse of North Korea, which was attended by former Secretary of Defense, Schlesinger, former U.S. Ambassador to Korea, Laney, former Assistant Secretary of State, Richard Solomon, and others. As revealed in the simulation, the U.S. prefers "democratization of North Korea" over "reunification of the peninsula" and "management through the United Nations" over "sole take-over by South Korea."[33]

Nye once expressed the idea of establishing a very loose confederation between the two Koreas within which the North would slowly be transformed to a pluralist system. "A very loose confederation," which sounds similar to that of the British Commonwealth of Nations, seems to stress

32. *JoongAng Ilbo*, 22 September 1997.
33. David S. Maxwell, "Bukhan-ui pagukjeok bunggoe-wa miguk-ui dae-eung" (The Collapse of North Korea and the U.S. Response), *Gyegan sasang* (fall 1997).

"management of the division" rather than unification per se. Also, such remarks that unification of the Korean peninsula "requires a lot of time and preparation," a phrase often expressed by Americans, emphasizes the necessity of "coexistence in division." The logic behind the U.S. stance that "we support the unification of the Korean peninsula but it requires time and preparation" is quite similar to that of the Allies at the Cairo Conference in 1943 saying "in due course Korea shall become free and independent." It is obvious that the U.S. does not want a forceful and speedy unification of Korea, even if the South leads the process.

Actually, not just the U.S., but other surrounding superpowers such as Japan and China, also prefer management of the division over a speedily unified Korea. After the Cold War, the basic principle of Japan's diplomacy switched from "small Japan," which focused on defending its territory, to "big Japan," which actively sought to make inroads to foreign nations.[34] As shown in the Guidelines for U.S.-Japan Defense Cooperation (Sep. 1997), Japan's defense principle expanded from defense actions in response to an armed attack against Japan to cooperation in situations in areas surrounding Japan that will have an important influence on Japan's peace and security,[35] including the Korean peninsula. In short, Japan's foreign policy aims for "big Japan" to make inroads into nearby nations, exploiting its alliance with the U.S. As for the Korean peninsula, Japan pursues balance in division by maintaining relations with both South and North Korea.

On the other hand, in the National Congress of the Communist Party held on September 1997, China turned away from the Third World line and adopted an "open diplomacy" to the rest of the world as the basic diplomatic principle in the post-Cold War period. China seeks to curb U.S. hegemony in Asia by restoring its relations with Russia on the one hand, and forming a strategic alliance with the U.S. on the other, as demonstrated by mutual visits by Jiang Zemin and Clinton. Aiming to be a hegemonic power in Asia and a leader in the world, China's policy vis-à-vis Korea can be summarized as the three "No"'s (no nuclear weapons on the Korean peninsula, no war in Korea, and no collapse of the North) and three "unwelcome developments" (further alliance

---

34. The turning point was the passage of the Cooperative Measures for UN Peacekeeping Operations in 1992.
35. In response to this, China criticized it as a threat to its territory, while North Korea rebuked it as a scenario of aggression against it.

between South Korea and the U.S., heightened competition between Korea and China, and Korea's reunification and surge of nationalism).

Taking into account concrete developments in the foreign policies of the surrounding superpowers, it is possible that the current "hostile South-North confrontation maintained by force" will be replaced with "peaceful coexistence and exchange with institutional guarantee." In this sense, time is a critical factor in the unification. It will take less time to achieve a unified Korea if we prepare for it with a long-term vision rather than hasten with a shortsighted view.

Depending on the capacity of the Korean people, peaceful coexistence can develop into peaceful unification faster than expected. For this, the South and the North need to recognize the advantages of peace and unification. Moreover, unification of the peninsula must be achieved in a manner that contributes to peace and prosperity in Northeast Asia and the rest of the world.

Government plays a crucial role in this process. How the unification movement conceives the role of the government is important. Considering the complex triangular relations among South Korea, North Korea, and the U.S., it would be difficult to fully utilize the resources of the nations if one of them becomes dominant or excluded in the process. Therefore, it is necessary for each of them to adopt a broad perspective and adjust its role with the others. Also, the unification movement must build a strong foundation at the societal level.

Conclusion

Since South Korea slipped into the foreign exchange crisis at the end of 1997, we always talk about the IMF crisis and hear news reports about what is happening on Wall Street. Swept up in the wave of change called globalization, we live in the "Age of Extremes" in which centrifugal force such as foreign influence is legitimized as advanced and what is national or traditional, based on centripetal force, is regarded as backward.

The Age of Extremes generally begins with a monistic view of the world. The monistic view of the world, remanent from the peninsula's partition after the liberation in 1945, was reinforced during the subsequent Cold War period, and has been reproduced until today. To take some examples,

(1) When Korea was liberated on August 15, 1945, most Koreans

were dreaming of a utopia, believing "everything will be fine once Japan retreats." But what befell on us in reality was a divided occupation by the U.S. and the former Soviet Union, left-right confrontation, and division into two nations. Looking back, what we should have been more watchful of was the question: "What kinds of foreign forces will flood into the peninsula after Japan?"

(2) After the collapse of the former Soviet Union in 1989, scholars were optimistic about the collapse of North Korea and unification of the nation.[36] But Korea still remains divided and furthermore, it is mired in the IMF crisis induced by the vanguard of U.S. financial capital. Since national division is a product of the U.S.-led Cold-War regime, we should have made strenuous efforts to figure out how international order around the peninsula will change in the absence of the Soviet Union and what we should do in preparation for the changing order, but instead we just idled away precious time.

(3) Because national division is grounded on the triangular relations among South Korea, North Korea, and the U.S., we South Koreans must clearly understand the other two nations to grasp the situation we ourselves are placed in. But such incidents as the IMF crisis and the satellite launching by the North only demonstrate the current situation in which we repeatedly fall into an intellectual vacuum or succumb to intellectual panic. What should be the issue in the satellite incident is not whether it is a ballistic missile or an artificial satellite, but that the U.S.-North Korea relations have entered a new era and the confrontation and compromise of the dual facets of peace and war have begun. Although Seoul can resettle the South Korea-U.S. relations reflected in the Memorandom of Understanding between U.S. and South Korea on Missiles, for example, a more fundamental solution to the current situation would be to stabilize the triangular relations to establish a normalized peace regime.

Columbus discovered America by accident in his voyage to the Orient and thus was recorded as a great adventurer in history. On the surface, Columbus's discovery sounds like an event of pure luck, but actually, what made Columbus's achievement possible was his scientific belief that the earth is round and his 'effort and courage to try new sailing techniques and routes.

---

36. Progressive groups, which were looking for a socialist alternative in South Korea, held the same view.

Today no one can give a timetable for the future of the division. However, the reunification of the Korean peninsula cannot arrive suddenly like the bridegroom of midnight, overpassing the preconditions of unification. Some of the external preconditions are 1) to stabilize the triangular relations into normal peaceful relations, 2) to recover the lost identity of being Asian through the reinforcement of solidarity with other Asian nations, and 3) to overcome the monistic view of the world and replace it with a diversified perspective.

Discourse in humanities and social sciences must not delineate on the preconditions of unification as an obligation to overcome national division. Rather, it must entail a self-reflective process overcoming sterile ideas which are divorced from reality and which will prepare us to take steps toward the globalizing era. The twenty-first century of the Korean peninsular begins at this point.

Index–Glossary

Abeno, Uchimaro (J.) 阿部內麻呂, 64

achan (sixth of the 17 official ranks), of Silla 阿湌, 224

administrative units, of Balhae: *bu* 府, 145; *dokjuju* 獨奏州, 145; *gyeong* 京, 145; *ju* 州, 145

administrative units, of Goryeo: *bugok* 部曲, 207; *hyang* 鄉, 207; *so* 所, 207; *gun* (county) 郡, 207; *hyeon* (sub-county) 縣, 207

administrative units, of Joseon: *myeon* 面, 207; *ri* 里, 210-211

Allen, Horace N., 509

allyeomsa (governors) 按廉使, 207

Amaterasu Omikami (J.) (Sun Goddess) 天照大神, 69

Amnokbu, of Balhae 鴨綠府, 144

An, Chang-ho 安昌浩, 465-466, 564

An, Jeong-bok 安鼎福, 143, 153. *See also Dongsa gangmok*

An, Jung-geun 安重根, 494

Anglo-Japanese Alliance 英日同盟 (1902), 490, 538-541, 543, 547

An Lushan (Ch.) Rebellion 安祿山亂, 144

annexation of Korea (1910), 491-494

anti-Japanese movement: by conservatives, 554-562; by Donghak peasant army, 556-556; by righteous armies,

558-559, 561-563; by patriotic enlightenment group, 559-560, 563, 567, 570-571; bases abroad, 565, 566; ideological foundation, 568-570; armed struggle, 571-572

Armistice Agreement. *See* Korean War Armistice Agreement

Baegeo, of Silla 伯魚, 144

Baegoin Sageon (Case of the One Hundred Five) 百五人事件 (1911), 466, 578

Baegyeong, of Silla 白永, 145

Baekchongang (river) 白村江: Silla's defeat at, 65; Japan's defeat at, 67

Baeksan Malgal 白山靺鞨. *See* Malgal

Bak, Eun-sik 朴殷植, 468, 469, 470, 471-472

Bak Geoseogan, king of Silla 朴居西干, 69

Bak, Yeong-hyo 朴泳孝, 481, 487

Balhae (Ch.: Bohai) 渤海: territory of, 133; relations between Balhae and Silla (Unified Silla), 134, 140-145, 147, 150, 152-158; Balhae Malgal, 136; relations between Balhae and Japan, 141, 143-144, 148; war among the Balhae, Silla, and Tang, 142; relations between Balhae and Goryeo, 146-147; culture, 147-151;

Balhae castles, 148; stone burial chambers, 148; Buddha statues, 148; "northern kingdom," 152-155. *See also nambukguk sidae*

Balhaego (On Balhae) 渤海考, 153

Basic Agreement between the North Korea and the U.S. (1994), 655

Basic Agreement between the South and North Korea, 654, 660

Bezobrazov, Alexander M., 517, 518, 519, 520, 542

bingdogo (icehouse) 氷都庫, 316. *See also gyeonggang sangin*

bin-gong gwa (civil service examination for foreigners) 賓貢科, 239

binsa (honorable master) 賓師, 254

bipahyeong donggeom ("violin-shaped bronze dagger") 琵琶形銅劍, 31

boat merchants, 313-314. *See also gyeonggang sangin*

bobusang (pack and back peddlers) 褓負商, 560

Bohai guozhi zhangpian (Ch.) (A Long History of Balhae) 渤海國志長編, 139

"Bohaizhuan" (Ch.) (Tales of Balhae) 渤海傳, 152

boksi (second-stage examination) 覆試, 235, 240-241. *See also hoesi*

bone-rank system. *See golpumje*

Book of Changes. See Yijing

Boxer Rebellion 義和團事件, 490, 517, 533

Boxer Uprising. *See* Boxer Rebellion

boyuron (the position that Catholicism can supplement Confucianism) 補儒論, 378

Bronze Age culture in Korea, 30-34. *See also* burial forms

bu 府. *See* administrative units, of Balhae

bugok 部曲. *See* administrative units, of Silla

bujok (tribe) 部族, 32

Bukjeop (Northern Assembly of Donghak) 北接, 416

Bukpunghoe (Northern Wind Society) 北風會, 598, 599

bumin goso beop (the law for filing grievances against magistrates' misdoings) 部民告訴法, 229

bummei kaika (J.) 文明開化, 481

Bungno Gunjeongseo (Northern Route Military Command) 北路軍政署, 571, 579

burial forms: in the Bronze Age, 31; in the Iron Age, 31

Buyeo, royal family of Baekje 扶餘(氏), 153

Buyeobu, of Balhae 扶餘府, 144

Byeolgigun (Special Skills Force) 別技軍, 479, 480

Byeongjo (Ministry of Military Affairs) 兵曹, 241

Carter, Jimmy, 647, 654

Catholic faith movement, 370-372. *See also* Yi Byeok

Catholic persecution of 1801 辛酉迫害, 373

Chaekseongbu 柵城府, of Balhae, 144. *See also* Donggyeong Yongwonbu

champan (vice-minister) 參判, 294. *See also champansa*

champansa (envoys to the vice-minister) 參判使, 293

chamsanggwan (officials of the third to the sixth grade junior) 參上官, 238

Changan (Ch.), capital of the Sui and the Tang 長安, 148. *See also* Balhae castles

che (sacrificial rites for royal family's ancestors) 禘, 380

cheokhwabi (anti-appeasement stele) 斥和碑, 481

cheoksaron ("rejection heterodoxy")

argument) 斥邪論, 366

Cheomseongdae Observatory 瞻星臺, 68

Cheonjeonggun (present Deogwon) 泉井郡, 142, 144

Cheontae Sect 天台宗, 179

cheosa (hermits) 處士, 246

Childe, V. G., 29

Chiljae (Seven Special Courses at Guk-jagam) 七齋, 232, 240. *See also Guk-jagam*

chiljido (a sword with seven branches) 七支刀, 87-88, 95

Chinese Communist Party, 586-587

Chiryu (J.) 智隆, 69

Choe clan, Goryeo 崔氏, 202. *See also* military regime

Choe, Chi-won 崔致遠, 139, 143, 145, 152

Choe, Eon-wi 崔彥撝, 146, 157

Choe, Han-gi 崔漢綺, 351-358; and optics, 352-353; and *monggi* 蒙氣, 352, 358; and wave motion, 353; and thermometer and hygrometer, 353-354; and view of the universe, 354-357; and rotation of the earth, 355; and *jugiron* 主氣論, 357; and *gihwa* 氣化, 358

Choe, Ik-hyeon 崔益鉉, 452, 554, 561

choja (a method of promotion which allowed one to advance several ranks at a time) 超資, 237

chojik (a method of promotion which allowed one to advance one rank at a time) 初職, 237

chosi (first-stage examination) 初試, 233

Chosun Ilbo 朝鮮日報, 604

Chungmok, king of Goryeo 忠穆王, 201, 212

Chungnyeol, king of Goryeo 忠烈王, 212

Chungseon, king of Goryeo 忠宣王, 201, 212

Chun-gyeongwondang (party) 春景園黨, 611

chwijae (examination for the selection of lower-level officials) 取才, 229

civil examinations. *See mun-gwa*

Clionton, Bill, 646, 647, 654, 661; Clinton adminstration, 647, 654

colonial Korea, 618; colonial industrialization, 621; food provision area, 622; single-crop production, 622; agricultural community, 622-628; landlord class, 623; tenant farmer, 623; right of ownership, 624; land-owner's exploitation, 624; owner-tenant, 624; land tax, 624; tenant right, 624, 627; Japanese landlord, 625; Korean landlord, 625; tenancy dispute, 627-628

comb-pattern pottery 빗살무늬土器, 29-30

Comintern, 582, 588, 589, 628; "December Theses," 628; "September Theses," 628

"communication embassy." *See tong-sinsa*

Confucianism: *gwageo* and Classics of Confucianis, 243, 250. *See also gwageo*

Convention of Tianjin 天津條約, 398, 483

"cultural politics" 文化政治, 574. *See also* colonial Korea

Dae, Bong-ye 大封裔, 145

Dae, Gwang-hyeon 大光顯, 147

Dae, Heum-mu 大欽茂, 135, 143-144, 158

Dae, In-seon 大諲譔, 146, 158

Dae, In-su 大仁秀, 145, 158

Dae, Jo-yeong (Ch.: Dazuoying) 大祚榮, 134-139, 142-144, 157-158; man of the Malgal race, 137; cultural background, 138

Dae, Mu-ye 大武藝, 143, 158

daechan (fifth of the 17 official ranks) of Silla 大飡, 143

Daedong jiji (Geography of Korea) 大同地志, 153

Daedong sugyeong (Rivers in Korea) 大東水經, 285-289; Joseon-centered notion of nature, 282, 287

Daedongbeop (Uniform Land Tax Law) 大同法, 314

daegan (primary mountain range) 大幹, 273

Daegok Castle, of Silla 大谷城, 143

daegwa (main examination) 大科, 232-233, 240-241

Daehan maeil sinbo (Korea Daily News) 大韓每日申報, 448, 469, 500

daenaema (the 10th of the 17 official ranks), of Silla 大奈麻, 224-225, 231

daero (the great authority) 大老, 253

daesa (the 12th of the 17 official ranks), of Silla 大舍, 231

daesaseong (head of Seonggyungwan) 大司成, 251

Daewongun 大院君, 476-477, 480, 481, 484, 485, 486, 487, 506; seclusionist policy, 385, 386, 397, 400, 401-403

Damheon yeon-gi (Beijing Diary of Travel by Damheon) 湛軒燕記, 331-332

danghagwan (officials of the third grade senior or lower ranks) 堂下官, 236-237

Dangun 檀君, 24, 29; Dangun Joseon 檀君朝鮮, 28-31; Dangun myth, 28, 30, 33, 43; "nation-founding," 29-30, 33; bear cult, 30

"Dangun bon-gi" (Chronological Narrative of Dangun) 檀君本紀, 24

Darwin, Charles, 441. *See also* Social Darwinism

Deunggwarok (Records of State Service Examinations) 登科錄, 212

Dohak (Learning of the Way) 道學, 363

dokjuju 獨泰州. *See* administrative units, of Balhae

dokseo sampum gwa ("three-gradation reading examination") 讀書三品科, 222, 224-225, 231, 239

Dongbuk Hangil Yeon-gun (Northeast Anti-Japanese Alliance Army) 東北抗日聯軍, 586-588

dongdanggamsi 東堂監試, 240, 247-250

dongdangsi 東堂試. *See dongdanggamsi*

dongdo seogi (Eastern Way and Western Technology) 東道西器, 361

Dongguk munheon bigo (Reference Compilation of Documents on Korea) 東國文獻備考, 265

Dongguk tonggam (Comprehensive Mirror of the Eastern Kingdom) 東國通鑑, 467

Donggyeong Yongwonbu, of Balhae 東京龍原府, 142, 144

Donggyeongseong, capital of Balhae 東京城, 141, 144

Donghak (Eastern Learning) 東學, 431

Donghak peasant army 東學農民軍. *See* Peasant War of 1894

Donghak Revolution (1894) 東學革命. *See* Donghak revolutionary movement

Donghak revolutionary movement: two main forces, 430, 556-558; process in four stages, 430-431; anti-feudal struggle, 433-434; anti-imperial struggle, 433-434; comparison with French Revolution, 434-445; and bourgeois reform, 435; and medieval *ancien régime*, 435-436

Dongmosan (Ch.: Dongmoushan) 東牟山, 135-136, 138-139

Dongnip Hyeophoe (Independence

Club) 獨立協會, 453, 454, 488, 493, 513, 530, 559-560, 573. *See also* patriotic enlightenment movement

Dongnip sinmun (The Independent) 獨立新聞, 453

Dongnipgun (Independence Army) 獨立軍, 571, 578, 580

dongpo (compatriots) 同胞, 13, 14

Dongsa gangmok (Annotated Account of Korean History) 東史綱目, 79, 143

Dongsa jimnyak (An Outline of Eastern History) 東史輯略, 153

Dongseong, king of Baekje 東成王, 58

doushi (J.) 道師, 68. *See also* eight-surname system

Dunhua (Ch.) 敦化, 144

East Asian international politics: structural features of the world-system at the 19th century, 527-528; Russo-Japanese confrontation over Korea, 529-531; Manchurian crisis and Russo-Japanese antagonism, 534-535; shift in Japan's foreign policy, 536-537; neutralization of Korea, 536, 539, 544-545; Anglo-Japanese Alliance, 538-541, 547; Forward policy of Russia, 542; international recognition of Japan's control of Korea, 544-558

Edo (J.) period 江戸時代, 290, 294

eight-surname system (J. *yatsuseisei*), 68

enlightenment movement 啓蒙運動, 487-490

Eulsa Treaty 乙巳條約 (1905). *See* Protectorate Treaty of 1905

eumseo 蔭敍, 222, 225-226. *See also gwageo*

eun (hermits) 隱, 255

farmers. *See* peasants

Five Dynasties, of China 五代, 146

formation of a (Korean) state, 27-28, 32-35; chiefdom, 33-35; tribal confederation, 32; tribal states, 32

Fukumoto, Kazuo (J) 福本和夫, 596 607

Furuhata, Toru (J.) 古畑徹, 137

Gabo Gaehyeok (Gabo Reform of 1894) 甲午改革, 430, 436, 487

Gabo Gycongjang 甲午更張. *See* Gabo Gaehyeok

Gabo Reform of 1894. *See* Gabo Gaehyeok

Gaegyeong, capital of Goryeo 開京, 209

gaegyeongsi 開京試. *See gaeseongsi*

gaehwa (enlightenment) 開化, 479

Gaehwadang (Progressive Party) 開化黨, 481-482

Gaehwapa (Enlightenment faction) 開化派, 430, 435, 442; and bourgeois reform, 436-445

gaekju (inland market brokers) 客主, 307, 319

gaeseongsi 開城試, 233, 241

gamchangsa (superintendents of granaries) 監倉使, 207

gamjo (rent reduction) 減租, 421

gamju (party leader) 監主, 249

gangsanggok (grain that is dealt by the Hangang river merchants) 江商斛, 319

gangsangmi 江商米. *See gongmi*

Gao, Biaoren (Ch.) 高表仁, 62, 65

Gaoli tujing (Ch.) (Illustrated Account of Goryeo) 高麗圖經, 174. *See also* Xu Jing

Gapsin Jeongbyeon (Coup d'Etat of 1884) 甲申政變, 397, 481-482; fourteen-point reform edict, 482

Gara 加羅, 59. *See also* Gaya

Gaya 伽倻, 71, 80, 85, 153; Dae Gaya 大伽倻, 73, 81, 105, 107; Geumgwan Gaya 金官伽倻, 81, 105

geojasi (Ch.: juzishi) 舉子試 , 240

Geolgeol Jungsang 乞乞仲象, 135, 137, 139

Geolsa Biu 乞四比羽, 137, 139

Geomundo affair 巨門島事件 (1885), 505-506

Geon-guk Dongmaeng (National Foundation League) 建國同盟, 590

geupchan (sixth of the 17 official ranks) 級湌, 144

gigaje (family-based system) 起家制, 224

Gija 箕子: "eastward movement of Gija," 30; Gija Joseon 箕子朝鮮, 29-30, 397

Go 高. *See* surnames of Balhae kings

Gobu uprising, 430. *See also* Peasant War of 1894

Gogeum gun-gukji (Notes on Old and New Countries in the Country) 古今郡國志, 142, 144

Gogi (Old Record) 古記, 34

gogwa beop (rule of performance rating) 考課法, 229

Gojong, king of Joseon 高宗: Ganghwa Treaty, 477; treaty with the United States in 1882, 489; his diplomatic moves for Korea's independence, 499-500; and Möllendorf, 504-505; his anti-Chinese and pro-Russian attitude, 507-508; his flight to the Russian legation, 529; and Ito Hirobumi, 548

golpumje (bone-rank system) 骨品制, 68, 188, 222-224, 226, 231

gongbeop (law of land rents and taxes) 貢法, 202

gonggeoje 貢擧制, 226, 228, 241

gongin (tribute men) 貢人, 307, 314

gongmi (tax rice) 貢米, 314-315

Gongmin, king of Goryeo 恭愍王, 201, 212

Goryeo 高麗: unification of the Later Three Kingdoms, 157-158, 225; slavery system, 185-197; class stratification, 190; landlord-tenant relationship, 206, 216-217; bureaucratic system, 223

Goryeo Gongsandang (Goryeo Communist Party) 高麗共産黨, 579-580

Goryeosa (History of Goryeo) 高麗史, 145, 187-189, 193-196, 211, 240

Goryeosa jeryo (Essentials of Goryeo History) 高麗史節要, 189

gosigwanje (system of selecting candidates by multiple judges) 考試官制, 228, 241

"government-employed painters," 303

Great Depression, 617-619, 637-638; and Japanese colonial policy, 619-622; Korean agricultural crisis, 622-627; Korean socialists' response, 628-631; Korean nationalists' response, 631-634

Griffis, William Eliot, 387-388; *Corea, the Hermit Nation*, 386-393; his view of Japan, 389-393

gujaesaksi 九齋朔試, 241

gukga (state) 國家, 32; *geundae gukga* (modern states) 近代國家, 21; *godae gukga* (ancient states) 古代國家, 21

Gukhak (National Academy), of Goryeo 國學, 232, 239

Gukhak (National Confucian College), of Silla 國學, 66, 224-225, 231, 239

Gukjagam (National University) 國子監, 178, 232-233, 240-241

gukjagamsi 國子監試, 232, 239-241

gun (county) 郡. *See* administrative units, of Goryeo

gunban (soldier order) 軍班, 234

gungmin (nation) 國民, 13, 17-18

Gun-guk Gimucheo (Deliberative Council) 軍國機務處, 486

gun-hyeon system (a system of centrally controlled local administration) 郡縣制, 23, 210, 226

gunjang (chief) 君長, 33

Guomindang (Ch.) 國民黨, 584

gwageo (Ch.: *keju*) (state examination system) 科擧, 212, 237, 247; introduction of China's *keju* system, 221; comparison with *eumseo* system, 222-226; centralized bureaucratic system, 225-226; *gwageo*-first policy, 226; qualifications for, 227, 231-236; relationship between *gwageo* system and school system, 238-243; corruption of the system, 239

gwageo samjeung beop (Ch.: *keju sanzhengfa*) 科擧三證法, 227, 241

gwajeon (rank land) 科田, 228, 230. *See also gwajeonbeop*

gwajeonbeop (Rank Land Law) 科田法, 217

Gwangbokgun (Restoration Army) 光復軍, 571, 585

Gwanggaeto, king of Goguryeo 廣開土大王: tombstone or tomb inscription, 72, 75, 77, 80, 82, 87, 89-91, 95, 112

Gwangju Student Movement 光州學生運動 (1929), 572, 629

gwansi (academy examinations) 館試, 237, 241

gwonnongsa (officer in charge of the encouragement of farming) 勸農使, 207

gyeol (unit of land area) 結, 203-206

gyeolbuje (system of taxation based on measures of yields and arable land) 結負制, 23

gyeong 京. *See* administrative units, of Balhae

gyeonggang busang (wealthy merchants on the Hangang river) 京江富商, 325

gyeonggang gobu (men of great wealth on the Hangang river) 京江巨富, 325

gyeonggang sangin (Hangang river merchants) 京江商人 308; accumulation of capital, 308-312; irregularities in shipping grain, 309-310; System of Oarsmen, 310-311; relation between government, 310-311; commercial activities, 312-316; wholesale trade, 314-317, 323-324; trade by ship, 312; salt trade, 313; wholesale rice trade, 314-315; wholesale trade in firewood, lumber and *bingdogo* (icehouse) 氷都庫, 316; method of possessing ships, 321-322; shipbuilding monopoly, 322-324. *See also* Hangang river boat

Gyeongguk daejeon (National Code) 經國大典, 188, 190, 193, 235

Gyeongheung, monk of Silla 憬興, 69

Gyeongjong, king of Goryeo 景宗, 203

gyeongwi (central government ranks) 京位, 223

gyeore (compatriots) 겨레, 14

gyesugwansi 界首官試, 232, 241

gyo (sacrificial rites for heaven) 郊, 380

gyunjak (equal tenant farming) 均作, 421

gyunjeon (equal possession of land) 均田, 421

gyunjeonsa (land surveyor general) 均田士, 421

Haedong yeoksa (History of Korea) 海東繹史, 79, 180

Haeyurok (Record of a Sea Voyage to Japan) 海遊錄, 292, 297, 301

Haircut Decree 斷髮令 (1895), 558

hakase (J.) (doctor) 博士, 66

Hakuho period (J.) 白鳳期, 69

hallyang (out of government service) 閑良, 207

Han (tribe) 韓, 5, 10-12

handang (*han* party) 漢黨, 251

Hangang river boats: *jinseon* (ferry boats) 津船, 323; *chamseon* (river boats) 站船, 323; *joseon* (coastal ships) 漕船, 323

Hanguk dongnip undong-ji hyeolsa (The Bloody History of the Korean Independence Movement) 韓國獨立運動之血史, 472, 591

Hanguk Dongnipdang (Korean Independence Party) 韓國獨立黨, 583, 585

Hanguk Gwangbok Undong Danche Yeonhaphoe (Union of Korean National Liberation Movement) 韓國光復運動團體聯合會, 584

hanjeon (limitation of land possession) 限田, 421

Hanseong sunbo (Seoul Thrice Monthly) 漢城旬報, 489

hanseongsi (a kind of preliminary examination conducted at the prefecture of Seoul) 漢城試, 237

Heondeok, king of Silla 憲德王, 144

hermit nation: hermit image of Korea, 385; promoted by Japan, 393-400, 407; Japanese writings on Joseon, 396-397

Heuksu Malgal 黑水靺鞨. *See* Malgal

Heungsadan (Young Korean Academy) 興士團, 459, 466

Hideyoshi invasion. *See* Japanese invasion of 1592

Hinayana (Skt.) 小乘佛教, 167

hoedap gyeom swaehwansa (envoys for returning courtesies and promoting the repatriation of kidnapped Korean) 回答兼刷還使, 294

hoeryesa (envoys for returning courtesies) 回禮士, 294. *See also heodap gyeom swae hwansa*

hoesi (second-stage examination) 會試, 241. *See also boksi*

Hong Gyeong-nae Rebellion 洪景來亂, 318

Hong, Dae-yong 洪大容, 338-345; interest in Western science, 339-342; Nongsugak 籠水閣, 340, 341; *Uisan mundap* (Dialogue on Mount Yishan) 醫山問答, 342

Hong, Myeong-hui 洪命熹, 603-605

Hongmungwan (Office of the Special Advisors) 弘文館, 249

Honil gangni yeokdae gukto jido (Unified Territorial and Chronological Map of National Lands) 混一疆理歷代國土地圖, 262

Honil yeokdae gukto gangni jido (Unified Chronological and Territorial Map of National Lands) 混一歷代國土疆理地圖, 263

hu, title of king 侯, 34. *See also wang*

Huang, Zunxian (Ch.) 黃遵憲, 555

Hwangguk Hyeophoe (Impcrial Association) 皇國協會, 560

Hwangseong sinmun (Imperial Capital News) 皇城新聞, 445, 469

hwarang ("flower boys") 花郎: in *Samguk sagi*, 120-124; its functions and ethics, 124-132

Hwayohoe 火曜會 (Tuesday Society), 581, 599

hyang 鄉. *See* administrative units

hyangdo (bier bearers) 香徒, 209-210

hyanggeoriseon (Ch.: *xiangju lixuan*) 鄉擧里選, 222

hyangni (clerks in local authorities) 鄉吏, 208

hyangsi (local examinations) 鄉試, 237, 241-242

hyangyak (village code) 鄉約, 229

hyeon (subcounty) 縣. *See* administrative units, of Goryeo

hyo (J.) 評, administrative or military unit of Japan, 66. *See also pyeong*

ibeolchan (the highest of the 17 official

ranks), of Silla 伊伐湌, 224

Ikeuchi, Hiroshi (J.) 池內宏, 136, 140

ikusanokimi (J.) 行軍元帥, 100

ilgilchan (7th of the 17 official ranks), of Silla 一吉湌, 144

Iljinhoe (Advancement Society) 一進會, 492

Imna 任那. *See* Mimana

Imo Gullan (Military Munity of 1882) 壬午軍亂, 395, 396, 398, 410, 480, 554

Independence Army. *See* Donggnipgun

Independence Club. *See* Dongnip Hyeophoe

indu (human smallpox) 人痘, 349

Inoue, Kaoru (J.) 井上馨, 450, 486

Iron Age in Korea, 31. *See also* burial forms

Irwolhoe (January Society) 一月會, 599, 608, 609

isagwan (Japanese Residence Executive Director) 理事官, 406

Ito, Hirobumi (J.) 伊藤博文, 483, 485, 491, 492, 494

iyonggam (official of utility and utilization) 利用監, 350

jachiron ("limited autonomy doctrine") 自治論, 599, 603

jagang (self-strengthening) 自强, 487

janban (ruined yangban) 殘班, 416

Jang 張. *See* surnames of Balhae kings

Jang, Ji-yeon 張志淵, 454

jangmokjeon (government-licensed lumber dealers) 長木廛, 316

Jangnyeongbu, of Balhae 長嶺府, 144

Japanese Government-General of Korea 朝鮮總督府, 618, 619-622, 634-637; agricultural policy, 632

Japanese invasion of 1592 壬辰倭亂, 290-292, 301, 302, 394, 398

Japanese-Russian relations: Lobanov-Yamagata Protocol, 494, 511, 512, 513; Komura-Waeber Agreement, 510, 513; Nishi-Rosen Convention, 496, 524, 529, 530; anti-Japanese sentiment, 529; Russia's concession to Japan, 529-530; Manchurian problems, 520-521, 530-535; anti-Russian sentiment, 534

japgwa (miscellaneous examinations) 雜科, 225, 234-236, 241, 243

Jegwan, monk of Goryeo 諦觀, 175

jeju (official post in Seonggyungwan) 祭酒, 252

jeokgi (accumulated air) 積氣, 347

jeokseokchong (stone mound tombs) 積石塚, 11

jeokseok mokgwakbun (stone mound tombs with wooden chambers) 積石木槨墳, 11

Jeon, Bong-jun 全琫準, 430-431, 486, 557. *See also* Peasant War of 1894

Jeonbeopsa (Office of Legal Administration) 典法司, 205

Jeong Yak-yong 丁若鏞, 277-283; his criticism on the state examination system, 247; and *sallim*, 254; and five elements, 346-347, 376-377; and optics, 347-348; and rotation of the earth, 348-349; and vaccination, 349-350; and *Magwa hoetong* (Comprehensive Treaties on Smallpox) 麻科會通, 349; and technology, 350-351; intellectual environment, 364-366; and introduction of Catholicism, 366-370; contact with Catholic doctrine, 370-371; Catholic persecution of 1801, 373; banishment in Gangjin, 374; literary writings, 374; religious books, 375; interpretation of the Neo-Confucian concepts, 376-381; rejection of the *yin* and *yang*, 376; rejection of the five elements, 376-377; concept of *cheon* (heaven),

377; interpretation of the *Doctrine of the Mean*, 378-379; science of divination, 380

Jeongchi Dogam (Office of Maladministration Reform) 整治都監, 201

Jeonghye, princess of Balhae 貞惠: tomb of, 135, 138-139, 151, 157

Jeonghyo, princess of Balhae 貞孝: tombstone of, 139, 151

jeongjeon (land allocated to male adults) 井田, 203, 421

Jeonguhoe (Righteous Fraternity Society) 正友會: Jeonguhoe Declaration, 596, 599, 605-606, 607

Jeonjinhoe (Advance Society) 前進會, 607; Review of Jeonjinhoe, 613-614; "two-party theory," 606, 608, 609-610

Jeonjo (Office of Personnel Administration) 銓曹, 249

jeonsi ("palace examination") 殿試, 241

jeopju (head of a local unit of Donghak) 接主, 416

jesureop (composition examination course) 製述業, 233

Jewang un-gi (Songs of Em-perors and Kings) 帝王韻紀, 135

Jibong yuseol (Topical Discourses of Jibong) 芝峰類說, 329

jin-gol (true-bone) 眞骨, 68, 223, 225. *See also golpumje*

Jinju Uprising 晋州民亂, 318

Jinmyeong hwiron (A Note on Progress) 進明彙論, 451

Jinpyeong, king of Silla 眞平王, 67

jinsa (literary licentiate) 進士, 235, 237, 241, 243

Jipgangso (Local Directorates) 執綱所, 418, 431, 432, 433, 434, 436; reforms implemented by, 433

jiseongmyo (dolmen tombs) 支石墓, 31. *See* burial forms

Jito (J.), emperor of Japan 持統天皇, 68

jiupin guanrenfa (Ch.) 九品官人法. *See* Nine Rank System

Jiutangshu (Ch.) (Old Book of Tang) 舊唐書, 135-136, 138

Jo, Jun 趙浚, 204-205

Joint Declaration of the Denuclearization of the Korean Peninsular (1992), 654

jokjeong 足丁, 205

Josa Sichaldan (Courtiers' Observation Mission) 朝士視察團, 479

Joseon Communist Party. *See* Joseon Gongsandang

Joseon Dongnip Dongmaeng (Korean Independence Alliance) 朝鮮獨立同盟, 587

Joseon Gongsandang (Joseon Communist Party) 朝鮮共産黨, 580-581, 596; "December Theses," 586; "one country, one party," 586; JCP reconstruction movement, 588-589, 599, 600-601, 609, 610, 613-614

Joseon Hyeongmyeongdang (Korean Revolutionary Party) 朝鮮革命黨, 583, 584

Joseon jeonsa (A Complete History of Korea) 朝鮮全史, 156

Joseon Minheunghoe (Korea People's Prosperity Society) 朝鮮民興會, 600-603

Joseon Minjok Hyeongmyeongdang (Korean National Revolutionary Party) 朝鮮民族革命黨, 583, 584

Joseon Minjok Jeonseon Yeonmaeng (Korean National Front Alliance) 朝鮮民族戰線聯盟, 584, 585

Joseon Nongminsa (Korean Farmers Group) 朝鮮農民社, 634

Joseon Sahoe Danche Jungang Hyeobuihoe (Korean Social Organizations Central Council) 朝鮮社會團體

中央協議會, 609-610

Joseon tongsa (A General History of Korea) 朝鮮通史, 5, 158

Joseon Uiyongdae (Korean Righteous Volunteers Corps) 朝鮮義勇隊, 584, 585

Joseon-ji gwang (The Light of Korea) 朝鮮之光, 608

josi (officials serving at the court and city offices) 朝市, 246

ju 州. *See* administrative units, of Balhae

Jun, king of Yemaek Joseon 準王, 34

jungin (middle people) 中人, 228, 243

jungsi (a special examination to encourage those who passed the state examination) 重試, 237

Jungyong gangui (Discourse on the Doctrine of the Mean) 中庸講義, 376. *See also* Jeong Yak-yong

Jurchens 女眞, 136

jwaju munsaeng je (system of the leader questioning the students) 座主門生制, 226, 228

Kanchi (J.) 觀智, 69

Kang, Hang 姜沆, 301

Karu Ouji (J.), prince of Japan 輕皇子 (Emperor Kotoku 孝德天皇), 63

Katsura-Taft Agreement (1905), 490, 547

Keinichi (J.) 惠日, 62

Keiun (J.) 惠雲, 67

keju (Ch.). *See gwageo*

Khitan (or Khitanese) 契丹, 141-142, 144, 146

Kim, Bu-sik 金富軾, 141, 154

Kim, Chun-chu 金春秋, 64-65, 67

Kim, Dong-eom 金東嚴, 68

Kim, Heon-chang 金憲昌, 145

Kim, Hong-jip 金弘集, 479, 480, 482, 485, 488, 493; Kim Hong-jip cabinet, 487

Kim, Ok-gyun 金玉均, 481, 484

Kim, royal family of Silla 金, 153

Kim, Yun-jung 金允中, 143

Kim, Yun-mun 金允文, 143

Kim, Yu-sin 金庚信, 65, 67, 121-122, 143

Komura, Jutaro (J.) 小村壽太郎, 510, 536, 543

Komura-Waeber Agreement, 510, 513

Korea's effort to open, 409-410

Korean culture: its origin, 27; prehistoric culture, 28

Korean envoys to Japan, 294-301; ties with Japanese Confucian scholar, 301; exchange of medical science, 302; activity of "government employed painters," 303; economic exchange, 304-305

Korean nationalist movement: "compromise" nationalist camp, 597, 598; "intransigent" nationalist camp, 598; improvement and enlightenment of rural community, 632-633

Korean Provisional Government (KPG), 572, 579-580, 583, 584, 593; republicanism, 578-579; in Shanghai, 583

Korean socialist movement, 628-629; revolutionary peasant unions, 630-631

Korean unification, 659-662

Korean War Armistice Agreement (1953), 643-644; Neutral Nations Supervisory Commission, 656

Korean-Japanese economic exchange: Japanese office in Busan, 304; private trade with Japan, 305; entry and transplantation of potatoes, 305

Korean-Japanese relations (17th-19th centuries). *See* Korean envoys to Japan

Korean-Japanese relations (ancient): Baekje-Japan relations, 57-63; Silla-Japan relations, 58, 63-69; Japan's introduction of Baekje Buddhism, 61; cooperative relations among Silla, Japan, and Tang China, 63-69; Japan's introduction of Silla Buddhism, 64, 67; Japan's introduction of Silla's educational system, 66-67

Korean-Russian relations: flight of the King Gojong to the Russian legation, 488, 508-509; Russia's initial involvement in Korea (1885–1887), 503-508; rise of Russian influence (1895–1897), 508-513; Li-Lobanov treaty, 511; Min-Lobanov agreement, 511; eclipse of Russian influence, 513-518; end of Russian intervention, 518-521; Manchurian issue, 520-521

Kwak, Won 郭元, 163

landlord-tenant relationship, of Joseon, 206, 216

Later Baekje 後百濟, 146

Later Liang (Ch.) 後梁, 146

Later Silla 後新羅, 157

Later Three Kingdoms 後三國, 145-147, 157

Li, Hongzhang 李鴻章, 479, 483, 503, 506, 507

Liang, Qichao (Ch.) 梁啓超: his writings translated in Korea, 445-449; his theory of the "new people," 460-461

lianhua (Ch.) (lotus flower pattern) 蓮華, 148

Liaoshi (Ch.) (History of Liao) 遼史, 145-146

Lixiang kaocheng houbian (Ch.), 355

Lord of Heaven 天主, 368, 378, 380

luyou (Ch.) (green glaze) 祿釉, 148

Maek (tribe) 貊. *See* Yemaek

Mahayana (Skt.) 大乘佛教, 167

main examinations. *See daegwa*

maje seokgeom ("polished stone dagger") 磨製石劍, 31

Malgal (Ch.: Mohe) 靺鞨, 134-139, 147-149, 152, 158: people, 134, 137-138; culture, 151; Baeksan Malgal 白山靺鞨, 136; Heuksu Malgal 黑水靺鞨, 143; Songmal Malgal 粟末靺鞨, 136, 148

Manbugyo Incident 萬夫橋 事件 (942), 147

Manjeok 만적, 194

ManKan Fukan (J.) 滿韓不換, 536, 537, 544

ManKan Kokan (J.) 滿韓交換, 530, 535, 536

Manmin Gongdonghoe (Convocation of Ten Thousand People) 萬民共同會, 560

March First Independence Movement 三一獨立運動, 554, 567-568, 570, 573-574, 605

Matsui, Hitoshi (J.) 松井均, 137

Meiji Restoration 明治維新 (1868), 290, 293, 306, 395, 400, 403, 404, 408, 475, 476

Meiso (J.) 明總, 69

Middle Kingdom, 169

military coup d'état (1170), of Goryeo, 200-202

military examinations. *See mugwa*

military regime, of Goryeo, 200-202

Military Revolt of 1882. *See* Imo Gullan

Mimana (J.) 任那, 59, 71, 397; in Japanese document, 72-74, 81-87; falsifications in the *Nihon shoki*, 95; Japanese domination of Mimana, 95-99; *mikotomoji*, 99-101

Min (Ch.), monk 旻, 62-64, 67

Minabuchi, Shoan (J.) 南淵請安, 63-64

mingdaoqian (Ch.) ("knife-shaped coin") 明刀錢, 31

mingjing (Ch.) (study of Confucian classics), of Tang dynasty 明經, 66

minjok 民族: and blood community, 4-9; formative period of the Korean *minjok*, 5-6; and cultural community, 9-12; ethnicity, 10-12, 17, 19-20; and nation, 16-22; ethnic group (*jok*) 族, 15-17; ethnies, 15; *injong* (races) 人種, 17; physical features of the Korean *minjok*, 7-9; and political and economic community, 12-16

"Minjokjeok gyeongnyun" (National Steering) 民族經綸, 598, 603

minjung (common people) 民衆, 424; emergence of *minjung's* power, 424

miscellaneous examinations. See *japgwa*

Möllendorff, Paul G. von, 480, 503, 504, 505

Mononobe Makibumuraji (J.) 物部麻奇武連, 57

muban (military officer order) 武班, 234

mugwa (military examinations) 武科, 229, 234-245

Mulsan Jangnyeo Undong (Campaign for the Encouragement of Native Products) 物産奬勵運動, 596

Mulsan Jangnyeohoe (Society for the Encouragement of Native Product) 物産奬勵會, 571

munban (civil official order) 文班, 233

mun-gwa (civil examinations) 文科, 225, 229, 233, 235, 237, 241, 243-244

Munjong, king of Goryeo 文宗, 214,

Munmu, king of Silla 文武王, 65, 68

Mun, king of Balhae 文王, 135

Munyeong, king of Baekje 武寧王, 58

Mu, king of Balhae 武王, 142

myeon 面. See administrative units, of Joseon

myeonggyeongeop (classics examinations course) 明經業, 233

myoje (shrine system for Confucius) 墓祭, 380

naema (the 11th of the 17 official ranks), of Silla 奈麻, 224

Naesa Munhaseong (Supreme Council) 內史門下省, 233

Naka no Oe (J.), prince of Japan 中大兄皇子 (Emperor Tenji 天智天皇), 63-65, 67

Nakatomi, Kamatari (J.) 中臣鎌足, 63-65, 67

Nakatomi, Murajikuni (J.) 中臣連國, 62

namban (court functionary order) 南班, 241

nambukguk sidae (Period of Southern and Northern Kingdoms) 南北國時代, 134, 152-158

Namgyeong Namhaebu, of Balhae 南京南海府, 152

Namhaebu 南海府. See Namgyeong Namhaebu

Namin (Southerners) 南人: Byeokpa (Party of Principle)辟派, 372; Sipa (Party of Expediency) 時派, 373

Namjeop (Southern Assembly of Donghak) 南接, 416

namseongsi 南省試, 240. See also *seonggyungwansi*

nanjeonin (owners of unlicensed shops) 亂廛人, 307

national division: division system 分斷體制, 643-644; compared to other historical divisions, 648-653; triangular relation, 653-659; peace agreement 平和協定, 645, 655, 656, 659

national liberation movement: socialist movement, 580; revolutionary labor and peasant union movement, 589, 590; revolutionary national movement, 600; peasant movement, 618

national united front movemen, 596, 598, 599, 628; the first half of the

1920s, 578-580; and Joseon Communist Party, 580-581; the second half of the 1920s, 580-582; Singanhoe, 581-582, 608; in China during the 1930s, 582-585; in Manchuria during the 1930s, 585-588; in Korea during the 1930s, 588-591

nationalism (Korean): nationalist historians, 467-472, 553-554, 573-574. *See also* anti-Japanese movement and Korean nationalist movement

nation-state, 4, 12-13, 15, 17-21

Neo-Confucianism: and agriculture, 217; Confucian "people-first" principle, 217

Neolithic Age in Korea, 29-30

newly rising scholar-officials, 199-201, 211-212, 216-217, 227

Niha river (present Yongheunggang river) 泥河, 140

Nihon shoki (J.) (Chronicles of Japan) 日本書紀, 58-59, 69-70, 71, 79, 80, 81, 88, 95; falsfication of Japanese history, 84-86, 95; Japanese domination of Mimana, 95-99; *mikotomoji*, 73, 99-101; regions to conceded to Baekje by Wai King, 101-105; Japanese governor of Mimana, 107-110; Wai military expedition, 111-113

Nine Rank System (Ch.: *jiupin guanrenfa*), 224

Nogajae yeonhaeng ilgi (Beijing Travelogue by Nogajae) 老稼齋燕行日記, 330

nongjang (manors) 農莊, 200

Nongsa jikseol (Straight Talk on Farming) 農事直說, 202, 204, 208-209

Nongsang jiyao (Ch.) (A Synopsis of Agriculture and Sericulture) 農桑輯要, 216-217

O 烏. *See* surnames of Balhae kings

Oberdorfer, Don, 646

Odong Castle, of Balhae 敖東山城, 135

odupum (head-rank five) 五頭品, 224, 231

oewi (provincial government ranks) 外位, 223

Office of Maladministration Reform. *See* Jeongchi Dogam

Ogwangchan, a son of Osodo 烏光贊, 146

ogyeong baksa (The Learned of the Five Confucian Classics) 五經博士, 57

Okjeo 沃沮, 143

Old Joseon 古朝鮮, 28, 30, 35

onggwanmyo (jar burials) 甕棺墓, 11

Open Door Policy, of the U.S. in China, 532-533, 537, 538, 541, 549

opening of Korea, 476-478

Oriental Development Company 東洋拓植株式會社, 491

Oruha, northeast of Baekdusan Mountain 奧婁河, 136

Osodo 烏炤度, 145-146

Paleolithic Age in Korea, 28

Palgwanhoe (Festival of the Eight Vows) 八關會, 181, 209

Pandosa (Office of Census Registration) 版圖司, 205

patriotic enlightenment movement 愛國啓蒙運動, 439, 563, 570; organizations, 459, 500-501; nationalist education, 563-565, 578; ideological foundation, 563-567; *See also* anti-Japanese movement

Peasant War of 1894 甲午農民戰爭, 413-414, 556-558; present state of research, 414-417; socioeconomic background, 417-424, 556; demands of the peasant army, 418, 420; anti-feudal character, 421-422; growth of reform force, 424-426; failure of the feudal system, 419-422; encroachment of imperialism, 422-424; Northern and Southern forces, 557 peasants: social status in the 19th century, 434-435

Period of Southern and Northern Kingdoms. *See nambukguk sidae*

popyeom beop (a method deciding promotion or demotion based on evaluation of an official's service) 褒貶法, 229

Portsmouth Peace Treaty, 547

preliminary examinations. *See sogwa* 小科

Progressives. *See* Gaehwadang

Protectorate Treaty of 1905, 546, 549, 563.

pungsu (traditional geomancy) 風水, 259, 260, 262, 283

pyeong, administrative or military unit of Silla and Goryeo 評: *naepyeong* 內評, 66; *oepyeong* 外評, 66; *takpyeong* 啄評, 66

Qingyibao (Ch.) 清議報, 445, 446

Queen Min, 432, 435, 480, 485, 487; murder of Queen Min, 397, 495, 508, 529, 558

Rank Land Law. *See gwajeonbeop* 科田法

Restoration Army. *See* Gwangbokgun

reunification. *See* Korean unification

Rhee, Syngman (Yi Seung-man) 李承晚, 488, 492, 500

ri 里. *See* administrative units

rice riot in 1883, 318-320. *See also gyeonggang sangin*

righteous armies. *See uibyeong*

rock art in Korea: grouping according to the motifs, 39; geographical distribution, 40-41; "x-ray style," 41-43, 52-53; "silhouette style," 43-44, 48, 52-53; techniques employed in rock art, 44-45

Ruishu kokushi (J.) (A Collection of Anecdotes in National History) 類聚國史, 137, 140

Rural Development Movement, 636

Russo-Japanese War of 1904 露日戰爭, 454, 489-490, 521, 526, 534, 544, 549

sa (a man devoted to learning and self-cultivation) 士, 255

sa (sacrificial rites for the state) 社, 380

sa jeong (four affections) 四情, 353

"Sabulheo bukguk geosangpyo" 謝不許北國居上表, 143

sadae (serving the great) 事大, 174, 396

sadae gyorin ("serving the great and maintaining amicable ties with neighboring states") 事大交隣, 651

sadaebu (scholar-officials) 士大夫, 211, 246

sadang (blood pledge party) 私黨, 256

sadupum (head-rank four) 四頭品, 224

saengjon gyeongjaeng ("struggle for existence") 生存競爭, 441

saengwon (classics licentiate) 生員, 235, 237, 241, 243

saengwonsi 生員試, 240

sa-eop (important position at Seonggyungwan) 司業, 250-251

Saganwon (Office of the Censor-General) 司諫院, 249, 253

Saheonbu (Office of the Inspector-General) 司憲府, 250

sallim (hermits): meaning, 246-248; political importance, 248-249; and new government system, 250-252; as a political faction, 251; change of role, 252-256

sallim hakja (scholars in hermitage) 山林學者, 248

sallim yangdeok jisa (gentlemen accumulating virtues in the mountains and forests) 山林養德之士, 248

Samguk sagi (Historical Records of the Three Kingdoms) 三國史記, 27, 58,

141-142, 144-145, 147, 152, 154

Samguk yusa (Memorabilia of the Three Kingdoms) 三國遺事, 28, 135, 142

sandang (mountain party) 山黨, 251

sangdukkun 상두꾼, 209

Sanggyeong Yongcheonbu, of Balhae 上京龍泉府, 144

sangje (Ultimate Being) 上帝, 378

Sanguozhi (Ch.) (The History of the Three Kingdoms) 三國志, 33

San-gyeongpyo (A Chart of Mountain Ranges) 山經表, 271-277, 286, 287

sanin (mountain people) 山人, 250

Sansugo (A Landscape Study) 山水考, 268-271, 276, 287

saok (Catholic persecution) 邪獄, 366

Sarimwon (Secretariat of Letters) 詞林院, 201

Secretariat of Letters. *See* Sarimwon

Security Maintenance Law, 599, 634

sehyeong donggeom ("slender Korean-style bronze dagger") 細形銅劍, 31

Seikanron (J.) (Conquest of Korea) 征韓論, 395-400, 404-405, 477, 534

Seja Sigangwon (institute for the education of the crown prince) 世子侍講院, 250

Sejong, king of Joseon 世宗, 203, 214-215, 217

Seo, Gwang-beom 徐光範, 481, 494

Seo, Jae-pil (Philip Jaisohn) 徐載弼, 453, 488, 560. *See also* Dongnip Hyeophoe

Seobuk Hakhoe (Northwestern Academic Association), 459, 563

Seogyeong, capital of Goryeo 西京, 209

seok 石, 204-205

seokgwanmyo (stone-cist tombs) 石棺墓, 31, 33-34

seoksil bongtobun (stone chambers covered with an earthern mound) 石室封土墳, 11

seonbi 선비, 247

Seondeok, queen of Silla 善德女王, 68

Seongdeok, king of Silla 聖德王, 163

seongeup gukga (walled-town state) 城邑國家, 33

seonggol (holy-bone) 聖骨, 68. *See also golpumje*

Seonggyungwan (National Confucian Academy) 成均館, 237, 241, 249, 250, 251,

seonggyungwansi 成均館試, 240. *See also namseongsi*

Seonghan 星漢, 69

Seongho school 星湖學派, 368-369; Gongseopa (Anti-Western Faction) 攻西派, 368; Sinseopa (Pro-Western Faction) 信西派, 368

Seoro Gunjeongseo (Western Route Military Command) 西路軍政署, 571, 579

Seou Hakhoe (Western Friends Academic Association) 西友學會, 440, 468

Seoul Cheongnyeonghoe (Seoul Youth Society) 서울靑年會, 597

Seoyu gyeonmun (Observations on a Journey to the West) 西遊見聞, 443. *See also* Yu Gil-jun

Service, E. R., 33

"serving the great." *See sadae*

seungbosi (promotion examination) 升補試, 232, 240

Seven Books of Martial Arts, 235

Seven Special Courses. *See* Chiljae

Shimonoseki Treaty. *See* Treaty of Shimonoseki

shinjin (J.) 眞人, 68. *See also* eight-surname system

Shiratori, Kurakichi (J.) 白鳥庫吉, 137

Shiwubao (Ch.) (China Progress) 時務報, 446, 447

Shixian (Ch.) calendar 時憲曆, 335

Shotoku (J.), prince of Japan 聖德太子,

62

Siheonnyeok. See Shixian calendar

sihyang (seasonal ancestral rites) 時享, 380

siin (markerteers) 市人, 307

Silhak (Practical Learning) 實學, 365

Silla 新羅: unification of the Three Kingdoms, 134, 142, 156

Silla gogi (Old Notes on Silla) 新羅古記, 135, 138-139, 157

"Silla Road," 147

Sin, Chae-ho 申采浩, 466-468, 471, 472

Sin, Don 辛旽, 187, 196

Sin, Gyeong-jun 申景濬, 265, 267, 268, 269, 270, 271, 274, 276, 286, 287

Singanhoe 新幹會: emergence, 581-582, 593, 603-604; dissolution, 582; national cooperative front movement, 595-600; Fukumotoism, 606; Yamakawaism, 606; organizational change, 612-614; formation of chapers, 612; organizational weakness, 613; and Cominterin, 613, 629

single national party movement 民族唯一黨運動, 581, 582, 593, 600

Sinhae Tonggong (Commercialization Equalization Enactment of 1791) 辛亥通共, 313

sinheung sadaebu 新興士大夫. *See* newly rising scholar-officials

Sinminhoe (New People's Association) 新民會, 465-466, 501, 564, 567, 578

Sinmun, king of Silla 神文王, 158

Sino-Japanese War (1894) 清日戰爭, 431, 484-487, 526, 529, 534, 535, 549

Sino-Korean relation, 177-182; "Sinic Zone," 161; tributary system, 162; "country of gentlemen," 163, 169

slavery system (in Goryeo): definition of a slave, 190; sources and conditions of slaves, 191-192; comparison with other countries, 192-193; biographies of base office holders, 195-196

so 所. *See* administrative units, of Goryeo

Social Darwinism 社會進化論: Theory of Evolution 進化論, 441-443; *The Origin of Species* 種의 起源 by Charles Darwin, 441, 453; acceptance of Darwinism in Korea, 441-452; influence of Liang Qichao's writings on Darwinism, 445-451; Korean writings on Darwinism, 449-452; exaltation of political consciousness, 452-460; appearance of political organizations, 457-460; advocacy of the ideology of "new people," 460-466; nationalistic view of history, 466-472

Soga clan (J.) 蘇我氏, 60, 62-63. *See also* Yamato government

Soganokura (J.) 蘇我倉, 63

sogwa (preliminary examinations) 小科, 235, 237, 239, 241, 243

Solbin, of Balhae 率濱, 143

Soldiers' Riot. *See* Imo Gullan

Son, Byeong-hui 孫秉熙, 557

Song, Si-yeol 宋時烈, 249, 250, 251, 252, 253, 254

Songmal Malgal 粟末靺鞨. *See* Malgal

Songmalsu, present Songhwagang river 粟末水, 138

Songmojiwen (Ch.) (Observations by Songmo) 松漠紀聞, 139-140

songsang (merchant of Gaeseong) 松商, 307

Sosen Meimei (J.) (Silla god) 素戔嗚命, 58, 69; and Izumo Kami, 58, 69

soshi (J.) 刺使, 490

Southern Dynasties, China 南朝, 60-61

Speyer, Alexis, 514-515

state conscription system, of Joseon, 206

Sungjeong, Silla period 崇正, 144

sunja beop (method of deciding promotion or demotion based on length of service) 循資法, 229

surnames of Balhae kings, 139; Dae 大, 139, 153; Du 竇, 139; Go 高, 139, 153; Jang 張, 139; O 烏, 139; Yang 揚, 139; Yi 李, 139

susinsa (trust cultivating embassy) 修信使, 479

swaeguk (seclusionist policy) 鎖國, 401, 402. *See also* Daewongun

Taebong 泰封, 146

Taehakgam (National Confucian University), of Silla 太學監, 224n6

Taejo, king of Goryeo 太祖, 211

Taengniji (Ecological Guide to Korea) 擇里志, 265, 286

Taigaku (J.), Japanese college 太學, 66

Taiho (J.), Japanese era 大寶, 70

Taika Reforms (J.) 大化改新, 59, 63-64, 66, 75, 99, 112

Takamuko, Kuromaro (J.) 故向玄理, 63-65, 67

Tanaka, Tomi (J.) 田中臣, 62

Tantian (Ch.) (Outlines of Astronomy), 360

Ten Admonition 訓要十條. *See* Wang Geon

Tenmu (J.), emperor of Japan 天武天皇, 65, 68, 69

Tenpyo (J.), Japanese era 天平, 69

Theory of Evolution 進化論. *See* Social Darwinism

Three Han 三韓, 28, 30, 32-33

"three-gradation reading examination." *See dokseo sampumgwa*

Tianyanlun (Ch.) (On Evolution) 天然論, 444-445, 448, 452

Tianzhu shiyi (True Principles of Catholicism) 天主實義, 366, 368, 370, 377

togwangmyo (earthern tombs) 土壙墓, 31, 33, 35. *See* burial forms

Tokugawa, Iyeyasu (J.) 德川家康, 292-293; Tokugawa shogunate, 290, 295, 297, 298

tongdeok rang (an honorific phrase for officials of fifth grade senior) 通德郎, 237

Tongni Gimu Amun (Office for Extraordinary State Affairs) 統理機務衙門, 479

tongsinsa (ambassadors to Japan) 通信使, 294, 485. *See also* Korean envoys to Japan

Toriyama, Kiichi (J.) 島山喜一, 136, 141-142

"traditional geography," 259-260, 286-287; Silhak geography, 260, 283; Baekdu Daegan (primary mountain range of Baekdu) 白頭大幹, 273; *jeonggan* (major mountain range) 正幹, 273; *jeongmaek* (secondary mountain ranges) 正脈, 273; classification system for nature, 276; Japanese classification system of mountain, 285-286; humanistic physical geography, 286. *See also* traditional view of nature

traditional view of nature (during the Joseon dynasty): overview, 261-266; mountain-based perception, 271-277; river-based perception, 277-283; its discontinuation, 283-287

Treaty of Ganghwa 江華島條約 (1876), 477-478

Treaty of Hanseong 漢城條約 (1885), 482

Treaty of Jemulpo 濟物浦條約 (1882), 480, 502

Treaty of Shimonoseki 下關條約 (1895), 495, 508

Treaty of the Year Giyu, 302

Triple Intervention 三國干涉 (1895),

487, 508, 522, 526

Tsuda, Sokichi (J.) 津田左右吉, 136

Twelve Private Schools, 228, 239-240

U.S. Forces in Korean (USFK), 646, 656; Second Korean War Plan, 646-648

uibyeong (righteous armies) 義兵, 486, 500, 553, 558-559, 561-563; leaders, 561. *See also* anti-Japanese movement

Uicheon 義天, 175, 179. *See also* Cheontae Sect

ui-eop (medical examination) 醫業, 234

Uijong, king of Goryeo 毅宗, 211-212

Uisang, monk of Silla 義湘, 69

Uiyeoldan (Righteous Brotherhood) 義烈團, 572, 583

Unified Silla 統一新羅, 157. *See also* Later Silla

Unyo (Japanese naval vessel) 雲揚號, 396, 400, 407, 408, 485

useung yeolpae ("triumph for the strongen and defeat for weaker") 優勝劣敗, 441

u-uijeong (a deputy prime minister) 右議政, 254

Wada, Kiyoshi (J.) 和田淸, 136

Waeber, Carl, 503, 507, 508, 509, 510, 512, 514, 515

waegwan (Japanese office) 倭館, 290, 335, 336, 402, 404, 476

Wai (J.) 倭, 71

Wang, Anshi (Ch.) 王安石, 238

Wang, Chengli (Ch.) 王承禮, 136, 149

Wang, Geon 王建, 225; Ten Admonition 訓要十條, 179

wang, surname of the Goryeo royalty 王, 147

wang, title of king 王, 34. *See also hu*

"we-consciousness," 10-11, 17, 19-20, 22-24

Wenti (Ch.), emperor of Sui Chian 文帝, 221

Western Powers' Eastern Advance, 363

wijeong cheoksa (defending orthodoxy and rejecting heterodoxy) 爲政斥邪, 424, 488

Wiman Joseon 衛滿朝鮮, 31, 34

Witte, Sergei, 501, 517, 520, 525, 533, 538, 541, 542

Woncheuk, monk of Silla 圓測, 69

Wonjong, king of Goryeo 元宗, 212

Wudai huiyao (Ch.) (An Outline of Five Successive Dynasties) 五代會要, 135

Xiaoxue (Ch.) (Lesser Learning) 小學, 235, 241

Xiedan guozhi (Ch.) (History of Khitan) 契丹國志, 146

Xinmin congbao (Ch.) (New Citizen's Journal) 新民叢報, 445, 446, 447, 460

Xintangshu (Ch.) (New Book of Tang) 新唐書, 135-136, 138, 142, 144, 152

Xu, Jing (Ch.) 徐兢, 163, 177, 179, 181

Xuanzong (Ch.), emperor of Tang China 玄宗, 143

Yamada, Ishikawamaro (J.) 山田石川麻呂, 63

Yamakawa, Histoshi (J.) 山川均, 596, 606-607

Yamato (J.) (government) 大和, 57-61, 63-65. *See also* Soga clan

Yan (Ch.) 燕, 31

Yang 楊. *See* surnames of Balhae kings

yangban 兩班: bureaucratic system, 191, 222, 226-228, 230-232, 234

Ye (tribe) 濊. *See* Yemaek

Yejo (Ministry of Rites) 禮曹, 241

Yemaek 濊貊, 10-12, 28-29, 143; Yemaek Joseon, 30, 34; Yemaek people, 31

Yeo, Un-hyeong 呂運亨, 590

yeogak (coastal trade brokers) 旅閣, 307, 319

yeokgwan (government translators and

interpreters) 譯官, 307

Yeondeunghoe (Lantern Festival) 燃燈會, 209

yeonghon (soul) 靈魂, 378

yeongmyeong (enlightened spirit) 靈明, 378

Yeonjeonghoe (Political Research Society) 研政會, 581, 598

Yi 李. *See* surnames of Balhae kings

Yi, Byeok 李蘗, 369, 370, 371-372, 376, 379

Yi, Hang-no 李恒老, 554

Yi, Ik 李瀷, 334-338; and western books, 335; and rotation of the earth, 336-338; and Catholic faith, 359-362

Yi, In-jwa 李麟佐, 294

Yi, Ja-gyeom 李資謙, 174

Yi, Je-hyeon 李齊賢, 203

Yi, Sang-jae 李商在, 560. *See also* Manmin Gongdonghoe

Yi, Sun-sin 李舜臣, 291

Yi, Wan-yong 李完用, 494, 508

Yijing 易經: *geon, gi* (heaven) 乾, 氣, 376; *gon, to* (earth) 坤, 土, 376; *gam, su* (water) 坎, 水, 376; *ri, hwa* (fire) 離, 火, 376; *cheon* (heaven) 天, 376

Yinbingshi wenji (Ch.) (The Collected Works of Liang Qichao) 飲氷室文集, 447-448, 465

Yingzhou (Ch.) 營州, 138-140, 144, 150

yoho bumin (local landed gentry and the wealthy) 饒戶富民, 425-426

yongbeom ("mold") 鎔范, 31

Yongwonbu, of Balhae 龍原府. *See* Donggyeong Yongwonbu

Yoro (J.), Japanese era 養老, 66

Yu, Gil-jun 俞吉濬 481, 488; his ideas on Darwinism, 441-444; *Seoyu gyeonmun,* 443

Yu, In-seok 柳麟錫, 554, 561

Yuan, of China (Ch.) 元: anti-Yuan group and pro-Yuan group, 201-202; anti-Yuan reforms, 202

Yuan, Shikai (Ch.) 袁世凱, 482, 483, 485, 506-507

Yuhyangso (local government advisory committee) 留鄕所, 229

yukdupum (head-rank six) 六頭品, 224, 231

Yun, Chi-ho 尹致昊, 560. *See also* Dongnip Hyeophoe

Zhang, Jianzhang (Ch.) 張建章, 139

Zhaoxian zhanlue (Ch.) (Korean Stratagem) 朝鮮策略, 555

Zhou Wenmo (Ch.) 周文謨, 372, 373

Zhu Xi (Ch.) 朱熹, 217

Zhuzi jiali (Ch.) (Family Rituals of Zhu Xi) 朱子家禮, 235, 241

Zizhi tongjian (Ch.) (General Mirror for the Aid of Government) 資治通鑑, 146

(Ch.: Chinese; J.: Japanese; Skt.: Sanskrit)